S0-AHN-426

Alter Orient und Altes Testament
Veröffentlichungen zur Kultur und Geschichte
des Alten Orients und des Alten Testaments

Band 204

Samuel E. Loewenstamm

Comparative Studies in Biblical and Ancient Oriental Literatures

Alter Orient und Altes Testament

Veröffentlichungen zur Kultur und Geschichte des Alten Orients
und des Alten Testaments

Herausgeber

Kurt Bergerhof · Manfried Dietrich · Oswald Loretz

1980

Verlag Butzon & Bercker Kevelaer

Neukirchener Verlag Neukirchen-Vluyn

Comparative Studies in Biblical and Ancient Oriental Literatures

by

Samuel E. Loewenstamm

1980

Verlag Butzon & Bercker Kevelaer

Neukirchener Verlag Neukirchen-Vluyn

CIP-Kurztitelaufnahme der Deutschen Bibliothek

Loewenstamm, Samuel E.:
Comparative Studies in Biblical and Ancient Oriental Literatures / by Samuel E. Loewenstamm. – Kevelaer: Butzon und Bercker; Neukirchen-Vluyn: Neukirchener Verlag, 1980.
(Alter Orient und Altes Testament; Bd. 204)
ISBN 3-7666-9147-3 (Butzon u. Bercker)
ISBN 3-7887-0651-1 (Neukirchener Verl.)

Herstellung: Breklumer Druckerei Manfred Siegel
Printed in Germany
ISBN 3-7887-0651-1 Neukirchener Verlag
ISBN 3-7666-9147-3 Verlag Butzon & Bercker Kevelaer

Preface

The present book owes its appearance to the initiative of Prof. Dr. M. Dietrich and Prof. Dr. O. Loretz who kindly suggested to me the publication of a volume collecting my articles and reviews in the field of Near Eastern Ancient Oriental research with the exception of studies in purely Biblical exegesis. In accordance with this guide-line the volume comprises in addition to the treatment of Ugaritic, Akkadian and Greek texts even investigations into Biblical writings in the light of their Ancient Oriental parallels.

However, some papers, though thematically pertinent, had to be excluded, to wit 1) Two articles in the field of Ugaritic research, composed together with my friend and colleague Prof. Dr. J. Blau. 2) Two articles on plene writing in Ugaritic whose revised results have been summed up in one of the papers by Blau-Loewenstamm. 3) Two popular surveys on the results of Ugaritic research. 4) Parabiblical articles in the *Encyclopaedia Biblica* as e.g. *miktāb* (letter), *^{ca}rebut* (suretyship), *šor naggāḥ* (goring ox) because of their extremely concise style. (It is not without misgivings that the present writer reprints here the short para *Taautos* out of an article *Sanchunjaton*, published in *Pauly's Realencyclopaedie der Classischen Altertumswissenschaft* in order to make up for a certain deficiency in his study of *Philon of Byblos*, at least to some degree). 5) Single passages, scattered in articles on Biblical exegesis, as e.g. the comparison of Nu. 16:15 and 1 Sam. 12:3 with *EA* 280:21-24 or the comparative discussion of different monetary systems in the review of R. de Vaux, *Les Institutions de l'Ancien Testament*, vol. 1. All these papers can conveniently be traced in the appended bibliography of those of the author's writings which are not reedited in this volume.

On the other hand, I took the liberty of reprinting my note on the law of murder and adultery in the Bible, since this note has been written in defence of another paper arguing the affinity of these laws to their Ancient Oriental counterparts. Not without hesitation I am including a discussion of the *Mishna Hagiga* 2:1. I am cognizant of the fact that some readers will be perplexed by a research delving into niceties of Talmudic exegesis. Nevertheless, a closer scrutiny may convince them that the confrontation of the current interpretation of the Mishna in the light of the Gnosis with its explanation on the ground of Ancient Oriental sources pertains to the subject-matter of this book.

The author strove for uniformity in presentation. Papers, originally published in Hebrew or in German have been translated into English. References to sources and secondary literature have been standardized. Additions to the original publications are enclosed in square brackets.

In the transcription of Hebrew texts quiescent letters have been omitted, except quiescent *'ālāp*. Aspiration of tenues by *dāgeš lene* has not been marked. Consonants strengthened by *dāgeš forte* have been doubled. *Ṣere* is rendered by *e* in contradistinction to *s*e*gol*, indicated by ä. Long *a* (*ā*) has been differentiated from a short one (*a*). The length of other vowels has not been indicated. The transcription of Hebrew titles has been left as in the original publication, e.g. Kirjat Sepher, not *Qiryat Sepär*. Talmudic titles are quoted in a simplified transcription, e.g. Mishna Baba Mezia, not *Mišnā Bābā' m*e*ṣi*c*a'*.

The arrangement of the papers follows the order of their first appearance.

At every stage of the preparation of this volume I enjoyed the untiring cooperation of my wife, Mrs. Ayala Loewenstamm. Her share in the completion of this volume can hardly be overestimated.

My best thanks are due to Mr. Victor Hurovitz, Dr. Michael Sokoloff and Dr. Raymond Westbrook for their part in translating a number of articles, which originally appeared in German or Hebrew.

I wish to thank also Mrs. Geulah Cohen for her meticulous work in compiling the main part of the indices.

Last not least, I wish to express to Prof. Dr. M. Dietrich and Prof. Dr. O. Loretz my sincerest feelings of gratitude for their proposal to publish the present volume.

Table of Contents

List of Abbreviations

AANL	Atti della Academia Nazionale dei Lincei, Rendiconti della Classe di Scienze morale, storiche e filologiche (Roma).
Aartun, Partikeln	Kjell Aartun, Die Partikeln des Ugaritischen, AOAT vol. 21/1, 1974
AASOR	Annual of the American Schools of Oriental Research
ABIU	Annual of Bar-Ilan University
ACF	L'Annuaire du Collège de France
AcOr	Acta Orientalia
AfO	Archiv für Orientforschung
Aistleitner, Texte	Die Mythologischen und Kultischen Texte aus Ras Schamra, übersetzt von J. Aistleitner^2, Budapest 1964
Aistleitner, UGU	J. Aistleitner, Untersuchungen zur Grammatik des Ugaritischen (Berichte über die Verhandlungen der Sächsischen Akademie der Wissenschaften zu Leipzig, Phil.-hist. Kl., Bd. 100, Heft 6, Berlin 1954)
Aistleitner, WUS	J. Aistleitner, Wörterbuch der Ugaritischen Sprache, ed. O. Eißfeldt (Berichte über die Verhandlungen der Sächsischen Akademie der Wissenschaften zu Leipzig, Phil. hist. Kl., Band 106, Heft 3)
AJA	American Journal of Archeology
AJSLL	American Journal of Semitic Languages and Literatures
Alalakh	D.J. Wiseman, The Alalakh Tablets, London 1953
ANET	Ancient Near Eastern Texts relating to the Old Testament, ed. J.B. Pritchard^3 Princeton 1969
AnSt	Anatolian Studies
AOAT	Alter Orient und Altes Testament. Veröffentlichungen zur Kultur und Geschichte des Alten Orients und des Alten Testaments, Neukirchen-Vluyn
AOH	Acta Orientalia Academiae Scientiarum Hungaricae
AP	A. Cowley, Aramaic Papyri of the Fifth Cent. BC, Oxford 1923
ARM	Archives Royales de Mari

ArOr	Archiv Orientálni
AS	Assyriological Studies (Chicago)
AuJBA	Australian Journal of Biblical Archaeology
BA	Biblical Archaeologist
Barth, Nominalbildung	J. Barth, Die Nominalbildung in den Semitischen Sprachen², Leipzig 1894
Barth, Pronominalbildung	J. Barth, Die Pronominalbildung in den Semitischen Sprachen, Leipzig 1913
BASOR	Bulletin of the American Schools for Oriental Research
Baumgartner, HAL	W. Baumgartner, Hebräisches und Aramäisches Lexicon zum Alten Testament 1, Leiden 1967
Ben-Yehuda, Thesaurus	E. ben Iehuda, Thesaurus Totius Hebraitatis, Berlin - Jerusalem 1910-1959
BH	Biblica Hebraica³, ed. R. Kittel, Stuttgart 1951
BIES	Bulletin of the Israel Exploration Society (= Yediot)
BiOr	Bibliotheca Orientalis
BJ	Le Bible de Jerusalem
BJPES	Bulletin of the Jewish Palestine Exploration Society (= Yediot)
BJRL	Bulletin of John Rylands Library
BM	Beth Mikra
BMAP	E. Kraeling, The Brooklyn Museum Aramaic Papyri, New Haven 1963
Brockelmann, Grundriß	C. Brockelmann, Grundriß der vergleichenden Grammatik der semitischen Sprachen, Berlin 1908, 1913
Brockelmann, LS	K. Brockelmann, Lexicon Syriacum², Halle 1928
BWANT	Beiträge zur Wissenschaft vom Alten und Neuen Testament
BZAW	Beihefte für die Zeitschrift für die Alttestamentliche Wissenschaft
CAD	The Assyrian Dictionary, published by the Oriental Institute, Chicago
Caquot-Sznycer, RPO	A. Caquot - M. Sznycer in Les Religions du Proche Orient, Paris 1970, Deuxième partie, Textes Ougaritiques, pp. 351-524

Caquot-Sznycer, Textes 1	A. Caquot - M. Sznycer in Textes Ougaritiques, Tome 1 Mythes et Légendes, pp. 1-480, Paris 1974
Cassuto, Anath	U. Cassuto, The Goddess Anath, Jerusalem 1971
Cassuto BOSt 2	U. Cassuto, Biblical and Oriental Studies, vol. 2, Jerusalem 1975
Cassuto, From Adam to Noah	U. Cassuto, A Commentary on the Book of Genesis, Part 1, From Adam to Noah, Jerusalem 1961
Cassuto, From Noah to Abraham	U. Cassuto, A Commentary on the Book of Genesis, Part 2, From Noah to Abraham, Jerusalem 1962
CBQ	Catholic Biblical Quarterly
CH	Codex Hammurabi
CIS	Corpus Inscriptionum Semiticarum, Pars 1, Paris 1881ff.
Cowley, AP	See AP
CRAIBL	Comptes rendus de l'Académie des Inscriptions et Belles-Lettres, Paris
CTA	Corpus des Tablettes en Cunéiformes Alphabétiques, par A. Herdner, Paris 1963
Dahood, UHPh	M. Dahood, Ugaritic-Hebrew Philology (Biblica et Orientalia 17), Rome 1965
Dalman, AuS	G. Dalman, Arbeit und Sitte in Palästina 1-6, Gütersloh 1927-1936
Driver, CML	G.R. Driver, Canaanite Myths and Legends, Edinburgh 1956
EA	Die El-Amarna Tafeln, ed. J.A. Knudtzon, Kristiania 1907
EB	Encyclopaedia Biblica, Jerusalem
EI	Eretz-Israel (Publications of the Israel Exploration Society)
Eißfeldt, Taautos und Sanchunjaton	O. Eißfeldt, Taautos und Sanchunjaton (Sitzungsberichte der Deutschen Akademie der Wissenschaften zu Berlin, Klasse für Sprache, Literatur und Kunst 1952, Nr. 1)
ET	Expository Times
Eusebius, PrEv	Eusebius, Praeparatio Evangelica
Friedrich, HW	J. Friedrich, Hethitisches Wörterbuch, Heidelberg 1952

Friedrich PPG	J. Friedrich, Phönizisch-Punische Grammatik, Rome 1957
Friedrich PPG²	J. Friedrich - W. Röllig, Phönizisch-Punische Grammatik, Rome 1970
FuF	Forschungen und Fortschritte
Gaster, Thespis²	Th.G. Gaster, Thespis², Garden City 1961
GB	W. Gesenius - F. Buhl, Hebräisches und aramäisches Handwörterbuch über das Alte Testament[17], Leipzig 1915
GK	W. Gesenius - E. Kautzsch - A.E. Cowley, Hebrew Grammar, Oxford 1910
Gesenius, Thesaurus	G. Gesenius, Thesaurus Philologicus Criticus Totius Hebraitatis, Leipzig 1858
Gevirtz, Patterns	St. Gevirtz, Patterns in the Early Poetry of Israel (Studies in Ancient Oriental Civilization No. 32, Chicago 1963)
Gilg.	Gilgamesh
Ginsberg, Keret	H.L. Ginsberg, The Legend of King Keret, BASOR, Supplementary Studies 2-3, New Haven 1946
Ginsberg, KU	H.L. Ginsberg, The Ugaritic Texts (Kitbe Ugarit), Jerusalem, 1936
GLECS	Comptes Rendus du Groupe Linguistique d'Études Chamito-Sémitiques, Paris
Gordon, UH	C.H. Gordon, Ugaritic Handbook, Rome 1947
Gordon, UL	C.H. Gordon, Ugaritic Literature, Rome 1949
Gordon, UM	C.H. Gordon, Ugaritic Manual, Rome 1955
Gordon, UT	C.H. Gordon, Ugaritic Textbook, Rome 1965
Gray, Krt	J. Gray, The Krt Text in the Literature of Ras Shamra, VTS 5, Leiden 1955
Gray, Krt²	J. Gray, etc., Leiden 1964
Gray, Legacy	J. Gray, The Legacy of Canaan, VTS 5, Leiden 1957
Gray, Legacy²	J. Gray, etc., Leiden 1965
HAT	Die Heilige Schrift des Alten Testaments
Herdner, CTA	See CTA
Herdner, Textes 1	A. Herdner, Textes Ougaritiques 1, Mythes et Légendes, Paris 1974, pp. 481 ff. (Keret)
Höfner, ASG	M. Höfner, Altsüdarabische Grammatik, Leipzig 1943

HTR	Harvard Theological Review
HUCA	Hebrew Union College Annual
ICC	The International Critical Commentary
IEJ	Israel Exploration Journal
IOS	Israel Oriental Studies
ISBR	Publications of the Israel Society for Biblical Research
JANES	Journal of Ancient Near Eastern Studies
Jastrow, Talmud Dictionary	M. Jastrow, A Dictionary of the Targumim, the Talmud Babli and Yerushalmi, and the Midrashic Literature, Philadelphia 1903
JAOS	Journal of the American Oriental Society
JBL	Journal of Biblical Literature
JCS	Journal of Cuneiform Studies
JEA	Journal of Egyptian Archaeology
Jean-Hoftijzer, DISO	Ch.F. Jean - J. Hoftijzer, Dictionnaire des Inscriptions Sémitiques de l'Ouest, Leiden 1965
JJS	Journal of Jewish Studies
JNES	Journal of Near Eastern Studies
JNWSL	Journal of North West Semitic Languages
Joüon, Gr.	P. Joüon, Grammaire de l'Hébreu Biblique, Rome 1947
JPOS	Journal of Palestine Oriental Society
JQR	Jewish Quarterly Review
JRAS	Journal of the Royal Asiatic Society
JSS	Journal of Semitic Studies
JTS	Journal of Theological Studies
KAI	H. Donner - W. Röllig, Kanaanäische und aramäische Inschriften, Wiesbaden 1962-1964
Kapelrud, Baal	A.S. Kapelrud, Baal in the Ras Shamra Texts, Copenhagen 1952
KAR	E. Ebeling, Keilschrifttexte aus Assur religiösen Inhalts, Leipzig 1919-1920
KBL	L. Koehler - W. Baumgartner, Lexicon in Veteris Testamenti Libros, Leiden 1958
Kraeling, BMAP	E. Kraeling, The Brooklyn Museum Aramaic Papyri, New Haven 1953

Lambert, BWL	W.G. Lambert, Babylonian Wisdom Literature, Oxford 1960
Lambert-Millard, Atra-ḫasis	W.G. Lambert - A.R. Millard, Atraḫasis, Oxford 1969
Landberg, Glossaire Dathinois	Comte de Landberg, Glossaire Dathinois, Leiden 1920-1947
LE	Lex Eshnunna
Luc.	Lucas
MAL	Middle Assyrian Laws
Mar.	Marcus
Matt.	Mattheus
De Moor, New Year	J.C. de Moor, New Year with the Canaanites and the Israelites, Kampen 1972
De Moor, Seasonal Pattern	J.C. de Moor, The Seasonal Pattern in the Ugaritic Myth of Ba^{c}lu, AOAT 16,1971
MT	Masoretic Text
MVAG	Mitteilungen der vorderasiatisch-ägyptischen Gesellschaft
NEB	The New English Bible, Oxford 1970
OLP	Orientalia Lovaniensia Periodica
OTL	Old Testament Library
OTS	Oudtestamentische Studien
PEQ	Palestine Exploration Quarterly
PRU 2	Ch. Virolleaud, Le Palais Royal d'Ugarit 2, Mission de Ras Shamra 7, Paris 1957
PRU 3	J. Nougayrol, Le Palais Royal d'Ugarit 3, Mission de Ras Shamra 6, Paris 1955
PRU 4	J. Nougayrol, Le Palais Royal d'Ugarit 4, Mission de Ras Shamra 9, Paris 1956
PRU 5	Ch. Virolleaud, Le Palais Royal d'Ugarit 5, Mission de Ras Shamra 11, Paris 1965
PRU 6	J. Nougayrol, Le Palais Royal d'Ugarit 6, Mission de Ras Shamra 12, Paris 1970
PS	Proto-Semitic
RB	Revue Biblique
REJ	Revue des Études Juives
RHR	Revue de l'histoire des religions

Rin, Aliloth	S. Rin, Aliloth ha-elim, Acts of the Gods, Jerusalem 1968
RLA	Reallexikon der Assyriologie, Berlin/Leipzig 1928 ff.
RSO	Rivista degli Studi Orientali
RSP 1	Ras Shamra Parallels 1, ed. L.R. Fisher, Rome 1972
RV	Revised Version
ScHi	Scripta Hiersolymitana
SCS	Septuagint and Cognate Studies
v. Soden, AHW	W. v. Soden, Assyrisches Handwörterbuch, Wiesbaden
v. Soden, GAG	W. v. Soden, Grundriß der Akkadischen Grammatik, Rome 1952
StOr	Studia Orientalia
ThLZ	Theologische Literaturzeitung
ThZ	Theologische Zeitschrift
TO	Targum Onkelos
TY	Targum Yerushalmi (= Pseudo Yonathan)
U 3	ed. C.F.A. Schaeffer, Ugaritica 3, Mission de Ras Shamra 8, Paris 1956
U 5	J. Nougayrol, E. Laroche, Ch. Virolleaud, C.F.A. Schaeffer, Ugaritica 5, Mission de Ras Shamra 16, Paris 1968
U 6	ed. C.F.A. Schaeffer, Ugaritica 6, Mission de Ras Shamra 17, Paris 1969
U F	Ugarit Forschungen 1 (1969) etc.
VAB	Vorderasiatische Bibliothek, Leipzig
VAT	Tafelsignaturen der Vorderasiatischen Abteilung der Berliner Museen
VT	Vetus Testamentum
VTS	Supplement to Vetus Testamentum
Wiseman, Alalakh	see Alalakh
WMANT	Wissenschaftliche Monographien zum Alten und Neue Testament, Neukirchen-Vluyn
WO	Die Welt des Orients
WZKM	Wiener Zeitschrift für die Kunde des Morgenlandes
ZA	Zeitschrift für Assyriologie
ZAW	Zeitschrift für die Alttestamentliche Wissenschaf
ZäS	Zeitschrift für ägyptische Sprache

van Zijl, Baal	P.J. van Zijl, Baal, AOAT 10, 1972
ZDMG	Zeitschrift der Deutschen Morgenländischen Gesellschaft

Read not *'^{a}rubbotenu* but *'arm^{e}notenu* (Jer. 9:20)*

To the Question of Biblical Textual Criticism on the Basis of Ugaritic Writings.

Ugaritic writings twice tell us in describing the building of Baal's palace how Baal forbade putting windows in his houses as long as he had not defeated his opponent Mot. He ordered his servant *Kṯr* and *Ḫss*: "Do not put an air-hole (*urbt*) in the house, an aperture (*ḥln*) in the midst of the palace" (CTA 4:V:120-127; VI:1-6). However, after he succeeded in dealing his enemy a decisive blow[1], he commanded "Let an aperture (*ḥln*) be opened in the house, an air-hole (*urbt*) in the midst of the palace" (CTA 4:VII:17-19).

The key to comprehending Baal's behaviour was found by Prof. Cassuto[2] in the verse: "For Death has come up to our apertures (*ḥallonenu*), he is

---

* It is my pleasant duty to express my sincerest thanks to my teacher Prof. U. Cassuto, who advised me in the composition of this note.

[1] U. Cassuto, *Orientalia* N S 7 (1938), pp. 285ff.; idem, *Tarbiz* 13 (1941), p. 208; idem, *JBL* 61 (1942), p. 54.

[There is no real proof of Cassuto's assertion that Baal's consent to the opening of apertures in his palace was preceded by a victory over Mot. Today the opinion clearly prevails that the apertures in Baal's palace symbolize rifts in the clouds through which the rain was supposed to pour down. cf. de Moor, *Seasonal Pattern*, pp. 162f. This interpretation leads to the conclusion that Baal changed his mind at the beginning of the season of rains in autumn. Against this fixation of time de Moor argues "that the early rains are impossible when very soon afterwards Ba^{c}lu succumbs to Motu and has to take his rains with him into the Nether World" (*CTA* 5: V). This difficulty compels de Moor to fix the opening of the apertures at March. His solution, then, tacitly supposes a concept that the early rain did not pour down through a rift in the clouds, but in some different way. Such differentiation between early and late rain, however, is unsupported and no possible reason for it can be shown.

De Moor gets entangled in this unsurmountable difficulty as a result of his thesis that the texts reflect a seasonal myth. But Baal's death does not indicate the beginning of the rainless period of the year, rather the failure of rain in the rainy season. On this supposition everything falls into place. Baal had completed his royal palace, opened apertures in it to pour down the rain and gave his holy voice, solemn inauguration of the rainy season. He had reached the height of his power. This situation, however, proved to be the turning-point of his fate. Immediately afterwards Mot starts his war against him and quickly succeeds in killing his adversary. This involves that the rains failed very soon with the consequence of an ensuing period of drought.]

[2] Cf. Cassuto, *ibid*.

entered into our castles (*'armᵉnotenu*), to cut off children from the street, and the young men from the broad place." According to an ancient Canaanite belief, Mot would come through the apertures.

Scholars after Prof. Cassuto[3] agreed with this interpretation. However, they found difficulty in the fact that in all the Ugaritic passages mentioned *ḥln* is parallel to *urbt*, whereas in Jer. 9:20 this parallel to *ḥallon* is conspicuously absent, and looked for this parallel in the Biblical verse too, since numerous examples have proven that Biblical writings received from the Canaanite tradition a wealth of word pairs which appear as parallels in the two stichoi of a verse.[4] Therefore it seemed reasonable to assume that the prophet who borrowed his imagery from the ancient Canaanite tradition - also borrowed the pair of parallel words *ḥallon* and *'ᵃrubbā*. H.L. Ginsberg and A. Singer therefore contended that *'armᵉnotenu* should be emended to read *'ᵃrubbotenu*.

Both of them claim that the emendation is minor. Singer[5] states that *'ᵃrubbā* is rare in the Bible and is therefore prone to corruption. He also sees no graphic difficulties in the emendation. The cause of the corruption is, in his opinion, that the phrase "was forgotten and obscured after the great rift of the Babylonian Exile". Ginsberg[6] points out that the Septuagint reads here *'admātenu* instead of *'armᵉnotenu* and that the same change is found in the Septuagint to Mi. 5:4 where the parallelism with *'arṣenu* proves that the Septuagint reading is superior. Although in Jeremiah the Septuagint reading is incorrect, the reading *'admātenu*, which is graphically equivalent to *'armatenu* stands midway between the original reading *'ᵃrubbotenu* and the Masoretic reading *'armᵉnotenu*. Therefore it is closer to the original than the Masoretic rendition.

However, the Septuagint proves nothing in the matter under discussion. In the two verses mentioned, the Septuagint renders the Hebrew *'armon* by the Greek χώρα and the same Greek word appears for the Hebrew *'armon* in

---

3 Cf. H.L. Ginsberg, *JBL* 62 (1943) pp. 113ff.; A.D. Singer, *BJPES* 11 (1944) pp. 18ff. *[But cf. note 1.]*

4 Cf. Cassuto, *Tarbiz* 14 (1942), pp. 1ff. *[= BOSt* 2, pp. 43-59*]*.

5 Cf. Singer, *op. cit.* (note 3), p. 19.

6 Cf. Ginsberg, *op. cit.* (note 3), p. 114.

four other verses[7], in which no one would cast doubt on the Masoretic reading. In addition, there is no proof that the Septuagint read *'ªdāmā* rather than *'armon* in the six mentioned verses. χώρα is not the usual Septuagint rendition of *'ªdāmā* (exceptions being Is. 1:7; 19:17; Dan. 11:39). Almost everywhere the Septuagint translates *'ªdāmā* with γῆ and in the books being considered with total regularity.[8] χώρα is not, therefore, a usual translation for *'ªdāmā* and it further seems that in the six mentioned verses the Septuagint engages in loose rendition of *'armon*. It does not retain the original imagery but is satisfied with relation to the general idea; viz. that disaster is imminent upon the land.[9]

Nor do Singer's claims remove the difficulties from the suggested emendation. *'ªrubbā* appears nine times in the Bible, and the Talmud proves that the word never disappeared from popular daily use.[10] There is also no proof that the Second Temple copyist did not understand the underlying idea. The Midrash demonstrates at every step of the way that the popular imagination retained mythological ideas for millenia and that even in the Amoraitic period we find an incident recalling the Ugaritic writings: "Raba closed the windows at the time of an epidemic as it is written 'for death is come up to our apertures'" (Baba Kamma 60b). We learn from here that Raba not only understood the outlook at the base of the imagery, but even shared it himself and therefore guarded himself against death in ways very similar to those of Baal. Even if we assume that the copyist did find difficulty in the imagery, we must then ask why did he change only the second member -- which did not remove the difficulty -- and not read for example *ᶜālā māwät bᵉḥelenu bā' bᵉ'armᵉnotenu* 'came up into our ramparts etc'.[11] It is also difficult to admit that a change of *bet* in *'ªrubbotenu* to *mem* in *'admātenu*

---

[7] Cf. Am. 3:9-11; 6:8.

[8] Cf. Septuagint Jer. 7:20; 8:2; 12:14; 14:4; 16:4,15; 23:8; 24:10; 25:5, 26,33; 27:10-11; 28:16; 35:7,15; 42:12; 52:27; Am. 3:2,5; 5:2; 7:11,17; 9:8,15. In Mi. *'ªdāmā* is not found in the Masoretic Text.

[9] χώρα serves as a translation for *'äräṣ* in sixty-four verses and for *mᵉdinā* in thirty-nine verses. Cf. also the loose translation of *'armon* in Is. 34:13.

[10] Cf. Mishna Beza 5:1, Ohalot 5:2; 7:2 etc.

[11] Cf. Ps. 48:14; 122:7.

is graphically very easy. We cannot equate this change to the prevalent changes such as *dalät* and *reš*, dittography, haplography etc.

Even were the emendation truly minor, we could still not accept it in that there is not sufficient reason to cast doubt on the Masoretic reading. Against *'armᵉnotenu* Singer claims "The prophet speaks about the danger impending on the people. Why does he make particular mention of the luxurious buildings of the nation's upper class? Does not Mot do his cruel work in the tents of the poor as well as in the palaces of the rich, without distinction?"[12] This argument is unconvincing for two reasons. First, in the literary tradition *'armon* is well attested to in descriptions of disaster encroaching upon a city. It is found ten times in the phrase "to set fire to the *'armonot* of a town".[13] Similarly, the word appears in numerous combinations particularly in descriptions of disaster.[14] Just as a traditional place was afforded to *'armon* in prophetic language and in lamentations which deal with disaster, so the same importance was afforded it in hymns of thanksgiving describing the joyous state of peace and prosperity.[15] Secondly, Singer was not precise in defining *'armon*. The word appears twice in parallelism with *mibṣār* (fortress)[16] once with *qiryā bᵉṣurā* (fortified city)[17], thrice with *ḥomā* (wall)[18] and twice with *ḥel* (rampart).[19]. In Proverbs *bᵉriªḥ 'armon* (bolt of a palace) parallels *qiryat ᶜoz* (a city of strength).[20] In Isaiah it is said that the enemy besieging the city *ᶜorᵉru 'armᵉnotähā* (have laid bare its *'armonot*).[21]

---

[12] Cf. Singer, *op. cit.* (note 3), p. 18.

[13] Cf. Jer. 17:27; 49:27; Ho. 8:14; Am. 1:4,7,10,12,14; 2:2,5.

[14] Cf. Is. 25:2; 32:14; Jer. 6:5; Am. 3:11; 6:8; Mi 5:4 (However, recent critics read here *'admātenu* in place of *'armᵉnotenu* along with the Septuagint and the Pešitta. cf. above note 8. But, *'ªdāmā* is in the Bible several times more freqüent than *'armon* and is not, therefore, prone to be corrupted to *'armon*. *'armᵉnotenu* is apparently a gradation of *'arṣenu* (to our land, even to our castles); similar are Am. 3:11; Thr. 2:5,7.

[15] Ps 48:14; 122:7.

[16] Is. 34:13; Thr. 2:5.

[17] Is. 25:2.

[18] Jer. 49:27; Am. 1:7,14.

[19] See note 15.

[20] Pr. 18:19.

[21] Is. 23:13.

These verses leave no room to doubt that *'armᵉnot* served as fortresses. Should the enemy successfully conquer the fortified palaces of the city, the implication is that they conquered the city itself. From this we can understand why these buildings play such a prominent role in the descriptions of a national tragedy.

The use of *'armᵉnotenu* in our verse therefore is appropriate in a fixed and well understood literary tradition. The meaning of *bā' bᵉ'armᵉnotenu* is clear. The murderous enemy (*Mot*) has entered our fortresses. Ginsberg and Singer claim against *'armᵉnotenu* that it is unsuitable as a parallel to *ḥallonenu*. To this general assertion they each add a more detailed claim. Singer says that *bᵉḥallonenu* means "through our windows" and asks how we can accordingly understand the *b* in *bᵉ'armᵉnotenu*. Ginsberg is of the opinion that the Masoretic Text expresses an "awkward hysteron-proteron". Death can go up into our windows only after it has come into our *'armonot*, i.e. our fortresses.

But, all of these proofs are not convincing. Joel describes the onslaught of the locusts: "They go up (*yaᶜᵃlu*) into the houses, they enter-in (*yābo'u*) at the apertures like a thief" (Joel 2:9). This verse is recognizably similar to ours both in its structure and content, and provides us with a clue why people believed that death comes into the houses through the windows. A welcome guest will enter the house through the doorway, while an unwelcome visitor will find the door closed and with no choice will enter like a thief through the windows; and it goes without saying that death is everywhere an unwelcome guest.[22] As for the structure, interesting here is the parallelism between the verbs *ᶜlh* and *b'* - precisely what is found in our verse. In addition we find *ḥallonenu*. This word is parallel to *bāttim* and we cannot ignore the similarity between the parallelism *ḥallonim* - *bāttim* and *'armonot* - *ḥallonim*. The locusts climb up on the houses. This does not mean that they climb up through the houses. They ascent on to the houses from outside and afterward come through the window. It is not explicitly stated into where they entered but even so the matter is under-

[22] Another interpretation has been suggested by Albright, *Archaeology and the Religion of Israel*, p. 198, note 45.
In his opinion, the source of this strange idea was the feeling that the night air is apt to cause damage in the instance of respiratory diseases. However, this interpretation has a suspicious air of modern science about it.

stood. Naturally they came into the houses on which they ascended. There is a similar picture in our verse. Death ascends in our windows, that is to say it climbs and ascends into the palace windows from outside, but it is not explicitly stated that it entered through them. The second half of the verse states explicitly that which we learned in Joel from the general intent of the matter. Death enters the building.

In Jeremiah it is not stated explicitly through what death entered just as in Joel it was not explicitly stated into where the locusts entered. But, as in the latter, so in the former it is easy to fill in what is lacking. Naturally death entered through the windows to which it had ascended.[23] Thus both Ginsberg's and Singer's claims are not convincing. In Biblical parallelism the two stichoi of the verse explain and complement one another and therefore the windows mentioned in the first stichos are none other than those of the palaces mentioned in the second stichos. So R. David Kimḥi already correctly explained the matter.[24]

We have tried to demonstrate that the alleged difficulties in the Masoretic Text provide no basis for emendation. Also the argument drawn from supposed Ugaritic parallels is fallacious. The Biblical Text provides us with a detailed description of an unwanted guest's entry into a building, while the Ugaritic writings tell us a strategic-architectural consideration.

In such a consideration there is room for an exact parallel tautologism. In a multistaged process, however, every step is deserving of special mention.

---

[23] Ginsberg also noticed the verse from Joel but he is so certain of the emendation to *'ᵃrubbotenu* that even this verse cannot add credibility to the Masoretic Text.

[[24] For an Akkadian parallel see now Sh. M. Paul, Biblica 49 (1968), pp. 373-376.*]*

New Light on the History of the Alphabet

In the fall of 1949 the French archaeological mission under the direction of C. Schaeffer resumed its excavations at Ras Shamra, ancient Ugarit, and immediately made an important discovery: A small tablet from the first half of the 14th cent. B.C.E. containing a list of the Ugaritic letters in order[1] as follows[2]: *a b g ḫ d h w z ḥ ṭ y k* $\check{s}_1$ [today transcribed *š*] *l m* $\check{s}_2$ [today transcribed by most scholars as *ḏ*] *n ẓ* s_1 ᶜ *p ṣ q r ṯ ġ t i u* s_2.

The agreement between the order of the letters in this alphabet and that in the Hebrew alphabet is self-evident, and even from a cursory glance it seems likely that here is a historical connection between the two alphabets. The exact nature of this connection will become clear from a detailed analysis of the Ugaritic alphabet.

It is known that in addition to its use in writing Semitic Ugaritic this alphabet was also employed to write non-Semitic Hurrian. This had led

---

[1] On this discovery, see: W.F. Albright, *BASOR*, 118 (1950), pp. 12ff.; 119 (1950), 23ff.; C.H. Gordon, *Orientalia*, 19 (1950), pp. 374ff. A facsimile and photograph of the tablet is given in the last-mentioned publication.

After this article was accepted for publication the following studies appeared: N.H. Tur-Sinai, *Ha-lashon we ha-sepher, Ha-sepher*[2], Jerusalem 1959, pp. 191-194 (in Heb.); Cassuto, *Anath*, pp. 11f. (in Heb.); [English edition, pp. 8-11]; E.A. Speiser, *BASOR* 121 (1951), pp. 17ff. The discussions of Tur-Sinai and Cassuto are of principal importance since they date the 22-letter Canaanite alphabet before the Ugaritic alphabet. This theory permits the possibility of explaining the problem of the alphabet in a completely different manner than has been done until now. Speiser tried to show that $\check{s}_2$ signified the Arabic consonant ḏ, even though this consonant is often written in Ugaritic with d as in later Aramaic. Speiser also tried to clarify the reason why ancient ṯ was kept in the Hebrew alphabet and not $\check{s}_1$[*š*].

[On the partially interrelated problem of the interpretation of the Ugaritic letter *d* and the sixteenth letter of this alphabet and on the occurrences where the sixteenth letter does not represent ḏ, but rather other phonems including perhaps Proto-Semitic *š*, see now: J. Blau, *JAOS* 88 (1968), pp. 523-525. Cf. also J. Blau - J.C. Greenfield, *BASOR* 200 (1970), p. 17].

[2] We employ here the accepted symbols for the Ugaritic alphabet even though it is better to designate ṯ as $\check{s}_1$, $\check{s}_1$ as $\check{s}_2$, and $\check{s}_2$ as z_2 as will become clear further on.

scholars to surmise that several letters which were invented to represent phones found in Hurrian- but not in Ugaritic - were added to the Ugaritic alphabet. This theory now receives decisive confirmation.

The three letters *i, u,* s_2 follow the letter *t* in the Ugaritic alphabet, and it is certain that the three were appended to the Canaanite alphabet which ended in *t*, just as several letters were added to the Greek alphabet following the letter τ. For some time scholars have seen in the plurality of the aleph-signs a clear sign of Hurrian influence on the shaping of the form of this alphabet. Now we may be more exact. It seems probable that the letter a (i.e. *'a*) originally stood for just *'*. Afterwards the letters *i, u* (i.e. *'i, 'u*) were invented and the *'* was restricted to *'a*. S_2 is extremely rare and until now has been found in only eight - apparently non-Semitic - words.[3] After the subtraction of the final three letters of the Ugaritic alphabet we are left with 27 letters. If we then take away the five letters *ḫ* $\check{s}_1$ *[š]* $\check{s}_2$ *[ḏ]* *ẓ* *ġ* we get the Hebrew alphabet without any modification. From the order of the letters it follows that the letters $\check{s}_1$ *[š]* $\check{s}_2$ *[ḏ]* have not been preserved in the Hebrew alphabet, and that from the point of view of the alphabet the Hebrew letter ש corresponds to Ugaritic *ṯ* and not to $\check{s}_1$ *[š]* as was supposed until now.[4] This mistaken view was based on the phonetic correspondence between Ugaritic $\check{s}_1$ *[š]* and the Hebrew letter representing *š* and *ś* since from a phonetic viewpoint Ugaritic $\check{s}_1$ *[š]* corresponds both to Hebrew *ś*[5] and *š* (= Proto-Semitic *š*).[6] On the other hand,

---

[3] See Gordon, *UH, Glossary*, Nos. 27; 297; 317; 428; 766; 950; 1420; 1433. Cf. now in this volume, *The Noun* $ṣ^c r$ *($K^e tib$)* $ṣā^c ir$ *($Q^e re$)*, pp. 249-255.

[4] The lack of alphabetical correspondence between Hebrew ש and Ugaritic $\check{s}_2$ is not surprising since there is no phonetic correspondence between the two letters. $\check{S}_2$ still does not have a clear correspondence in any other Semitic language. Some scholars therefore tend to include it among the Hurrian phonemes. However, this opinion does not fit the place of this letter in the middle of the 27-letter Canaanite alphabet. Gordon has recently suggested that $\check{s}_2$ is a Proto-Semitic phoneme which has become known for the first time from Ugaritic, but Albright disputes this point. Nevertheless, the affinity of this letter to z in the Hebrew alphabet is clear. Cf. $br\check{s}_2 l$ = *barzäl* 'iron'; $\check{s}_2 r^c$ = $z^e ro^{ac}$ 'arm'. Therefore it is preferable to designate this letter by the sign z_2. Contrast now note 1.

[5] E.g. ${}^c\check{s}_1 r$ *[^{c}šr]* = ^{c}äśär 'ten'.

[6] E.g. $\check{s}_1 m^c$ *[šm^c]* = Hebrew and Aramaic $\check{s}m^c$ 'to hear'.

whenever we have Ugaritic ṯ we find Hebrew š.[7] It follows that there is no phonetic correspondence between Ugaritic ṯ and Hebrew ś, but nevertheless Hebrew ś is written with the same graph which was originally used for ṯ. This anomaly suggests the assumption that the Hebrew alphabet was invented by speakers of a Canaanite dialect who did not distinguish between ś and š. The Bible apparently alludes to such a dialect in the story of the Ephraimites who were unable to pronounce š and said *sibbolät* instead of *šibbolät*.[8] Marcus' theory[9] that the Ephraimites did not actually pronounce *sibbolät* (with *s*) but *śibbolät* (with ś)[10] seems probable. This indicates that in the Ephraimite dialect *š*$_1$ *[š]* shifted everywhere to ś, and it seems probable that the same occurred with ṯ. It appears that in just such a dialect ṯ could take the place of *š*$_1$ *[š]*[11]; *[That is to say that in this dialect the opposition between Proto-Semitic ṯ, š and ś had disappeared.]* If we assume that the name of the letter *šin* is ancient[12] then *šin* was originally just *ṯin*, and the possibility of explaining the name of the letter from *šen* 'tooth'[13] is invalid. It is possible that *šin* is simply the word *ṯn* meaning 'two' in Ugaritic, and this meaning fits the form of the letter in the Ca-

---

[7] E.g. *ṯr* = Hebrew *šor*, Aramaic *torā'* 'ox'.

[8] Ju. 12:6.

[9] R. Marcus, *JBL* 60 (1941), p. 149; id., *BASOR*, 87 (1942), p. 39. Marcus rightly states that in ancient Hebrew orthography there was no way of distinguishing between š and ś.

[10] *šibbolät* = Ugaritic *š*$_1$*blt [šblt]*.

[11] According to Harris (Z. Harris, *The Development of the Canaanite Dialects*, New Haven 1939, § 4). the letter *š* (= *š*$_1$) was pronounced in Ugaritic and Phoenician in all cases as š. Friedrich, *PPG*, § 44 correctly argues against him that the spelling *ᶜsr* in the Eshmunezer inscription refutes this assumption.
[The opposition between š and ś does not occur in the reading tradition of the Samaritan Pentateuch since both are pronounced as š.
J. Blau, *On Pseudo-Corrections in some Semitic Languages*, Jerusalem, 1970, p. 44, note 8 considers the possibility that "ṯ might have been used, by pseudo-correction, in additional cases as well instead of original š. Thus, at first, ṯ might have prevailed and, finally, ousted š altogether, taking over its whole function, that is denoting both š and ś". He admits, however, that "Loewenstamm's explanation is simpler."*]*

[12] This assumption is uncertain. Cf. the name of the letter Σιγμα in Greek and the bi-form Σα .

[13] The š in the word *šen* 'tooth' goes back to Proto-Semitic š.

naanite alphabet well.[14]

With regard to the names of the letters of the alphabet, we should recall that from the antiquity of the order of the letters Albright concluded that all (or at least most) of their names were ancient. Proof for this assumption may be found in the restriction of the value of the first letter which strengthens the opinion that the name of this letter in Ugaritic was *alpu* 'ox'.[14a]

We now come to the clarification of the nature of the historical connection between the Ugaritic and Hebrew alphabets. The opinion put forth by Albright and Gordon that the two alphabets are descendants of a 27 - letter Canaanite alphabet except that the Ugaritic alphabet added three letters while the Hebrew alphabet deleted five letters seems probable. Gordon has correctly claimed that we should not reverse our reasoning and see in the Hebrew alphabet the source of the 27-letter Canaanite alphabet. If this were so then the five letters would have been placed at the end of the alphabet after *ṯ* [as the letters added to the Greek alphabet after ταυ] and would not have been scattered throughout the alphabet without any clear reason in the meaning of the letters or in their graphic similarity.

Gordon looks for the reason for the loss of the five letters from the Hebrew alphabet in the phonetic shifts which occurred. The following phonetic shifts took place: *ḫ* > *ḥ*; *š*$_2$ [*ḏ*] > *z*; *ẓ* > *ṣ*; and *ǧ* > ^{c} (On the problem

---

[14] From a phonetic point of view it is possible to derive the name of the letter *š* from the Ugaritic root *ṯ y n* 'urine'. Cf. the *K^{e}tib* in 2 Reg. 18:27, and Gordon, *UH*, p. 77. However, it does not seem likely that a letter would be given such a strange name.

[[14a] W.W. Hallo, *JBL* 78 (1958), pp. 324-338 has explained Is. 28:10 as a description of a school-lesson in which the instructor teaches the children the letters *ṣ* and *q* in their alphabetical order. He concludes from this that the ancient names of these letters were *ṣaw* and *qaw* which were later replaced by the names *ṣade* and *qop*. His proposal however is unconvincing. We may speak of a lesson on the alphabet, but it seems far-fetched to refer to a lesson on *ṣade* and *qop*. Moreover, the name *ṣaw* has the clear meaning 'command' in Hebrew, whereas the name *ṣade* yields no sense whatsoever. It is hardly likely that an established and well understood name would be exchanged for a merely invented and obscure one. The antiquity of the name *qop* is shown by the Greek name *Koppa*. This letter was no longer in existence in classical Greek and was apparently borrowed by the Greek from the Phoenicians together with the rest of the alphabet, i.e. in the eighth century BCE and in any event no later than Isaiah].

of $\check{s}_1$ - *ṯ* > ש, see above). Therefore, the redundant letters were eliminated. This explanation seems probable even though we have some proof for the preservation of the phone *ġ*.[15] For example, the standard transcription of the name *ᶜazzā* in the Septuagint is Γάζα, and to this day the Arabs pronounce the name of the city with *ġ* and not with *ᶜ*. The same applies to many other names such as *ᶜᵃmorā* - Γομοῤῥα etc. Even if we assume that *ġ* was kept in the dialect of Gaza[16], it is possible that it shifted to *ᶜ* in other dialects, and these dialects fixed the new alphabet.

In short, the discovery at Ras Shamra has considerably advanced the study of the development of the Hebrew alphabet from the Canaanite and Ugaritic alphabet. For the moment however the study of the alphabet has come to a dead end until we discover inscriptions in the ancient 27-letter Canaanite alphabet[17] and can clarify where and when the five letters were eliminated from this alphabet. At the moment no Phoenician-Hebrew inscription may be dated prior to the 10th cent. BCE. It is true that there are inscriptions from the 13th - 14th cent. BCE in a Canaanite script. But unfortunately these Proto-Canaanite inscriptions are short and do not contain words which could be written in one of the five letters which differentiate between the two alphabets.[18] It is therefore impossible to decide which alphabet was employed at the time when these inscriptions were written.

There is also an additional problem. Can we find a connection between the graphic forms of the letters in the Ugaritic and Phoenician Canaanite alphabets? The suggestion to see a common origin of the Ugaritic and Canaanite letters is based on the similarity in form of eight letters in Ugari-

---

[15] On the problem of *ḫ* and *ġ* in the Septuagint, see M. Flashar, *ZAW* 28 (1908), pp. 211ff. and for a different view R. Ruzicka, *ZA* 21 (1907/8), pp. 293ff.

[16] And perhaps in the south Judean dialect in general. See EB, s.v. *'arbaᶜ* (in Heb.).

[17] According to a hesitant proposal put forth by Albright the Proto-Semitic inscriptions were written in this alphabet.

[18] E.g., the inscription *šlšt* (Lachish 3, 13th cent. BCE) is not conclusive here. The word would have to have been written in the same way (*šlš* = *ṯlṯ*) in the ancient alphabet also. If instead the text were *bḥmšt*, then we could learn from it that the new alphabet was already in existence (*ḥmš* < *ḫmš*$_1$).

tic (*g*, *h*, *w*, *z*, *i*, s_2, ^{c}, $\check{s}_1$ [*š*]) with the forms of eight letters in Canaanite (*g*, *h*, *w*, *z*, *y*, *s*, ^{c}, *š*).[19] But it is clear that we should only compare the forms of those letters which correspond to each other as far as the alphabet is concerned. From the new discovery it is clear that there is no room to compare the forms of the letters *y*, *s*, *š* in the Phoenician-Canaanite alphabet with the forms of the letters *i*, s_2, $\check{s}_1$ [*š*] in the Ugaritic alphabet. As we have seen Canaanite *y* corresponds to Ugaritic *y* and not to *i*; *s* corresponds to s_1, and not s_2; *š* corresponds to <u>t</u> and not to $\check{s}_1$ [*š*]. We see from this that the similarity between the three letters *i*, s_2, and $\check{s}_1$ [*š*] in the Ugaritic alphabet with the three letters *y*, *s* and *š* in the Canaanite alphabet is purely coincidental, and on this basis we should not come to any conclusions as to the common source of the graphic forms of the letters. This consideration raises the doubt that the similarity between the other five letters is also coincidental.

---

[19] Tur Sinai in *EB*, s.v. *'aläpbet* col. 394 (in Heb.).

The Development of the Term "First" in the Semitic Languages

In the creation story the concluding formula of the first day: "And there was evening and there was morning, one day" (Gen. 1:5) is paralleled by the endings: "And there was evening and there was morning, a second day" (v. 8), "a third day" (v. 13), "a fourth day" (v. 19), "a fifth day" (v. 23), "the sixth day" (v. 31). Thus in every instance the text employs ordinal numbers. Only the first day is indicated by a cardinal number.

In his commentary on the Book of Genesis my late teacher, U. Cassuto, paid attention also to this linguistic phenomenon and explained it as follows[1]: "The use here of the cardinal instead of the ordinal number, as for the other days, is to be explained, with Naḥmanides, as follows: 'First implies precedence over another in number or grading, when both are in existence', but in our case there was only one day, for the second had not yet been created ... But verses like Gen. 2:11: The name of the first literally, 'one' is Pishon compel us to extend the rule of Naḥmanides and to state that even when all the objects enumerated together exist at the same time, we are able, momentarily, to pay attention only to the first object, and to designate it therefore one."[1a]

This explanation which is satisfactory from a logical viewpoint can also explain a parallel phenomenon in Akkadian. In Akkadian the cardinal number *istēn* occasionally indicates the concept "first". It is instructive that we find this usage in a text quite similar to the creation story in its literary structure.

---

1 Cassuto, *From Adam to Noah*, p. 30.

[1a In a note upon the use of *'äḥād* instead of *ri'šon* J. Blau (*Shnaton* 1 [1975], pp. 29-31) points out that this use is more easily understood in the report on the four rivers than in the story of creation since the sequence of the counted rivers is an arbitrary one and it was possible to begin their enumeration with any of them. To Blau's mind it is for this reason that the speaker is inclined to designate the river which he mentions first, with a cardinal rather than an ordinal number.]

We refer to what is related in the Gilgameš Epic that Mount Niṣir held the boat fast (Tablet XI; 141-145). Here too we are confronted with a Seven-day pattern where an action lasts six days until on the seventh day the decisive new event takes place. This framework is stressed in the following words: *ištēn ūma, šanâ ūma ... šalša ūma ribâ ūma ... ḫanša šešša ... sibâ ūma*. 'One day, a second day, a third day, a fourth day ... a fifth, a sixth ... a seventh day'. We may say also for Akkadian that "we are able, momentarily, to pay attention only to the first object and to designate it therefore one".

The prehistory of this phenomenon can be traced back to much earlier periods. Scholars have noted for a long time that the first ordinal number is unlike the others.

Brockelmann in his comparative grammar of the Semitic languages[2] already called attention to the special character of this number. Even if his survey needs to be supplemented today, he must be credited with a presentation of the main points. Brockelmann stated differences between the numbers which express the concept "first" and the other ordinal numbers. 1) The roots of the other ordinal numbers are common to all the Semitic languages, which is not the case with the concept "first" which in the various Semitic languages is derived from different roots having no connection between them; 2) All the other numbers are derived from the same root as the corresponding cardinals, whereas this is extremely rare for the concept "first". In no Semitic language do we find an ordinal number which is derived from the Proto-Semitic root *'ḥd*. There are only two examples of the derivation of an ordinal number from the Proto-Semitic root *ᶜšt*: 1) The form *ištijûm* attested rarely in Old Babylonian[3] and derived from the ordinal *ištēn*; 2) The South Arabian form *ᶜstm* derived from the ordinal *ᶜstn* and appearing once in a Qatabanian text.[4] All the other words which express the concept "first" in the Semitic languages are not connected with the cardinal, e.g., Arabic *'awwalu*, replaced in the ᶜOmān dialect by *qabli*; Ethiopic *qadāmī*, Tigrina *falamāï*, Amharic *fitanā* and *mağammariya*; Aramaic *qadmaya*; South Arabian *qdmn*; and Akkadian *maḫrū* and *panûm* used alongside

---

[2] Brockelmann, *Grundriss* 1, p. 490.

[3] v. Soden, *GAG*, § 70a.

[4] Höfner, *ASG*, §§ 117, 121.

ištēn and *ištijûm*.

In order to explain this linguistic phenomenon we are left with the choice between the following two contradictory assumptions: 1) either that Semitic had a word expressing the concept "first" which for some reason disappeared later on from all or most of the Semitic languages and was replaced by newly created words; 2) or that Proto-Semitic had no word for this concept at all. Logically the second assumption seems more probable. It is hard to understand why the Proto-Semitic root expressing the concept "first" should disappear from the Semitic languages while the ancient roots of the other numerals remain intact. On the other hand we may easily account for the large number of roots employed to express this concept, if we accept the assumption that each language invented its own word for a concept which was lacking in Proto-Semitic.

Fortunately we need no longer rely solely on assumptions in this matter, but we may point to the concrete example of one Semitic language, viz. Ugaritic, which preserved the Proto-Semitic usage and did not possess the concept "first". As is well-known, the same scheme of action which lasts for six days and ends on the seventh has also been discovered in Ugaritic. The schematic framework takes here the following form: *ym wṯn ... ṯlṯ rb*^{c} *ym ... ḫmš ṯdṯ ym ... bšb*^{c} *ymm*[5], or in the abridged form: *ym wṯn ṯlṯ rb*^{c} *ym ḫmš ṯdṯ ym ... špšm bšb*^{c}.[6] As in Hebrew and in Akkadian so also in Ugaritic the days are indicated by ordinal numbers, as proved by the number *rb*^{c} ("Four" in Ugaritic is *arb*^{c}). But we immediately recognize the telling difference between the Ugaritic way of counting and that of the other languages. The first day is indicated just by the word *ym*. This implies that Ugaritic had no need at all to express the concept "first", but counted according to the pattern: "day, a second day, a third day, etc."

This usage apparently has its basis in the primitive thought process. Ancient man did not know ordinal numbers as abstract entities but only when they were attached to objects. When he wished to count similar objects in order, it was sufficient to designate the object which stood at the head of the line by its mere name. Only when he wished to designate the second ob-

---

[5] *CTA* 4: VI: 24-32; 17: I: 6-16; 17:II:32-39; 22B:21-26.

[6] *CTA* 14: 106-108, 114-119.

ject did he feel a need to add an ordinal number to its name in order to distinguish this object from its predecessor. However, with the development of human thought the desire arose to define the place of the object preceding the other objects in the numbered row as well; then - and then only - did the time come to invent words in the various Semitic languages to express this concept.

After this principal discussion we return to the phrase "one day" which was the starting point of our study. It seems that the use of a cardinal instead of an ordinal number is also evidence for the struggle of the language in creating the concept "first". To be more exact: The use of the phrase "one day" for "a first day" stands midway between Proto-Semitic which did not express the concept "first" at all, and the developed language which assigned a special word for this concept. This usage testifies to hesitation of the thought process in conceiving of the first in a series of counted objects as a link connected to what follows.

*[*In the foregoing study we tacitly took for granted that the numbers of the Seven-Day Unit should be regarded as ordinals throughout and consequently treated the second *m* of *ymm* in the phrase *bšb*^{c} *ymm* as enclitic. A closer scrutiny, however, reveals a more involved picture.

As demonstrated by M. Liverani with a high degree of probability, in the phrase *bšb*^{c} *ymm, šb*^{c} is a cardinal number, *ymm* a plural. See in this volume, *The Seven-Day-Unit*, p. 194, note 4a. Nevertheless the preceding numbers are ordinals as borne out by the unequivocally ordinal number *rb*^{c} (not *arb*^{c}!). It is therefore that the two pairs of numbers *t̲lt̲ rb*^{c} and *ḫmš t̲dt̲* are connected with the singular *ym*. (The connection of cardinals between three and ten with the singular of nouns is extremely rare. See in this volume, *The Numerals in Ugaritic*, pp. 318f.). The formula *bšb*^{c} *ymm* is then unique within the framework of the Seven-Day-Unit. This variegation in style serves the patent purpose of throwing into relief the decisive importance of the last day in a climactic pattern. Compare also the formula of the Krt epic *špšm bšbʿ*. Here *šb*^{c} is an ordinal number referring back to the preceding noun *ym* and admits the verbal translation 'on the seventh (day)'. and the task of laying special stress upon the seventh day is fulfilled by the addition of the (adverbial?) expression *špšm.]*

Notes on the Alalakh Tablets

A Comparison of the Alalakh Tablets with the Ugaritic Documents

The proper names contained in the recently published Alalakh Tablets[1] give evidence of a population in which the Hurrian element was predominant. Second in number are names from Asia Minor[2] and of West Semitic extraction, the latter chiefly names of kings. This proportion, which is seen equally in post-Hammurabian documents[3] and in those dating from the 15th century BCE indicates an ethnical continuity only slightly impaired by a few Indo-Aryans in the documents of the 15th century.[4] Their presence is not surprising in a kingdom dependent, as Alalakh was at that time, on the Indo-Aryan dominated Mitanni; it is, moreover, paralleled by the Indo-Aryan names in the roughly contemporary El-Amarna letters.

These facts confront us with a striking similarity between the composition of the population of Alalakh and that of Ugarit[5], as known from documents of the 14th and 13th centuries BCE. In these Ugaritic texts we find exactly the same elements, the only difference being that the western Semitic and not the Hurrian element predominates. We may therefore reasonably conjecture that the ethnic structure of the populations both of Ugarit and Alalakh can be explained as a result of the same migration of peoples. In Ugarit, too, we may assume that the historical processes leading to the union of the three *[rather two]* main elements came to their conclusion not later than the beginning of the period of Hammurabi.

---

[1] D.J. Wiseman, *The Alalakh Tablets*, (in the following Alalakh) London 1953; id., *JCS* 8 (1954), pp. 1-30.

[2] A. Goetze, *ibid.*, pp. 74-81; B. Landsberger, *ibid.*, pp. 56, 120ff.; A. Alt, *ZDPV* 71 (1955), pp. 60-69.

[3] Landsberger, *op. cit.* (note 2), p. 52.

[4] id., *ibid.*, pp. 56f., 129f.

[5] M. Noth, *ZDPV* 65 (1942), pp. 60f.; Landsberger, *op. cit.* (note 2), pp. 56, 129f.

The ethnic resemblance and local proximity between Alalakh and Ugarit raises the question as to what extent the documents from one kingdom are likely to illuminate the other. Further investigation may help us to determine how far the historical background of the two kingdoms is identical.

Of paramount interest is the question already raised of the recurrence of terms denoting social classes in the Alalakh texts of the 15th century and the somewhat later Ugaritic texts. In an Akkadian document from Ugarit a certain ^{awil}*na-mu-û* pays 20 shekels for the manumission of a slave-girl in order to marry her[6] *[*In another document the king of Ugarit invests a man with the heredital possession of a landed agricultural property and imposes upon him the servitude of the *namū*-people in (or to ?) a certain town[6a]*]*. The term *ṣābu namē* occurs frequently in the Alalakh documents.[6b] In one document it stands for *42 ṣābu*^{meš} *ḫu-up-še-na* and *13 māre*^{meš} *ḫania=ḫena*[7], and in another document[8] *ḫupšu* and *namē* are synonymous terms. Obviously the term *ṣābu namē*, unqualified, is synonymous with *ṣābu ḫupšu*.

Similarly the word *ḫupšu*, denoting a social class, is common to both Ugarit and to the Alalakh writings. In the Keret legend *ḫpṯ* and *ṯnn* designate the main, if not the only, units of the king's army.[9] In the Alalakh documents the *ḫupšu* are referred to several times as householders[10], and once as vineyard owners.[11]

There is also a list of *42 ḫupšu* where the note *GUD.NU.TUK*[12], i.e. having no ox, is appended to 13 of the names. This implies that the remaining

---

6 F. Thureau-Dangin, *Syria* 18 (1937), pp. 248, 253ff.

[6a *pīl-ka-ma ša* $^{amil\ meš}$*na-mu-ti [i-na?]* ^{al}*maḫsisi û-bal* (*PRU* 3, RS 16. 148+254B: Verso: 10-11, p. 116)*]*

[6b Wiseman and *CAD, s.v. ṣābu* f 4' render *na-me-(e)*, i.e. *namē*. Contrast v. Soden, *AHW, s.v. namû* I who reads *NA.ME (namû(tu?)* and explains the word: *namû (nawûm - i)* 'in der Steppe wohnend!'*]*

7 *Alalakh*, text 129; cf. text 131 which combines in the total as *ṣābu namē*: *133 ṣābu*^{meš} *ḫupšena 3 māru*^{meš} *ḫaniaḫena*.

8 *ibid.*, text 136.

9 *CTA* 14:II:90-91.

10 *Alalakh*, texts 186, 187, 202.

11 *ibid.*, text 211.

12 *ibid.*, text 136.

ḫupšu mentioned in the list were cattle owners. If we were to add the abovementioned Ugaritic documents concerning the *namē*-people to these documents, Mendelsohn's[13] contention (based on the El-Amarna letters) that the *ḫupšu* were freeborn, householders and landowners, would be fully confirmed.

With reference to the parallelism between *ḫpṯ* and *ṯnn* mentioned above, Albright's identification[14] of the *ṯnn* with the *ša-na-nu* or *ša-na-an-nu* seems well founded, and one can hardly agree with Speiser[15], who repudiated this identification on the strength of the spelling *sa-na-nu-ḫe* in one of the Alalakh documents. In his opinion, the variant spelling testifies that the *š* in the noun *šanannu* derives from Proto-Semitic *š* and not from Proto-Semitic *ṯ*, which would make it impossible to identify the Ugaritic *ṯnn* with the *ša-na-nu* of Alalakh. This nicety, however, is not convincing. *Awil ša-na-ni* are also mentioned[16] in the Akkadian texts from Ugarit and it is difficult to separate the *ṯnn* from the *ša-na-nu* in the Akkadian text of Ugarit on the one hand, and the *ša-na-nu* of Ugarit from the *ša-na-nu* of Alalakh on the other hand. Besides, the information on the *ša-na-nu* from Ugarit tallies with that from Alalakh. At the time when Speiser wrote, Virolleaud[17] had already stressed the fact that the *ṯnn* in a Ugaritic document were mentioned along with the *nqdm*, i.e. the shepherds. This juxtaposition is well understood in the light of the Alalakh tablets. In some of these documents the *ša-na-nu* are mentioned along with the *SA.GAZ*.[18] In one document we learn that both the *ša-na-nu* and the *SA.GAZ* were owners of sheep.[19] Further evidence is afforded by a document in which sheep and asses are mentioned (apparently as a tax paid in kind) in connection with the *ša-na-nu*.[20] One may therefore state with confidence that the *ša-na-nu* as a class (apparently of semi-nomadic origin) made their livelihood by sheep-

---

13 J. Mendelsohn, *BASOR* 83 (1941), pp. 36ff.; cf. also id., *ibid.*, 140 (1955), p. 186.

14 W.F. Albright, *HUCA* 23 (1950/51), p. 25, id., apud Wiseman, *Alalakh*, p. 11, note 4.

15 E.A. Speiser, *JAOS* 74 (1954), p. 21, who points to text 350:9.

16 PRU 3, p. 194, ll. 5-6.

17 Ch. Virolleaud, *Syria* 21 (1940), p. 151.

18 *Alalakh*, texts 183, 226, 350.

19 *ibid.*, text 350.

20 *ibid.*, text 341; cf. text 352.

raising.[20a]

It is, however, more difficult to ascertain from these documents the exact nature of the *ša-na-nu*'s functions in the army. One document enumerates[21] *1006 ṣābu^{meš} ša-na-an-nu 76 GIŠ.GIGIR.ḪI.A*, i.e. 1006 *šananu* warriors and 76 charioteers. The affiliation of the 76 charioteers to the *šananu* class is clear from a parallel text[22]: *napḫar 1006 ṣābu^{meš} ša-na-nu ga-li-ma ù 76 GIŠ.GIGIR^{meš} GIŠ.GIGIR.ḪI.A a-na napḫaru^{meš} la-a i-ru-bu*, i.e. a total of 1006 *šananu* warriors altogether and 76 charioteers not entered in the totals. The last statement is not clear unless we assume that the charioteers belonged to the *šananu* class.[23] It is plain from these facts that only an insignificant minority of *šananu* had anything to do with chariots, while the military function of the majority remains obscure. Furthermore, the Ugaritic parallelism between *t̠nn* and *ḫpt̠* indicates that the noun *t̠nn*, too, fundamentally designates a certain class of civilians and does not mean any specific type of military unit. Albright's[24] and Speiser's[25] explanation of the word as a military unit, the former basing his argument on Semitic and the latter on Hurrian etymology, should therefore be taken with some reserve.

It is hardly necessary to emphasize that the *mariannu* class, a class of warriors prominent in Canaan and Mitanni during the days of the New Egyptian Kingdom[26], is also mentioned in the Ugarit[27] and Alalakh[28] texts.

[[20a] The explanation of the Hurrite hapaxlegomenon *sa-na-nu-ḫe* remains an open question. The change between *s* and *š* in the Akkadian rendering of Proto-Semitic *t̠* is attested so far only in the different spellings of the name *^{c}mt̠tmr* in Ugaritic documents. Consult J. Nougayrol *PRU* 3, p. 239.*]*

[21] *ibid.*, text 183.

[22] *ibid.*, text 226.

[23] Wiseman translates Text 183 as follows: "1006 *šananu* warriors, 76 of whom fight from (or are owners of) chariots". Text No. 226, however, proves that the 76 charioteers are not incorporated in the figure of 1006 *šananu*. Wiseman's translation of *76 GIŠ.GIGIR^{meš}* in text 226 is 76 chariots, whereas a comparison of the two texts shows that the expression is an abbreviation of *ṣābu GIŠ.GIGIR^{meš}* and should be rendered as 76 charioteers.

[24] W.F. Albright apud Wiseman, *Alalakh*, p. 11

[25] Speiser, *op. cit.* (note 15), p. 25.

[26] E. Meyer, *Geschichte des Altertums 2*^{2}, Stuttgart 1928, p. 34

[27] Gordon, *UT, Glossary* No. 1551.

It may be worth while, however, to mention that the Alalakh texts shed additional light on their status, and confirm the conjecture that the larger number of chariots was in the possession of the *mariannu*.[28] There is one text of special interest in which the king confers on somebody hereditary mariannuship, which also entails hereditary priesthood.[28a] This document is paralleled by a text from Ugarit where the king raises a slave to the high status of *mariannu*.[29]

Needless to say, parallels in Ugarit and Alalakh are not confined to social organization. A cursory glance at the Alalakh tablets reveals the names of no less than four Ugaritic kings[30], namely Ammurapi (in Alalakh *Ḫammurapi*), *Niqmepa*, *Niqmadu* and *Iaqarum* (in Alalakh *Iaqaru*), of which the first two are also royal names in the Alalakh tablets. The resemblance between the proper names of the two towns provides a new key to the correct reading of proper names in the Akkadian texts from Ugarit. In one of these texts, Virolleaud[31] identifies the name *I-ši-^{d}ba^{c}alu* with the Biblical name *'äšba^{c}al*, but this transcription overlooks the possibility that the name may be read *I-li(m)-^{d}ba^{c}alu*. It is precisely this latter reading which proves to be correct in the light of the Alalakh tablets, where the name *I-li(m)-i-li(m)-ma*, which is also spelled *AN.AN.ma* and *AN-li(m)-AN-li(m)-ma*, occurs frequently.[32] This alternative spelling proves beyond doubt that it is not possible to transcribe the name *I-ši-i-lim-ma*, and makes it virtually certain that the Ugaritic name, too, should be read *I-li(m)-^{d}ba^{c}alu*.

One comes across similar enlightening parallelism in the language and style of the tablets. The Ugaritic noun *šd* is generally rendered as

---

[28] *Alalakh*, texts 128, 131, 138, 143, 144, 149, 150.

[[28a] *ibid.*, text 15.]

[29] Cl. Schaeffer, *Syria*, 31 (1954), p. 31. In the Alalakh document, too, the newly appointment mariannu may have been a former slave, as perhaps hinted by the formula: *a-na ma-ri-an-na ut-aš-šar-šu*, literally: freed into a *mariannu*.

[30] id., *ibid.*, pp. 35f.; Wiseman, *Alalakh*, pp. 135, 136, 143.

[31] Ch. Virolleaud, *Syria* 28 (1951), pp. 49ff.

[32] Wiseman, *Alalakh*, p. 137. The sign *AN* stands for *ilum* in Akkadian. Attention should also be drawn to the Ugaritic name *idrm* (in Ugaritic cuneiform script). M.D. Cassuto: *World Congress of Jewish Studies*. Jerusalem 1952, p. 138 (in Heb.) proposed the reading *addir(im)*. In view of the name *Id-ri-mi* in the Alalakh Tablets this proposal should be abandoned.

'field' (*šādä(h)* in Hebrew). This interpretation, however, is unsatisfactory in those verses where the word *šd* is parallel to *kmn*.[33] The Ugaritic noun *kmn* has for some time been identified with the word *kumanu* of the Nuzu documents, as a measure of area.[34] As to the word *šd*, Cassuto asserted that it means 'field' in the above verses too.[35] Gordon, on the other hand, while conceding that it is a measure of area on the strength of its parallelism to *kmn*, maintains that it differs from the *kmn* unit. Now, with the discovery of the Alalakh tablets where the words *kumanu* and *šidum* appear as synonymous terms for the same measure of area, the question seems to be finally settled.[35a]

The word *ma-ḫi-zi* in the Alalakh documents provides a further example of the importance of comparing the Alalakh and Ugarit vocabularies. The *ma-ḫi-zi* appear in lists of recipients of rations issued by the palace; the recipients are designated by their calling. Wiseman[36] translates the word as 'sick, wounded', but this is hardly appropriate if the position of the word in the list of craftsmen is considered. The *ma-ḫi-zi* should certainly be identified with the *mḫṣm* of the Ugarit documents[36a], where they appear in the list of craftsmen's guilds.[37] With regard to the calling of members of the *ma-ḫi-zi* guild, attention should be drawn to Virolleaud's remarks on the Akkadian word *māḫiṣu*, which designates both butcher and weaver of flax.

The names of the months *ḫiar* and *pagri* (*ḫyr, pgrm* in Ugaritic)[38], are also common to both Ugarit and Alalakh. This subject, however, cannot be properly treated until a thorough study of the names of the months in both towns is made.

---

[33] Gordon, *UT, Glossary* Nos. 1256, 2386.

[34] Wiseman, *Alalakh*, p. 15, note 2.

[35] Cassuto, *Anath*, p. 139.

[[35a] Cf. M. Dietrich - O. Loretz, *UF* I, pp. 61f., who point to the Babylonian measure of land *šiddum*.]

[36] Wiseman, *Alalakh*, p. 158.

[[36a] Cf. v. Soden, *AHW*, s.v. *māḫisu* who reads in the Alalakh documents *ma-ḫi-si*(!). On the guild of Ugaritic *mḫṣm* see also M. Held, *JAOS* 79 (1959) p. 175.]

[37] Gordon, *UT, Glossary* No. 1456; Ch. Virolleaud, *Syria* 21 (1940), p. 150; id., *ibid.* 28 (1951), pp. 33f., 170.

[38] Ch. Virolleaud, *CRAIBL* 1952, pp. 230f.

A systematic comparison of the legal vocabulary in the Ugarit and Alalakh texts also requires special research. Here too a few remarks on the subject will have to suffice. *[*The following section has been deleted. See instead in this volume, The formula *me^c^attā w^ec^ad ^c^olām*, pp. 166-170*]*.

The analogy between the legal texts of Ugarit and Alalakh is not limited to details of style alone. We also find analogies in the types of legal documents. However, the small number of legal documents from Ugarit so far published compels us to defer analysis and to content ourselves with Nougayrol's[39] statement that the legal phrase *ana pāni X šarri* 'before the king so and so', found in Alalakh documents[40], appears likewise in the Ugaritic texts.[41]

Legal Documents from Alalakh.

Among the Alalakh documents two legal texts from the period of Hammurabi stand out, They are records of lawsuits conducted in the presence of the king. Wiseman's translation of these documents is not sufficiently clear on all points. The first[42] of these documents deals with a case in which a woman by the name of Bittatti claimed a share of part of the property of her brother Abban. After each side has presented its case, the record goes on as follows[43]: *iṣ-ṣa-ab-tu a-na ma-ḫar Ni-iq-mi-e-pa šarrim i-ru-bu-ma ^m^A-bi-a-du ki-ma ^f^Bi-it-ta-at-ti i-na bītim zi-it-tam i-šu-û ši-bu-us-sû ma-ḫar Ni-iq-mi-e-pa šarrim iq-bi-ma um-ma šar-rum-ma i-na bītim^tim^ ^m^Ab-ba-an bītam ša i-ra-am-mu li-is-sû-ûq-ma li-il-qi bītam ša i-zi-ir-ru ^f^Bi-it-ta-at-ti li-il-qi an-ni-tam šarrum iq-bi-ma*. Wiseman translates: 'The matter was taken up (legally) and before Niqmepa the king they went. Abiadu testified that Bittatti had a share in the bequeathed property. His witness before Niqmepa the king spoke: "Thus (says) the king, 'From the property let Abban choose and take the part he prefers and the part which he does not like let Bittatti take." The king spoke (gave judgment) accordingly.'

---

[39] J. Nougayrol, *CRAIBL* 1952, p. 153.

[40] Wiseman, *Alalakh*, p. 17.

[41] E.g. *PRU* 3 16.140:2-3, p. 45; 15.90:2-4, p. 54; 15. 146+161:2-3, p. 58; 16. 133:2-4, p. 59.

[42] *Alalakh*, text 7.

[43] *ibid.*, ll. 13-24.

This translation makes it appear that the witness of a witness pronounced the verdict, which the king afterwards upheld. No such procedure is known in the history of law. The correct translation should read: 'They took the matter up (legally)[44], and before Niqmepa the king they went. Abiadu testified (literally: 'told as his testimony') before Niqmepa the king[45] that Bittatti had a share in the house (or landed property).[46] Thus (said) the king, "Let Abban choose and take the house (or landed property) he prefers and the house (or landed property) which he does not like let Bittatti take", Thus spoke the king.'[47] The structure of the record is logical and clear. It opens by presenting the quarrel of the litigants, adds that the case was brought before the king, brings in the testimony which confirms the complaint of one of the parties, and finally the king's verdict, based on the witness' testimony, is pronounced.

There is another record[48] with a similar structure, as may be seen from the following extract from this document[49]: *V me-tim kaspam [š]a a-li ... i-na* $^{\bar{a}l}$*A-i-ir-ra-še*^{ki} *[ni-i]d-di iz-zab-tu a-na ma-ḫar Ia-ri-im-li-im šarrim i-ru-bu-ma. ki-ma V me-tim kaspum i-na* $^{\bar{a}l}$*A-i-ir-ra-še*^{ki} *la na-du-ú ši-bu-šu-nu iq-bu-ú*. Wiseman renders the text as follows: '(this) 500 (shekels) of silver which ... we had then deposited in Airraše (but) they have taken (it). They came as litigants before Iarimlim the king. That the 500 (shekels) of silver were not deposited in Airraše their witnesses stated'. Only the translation of the formula *izzabtu ana maḫar Iarimlim šarrim iru=buma* in the above text requires correction, in view of its obvious identity with the formula *iṣṣabtu ana maḫar Niqmepa šarrim irubuma*. The translation

---

44 Compare the formula *iṣṣabtu* with Alalakh, text 112:5-6 *it-ti-ka a-na pa-ni šarri di-nam iṣ-ṣa-bat* 'he took the matter (legally) up with you before the king' *[*On the phrase *ṣabātu dīna itti* ... 'to sue somebody' consult *CAD*, s.v. *ṣabātu 8 dinu*. The phrase is attested in Alalakh, Ras Shamra and Nuzi only and may be a loan from Hurrian.*]*. *Iṣṣabtu* should be interpreted as perfect (or Gt) of *ṣabātu [*i.e. as *iṣṣabtu (dina)]*, and not as N. *[*Cf., however, also *ṣabātu* N 'to quarrel' and see *CAD*, s.v. *ṣabātu* 13b*]*.

45 For the construction of object sentences after *kīma* see v. Soden, *GAG* § 177.

46 Cf. E.Y. Kutscher, *JAOS* 74 (1954), pp. 234f.

47 In the Mari documents, too, a sentence starting with *annītam marks* the end of a quotation. Compare, for instance *ARM* 2, text 82:24; 3, text 38:23.

48 Wiseman, *JCS* 8 (1954), pp. 1f.; text *455:21-24.

should therefore read: 'They took the matter up (legally) and came (as litigants) before Iarimlim the king', and not 'but they have taken (it). They came as litigants before Iarimlim the king.'

From the standpoint of the history of the King's Law, Text 17 from the 15th century BCE is of special interest. Here too there is a flaw in Wiseman's rendering, and the document should be read in the light of Landsberger's[50] corrected translation. The contents in brief are as follows: S. had asked for the hand[51] of A.'s daughter (for his son)[52] and he made the betrothal payment in accordance with the edict of Aleppo. Subsequently A. turned into an evil-doer (*bēl-mašikti*) and was put to death and his property was confiscated by the king (literally: came to the palace). S. demands from the king the return of the betrothal payment and gets it.

Is is difficult to guess the crime for which A. was put to death. Nevertheless, it is worth drawing attention to the Idrimi inscription, where the word *mašiktum* stands for political upheavals which compelled Idrimi to flee from the country. This yields material on which to base the conjecture that A. too had been involved in a rebellion against the kingdom for which

---

49 *ibid.*, lines 21-27.

50 Landsberger, *op. cit.* (note 2), note 129, cf. also Speiser, *op. cit.* (note 15), p. 23.

51 Attention should also be drawn to the use of the verb *šâlu* in this document, which indicates 'to ask for the hand of a woman and cf. Elephantine *'nh 'tyt ᶜl [by]tk wš'lt mnk lnšn yhwyšmᶜ šmh 'htk l'ntw* 'I have come to thy house and asked of thee the woman Yehoyishmaˈ (by name) thy sister in marriage' (*BMAP*, text 7:3). The use of the verb *š'l* is also attested by the Biblical phrase *wayyiš'al hᵃmon nāšim* (2 Chr. 11:23). It is true that most scholars follow in Perles' footsteps and correct the text to read *wayyiśśā' lāhäm nāšim*, but the Alalakh and Elephantine documents disprove this emendation. Compare too in this volume, *The formula meᶜattā weᶜad ᶜolām*, pp. 166-170 and the recurrence of a legal formula of the documents of Alalakh, in the Elephantine papyri pointed out in the author's article in *BIES* 20 (1956), p. 15, note 14 (in Heb.) [In this note attention has been drawn to the similarity of the formula of satisfaction *wṭyb lbbn*, which is very common in the Elephantine documents, to *ap-lu li-ib-ba-šu-nu ṭa-a-ab* (*Alalakh*, text 52:16-17) and to *li-ib-ba-ša ú-ṭa-ab-bu* (*CH* § 178). Since then the formula of satisfaction in Ancient Oriental (including Demotic) documents has been made the subject of a comprehensive study by Y. Muffs, *Studies in the Aramaic Legal Papyri from Elephantine*, Leiden 1969.]. See also Kutscher, *op. cit.* (note 46), on the origin of the legal terms found in Hellenistic Egypt.

52 *E.GI.A. šu*, i.e. *kallatušu*, and cf. *CH* § 166.

he was put to death, and the king, in compliance with the law, confiscated his property, but had to pay off the dead man's debts. The same law was practised in Israel, as the story of Naboth testifies.[53] The king, desiring to take possession of Naboth's property, put up false witnesses to accuse Naboth of blaspheming God and the king[54], and had him stoned to death.

[53] 1 Reg. 21:1-16.

[54] *ibid.*, v. 10.

The Cypress as a Symbol of the Life Giving Force

The chief concern of Hosea's prophecy is the severe crisis in God's relationship with His people Israel who trespassed against him and strayed after the Baal. The words of the prophet present the quarrel between God and Israel in all its bitterness. But, as is customary in Biblical books, Hosea ends with words of comfort and pacification. The people return to their God and the Lord receives the penitent with words of love and says, among other things *'äprayim ma-lli ᶜod lāᶜaṣabbim 'ᵃni ᶜāniti wa'ᵃšurännu 'ᵃni kibroš raᶜanān mimmänni päryᵉkā nimṣā'* (Ho. 14:9).

'Ephraim what have I to do any more with idols? I have responded and will regard him. I am as a leafy cypress, from me your fruit is found.'

The metaphor of God as a tree is unique in the Bible and consequently raised difficulties for early and recent scholars alike. The struggles of the early exegesis are attested to in the Syriac translation which reads 'Ephraim shall say' resulting in Ephraim, rather than God, being equated to the cypress. The extra word- *wne'mar* in the Pešitta is an exegetical gloss, which solves one problem, and raises yet another of more serious difficulty: *mimmänni päryᵉkā nimṣā'* makes no sense except in the mouth of God. There is no convincing force, therefore, to Nyberg's suggestion[1] to emend the Masoretic text on the basis of the Syriac version.

Similarly, Ibn Ezra attempted to escape from the metaphor of God as a tree. He writes "*'ᵃšurännu* - I will gaze upon him, setting my eye favourably upon him until I shall see him as a leafy cypress. Don't fear that a cypress bears no fruit because your fruit is found from me." Ibn Ezra then explains the verse as if it were written *'ᵃni ᶜāniti waᵃ'šurännu kibroš ra=ᶜanān* ignoring the *'ᵃni* before *kibroš* and resulting in failure to explain that which is written. There is no evading the question: What is meant by comparing God to a leafy cypress?

Thus far, modern scholarship has offered two solutions to the problem. Harper[2], in his commentary to Hosea, suggests "(the Lord's) shelter and pro-

---

[1] H.S. Nyberg, *Studien zum Hoseabuche*, Uppsala 1935, *ad loc.*

[2] W.R. Harper, *Amos and Hosea*, Edinburgh, 1936, *ad. loc.*

tection of His people are likened to the refreshing shade of the cypress". But this exegesis inserts a foreign idea into the verse which does not even suit the continuation "from me your fruit is found". A different path was followed by Guthe[3] who looked among the other sacred trees of the Bible for the key to understanding our verse. However, his suggestion does not solve the problem in that the cypress is not one of the trees mentioned in the Bible in a cultic context. Not only this, but one would hardly expect that Hosea would compare God with a tree whose holiness is rooted in the detested Canaanite cult and the prophet's complaint proves this: "They sacrifice upon the tops of the mountains, and offer upon the hills, under oaks and poplars and terebinths, because the shadow thereof is good; therefore your daughters commit harlotry, and your daughters-in-law commit adultery." (Ho. 4:13) Harpers's and Guthe's suggestions are, therefore, not borne out by the context, and without support from present knowledge of the significance of the cypress in the ancient Near-East.

The cypress's significance is known to us from one letter among a collection of Assyrian letters[4] which were composed in the last century of the Assyrian Empire, namely in the seventh or at earliest the late eighth century BCE. In one of these letters, a priest of Assyria turns to his king saying ^{iṣu}*burāšu šarru be-li mu-bal-li-ṭu ša nīši ma-a-du-te* 'My lord the king is a cypress, giving life to many people'. The closeness of the Assyrian metaphor to that of Hosea is clear. Just as the Bible drew a comparison between God and a cypress, so the Assyrian letter compares the king to the very same tree. Furthermore, both of the sources juxtapose to the cypress metaphor the idea that the object of the metaphor is the basis of life- a life-giving, fertilizing power. The general intent of our verse therefore becomes clear: "I am the power that gives life and therefore from me your fruit is found".

But, in order to fully understand the prophet we must investigate the roots of the Assyrian imagery and also consider the Babylonian incantation texts which couple every cultic object with a certain divinity. Among these cultic objects appears ^{iṣu}*burāšu* as an incense likened to the fertility

---

[3] D. Guthe, in Kautzsch-Bertholet, *Die Heilige Schrift des Alten Testaments*, 4. Aufl., Tübingen 1923, *ad loc.*

[4] R.H. Pfeiffer, *State Letters of Assyria*, New Haven, Connecticut 1935 n°-318 l. 6.

god Adad[5] - identical in Ugaritic writings to Baal, the god of life. It seems reasonable that the cypress was a symbol of Baal or, more exactly, of his life-giving power. We should add that the symbol is fully understood in the light of the Akkadian medical literature. We learn from this literature that the resin of the cypress and its ashes were the most widespread medicines in the ancient Near-East.[6] The life-giving power of the cypress was not, therefore, an empty imagery, but a fact of life. In the light of these Akkadian sources, Hosea's words are understood exactly. "I am a leafy cypress", says the God of Israel meaning I and not Baal am the life giving force. "From Me your fruit is found" implies that it is the Lord who provides for Israel grain and wine and olive oil (Ho. 2:10) and not Baal who was by many of the people considered to be the giver of the fruit of the earth.

---

[5] H. Zimmern, *Beiträge zur Kenntnis der Babylonischen Religion*, Leipzig 1896, *Ritualtafeln für den Beschwörer (āšipu)* Nr. 27 Col. II.

[6] R.C. Thompson, *A dictionary of Assyrian Botany*, London 1949, p. 258ff.

Review of Cyrus H. Gordon, Ugaritic Manual, Rome 1955

The *Ugaritic Manual* published by Cyrus Gordon in Rome has a long and distinguished history. In 1940 the same author's *Ugaritic Grammar* appeared, being the first attempt to summarize the results of Ugaritic grammatical study. In 1947, Gordon published his *Ugaritic Handbook* which included besides a corrected grammar also a complete collection of all the known Ugaritic texts in Latin transliterations as well as the first dictionary of the Ugaritic texts. It is thus easily understood, that this book was the only publication among the thousands in this field to which every scholar of Ugaritic studies had recourse in his everyday work.

Thus we may say that the *Ugaritic Manual* by the same author is assured the same full attention of the scholarly world. The new book adds to the *Handbook* a selection of texts in Ugaritic cuneiform which permits every student to become quickly accustomed to reading the texts in the original. He also brings in transliteration the few new texts which were published in 1951. In addition the author reworked the grammar and the glossary and was aided in his work not only by the large numbers of new studies, but also by unpublished texts. It goes without saying that his new book will become the main reference work for all those engaged in research of the Ugaritic language, literature, culture, and religion, including all Biblical scholars.

In his new grammar the author assigns a conspicuous place to the most important of the new texts, viz. the tablet containing the Ugaritic alphabet, and comes to conclusions concerning the history of our alphabet.[1] The phonetic section has been greatly expanded and contains many points of detail. Gordon concludes for example, from the interchange of the Caphtorian noun form *ḥkpt* with the alternating form *ḥqpt* that the non-semitic palatal consonant did not exactly parallel phonetically either *k* or *q*, but was a sort of phone midway between them. He immediately puts forth the reasonable hypothesis that we should explain the interchange of the forms *koba*^{c} - *qoba*^{c} in the Bible in the same manner, i.e. that this name is a foreign word in

[1] § 3. A bibliography on this subject may be found in this volume, *New Light on the History of the Alphabet*, pp. 7-11.

Hebrew borrowed from the Philistine language.[2] Less convincing is his hypothesis which establishes the following evolution for Ugaritic *špš* : *šmš* > *šmpš* > *špš*. The author finds support for his opinion in the English name *Sampson* which has its origin in *Samson*[3], to which we may add the Hellenistic name Ἰαμβλιχος from the Semitic name *Yamlik*, as well as the examples collected by Brockelmann, *Grundriss*, 1, pp. 208-209. However, in none of the examples is there assimilation of a nasal consonant to a plosive.[4] Therefore, it is far-fetched to assume this also for *špš*. It thus seems that the Ugaritic noun may only be explained on the basis of the well-known interchange of *m* with the labials.

In the morphology of the noun, Gordon returns to his claim that the suffix -*ā(h)* added to the construct of Biblical phrases, such as *'arṣā(h) k^ena^can* 'to the land of Canaan', belongs to the early stage of Hebrew.[5] However, he did not note the fact that an exact parallel to this phrase is now found in one of the new Ugaritic texts, viz. text 143:2-4 *^crbt špš ṯġrh ršp*. Gordon apparently accepted Virolleaud's interpretation[6]: 'The sun set, Ršp is its gatekeeper', i.e. the sun set while Ršp serves as its gatekeeper. But according to this interpretation the language of the document is awkward. On the other hand, the structure of the sentence is simple and clear if we translate: 'The sun came to Ršp's gate', i.e. the sungoddess entered the temple of Ršp, which testifies to the ceremony of bringing its statue into Ršp's temple, like the similar ceremonies known from Akkadian literature.[7] It does not seem coincidental that this Biblical use of *h* directionis

[2] *Grammar*, 5. 34.

[3] *Grammar*, 5. 25.

[4] Brockelmann, *Grundriss* 1, p. 174, quotes an isolated instance of *mp* > *pp* from the Iraqi Arabic dialect.

[5] *Grammar*, 8. 13.

[6] Ch. Virolleaud, *Syria* 28 (1951), p. 51.

[7] To the term *^crbt ṯġrh*, cf. Akkadian *bāb nīribu* (from the root *erēbu* 'to enter') which refers to temple gates. See on this: E. Unger, *Babylon*, Berlin-Leipzig 1931, pp. 201ff. And cf. also in the Bible: "Enter his gates in thanksgiving" (Ps. 100:4). Further on in this Ugaritic document we should probably read: *wd(!)dm tbqrn* 'and visit him with love'. On these visits which were for the purpose of the *hieros gamos*, see especially: D. van Buren, *Orientalia* 13 (1944), pp. 1ff. On the Ugaritic verb *bqr*, cf. Ps. 27:4 and the phrase *biqqur holim*, 'visiting of the sick', in Mishnaic Hebrew. [On this text see now M. Dietrich - O. Loretz - J. Sanmartín, *UF* 6, pp. 464f. who read 1) *bṯṯ ym ḥdṯ* 2) *ḫyr ^crbt* 3) *špš ṯġrh* 4) *ršp*

is found in one of the few prosaic texts which have come down to us from Ugarit, since in the Bible, too, it only occurs in prose.

In the morphology of the verb Gordon re-iterates his hypothesis that we find in Ugaritic *qatala* alongside *qatila*.[8] However, now he was in the position to add in his glossary a proof for his assumption, viz. the personal name *TUR-^{m}ša-bi-ili* in an Akkadian text from Ugarit, which clearly shows that the perfect of the verb *ṯwb* (Hebrew *šwb*) was pronounced *ṯab* (and not *ṯib* or *ṯeb*).[9]

Gordon's exhaustive grammar is incomplete especially in the section of the vocative[10], in which the author simply repeats what he wrote in the *Handbook* without taking into consideration the brilliant monograph which the late A.D. Singer devoted to this interesting problem.[11]

The Biblical scholar will be thankful to the author for attempting to come to warranted conclusions from Ugaritic to Biblical studies. It is even natural that occasionally he overshot the mark. I refer, for instance, to his attempts to discover also in the Bible (as in Ugaritic) verses in which the preposition *b-* means 'from'.[12] Following this tendency the author interprets, for example, the verse *b^{ec}ebär hayyarden yammā* (Jos. 5:1) as 'from

---

5) *kbdm*(!) *tbqrn*(!) 6) *skn* and translate: *Der Neumondstag des Monats Hjr wurde zu Schanden. Die Sonne ging unter, Ršp war ihr Pförtner. Die Leber überprüfte man. Gefahr.*
We concur with the general tenor of this rendering, take, however, exception to the representation of *Ršp* as gatekeeper of *Špš* which lacks corroboration and stick to our translation: 'came *Špš* into the gate of *Ršp*', i.e. entered the Netherworld. On the identification of *Ršp* with *Nergal*, see J. Nougayrol, *U* 5, p. 57. That is to say that the eclipse of the sun is here explained as the entering of *Špš* into the Netherworld.*]*

[8] *Grammar*, 9.3.

[9] *Glossary* No. 2013 *[*Cf. now A.F. Rainey, *UF* 3, p. 164*]*.

[10] *Grammar*, 12.6.

[11] A.D. Singer, *BIES* 14 (1949), p. 98ff. *[*Cf. idem, *JCS* 2 (1948), pp. 1-10*]*.

[12] *Grammar*, 10.1. *[*Compare now Z. Zevit, *JANES* 7 (1975), pp. 103-112 (with bibliography)*]*.

Transjordan to the sea', but verses such as *b^ec^ebär hayyarden mizr^e^ḥā haššāmäš* (Jos. 12:1) leave no doubt as to the correctness of the accepted explanation: 'in the land which is west of the Jordan'. A further example is furnished by the verse: "or from whose hand have I taken a ransom to blind my eyes *bo*" (1 Sam. 12:3), i.e. to blind my eyes from it. But the text of this verse is in doubt in the light of the Septuagint translation and Ben Sira 46:19[13], and no proof should be adduced from unsure readings.

The glossary is brimming over with new interpretations, arrived at by the author and some of his colleagues in the course of their studies. I shall adduce here only a few examples which are relevant for Biblical research.

The phrase *yṣq baph* found in a text on the treatment of horses has been explained until now as meaning the pouring of a medicine into the horse's nostrils. It has now become clear to the author on the basis of parallel Akkadian texts that this phrase means 'to pour in front of it'.[14] On the basis of this, Gordon puts forth the interesting hypothesis that we should also understand the verse: *yāšimu q^e^ṭorā b^e^'appäkā* 'and burnt offering upon your altar' (Deut. 33:10), as 'they shall put incense before you'. Under *spl*[15] Gordon points to the noun *saplu* which in Akkadian texts from Ugarit refers to very heavy vessels. In this regard, we should mention the study of the late Prof. Sukenik who was the first to claim that we should not interpret the noun *sepäl* in the Bible as 'cup'.[16] Under *šyt*[17] Gordon - following Virolleaud - translates the end of a new letter: *aṯr iṯ bqṯ wštn ly* 'What is seek and put it to me = investigate the situation and put findings in a letter to me'. If this interpretation is substantiated by the publication of the full letter, this text will strengthen the unsure hypothesis that the Hebrew conjunction *'^a^šär* should be connected with Aramaic *'tr*.[17a]

---

13 Cf. e.g. R. Gordis, *JNES* 9 (1950), p. 44ff., who reads *kopär w^e^na^ca^lam* (i.e. a bribe) *^c^änu bi*.

14 *Glossary* No. 184; Cf. *Grammar*, 10.4, note 1.

15 *Glossary* No. 1352.

16 See E.L. Sukenik, *PEQ* 1940-1941, pp. 59ff. See also the inscription of Shalmaneser on the tribute of Jehu, quoted in *ANET*, p. 281.

17 *Glossary* No. 1826.

[17a But cf. now A.F. Rainey, *UF* 2, pp. 160-162 who proved that *aṯr* should be translated 'everywhere'.]

Because of the difficult problems which are connected with the study of the Ugaritic vocabulary, there is room here and there for criticism of the author's explanations. The noun *plṯt*[18] is explained as 'wallowing' in accordance with the prevalant interpretation of the Biblical phrase *hit=palleš b*^{ec}*āpār*. However, already the late Prof. Cassuto[19] and Driver[20] showed that there is no sense in the strange assumption that the mourner wallowed in the dust, and they proved that the root *plṯ* (Hebrew *plš*) refers to pouring dust upon the head. The author explains the noun *dqn*[21] everywhere as 'beard'. But, the late Prof. Cassuto already realized that this explanation did not fit the phrase *šbt dqn*, and noted that it was perhaps better to explain *dqn* here as 'old age'.[22] This suggestion is confirmed by a study of Biblical expressions. There is not one verse in the Bible which connects the root *śyb* with *zāqān* 'beard'. On the other hand, there are clear examples of the connection of the root *śyb* with the root *zqn* in the meaning 'old age'. The noun *śebā* is parallel to *zāqen* (Lev. 19:32) and also to *ziqnā* (Is. 46:4; Ps. 71:18). The verbs *zāqanti wāśabti* (1 Sam. 12:2) form a word pair. Cf. also *wah*^{a}*dar z*^{e}*qenim śebā* (Pr. 20:29); *b*^{e}*śebā ṭobā zāqen w*^{e}*śābe*^{ca} (Gen. 25:8). These examples prove clearly that the Ugaritic phrase *šbt dqn* should be translated as 'hoary old age'. It is not the hoariness of his beard which afflicts Il and makes him wise, but the hoariness of his old age.[23] Gordon rightly notes that it is sometimes difficult to distinguish between the forms of the verb *ṯwb* and *yṯb*.[24] In this respect also not all of the possibilities inherent in the comparison of Ugaritic and Biblical phraseology have been utilized. In the Baal epic, Il says after the resurrection of his son: *aṯbn ank wanḫ wtnḫ birt npš*.[25] According to Gordon: 'I will dwell and I will rest, and my soul will rest within me' (literally 'in my breast'). But the same combination of roots recurs in the Karatepe inscription in which Azitawadda boasts that in his

---

[18] Glossary No. 1547.

[19] U. Cassuto, *Tarbiz* 12 (1941), pp. 179 *[= BOSt* 2, p. 164*]*.

[20] G.R. Driver, *Biblica* 35 (1954), pp. 167ff.

[21] *Glossary* No. 503.

[22] Cassuto, *Anath*, p. 86.

[23] Text 51:V:65-66.

[24] *Glossary* No. 878.

[25] Text 49:III:18-19; cf. also 2 Aqht: II:12-14.

time there was in the land *šbt n*^{c}*mt wnḥt lb*.[26] A short form of this phrase is found in the Book of Isaiah as well "*b*^{e}*šubā wānaḥat* you will be saved" (Is. 30:15), where the prophet's phrase is simply an abbreviated form of the Phoenician one. From this it is clear that we should translate in the Karatepe inscription: 'in pleasant withdrawal and comfort of heart', and in the Ugaritic poetical text: 'I will return and rest'.[26a] The author retains in the *Manual* his well-known opinion that Ugaritic has a verb *prr*[27] which means 'to flee'. This verb occurs in the Aqht epic, where his father Dnil asks Baal to repair the broken wings of the eagles, and adds to his request: *nšrm tpr wdu*[28] 'eagles ... and soar'. But the context requires here a verb synonymous with *d'y* 'to soar', and therefore Ginsberg translated 'flutter'.[29] This explanation is confirmed in the light of the verse in the Baal epic: *širh ltikl* ^{c}*ṣrm mnth ltkly npr[m]*[29a] 'his flesh (or his remnant?) the birds will eat, his portion ...'. Ullendorff devoted a special study to *npr*[30] in which he explained *npr* by the parallelism with ^{c}*ṣrm* (= birds), in the sense 'bird', and he supported his explanation from Tigrina in which the root *npr* refers to any flying movement. From this we may conclude that the word *pr* should be derived from the verb *npr*, which is related to the noun *npr* as the Hebrew verb ^{c}*wp* 'to fly' is related to the Hebrew noun ^{c}*op*

---

26 Karatepe inscription II:7-8.

[26a The same texts have been compared by M. Dahood, *CBQ* 20 (1958), pp. 41-45, who concludes that all are expressions of sitting, including the noun *šūbā* which he derives from the root *yšb*. Dr. Y. Avishur has pointed out to me that Dahood's proposal is corroborated by the pair of roots *yšb* and *nu*^{a}*ḥ* in Ps. 132:14 and by Akkadian *šubat neḫti(m) šūbu=bam* Wohnung der Ruhe wohnen lassen (v. Soden, *AHW* s.v. *neḫtu*), Cf. also Ugaritic *nḫt* as an epithet of the throne. Nevertheless and in spite of a certain similarity between Hebrew *šūbā* (with a long vowel) and Akkadian *šubtu* (with a short vowel) I prefer to derive *šūbā* from *šwb* and to differentiate between two homonymous roots *šwb* 1) return, 2) sit, a by - form of *yšb*. Cf. *w*^{e}*šabti b*^{e}*bet YHWH* 'I shall sit in the house of YHWH' (Ps. 23:6). This *šwb* II may also be recognized in: *uwnuho yo'mar šubā YHWH*. 'And when it rested he said sit YHWH' (Nu. 10:36).]

27 *Glossary* No. 1531.

28 1 Aqht: 119-120; cf. ibid., ll. 133-134.

29 H.L. Ginsberg, *ANET*, p. 154.

29a [Text 49:II:35-37].

30 E. Ullendorff, *Orientalia* 20 (1951), pp. 273-274.

'bird'.[31] In the entry *dll* II[32], Gordon limits himself to the short note: "// ^{c}*dd*. cf. *dalilu*". The meaning of this Akkadian noun, which according to von Soden[33] is '*Huldigung*', i.e. praise, which contains the acceptance of the yoke of a king or a god should have been mentioned. This connotation fits the text.[34] It means that Baal, who refuses to surrender to Mot declares that he will not send to his rival *dll*, i.e. a declaration of surrender. When Baal finally surrenders, his messengers inform Mot in the name of their master: "I am your servant forever."[35] In the entry *kll*[36] Gordon brings the word *kl* which means 'every(body), without discussing the difficult phrase *il klh*. This phrase is found twice: 1) In the ^{c}*nt* epic: *idk al ttn pnm ḥqpt il klh kptr ksu ṯbth* etc.[37] 'Do not place (your) face forwards *ḥqpt* ... Caphtor is the seat of his dwelling etc.' The continuation of the story makes it clear that *il klh* here is simply epithet of the god *Kṯr-wḫss*, the friend of Baal, his architect and craftsman. The late Prof. Cassuto already suggested identifying this epithet of *Kṯr-wḫss* with the name of the Sumerian god *Kulla* who served in Mesopotamia as the architect of the palace of the gods[38]; 2) The phrase *il klh* recurs in the Baal myth in the story of ^{c}*ṯtr*. After the death of Baal, Il and *'ṯrt* (i.e. Ashera) made the despotic ^{c}*ṯtr* king instead of Baal. The new king went up on Baal's throne in the North. However, his legs did not reach the footstool, and his head did not reach the upper edge of the throne. Therefore, he proclaimed that he would not reign in the northern reaches, and descended from Baal's throne. The portion of the story which is preserved ends with

---

[31] Perhaps we should connect here the verse in the thanksgiving Scroll: *bht^{c}wpp kl ḥṣy šḥt l'yn ḥšb wyprw l'yn tqwh*. 'when all the arrows of the netherworld flew not to be returned and they ... without hope'. (E.L. Sukenik, *Oṣar hamegillot hagenuzot*, Jerusalem, 1955, pl. 37, l. 27; cf. also *ibid*. pl. 36. However, see: H. Yalon, *Kirjath Sepher*, 26 (1950), p. 243, who connects *wyprw* with the Aramaic root *pr'* 'to run'.

[32] *Glossary* No. 478.

[33] v. Soden, *GAG*, § 551.

[34] Text 51:VII:45-47. *[For other interpretations of dll see de Moor, Seasonal Pattern, p. 168.]*

[35] Text 67:II:12.

[36] *Glossary* No. 915.

[37] ^{c}nt VI:12-15.

[38] Cassuto, *Anath*, p. 89.

the words: *wymlk barṣ il klh.*[39] According to the accepted interpretation, this means that ^{c}*ṯtr* reigned in the whole land of Il. But there is no reason to suppose that ^{c}*ṯtr* reigned in the whole land after he himself realized that he lacked the required stature and descended from the throne. Therefore, the following explanation presents itself: 'and in the land reigned the god (whose name is) *Klh,* i.e. the god *Kṯr-wḫss,* Baal's companion, who replaced Baal after the failure of ^{c}*ṯtr*. This also sheds new light on what Philo of Byblos records concerning Χουσωρ, viz. *Kṯr-wḫss,* i.e. *il klh,* that he is also called Ζεὺς μειλίχιος[40], i.e. Zeus who does good deeds. In Philo of Byblos, Zeus is simply Ba^{c}l whose place was temporarily filled by *il klh.*

The noun[41] *šd // kmn* is explained by Gordon as a land measure differing from the *kmn*. However, in the Alalakh Tablets, the words *kumanu* and *šidum* are synonyms for the same land measure[42], and this proves that these two words should be explained in Ugaritic too as synonyms.

In his reworking of the glossary the author increased the number of comparisons with the other Semitic languages, but there is still room for interesting additions. In the entry *uzr*[43] the author translated simply 'food or drink offerings', without mentioning the Punic noun **'zrm*[44], which is found in the spelling ^{c}*zrm* in a Neo-Punic inscription with an accompanying Latin translation: *'dr* ^{c}*zrm - prae[fectus] sacr[orum]*[45], i.e. the one appointed over the holy offerings.[46]

---

[39] Text 49:I:37. *[*On the god Kulla and the writing of his name in Ugaritic cf. also J. Blau - S.E. Loewenstamm, *UF* 2 (1970), p. 33, on the use of il as determinator before the name of a god J. de Moor, *ibid.*, p. 226*]*.

[40] Eusebius, *Pr Ev,* I:10:11-12.

[41] *Glossary* Nos. 929, 1809.

[42] Wiseman, *Alalakh,* p. 15. See now M. Dietrich - O. Loretz, *UF* 1, pp. 61-62.

[43] *Glossary* No. 89.

[44] See J.G. Février, *Journal Asiatique,* 143 (1955), p. 15.

[45] Leptis 4. See: Friedrich, *PPG,* § 277.

[46] Février, *loc. cit.* (note 44), cautiously suggests translating the Punic word as *'agneau'*. But the Ugaritic texts and the neo-Punic text Leptis 4, all unknown to him, contradict his proposal.

To these notes I would like to add a basic request for the plan of a new edition. Every scholar of Ugaritic would be thankful to the author if he would append to his book a list of the Ugaritic words which have come down to us only in Akkadian transcription. The importance of such a list for the study of the Ugaritic personal names needs no explanation. But even other Ugaritic words are apt to be found in Akkadian texts. We may mention here as an example the phrase *aweli marziḫi* found in an Akkadian contract from Ugarit[47] which testifies to the existence of a (non-Akkadian) institution of the *mrzḥ* at Ugarit.

It is in the nature of a review that the subjects on which the reviewer is in disagreement with the author are highlighted. Therefore, the reviewer occasionally must correct the negative impression. However, with regard to a basic book like that of Gordon's, this is unnecessary. One may disagree on one point or another, but, in general, this is a valuable tool in the hands of every Ugaritic and Biblical scholar.

---

[47] Ch. Virolleaud, *Syria* 28 (1951), p. 173ff.

Review of A. Goetze, The Laws of Eshnunna.

AASOR, 31. New Haven, 1956. X - 197 pp. 4 Plates, Glossary, Autographs.

When Goetze first published in 1948 the laws of Eshnunna[1], found at Tell Abu Ḥarmal, a small site on the outskirts of Baghdad, their importance for research into old Oriental law was immediately recognized by competent scholars. The lively discussion which followed the publication of the laws has now been critically summed up by Goetze in the last volume of *AASOR*, which will remain for many years to come the basis of all discussion in this field of research. The new publication contains everything necessary for a ready and thorough study of the texts: photographs and autographs of the tablets, their transliteration and translation, detailed philological and legal notes, and a complete glossary.

The book is introduced by general remarks illustrating the historical background of the laws. Tell Abu Ḥarmal turned out to have been a small rural outpost of the Old Babylonian kingdom of Eshnunna, destroyed by Hammurabi in the 31st year of his reign. The town flourished between the end of the third dynasty of Ur and Hammurabi. In a detailed discussion of the two copies of the law found, Goetze reaches the conclusion that tablet B belongs to the age of Dadusha, king of Eshnunna, who reigned a generation before Hammurabi, whereas tablet A is somewhat older. The archetype from which both remains were derived already contained some corruptions, which presupposes the existence of still older copies. The law is therefore considerably older than Codex Hammurabi (*CH*), which it antedates close to 200 years.[1a]

In this review we cannot give an account of the philological and legal problems raised by the study of these laws, and will therefore confine ourselves in the main to an indication of its importance for the study of old

---

* I wish to thank Prof. E.A. Speiser, who read a proof of this review, for his helpful remarks.

[1] A. Goetze, *The Laws of Eshnunna, Sumer* 4 (1948), pp. 63-102, Pls. I-IV.

[[1a] We cannot be sure about the exact time when these laws were issued. Anyhow, they precede *CH*. See R. Yaron, *The Laws of Eshnunna*, Jerusalem 1969, pp. 1-2].

Oriental law in general and Biblical law in particular, by picking out some striking examples.

The Laws of Eshnunna (hereinafter to be called *LE*) begin significantly with a list of prices of basic commodities - barley, oil, wool, etc. (§§ 1, 2) - which are apparently meant to be maximum prices. They continue with wage and hire tariffs (§§ 3, 4, 7-11). We know from our own experience that it is easier to proclaim than to enforce prices, and we are regrettably unaware how these laws worked in practice, but they admirably typify the Old Babylonian desire to bring economic life under close and all-embracing control, an ideal utterly foreign to Biblical law. *CH* does not reveal this tendency with the same clarity, as it contains only wage and hire tariffs (§§ 215-217, 221-224, 228, 234, 239, 242, 243, 257, 258, 268-272) and there are no lists of commodity prices. We have only a hint in *CH* § 51, which obliges the moneylender to accept from a moneyless debtor grain instead of money, at rates fixed by royal ordinance. But we may conjecture that such ordinances generally fixed the prices of basic commodities, for, as Goetze points out for *LE*, only the fixed prices of commodities set the economic standard by which the wages decreed can be evaluated.

The well-known tendency of Babylonian law to obviate any unclear legal situation is evident in *LE* too. A case in point is *LE* § 27: 'If a man takes a man's daughter without asking the permission of her father and her mother(!) and concludes no formal marriage contract with her father and her mother, (even) though she may live in his house for a year, she is not a "housewife".' § 28 adds immediately that if such a contract is concluded, the wife is liable to the death penalty if caught in adultery. *LE* §§ 27, 28 are paralleled by *CH* §§ 128, 129. But *CH* § 129, which deals with adultery, does not expressly refer to the marriage contract, and therefore the connection between the two paragraphes is less evident in *CH* than in *LE*.

The same marked tendency found in family law prevails in commercial law as well. *LE* § 40 runs: 'If a man buys a slave, a slave girl, an ox or any other valuable goods but cannot prove who is the seller, he is a thief'. That is to say that the buyer of a valuable stolen object is liable to be punished for theft if he cannot bring witnesses to prove the identity of the seller to the court's satisfaction. Goetze correctly points to the affinity of this paragraph with the widely-discussed *CH* § 7, which decrees: 'If a man buys silver or gold or a slave or a slave girl or ox or sheep or anything else from a free man (*mār awīlim*) or a free man's slave, or has them received for safe custody without witnesses and written contract (signed by witnesses), that man is a thief; he shall be put to death'. Koschaker[2], in an incisive analysis of this paragraph, reached the bold conclusion that it postdates an older Babylonian law which omitted all mention of the deposit and contented itself with proof by witnesses without requiring proof by written document. Hammurabi interpolated the reference to a deposit and the excessively rigid requirement of a written document. This latter stipulation rendered the old law nugatory, as nobody could be expected to draw up a tablet when buying an object of small value. This was the point that aroused the opposition of Rabinowitz[3] and Miles[4], who argued against Koschaker that we cannot impute to the Babylonian lawgiver such an impracticable ruling. They proposed to translate *mār awīlim* by 'the son of a free man', i.e. a minor. Rabinowitz adduces in corroboration of his view a Talmudic law[5] which forbids the acceptance of deposits from wives, slaves and minors. Miles cites the Gortynian Code[6] which forbids a man to receive the property of a father by way of sale or pledge from his son, and even *LE* §§ 15, 16 which prohibit certain financial transactions with slaves. These parallels are not convincing. Neither Rabinowitz nor Miles[7] was in a position to point to a law which, while allowing the acquisition of goods from slaves and minors,

---

[2] P. Koschaker, *Rechtsvergleichende Studien zur Gesetzgebung Hammurapis*, Leipzig 1917, pp. 73-84.

[3] J.J. Rabinowitz, *Section 7 of the Code of Hammurabi in the Light of a Legal Proposition in the Talmud, BIES* 16 (1951), pp. 26-28 (in Heb.).

[4] G.R. Driver & J.C. Miles, *The Babylonian Laws*, Oxford 1952, pp. 82-86.

[5] Bab. Talmud, Baba Batra 51 b.

[6] J. Kohler & E. Ziebarth, *Das Stadtrecht von Gortyn*, Göttingen 1912, pp. 12-15, VI:2-7.

[7] It should also be pointed out that *lex Gortynia* forbids only the purchase from a son of the property of his father who is still alive, but concedes to the son *expressis verbis* the right to sell his own property to whomever he wishes. This law moreover states that the father, too, is not entitled to dispose of the property of his children (*ibid.*, ll. 7-9).

requires in these cases a special legal form. The view of Koschaker, on the other hand, has been strikingly confirmed by *LE* § 40, which actually contains the Old Babylonian law whose existence he surmised. We should, however, add that *CH* § 7 is not so impracticable as the above-mentioned scholars supposed, since the words 'anything else' refer in the light of *LE* § 40 to valuable goods only, which are comparable to the goods enumerated in *CH* § 7 *expressis verbis*.

The paragraphs of *LE* discussed above show a close affinity to *CH*, whereas Eshnunna's laws concerning bodily injury are very different from *CH*. The subject will be easier to understand if we begin with a brief glance at Biblical law. The Biblical principle of an eye for an eye, a tooth for a tooth has long been denounced as archaic, inhuman and cruel, as opposed to the progressive and humane Talmudic law which replaces bodily mutilation by fine. When the law of Hammurabi was discovered, scholars were not surprised to find the archaic principles of Biblical law again in *CH* §§ 196, 197, 200, which antedate Biblical law by hundreds of years. But they were astonished to detect that the corresponding paragraphs of the still older *LE* (§§ 42-48) were in accordance with the modern and progressive principles of the Talmud. In the meantime a fragment of the code of Urnammu, founder of the third dynasty of Ur, had been published[8] and this old Sumerian law, which antedates *LE* by some hundreds of years, likewise fixes fines for bodily injuries (§§ 16-18). It may therefore be regarded as an established fact that in Mesopotamian law the *jus talionis* was an innovation of *CH*, which partially superseded the old Sumerian principle of fine. It superseded fine in cases of injury upon an *awīlum*, a fully free man, while retaining fine in the laws concerning injuries inflicted upon a *muškēnum*, a dependent man (§§ 198, 201) and upon a slave (§ 199). *CH* apparently deemed it intolerable that a rich man should be in a position to mutilate his fellow-citizen wilfully and then get away with a mere fine. Even today the ethical and progressive character of such a law should not be left unquestioned. Goetze remarks that the archaic principle of jus talionis has been replaced in *LE* by fines. The opposite seems to be the case. *LE* simply retains the old Sumerian principle of fines for bodily injury, whereas *CH* replaces it in part by the prin-

[8] S.N. Kramer, *Ur-Nammu Law Code, Orientalia* 23 (1954), pp. 40-51, see esp. p. 48; *[*J.J. Finkelstein in *ANET*[3], p. 524, §§ 15-19*]*.

ciple of bodily retaliation, perhaps under the influence of the West Semitic class of conquerors to which Hammurabi belonged (so B. Mazar).[8a] In his detailed survey of the laws of bodily injury in the ancient East, Goetze puts forward a rather surprising interpretation of the Biblical principle (*näpäš taḥat näpäš*); in his opinion it means 'a nose for a nose'. According to Goetze *näpäš*, usually translated soul, was originally breathing organ > breath, cf. Acc. *napištu*, 'throat and soul'. It is hardly necessary to point out that in Hebrew (and Ugaritic) too *näpäš* means throat or soul and not nose.

The close connection between Biblical law and *CH* as against *LE* does not mean that parallels between *LE* and the Bible are lacking. *LE* § 13 distinguishes between a thief who comes in the daytime and a thief in the night: the former is liable to a fine whereas the latter may be killed if caught. Goetze correctly remarks that Ex. 22:1-2 is based on the same principle, viz. that unlawful entry in the night places a man outside the rules governing manslaughter. Another parallel pointed out by Goetze is to be found in *LE* § 26, which prescribes the death penalty for a man who forcibly deflowers a virgin for whom another man has already paid the bride-price. The apparent affinity of this law with *CH* § 130 and with Deut. 22:25-27 is striking. Compare in this volume, Review of R. Yaron, *The Laws of Eshnunna*, pp. 385-387.

According to Goetze's translation, which is probable but not absolutely certain, *LE* § 25 illustrates the relations between Jacob and Laban, as it apparently refers to a father-in-law who takes his son-in-law into bondage so that the latter may work off the equivalent of the bride-price.[8b]

The best-known and most striking parallel to Biblical law is the law of the goring ox, which we would like to quote in full. § 53: 'If one ox gores a(nother) ox and causes its death, both ox owners shall divide (between them) the price (realized from the sale) of the live ox and the value *[read instead of value, 'carcass'. See Yaron op. cit. (note 1a), pp. 48-49]*

[[8a] The first to sense this problem of legal history was A.S. Diamond, *The Evaluation of Law and Order*, London 1951, pp. 288ff.; cf. also idem, *Iraq* 19 (1957), pp. 151ff.*]*.

[[8b] Contrast R. Yaron, *op. cit.* (note 1a), pp. 123-128*]*.

of the dead ox'. § 54: 'If an ox is known to gore habitually and the ward authorities have had (the fact) made known to his owner, but he does not have his ox dehorned(?), it gores a man and causes (his) death, then the owner of the ox shall pay 2/3 of a mina of silver'. § 55: 'If it gores a slave and causes (his) death, he shall pay 15 shekels of silver'. *LE* § 54, 55 are paralleled by *CH* § 251, 252. There is no parallel in *CH* to *LE* § 53. On the other hand, we find in *CH* § 250 the additional provision that the owner of an ox which is not known as a gorer is free from responsibility, if the ox kills a man. The affinities between these laws and the laws in the book of Covenant are obvious. All the three laws make a distinction according to whether the owner of the goring ox was officially warned or not. The owner of an ox not known as a gorer is free of any liability, as expressly stated in *CH* § 250 and Ex. 21:28. The same ruling is implied in *LE*, which never includes cases where there is no punishment, as Goetze remarks. When the owner has been warned beforehand, his punishment is a fine in *LE* § 54 and *CH* § 250, while in Ex. 21:29 it is the death penalty.[9] But the Biblical law adds in Ex. 21:30 that the death penalty may be converted into a fine, a conversion expressly forbidden in the event of murder (Nu. 35:31). We may conclude that the Hebrew law only hesitatingly deviated from the old established rule of imposing a fine in this case. If a slave is killed, Ex. 21:32 imposes a fine in accordance with the principles laid down in *LE* § 55 and *CH* § 252. The Book of Covenant goes on to deal with the owner of an ox not known as a gorer which kills another ox (Ex. 21:35), in striking conformity with *LE* § 53.[10] *CH* lacks a ruling for this case, but we should

[9] It appears from *LE* that the law of the goring ox whose owner has been warned by competent authorities, emanates from a more general principle which imposes upon the authorities the duty of warning the owner of any dangerous object. This warning in effect lays upon the owner a responsibility which otherwise does not exist. Cf. *LE* §§ 56, 57, dealing with the punishment of the owner of a vicious dog and of a wall threatening to fall, who failed to take the necessary precautions though officially warned. In *CH* and the Book of Covenant, only the case of the goring ox has survived.

[10] D. Daube, *Studies in Biblical Law*, Cambridge 1937, pp. 85-88, has drawn attention to the fact that the Biblical laws of the goring ox are interrupted by the law of the pit (Ex. 21:33-34) and has denounced the law of the ox-killing ox as a late addition. As corroborative evidence he cites the *CH*, which contains laws about a man-killing ox without mentioning the ox-killing ox. His argument, now definitely refuted by *LE*, displays two faults of method: (1) The law of the pit mentions the death of an ox through falling into the pit. The principle of loose association of

not conclude that the principle was foreign to legal practice in Babylon. Like all old Oriental laws, *CH* cannot claim to be a complete compendium of the principles behind the law and the astonishing agreement between *LE* § 53 and Ex. 21:35 makes it most probable that they reflect common Oriental law.

The last Biblical provision dealing with a habitually goring ox which kills another ox (Ex. 21:36) has no parallel whatever in Mesopotamian laws. But as it is definitely proved that the Mesopotamian law distinguished between a habitual and a non-habitual gorer, the distinction must have been in force equally in the case of an ox killing another ox. Furthermore it is obvious that the ruling given in the case of the less dangerous ox (viz. the even division of the loss between the owners of the two oxen) does not make sense in the case of a habitual gorer, whose owner should bear the entire loss and be liable to some kind of fine. For all these reasons we may conjecture that the law of Ex. 21:36 also reflects old Oriental tradition. The only basic difference between the Biblical and Mesopotamian rulings is to be found in the actual legal responsibility of the ox who kills a man (Ex. 21:28, 29). This responsibility of the ox conforms to the principle: 'And surely your blood of your lives will I require: at the hand of every beast will I require it' (Gen. 9:5). It goes without saying that the religious cast of thought reflected in the legal responsibility of beasts is quite foreign to the secular spirit of Mesopotamian law.

To this general survey we may add a few words of criticism. As is well known, the translation of many words in *CH*, which was discovered in 1902, is still open to discussion. It is hardly surprising that the same applies to *LE*, discovered only in 1948. We venture here to propose a new translation of §§ 19, 21, both of which belong to the laws of loan (§§ 18A-21). As all the laws of loan in *LE* form a logical unity in which one paragraph completes and explains another, we shall cite them all in the translation of Goetze, adding the Babylonian text in §§ 19, 21, for which we shall propose a new interpretation.

---

thoughts underlying the order of Biblical laws fully justifies the placing of the law of the pit between the laws of the goring ox. (2) The fact that the law of the ox-killing ox is not contained in *CH* does not prove that this law was not in existence at that time.

§ 18A: 'Per 1 shekel (of silver) he (the debtor) will add one sixth of a shekel and 6 grains as interest; per 1 kor (of barley) he will add 1 (pan) and 4 seahs of barley as interest.' § 19: *awîlum ša a-na me-eḫ-ri-šu i-na-ad-di-nu i-na maškanim*^{nim} *u-ša-ad-da-an*. According to Goetze: 'A man who lends out (valuta) in terms of his retake shall be made to pay (his debt) on the threshing floor.' § 20: 'If a man lends out money to the amount recorded, but has the corresponding amount of barley set down to his credit, he shall at harvest time obtain the barley and its interest, (namely) 1 (pan) (and) 4 seahs per 1 kor'. § 21: *šum-ma awîlum kaspam a-na pa-ni-šu id-di-in kaspam u ṣibat-su 1 šiqlum šadištam ù [6 utteti] i-le-eq-qe*. According to Goetze: 'If a man lends out money in terms of its initial (amount), he shall obtain the silver and its interest, (namely) one sixth (of a shekel) and 6 grain per 1 shekel.'

Upon § 18A Goetze comments correctly: 'The rate of interest set by § 18A is 1/6 shekel - 6 grains, or 36 grains, of silver on the shekel of 180 grains, i.e. 20 per cent, and 1 pan - 4 seah or 100 qa of barley on the kor of 300 qa, i.e. 33 1/3 per cent.' In § 19 Goetze makes the money-lender repay the debt on the threshing floor. But it can scarcely be doubted that it is the debtor who has to repay the loan, not the creditor. Actually the words *ša... inaddinu* do not mean 'a man who gives' - lends out (valuta), i.e. the creditor, but 'a man who has to give' - who is obliged to pay, i.e. the debtor.[11] Another objectionable interpretation is put forward by Goetze for the difficult words *ana meḫrīšu*, literally 'in terms of equivalent'. Goetze remarks: 'In para 19 no interest at all is mentioned ... the conclusion must be drawn that the interest is from the outset added to the amount owed, be it money or barley'. This is not a cogent conclusion, as the rates of interest had already been fixed in § 18A. § 19 adds that the term of repayment is harvest time - i.e. when the peasant is in a position to repay.

[11] *[*Contrast Yaron, *op. cit.* (note 1a), pp. 31, 153-154 who correctly renders: "... who will give ... will collect." The explanation of *ana meḫ=rīšu* remains a matter of speculation even after Yaron's discussion*]*. The difference between the rate of 20 per cent. for loans of money and 33 1/3 per cent. for loans of grain may be explained by the fact that the price of grain is at its lowest at harvest time. When the creditor gets back his grain, it is less valuable than it was when he gave it; cf. *CH* § 51 mentioned above. Cf. also Bab. Talmud, Baba Batra 90 b, which distinguishes between *tr*^{c}*' ḥrp'* the early market-price (i.e. the low price when the corn is on the threshing floor), and *tr*^{c}*' 'pyl'* the late market-price (i.e. the high price afterwards).

The clue to the translation of the difficult term *ana* meḫrīšu may be found in the Latin word *mutuum*, which means literally equivalent. It is, however, used as a legal term for a loan, especially in the expression *mutuum fit*, a loan is paid back. § 19 may therefore simply be translated: 'A man who has to repay a loan should be made to repay his debt on the threshing floor'.[11] § 20 is distinct from the general rules for loans formulated in §§ 18A and 19. It deals with the special case in which the debtor has received money but is to repay it in grain. In such a case the sum of money has to be converted into grain and the debtor is obliged to add 33 1/3 per cent., as correctly observed by Goetze. In § 21 Goetze interprets the difficult words *ana pānīšu* - literally 'in terms of its first (initial) amount' - as meaning: 'the actual amount lent is recorded'. In his opinion *ana pānīšu* is the opposite of *ana meḫrīšu* in § 19, which refers, according to the interpretation rejected above, to a loan where only the sum to be repaid is recorded. But § 21, which begins like § 20 with *šumma* should be understood to refer to this immediately antecedent paragraph and not to § 19. It stresses that if the money has not been converted into grain, but is to be repaid in kind, the rate of interest should not exceed 20 per cent., the rate fixed for money loans in § 18A.[12]

The typical debtor envisaged by this law is apparently the tenant farmer, cf. Mishna, Baba Mezia 5:8-9. It is true that the law of the tenant farmer is not treated in *LE*, but it is dealt with in detail by *CH* (§§ 42-47; 60-65), and it may be supposed that similar laws were in force in Eshnunna too. Cf. also *CH* § 113, which presupposes the type of loan regulated by *LE*. In the Bible, both laws of land-tenancy and loans repayable on the threshing floor are conspicuously absent, and it may be concluded that there was no land-tenancy in Israel, at least not in the early days which the Biblical laws reflect.

The transliteration of the text is generally most reliable. Nevertheless, some typographical errors have crept in. In § 39 the words *u₄-um ša-a-ia-ma-nu i-na-ad-di-nu* have been omitted before the word *be-el* in both A and B. In § 37 A III, 18 the words *bu-še-e awīl* should be deleted, and in § 38 A III, 23 - the words *a-na kaspim*. In § 37 A III, 20, B III, 3 read *ilim* instead of *i-lim*.

[[12] Yaron, *op. cit.* (note 1a), pp. 162-163 proposes for *ana pānīšu* the rendering 'at his disposal', but does not adduce any evidence for the existence of such a type of contract in ancient law.*]*

"Beloved is Man in that he was created in the Image"

The creation story emphatically stresses that Man was created in the image of God (Gen. 1:26-27). The corporeality of the description which ascribes a form to God, as if is were, caused considerable perplexity, and to this day scholars are divided on the question of whether the concepts in the Pentateuch should be explained according to their original corporeal sense, or perhaps the intention of the Pentateuch was to a spiritual figure of the godhead. But even according to the spiritual explanation, "there is no doubt that the original signification of this expression in the Canaanite tongue was, judging by Babylonian usage, corporeal in accordance with the anthropomorphic conception of the godhead among the peoples of the ancient East".[1]

In this article I do not intend to deal with the problem of whether this expression is spiritual in the Pentateuch, but only with an attempt to uncover its source in Ancient Near Eastern literature. And, in fact, there exists literary evidence which permits us to arrive at the source of this expression. I refer to two letters which are included in the collection of letters sent to the kings of Assyria in the 8th-7th cents. BCE.[2] In one of the letters the writer praises the king as follows: *abu-šu ša šarri be-li-ia ṣa-lam* ^{d}*bel šu-u ù šarru be-li ṣa-lam* ^{d}*bel šu-u*.[3] 'The father of my lord, the king, is the statue of Bel, and my lord, the king, is the statue of Bel'. In another letter the author adduces evidence for the deification of the king whom he addresses by quoting an Assyrian proverb: *ṣil ili a-me-lu [u] ṣil* ^{amelu}*a-me-li-e [qu]l-lu. šarru: su-ù [a-ke]-e mu-uš-šu-li ša ili*.[4] 'The shadow of the god (is) a free man. *[And]* the shadow of a free man (is) a slave. The king: He is li*[ke]* the image[5] of a god.'[5a] It is clear from this that in Assyrian

---

[1] Cassuto, *From Adam to Noah*, p. 56.

[2] Robert H. Pfeiffer, *State Letters of Assyria*, New Haven 1935.

[3] Id., *ibid*. no. 161, ll. 18-19, pp. 119-120.

[4] Id., *ibid*. no. 344, rev., ll. 10-13, p. 234.

[5] *mašālu* 'to be similar'; *muššulu* 'image'.

[[5a] On the different interpretations of this difficult passage see Lambert, *BWL*, pp. 281f. with bibliography; *CAD*, s.v. *amīlu* 1 a 1'. Anyhow the characterization of the king as the *muššulu* (simile) of a god is fairly sure.*]*

court language it was customary to compare the king to the statue of the god or his image in order to exalt him and to raise his rank above that of the common man which only reaches that of the shadow of the godhead. In clear contrast to this point of view, the Pentateuch emphasizes that every person is created in the image by the very fact that he is a human being. The language of a court compliment turns into a praise of the human race which is beloved by God above all his other creatures.

We have thus seen that a title specifically coined for the kings of Assyria was attributed in the Pentateuch to the whole of the human race. A similar process is found with regard to another expression which is also a term of relationship with the godhead. In the Ancient Near East it was customary to regard the king as the son of the god. Thus, for example, Hammurapi, king of Babylon, states of himself that he is "the seed of kingship to whom (the god) Sin gave birth".[6] In the Ugaritic writings, King Krt bears the title *bn il*.[7] We even find traces of this court phrase in the Bible. In Ps. 2:7, the king boasts that God said of him: "You are my son. This day I have begotten you". In the Pentateuch this term of honour and affection is transferred to the people of Israel: "You are sons to YHWH, your God" (Deut. 14:1). Here also the Pentateuch thus devoided a court term of its original sense and transferred it - if not to all of humanity - to at least an entire people with a special closeness to God because of the covenant between this people and God.

Both, the idea that man is created in the image of God, and that the people of Israel are the sons of their God, have their common origin in court language which attributes to the king a special relationship with the godhead. These terms developed in the Pentateuch in similar, but nevertheless somewhat different, directions. The first idea was transferred to all of humanity, the second to the people of Israel. However, this does not amount to the absolute separation of the two related motives. It is not for naught that R. Akiba placed them side by side in his beautiful homiletic sermon: "Beloved is man in that he was created in the image (of God). (It is a mark of) superabundant love (that) it was made known to him that he had been created in the image (of God), as it is said: 'For in the image of

---

[6] *CH* Col. II,a:13-14.

[7] *CTA* 16:I:20-22.

God he made man'. Beloved are Israel in that they were called children of the all-present, as it is said: 'Your are children of the Lord Your God.'" (Mishna Abot 3:14).[8] *[*Compare now S. Herrmann, *ThLZ* 86 (1961), pp. 419f. who stresses that the Egyptians regarded Pharaoh as the son of a god and as his image: *So war es ein möglicher Schritt, die Menschheit überhaupt zu Abbildern der Gottheit zu machen*. This step was taken in the Meri-ka - Re text where mankind is qualified as "they who have issued from his (i.e. the god's) body as his images." (see *ANET*, p. 417 b). In the same way Herrmann explains Gen. 1:26 as the democratisation of a royal ideology. Cf. also W.H. Schmidt, *Die Schöpfungsgeschichte der Priesterschrift, WMANT* 17 (1964), pp. 136-144; H. Wildberger, *ThZ* 21 (1965), pp. 253-255, 484-485. Contrast M. Weinfeld, *Tarbiz* 37 (1968), pp. 113-116 who argues 1) that the earliest attestations of Pharaoh's descriptions as the image of a god belong to the period of the eighteenth dynasty and thus are later than the Meri-ka-Re text. Therefore it can not be demonstrated that the anthropology of that text had been preceded by a theology of kingdom. 2) that the anthropology of Gen. 1:26 may have been influenced directly by the concept of the Meri-ka-Re text.

Weinfeld's arguments show that the traditio-historical background of Gen. 1:26 can not be determined with certainty. Nevertheless the striking identity of Hebrew *ṣäläm* with Akkadian *ṣalmu* should be taken into account as an indication of Akkadian origin. In Akkadian literature, however, man is never qualified as a god's image.*]*

---

[8] The Hebrew text was taken from the Albeck-Yalon edition. Variae lectionis are irrelevant.

Review on Ugaritica 3

Schaeffer, C.F.A.: *Ugaritica*, III (Mission de Ras Shamra, tome VIII.) Paris: Librairie orientaliste Paul Geuthner, 1956. Avec des contributions de C. Desroches-Noblecourt, H.G. Güterbock, P. Krieger, E. Laroche, O. Masson, J. Vandier. 302 pp., 10 Plates. Figs., Index. 4,000 fr.

The new volume of *Ugaritica*, edited by the indefatigable excavator of Ugarit, C.F.A. Schaeffer, offers the reader an abundance of varied material, representative in its richness of the different civilizations that met in this famous centre of the Middle and Late Bronze Ages. The 242 excellent reproductions are comprehensively surveyed and competently evaluated by the editor, while his well-known staff of experts contribute detailed analytical studies in their several fields of research.

More than half the volume is devoted to seals impressed on documents of the southern Archive of the Palace of Ugarit, which contained documents emanating exclusively from the Hittite kingdom and its vassals in the 14th and 13th centuries BCE. To this collection of seal impressions we now add the matrix of the Hittite King Muršili II (Figs. 109-112), the first royal Hittite seal matrix ever found. This corpus of seals of kings and high officials is a valuable and welcome supplement to H.G. Güterbock's fundamental work: *Siegel aus Boğazköy*, I-II (*AfO, Beihefte* 5, 7) Berlin, 1940, 1942.

The images on the seals are extremely interesting to the student of religious ideas. The seal of the Hittite King Tudḫaliya IV (Figs. 24, 26) shows the weather-god embracing with his left arm a smaller man, evidently the king, and supporting with his hand the king's fist and his weapon. The weapon in the king's fist is exactly like the rod shown on many other seals in the fist of the weather-god himself. This suggests the idea that the king holds the god's rod, and the god helps him to carry it. The scene recalls similar seals of the Hittite King Muwatalli.[1] It is also reminiscent of the Biblical report about God, who caused His glorious arm to go at the right hand of Moses 'dividing the water before them' (Is. 63:12, 13), i.e. Who

[1] Cf. e.g. O.R. Gurney, *The Hittites*, Pelican Books, 1954, Fig. 16. Nos. 1, 2.

divides the water by transferring the power of His arm into the right hand of Moses, holding the rod of God which parts the sea (cf. Ex. 4:20; 14:16).

In both a seal of Carchemish (Fig. 32) and a seal of Amurru (Fig. 46) we find an ornament consisting of an inner circle surrounded by six outer circles. The form of this ornament strikingly recalls the structure of the offering bowls found at the Nahariyah excavations[2], and may quite well symbolize the idea of perfection inherent in the holy figure seven.[3] The seal inscriptions are mostly in both Hittite hieroglyphs and Akkadian cuneiform, but sometimes in Hittite hieroglyphs only. Even in the latter cases the name of the bearer is ascertained by the Akkadian text of the document to which it is attached. E. Laroche, in a painstaking monograph, fully utilizes the bilingual character of the inscriptions to make progress in the deciphering of Hittite hieroglyphs. In this paper Laroche once more displays his well-known skill in making problems clear even to the uninitiated reader. The latter will be particularly grateful for the list of hieroglyphic signs which Laroche has added to the book - a very thorough compilation in which the reviewer missed only three signs, viz. G.8 = M.33 (*op. cit.*, p. 112), G. 42 (p. 131), and G. 189 (p. 147).

Güterbock, in an appendix to Laroche's study, finally established the fact that the Hittite King Urḫi-Tešub adopted the throne-name Muršili. The seals of the Hittite kings cover the period from Šuppiluliuma to Muršili II, and from Hattušili III to Tudḫaliya IV, whereas the seals of Urḫi-Tešub = Muršili III and Muwatalli are lacking. This gap is hard to explain, especially when we remember that the last-mentioned ruler, who was very powerful, forced the Ugaritic army to take part in his battle against Ramses II at Kadesh. The absence of the seals of the last Hittite kings after Tudḫaliya IV raises no problem, if we accept Nougayrol's plausible suggestion that the destruction of Ugarit coincided with Tudḫaliya's death in the fourth year of Pharaoh Mernephtah.[4] The three royal seals of Ugarit are

---

[2] M. Dothan, *The Excavations at Nahariyah*, *IEJ* 6 (1956), p. 19, Fig. 3.

[3] Cf. ibid., p. 23.
[But compare now also D. Collon, *The Seal Impressions from Tell Atchana/Alalakh*, *AOAT* 27 (1975), Astral and other Symbols (pp. 194f., Pl. LIII) where the inner circles are surrounded by seven, eight or ten outer circles.]

[4] Cf. Nougayrol, *PRU* 4, p. 206.

clearly distinct from the Hittite seals and those originating from the kingdoms of Carchemish and Amurru. These royal seals are (a) the seal of Iaqarum from the Old Babylonian period and its copy (Figs. 92-99)[5], which served as the dynastic seal of all kings of Ugarit; (b) the private seal of Niqmadu (Figs. 100-102), a contemporary of Šuppiluliuma; and (c) the private seal of Ammistamri II (Fig. 103), a contemporary of Tudḫaliya IV. Their outstanding feature is the complete absence of Hittite hieroglyphic signs, which tends to show that the influence of Hittite civilization was less felt at Ugarit than in the other North Canaanite kingdoms. The two older seals bear purely Akkadian inscriptions, the seal of Ammistamri bearing in alphabetical Ugaritic the words *mišmn* ^{c}*myṯtmr mlk ugrt*, i.e. seal of Ammistamri, king of Ugarit.[6] The name ^{c}*myṯtmr* as compared with its well-documented[7] Akkadian form Ammistamri (seldom Ammištamri) shows that y served in atypical late Ugaritic texts as *mater lectionis*.[8]

The second place in *Ugaritica* 3 is taken by Egyptian or Egyptianizing material. The first item discussed is a fragment of a bowl (Figs. 118, 126), on which the name of the Ugaritic King Niqmadu is recorded in Egyptian hieroglyphs. The picture on the bowl has been studied by Mme C. Desroches-Noblecourt. In a full comparative analysis she reaches the conclusion that the style of the picture points to the very last days of the 18th dynasty of Egypt, and that the scene represents the marriage of the Ugaritic king to an Egyptian princess. The authoress goes a long way to prove that the headdress worn by the woman was the exclusive privilege of Pharaoh's wives and asserts that Pharaoh gave one of his concubines in marriage to the Ugaritic king. But this rather bold assumption still needs corroboration by documentary evidence if we are to believe that marriages of kings with the concubines of foreign rulers really took place in the ancient Near East.

---

[5] Cf. Nougayrol, *PRU* 3, pp. XL-XLIII.

[6] Cf. now also the seal bearing the pure Ugaritic inscription *mašmn ytn*, Virolleaud, *PRU* 2, pp. 197-198.

[7] Cf. Nougayrol, *PRU* 3, p. 239.

[8] Apparently only at the end of words. Cf. Gordon, *UM*, text 138, and *Glossary* No. 108 end, and cf. now also Virolleaud, *PRU* 2, pp. 30-31. For analogous developments in Old Phoenician and Old Aramaic writings, cf. Friedrich, *PPG*, § 101; F.M. Cross & D.N. Freedman, *Early Hebrew Orthography*, New Haven 1952, pp. 31-32.

Additional light on the relations between Ugarit and Egypt is shed by the fragment of a scarab of Amenhotep III, studied by P. Krieger. Of paramount historical interest is the sword giving the name of Pharaoh Merneph-tah in Egyptian hieroglyphs, the latest Ugaritic document to be approximately datable. Schaeffer suggests that this sword is of non-Egyptian type and was manufactured at Ugarit for a consignment of weapons destined for Egypt.

To this material Schaeffer adds a report about the Cypro-Minoan inscriptions found at Ugarit, which for the time being defy all efforts to decipher them, as is shown in a comparative study by O. Masson. The book concludes with a corpus of Ugaritic bronze weapons and utensils, carefully described by Schaeffer with a view to defining their place in the development of these instruments.

Notes on the Pronouns in Ugaritic in the Light of Canaanite*

It is common knowledge today that the pronouns are the oldest elements of a language. Similarly, scholars have correctly seen that - at least in the Semitic languages - these ancient pronouns were formed through combinations of monosyllabic elements with a deictic character.[1] It has also been rightly established that the pronouns in the Semitic languages change their forms through a free interchange in the composition of these deictic elements.[2] Among the studies devoted to this subject, Barth's monograph on the pronouns in the Semitic languages[3] still holds first place, even though notable additions to his work have been made here and there, e.g. Tur-Sinai's discovery that the Biblical word *k^{e}yom* should not be analyzed as *k^{e}-yōm*, but that this particle is composed of a deictic *kap* with an additional *mem*.[4] Moreover, since Barth's book was written new sources have been discovered which, on the one hand, must be investigated in the light of previously known linguistic phenomena, and which, on the other, contribute to the understanding of the older material. The most important sources are the Ugaritic writings and the El-Amarna letters in whose Akkadian text we occasionally find pronouns of a clear Canaanite nature. In this article we will at-

* It is my pleasant duty to express here my thanks to Prof. J. Blau whose advice I received in writing this article.

[1] See recently: F. Rundgren, *Über Bildungen mit s- und n-t Demonstrativen im Semitischen*, Uppsala 1955, pp. 8f.

[2] C. Brockelmann, *Anthropos*, 27, p. 38 quoted by Rundgren, *op. cit.* (note 1), p. 318.

[3] Barth, *Pronominalbildung*.

[4] N.H. Torczyner, *[Tur-Sinai] The Lachish Ostraca*, Jerusalem 1940, pp. 148-153 (in Heb.)
*[*Torczyner pointed to the writing *kym* in the Lachish Letters 2:3; 4:1; 5:3; 8:2 and argued that *kym* cannot be explained as a defective spelling of *yom* 'day' since its plene spelling *ywm* is attested in the word *byw[m]* in the Lachish letter 20:1. Contrast, however, now the consistently defective spelling *ym* in the Arad letters, 1:4; 24:19; 40:11. As the Lakhish and Arad letters were both written at the end of the first temple period Torczyner's argument has been seriously weakened*]*.

tempt to further the understanding of the Ugaritic pronouns in the framework of the pronouns in the Semitic languages as a whole, with particular attention to the language of the El-Amarna letters and Hebrew. Their parallels with the Ugaritic writings justify the claim that, at least from the point of view of its pronouns, Ugaritic may be considered as one of the Canaanite languages.

A. The Interrogative Pronouns *my, mh, mn*

1. The interrogative pronoun *my* is known in most of the Semitic languages, whether in its short form, or in forms enlarged by additional deictic elements. In Ethiopic, *mi* means 'what', and this meaning is paralleled by the meaning of the Akkadian interrogative pronoun *mīnum* 'what'. In Babylonian Aramaic the interrogative pronoun *mi* is commonly found in the meaning 'Is there ...?, does he?'[5] In many modern Arabic dialects the interrogative pronoun *mīn* is attested in the sense 'who'[6], and it goes without saying that this is the ordinary use of the Hebrew interrogative pronoun *mi*.[7] Here belongs also the interrogative pronoun *mi-ia* which appears in the El-Amarna letters, generally in the expanded forms *mi-ia-mi* or *mi-ia-ti* whose usage agrees in every instance with that of the Hebrew interrogative pronoun *mi*. True, Ebeling's glossary - following Knudtzon's translation - translates *mi-ia* as 'wer, was'[8] and this translation is apt to create the impression that the word encompasses the whole semantic range of 'who' and 'what'. This impression is, however, misleading since the interrogative pronoun admits the translation by Hebrew *mi* even in those letters where Knudtzon translated it 'was', e.g.: *mi-ia-mi šu-nu marē Abdi-a-šir-ta u [l]a-qu māt šarri ana ša-šu-nu* (*EA* 116:67-69) 'Who are the sons of Abdiaširta that they should take the land of the king for themselves?' The interrogative pronoun *mi-ia-mi* asks here about the character of a person, and in this meaning the Hebrew

---

[5] According to Barth, *Pronominalbildung*, p. 42, *mi* in Am. 7:2, 5 should also be explained with this meaning.

[6] Barth, *Pronominalbildung*, pp. 137f.

[7] *my* seems to be attested in this meaning also in Phoenician-Punic, but the matter is not entirely clear. See Friedrich, *PPG* § 120.

[8] E. Ebeling in J.A. Knudtzon, *Die El-Amarna-Tafeln*, Leipzig 1915, Zweiter Teil, p. 1469. On *t* as an additional deictic element, see infra *E*, end. We should point out here the incorrect use of the Akkadian pronoun *mi-nu(-um)* in the meaning 'who' (EA 126:14; 130:51). It is clear that the source of the error is Canaanite. Cf. F.M.Th. Böhl, *Die Sprache der El-Amarnabriefe*, Leipzig 1909, p. 29.

pronouns *mi* and *mā* occur in free variation. Cf., for example, sentences employing *mi*, such as: *my* ᶜ*bdk klb ky zkr 'dny 't [*ᶜ*]bdh* (Lachish letters, 2:3-5) 'Who is your servant, a dog, that my lord should remember his servant'[9]; *mi 'ānoki ki 'elek 'äl par*ᶜ*o* (Ex. 3:11) 'Who am I that I should go to Pharaoh'[10], with sentences employing *mā*, such as in *ki mā* ᶜ*abd*ᵉ*kā hakkä=läb ki ya*ᶜᵃ*śä haddābār haggādol hazzä* (2 Reg. 8:13) 'But what is your servant the dog, that he should do this great thing?', *mā 'imm*ᵉ*kā l*ᵉ*biyyā* (Ez. 19:2) 'What is your mother, a lioness'. The interrogative pronoun *my* is found twice in Ugaritic in epic texts. It is an accepted rule that in these texts *y* is employed as a consonant and not as a mater lectionis, even when it occurs in word-final position.[11] We may suppose that *my* was pronounced in Ugaritic *miya*, just as in the El-Amarna letters. Barth already dealt with *ya* as a deictic element which is appended in the Semitic languages to

---

[9] Cf. Torczyner, *op. cit.* (note 4), pp. 32f. *[*who compares the letters 5: 3-5; 6:2-4 and stresses the absence of the article before *klb* in all three instances. This perplexing lack, he argues, excludes the translation: 'Who is your servant the dog that ...' Therefore the word *klb* should be understood as an answer to the question: 'who is your servant' and be enclosed in brackets, since it interrupts between the protasis *my* ᶜ*bdk* and the apodosis *ky* ... In other words: The sentence *my* ᶜ*bdk klb* has been blended with the sentence *my* ᶜ*bdk ky.]*

[10] The interchange between *mi š*ᵉ*mäkā* (Ju. 13:17) verbally 'who is your name' and *ma-šš*ᵉ*mo* (Ex. 3:13) 'what is his name' is apparently of another type. Here the pronoun *mā* is normal according to our way of thinking, and it seems that the interchange with *mi* derives from the identification of the name with the person. On this and parallel phenomena in Ethiopic languages, see: Rundgren, *op. cit.* (note 1), p. 153. *[*Cf. with M. Sokoloff (orally) also Ezr. 5:4*]*.

[11] This rule which holds for the ancient orthography of the Ugaritic epic texts does not hold for the later orthography which is evident in the letters from Ugarit in which *y* in word final position already acts as a *mater lectionis*; for example, in the phrase: *aḫy bny yšal* (*UT* 138:10-11) in which the spelling *aḫy* is used in the nominative. Cf. for example, the phrase *ily ugrt tġrk* (*PRU* 2, text 15:4-6) 'may the gods of Ugarit protect you' in which the phrase *ily ugrt* is in the nominative. This shows that the nominative ending *u* in the pl. construct had already disappeared and was replaced by the *obliquus*, exactly as in Hebrew. Cf. also: Claude F.A. Schaeffer, *U* 3, p. 81, who quotes the seal of king Ammištamri in which the king's name is written in the partially plene spelling ᶜ*myṯtmr*. See also in this volume, Review on *U 3*, p. 53, note 8. *[*J. Blau - S.E. Loewenstamm, *UF* 2, pp. 25-30. Contrast Aartun, *Partikeln*, pp. 44-47*]*.

personal and demonstrative pronouns.[12] Comparison of the Ugaritic writings to the El-Amarna letters makes it seem plausible that this same deictic element is attached also to the interrogative pronoun *my*. The meaning of *my* is evident in the sentence: *my bilm ydy mrṣ gršm zbln*[13] 'Who among the gods will remove illness (and) will expel sickness?' The sense of the word is less obvious in the sentence *bᶜl mt my lim bn dgn.*[14] Following Gray's proposal[15] we are of the opinion that the Ugaritic verse should be viewed together with the biblical verse 'And when she came to her mother-in-law, she said *mi 'at bitti*. Then she told her all that the man had done for her' (Ruth 3:16). Here the exact meaning of Naomi's question may be ascertained by an analysis of the story. Naomi had sent Ruth to Boaz to find out whether he was willing to marry Ruth, and on her return she asks her: "What happened to you? What is the matter with you?" The use of *mi* in this verse is not different then from the use of *mā* in the question which the Danites posed to their returning spies: *mā 'attäm* (Ju. 18:8), i.e. 'What do you have to say? What have you clarified?'[16] In the light of these biblical passages we should interpret the Ugaritic verse *my lim bn dgn* in the sense 'what has happened to the people of Dagan's son?' i.e. 'what is their fate?' It is not surprising that this question expresses a lament if we note the parallel use of the word *'ek* 'how' in biblical Hebrew.

2. The interrogative pronoun *mh* exists in all the Semitic languages[17] except for Akkadian and Ethiopic. Its use in the Ugaritic epic texts is easi-

---

[12] Barth, *Pronominalbildung*, pp. 3, 7, 10, 116.

[13] *CTA* 16:V:10-21.

[14] *CTA* 6:I:6.

[15] Gray, *Legacy*, p. 52. For a different opinion: Gordon, *UT, Glossary* 1470 who distinguishes between the interrogative pronoun *my* and the interjection *my* meaning 'woe'.

[16] Ginsberg, *Keret*, p. 35 already hinted to the closeness of the verses in Ju. 18:8 and Ruth 3:16.
[On *my* as an interrogative particle (not pronoun), cf. now also M. Tsevat, *Biblica* 46 (1965), pp. 355f., who adds *inter alia* Gen. 33:8; Am. 7:2, 5 (cf. note 5) and the doubtful border case 2 Sam. 7:23 where he translates: "Is then on earth a single nation etc."].

[17] This apparently applies also to South Arabian, but because of their special style no interrogative pronouns are found in the South Arabian inscriptions. And cf.: Höfner, *ASG*, p. 54.

ly understood[18] and requires no explanation.[19] Its pronunciation in Ugaritic is not entirely clear, and all we are able to establish with a large degree of probability is the audibility of the final *h*.[19a] On the other hand, it is impossible to determine whether - unlike the other Semitic languages - a vowel was pronounced after the *h*. No certain results may be concluded from the form *mhy* in a Ugaritic letter.[20] True, it may be hypothesized, that the *y* in this word is a mater lectionis[21], and that this plene spelling gives us the pronunciation of *mh*. But this hypothesis is disputable and does not rule out Gordon's explanation of *mhy* as *mh* - *hy*.[22]

3. The interrogative word *mn* has various meanings in Ugaritic and there is no reason to exclude the possibility that the spelling *mn* represents more than one word. Cf. for example, Akkadian *mannu* 'who?' with *mīnu* 'what?' The element *mn* with the meaning 'who' is known in Arabic, Aramaic, Ethiopic, and Akkadian. There is no certain proof for the use of *mn* in this meaning in Ugaritic. Consider *mn ib yp[*^{c}*] lb*^{c}*l*[23], and similarly *mnm ib yp*^{c} *lb*^{c}*l*.[24] The accepted translation of the line is: 'which enemy has arisen against Baal?' This translation supposes then that *mn* is employed in Ugaritic in the sense 'which'. But this usage of *mn* is unknown from the other Semitic languages, and, therefore, it is perhaps better to explain the words *yp*^{c} *lb*^{c}*l* as an asyndetic subordinate clause: 'who is the enemy (who) has arisen against Baal?' In the meaning 'what' *mān, mānā'* is common only in Aramaic, and the originality of this form is open to doubt and some scholars derive it from *ma-den*.[25] The disputable Aramaic evidence is however, supported by the Biblical *mān hu'* (Ex. 16:15), and also from an El-Amarna letter where

---

[18] Gordon, *UT, Glossary*, No. 1437.

[19] But cf. Ginsberg, *Keret*, p. 35, and against him: Gordon, *UT*, Krt, l. 38, who reads *mn*(!) instead of *mat*.
[Herdner, *CTA*, p. 62 note 10: *matériellement m'at ne fait aucun doute.]*

[[19a] On this question cf. now J. Blau - S.E. Loewenstamm, *UF* 3, pp. 31f.*]*

[20] *UT*, 138:9.

[21] Cf. note 11.

[22] Gordon, *UT, Glossary*, No. 1437.

[23] *CTA* 3:III:34.

[24] *CTA* 3:III:48.

[25] Definitely, see: Barth, *Pronominalbildung*, p. 140; hesitantly, see: C. Brockelmann, *Syrische Grammatik*. Leipzig 1955, § 28.

ma-an-na is used for 'what' (*EA* 286:5). Thus it seems that Ugaritic *mnm* in the meaning 'what?' should be connected to the above-mentioned forms, and not to Akkadian *minum*. Ugaritic *mn* in the meaning of 'what?' is found in sentences, such as: *ṯmny ᶜm adtny mnm šlm rgm ṯṯb lᶜbdk*[26] 'What is the welfare there with our Lady? May you send back word to your slave.' The use of *mn* as an interrogative adverb in the meaning 'how much' in the following lines is surprising: *mn yrḫ km[rṣ] mn kdw kr[t], wyᶜny ġzr [ilḥu] ṯlṯ yrḫm km[rṣ] arbᶜ kdw k[rt]*[27] 'How many months is it that Krt is si[ck]? How many that Kr[t] is ill? And the hero [Ilhu] replies: Three months that he is si[ck], four that K[rt] is ill.' I have found a parallel to this use of *mn* only in the El-Amarna texts where we meet with the question *ma-ni ūmē*, i.e. 'How many days?, How many times?'[28] This expression seems to be based on old Canaanite since Akkadian employs other words to express the concept "how many".[29] It should be noted that in Ugaritic the noun following *mn* is in the singular, whereas after *mani* in the El-Amarna texts it comes in the plural. Interchanges of this sort are known in the Semitic languages not only after adverbs of quantity. Above all we should compare Hebrew *kammā* with the following plural noun to Arabic *kam* which takes the following noun in the accusative singular.

B. The Indefinite Pronouns *mnm, mnk, mhk*

According to a well-known rule the indefinite pronouns tend to develop from the interrogative pronouns. The following verse gives a clear example: *ṯlḥn il dmla mnm dbbm*[30] 'Il's table which is filled with all kinds of ...'[31]

---

26 *CTA* 51:14-18. A parallel phraseology is employed in the Akkadian letters from Ugarit. Cf. for example *PRU* 4, RS 17.383:7-9, p. 222: *aš-ra-nu itti šar-ri bēli-ia mi-nu-me-e šul-ma-nu ṭè-ma li-te-er-ru-ni* 'What is the welfare there with the lord my king? May he send me back word'. [Contrast in this volume, *Lexicographical Notes*, p. 451, note 7a, where Ugaritic *mnm*, Akkadian *mīnummē* in the formula under discussion have been interpreted as indefinite pronouns].
The Akkadian word *mīnummē* exactly parallels here Ugaritic *mnm*, but, of course, nothing may be learnt from here of the pronunciation of the Ugaritic word.

27 *CTA* 16:II:81-85.

28 Ebeling, *op. cit.* (note 8), p. 1463. [Cf. now also W. v. Soden, *VTS* 16 (1967) pp. 294f.]

29 v. Soden, *GAG* § 120a.

30 *CTA* 4:I:39-40.

31 The noun *dbbm* is obscure. For a suggested explanation, see: Driver, *CML*, p. 154.

Here *mnm* is employed as an indefinite pronoun. Scholars have seen for some time that this is the meaning of *mnm* also in Phoenician and Punic.[32] We can now add to this previously known word new evidence on indefinite pronouns. In two new letters we find the expression: *waḫy mhk blbh al yšt; wap mhkm blbk al tšt.*[33] Virolleaud determined the meaning of the new word *mhk* from the context as 'travail, worry'; however, he did not deal with the etymology of the word. Here also we may be aided by the El-Amarna texts where we find parallel expressions, such as: *bēli-ni mi-im-ma-am-ma i-na lib-bi-ka la ta-šak-kán* (*EA* 170:7-8) 'Our master, do not place anything in your heart'. Here also, *mimmamma* means 'travail, worry', according to the context, and Knudtzon correctly translates 'irgend welchen (Kummer)'. Similarly in another letter: *la-a ti-š[a]-k[á]n mi-ma i-na lib-bi-ka* (*EA* 34:12-13) 'Do not put anything in your heart', i.e. 'Do not worry, do not be troubled'. From here we see that Ugaritic *mhk* is simply *mh* with the addition of a deictic *k*. The enlarged *mhkm* is of course, *mhk* + enclitic *-ma*; cf. above *mn ib* with *mnm ib*.[33a] This also clarifies the Ugaritic phrase *mnk mnkm lyqḥ* 'whosoever shall not take'.[34] Gordon already recognized in the word *mnk* the element *mn*, but he explained the *k* as the suffixed pronoun of the 2 sg. and the *m* of *mnkm* as the plural ending. But it is obvious that the structure of *mnkm* is like that of *mhkm*. In both indefinite pronouns the *k* as well as the *m* act as additional deictic elements.[35]

---

32 J.N. Epstein apud Maisler-Ginsberg, *JPOS* 14 (1934), p. 250; Friedrich, *PPG*, § 124 a; H.L. Ginsberg, *JBL* 56 (1937), p. 140 (note of Prof. Z. Ben-Ḥayyim).

33 Ch. Virolleaud, *CRAIBL* 1955, p. 177; The second of these texts has now been published in *PRU* 2, text 13, *[*the first in *PRU* 5, text 5*]*. *[*But cf. now: Virolleaud, *GLECS* 8 (1959), p. 65; *PRU* 5, p. 83. Here Virolleaud correctly analyses *mhk* as *mh - k*, *'quoique ce soit'* and *mnk* as *mn - k*, *'qui que ce soit'*]*.

*[*33a Add *mm* 'something' in the phrase *in mm* (*CTA* 53:9) '(there is) nothing'. W.F. Albright, *BASOR*, 82 (1941), p. 47 correctly compared Akkadian *mim=ma*. Ugaritic *mm* may be a loan from Akkadian.*]*

34 Gordon, *UT, Glossary*, No. 1503. *[*Text 1009:12-13*]*.

35 I pose with hesitation the question whether it is possible to find in Babylonian Aramaic a trace of the interrogative pronoun *m'nky* which parallels the indefinite pronoun *mnk* in Ugaritic. Cf. in Baba Batra 110 a-b the question: *'l' m'n kw lyrwt*. On the obscure word *kw* the *Massoreth hashas* notes: "Another manuscript *bw*." The *Bah* notes: "*m'n lyrwt*. Thus should it be and the word *kw* is to be delected." Ms. Munich reads: *m'n ky*. Jastrow, *Talmud Dictionary*, *s.v. qašša'* II notes: "*m'n kw lyrwt* (*ku* = *k*^{e}*hu*, not *bw*) who else should be the heir?" Yet, this does not

Neither is the reduplication of *mnk mnkm* surprising since it has its exact Akkadian counterpart in the indefinite pronoun *mamman* 'whosoever' which derives from *manman*, i.e. a reduplication of the element *man*. Here also we may adduce final proof from Akkadian documents, this time from Ugarit itself, such as: *ma-am-ma-an la i-le-qi*[36] 'no one shall take' or from the synonymous phase: *ma-an-nu-um-ma ... ú-ul i-laq-qi*[37], etc. Gordon correctly compared the expression *mnk mnkm* with the Ugaritic synonymous expression *bnš bnšm* in the sentence *bnš bnšm lyqḥnn bd ...*[38] 'no one shall take him from the hand of ...' Here we should accept Virolleaud's opinion that *bnš* is a combination of *bn - nš*, i.e. Hebrew *ben 'ä̆noš*. However, here too the *m* of *bnšm* should not be analyzed as the plural ending, but as the additional deictic element attested in *mnk mnkm*. Cf. also in Hebrew sentences such as *'iš 'iš 'äl kol š'er bešāro lo' tiqrebu* (Lev. 18:6) Verbally: 'Man, man, i.e. whosoever, you shall not come near to his kin', where *'iš 'iš lo'* denotes a strongly emphasized 'none', the negation of whosoever. Here the reduplication of the noun *'iš* creates an indefinite pronoun which is equivalent to Ugaritic *bnš bnšm*. We should also compare the evolution of the noun meaning "man" in Indo-European languages into the indefinite pronoun, e.g., Latin *ne-homo* > *nemo*, German *Mann* > *man*, or French *on* (from Latin *homo*). The situation is similar in the Slavic languages.[39]

C. *k* as a Deictic Element in Ugaritic

It was shown above that deictic *k* is employed in Ugaritic to form the indefinite pronouns *mhk*, *mnk*. This phenomenon is of considerable interest.

---

seem to be correct. Should we not perhaps read: *m'nkw*, or *m'nky* as one word, this being an extended form of *m'n*? There is, however, no possibility of arriving at a definite conclusion on the basis of one doubtful example.
[The question has been clarified by J.N. Epstein, *A Grammar of Babylonian Aramaic*, Jerusalem 1960 (in Heb.), p. 141. Epstein adduces many examples of *m'n kw* 'who then' and *my kw* 'what then' and points to the analogous use of *kai* in Syriac. It should, however, be remarked that in the abovementioned passage MS. Munich clearly reads *m'n ky* in accordance with Syriac. Could the reading *kw* be a misspelling of *ky*?]

36 *PRU* 3, RS 16. 248:15-17, p. 49.

37 *PRU* 3, RS 16. 140:14-15, p. 46.

38 Gordon, *UM*, *Glossary*, No. 335. See now: *PRU* 2, text 8:16-17.

39 Note of Prof. Z. Ben-Hayyim.
[Concerning the indefinite pronouns in Ugaritic, see now also: M. Liverani, *RSO* 39 (1964), pp. 1-4. In this connection the enigmatic *imt imt*

Though the function of *k* as a deictic element had been established long ago[40], until now *k* had not been attested in the Semitic languages as a component of the indefinite pronouns. The words *mhk, mnk* thus once again show the freedom which exists in the Semitic languages in forming pronouns from deictic elements. Similarly, only in Ugaritic do we find an example of the enlargement of a presentative word by *k*. In Ugaritic this category is represented by two synonyms *hl* and *hn* which both mean 'behold' and correspond to Hebrew *hen, hinne*.[41] Now a deictic *k* may be appended also to *hl*. We refer to the text: *hlk kṯr ky^{c}n wy^{c}n tdrq ḫss hlk qšt ybln hl yšrb^{c} qṣ^{c}t apnk dnil mt rpi aphn ġzr mt [h]rnmy gm laṯth kyṣḥ*.[42] 'He spies the going of Kṯr, and spies the course of Ḫss. Lo, he brings a bow, behold, he carries arrows. Thereupon Dnil, Man of Rp^{c}, straightaway the Hero, Man of Hrnmy, shouts aloud to his wife'. The parallelism between *hlk* and *hl* shows clearly that *hl* = *hlk*.[43] In the same text we find the adverb *apnk* parallel to *aphn*. Following Gordon[44], *apnk* should be analyzed as a combination *ap - hn - k [*with syncope of the *h]*, i.e. 'also behold' resulting in meaning 'then, thereupon'. There is no example in the other Semitic languages for this use of *k*. This does not, of course, mean that the use of deictic *k* in Ugaritic always dif-

---

(*CTA* 5: I:18) may be reconsidered. It is generally explained as 'indeed' based on Hebrew *'ämät*. A translation 'at any time, always' would be more satisfactory. We tentatively propose to compare Akkadian *immati* 'when?' and *immatima* 1) 'whensoever' 2) 'at any time, always'. True, in this case we should expect *imtm* in Ugaritic rather than *imt*. But possibly the duplication of *imt* has the same function as affixed *m]*.

40 See, e.g. Barth, *Pronominalbildung*, pp. 78-83; 108; 110. Torczyner, *op. cit.* (note 4), ibid.

41 The synonymy of the elements *hl* and *hn*, which are close to each other from a phonetic point of view, is assured in the light of the comparison of the adverbs *hnny* and *hlny* which are used indiscriminately for 'here'. See Gordon, *UT, Grammar* 11. 3 *[hnny / hlny* are attested in a more or less stereotyped Ugaritic letter formula. A comparison of this formula to its Akkadian counterpart shows that *hnny / hlny* correspond to Hebrew *hinne*, 'now, here is, (French *voici*)', not to Hebrew *hennā* 'here'. Cf. also in this volume, *Lexicographical Notes* on *hnny/hlny*, pp. 451-454.

42 *CTA* 17:V:10-15.

43 The composition of *hlk* from *hl - k* is already known. However, Gordon, *UT, Glossary*, No. 55, explains the *k* also here as the attached 2 sg. pronoun. But here too his explanation is not convincing.

44 Gordon, *UT, Glossary*, No. 308 *[*The explanation is not given explicitly*]*.

fers from the framework of previously known phenomena. It goes without saying, that just as in the other Semitic languages, *k* in Ugaritic serves as the suffixed 2 sg. pronoun. As is well-known Ugaritic has besides the pronoun *an* the expanded form *ank*, with the attached deictic *k*, as in Hebrew, Phoenician, and Akkadian.[45] Like in Hebrew, Ugaritic employs the word *ky* (in poetry always spelled defectively *k*) as an intensifying particle. Again as in Hebrew, this intensifying particle turns into a subordinating conjunction. Therefore, we find it hard to accept Gordon's opinion[46] that the two functions should be completely separated. He even formulates the rule that intensifying *k* always precedes the verb which is removed to the end of the sentence. This rule is quite doubtful. We find the verse introducing direct speech: *ky*^{c}*n lṭpn il dpi[d]*[47] 'And the kind one, god of understanding declared', or 'in fact declared'. This means that *k* acts here as a clear intensifying particle even though the verb remains at the beginning of the sentence. On the other hand, *k* may be sometimes explained as a subordinating conjunction also where the verb is moved to the end of the sentence, such as: *hlk b*^{c}*l aṯ[t]rt kt*^{c}*n ... bh p*^{c}*nm [tṭt]*.[48] The probable explanation here is: 'When Asherah saw Baal's going ... her (literally: on her) feet wobbled'. We can at least recognize here the transition from an intensifying particle to a subordinating conjunction. Also the interrogatory adverb *ik*, which apparently means 'why'[49], parallels in form Hebrew *'ek*. It should be pointed out that sometimes the meaning of the Hebrew word is also close to 'why', e.g., "Why (*'ek*) were you not afraid" (2 Sam. 1:14). We should also mention here the Ugaritic adverb *idk* = Hebrew *'az*, whose connection with Arabic has already been pointed out.[50] We may add to the list of Ugaritic words ending

---

[45] Rundgren, *op. cit.* (note 1), p. 319.

[46] Gordon, *UT, Grammar* 9. 17; 13. 51.

[47] *CTA* 16:IV:10 [but note that Herdner, *CTA* p. 75 prefers the reading: *wy*^{c}*n]*; and cf. C. Brockelmann, *Orientalia* 10 (1941), p. 238, who rightly states that the role of the particle *k* is occasionally limited to emphasis of the verbal object.

[48] *CTA* 4:II: 13-17.

[49] Cassuto, *Anath*, p. 131.

[50] Gordon, *UT, Glossary*, No. 79; Driver, *CML*, p. 135. [This comparison has been refuted with cogent reason by Aartun, *Partikeln*, p. 5, note 6. Cf. now also the basic form *id* (*U* 5, p. 586, RS 24. 260:1)].

in deictic *k* the demonstrative pronoun *hnk*, found in the line: *wmlk b*ᶜ*ly lm škn hnk l*ᶜ*bdh*[51] 'And king, my master, why has he imposed[51a] these upon his servant?' Note the resemblance between this form and the demonstrative pronoun *hnk* in Babylonian Aramaic and Mandaic, which parallels Christian Palestinian Aramaic *hlyk*. It is evident that *hnk* is composed of the elements *hn - k*.

D. Demonstrative Pronouns

We now come to the question of the demonstrative pronouns in Ugaritic. Our knowledge of these pronouns is extremely limited. Not a single example exists in the Ugaritic epic texts, and it appears that their use was alien to poetic style.[52] In the prose texts there has been found - besides the

---

51 Gordon, *UT, Glossary*, No. 787. See now *PRU* 2, text 12:22-24, and cf. also the *Glossaire* in which the author states correctly: *hnk* (= *hn* + *k*) *'cela'*. *[hnkt* points proleptically to the direct object *alpm* s_2*[*s_2 *w]m* 'two thousand horses' which follows the indirect object *l*ᶜ*bdh*. Cf. now *wbny hnkt yškn anyt ym* (*PRU* 5, text 61: 11-13) 'and my son may this equip (or: provide) a ship of sea'. On the free interchange of the forms *hnd* and *hndt*, see note 53. Contrast M.S. Astour, *AJA* 69 (1969), p. 255 who renders *hnkt* 'in the same way' and Gordon, *UT, Glossary*, No. 787 where Gordon translates *hnk* 'levy' *hnkt* 'levies'. Aartun, *Partikeln*, p. 50: *'siehe'*.

[51a Contrast M. Dietrich - O. Loretz - J. Sanmartîn, *UF* 6, p. 51, who analyze *škn* as *kūn* (*Š*) and render *'bereitstellen'*. However, the explanation of *škn* has no bearing on the interpretation of *hnk]*.

52 For another opinion, see Aistleitner, *UGU*, p. 31ff. Aistleitner thinks that *hn, ht* are demonstrative pronouns. Cf. H. Goeseke, *Wissenschaftliche Zeitschrift der Martin Luther Universität*, Halle Wittenberg, VII. 3 (1958), p. 635, who translates *t̠nm tšqy msk hwt* (*CTA* 19:224). 'Twice she will drink this mixture'. But we should translate following Ginsberg (*ANET*, p. 155) 'A second time she gives the mixture to him to drink'.
[Aistleitner distinguishes between *hn* 1 a demonstrative pronoun and *hn* 2 a local adverb. His treatment of the alleged pronoun may be exemplified by his translation of the first words of the Seven-Days-Scheme: *hn ym wt̠n* (*CTA* 4:VI:24 et passim) *'an diesem Tage und am zweiten!* He then renders *hn ym* 'this day' although *ym* does not refer to a day mentioned before and *hn* rather introduces the series of the first six days. M. Liverani (*AANLR* 8, 19, 5-6 (1964), pp. 9f. goes a step further in this direction and even supposes an attenuation of the alleged demonstrative pronoun *hn* to a definite article in the difficult passage: *tmġy {y} hn alpm* s_2*sm hnd* (*PRU* 2, text 12:30), *in cui il valore originario "questi 2000 cavalli questi qui" e evidentemente alternato in "questi 2000 cavalli"*.
Aartun who regards *hn* as *Hervorhebungspartikel* everywhere, translates it in this way even in the passage under discussion and renders: *Sie*

afore mentioned *hnk* - the demonstrative pronoun *hnd* in the phrase *lym hnd*[53] 'from this day'. *[*Add now: *ḫpṯ hndn* 'this ḫupšu'*]*.[53a] There is no doubt that *hnd* is composed of the elements *hn* - *d* and that *d* is the deictic element *ḏ* known from all the Semitic languages with the exception of Akkadian. In Hebrew *hnd* is paralleled by *zä, hallāz(ä)*. The interchange between Ugaritic *hn* and Hebrew *hal* - is better understood in the light of what was previously mentioned concerning the nature of the synonymous elements *hl* and *hn* in Ugaritic. Barth analyzed *hallāz* as a combination of *h* + *z* with an additional *l* in the middle.[54] But in the light of Ugaritic this analysis seems artificial. It is better to explain *hallaz* as simply a combination of *hl* + *z*. The two elements which make up the demonstrative pronouns *hnd* and *hallāz* are apt to serve in the Semitic languages as demonstrative pronouns even when they stand alone. The possibility of *ḏ* serving as a demonstrative pronoun needs no proof. But the assumption that the element *hl* = *hn* serves the same function has not until now been generally accepted in spite of the

---

sollen dahin kommen, siehe diese 2000 Pferde (*Partikeln*, pp. 46, 64, 69). However, the position of presentative *hn* (Hebrew *hinne*) between the predicate and the subject of a verbal clause differs from Hebrew usage and is therefore suspect.
The most commendable solution remains after all Aistleitner's proposal: *Sie sollen daher kommen*. Cf. Hebrew *hennā* 'thither'*]*.

53 Gordon, *UT, Glossary* No. 786; and cf. also in this volume, *The Formula meᶜattā wᵉᶜad ᶜolām*, p. 167; and cf. now the phrases *spr hnd, ᶜbdh hnd, spr mlk hnd* (*PRU* 2, text 5:9, 13), and especially the phrase *mlakty hnd* (*ibid.*, 12:35) in which the word *hnd* is used after a feminine noun. The form *hnd* is thus common gender like Phoenician *z*, see Friedrich, *PPG*, § 289 and the Hebrew form in which masculine *zä(h)* and feminin *zo(h)* are distinguished only by their vocalization. The opinion that *hnd* is a demonstrative pronoun is confirmed by parallel Akkadian texts. See in this volume, *Review of PRU 2*, p. 84.
*[*Cf. now *hndt* which takes up the preceding subject after a subordinate clause: *any kn dt likt msrm hndt bṣr mtt by gšm adr nškh* (*PRU* 5, text 59: 10-15) 'and the good (? cf. *PRU* 3, RS 16. 166:16, p. 48) ship which you sent to Egypt that one capsized near Tyre. In a strong rain it was ...' Ch. Virolleaud, *GLECS*, 8 (1959), p. 65 remarks that *any* is referred to as a masculine noun in *kn* and *nškḥ*, however, as a feminine noun in *dt, hndt* and *mtt*. But *dt* and *hndt* are common gender and *mtt* may be *Polal*. Cf. Hebrew *Polel motet*. Cf. also: *wtdᶜ ilm* (!) *kmtt* (*CTA* 5:V:16-17), which should be rendered: 'And know, god, that you are killed'. The following lines: *w anyk ṯt by ᶜky ᶜryt* (*ibid.*, ll. 24-25) are unclear and Virolleaud's proposal to parse *ṯt* and *ᶜryt* as 3. f. perfect of the verbs *ṯwy* and *ᶜry* is highly problematic.*]*

*[*53a RS 34. 124 Recto l. 7'. See A. Caquot, *ACF* 75 (1974-75), p. 430*]*.

54 Barth, *Pronominalbildung*, pp. 78, 105.

demonstrative pronoun *hallā* in Mishnaic Hebrew. Barth[55] explained the plural form *hānē* (*hny*) found in Babylonian Aramaic as resulting from *hā'illēn* (*h'lyn*) > *hālēn* (*hlyn*) (found in Galilean Aramaic, Samaritan Aramaic, Mandaic, and in the Babylonian Talmud only in the tractates Nedarim and Nazir) > *hānē* (*hny*). On the other hand, he derives the Syriac singular form *hān, hānā* (*hn'*) from *hāden, hādenā* (*hdn, hdn'*) by assimilation of the *d*. Thus according to him, the two forms *hānē* (*hny*) and *hān, hānā* (*hn, hn'*) have completely different histories. However, the situation in Ugaritic opens the way for a simpler hypothesis: The Syriac demonstrative pronoun *hn(')* is just the direct descendant of the deictic element *hn*, and the plural form *hny* is formed directly from the singular.[56] This supposition is supported by the Akkadian demonstrative pronoun *anniu* 'this', found in Neo-Assyrian also in the form *ḫanniu*. Von Soden has already dealt with the possibility that this interchange reflects a pronunciation *hanniu*[57], and on this supposition, *hn* as a demonstrative pronoun is attested also in Akkadian. But even if we assume that Neo-Assyrian was influenced here by Aramaic and that the original Akkadian pronunciation was *anniu*, we should not disregard the closeness of the elements *'n* and *hn*; cf., for example, in Ugaritic the interchange between *hm* and *im*[58], in Aramaic the interchange of the forms *'ān* and *hā(')n* 'where', and in South Arabian the interchange of the Maonite relative pronoun *hl* with the relative pronoun *'l* in the other dialects.[59]

E. *d, dt, dtm*

We have already recognized in the demonstrative pronoun *hnd* the ancient Semitic element *ḏ* which plays an important role in forming pronouns in all the Semitic languages with the exception of Akkadian. This element is also found in Ugaritic without the addition of another consonant in the particle *d*. This particle is, however, not used as a demonstrative pronoun, but only as: (1) the relative pronoun, and (2) the particle of possession. Clear vestiges of this usage of *ḏ* in Hebrew remain in the relative pronoun *zu* which

---

[55] id., *ibid*. pp. 107, 119.

[56] Cf. also the famous dispute on the history of the demonstrative adjective *hal* which is used in many modern Arabic dialects. And see id. *ibid*., pp. 116f.

[57] v. Soden, *GAG*, § 24a.

[58] Gordon, *UT, Glossary* No. 216. See now *PRU* 2, text 20:8.

[59] Höfner, *ASG*, § 43 (p. 51).

is preserved in poetry and which occasionally interchanges with *zä* in the same function.[60] According to many scholars there are a few traces in the Bible of the use of *zä* as a particle of possession.[61] The question of the Ugaritic particle *d* is complicated by the fact that it occasionally interchanges with *dt(m)*.[61a] Gordon at first tried to establish that *d* is employed for m. sg. and *dt* for f. sg. and pl.[62] He afterwards retracted this rule and proposed the theory that *d* has a personalized use while *dt* is used impersonally.[63] But lately he has also abandoned even this distinction.[64] Aistleitner argued that *d* and *dt* are used indiscriminately as particles of possession, whereas *d* alone is used as a relative pronoun.[65] But this distinction also has not been established.

d is used as a relative pronoun for m. sg., e.g., ... *[i]l mlk dyknnh*[66] 'King Il who brought her into being'. Similarly, it refers to an impersonal expression: *pdin bbty ttn*[67] 'But what is not in my house shalt thou give', and similarly for the feminine, e.g. *tn ly mṯt ḥry ... dk nᶜm ᶜnt nᶜmh ... dᶜqh ib ... dbḥlmy i[l] ytn*[68] 'Give me Lady Ḥry ... whose charm is like ᶜAnat's charm ... whose eyelids(?) are a precious stone whom in my dream Il has granted'. Similarly, *d* refers back to the plural: *ṯṯm ḫzr wᶜšt ᶜšr ḥrš d tbᶜln bugrt*[69] 'Twelve ... [70] and eleven craftsmen who work in Ugarit'.

---

60 Besides the dictionaries, cf. Barth, *Pronominalbildung*, p. 153.

61 C. Brockelmann, *Hebräische Syntax*, Neukirchen 1965, § 75, with literature. See also J.M. Allegro, *VT* 5 (1955), pp. 309ff.

[61a Aartun, *Partikeln*, p. 60 regards even dm in *CTA* 12:II:47-48 as a variant of *d*, not as the well-known noun blood.]

62 Gordon, *UH, Grammar* 6.38.

63 Id., *UM, Grammar* 6.21-23.

64 Id., *UM, Glossary* No. 449 [Cf. now *UT, Grammar* 6. 23-26].

65 Aistleitner, *UGU*, pp. 32f.

66 *CTA* 4:IV: 48.

67 *CTA* 14:142.

68 *CTA* 14:143-150.

69 Gordon, *UM, Glossary* No. 449. [See now *PRU* 2, text 24 Rev. 7-8 Virolleaud reads *d(t)* because of *dt tbᶜln* in ll. 6 and 10. But this emendation is gratuitous.]

70 See now *PRU* 2, text 24: 7-8. The exact meaning of the noun *ḫzr* is unknown. In any event it is clear that it refers to some type of craftsmen. The problem of the translation of the text which describes the descent of Baal to Mot comes up again here. The text reads: *ᶜmk šbᶜt*

The antecedent may thus be a m. or f. sg. noun or a m. pl. noun, and it appears that it is just a coincidence that up until now the pronoun *d* has not occurred with a f. pl. noun. On the other hand, we find sg., m. and f. pl. nouns with the pronoun *dt*. Here are the examples: *šd ... dt bd skn*[71] 'the field ... which is in the hand of the governor'; *t̲t̲tm ḫzr dt tbᶜln bgt hrt̲m*[72] 'Twelve ... who will work in the press of hrt̲m'; *t̲mn mrkbt dt ᶜrb bt mlk*[73] 'eight chariots which came to king's palace'. These texts which were not available to Aistleitner when he wrote his book completely refute his assumption that *dt* does not act as a relative pronoun. In addition, it is clear that we should not draw any conclusions from the fact that we have not found until now a f. sg. noun with *dt*. Consequently *dt* is a free variant of *d*.[73a] This phenomenon itself requires explanation.

ġlmk t̲mn ḫnzrk (*CTA* 5: V:8-9). According to the accepted translation: 'With thee thine seven lads, thine eight boars.' But perhaps *ḫzr* = *ḫnzr* and the texts refers to a type of craftsman, servitors of Baal. [Cf. now CAD s.v. *ḫaziru* for the free interchange of *ḫaziru* and *ḫanziru* in Akkadian].

71 *UT* 146: 1-2.

72 *PRU* 2, text 24: 9-11.

73 *PRU* 2, text 121:1-2.

[73a Cf. now text RS. 24.277, published and discussed by M. Dietrich - O. Loretz, *Beschriftete Lungen- und Lebermodelle aus Ugarit, U 6* (1969), pp. 165-172. The first inscription on this liver begins with the words: *dbḥ kljrḫ* 'slaughter (for sacrifice) of *kljrḫ*.' In the second inscription on the same liver the words: *dt* ***nat*** correspond to this formula. The authors interpret: '(the slaughter for sacrifice) of *nat*' and explain: "*dt stellt den Anschluss an Zeile 1 mit Bezug auf dbh das hier offensichtlich als Fem. konstruiert wird (Cf. Pl. dbḥt sub Ḃ. Z. 1) her.*" According to this analysis we are dealing here with a split construct phrase in which the *regens* can be supplied from a previous text. On this supposition, however, *dt* should be explained as masc. sing., since Ugaritic *dbḥ* is masc. like Hebr. *zäbaḥ*. Cf. *t̲n dbḥm* (*CTA* 4: II:17). The pl. *dbḥt* does not disprove our point. Cf. e.g. in Hebr. the masc. pl. *dorot*. But on the other hand, we can not state with certainty that *dt* here is a particle of attachment, grammatically related to *dbh* in the preceding text. Cf. the independent use of *dt* in the phrase *dt ẓrh* (*CTA* 3:III:32) 'the muscles (or the like) of his back', where no *regens* can be supplied from the context and *dt* functions as a noun substitute. This construction, however, is rare in Ugaritic, and the dependence of *dt* on *dbḥ* seems more probable.]

But before we turn to this problem, let us first survey the uses of *d* and *dt* as particle of attachement used to break up construct phrases. Here is a simple example from a list: *šb^{c} kbd d ṯbṭ wḫmšm yn diḫh*[74] 'seven heavy (shekels) of *ṯbṭ* and fifty (jars) of wine of his brothers'. Particularly interesting are the lines in which we find the broken-up construction with *d(t)* in parallel with a construct phrase, e.g., *yip lḥm dḫmš mġd ṯdṯ yrḫm*[75] 'He baked bread for five, provisions of six months' *[*if we do not assign to *d* before *ḫmš* a double-duty and explain *mġd (d)ṯdṯ yrḫm]*. The same parallelism between the broken-up construction and the construct phrase is found in the verse *tqḥ mlk ^{c}lmk drkt dt dr drk*[76] 'Thou wilt take thine eternal kingdom, thine everlasting sovereignty'. The possessive pronoun in the genitive phrase *mlk ^{c}lmk* is attached to the *nomen rectum* as in Hebrew. But also in the broken-up construct phrase *drkt dt dr drk* the possessive pronoun remains attached to the *nomen rectum*. The preceding verse gives us the key to the analysis of the difficult verse: *^{c}bdk an wd^{c}lmk*[77], i.e., in simple Ugaritic: *^{c}bd d^{c}lmk an*, but the predicate *^{c}bd d^{c}lmk* is divided into two parts in order to emphasize the concept *d^{c}lmk*. Therefore, we cannot agree with Gordon who distinguishes between the broken-up construction *drkt dt dr drk* and the independent use of *d* before a noun in *wd^{c}lmk*[78], since the second usage is just a direct derivation from the first. The broken-up construction may indicate place of origin: *adr ^{c}qbm d lbnn*[79] 'The mightiest of sinews(?) of the Lebanon, from the Lebanon'. *dt* precedes especially the indication of the material from which the article is made. A phrase of this type is formed in the verse *kt il dt rbtm*[80] 'Il's ...[81] of two myriads (of shekels)'. Similarly: *št gpnm dt ksp dt yrq nqbnm*[82] 'Puts on a harness of silver, trappings

---

[74] *UT* 145 : 22-23. *[*Correct the translation in accordance with M. Liverani, *UF* 2, pp. 89-108, who has demonstrated, that *kbd* means *'totalità, in tutto']*.

[75] *CTA* 14: 83-84.

[76] *CTA* 2:IV:10.

[77] *CTA* 5:II:12.

[78] Gordon, *UT, Grammar* 13. 71, 75.

[79] *CTA* 17:VI:20-21.

[80] *CTA* 4:I:31.

[81] The meaning of the word *kt* is in the nature of guesswork. See Gordon, *UT, Glossary* No. 1318; Driver, *CML*, p. 145; P. Fronzaroli, *La Fonetica Ugaritica*, Roma 1955, p. 73.

[82] *CTA* 4:IV:10-11.

of gold'.[83] The chiastic structure of the sentence which leads to the wording *dt yrq nqbnm* instead of *nqbnm dt yrq* should especially be noted. This word order removes the phrase with *dt* even further from the construct phrase. This distance still more increases in the verse: *bhty bnt dt ksp hkly dtm ḫrṣ*[84] 'My house[85] I have built of silver, my palace of gold'. We must suppose that this usage derives from sentences such as: *bhty dt ksp bnt*. But in the actual Ugaritic text the *nomen rectum* is so far removed from the *regens* that when we translate it into Biblical Hebrew we have to change it into an apposition: *bāttay bāniti käsäp* ...[86] *d(t)* comes also in place of a noun in phrases such as: *ᶜglm d[t] šnt*[87] 'One year old calves'; *šlyt dšbᶜt rašm*[88] 'ruler(?) of ...', i.e., 'possessing seven heads'; *il dpid*[89] 'Il of heart, (full of understanding)' and apparently also: *hyn dḥrš yd[m]*[90] '(The god) Hyn of the handicraft'. We find it in an independent phrase: *dt*

[83] For the word *nqbnm*, we should compare *nqb* (Ez. 28:13) the meaning of which is not known. Cf. also: Driver, *CML*, p. 156.

[84] *CTA* 4:VI:36-38.

[85] Gordon rightly notes (*UT, Glossary* No. 463) that the house of a god is occasionally mentioned in Ugaritic in the plural form *bhtm*. Höfner, *ASG*, pp. 106f., has also noted the same phenomenon in South Arabian. My late friend, Akiba Schlesinger, noted the Ugaritic parallel on the margin of his copy of the South Arabian grammar. Gordon explains that the god's house is composed of various buildings. Höfner similarly translates the South Arabian plural *'byt* 'Tempelanlage'. But perhaps we should explain the plural here as a *pluralis majestatis* whose usage is not limited to persons (such as *'ᵃdonim, bᵉᶜālim* in Hebrew), but is employed also for an object which belongs to the god or the king. Cf. Böhl, *op. cit.* (note 8), pp. 35ff.

[86] It may be pointed out that Friedrich, *PPG*, § 309, states that in Semitic languages the material from which an object is made is always in apposition. Therefore, he has difficulty with Punic which occasionally places the material after the particle of attachment *š*. But the problem which he deals with is not a real one, since there is no obligatory rule that the material must be attached to its object in apposition, but it may as well be connected with it as a *nomen rectum*. This type of construction of course may be broken up.

[87] *CTA* 4:VI: 42-43.

[88] *CTA* 5:I:3. For *šlyṭ*, see on the one hand Gordon, *UT, Glossary* No. 423 and on the other Cassuto, *Anath* p. 134 [Cf. now J. Blau - S.E. Loewenstamm, *UF* 2, p. 28].

[89] *CTA* 6:III: 14.

[90] *CTA* 17:V: 24-25.

ẓrh.[91] '(The muscles or the like) of her back'.

The historical development of the various usages of *d(t)* as a particle of attachment is open to discussion. Following Barth[92], we may emphasize the fact that besides its use as a particle of attachment, *d(t)* is used in Ugaritic as a relative pronoun only, and not as a demonstrative pronoun[92a], and we may conclude from this that the particle of attachment developed from the relative pronoun. According to this view, *gpnm dt ksp* means originally 'a harness which is silver' and from this 'a harness of silver'.[92b]

---

[91] *CTA* 3:III:32; *CTA* 4:II:20.
[J.C. de Moor, *JNES* 24 (1965), p. 356; *Seasonal Pattern*, p. 241 supposes the same nounlike use of *d* in *š^cly dġṯh bšmym // dġṯ hrnmy dkbkbm* (*CTA* 19: IV: 185-187; 192-193). According to him, "the parallel *dkbkbm* 'those-of-the-stars' simply requires 'those-of-the-heaven'". In our opinion the possibility of this interpretation is remote. The fact that the use of *d* as a quasi-noun is extremely rare in Ugaritic in contrast to its frequent attestation in the genitive construction should be taken into consideration. Therefore, we should rather translate: 'He made his incense ascend to heaven, the star-incense of the *hrnmy*', i.e. his incense for the stars. For another possible case of noun - like use see note 73a].

[92] Barth, *Pronominalbildung*, pp. 166ff.

[[92a] Cf. the Old-Aramaic relative pronoun *zi/di* which is clearly distinct from the demonstrative pronouns *znh, z' 'l, 'ln*. Therefore it is not exact to state that "... *die altaramäischen Inschriften ... das Demonstrativpronomen zi/di zur Einleitung von Relativsätzen benutzen*" (H.S. Schuster, *Studies in Honor of B. Landsberger*, Chicago 1965 p. 441). There is even no proof for the less sweeping statement that "*zy* as a relative pronoun goes back to a demonstrative pronoun" (E.Y. Kutscher, *Current Trends in Linguistic* 6 [1969], p. 352), since this statement cannot be verified by any text extant.]

[[92b] Such development of *d* phrases may easily be understood, if the *rectum* is undeterminated, i.e. in instances of *genetivus materiae* or *genetivus partitivus*. The development is less perspicuous, however, when the *rectum* is determinated, e.g. in the phrase *^cqbm d lbnn* 'tendons from the Lebanon'. The origin of that phenomenon could be explained by either of two ways or by both together 1) That the expression arose from a nominal phrase of attribution with a prepositional complement after *d*, e.g. *^cqbm d llbnn* 'tendons (?) which (are) from the Lebanon'. This possibility has been mentioned by M.Z. Kaddari in his discussion of the origin of Aramaic *zi/di* in genetive construction, but appears to him rather improbable (*Proceedings of the International Conference on Semitic Studies*, Jerusalem, 1969, p. 67). 2) that the expression originated from the analogous expansion of that genetive construction in which the *rectum* is undeterminated.
Anyhow the clear fact should not be overlooked that the use of Aramaic *zi/di* exactly corresponds to that of Ugaritic *d*. Therefore there is no cogent reason, to consider this Aramaic construction as loan translation

Furthermore, following his line of thought, the elimination of the noun preceeding the particle of attachment is the origin of an expression such as *dt ẓrh* paralleling Hebrew expression such as *šäl bet Gamli'el.*[93] Friedrich[94] takes the opposite point of view in explaining Phoenician - Punic *š*, which in its use parallels Ugaritic *d(t)* and Akkadian *ša*. According to him the original demonstrative force of *š* is kept in those phrases in which *š* does not refer to an anteceding noun, e.g. in the Punic phrase. *š^{c}zrb^{c}l* '(the grave) of ^{c}*zrb*^{c}*l*', literally 'that of ^{c}*zrb*^{c}*l*'. We should add that this linguistic usage is already found in Aramaic grave inscriptions in Syria from approximately 600 BCE in which the words *š'gbr, ššnzrbn*[95] occur meaning '(the grave of) *'gbr* (or of *šnzrbn*)'. Against this we should view the use of *š* in breaking up a construct phrase as well as its function as a relative pronoun as a result of the weakening of the original deictic meaning of

---

from the Akkadian. Contrast Schuster, *loc. cit.* (note 92a), p. 442 who argues that this use should be considered as "*Lehnübersetzung aus dem Akkadischen*" and Kutscher, *op. cit.* (note 92a), pp. 352f., who reaches at the same result in an independent discussion of the problem. Both scholars stress *inter alia* that the only attestation of this construction in documents from the Old-Aramaic period (10-8th century BCE) is found in Sfiré III: 7-8 (Cf. however R. Degen, *Altaramäische Grammatik*, Wiesbaden 1969, § 68 for possible additional examples in Sfiré) and Kutscher adds the short remark that even Sfiré III: 7-8 "can be explained differently". Cf. also Kaddari (*loc. cit.*), who holds the view that the Akkadian influence was the reason of the Aramaic *zi/di* construction with determinated *rectum* whereas this construction with undeterminated *rectum* might be explained as the result of an internal development. Without entering into the details of this discussion, we want to point out that an alternative solution is suggested by Ugaritic. True, even in Ugaritic texts the possibility of Akkadian influence cannot be excluded as far as administrative texts are concerned. But the genitive construction under discussion is found in the clearly genuine Ugaritic style of the epic poem as well, irrespective of whether the *rectum* be determinated or not. Therefore the Aramaic usage could have developed on the same lines. This argument gains additional force if we accept the thesis that Ugaritic *d* as a relative pronoun preceded *d* in the circumscription of the genitive. On the supposition that the same happened with Aramaic *zi/di* in a later period, the rareness of its use in Old Aramaic genitive constructions could satisfactorily be accounted for.*]*

93 Mishna Shekalim 3:3 *[*Cf. also *šäl hakkohānim* 'those of the priesthood' (Mishna Pesaḥim 1:6) and especially well-known Akkadian expressions like *ša reši*. Cf. also in Gilg. XI: 282 the variant readings *ša ṣuḫrijama* 'the state of my youth' and *ṣuḫrij[ama]* 'my youth'.*]*

94 Friedrich, *PPG*, § 310.2.

95 G.A. Cooke, *North-Semitic Inscriptions*, Oxford 1903, text 64:1; 65:1 (Note of Prof. Z. Ben-Ḥayyim). *[*E.Y. Kutscher, *op. cit.* (note 92a), p. 353 holds the view that this *š* "is Akkadian *ša* pure and simple". The isolated character of this *š* in Aramaic recommends his proposal.*]*

š. If we apply this to Ugaritic we must say that a phrase like *dt ẓrh* kept the original deictic force of *d*, and that the other usages of *d(t)* belong to later phases of the language. In any event, *d(t)* completely parallels Aramaic *zy, dy, d*, Akkadian *ša*[95a], and Phoenician-Punic *š*, all of which are undeclined for case, gender, and number, and are used both as relative pronouns and as particles of possession, whether in the meaning of 'the one of, possessor of', or to break up a construct phrase. There is, therefore, no basis for the accepted comparison of Ugaritic with Classical Arabic which formed from the element *ḏ* the noun *ḏu* declined according to case, gender, and number in the specialized meaning of 'the one of, possessor of'. Arabic does not use this noun either as a relative pronoun or in order to break up a construct phrase.[96]

After this discussion of *d(t)* as a particle of possession we now return to the question of how to explain the phenomenon that *d* and *dt* are synonymous in Ugaritic. It should be pointed out immediately that this is not a unique phenomenon. We find similarly in Punic that the demonstrative pronoun *z* interchanges with *zt* with both masculine and feminine nouns. Friedrich in his grammar of Phoenician and Punic states: "*Ein deutlich durch -t charakterisiertes Femininum* (of the demonstrative pronoun) ... *hat erst das Vulgärpunische in zt, st, syth, und dieses wird seinerseits als Maskulinum*

[[95a] In Old Akkadian, however, the determinative pronoun is inclined for case, gender and number.]

[96] South Arabian holds a special place. In this language the particles of possession are: *ḏ* (m. sg.), *ḏt* (f. sg.), *'lw* (pl. nominative), *'ly* (pl. obliquus). The singular forms *ḏ, ḏt* serve also as relative pronouns, but the plural forms *'lw, 'ly* do not. This implies that in South Arabian we should distinguish between the relative pronoun and the particle of attachment. The fact that the particle of attachment distinguishes in the plural between cases, establishes the assumption that the same distinction existed also in the singular, and that the declination of this particle in the singular was like that of Arabic. From this it may be concluded that the possessive particle *ḏ* acts like a noun like Arabic *ḏu* (Barth, *Pronominalbildung*, p. 168, note 2; Höfner, *ASG* § 37). The trouble is that the function of South Arabian *ḏ* is wider than that of Arabic *ḏu* and includes also the breaking up of the construct phrase, such as in the expression: *brktn ḏt ᶜrn* 'the cistern of the fortress'. This usage which diverges from the regular usage of the Arabic noun *ḏu* appears to be secondary, even if we do not accept Friedrich's opinion quoted above that the usage of the article of attachment is secondary also in the other Semitic languages.

verwendet".[97] From the references he quotes it is clear that the typical feminine form *zt* is known from seven examples as masculine, and from three as feminine. But his assumption that a typical feminine form may be used in most cases as a masculine one is strange, and it is evident a priori that it is not a feminine form at all. Barth already pointed the way to a solution of the problem in his thorough discussion of the Hebrew demonstrative pronoun *zo't*.[98] There he claimed that the *t* in *zo't* was not a feminine *t* but an additional deictic element. He brought proof from the short forms *zo* (*zw, zh*), which show that here it is the vowel which determines the feminine gender. He strengthened his proof by comparing the Hebrew demonstrative pronouns *zä, zo't* with their Ethiopic counterparts *ze-n-tū, zā-tī* which attach the deictic elements *tū* (m.), *tī* (f.) to the demonstrative pronouns. In his opinion the *t* of *zo't* is just a shortened form of the deictic element *tī* which is attached to the feminine. Barth, however, was aware of the difficulty that final long *i* in Hebrew should have remained. He answered that with the disappearance of deictic *t* from Hebrew, the ending *-ty* of *z'ty* was felt to be a feminine ending and was adapted to it. This answer seems at first sight somewhat far-fetched. One may additionally argue against him that *t* could have been appended to *zo* as a pleonastic feminine ending. But the forms *zt* and *dt* of Punic and Ugaritic - unknown at the time of Barth - prove conclusively that at least in the main point he had deep insight, namely, that the *t* of *zo't* is an additional deictic element. Perhaps we may strengthen his opinion by assuming that the *i* of the deictic element *ti* in Proto-Semitic was anceps, and that the Hebrew form developed from *zo'ti* with short *i*.

F. *hn, hm, hmt*

Virolleaud's new publication on which we have based our previous discussion adds to our knowledge also in the realm of the independent personal pronouns. It should be pointed out that we find here in Ugaritic for the first time the 3 f. pl. independent pronoun *hn* which until now was only known as a suffixed pronoun.[99] This pronoun is found in an account text:

---

[97] Friedrich, *PPG*, § 115.

[98] Barth, *Pronominalbildung*, pp. 83ff.; pp. 104f. *[*Cf. now Ch. Krahmalkov, *JSS* 14 (1969), pp. 201-204, who stresses the expression *mija-ti* in the El-Amarna letters.*]*

[99] Gordon, *UM*, *Grammar* 6. 13.

ṯt ktnm ḫmšt wnṣp ksp hn[100] 'Two garments are 5 (shekels) and a nṣp of silver'.

The pronoun *hmt* in a document on the responsibility of sureties also raises interesting questions. It is stated: *mnm šalm dt tknn ^{c}l ^{c}rbnm hn hmt tknn.*[101] Virolleaud translates: '*Et tous les enquêteurs qui doivent faire la preuve concernant (ces) ^{c}rbnm, voici ceux (qui) feront cette preuve.*' Perhaps it is better to translate: 'The guarantors shall be responsible for all claims which shall arise' (lit. whatever claims shall arise, upon the guarantors they shall arise).[101a] In any event, this document at first glance seems to permit the statement that the pronoun *hmt* is used here in the nominative case unlike the previously known texts in which the form *hmt* was used only for the *casus obliquus* while *hm* was used for the nominative.[102] It follows that *hm* and *hmt* freely interchange in Ugaritic. This claim is strengthened by the accepted assumption of the free interchange of these two forms in Proto-Semitic, especially the nominative use of *hmt* in Phoenician.[103] Z. Ben-Ḥayyim, however, has rightly pointed out to me that the form *hmt* in our text is preceded by the presentative particle *hn* whose Arabic parallel *'inna* attracts after it the accusative. Unfortunately, it

---

[100] *PRU* 2, text 110:6. Virolleaud unfortunately forgot to include the word *hn* in this text in his *Glossaire*.
[Gordon, *UT, Glossary* No. 781 records such *hn* in *PRU* 2, text 2:49. But there the context is broken and *hn* cannot be explained with certainty.]

[101] *PRU* 2, text 161: 5-9.

[[101a] Contrast M. Liverani, *U* 6, pp. 375-378 who renders: '*E tutti i debiti che verranno stabiliti a carico dei loro garanti serranno stabiliti.*' From a legal point of view, this interpretation is identical with our proposal. But in our opinion *hn hmt* refers back to *šalm* while in Liverani's opinion to *^{c}rbnm*, as stressed in his remark: "*^{c}rbnm hn hmt litteralmente i garanti, quelli loro*". His explanation is based upon the concept discussed *supra* note 52, that Ugaritic *hn* may approximate in its use the Hebrew article. Moreover, Liverani's proposal implies here that an indeterminated noun *^{c}rbnm* had been followed by a determinated attribute. Such a Ugaritic construction would be strikingly different from both the Hebrew pattern *haddābār hazzä* and the Phoenician pattern *haddabar zä*. For the same reason we cannot accept the translation of M. Dietrich - O. Loretz - J. Sanmartîn (*UF* 6, p. 467): '*und werden alle Forderungen, die festgestellt wurden, zu Lasten der Bürgen selbst festgestellt.*' Cf. also A.F. Rainey, *UF* 3, pp. 159f.; Aartun, *Partikeln*, p. 70.]

[102] Gordon, *UT, Grammar* 6.3.4.

[103] Friedrich, *PPG*, § 111. Cf. J. Blau, *H. Yalon Memorial Volume*, Jerusalem 1974, p. 20 (in Heb.).

is not possible at present to establish whether this rule applied also to Ugaritic *hn*. This assumption finds some support in the well-known fact that as of yet we have not found in Ugaritic the m. and f. pronouns *hw, hy* except in the nominative, unlike the pronouns *hwt, hyt* which are limited to the *casus obliquus*.[104] At present it is impossible to decide whether the document under discussion testifies to the free interchange between *hm* and *hmt* in the nominative, or whether we should conclude from it, that the interjection *hn* attracts after it the accusative.

---

104 Gordon, *UT, Grammar* 6. 4.
[*hm* is attested as an accusative in *b^cl ymšḥ hm* (*CTA* 10:II:23) 'Baal will anoint them' and in *lm lytn hm mlk* (*PRU* 2, text 12: 25-26) 'Why does the king not provide them'. The question is complicated, however, since *ymšḥ hm* and *ytn hm* stand here for *ymšḥhm* and *ytnhm*. Therefore, we touch here upon the problem of the possible origin of the suffixed pronoun from the separate one. The first scholar to raise this problem was Chr. Sarauw, *Über Akzent und Silbenbildung*, København 1939, p. 23. Sarauw stressed that the forms of the noun with a heavy suffix agree with the construct forms and offered the explanation that these suffixes were originally independent words with a genitive function. Recently his idea has been taken up by J. Blau, *Remarks upon the Change of Stress in Ancient Hebrew, Schirman Jubilee Volume*, Jerusalem 1970, p. 33, note 19 (in Heb.). Blau noted *inter alia* that *hm* is attested as an independent word after nouns in the Old Aramaic inscriptions of Zakur A l. 9 and Bar Rekab l. 19 and drew attention also to *w'sḥb hm* 'and I dragged them' in the Meša^c inscription, l. 18, where independent *hm* appears after *yaq=tul*. In Ugaritic we are confronted with *diy hwt, diy hyt* and *diy hmt* (*CTA*, 19:III:133, 137-138, 149-150) his, her, their pinions instead of *diyh, diyhm* and with the above mentioned *ymšḥ hm*. The pronouns *hwt* etc. then appear in the regular genitive form, in spite of the fact that they fulfill the function of suffixes. In constrast to this *hm* in *ymšḥ hm* and *ytn hm* show the form of a verbal suffix, and not the usual form of the independent pronoun *hmt* in the *casus obliquus*. This points to the secondary character of the differentiation between *hm* and *hmt*.]

The Hebrew Root ḥrš in the Light of the Ugarit Texts

Hebrew lexicography, like that of any other language, is necessarily based on the assumption that within the compass of a single root there are semantic transitions leading from a first to a second meaning. Consequently the temptation to build arbitrary semantic bridges is particularly great in a language like Hebrew, where research must always take into account the possibility of several different primitive Semitic roots coinciding in a Hebrew word. Hence the essential rule, undisputed in principle, that the theory of semantic transition needs constantly to be checked in its application by a comparison of Hebrew with those Semitic languages which have to a greater extent preserved the original phonetic structure of Proto-Semitic. Among these languages a significant place has, for several decades, been occupied by Ugaritic. We propose to show that the rule has not always been adequately observed, taking as an example for discussion the unequivocal example of the Hebrew root *ḥrš*.

This Hebrew root denotes, among other things, the activities of: (1) the ploughman (e.g. in Deut. 22:10), (2) the cutter and engraver (Jer. 17:1), (3) the craftsman. For the latter meaning we twice find the participle *ḥoreš* with the objective genitive of the raw-material fashioned (Gen. 4:22; 1 Reg. 7:14), but more frequently the substantive form *ḥārāš*, which stresses the professional character of the activity. This form also can be complemented by reference either to the raw material (e.g. Is. 44:12) or alternatively the finished product (e.g. Is. 14:16).

It has long been correctly observed that the Hebrew verb *ḥrš* = plough has an exact conterpart in the Arab verb *ḥrṯ* which has the same meaning. It is thus natural not only to connect the two meanings to plough and to engrave, but also to suggest a link between the meaning cutting, engraving and the meaning craftsman. And indeed, we find that the older dictionaries of Gesenius-Buhl and Brown-Driver-Briggs as well as Koehler's new lexicon trace all three meanings back to the same Proto-Semitic root *ḥrṯ*. Among still earlier views we may mention the opinion of Mandelkern who, in his concordance, lists the expressions for ploughing separately and suggests a second root comprising the two meanings of engraving and craftsman. In opposition to the above mentioned opinions we shall try to show that it is only the expressions for ploughing and engraving which are derived from the Proto-Semitic root *ḥrṯ*, but not the expressions for craftsman.

The verb *ḥrš* = to engrave is found in the parallel form *ḥrt* in the Bible itself. (Ex. 32:16), [mostly explained as a North Israelite Aramaism]. This parallel is obviously the same as the Aramaic verb *ḥrt*, which in the TO to Lev. 19:18 is used in the combination *rušmin ḥ^aritin* to translate *k^etobät qa^ca qa^c* and denotes tattoo cuts. The alternation of the two synonymous forms *ḥrš* and *ḥrt* suggests a common origin from a Proto-Semitic *ḥrṯ* or *ḫrṯ*. We have, however, no evidence that a root *ḫrṯ* exists. We may therefore accept the usual interpretation that derives *ḥrš* = to engrave from the Proto-Semitic root *ḥrṯ* which means cutting in general and the cutting up of the ground by the plough in particular. This interpretation is further confirmed by a Ugaritic text which says of a mourner: *yḥrṯ kgn aplb*[1] - 'he ploughs his breast as if it were a garden', i.e. he makes cuts in his body. The close relation of the meanings to make cuts and to plough is spotlighted by this expression, which recalls the usage of the Targum quoted above.

So far the Ugaritic text has served as no more than a welcome confirmation of a conclusion convincing enough in itself. It assumes, however, a decisive significance in the elucidation of the root *ḥrš* in the meaning of craftsman. The Ugaritic word-combinations *ḥrš anyt* = shipbuilder, *ḥrš mrkbt* = chariot-builder etc.[2] provide an entirely new and conclusive proof that the Hebrew world for craftsman is derived from an independent Proto-Semitic root, not identical with *ḥrṯ*.

It would be easy to distribute the various references between the two roots, were it not for certain difficulties which arise in those cases where the Hebrew verb *ḥrš* is used figuratively as, for instance, in the saying: *'al taḥ^aroš ^cal re^cakā rā^cā w^ehu' yošeb lābäṭaḥ 'ittāk* (Pr. 3:29). It would here seem possible to make the verb *ḥrš* mean to work evil and thereby to assume, with Mandelkern, that the verbal image is taken from the activity of the craftsman. It is, however, more plausible to assume that the reference

[1] *CTA* 5:VI:20-21.

[2] Gordon, *UT, Glossary* No. 668; Virolleaud, *PRU 2, Glossaire*, p. 208.

is not to a completed evil action but to wicked plans or preparations for bad deeds. An analogy to such plans and preparations may be seen in the ploughing which precedes sowing and reaping and thereby clearly symbolizes a future-directed beginning. This aspect of the metaphor was already recognized by Rashi who remarks to Pr. 3:29 "Devise not. Devising is represented by the metaphor of ploughing; just as the ploughman makes the ground ready for the time of sowing, so the man who devises wickedness prepares the ground in his heart for crooked scheming which he intends to realise". This explanation of Rashi's holds good even more, of course, for a turn of phrase such as: *leb ḥoreš maḥšᵉbot 'āwän* (Pr. 6:18), which concerns wicked thoughts *expressis verbis* and which is indeed formulated in such a way as to suggest the comparison with *ḥorᵉše 'āwän wᵉzorᵉᶜe ᶜāmāl yiqṣᵉruhu* (Job 4:8), where the images of sowing and reaping make it quite clear that evil intention is indicated by the image of ploughing.

Review of Charles Virolleaud - Le Palais Royal d'Ugarit II, Paris 1957

From the first text discoveries at Ugarit the *editio princeps* has been entrusted to the sure hands of Virolleaud who has made important contributions both to the decipherment of the Ugaritic alphabet and to the interpretation of the new texts. He has even specialized in making autographs of the cuneiform texts as no other scholar has. This experience has stood by this distinguished scholar in the edition of the new texts which were found in the palace of the kings of Ugarit, and we may state that this new book continues a tradition of the highest standing.

Most of the texts were discovered during the years 1951-1953. To these were added some tablets from the excavations of the years 1935, 1948, 1949, and even two tablets from the excavations of 1955. Not all of the material presented here is new to Ugaritic scholars. Some of it has already been published in *Syria* in 1951, while as for the rest of the material, there were some notices in the recent annuals of *CRAIBL*. Furthermore, Virolleaud generously permitted Gordon to utilize the new material in the preparation of the Glossary of his *Ugaritic Manual*. Nevertheless, it must be stated that most of the tablets are published here in their entirety for the first time. The texts are given in Virolleaud's cuneiform hand copies and in transcriptions into latin characters which - in spite of the printer's errors which have occasionally crept into the transcription - make the reading of the copies easier.

Photographs of some of the texts have been included, and Virolleaud has added interesting commentaries, and when necessary and possible - also translations. Similarly, he has appended a glossary and indices of personal, divine, and geographic names. A general survey by Claude Schaeffer, the director of excavations at Ugarit, facilitates study of the texts.

The table of contents shows that the book contains a collection of almost all the types of texts which have ever been found at Ugarit. There are fragments of the Baal Epic, royal documents, private letters, lists of court personnel and of various craftsmen, texts listing the produce of vineyards and olive groves, garments, weapons, Ugaritic ABC's, including two fragments of a list which adds to each Ugaritic letter the parallel sign in Akkadian cuneiform, etc.

The new fragments of the Baal Epic were not known until now, but they are so fragmentary and difficult that the possibilities establishing their content are very slim. However, it should be pointed out that new everyday texts provide considerable help in clarifying previously known obscure passages in the epic. An exemplary case, is the word *ištir* which is found once in the Aqht Epic in a difficult context: *n[ᶜ]mn. ġ̇zr. št. ṯrm. w[...] ištir. bḏdm wnᶜrs[...].*[1] Ginsberg translates: 'The darling Youth has set meat and *[drink]*. He is left in the fields and ... *[...]*'.[2] This implies that he took *ištir* as *š'r* (*Gt*). Driver, following Gaster, divides *ištir* into two words: *išt ir*, and translates: '(when) the gracious one, the hero puts on a meal and I *[myself]* I will put moisture(?) on the fields and lo! *[they shall]* indeed be tilled'.[3] He explains that this is a magic text which preserves the earth's fertility. Gordon[4] interpreted *ištir* as a *št* form of *'wr* and offered the translation: 'I shall provide myself with light'. All of these theories have been proved false now that we find in no. 83:3 *kd ištir*, mentioned after 14 (jars) of oil. This implies that *ištir* is the name of a victual (pure oil?)[4a] which is mentioned in the epic during the description of the meal.

---

1 *CTA* 18:IV: 14-15.

2 H.L. Ginsberg, *ANET*, p. 152.

3 Driver, *CML*, pp. 57, 135, 141.

4 Gordon, *UM*, *Glossary* No. 76.
*[*But cf. now id., *UT*, *Glossary* No. 404: a liquid.*]*

*[*4a Contrast J. Hoftijzer, *UF* 3, pp. 361-364 who parses *ištir* as Gt of *š'r*, meaning 'to be left over' and translates *arbᶜ ᶜšrh šmn d lqḥt ṯlġ̇ḏy w kd ištir ᶜm qrt* as follows: 'fourteen jars of oil, which *T.* has taken (with her) and an (other) jar (containing oil) are still owed by the city'. With his translation of *ᶜm* as synonym of *ᶜl* contrast Gordon, *UT*, *Grammar*, 10.14, note 2, who renders *ᶜm* 'to the credit of'. Anyhow the possibility can not be excluded, that the text opposes the fourteen jars of oil, taken away by *T.* to one jar (of oil) which remains with the city, whether this implies that that one jar remained to the debit or credit of the city or not.*]*

Sometimes the texts add to our knowledge of typical word combinations. We find in the Anat Epic: *ybrd ṯd lpnwh bḥrb mlḥt qṣ mri*[5] 'He cut up a slice of a breast before him with ... knife the breast of a fatling'. *mlḥt* is generally related to Arabic *maliḥ* 'good', yielding the translation: 'with a good sword', i.e., 'with a good knife'. But this epithet for a knife is somewhat colourless. Therefore, Gordon explains: 'with a good / sharp sword'.[6] Cassuto, basing himself on another meaning of the root *malaḥa* translates: 'with a nursing sword'.[7] Driver, following de Vaux translates: 'with a shining sword', and finds support for his translation in Arabic *lamiḥ* 'shining'.[8] We now find in no. 128:19-20 *alp uz mrat mlḥt* 'a thousand fat geese of good appearance'. It is the same pair of roots, *mr'* and *mlḥ* which is found in the epic. Here, however, the adjective *mlḥ* is figuratively transferred from a description of meat to a description of the knife which cuts it.[8a]

Sometimes a simple administrative text adds both to our understanding of the epic and to the study of Hebrew lexicography. Some scholars already connected the word *nṯq* in the Baal epic[9] with the Hebrew word *nešäq*[10], but this opinion has not been generally accepted.[11] We now find in no. 123: 1-3 *arb*^{c}*m. qšt. alp ḥ̈zm. walp nṯq. ṯn. ql*^{c}*m.* This shows that the noun *nṯq* stands for a weapon or a part of one. Even though its exact meaning is unknown to us, it is nevertheless clear that those scholars who connected the word *nṯq* in the Ugaritic epic with Hebrew *nešäq* - whose Proto-Semitic root is now finally clarified - were right.

---

[5] *CTA* 3:I: 6-8.

[6] Gordon, *UT, Glossary* No. 1482.

[7] Cassuto, *Anath*, p. 108.

[8] Driver, *CML*, p. 162.

[8a] *[*But cf. now J. Blau - S.E. Loewenstamm, *UF* 2, p. 21, note 9.*]*

[9] *CTA* 4:VII: 39.

[10] U. Cassuto, *Dinaburg Jub. Vol.*, Jerusalem 1949, p. 66 (in Heb.) *[= BOST* 2, p. 190*]*; *KBL*, s.v.

[11] Gordon, *UM, Glossary* No. 1303, does not offer any translation. *[*But cf. now id., *UT, Glossary* No. 1721: a kind of weapon*]* and similarly Ginsberg, *ANET*, p. 135; Driver, *CML*, p. 157: 'clash'.

In his explanation of the Ugaritic legal documents Virolleaud made use of the legal texts from Ugarit - which were drawn up in Akkadian. For example, he explains the expression *šḥr ᶜlmt* (No. 8:15) as being parallel to the term *urra šera* 'in the future' which is well-known from the Akkadian of Mari, Alalakh, and Ugarit.[12] It is possible to continue in this manner in order to clarify these documents more fully.

We will limit ourselves here to one instructive example, text no. 5, whose beginning is broken. After the break it reads: (2) *bunṯ km. špš* (3) *dbrt. kmt* (4) *br. s̈tqšlm* (5) *bunṯ. ᶜd ᶜlm* (6) *mišmn. nqmd* (7) *mlk ugrt* (8) *nqmd mlk ugrt* (9) *ktb spr hnd* (10) *dt brrt. s̈tqšlm* (11) *ᶜbdh. hnd* (12) *wmnkm. lyqḥ* (13) *spr. mlk. hnd* (14) *byd. s̈tqšlm* (15) *ᶜd ᶜlm*. Virolleaud translates: '( ) *sur le peuple* (?), *comme le soleil* (3) *qui brille, ainsi (que)* (4) *brille S̈tq-šlm* (5) *sur le peuple*(?) *à jamais,* (6-7) *Sceau de Niqmad, roi d'Ugarit* (8) *Niqmad roi d'Ugarit* (9) *a écrit cette lettre-ci* (10) *qui (est) la ... de S̈tq-šlm,* (11) *ce sien serviteur,* (12) *et que les ... ne la saisissent pas.* (13) *Cette lettre royale-ci* (14) *(qu'elle demeure) dans les mains de S̈tq-šlm* (15) *à jamais*." Virolleaud thus explained *unṯ* as cognate with Hebrew *'ănoš*. However, Nougayrol has already pointed out that in the Akkadian texts from Ugarit the term *unṯ* parallels *unuš(š)u* which is synonymous with *pilku* or *ilku*, both denoting feudal servitude connected with land tenure.[13] Let us add that Speiser has offered even closer definitions and suggested that *pilku* refers to payments, *ilku* to services and has tentatively equated *unuš(š)u* with *pilku*. In addition Speiser has rightly connected *unuš(š)u = unṯ* with Hurrian *LÚ.MEŠ u-nu-šu-ḫu-li* 'people who are required to do) *unuš(š)u*" which is found in the Alalakh tablets, and assigned to the word a Hurrian origin.[14] Furthermore, we should not overlook the ob-

---

[12] On this expression, see: J. Nougayrol, *PRU* 3, p. 230, and especially: E.A. Speiser, *JAOS* 74 (1954), p. 23, who establishes that the literal meaning of the word *šēra* is 'day dawn'. The same word *šḥr* 'dawn' is found in the Ugaritic expression, but *ᶜlmt* is obscure.

[13] J. Nougayrol, *PRU* 3, p. 227.

[14] E.A. Speiser, *JAOS* 75 (1955), pp. 161ff. Speiser admits that his equation of *unuš(š)u* with *pilku* - and not with *ilku* - is uncertain. Unfortunately, the Ugaritic texts do not permit a definite decision on the matter. [R. Yaron, *VT* 10 (1960), pp. 83-90 argues that in *PRU* 2, text 6 *unṯ* rather denotes 'landed property' and that Hurrian *unuššuḫuli* should rather be rendered 'landowner'. His criticism overshoots the mark. *Unuṯ*, like *ilku* and *pilku*, designates both feudal servitude connected with land-te-

vious similarity between the Ugaritic text: *br ṣṭqšlm bunṯ* and Akkadian: *ištu pilki zakî*[15] 'he is pure (i.e., free) from the feudal payment'. Moreover, in Akkadian texts, *zakî* is sometimes expanded into expressions such as[16]: *kīma šamši zakīti / zakî* 'like the sun is clear so is N clear', i.e. there are no legal claims whatsoever against him. This clarifies the beginning of the document as follows: '... (2) from servitude, like the sun (3) which is clear, so (4) Ṣṭqšlm is clear (5) from servitude forever. (6) Seal of Nqmd. (7) king of Ugarit. (8) Nqmd king of Ugarit (9) has written this document (10) of 'clarity' (i.e., freedom from servitude) of Ṣṭqšlm (11) his servant'.

This document contains therefore a royal privilegium which frees Ṣṭqšlm from servitude - apparently payments - on the lands which he held. The meaning of the conclusion of the document also may be determined with certainty in the light of the regular closing formulae in the Akkadian documents from Ugarit, e.g.: *amīlum*^{lum} *ma-am-ma-an la-a i-laq-qì eqla*$^{ḫi-a}$ *an-na-a iš-tu qā-ti amīlu kur-wa-na*[17] 'No one shall take these fields from the hand of Kurwana'. Also: *ma-am-ma-an la i-le-qi iš-tu qāti*^{ti}*-šu-nu ni-id-na an-na-am*[18] 'No one shall take this gift from their hands'. This same scheme is found here: "(12) and no one[19] shall take (13) this document of the king (14) from the hand of Ṣṭqšlm (15) forever".[20]

---

nure and land-tenure connected with feudal servitude. On *ilku* and *pilku* see M. Dietrich - O. Loretz, *UF* 4, pp. 165f. who deny any differentiation between them and consider *pīl - ku* as a variant orthography of *il-ku* which should be read *jil-ku.]*

[15] J. Nougayrol, *PRU* 3, p. 227.

[16] id., *ibid.*, p. 231.

[17] *ibid.*, RS 15.136:13-15, p. 122.

[18] *ibid.*, RS 15. Z. 10-12, p. 59.

[19] *mnkm* is an indefinite pronoun composed of the elements *mn* + *k* + *m*. cf. in this volume, *Notes on the Pronouns in Ugaritic*, p. 61. Virolleaud did not translate the word, but in his *Glossaire* he notes that it means '*quelqu'un, personne.*'

[20] After this article was submitted for publication Albright's important study (W.F. Albright, *BASOR* 150 (1958), pp. 36-38) appeared. In note 11 Albright also deals with *PRU* 2, text 5. On the whole, his translation conforms to the translation offered here even though Albright does not utilize the Akkadian parallels. Only two points of his explanation should be challenged: 1) Albright did not translate *unṯ*. He therefore considered the text to be a document of manumission, whereas study of the word *unṯ* shows that the text deals with exemption of payments incumbent on a ser-

Even after the translation of this document there still remains room for linguistic notes. For the first time we find in this document the correlative use of the words *km-kmt* 'like', synonymous with the phrase *k-km* in the epic texts[21] and paralleling *kama-kama* in Palestinian Arabic.[22] We learn from this that Ugaritic *km* interchanged with an enlarged form *kmt* which is similar to *k*^{e}*mot* in Mishnaic Hebrew. This Hebrew word was usually explained as a combination of *k*^{e}*mo* + *'ot* (as in *'oto hā'iš* 'that man') until Barth explained the *t* of *k*^{e}*mot* as an adverbial suffix.[23] The absence of the pronominal element *'ot* in Ugaritic gives final confirmation to Barth's explanation. As to the history of Biblical style, the use of the adjective *br* in reference to the sun is interesting. Cf. the verse: "bright (*bārā*) as the sun" (Cant. 6:10).[23a]

There is occasionally room for alternative translations even of texts which cannot be elucidated by Akkadian parallels. No. 107: 5-8 reads: *mlbš. ṯrmnm* (6) *k. yṯn, w. b. bt* (7) *mlk. mlbš* (8) *ytn lhm*. Virolleaud translates: '*Les vêtements des šrmnm, quand ils sont usês et que (les šrmnm) (couchent) dans la maison du roi, (le roi) leur donne un vêtement (neuf)*'. Noting the fact that the preposition *b* in Ugaritic is often used in the meaning 'from' we should perhaps translate: '(5) when the garment of the ṯrmnm (6) is old

---

vant of the king, i.e. a freeman; 2) He is of the opinion that *hnd* should be translated 'here'. But in the light of the Akkadian parallels we should accept Virolleaud's opinion that *hnd* is a demonstrative pronoun. In addition to the Akkadian texts quoted above, compare also with Gordon, *UT, Glossary* No. 786 the expression *lym hnd* with the very frequent Akkadian formula *ištu ūmi annī(m)* 'from this day'.

21 *CTA* 6:II: 28-30.

22 G. Kampffmeyer, *Glossar zu den 5000 Arabischen Sprichwörtern aus Palästina*, Berlin 1930, p. 62. I should like to thank Dr. J. Blau who called my attention to this parallel.

23 Barth, *Pronominalbildung*, pp. 87ff.

[23a Cf. also Ps. 19:9, where the epithet *bar* has been transferred from the sun to the Torah. See N. Sarna, *Fourth World Congress of Jewish Studies* 1, Jerusalem 1967, p. 174. In Akkadian *barīru* denotes the rays of the sun.]

(i.e., worn out), from the house (7) of the king a (new) garment (8) should be given to them'.[24] Also in no. 19:7-8, Virolleaud's translation is doubtful. The text reads: *iršt* (8) *aršt laḫy lr^{c}y*. Virolleaud translates: *'Que le désir des désirs (le plus cher de ses désirs) soit accordé, (par les dieux?) à mon frère à mon ami'*. This implies that he took *aršt* as the plural of *iršt*. But this assumption does not give a satisfactory explanation for the interchange of *i* and *a*, and we should perhaps translate: 'I made a request of my brother, my friend'.

In No. 10 Virolleaud gives up in his attempt to translate the words *iky aškn*. The document reads as follows: (1) *ṭhm. rgm* (2) *mlk.* (3) *l ḥyil* (4) *lm. tlik.*[25] *^{c}my* (5) *iky. aškn* (6) *^{c}ṣm. lbt. dml* (7) *pank. atn* (8) *^{c}ṣm. lk*. Here also a quite simple translation is required: (1) 'The message[25a]: (2) The king spoke to (3) Ḥyil: (4) Why did you send to me (saying): (5) How should I place (6) wood in the house of Dml? (7) (Behold) I shall give (8) wood to you'. The use of the interrogatory pronoun *iky* parallels here exactly the Hebrew interrogatory pronouns *'ek, 'ekā* which also introduce questions in which the speaker points out the impossibility of carrying out the action, e.g.: "How (*'ekā*) can I bear alone the weight and burden of you ...?" (Deut. 1:12). We should not be surprised to find alongside the Ugaritic interrogatory pronoun *ik* the secondary form *iky*. Barth already pointed out the rule that deictic elements may be attached to the interrogatory element *'ay > 'e*, and he even noted the deictic force of the elements *k* and *y*.[26] Furthermore, it seems that the verb *škn* here fits the meaning of Akkadian *šakānu* 'to place', used in the same meaning in No. 12:22-24.[26a]

---

[24] As in Hebrew *w* introduces here the apodosis. For Ugaritic cf. *PRU* 2, text 13: 16-20. *[*Ugaritic *yṯn* proves conclusively that Hebrew *yāšān* 'old' derives from Proto-Semitic *yṯn* and not from Proto-Semitic *yšn* as was generally supposed. Cf. the standard dictionaries.*]*

[25] *tlik* is a secondary form of *tlak* and up until now it has no parallel in the Ugaritic texts.

[[25a] I would now take *ṭhm* as object of *rgm* 'A word spoke the king to ...'*]*

[26] Barth, *Pronominalbildung*, pp. 80ff.; 83ff.; 144ff. *iky* already appeared in an obscure passage. See: *UT* 138:6; *Glossary* No. 1222, Gordon derives this word from the verb *kyy* and translates 'I read'. This explanation is however too daring, and perhaps we should explain *iky* in this passage also as an interrogatory pronoun.

[[26a] Contrast M. Dietrich - O. Loretz - J. Sanmartín, *U* 6, p. 51 who parse *aškn* as *Š* of *kūn* and render *'bereitstellen'*. In our opinion H. has received a royal order to perform certain woodworks in the temple and complains of lack of wood.*]*

The salutatory formula in No. 19 has special interest for Hebrew. The text reads: (2) *ilm* (3) *tġrk. tšlmk* (4) *t^{c}zzk. alp ymm* (5) *wrbt šnt* (6) *b^{c}d ^{c}lm* (2) 'May the gods (3) protect you, give you peace, (4) give you strength for a thousand days (5) and for a myriad of years, (6) forever.' Scholars usually derive the form *tġrk* from the root *nġr* 'to guard, protect', implying that Ugaritic *ġ* parallels here Proto-Semitic ẓ. However, we should not overlook the fact that the *Hiph^{c}il* of ^{c}*wr* in Hebrew (or the *Qal* of ^{c}*yr*?) is used in the meaning 'watch, guard' in the verse "If you are pure and upright, surely then he will guard (*yā^{c}ir*) you, and give welfare (*w^{e}šillam*) to your rightful habitation" (Job 8:6). It is difficult to separate the Ugaritic phrase *tġrk tšlmk* from the Hebrew parallelism *yā^{c}ir // w^{e}šillam*. We may therefore derive also the Ugaritic verbal form *tġrk* from either *ġyr* or *ġwr* and assume that the verse in Job is based on a poetic development of an ancient salutatory formula.[26b] The parallelism "thousand // myriad" has been known for a long time from both the Ugaritic texts and the Bible[27], but we find here for the first time in Ugaritic the parallelism *ymm // šnt* which is common in the Bible (Deut. 32:7; Ps. 61:7; 77:6; Pr. 3:2; 10:27; Job 32:7). It should also be pointed out that the Ugaritic phrase *alp ymm* is close in meaning to "a thousand years", and we may now easily understand how the word "days" in the Bible is employed also in the meaning "year" (Lev. 25:29; Ju. 17:10; etc.). The phrase *b^{c}d ^{c}lm* which replaces the usual expression *^{c}d ^{c}lm* is strange. However, we should compare the verse "Evil shall not draw near and come to us (*ba^{ca}denu*)" (Am. 9:10) which is usually emended to *^{ca}denu*. The Ugaritic text shows that *b^{c}d* may also be employed in the meaning *^{c}d*[27a], and this confirms the massoretic reading.

No. 189 which is a joint of two pieces of a broken tablet containing a Ugaritic-Akkadian syllabary is a fundamental discovery. The following is the content of the fragmentary tablet: *a a ; b be ; g ga ; ḫ ḫa ; d di ;*

[[26b] Cf. now in the present volume *Ugaritic Formulas of Greeting*, pp. 362-365, and *Who is afraid of the Linguistic Method*, pp. 433-439.]

[27] U. Cassuto, *Tarbiz* 14 (1943), pp. 4-5 [= *BOSt* 2, p. 50].

[[27a] Cf. also the difficult passage *^{c}opäl wābahan hāyā b^{ec}ad m^{ec}ārot* (Is. 32:14). Perhaps even here *b^{ec}ad* may be synonymous with *^{c}ad* and denote 'like'. For *^{c}ad* denoting 'to the degree of, even like' in comparisons see Na. 1:10; 1 Chr. 4:27.]

h û ; *w wa (wi, wu)* ; *z zi* ; *ḥ ku* ; *ṭ ṭi* ; ... *[p] [p]u* ; *ṣ ṣa* ; *q qu* ; *r ra* ; *š sa* ; *ġ ḫa* ; *t tu* ; *i i* ; *u u* ; s_2 *zu*. In general, these transcriptions employ the transcription method known from personal names found both in the Ugaritic and Akkadian scripts. It should be especially noted that *a, i, u* are always transcribed by *a, i* (or *e*)[28] and *u* without indicating the *'*, which is possible in Akkadian writing. Similarly, the transcription of *ġ* by *ḫa* is not surprising, since Ugaritic *ġ* is always transcribed in Akkadian by a sign which indicates *ḫ* + a vowel. The transliteration of s_2 by *zu* is new. *[*But the sign may also be transcribed *sú]*. The rare letter s_2, which interchanges in Ugaritic with s_1, has not yet been found in transcriptions from Ugarit. Virolleaud however correctly compares the Ugaritic spelling s_2s_2w 'horse' with the Canaanite gloss in the El-Amarna tablets (*EA* 263:25) which explains Akkadian *sise* 'horses' by *zu-û-[zi-ma] [*or *sú-û [sî-ma]]*. The transcription of *h* by *û* is somewhat difficult.[28a] In the few transcriptions of Ugaritic words containing *h* this letter is not transcribed at all. Cf. *ulnhr*[29] with *u-lu-na-a-ri*[30], *hzp* with *^{âl}izpi*[31], and perhaps also *ḏmrhd*[32] with *Zi-im-rad-du*.[33] But we should note that there is no *h* in the Akkadian writing system, and that any transcription attempt into Akkadian is doomed to failure.[33a] More puzzling is the transcription of *ḥ* by *ku*. Virolleaud rightly points out that in the Akkadian transcription system used in practice there is no difference between *ḥ* and *ḫ*[34], and we should probably

[28] There are so far two examples for the rare transcription of *i* by *e*: 1) *iryn* = *e-ri-ia-na*; 2) *iġyn, iḫyn* (sic!) = *e-ḫi-ia-nu*. See: *PRU* 3, pp. 243ff.

[[28a] Cf. now A. Jirku, *ArOr* 38 (1970), pp. 129; A.F. Rainey, *Lĕšonēnu* 34 (1969/70), p. 181 (in Heb.)*]*

[29] Gordon, *UT, Glossary* No. 195.

[30] J. Nougayrol, *PRU* 3, p. 259.

[31] Gordon, *UT, Glossary* No. 757.

[32] Gordon, *UT, Glossary* No. 727.

[33] J. Nougayrol, *PRU* 3, p. 262.

[[33a] In transcriptions Akkadian *û* represents the three Ugaritic Laryngals *'*, *h* and ^{c}, when vocalized with *u*. See A. Jirku, *ArOr* 38 (1970), pp. 129f.*]*

[34] *[*See Gordon, *UT, Glossary* Nos. 836, 843, 890, 1088, 1634, 2398. Cf. also Ugaritic *ḥnn* with its Akkadian transcription *ḫa - na - (an) - nu* (*PRU* 3, p. 244)*]*. But cf. also the personal name *nḥbl* (Gordon, *op. cit., ibid.*, No. 1632) with the name *na-'a-pa-li* (Nougayrol, *op. cit.*, p. 251), which may also be read: *na-'a-ba-li*. This implies that *ḥ* may also be transcribed by *'*. This is not, however, proof for the possibility of the transcription of *ḥ* by *ku*.

treat the exceptional transcription *ku* as a scribal error and not as proof for a fricative pronunciation of the Akkadian sign *ku*.[34a]

Gelb has recently dealt with this syllabary[35] from another point of view. He looks in it for a support of his theory that the Canaanite alphabet was composed of syllables and not of consonants. Gelb does not, of course, ignore the clear fact that Akkadian does not possess signs to indicate simple consonants, and that the Ugaritic transcriber had to choose Akkadian signs representing a consonant + a vowel; however, he bases himself on the interchange of vowels found in the Akkadian signs in the syllabary tablet. This proof is not convincing since it is possible that the Ugaritic scribe disregarded the vowels which follow the consonant in the Akkadian signs.

[34a] *[*So also F.M. Cross - T.O. Lambdin, *BASOR* 160 (1960), pp. 21-25. Contrast E.A. Speiser, *BASOR* 175 (1964), pp. 42-47, Speiser supposes that the author was desirous of indicating the difference of *ḫ* and *ḥ* beyond any possibility of confusion. Since the *[ḫ]* group was the proper and traditional mean of transcribing *[ḫ]*, another sign class was required for the rendition of *[ḥ]*. The *[k]* group offered the only possible opportunity because of the inner - Akkadian changes between the writing of the same word with *k* and with *ḫ*. The author of this tablet under discussion, however, rendered both *[ḫ]* and *[ġ]* with the same Akkadian sign *ḫa*. Furthermore, Akkadian *ḫ* was the usual means even of transcribing *[ḥ]*. See supra note 34.*]*

[35] I. Gelb, *BiOr* 15 (1958), p. 6. Against Gelb's theory, see: S. Segert, *ArOr* 26 (1958), pp. 243-247.

The Muzzling of the Tannin in Ugaritic Myth*

One of the sources for our knowledge of Ugaritic myth is the detailed description given by the goddess Anat of a series of victories won by her over the god of the sea and a host of monsters allied to him. These are enumerated one by one (*CTA* 3:III:35-44). Most of the verbs describing the action mean 'to destroy', as for instance *mḫš* (ll. 36,38,40,42) and its synonyms *kly* (ll. 36,43) and *ṣmt* (l. 41). To these we may add the verb *mḫṣ* (l. 43), 'to beat', 'to fight'. It concludes the description as a general term referring to Anat's action against all the enemies mentioned before. The only verb which does not seem to fit into this picture is *šbm*, which appears in the verse: *lištbm tnn išbmnh* (l. 37). The commonly accepted explanation of this verb is 'to muzzle', based on the Arabic *šabama - šibām*. The verse has therefore been translated: 'I muzzled the Tannin, I muzzled it.' It may be doubted, however, whether this meaning is acceptable in a context where another Ugaritic synonym of 'destroy' would be expected. For this reason, apparently, Gordon proposed to render *šbm* by 'to check', 'to annihilate'.[1]

But such doubts regarding the Arabic etymon should be dismissed in the light of a striking Akkadian parallel. At the beginning of the second column of the fourth tablet of Ludlul, as reconstructed by Landsberger from two copies, we read.[2] *im-ḫa-aṣ rit-ti ma-ḫi-ṣi-ia ú-šad-di kakka-šu* ^{d}*Marduk. i-na pi-i gir-ra ākili-ia*[3] *id-di nap-sa-ma* ^{d}*Marduk*. 'Marduk beat the hand of my beater, caused his weapon to fall down' (i.e. 'Marduk knocked the weapon out of the hand of my aggressor'). 'Upon the mouth of the lion about to devour me put a muzzle Marduk'. This Akkadian text combines the conceptions of beating and muzzling in a way analogous to our Ugaritic text. It

---

* Compare in this volume, *Anat's Victory over the Tunnanu*, pp. 465-470.

[1] Gordon, *UM, Glossary* No. 1801.

[2] B. Landsberger, *AfO* 18 (1958), pp. 378f.

[3] In the parallel text: *ḫa-[ni-]qui-ia* - 'about to strangle me'. Cf. Na. 2: 13: "The lion ... and strangled (*umḥanneq*) for his lioness".

should be noted moreover that the Akkadian noun *napsamu*, derived from the stem *psm*, is most probably cognate with Arabic and Ugaritic *šbm* [more precisely Arabic *šbm*, Ugaritic *śbm*], notwithstanding the irregular correspondence between Arabic *š* and Akkadian *s* which is, however, attested several times, especially near *b/p*. Cf. e.g. Akkadian *b(p)ussuru* with Arabic *baššara*, Hebrew *baśśer*, Akkadian *kabsu* with Arabic *kabš*, Hebrew *käbäś*.[4] The interchange between *b* and *p* is a wellattested phenomenon[5] as for example in the Hebrew *d^ebaš*, Akkadian *dipsu* - 'honey'. It appears therefore, that the Akkadian root *psm* developed from a metathesis of the Proto-Semitic root *sbm* in a way that reminds us of the well-attested change between Hebrew *käbäś* and *käśäb*. In addition to this it may be pointed out that the verb *mḫṣ* is common to both the Akkadian and Ugaritic texts quoted above.

The idea of muzzling a monstrous enemy by a victorious god is well founded in oriental literary tradition.

Note. - In a paper '*mḫṣ/*mḫš* (*JAOS* 79,[1959], pp. 169-176), M. Held contests the existence of a Ugaritic verb *mḫš* and advances the proposal that the first singular perfect **mḫṣt* became *mḫšt* through partial assimilation of the emphatical *ṣ* to the following *t*. This opinion relies on the shift from *ṣ* to *š* which occurs in Akkadian before *t* according to a view held by some authorities. But the supposed applicability of Akkadian phonetics to Ugaritic lacks corroborative evidence. Albright's proposal to connect Ugaritic *mḫš* with Akkadian *ḫamāšu* (with metathesis), disputed by Held, still deserves serious consideration. *Ḫamāšu* is well attested in the meaning break (a reed), (cf. *CAD* s.v.) which is quite near to the sense 'crush' required here.

---

[4] For the irregular correspondence between Proto-Semitic *š* and *ś* with Akkadian *s*, cf. Brockelmann, *Grundriss* 1 § 58 i, and furthermore E.A. Speiser, *BASOR* 121 (1951), p. 19; v. Soden, *GAG*, § 30 d.

[5] Brockelmann, *ibid.*, 1 § 54 e ζ; Gordon, *UM*, *Grammar*, 5. 25.

The Flood

The story of the flood which destroyed the world in the days of Noah occupies the central position in the Israelite prehistory which commences with the creation and concludes with the genealogy of Abraham. It is no coincidence that the ten generations from Adam to Noah parallel the ten generations from Noah to Abraham. The flood brings to a close the age of the Creation, in which the descendants of the first creatures were fruitful and multiplied, and it opens a new age in which all the inhabitants of the earth are descended from Noah and his companions in the Ark. Accordingly, the flood story serves as an introduction to the Table of Nations, which gives in detail the relationship of every people to Noah and his sons. At the time of this second beginning of life upon the earth, the Creator, according to the Pentateuch, establishes His relationship with His creatures on a new basis, more secure than the previous one. Not only does God renew the blessing of fruitfulness and numbers with which He blessed mankind at the time of creation, but He also puts His bow in the clouds as a sign of the covenant with mankind, never again to destroy the world with a flood.

Whoever enters to-day into the research of this central section finds himself confronted with a consolidated and firmly established system, propounded as *causa judicata* which is not subject to discussion, namely, the division of the story into the documents *J* and *P*. Gone are the days when the advocates of this approach at least argued about the minutia of the division. Every verse and half verse has obtained its proper position either in *J* or in *P*, the sole exception being the account of the raven (Gen. 8:7). This raven has not found a resting place for its foot and is still wandering aimlessly to and fro among the two documents, except when one critic despairingly offered it a source of its own which may even be the most ancient one.[1] Critics naturally supplement the division into sources with a description of the vast, cognate material found in Mesopotamian documents. However, study of this material has not made the slightest imprint on source criti-

---

[1] E.G. Kraeling, *JBL* 66 (1947), p. 286.

cism, and even though it has been exploited in clarification of the story's background, this exploitation has not been made to its full extent. There has been near-total disregard of the later Jewish literature which deals with the flood such as the *Book of Jubilees, the Book of Sibyllines,* Josephus's *Antiquities*, and the Midrash. This literature has remained outside the realm of interest of critical scholarship and it has been considered a matter of course by critical scholars that it can add nothing to understanding the history of the Masoretic Text.[2]

My teacher the late Prof. Cassuto[3], took a different course by disputing source criticism, explaining the story of the Flood as a unity, incomparably broadening the comparison of the Pentateuch and the Mesopotamian sources, and considering at least the Jewish traditions embodied in the Midrash collections. His investigation is a most important contribution to the understanding of the section in that he demonstrates unity where it is found, and greatly adds to clarifying the history of the tradition. However, even while revealing unity in the story where it is to be found, he attempted to find it even where it is absent, and was thus compelled to forced explanations - his harmonistic tendencies even impairing at times his brilliant ability of comprehensive and penetrating analysis.

This study has been written with regard neither to source criticism nor to the harmonistic approach. It aspires to clarify the question, what may be learned from existing texts about the history of the formulation of the Masoretic text. This study will verify certain already agreed upon conclusions, and will also suggest other new solutions both in generalities and details. However, let us not forget even momentarily that Pre-Pentateuchal Hebrew texts are not available, and that deficiencies in our knowledge put substantial limits to our research and prevent us from analyzing the prehistory of the text in every detail. He who strives for the impossible will not even achieve the attainable, and his elaborate hypothesis will turn into a procrustean bed and do violence to the facts. As is appropriate

---

[2] Characteristic of this line of research are: G. Lambert, *Nouvelle Revue Théologique* 77 (1955), pp. 581-601; 692-724; A. Parrot, *Déluge et Arche de Noé*, Neuchâtel - Paris[3] 1955, pp. 1-35.

[3] Cassuto, *From Noah to Abraham*, pp. 3-140; id., *La Questione della Genesi*, Roma 1934, pp. 335-353.

to a historio-analytical study, we will begin with a survey of the remnants of the ancient Mesopotamian tradition. In their light, we will then deal with the Pentateuchal account, and finally, we will consider later Jewish sources. Only in the end will we turn to the accepted source-critical method and to the harmonistic approach - both of which are disputed.

Flood traditions are known among many peoples. However, scholars have long realized that only the Mesopotamian stories resemble the account in Genesis, if we disregard the tenuous similarity to the late Greek tradition and, in particular, the Greco-Syrian tradition which Lucian mentions in his book *De Dea Syria* (chap. 11, 13)[4] and which is apparently dependent on Mesopotamian or even Israelite or Pre-Israelite, Canaanite traditions.

---

[4] C. Clemen, *Lucians Schrift über die syrische Göttin*, Leipzig 1938, pp. 10ff.
[In the short report of *Apollodorus* (I:VII:2) the flood was brought on by Zeus who wanted to destroy man of the Bronze Age. Deucalion, son of Prometheus constructed by his father's advice a chest, embarked in it with his wife Pyrrha, drifted to the Parnassus, landed there when rain ceased and sacrificed to Zeus. So far the basic structure of the story resembles the Biblical report. But in contrast to it the extent of the flood is not universal, but restricted to Greece. Furthermore Deucalion and his wife are not the only people of Greece to be saved, but some other people managed to flee to the high mountains in the neighbourhood (of Greece?). After the flood men and women were created by Deucalion and Pyrrha from stones. In addition Deucalion had children by Pyrrha. The fate of animals is not mentioned at all. The story apparently blended traditions. According to one some men escaped to the high mountains, according to another only a chest could save people. If it were possible to flee to the high mountains on foot there was no point in building a chest. Neither was there any necessity of procreating men from stones, if Deucalion begot afterwards children by Pyrrha in the normal way.
Ovidius, *Metamorphoses* I: 125-437 postpones the flood to a time posterior to the beginning of the Iron-age. At that period mankind had become thoroughly perverted. After Jove had descended from heaven to earth in human disguise and verified the correctness of the rumours about the utmost demoralization of man, he announced to the gods his intention to annihilate man (128-243) and to create instead another race of wondrous origin (244-252). Then he destroyed earth by pouring down heavy rain (253-273) assisted by his brother Neptun with the auxiliary waves of the rivers (274-293). All living things perished (293-312). It is only at this point of the story that Ovidius introduces Deucalion and his wife who, borne in a small skiff had come to land at Mount Parnassus and immediately worshipped the mountain deities, since both were righteous and godfearing people. When Jove realized that only two innocent persons were left, he caused the flood to subside (313-346). Here follows the narrative that Deucalion and his wife created men and women from stones (348-415). The other forms of life were reproduced by the earth spontaneously (416-437). According to this version the flood covered the whole earth and exterminated every living

The most famous and complete Mesopotamian text is included in the eleventh tablet of the *Gilgamesh epic*[5], which has reached us in a late Assyrian version based on an Old-Babylonian text. The hero of the story in the epic is Utnapishtim, son of Ubar-Tutu, man of Shuruppak, who is also called Atrahasis - 'the exceedingly wise' - who was taken up among the gods after the flood. Gilgamesh approached him to inquire as to how he attained immortality, and his answer is the flood story. Utnaphishtim, therefore, told the flood story from his strictly personal view, without concerning himself with its place in world history. He, therefore, contented himself with a short, cryptic hint of the gods' decision to bring the flood, and did not mention at all the period during which the flood occurred. He also ignored the fate of the rest of those saved from the flood who continued to live on the earth. Besides this account there exist sources, most of them very fragmentary, which describe the flood in its original framework of the mythological prehistory of mankind. These sources include 1) Sumerian lists of kings who ruled at the dawn of history[6] which parallel the lists of the

---

being, like in the story of Genesis. Even the systematic moral motivation reminds of the Biblical text. But as in the report of *Apollodorus* the flood did not cover the highest mountains and again in accordance with *Apollodorus* the life-boat was a small skiff just enough to shelter a man and his wife. No children of this pair were taken aboard and especially no animals. Whereas *Apollodorus* passes them over in silence, *Ovidius* states that all of them perished and regards the existing animals as being descended from generations created by the earth after the flood (416-437).

Lucianus, De Dea Syria 11 reports the myth of Hierapolis in Syria. The building of its temple was attributed to ΔευΚάλιον Σισύθενς. The name Σισύθενς is regarded as a corruption of the Sumerian name Xisouthros (Cf. Meunier, *La Dèesse Syrienne*, Paris 1947, p. 55). *Lucianus* reports the myth that the first race of man was destroyed on account of its sinfulness. Only Deucalion his wife and his children were saved because of his wisdom and his righteousness. He had a large skiff and brought into it all kinds of animals which came in pairs. *Lucianus* takes care to stress that by a command of Zeus those animals did not do any harm to him and that the best relations prevailed between all of them. All travelled together in the skiff as long as the flood lasted. Deucalion became the founder of new mankind and the general tenor of the story makes it perfectly clear that the existing animals, too, were derived from those who were in the skiff. It is most astonishing that this version does not report the landing of the boat at a mountain. On the other hand the story of the skiff and its inhabitants strikingly resembles Genesis. This applies especially to the detail that the animals came in pairs, a feature not found in Mesopotamian texts.*]*

[5] E.A. Speiser, *ANET*, pp. 93-95. For additional literature cf. *ibid.*, p. 73.

[6] S. Langdon, *JRAS* 1923, pp. 251-259; Th. Jacobson, *The Sumerian King List*, Chicago, 1939.

primeval patriarchs in Genesis. These lists specify the time of the flood in the framework of mythological chronology. The king contemporary with the flood is not the same in every list, and beside the tradition which identifies him with Ubar-Tutu, king of Shuruppak, there exists also another tradition which makes his grandson, Ziusudra[7] the hero of the flood. There is even a list in which the last king is Ziusudra the *son* of Ubar-Tutu. In this list there have been preserved meagre remains of the flood description in Sumerian and in Akkadian. 2) Remnants of a Sumerian epic[8] which predates the Gilgamesh Epic. This source, which opens with the creation of the world and the descent of kingship from heaven, preserves from the flood story only a small account of the actual event, while the whole background is lost. 3) A few paragraphs from one or two Akkadian epics[9] from the end of the Old Babylonian period. Here the hero of the flood bears the name Atraḫasis. This source is the only one which preserves an explanation for the reason of the flood, according to Mesopotamian tradition. 4) A summary by Berossus[10], priest of Babylon, which was written in Greek at the beginning of the third century BCE. This source alone provides details concerning the fate of the men who were in the ship with the hero, Ξισοῦθρος.

On the basis of these sources, the following picture can be drawn of the Mesopotamian tradition: The Sumerian king lists tell first that kingship descended from heaven, and, afterwards, list the number of years of every king's reign. When the lists reach the king in whose days the flood occurred, they add to the mention of his regnal years the total of the years of all the kings who ruled until then, and note the coming of the flood. After the flood, it is again stated in some of the lists that kingship came down from heaven. It is therefore clear that the flood divided between two periods in

---

[7] The ancient tradition apparently considered him to be the son of Ubartutu, and by a misunderstanding he was changed into his grandson. Cf. Jacobsen, *ibid.*, pp. 75f., note 32.

[8] S.N. Kramer, *ANET*, pp. 42-44 (additional literature listed).

[9] E.A. Speiser, *ANET*, pp. 104-106. (Additional literature listed): J. Lassoe, *BiOr* 13 (1956), pp. 90-102. [Cf. now: W.G. Lambert-A.R. Millard, *Atraḫasis*, Oxford, 1969.]

[10] C. Müller, *Fragmenta Historicorum Graecorum*, II, Paris 1848, pp. 501ff. [F. Jacoby, *Die Fragmente der Griechischen Historiker*, N. 680 (dritter Teil, Leiden 1958, pp. 364ff.)]

the primeval history of the world.[11] As to the number of predeluvian kings and the number of years of their reigns, there are varying systems. Special attention is called to the fact that the list which considers Ziusudra, the grandson of Ubar-Tutu, as the flood hero, lists him as tenth king, and his regnal years as 36,000. Similarly, Berossus lists Ξισοῦθρος as tenth king even though his years are listed as 648,000. The cause of the flood becomes known from a reconstruction of the Atraḫasis epic. The noise of men deprived the gods of their sleep[12], and, at Enlil's instigation, they decided to obliterate mankind. This rationale for the flood apparently entered the Akkadian epic from the Sumerian tradition, as can be learned from the hints to the story of the flood incorporated into one of the king lists. There some letters of the Sumerian and Accadian versions have been preserved which allow the conclusion that the text included the two words "noise" and "Enlil".[13] The Atraḫasis epic adds that at first the gods smote mankind with various plagues but they did not achieve their goal until they decided to bring a devastating flood. However, the god Ea confounded the designs of the other gods by revealing them to Atraḫasis, convincing him to abandon his property and save his life, telling him to build a ship named "Life Preserver", describing how to build the ship, and hastening him to enter it some date he would tell him, and to shut the door after storing grain, possessions, his family, the artisans who built the ship, animals, and birds. Atraḫasis replied that he had never built a ship and asked Ea to draw a ship on the ground. At this point the tablet terminates. Also in the Gilgamesh epic, Ea turns to Utnapishtim in similar words, which include a short description of a ship. Utnapishtim declares his obedience but asks Ea, what to tell those who ask for an explanation of his deeds? The god provides him with a reply and, with the help of artisans, Utnapishtim proceeds to build the ship. From the detailed description of the building, it appears that the ship was cube-

---

[11] The problem of the history of the Sumerian tradition which brought about the compiling of king lists from various sources is dealt with at length by Jacobsen, loc. cit. (note 6). However, this problem does not concern us, it being clear that the Sumerian tradition influenced the Israelite tradition only in its final form.

[12] Concerning parallels to this motif in Mesopotamian literature cf.: A. Heidel, *The Gilgamesh Epic and Old Testament Parallels*, Chicago, 1945, p. 226, E. Kraeling, *JNES* 6 (1947), p. 194.

[13] Jacobsen, *op. cit.* (note 6), pp. 59f., note 13.

shaped with an edge of sixty meters and that it was partitioned into seven stories and thirty-three compartments. Among the details, we are told that he pitched the ship with *kupru*. After a luxurious banquet for the artisans, he loaded the ship with his silver and gold and put aboard his family, the beasts of the field, and the artisans. At the time predetermined by the god Šamaš, he boarded the ship, shut the entrance, and intrusted the navigation of the ship to the boatman.

Berossus tells how the god Κρόνος revealed the coming of the flood to Ξισοῦθρος. He commanded him to bury in the ground of Sippar books ancient and recent ones alike, to build a ship, to enter it along with his family and close friends, to bring aboard food and drink, living creatures, birds, and four footed animals, and to depart. Also to Ξισοῦθρος the god provides, upon request, an explanation to give to those curious about the aim of his voyage. Ξισοῦθρος builds a ship whose length exceeds ninehundred meters and whose breadth approaches four-hundred meters (its height is not stipulated). The parallel Sumerian text is very fragmentary. However, in the light of comparison of the fragments to the other source, it seems likely that also here one of the gods revealed the coming of the flood to Ziusudra, the hero, and told him to construct an immense ship. The hero is explicitly described as a righteous fearer of the gods.

The description of the flood proper is preserved nearly completely in the Sumerian epic. All the winds pounded with awesome strength for seven days and seven nights. When the wind subsided, Ziusudra opened the window(?) of the ship and the sun god sent his rays. Ziusudra prostrated himself and sacrificed an ox and a sheep. Following a lacuna in the text, his ascent to the gods is mentioned. The description of the flood in the Gilgamesh epic is more detailed and more complex. The epic describes, in awesome mythological pictures, the deeds of the god Adad and his helpmates the starters of the flood, the lament of Ishtar for the destruction of mankind, and the bewilderment of the terror-stricken gods who fled into the highest heavens, cowering in fear like dogs, crying by the walls. The flood raged for six days and seven nights[14] and abated on the seventh day. In agreement with

[14] We have completed the lacuna with VII after R.C. Thompson, *The Epic of Gilgamesh*, Oxford, 1930, p. 62, and in opposition to Speiser, *op. cit.* (note 5) p. 94, who filled in VI. Thompson's reconstruction is preferable for two reasons: (a) It is in accordance with the pattern of six days

the Sumerian epic, here too, the hero opens the window at this time and, just as the Akkadian epic previously added to the Sumerian epic the description of the trauma of the gods, so it adds here a description of the emotion of Utnapishtim who breaks out crying upon seeing the devastation. The story of the lot of those who set out on the ship becomes increasingly complex in the Akkadian epic. While the Sumerian epic links the sacrificing to the opening of the window and concludes by describing the results of the flood, the Akkadian epic specifies that when the hero looked out he only saw twelve mountainous regions and his ship was still floating and continuing on its way until it was stopped by Mount Niṣir. On the seventh day after the ship landed on the mountain, Utnapishtim sent fort a dove[15], but the dove, finding no resting place, returns. The subsequent sending forth and return of a swallow are described in exactly the same words. Finally, Utnapishtim sends forth a raven which does not return. Only then does Utnapishtim leave the ship with all his companions and offers a sacrifice, pours a libation and burns incense. The gods, smelling the sweet savor, gather around like flies, and immediately a stormy argument erupts about the flood and saving Utnapishtim at which time Ea bitterly condemns the flood and claims that punishment should be meted out to the sinner alone. The story concludes with the ascent of Utnapishtim and his wife to the gods. Berossus shortly indicates that the flood came and immediately abated. Ξισοῦθρος sends forth birds which return the first time as they went out, the second time with mud on their feet, and the third time do not return at all. Ξισοῦθρος then unstopped the seams of the ship, realized that it had landed in the Kardu mountains (known also from Rabbinic literature as the Ark's resting place in Armenia), left the ship with his wife, daughter, and boatman, built an altar and sacrificed to the gods. His friends who left the ship later to search for him hear his voice calling to them from above, admonishing them to fear the gods. He who walked in fear of the gods now lives among them, and his wife, daughter, and boatman participate of the same honour. He also tells them to remove the books from the ground of Sippar and to bring them to people in Babylon and so they did. It appears

---

and seven nights found in *Gilgamesh*, Tablet I, col. IV:21, and Tablet XI: 199. (b) It is a logical necessity. The seventh day (i.e. the seventh day-light) appears only after six days and seven nights.

[15] On the ancient seafaring custom of sending out birds to search for nearby dry land, see, for example: H. Heras, *CBQ* 10 (1945), pp. 131-139; M.V. David, *VT* 7 (1957), pp. 189f., [R.D. Freedman, *JANES* 5 (1973), pp. 123-127.]

from all this that Berossus's chief motive is to prove that the Babylonian priestly tradition is established on traditions written before the flood, and to emphasize the holiness of this ancient tradition.[15a]

The parallels between the Biblical and the Mesopotamian tradition are clear. Just as in one Sumerian tradition, so in Genesis, the hero of the story is of the tenth generation of primeval patriarchs. Cassuto correctly pointed out that the 36,000 years of this king are, according to Mesopotamian calculation, six-hundred *šars* and that these six-hundred *šars* are parallel to Noah's age at the start of the flood, but the Pentateuch, as is its custom, scaled down the mythological number to make it more realistic. The Pentateuch behaved similarly in specifying the size of the ark. An ark measuring 150x25x15 meters is unrealistic in the ancient world but is still modest in comparison to the tradition in the Mesopotamian myth. Utnapishtim's ship had a volume four time as great as Noah's ark, and the ship of Ξισοῦθρος even exceeded this several times. Just like Noah, the Mesopotamian hero is also commanded what he shall bring into the ship and again, just like in Genesis, the command, in all versions of the story, includes living creatures. Furthermore, both versions of the Akkadian epic tell that the hero was informed by a god of the day of the flood, and both describe the closing of the door before sailing. As to the account of the flood proper, the parallels to the Biblical text are most striking in the Gilgamesh epic, which describes like Genesis such details as the appearance of the mountains, the landing of the ship on a mountain, the opening of a window, and the sending forth of the birds. We also find in all versions of the Mesopotamian story that the hero offers sacrifices upon leaving the ship, and the Gilgamesh epic adds, in words reminiscent of Genesis, that the gods smelled the sweet savor. While these similarities are obvious, it is doubtful whether, along with Kraeling[16], we may find a tradition akin to that of Genesis in the report of Berossus, that the survivors of the flood travelled to Babylon - and explain in this

---

[[15a] Documents composed in the period preceeding the flood are already mentioned in Neo-Assyrian documents. Cf. P. Schnabel, *Berossos*, Berlin 1923, p. 175. Cf. also *Enoch* 92:1; *Jub*. 4:17; 10:14; 21:10; 45:16.]

[16] Kraeling, *loc. cit.* (note 1), pp. 279-283. Even more dubious is the suggestion of J. Martin, *JBL* 45 (1926), pp. 129-133, who finds in Gen. 8:22 a hint to the famine which is listed in *Atraḫasis* among the plagues which visited mankind before the flood.

way the fact that the story of the flood is followed in Genesis by that of the Tower of Babel. Anyhow, it seems appropriate to point out that, according to Josephus, the flood survivors dwelled at first in the land of Shinar, i.e. Babylon (*Ant*. I:4:1).

In any case, these obvious similarities prove, in everyone's opinion, a historical connection between the flood story in Genesis and the Mesopotamian tradition influenced the younger Israelite tradition. This assumption is supported by the well known considerations that the landing of the ark in the mountains of Ararat makes sense only in a Mesopotamian background and that, as opposed to Israel, destructive floods are a common sight in Mesopotamia. (However, there is no basis to attempts to find the flood story's historical antecedant in one of the floods whose traces have been found in excavations of certain Mesopotamian cities).[17] Even though the Mesopotamian influence is apparent, there is still considerable disagreement as to the time and circumstances of the influence. Meyer[18], Mowinckel[19], and with some qualification, even Kraeling[20] expressed the opinion that the Mesopotamian tradition entered Israel in the late Assyrian period (the seventh century BCE). Albright[21] correctly argued against this opinion that a nation's mythological traditions crystallize at the dawn of its history, and his claim is supported by the fact that the flood story in Israel was first formulated in epic form. We must therefore acknowledge the antiquity of a flood tradition in Israel, but we cannot determine whether the patriarchs brought it with them from Ur of the Chaldeans or whether it entered by way of Canaanite literature.

Scholars have for a long time realized that most of the differences between the Mesopotamian and the Genesis traditions are to be explained as resulting from the development of Mesopotamian motifs in an Israelite spiritual environment, but they have yet to properly evaluate the fact that

---

[17] L. Woolley, *PEQ* 1956, pp. 14-21; Parrot, *op. cit.* (note 2), pp. 43-55; B. Bright, *BA* 5 (1942), pp. 53-62.

[18] Ed. Meyer, *Geschichte des Altertums* II, 2, Stuttgart 1931, p. 186.

[19] G. Mowinckel, *The Two Sources of Predeuteronomic History*, Oslo 1937; id., *JBL* 58 (1939), pp. 87-91.

[20] Kraeling, *loc. cit.* (note 1).

[21] W.F. Albright, *JBL* 58 (1939), pp. 91-99; Woolley, *loc. cit.* (note 17), p. 19.

this explanation does not suit the image of Noah.[22] The Mesopotamian hero ascends among the gods, but Noah continues to live among mortals with no hint of deification neither in Genesis nor in the Apocrypha and in the midrashic literature in contrast to Enoch. Furthermore, Noah is the father of renewed mankind - a matter not mentioned in Mesopotamian literature, which does not contain any clear statement on the origin of Humanity after the flood. In addition, the story of Noah's life continues on past the flood and includes not only the covenant which God made with man by placing His bow in the clouds - a motif absent in the Mesopotamian flood tradition - but also a lengthy description of events totally unrelated to the flood. From all this, it seems that the Noah tradition had independent roots and that Noah was known in the most ancient Hebrew tradition (perhaps even in Canaanite tradition), and that under Mesopotamian influence he became the flood hero. However, the process by which the West-Semitic tradition mixed with the Mesopotamian tradition is obscured from us and we cannot know its details; we cannot even determine whether the mixing was Israelite or Pre-Israelite.

Neither have scholars so far paid attention to the fact that certain differences are imbedded in the Pentateuchal historiography which relates all men after the flood to Noah's sons. From this it becomes clear why Noah took with him only his wife, his sons, and his daughters-in-law but neither his non-immediate family, nor his friends, nor a boatman, nor even artisans who built the ark. We can also understand why Genesis makes no mention of such artisans; it not being easily imagined that the very men who built the ark would not be saved in it.

Additional divergences originate in free development of literary motifs and in theological differences. A striking example of independent development and increasing complexity of a simple Mesopotamian motif is found in the animals which entered the ark. The Mesopotamian accounts briefly

---

[22] Most scholars pass over this matter silently. An exception is Kraeling, *loc. cit.* (note 1), who sensed a difference between Noah, the father of mankind, the planter of a vineyard, and a drunkard, and the Mesopotamian flood story hero. However, even he did not realize that the absence in the Hebrew tradition of an ascent of Noah to the gods proves the antiquity of the blending of the Mesopotamian tradition with the Israelite or even Pre-Israelite tradition.

describe the matter: Utnapishtim was commanded, in the Gilgamesh epic, to bring into the ship all living things, while in the execution of the command, the beasts of the field are mentioned. In the rest of the sources, along with the beasts of the field, only fowl are recorded. As opposed to this, it seems from evidence in Genesis that the Israelite tradition strived for greater precision. First of all, in addition to mentioning the beasts and the fowl, there appears an all encompassing formula "every creeping thing that creepeth upon the earth after its kind" (Gen. 6:20; 7:8,14). It is always mentioned that the living creatures came in pairs (Gen. 6:19-20; 7:2-3,9,15-16). Furthermore, in every passage we find the number of animals of every kind and in certain places we even meet with a distinction made between clean and not clean animals. The number is given in Gen. 6:19, 20; 7:15,16 as "two and two" - just as in the Greco-Syrian tradition recorded by Lucian. The same number occurs in Gen. 7:8,9. Only there, when referring specifically to beasts, the lack of distinction between the clean and those which are not clean is especially mentioned: an additional definition which is not repeated concerning other living creatures. The distinction with regards to cleanliness recurs, again referring to beasts, in Gen. 7:2 which speaks about "seven and seven" of the clean beasts, and "two and two" of those which are not clean. No differentiation is made concerning the other living creatures, their number being given simply as "seven and seven" (Only the Septuagint extended the distinction between clean and not clean outside the realm of the beasts). These discrepancies testify to a conflict and an intermingling of traditions. It seems that the aspiration to be exact in the numbers of animals resulted, in Israel, in two ancient solutions - one solution calling for pairs, which is the minimum possible, and the other calling for seven which is the typological number of completeness.[23] To the first solution, the text adds, in Gen. 7:8,9, the expressly formulated statement that among the animals saved, there were both clean and not clean. This statement is only added concerning beasts of the field but from it we can learn about the other animals. In the final stage, the distinction with respect to cleanliness served as ground for compromise between the two opposing number traditions. The number seven was set aside for clean beasts, the number two for those which are not clean, and again from

[23] This number appears in *Jubilees* 5:24 as a number both of the apertures of heaven and the wells of the deep.

beasts of the field we can learn about the rest of the animals. In this way, a solution is also provided to the problem, where did Noah acquire clean animals for the sacrifice without exterminating the species, even if this alone does not justify increasing the number of clean animals from two pairs to seven.

A trend towards abstract and schematic exactness is present also in the story of Noah's sacrifice. Ziusudra sufficed at offering an ox and a sheep. Utnapishtim is said simply to have brought sacrifices. However, about Noah it is written that he sacrificed from *every* clean animal.

Free development of literary motifs also marks the description of events between the end of the flood and the hero's exodus from the ark. In Genesis continues the process of enlargement already discernable in the Mesopotamian tradition itself. We have seen that in the Sumerian epic, Ziusudra offers his sacrifice immediately upon opening the window of the ship, while the Gilgamesh epic expands the story and describes the event as follows: 1) Opening the window of the ship through which Utnapishtim sees the mountain tops. 2) Landing of the ship on the mountain. 3) Sending forth of the birds. 4) Leaving the ship and offering sacrifices. The same motifs appear in Genesis with slight variations in their interweaving and with addition of new motifs which separate the sending of the last bird from the exodus and sacrifice. A schematic survey of the development of the story shows the following stages: 1) Landing of the ark on the mountain. 2) Appearance of the mountain tops. 3) Opening the window and sending forth the birds. 4) Disappearance of the water from the face of the earth, removal of the cover of the ark, and looking out of the hero. 5) Drying up of the face of the earth. 6) Leaving the ark and offering of sacrifices. This part of the story evolved from brevity to elaboration and from simplicity to complexity.

The sending forth of the birds demands a special literary analysis. In the *Gilgamesh epic* we found a primitive three part climax. The sending forth of the dove and the swallow are told in identical language, and the change comes with the sending forth of the raven which does not return. A three part climax is also found in *Berossus*, but there it has taken on the late form of a phased climax in which every phase expresses a change. The birds also return the second time, but this time with mud on their feet, implying that the water has abated and that the birds had been able to rest briefly on wet ground. The account in Genesis of three sendings forth of birds reflects the same pattern, but an olive branch in the dove's mouth replaces the mud on the feet of the birds. It seems, however, that even the Hebrew tradition knew about mud on the feet of the birds in addition to the olive branch in the mouth, because in the first sending of the dove it is told that the dove found no resting place for its foot, implying that the second time it landed on wet ground. The *Book of Sibyllines* explicitly states that it did so before returning with a splinter[24] of olive wood in its beak. (I:247-255) Similarly, *Josephus* supplements the description of an olive branch[25] in the dove's beak with the detail that it returned dirty[26] (*Ant.* I:3:5). The phased climax of sending forth the dove is preceded in Genesis by the verse - "And he sent forth a *raven*, and it went forth to and fro, *until the waters were dried up from off the earth*" (Gen. 8:7), an addition which is unparalleled in the previously mentioned stories which suffice with a three phased climax alone. Comparison of this surprising verse to its parallel in the *Gilgamesh epic* immediately lends validity to the conjecture that the Israelite tradition at one time also considered the raven to be the third bird which did not return. This conjecture is also supported by the *Book of Sibyllines* which tells that Noah sent forth the dove twice but the third time sent a black winged bird (I:254-256), apparently the raven. Furthermore, we should pay attention to the surprising Septuagint version which reads "and it went forth and returned not until the water was dried up from off the earth". This strange, and obviously unsatisfactory reading makes sense if we discern in it a confusion of two versions: 1) A short version: "And it went forth and did not return", with no elaboration. 2) The Masoretic version on the basis of which were added the words

---

[24] In Greek κάρφος.

[25] In Greek θάλλος.

[26] In Greek πεπηλωμένη. There are those who contend that *Josephus* received this detail from *Berossus* who says similarly about the birds which returned a second time τοὺς πόδας πεπηλωμένους ἔχοντα. But, this contention is not cogent because a) It is hinted at in Genesis and explicitly stated in the *Book of Sibyllines* that the dove rested the second time on wet ground before returning. b) *Josephus*' statement that the bird brought back the second time an olive *branch*, is more similar to that told in *Sibyllines* than to the Pentateuchal description, indicating that in the matter there was an independent tradition.

"until the waters dried up from off the earth". On the basis of these considerations, it seems that the Masoretic version compromises between two variant traditions; one which said that the dove was sent three times, and the other, that the third time the raven was sent. The blending was justified by explaining that the raven refused to distance far from the ark and his fearful, hesitant behaviour did not permit reaching any conclusions, finally necessitating sending forth the dove three times.[27]

---

[27] For varying opinions in this matter cf. A. Schulz, *ZAW* 59 (1942/3), pp. 184-186, who disputes the suggestion to see in the passage about the raven a later addition based on a tradition which grew out of the passage about the dove. In his opinion, just the opposite occurred. The older passage only mentioned a one-time sending forth of the raven which did not return. The original text was preserved in the Septuagint which indicates that the raven did not return until the water had dried up from off the earth and even afterwards did not return; in other words, it did not return at all. In place of this short, simple story, a late redactor inserted the long, detailed account of the three-time sending forth of the dove. But, Schulz's interpretation of the Septuagint is tortuous and it is difficult to assume that an Israelite tradition would be satisfied with only a one-time sending forth of the raven in contrast to the Mesopotamian tradition. A three phased climax is absent only in Josephus. According to his description (*Ant.* I:3:5). Noah sent the raven and it returned. Subsequently, he sent the dove which returned with a branch of olive wood in its mouth and from this Noah knew that the waters had abated and sent no other bird. From Josephus's words, it becomes clear that he found difficulty with the sending forth of the raven and solved the problem with the simple assumption that it returned. To this "improved" account of the sending forth of the raven, he added a summary of the dove incident and it is no coincidence that he chose the second sending forth of the dove which contains interesting material.
[Cf. now also Freedman, *loc. cit.* (note 15) who disregards the questions of literary analysis involved. He simply finds in Genesis the order raven - dove and compares this order with the Akkadian sequence dove - swallow - raven. In his opinion the Biblical version is more ancient and in complete accordance with maritime practice, whereas its allegedly later Akkadian counterpart obscures the original motif. Freedman, however, fails to adduce any source attesting to a practice of seafarers sending doves in order to scout land. Nor can he point to a seafarer's usage of sending different kinds of birds in certain intervals. The unique character of the situation described in the story of the Flood should not be glossed over, still less the literary patterns, used in its description.]

Even more important are variations reflecting differing theological outlooks. The polytheistic, Mesopotamian view saw the flood as resulting from the conflict between the gods' decision to obliterate mankind and the guile of one god who confounded their intentions. Obviously, such a motif is out of place in Israelite monotheism, but it must be pointed out that the echo of this ancient tradition still resounds in the Pentateuch version. The gods' decision to put an end to mankind is paralleled in Genesis by the passage that the Lord regretted having made man. He was saddened and planned to destroy all existence (Gen. 6:5-7). The decision of the god who foiled the intentions of the other gods, is transformed to the passage "And Noah found favour in the eyes of the Lord" (Gen. 6:8). The exalted image of the Lord is fundamentally different from that of the Mesopotamian gods. It is unthinkable that He should be said to be frightened by the flood and to cower like a whimpering dog, and Cassuto correctly pointed out that even the most anthropomorphic passage, which speaks of God smelling the sweet savor of the sacrifice (Gen. 8:21) is a long way from the Gilgamesh epic parallel which pictures the gods swarming about like flies. Furthermore, in the pagan myth, smelling the sweet savor preceeds a stormy feud between the gods, while in the Pentateuch it introduces a solemn covenant between the Lord and mankind. God's exaltation pervades the entire story. God does not offer Noah good advice but He commands; and, in place of relating Noah's reply, Genesis states in concise brevity: "And Noah did according to everything God had commanded unto him, so he did" (Gen. 6:22). Such conclusions recur in Gen. 7:5,9,16. Similarly, Divine Providence is emphasized in God Himself closing the ark (Gen. 7:16), unlike the Mesopotamian tradition in which it is the hero of the story who closes the ship. This provides us with an additional explanation why Noah did not need a boatman: Divine Providence was sufficient. Again, in contrast to the Mesopotamian tradition, the flood did not stop by itself, but only because God remembered Noah and sent a wind to dry up the waters (Gen. 8:1). Emphasis of Divine Providence which Noah depends on, without a word being uttered, even without excitement is also felt in the motif that Noah waited for the express command of God before leaving the ark (Gen. 8:15-17). Biblical theology, as opposed to the Mesopotamian tradition, is imbued with the idea that the reason for the flood was a purely moral one. This, however, does not imply that the Mesopotamian tradition was entirely oblivious to moral problems. Utnapishtim acts out of the fear of heaven, and it is explicitly stated that Ziusudra and Ξισοῦθρος were exceedingly god-fearing. Furthermore, we find that Ea harshly criticized the act of the gods who punished the righteous along with the wicked, and one cannot ignore the similarity to Abraham's claims in his argument with the Lord prior to the destruction of Sodom and Gomorrah (Gen. 18:23-32). The possibility that a natural catastrophe should destroy the righteous with the wicked is rejected explicitly in the tale of Sodom and Gomorrah and implicitly in the flood story. There was no righteous man except for Noah, similar to what Lucian said about Δευκάλιον. However, even this explanation in the spirit of rationalistic ethics did not quell the fear of a repetition, as is shown by the end of the story which describes God's decision never again to bring a flood upon the earth "for the imagination of man's heart is evil from his youth" (Gen. 8:21). This theological criticism, which meditates about a wholesale destruction wrought by a merciful and compassionate God, left its mark on the exegesis of Gen. 6:3 which limits man's life span to one-hundred and twenty years. The Midrash already expresses the idea that this verse refers to the flood, namely, that the Lord restrained Himself for one-hundred and twenty years in order that the wicked might leave their evil ways (TO on Gen. 6:3), and to this was added the idea that Noah in vain warned the wicked[28] (Sanhedrin 108a,b). This idea was extensively developed in the *Book of Sibyllines* I:127-135, 147-199, and even today there are scholars who adhere to this Midrashic approach.[29]

---

[28] Cassuto, *op. cit.* (note 3), pp. 26f., made special mention of the Midrash in Sanhedrin 108b in which we find that the generation of the flood "derided him. Said they to him, 'Old man, what is this ark for you?', - He replied, 'The Holy one, blessed be He, will bring a flood upon you etc." In his opinion, this story is a continuation of the Babylonian tradition according to which the generation of the flood asked the hero, while building the ship, as to the meaning of his deeds. This incident has been preserved in the Israelite tradition and only the replies have been changed. The Mesopotamian hero replies slyly and evasively but Noah rebukes the men of his generation and warns them. This explanation of the background of the Midrash is plausible and attractive. However, the Midrash can be understood even without resort to Cassuto's conjecture. The Talmudic principle, that a sinner is not to be punished unless he has been legally warned necessitates the assumption that the Holy One, blessed be He, did not punish mankind without such a warning. This is sufficient to explain the Midrash. Even if we accept Cassuto's proposal, we cannot account for the changes in the Mesopotamian motif except in view of the Midrash's desire to justify an act of God.

[29] Heidel, *op. cit.* (note 12), p. 230 (additional literature listed.)

The chronology of the flood is one of the elements which differs from the Mesopotamian tradition. The Pentateuchal account increases the duration of the flood many times over the Mesopotamian tradition. Ziusudra spent one week in the ship. How much time Utnapishtim was in the ship cannot be precisely determined, but it is clear that in no case was it for more than one month. Noah, on the other hand, floated for an entire year. At first glance this is surprising, if we consider the fact that the age of the hero and the dimensions of the ark are considerably *less* than the huge numbers in the Mesopotamian accounts. We have here, in the duration of the event, just the opposite of the scaling down process of imaginary legendary numbers to realistic proportions. Yet, this difference can be accounted for. The human life span and the dimensions of a ship were common knowledge, known to the Hebrew story-tellers, and they therefore found difficulty in the enormous, unrealistic numbers and reduced them. The flood, however, was an event foreign to the Israelite experience and in the realm of miracles. Exaggeration, therefore, marked the description of an event which could not be conceived of empirically. The general line of development in the chronology traditions is now clear. But, the details of the chronology demand further, comprehensive review.

A survey of the chronological data in the flood story shows that these data can be placed into three categories which are apparently also distinguishable from the standpoint of the history of the traditions. We distinguish between three systems of time division in the story, viz. 1) Typological time periods. A period of seven days (Gen. 7:4,10; 8:10,12), which is also found in the Mesopotamian account, is of clear typological nature. In Israelite literature, a forty day period (Gen. 7:17; 8:6) is also typological, as we can learn from the many passages which mention periods of forty days or forty years (Ex. 34:28; Nu. 14:34; Ju. 3:11,5:31; 8:28; 1 Sam. 17:16; 1 Reg. 19:8; Jon. 3:4; etc.).[29a] It can therefore be assumed that periods of seven or forty days were already found in the ancient Hebrew epic (see below). 2) A period of one hundred and fifty days (Gen. 7:24; 8:3) which is supposed to represent a period of five months, and so it is explicitly stated in *Jub.* 5:27.[30] This number, which indicates the duration of

[[29a] A typological period of forty years is attested in *Atraḫasis* I:37.]

[30] Unacceptable is the approach of A. Jaubert, *VT* 3 (1953), p. 260, who opposes the prevalent opinion that the time period of one hundred and

the flood, is an alternative to the older number, forty. 3) Dates. These dates are foreign, not only to the epic style, but also to the ancient historiographic style such as is found in the book of Samuel. Their origin is in the chronistic style which joined the epic story at a later date; similar to the development within the Mesopotamian tradition which does not specify dates except in the late version of *Berossus*. The question of the combining of the dates with the typological time periods and with the one-hundred and fifty day period is one of the most difficult problems of the flood story. But, before we deal with the interweaving, we shall deal with the dates themselves. These are the dates given in the Pentateuchal account:

Verse	Year	Month	Day	Event
Gen. 7:11	600	2	17	Entering the ark and beginning of flood
Gen. 8:4	-	7	17	The ark rested on the mountain
Gen. 8:5	-	10	1	The mountain tops were visible
Gen. 8:13	601	1	1	The earth was drying
Gen. 8:14	-	2	27	The earth was dry and Noah left the ark on God's command.

Our Sages already noticed that the day of Noah's exit from the ark was not the anniversary of his entering it and said: "Now should not Scripture have said: 'On the sixteenth day of the month was the earth dry': why then is it stated. 'And in the second month, on the seven and twentieth day of the month, was the earth dry'? Because of the eleven days by which the solar year exceeds the lunar year". (*Genesis Rabba* 33:7). Accordingly, many critics are of the opinion that the verse is hinting at the difference between the solar year of three-hundred and sixty-five days and the lunar year of three-hundred and fifty-four days. However, there are those who claim

---

fifty days refers to the dates 17/II and 17/VII. She contends that this calculation corresponds neither to the lunar nor to the solar year, in that five months of a lunar year contain only 147-148 days and of a solar year 152 days and suggests that the flood lasted exactly one-hundred and fifty days and that two days after the end, i.e. five solar months after the start, the ark rested on the mountain. However, a period of two days is not found in the entire flood story, and Jaubert's overexact chronology does not suit the story's style. We will see further on that a least the final redaction speaks precisely about lunar months.

against them that the lunar year ended on the seventeenth of the second month and not on the sixteenth, implying that the story of Genesis only added ten days to the lunar year and envisioned a solar year of three-hundred and sixty-four days[31] which is known to us from *Jub.* 6:32 and *Enoch* 74:6. However, no conclusion can be reached because the customary counting in the Bible includes both the first and the last days.[32] It seems, therefore, that the verse is referring to a three-hundred and sixty-five day period, even though the specified period covers only three-hundred and sixty-four days.[32a]

There is support for the assumption that emphasizing the discrepancy between a solar and lunar year was not present in the first redaction to add the dates. A hint of an earlier system of dates is found in *Jubilees* which says "And on the new moon of the first month he was bidden to make for himself an ark and on that (day) the earth became dry and he opened (the ark) and saw the earth (*Jub.* 6:25). The relative antiquity of this approach is a limine plausible, it being easy to understand that in the system of dates the beginning of the year of the flood was New Year's day but no reason is recognizable which possibly could justify the queer date of the seventeenth of the second month as the date of the beginning of the flood.

This general consideration is also supported by analysis of the Pentateuchal version. Noah's entry in the ark on the seventeenth of the second month was preceeded by the completion of the ark on the tenth of that month (Gen. 7:4,10). If we make an assumption appropriate to the system of typological numbers, that the building of the ark took forty days, we reach the first day of the first month, namely the same date specified in the verse: "And it came to pass in the six hundred and first year in the first month, the first day of the month, the waters were dried up from off the earth; and Noah removed the covering of the ark, and looked, and, behold, the face of the earth was dried" (Gen. 8:13). The solemnity of this verse indicates that it once served as a direct introduction to God's commanding Noah to leave the ark. However, in the Masoretic version interrupts here the short,

---

31 Most recently J.B. Segal, *VT* 7 (1957), pp. 189f.

32 Cf. Cassuto, *op. cit.* (note 3), pp. 113f.

[32a But, cf. 32b.]

colourless verse which adds nothing but a date: "And on the seven and twentieth of the month was the earth dry" (Gen. 8:14).[32b] From all this, it seems likely that according to a previous edition, the Lord commanded Noah on the first day of the first month to build an ark and on the same date He commanded him to leave it. The final redaction deleted the original date and substituted a new date. This final redaction is only understood in the light of the conjecture that at the time there was a debate in Israel about calculating the year and that the final redactor wanted to lend support to his own calendrical system. We must here consider the well-known fact that as late as the days of the Qumran Sect, bitter arguments raged over this very question.[33] After this clarification we can, in the wake of Cassuto's investigation which showed the way to solution of the problem, return to the question, how were the old systems which indicated only periods of time, incorporated with the date system? These are the data: *[Explicitly stated dates are underlined.]*

Verse	Year	Month	Day	Increment	Event
-	600	1	1	-	The Lord commands Noah to build an ark (see above)
Gen. 7:4,10,11	-	2	10	+40 days	The building was completed
Gen. 7:11	-	2	17	+ 7 days	Noah entered the ark.
Gen. 7:17	-	3	27	+40 days	The end of the flood.
Gen. 7:24;8:3-4	-	7	17	+150 days from start of flood	The water had disappeared and the ark rested.
Gen. 8:5	-	10	1	-	The mountain tops were visible.

[32b] It is plausible to assume that the dates of the first month, until the corresponding date in the following year intend to indicate just a full lunar year and not a year plus one day. This assumption would imply that the author reckoned the time from the middle of the first day to the middle of the last day. If we transfer this system of counting to the version which substitutes the date of the first day of the first month by the seventeenth day of the second month, this would mean that the lunar year terminated on the seventeenth of the second month rather than on the sixteenth. Furthermore, it would follow that the last redactor added only ten days to the lunar year of three-hundred and fifty-four days; implying that he accepted the sectarian calendar.]

33 See e.g. S. Talmon, *Studies in the Dead Sea Scrolls* (in Heb.), Jerusalem, 1957, pp. 24-39; id., *ScHi* 4 (1958), pp. 162-199.

Gen. 8:6,7	-	11	10	⊥40 days	Noah sent forth the raven
Gen. 8:8,9	-	11	17	⊥ 7 days	Noah sent forth the dove for the first time
Gen. 8:10	-	11	24	⊥ 7 days	Noah sent forth the dove for the second time
Gen. 8:12	-	12	1	⊥ 7 days	Noah sent forth the dove for the third time
Gen. 8:13	601	1	1	-	The water was dried up.

The calculated dates - the first, the tenth, and the seventeenth of the month - appear in other places as explicit dates. There are only two exceptions, viz.: 1) The date of the second sending forth of the dove on the twenty fourth of the month. However, this deviation is not serious because it is half way between the seventeenth and the first of the (following) month; 2) The date of the end of the flood on the twenty-seventh of the third month, which is tied to the forty days of the flood and serioussly deviates from the system of dates. The end result is that the date sytem was successfully and harmoniously incorporated, not only into the time period of one hundred and fifty days, but also into the typological numbering system, with the exception of the forty day period of the flood. In the overall scheme, this period of time was replaced by a one-hundred and fifty day period, even though the compiler of the date system, not daring to ignore the tradition that the flood lasted forty days, with certain difficulty mentioned it in his version.

In Summary: The chronology of the flood developed approximately as follows: The most ancient tradition recognized only typological time periods, one of which was the forty day period of the flood. A late tradition fixed the duration of the flood at one-hundred and fifty days. The adder of dates incorporated into his system all the time periods which he had before him, and built a system according to which the flood lasted - from the Lord's command to Noah until Noah's leaving the ark - from the first day of the first month until the corresponding date of the following year. After slight alterations, the existing text was formed.

These detailed discussions of the development of certain facets of the flood story demand elaboration by way of a general discussion of the development of the Israelite flood tradition. Scholars have for a long time realized that the Biblical flood story contains remnants of an ancient flood epic. Ascribed to the epic is the verse: *nibq^{ec}u kol ma^{c}y^{e}not t^{e}hom rabbā wa'^{a}rubbot haššāmayim niptāḥu* 'All the fountains of the great deep (were) broken up / And the apertures of heaven were opened'. (Gen. 7:11). To this verse, which is written in the purest Hebrew poetic style, there is an apocopated parallel in the continuation of the story - *wayyissākru ma^{c}y^{e}not t^{e}hom wa'^{a}rubbot haššāmayim.* 'There were stopped the fountains of the deep and the apertures of heaven ...' (Gen. 8:2). The verse concludes with the prosaic words: *wayyikkāle' haggäšäm min haššāmayim.* 'And the rain from heaven was restrained'. The full form of the verse is indicated in the passage from *Jubilees*: "In the fourth month the fountains of the great deep were closed and the apertures of heaven were restrained" (*Jub.* 5:29), from which we can reconstruct *wayyissākru ma^{c}y^{e}not t^{e}hom (rabbā) wa'^{a}rubbot haššāmayim niklā'u.* We cannot definitely determine to what extent the epic is reflected in the Pentateuchal story. But we have already noted that we might ascribe to this epical version the typological periods in the Pentateuchal story. Likely is Cassuto's conjecture that it was the source of rare and poetic words such as *mabbul, gopär, kopär, ṣohar, ṭārāp*[34], *y^{e}qum.* Cassuto was furthermore right in finding in this poem the origin of the rainbow-motif. In any case, it is clear that the text of this epic was known to the Israelite prose story-teller and that it strongly influenced him.

---

[34] In Cassuto's opinion, we should include the noun *qinnim* (Gen. 6:14), meaning compartments, which is peculiar to the flood story. However, E. Ullendorff, *VT* 4 (1954), pp. 95f., claimed against the traditional explanation: 1) There is no philologic support. 2) Were this explanation valid, the text should be *qinnim qinnim* (so many emend). 3) Gen. 6:14 speaks about the materials for the ark and not about its structure. He therefore suggests reading *qānim* (reeds) and strengthens his suggestion with the proof that *qānim* (reeds) played an important role in ship-building; and the same was suggested by Gordon, *UL*, p. 6. Further support can perhaps be found in a fragment of a Babylonian story which may either belong to the *Atraḫasis* epic or to an independent source. The source is brought here according to *CAD*, s.v. *ḫuppu* A. It reads *[...] GIŠ. MÁ ra-bi-tam bi-ni-ma [kīma] qá-ne-e ḫúb-bi lu bi-nu-us-sà.* The dictionary translated: 'build a large ship: its structure should be like the ... of a huppu-basket'. The restoration of *kīma* and the translation assume that the structure of the ship is being spoken about. The word *qa-ne-e* is left untranslated because it is impossible to say that the ship will be like 'a reed of a basket'. But, perhaps the reference is to the material from which the ship will be built and the restoration of *kīma* is incorrect. If so, there is room to conjecture that we may translate 'basket reeds', i.e. that the type of reed used in basket weaving will be used for the ship.
[Contrast Lambert-Millard, *Atraḫasis*, pp. 126-127, l. 7 (Reference by cour-

After this survey of the problems of the flood story, in which we have attempted to explain the tradition's development in general lines and, to the best of our ability, even in detail, we should turn to Cassuto's harmonistic approach and to source criticism. Source criticism thrives on real or imaginary difficulties in the story's structure. To the later category belongs the contradiction between the prose text which sees only rain as a source of the flood water, and the poetic lines which add to the rain water the water of the great deep. There is no contradiction here but the poetic text has only supplemented the prose description. As opposed to this, there is a real contradiction in the number of animals of every type that entered the ark, and the text does not support Cassuto's explanation that one part of every species of animals came aboard of its own accord while the rest of the animals were taken aboard by Noah. We have already pointed out the contradiction between the tradition according to which the flood lasted forty days and the tradition according to which it lasted one hundred and fifty days. Cassuto here explained that according to Genesis the water rose only for forty days but remained stationary upon the earth for the hundred and fifty days, interpreting *wayyigb^eru hammayim* as connoting a continuing state rather than an activity.[35] However, this explanation does not solve

---

tesy of Prof. M. Weinfeld) who read: ...*]* *qà-ne-e gáb-bi lu bi-nu-us-sà* and translate 'Let its structure be *[...]* entirely of reeds'. Ships, entirely built of reeds existed in Mesopotamia. See A. Salonen, *StOr* 8 (1939), pp. 71-72. The supposition of such a vessel in Gen. 6:14 is, however, contradicted by the explicit mention of wood as building-material. Therefore Ullendorff argues that Gen. 6:14 should be interpreted in the light of the wide-spread practice of using both trunks and reeds in the construction of ships. But this interpretation yields the perplexing rendering: "Make thee an ark (of) gopher-wood; of papyrus reeds thou shalt make the ark" and this passage has a self-contradictory sound. True that difficulty is less blatant in Ullendorff's rendering: "with papyrus reeds", and even entirely disappears in the translation of *NEB* "... cover it with reeds", which smoothes away the supposed awkwardness of the Hebrew text. The attempt to evade the dilemma of the reading *qinnim* (attested already in the rendering of the Septuagint (νόσσιάς) then entangles us in new difficulties. Should the Biblical report reflect two traditions about the material used for the construction of the ark? On this supposition we could consider Gen. 6:14b as an addition from a source which depicted the ark as made of reeds only and hypothesize that *qānim* was explained as *qinnim* in order to harmonize v. 14b with v. 14a.*]*

35 On the same view apparently is based the Vulgate translation of Gen. 7:24. *Obtinueruntque aquae terram centum quinquaginta diebus*.

the problem. We have already seen that only with difficulty does the forty day duration of the flood find a place in the original system of dates. It must furthermore be pointed out that the flood chronology can be rectified only if we assume that the number one hundred and fifty includes the forty days of the flood. Yet we have no other instance of a smaller unit being included in a larger unit, but all time periods are subsequent to one another.[36] We must therefore accept the opinion of the critics that the Biblical account reflects two traditions about the duration of the flood, and of second importance is the question, did the compiler of the two traditions try to resolve them as did Cassuto? In addition, we cannot disregard strange

---

[36] In the light of what has been said, it is not surprising that Josephus (*Ant.* I:3:5) places the one hundred and fifty day time period after the elapse of the forty days. According to this account, the flood lasted forty days and afterwards, for one hundred and fifty days, the waters subsided nearly indiscernably (μόλις).
However, the artificiality of this solution is obvious. A tradition similar to that of Genesis is hinted at in the *Book of Sibyllines* which tells that Noah left the ark δὶς ἐίκοσι μίαν ἦῶ πληρῶσας ὑδατέσσι (I: 280-282), i.e. after two hundred and one days of water. Clearly, this time period is in no way typological but is based on a chronological calculation in the book's source. This calculation can be convincingly reconstructed if we pay attention to the story line in the book. It reads that when the flood abated Noah removed the covering from the ark, saw the sun (compare the Sumerian epic!) and sent forth a dove (I:230-247) according to our hypothesis on the one-hundred and eightieth day i.e. six months after the start of the flood. The second sending forth of the dove (I:248-250) occurred, according to our hypothesis, seven days later on the one-hundred and eighty-seventh day. Finally, the raven was sent forth (I:254-256) after seven additional days on the one-hundred and ninety-fourth day. After a period of time, the ark reached the mountain (The sending forth of birds preceded the landing of the ark just as in Berossus!) and Noah left the ark (I:257-282) after seven more days on the two-hundred and first day, as stated in Sibyllines. *[Cf. the Samaritan chronicle* *Tolida* *which reads: "We read: 'And the waters prevailed upon the earth one hundred and fifty days' until His word: 'And the ark rested in the seventh month on the seventeenth day of the month' And we took the number of days and calculated them into months and found them six", 'J. Bowman,* *Transcript of the Original Text of the Samaritan Chronicle Tolidah*. Leeds, 1954, p. 1.) It is obscure how the author reached at the number of six months. Possibly his perplexing statement originates in an apocryphal tradition already obfuscated in his book.*]*

repetitions: The Lord commands Noah twice about what to bring into the ark (Gen. 6:18-21; 7:1-3), and these two directives are not identical in all their details. There are two beginnings to the flood (Gen. 7:6; 10-12) and twice Noah enters the ark (Gen. 7:7-9; 13-15). Cassuto explained these repetitions as literary effects, characteristic of the ancient Oriental style. However, this does not solve the problem. It is true that story telling among ancient Oriental peoples was laden with repetition. However, this rule may cause error as long as we do not deal with the typology of the repetitions, which can be clearly and simply summarized, viz.: 1) A recurring event is told at length every time that it occurs. 2) A one-time event can be told several times, once by the narrator and one or more times by the characters in the story. However, in the flood story the narrator himself repeats the beginning of the story which is a one-time event, and such a repetition is not typical of the ancient Oriental style. These obvious contradictions gave rise to separation of sources in the story. We will here very briefly summarize the source-critical approach: According to this approach, the flood story is composed of the late source *P*, whose style is dry and learned, and the earlier source *J*, whose style is fresh and naive. The redactor chose *P* as a main stratum for his account, and he transmitted it in its entirety without changing the order of the passages. However, he inserted verses from *J* in places where they were more or less similar to *P* but without regard to their order in the original *J* document. The following verses are attributed to *J*, and we have listed them in their conjectured original order: Gen. 6:5-8; 7:2,3b-5,10,15b,12,17b,23a,22,23b; 8:6a,2b,3a, 6b,7-12,13b,20-22. There are those who attribute to *J* the passage about the raven (Gen. 8:7). To *P* are attributed the remaining verses in the order in which they appear in the Masoretic text.[37]

---

[37] Opinions contesting this approach have been largely ignored, e.g. P. Romanoff, *JBL* 50 (1931), pp. 304-307, claimed that even after dividing the story into its component documents, there remain repetitions, and on this consideration he bases his own division of the story into three sources. On similar claims G. von Rad, *BZAW* 65 (1934), pp. 1-11 based his suggestion to divide the *P* document into two sources. Also worthy of mention are Mowinckel, *op. cit.* (note 19) who considers the Mesopotamian material an addition from the Assyrian period, which should be ascribed to *E* and, especially, P. Volz, *BZAW* 63 (1933), pp. 140-142, who took issue with the very basis of source criticism, i.e. with the thesis that various sources were combined here by a redactor. In his opinion, the Pentateuchal text was formed by a re-working of *J*; implying that the story attributed to *P* never led an independent existance. Volz further claims that *J* contains a number of verses generally attributed to *P*.

The source-critical approach, which strives to explain the development of the existing text, in actuality blocks the way to understanding it. We have already brought the example of the sending forth of the raven which has wearied supporters of source-criticism while comparison of traditions has fully solved the problem. The chronological problem is solved by the accepted approach with the assumption that *J* only used typological numbers while *P* used dates and the one-hundred and fifty day periods with the combination of the two systems having been done by the redactor. However, we have already dealt with the combining process and have seen that the adder of dates incorporated into his work the time periods which he had before him. Furthermore, we have dealt with the matter of the animals which entered the ark and have pointed out that the distinction between clean and not clean animals is foreign to all Mesopotamian texts and belongs to the latest stages of the development of the Pentateuchal tradition in which it served ultimately as a compromising measure between varying ancient traditions regarding the numbers of animals and it should be pointed out here that even Lucian and the Books of Sibyllines do not mention this distinction.[38] The accepted approach disregards comparison of Genesis with ancient texts. In addition, this approach makes the most peculiar assumption that *J* innocently attributed the distinction between clean and not clean animals to the primeval period while the learned, priestly source saw the distinction originating at Sinai. Common sense demands that this purely legal and peculiarly Israelite distinction should have originated in the priestly way of thinking which was concerned with laws of cleanliness and uncleanliness, and assumed that these laws were natural, originating in the creation. The same non-historical approach is evident in attributing to *P* the description of the ark on the basis of its dry, technical nature. Volz[39] correctly claimed that the description of the ship in the Gilgamesh epic is no less detailed and exact than the description in Genesis, implying that a technical description of the wonderous ark aroused the interest, admiration, and

---

[38] Josephus (*Ant.* I:3:2) tells that Noah took male and female of every species but from some of them seven pairs. It cannot be determined whether he intended to hint at the distinction between clean and not clean or whether he tried to reconcile the tradition which read "two and two" with the tradition which read "seven and seven".

[39] Volz, *loc. cit.* (note 37).

astonishment of the ancient audience, unlike the modern audience who is stricken with boredom. We have already indicated that the nouns *ṣohar* and *kopär* in the description of the ark are of epic origin.

A crucial problem is raised by the verses borrowed from the epic. Those verses are attributed to *P* on the assumption that *J* considered only rain to contribute to the flood waters, while *P* adds to them the waters of the deep (*tᵉhom*). Seemingly, this division can be supported by the Mesopotamian tradition which does not mention the waters of the deep, implying that the rain-water motif antedated the motif of waters of the deep. But, all we can deduce from this is that the younger Israelite epic innovated the waters of the deep motif. However, this innovation occurred at the outset of the Hebrew tradition[40], because development of epics precedes in all cultures the development of prose and we can safely state that there is nothing between the fresh, mythology laden remnants of the Hebrew epic and the later priestly erudition.[40a] Another shortcoming of the source critics is their tendency to find in every verbosity evidence of a plurality of sources. However, Volz[41] has already pointed out that this criterion should be used with extreme caution since verbosity might serve as a stylistic device, and he even correctly indicated that repetition of certain expressions in Genesis 7:17-20 makes the listener actually feel the constantly rising waters. We should add Cassuto's admonition that when dealing with the development of traditions, rationality should be used cautiously. He is referring to the famous claim that according to *J* Noah left the ark after ascertaining

---

[40] It is fitting to mention here a striking parallel between the *Book of Jubilees*' and Lucian's account. The *Book of Jubilees* tells that after closing of the fountains of the great deep, they were reopened, only this time, not to release water but to swallow up the flood water which then descended into the earth (*Jub*. 5:29). A similar incident appears in Lucian who tells about a fissure through which the flood waters disappeared into the ground, and perhaps in both stories there is an echo of an ancient Canaanite tradition.

[The opening through which the floods of the Deluge entered into the bowels of the earth in the days of Deucalion, was shown at Hierapolis within the temple of the Syrian goddess (Lucianus, *De Dea Syria* 12-13), at Athens within the precints of the Zeus' sanctuary (*Pausanias* I:18:91). The origin of the underlying myth remains obscure.]

[[40a] My student, G. Kravitz, pointed out that the author of the prosaic text added the word *rain* to the epic verse Gen. 8:2 and therefore should be identified with *J*. If we maintain the division of the text between *J* and *P*, this argument seems to be decisive.]

[41] Volz, *loc. cit*. (note 37).

the proper time with the help of the birds and after removing the ark's cover, while according to *P* he checked nothing but waited for the Lord's command. Each of the stories, so claim the source critics, is logical. The redactor came and created an internal contradiction by combining the stories. However, Cassuto correctly rebutted that the redactor of a sanctified tradition is not free to wantonly abandon the tradition, his job being restricted to what seems, from his subjective point of view, to be a mere interpretation of the story. To this end he attached to the ancient story God's command to Noah to leave the ark, again emphasizing Divine Providence which had already been strongly emphasized in the passage attributed to *J* about God's closing the ark for Noah. It is not surprising that a God-fearing man would wait for the Lord's command to open the door that He, Himself had closed. We should add that also according to the description in the Book of Sibyllines, Noah sent forth the birds even though he did not leave the ark until after the direct command of God (I:267-281); and with all this the unity of the story is apparent.

In Conclusion: The flood story bears all the markings of an ancient tradition which developed in many phases until it crystallized into the form now existing in the Pentateuchal account. It is possible to investigate in it the Hebrew theological struggle with the ancient mythological epic, and to follow the long, complex development of various literary motifs. When doing such an analysis, it is forbidden to ignore the differences of traditions which were incorporated into our text. However, one may not look for such differences in every instance so as to justify the mechanical, undiscriminating dogma which is source criticism, and only an unbiased analysis, free from such dogmatism, can lead the way to understanding the dialectic which formed the flood story.

"What is Above, what is Beneath, what Before, what After."

The Mishna in Hagiga 2:1 reads: *Kol hammistakkel b*^{e}*'arbā*^{c}*ā d*^{e}*bārim rātuy*[1] *lo k*^{e}*'illu lo' bā' lā*^{c}*olām ma l*^{e}*ma*^{c}*lā uma l*^{e}*maṭṭā ma l*^{e}*pānim uma l*^{e}*'āḥor.*[2] 'Whoever speculates upon four things, a pity for him! He is as though he had not come into the world, (to wit), what is above, what is beneath, what before, what after'.

This Mishna which suggests a feeling of recoil from mystic lore is one of the most famous in Judaism; even as famous is its interweaving into most perplexing and wondrous Talmudic discussions, whose mythological and Gnostic character impresses itself on the reader's mind. Anyone, however, who attempts to interpret it will quickly realize that its exact meaning is shrouded in obscurity and that there is no accepted interpretation for any one of the notions which the Mishna employs. Not only are the interpreters of the Mishna divided on the question of what are the places referred to in the words 'above' and 'below', but they even differ on the basic question of whether the words 'before' and 'after' are to be taken in a spatial or temporal sense. From the very subject of the Mishna it is *a priori* clear that the differences in interpretation have their basis in different religious outlooks, i.e. that the history of the interpreta-

---

1 On *rātuy*, see: M. Jastrow, *Talmud Dictionary, s.v. rtwy.*

2 The text is quoted here according to the Vilna edition. From the many variants we will mention only two. Ms. Kaufmann reads: *Kol hammistakkel b*^{e}*'arbā*^{c}*ā d*^{e}*bārim rātuy lo killu lo' bā' lā*^{c}*olām ma l*^{e}*ma*^{c}*lān umā l*^{e}*maṭṭā ma b*^{e}*pānim uma l*^{e}*'āhor.* On the other hand Ms. Munich reads: *Kol hammiṡtakkel b*^{e}*'arbā*^{c}*ā d*^{e}*bārim rā'uy lo šällo' bā' lā*^{c}*olām ma l*^{e}*ma*^{c}*lān uma l*^{e}*maṭṭān ma l*^{e}*pānim uma l*^{e}*'āhor.* On the spelling *killu*, see: J.N. Epstein, *Mābo' le-Nosaḥ ha-Mišnā*, Jerusalem, 1948, p. 1236. On the variant *b*^{e}*pānim* - *l*^{e}*pānim*, cf. id., *ibid.*, pp. 1110-1129. On the variant *ma- umā*, cf. id., *ibid.*, pp. 1050-1076. The reading in Ms. Kaufmann: *ma l*^{e}*ma*^{c}*lān umā l*^{e}*maṭṭā* probably is a mixture of the reading: *ma l*^{e}*ma*^{c}*lā uma l*^{e}*maṭṭā* with *ma l*^{e}*ma*^{c}*lān umā l*^{e}*maṭṭān*. However, cf. also in the Aramaic of *Genesis Apocryphon* (ed. Avigad-Yadin, Jerusalem, 1957) the variation between *kmn* (XXI 14) with the forms *kmh* and *km'* (XX 2,4).

tion of our Mishna comprises a major chapter in the history of Jewish belief in the studies of which the recipient of this *Festschrift*, Prof. Y. Kaufmann, takes a foremost place. In this article we will attempt to make a contribution to the clarification of these fundamental questions. However, before we turn to them, we must pave the way through the methods of dry philological investigation which scrutinizes phrases *per se* and juxtaposes one exegetical reading with another in order to determine which is earlier and which is later.

This investigation should start with the clarification of the basic question whether the plain meaning of the formula 'what is above, what is beneath, what before, what after' is intended entirely to the dimensions of space or whether perhaps the words 'before and after' are related to the contemplation of the boundaries of time. From a lexical point of view both interpretations are equally possible. However, it should be immediately pointed out that the linguistic context tips the scales in favour of the spatial interpretation. The juxtaposition of the two double phrases 'above and below' and 'before and after' suggests that the second should be understood in the same way as the first, i.e. in a spatial sense. If the writer of the Mishna had wanted to change the subject he should have clarified this by using unambigious words. We are therefore disposed *a limine* to accept Rashi's simple explanation: "'What is before' - Outside the partition of the firmament to the east; 'and what is after' - To the west" (Hagiga 11b, on the Mishna). However, many commentators on the Mishna disagreed with him basing themselves on Talmudic passages which prefer the temporal explanation. Thus, anyone who attempts to clarify the plain meaning of our Mishna must first of all consider the Talmudic discussions and their development.

The Palestinian Talmud states: "R. Jonah (said) in the name of R. Ba': It is written: 'For ask now of the first days which were before you' (Deut. 4:32). I might have thought (the enquiry concerns the time) before the creation of the world. Therefore scripture states: "Since the day that God created man upon the earth.' (ibid.) I might have thought from the sixth (day) onward. Therefore scripture states: 'First' (ibid.). After scripture made a general statement it made a specific one. Therefore we learn from the sixth (day), as the sixth (day) is special in that it is one of the six days of creation, so you too should only include something which is like the sixth (day). (i.e. the first five days of creation. It follows that the enquiry into all the days of creation is permitted.) I might think that this refers to knowing what is above heaven or below the abyss. Therefore scripture states: 'From one end of heaven to the other' (ibid.). But (concerning time) before the world was created you interpret scripture and your heart agrees, but (concerning the time) after the world was created you walk and your voice travels from one end of the world to the other" (Hagiga ch. 2, halakha 1, p. 77c). This interpretation begins with a halakhic midrash, which concludes with the words: "Therefore scripture states: 'From one end of heaven to the other'". This midrash interprets three phrases in Deut. 4:32 one after the other: 1) "For ask now of the first days which were before you"; 2) "since the day that God created man upon the earth"; 3) "from one end of heaven until the other." The dry and technical language of the midrash is joined to the words of the verse which interprets it according to the system of generalizations and particularizations which, as stated in the Babylonian Talmud, R. Akiba received from his teacher R. Nahum of Gimzo (Shebuot 26a). The midrash connects the prohibition of asking what precedes the creation of the world with merely the first two phrases of the verse whose temporal meaning is clear. As far as these two phrases go the midrash does not bear on the text of the Mishna. Only when proceeding to the third phrase of the verse, whose spatial interpretation is self-evident, the midrash mentions the first part of the formula in our Mishna ('What is above and what is below'). This supports the assumption that the midrash did not recognize the connection between the formula of our Mishna and between the prohibition of asking what preceded the creation of the world, and understood the words 'what is before and what is after' as having a spatial meaning, since otherwise the midrash would most likely have said: "I might have thought: (One may ask) 'what is before and what is after', therefore scripture states: 'From the day etc.'". The Palestinian Talmud appends to this complete and understandable halakhic midrash another interpretation, which does not appeal to scripture, which is full of mystic tension and clearly distinguished from the simple and schematic style of the halakhic midrash: "But before the world was created you interpret scripture and your heart agrees, but after the world was created you walk and your voice travels from one end of the world to the other". This interpretation limits man's permission to speculate what preceded the creation of the world to speculation in the heart only[3], and permits, on the other hand, the speculation aloud of everything which is found on the world which was created from one end to the other - an allusion to the phrase "from one end of heaven etc.". Moreover it seems that the author of the addition to the halakhic midrash was of the opinion that the spatial prohibition included as a matter of course also a temporal prohibition, i.e. that the limitation of permission to speculate aloud on the area "from one end of the world to the other" carries with it logically the prohibition against speculation on what preceded its creation. But it is clear that this interpretation does not give the words 'before' and 'after' a temporal meaning and does not detract from their spatial interpretation as indicated in the halakhic midrash.

The spatial interpretation of the words 'before and after' is even clearer in the halakhic midrash in the Babylonian Talmud: "For the Rabbis taught: 'For ask thou now of the days past'. A single person may enquire, but two may not. One might have thought that one might enquire concerning the pre-creation period, therefore scripture teaches: 'Since the day that God created man upon the earth'. One might have thought that one may (also) not enquire concerning the six days of creation, therefore scripture teaches: 'The days past which were before thee'. One might have thought one may (also) enquire concerning what is above and what is below, what before and what after, therefore the text teaches: 'And from one end of heaven un-

---

[3] Perhaps the intention of the editor of the Mishna in the reading: *Kol hammistakkel* etc. was not simply "speculation" but expounding aloud, in accordance with the first portion of the Mishna: *'en dor^{e}šin ba^{ca}rāyot bišlosā w^{e}lo' b^{e}ma^{ca}śe b^{e}re'šit bišnayim w^{e}lo' bammärkābā b^{e}yāḥid 'ällā' 'im ken hāyā ḥākām umebin midda^{c}to*. 'The forbidden degrees may not be expounded before three persons, nor the story of creation before two, nor (the chapter of) the chariot before one alone, unless he is a sage that understands of his own knowledge.

*[*E.E. Urbach, *The Sages, Their Concepts and Beliefs*^{2}, Jerusalem, 1975, p. 772, note 37, negates the possibility of such a harmonistic interpretation. Our opinions are close. To my mind, too, the Mishna is composed of two sources, the first of which refers to speculation aloud, the second to contemplation in the mind. Moreover, even according to Urbach the difference between the first and second parts of the Mishna is eliminated in Hagiga 11b in which the term "looking" is replaced by the phrase: "One might have thought one may enquire". The question remains whether by the arrangement of his sources the editor of the Mishna wished to point to a harmonistic interpretation that the looking which is prohibited is not a simple "looking", but a "looking" which leads to questioning.*]*

to the other. (Concerning the things that are) from one end of heaven unto the other you may enquire, but you may not enquire what is above, what is below, what before, what after'" (Hagiga 11b). Therefore, this midrash also refrains from connecting the temporal limitations of the permission to speculate with our Mishna. Moreover, it quotes the formula 'what is above, and what is below, what is before, what after' in its entirety, as a formula applied to the dimensions of space and which is connected with the Biblical verse "from the end of etc."[4] But the continuation in the Babylonian Talmud is based on the opposite viewpoint, i.e. that the verse "from the end of etc." establishes temporal boundaries for speculations, as is clear from the question in the Babylonian Talmud: "But now that this is inferred from (the expression) 'from one end of heaven unto the other', why do I need (the expression), 'since the day that God created man upon the earth'?" (Hagiga 12a). There is no point here in dwelling on the Talmud's reply which goes into the realm of God's "body" which is irrelevant here. But the very fact that the Babylonian Talmud brings here in a halakhic midrash the spatial explanation of the expression "from the end of etc." and then poses a question on this midrash as if the midrash gave a temporal explanation, is strange. This may even raise the suspicion that the editor of the Babylonian Talmud combined here two sources which deal with one subject according to different methods. However, we have seen above that even the Palestinian Talmud goes from the spatial explanation to the temporal one. This similarity between the Babylonian and the Palestinian Talmud may serve as a warning that we should not be attracted to a hasty criticism of the Babylonian Talmud, but we should pay full attention to the traditional harmonistic exegesis. According to it, it was obvious also to the Babylonian Talmud that the spatial explanation carried with it as a matter of course also the temporal one, as Rekanati[5] states in *The book of the Commandments*, in which he summarizes the view of Hai Gaon as follows: "'What is above, and what is

---

[4] We are left with just the logical difficulty that the verse refers to one measure ("the distance between one end of the heaven to the other"), whereas the Mishna refers to two measures ("the distance between above and below and the distance between before and after"). R. Hananel already noted this and explained: "The distance between one end of the heaven to the other is like the distance from earth to heaven and both are one measure." Cf. also Tamid 32a.

[5] Rekanati's *Ṭaᶜᵃme hammiṣwot*, Basilea, fol. 21b, section 72. This is quoted here from M. Levin, *Otzar ha-Geonim*, Jerusalem, 1931, p. 53.

below, what is before, what after' - The reason is that it is forbidden to speculate. One can picture in one's mind only perceptible things ... for outside the boundary of the world nothing was invented in the creation of the world from what there was and what there will be. And if so, what is the meaning of 'what is above, and what is below, what is before, what after', i.e., before the invention and after it ... Thus I understood these words by tradition from R. Hai Gaon, of blessed memory." The same explanation is given by Rashi in a clearer fashion without recourse to philosophical terms. "Now that we know from the verse 'and from the end of heaven' that it is forbidden to ask what is outside of the boundaries, then it immediately follows that it is forbidden to enquire what was before it was created. For they are the same thing. What was before its creation is now out of its boundary."

The same problem of the ambiguity in the Biblical verses which comes to teach about the temporal limitation of speculation has left its mark also in the Tosefta; however, the Tosefta does not know the spatial explanation at all. The text reads as follows: "Anyone who speculates on four things would have been better not to have been born: What is above, and what is below, what was, and what will be. I might think that one might ask of what preceded the creation of the world? Thus scripture states: 'When you ask of the first days'. I might think that one may ask of what was before the cosmogony. Thus scripture states: 'From one end of heaven to the other'. What does scripture mean by 'from the day which God created man on the earth'? From the day on which God created man on the earth you may ask, but you may not ask what is above, and what is below, what was, and what will be."[5a] As to the discussion of this text we should note, to begin with, that several corruptions have crept in. S. Lieberman has already pointed to the need for comparing it with the text of the Palestinian Talmud, and of Ms. L which lacks the words "before the creation of the world. Thus scripture states: When you ask of the first days. I might think ...".[6] The question in the Tosefta: "I might think that one may ask what was before the cosmogony" is simply a variant reading of its preceding question: "I might think that one may ask what preceded the creation of the world." The duplication is not in Ms. L, but this manuscript also leaves out the words "Ask thou etc.", which are found in the Talmudim, and without which it is impossible to understand

---

[5a] Tosefta, Hagiga 2:7.

[6] S. Lieberman, *Tosepeth Rishonim* I, Jerusalem, 1938, p. 246.

the Tosefta's questions which begin "I might think that one may ask." This seems to show that the text should be restored approximately as follows: "Ask thou, etc., I might think that one might ask concerning what preceded the creation of the world (var.: before the cosmogony), Thus Scripture states: "From one end of heaven etc.", i.e. man's permission to ask is limited to the period between the creation of heaven and its destruction which are the temporal "ends of heaven". Thereupon the Tosefta asks, like the Babylonian Talmud, from the verse "from the day which he created etc." Even though its answer is different from that of the Babylonian Talmud - since as opposed to the Talmudim the Tosefta is stricter and forbids even to ask about the days of creation which preceded the creation of man. Furthermore, the editor of the Tosefta felt the need to strengthen his temporal explanation of the words of the Mishna, and replaced the ambiguous phrase 'what is before and what is after' with the clear temporal phrase 'what was and what will be'.[7]

A comparison of the preceding three sources presents the following picture: the halakhic midrash in the Palestinian Talmud derives the prohibition of temporal speculation from the first two phrases of the verse; the spatial prohibition - from the third phrase. The Palestinian Talmud adds, as an appendix, the idea that the spatial prohibition implies also a temporal one. The Babylonian Talmud quotes the same halakhic midrash in a shorter version and is also of the opinion that the spatial prohibition carries with it the temporal one, and asks on the strength of this viewpoint from the third phrase of the verse on the second one: "Now that etc." In the Tosefta this appendix of the halakhic midrash intruded into the text of the midrash itself. The midrash in the Tosefta skips over the second phrase in the verse, connects the temporal prohibition directly to the third phrase, and concludes by asking from the third phrase on the second. The halakhic midrash in the Talmudim, which expound the phrases of the verse in their order and give the reasons for the temporal prohibition as deriving from the verses which speak of time, and the spatial prohibition from the verse which speaks of place, may be supposed to reflect old

---

[7] This variant is not found in all of the manuscripts of the Tosefta and some of them keep the reading of the Mishna. But these manuscripts most likely corrected the less well-known text of the Tosefta in accordance with the famous text of the Mishna. Cf. also note 8.

tradition. The opposite applies to the halakhic midrash in the Tosefta which does not expound the phrases of the verse in their order and even deviates from the plain meaning of the verse "from the end of etc." by inverting a secondary temporal exposition of the verse to its primary and only explanation. We should point out an additional strange point in the difficult exposition of the Tosefta: "'From the day which God created man on earth', you ask, and you don't ask what is above and what is below what was and what will be". For it is clear that the words 'what is above and what is below' are completely functionless here and were inserted by mere routine. This also strengthens the claim that the midrash in the Tosefta does not correspond to the plain meaning of the Mishna.

On this interpretation of the Mishna, which in our opinion is a late one, are based two passages in the Talmudim. It is a matter of course with them that our Mishna prohibits first and foremost investigation into what preceded the creation of the world. The Palestinian Talmud (ibid.) brings as an interpretation of R. Jonah in the name of R. Levi the following reason for the creation of the world with the letter *beth*: "just as *beth* is closed on all sides and open on one side, so you do not have permission to enquire after what is above and what is below, what is before and what after, except from the day on which the world was created onward." This midrash is found with variants also in Genesis Rabba, chap. 1. The question raised on our Mishna by the Babylonian Talmud is based on the same point of view.: "Granted as regards what is above, what is below, what (will be) after, that (= the prohibition) is well. But as regards what was before - what happened, happened!" (Hagiga 16a). These quotations only prove that their propounders followed the later interpretation of the formula 'what is above, and what is below, what is before, and what is after'. No proof can be adduced from them regarding the plain interpretation of the Mishna.[8]

---

[8] Of course, the contradictions between the Talmudic sources caused perplexity among the commentators. The Tosaphists (Hagiga 11b, s.v. *yākol*) oppose to Rashi the Talmud in Hagiga 16a and they conclude: "And we should say that one may say this or one may say that". Cf. also the Tosaphists in Megilla 25b, s.v. *ma l^{e}pānim* who add to the spatial interpretation the temporal interpretation introduced by the words: "An alternative explanation". R. Isaia of Trani (See: *Häḥālus* 5, *[*1860*]*, p. 55 *[*in Heb.*]* goes to an extreme in opposing Rashi's opinion entirely, adducing in addition to Hagiga 16a - also the clear text of the Tosefta which he quotes as follows: *mä hāwā umä ^{c}ātid lihyot*.

Rashi's interpretation of the Mishna, which we strengthened by an analysis of the Talmudic material, is corroborated by an investigation of the prehistory of the formula 'what is above, and what is below, what is before, and what is after'. In this investigation we will be guided by the consideration that the same speculation which man is commanded to stay away from, is fitting for God, who by His very nature is praised in that nothing in the world is hidden from His glance. The question, therefore, may be posed whether the source of the formula under discussion is not in the glorification of God which turns into a disgrace for a man, when he has the audacity to try to liken himself to Him. Some support for this hypothesis may be found in the Bible. The Psalmist says: "Whither shall I go from Thy spirit? Or whither shall I flee from Thy presence? If I ascend up into heaven Thou art there! If I make my bed in Sheol, behold, Thou art there! If I take the wings of the morning and dwell in the uttermost parts of the sea, even there shall Thy hand lead me, and Thy right hand shall hold me" (Ps. 139:7-10). This implies that one cannot flee from God who is found everywhere and looks at every place, in heaven above and Sheol below, and even at the "uttermost parts of the sea" before and behind: "For He looks to the ends of the earth" (Job 28:24). If one argues that no proof may be adduced from the poetic style of the Bible to the dry and systematic phraseology of the Mishna, we may add an additional proof from an Akkadian text which has a most remarkable resemblance to our Mishna. I refer to the letter of the king of Urartu to the king of Assur in which the sender glorifies: *ša pa-ni ar-ki im-na šu-me-lu e-la-nu u šap-la-nu i-ḫa-ṭu šar ilâ-ni*[meš] *ša-qu u mu-tal-lu*[9] 'who orders what is before and what is behind, what is to the right and what is to the left, what is above and what is below, king of the gods, the lofty and elevated one'. This text clearly speaks of the six dimensions which the high god, apparently Marduk, commands. The spatial meaning of the words *pāni, arki* 'before, behind' is not in the slightest doubt. The resemblance of the text to the formula 'what is above, etc.' of our Mishna is obvious, even though the Mishna mentions only four dimensions. However, the Tosaphists already added to Rashi's interpretation: "The same applies to north and south" (Hagiga 11b, s.v. *yā-kol*). This implies that the difference between the Hebrew formula and the Akkadian formula is limited to just what medieval scholars added to our

---

[9] R.F. Harper, *Assyrian and Babylonian Letters*, No. 1240, ll. 11-13.

Mishna by way of interpretation. True, it is no coincidence that our Mishna mentions only the four dimensions, as we may learn from the midrash concerning the questions which Alexander the Great posed to the scholars of the south: "He asked: Which is further, from heaven to earth or from east to west? They replied: From east to west. The proof is that when the sun is in the east all can look at it, and when it is in the west all can look at it, but when the sun is in the middle of the sky no-one can look at it. The sages, however, say: The distance in both cases is the same, as it says: 'For as the heaven is high above the earth etc.' (Ps. 103:11); 'as far as east is from west' (ibid. 12). Now if one of the distances is greater, the text should not write both but only the one which is greater" (Tamid 31b-32a). Even the Biblical verses on which the Rabbis base themselves mention only four dimensions: "For as the heavens are high above the earth, so great is His steadfast love toward those who fear Him; as far as the east is from the west, so far does He remove our transgressions from us" (Ps. 103:11-12). Similarly we find that the phrase 'from east to west' is used in Biblical poetry as a *formula exhaustationis* in verses which indicate God's rule over the whole world, e.g. "that men may know, from the rising of the sun and from the west, that there is none besides Me" (Is. 45:6); "So they shall fear the name of the Lord from the west, and His glory from the rising of the sun" (Is. 59:19); "For from the rising of the sun to its setting my name is great among the nations" (Mal. 1:11); "The Mighty One, God the Lord, speaks and summons the earth from the rising of the sun to its setting the name of the Lord is to be praised!" (Ps. 113:3). Compare also the Phoenician inscription of Azitawadda in which this king boasts that he expanded the boundaries of his land *lmmṣ' šmš wᶜd mb'y* 'from the rising of the sun and until its setting' (A:4-5). In the light of this literary tradition we should not wonder at all about the fact that the Mishna skips over the north and the south. However, on the other hand it is clear that this omission opened the way for an explanation of the words 'before and after' as referring to time.

We have followed as much as possible the course of the change in the interpretation of the Mishna, even if these possibilities are limited, even more so since the time of the formulation of our Mishna is unknown. Nevertheless it seems that the new explanation did not quickly supersede the old one, for we find that the same R. Jonah who in the 4th cen. CE quotes in the name of R. Levi the midrash of the creation of the world with the letter *bet*, which is based on the later explanation, quotes also the halakhic midrash which reflects the earlier interpretation in the name of Rabbi. On the other hand the reasons which led to the change in the understanding of the formula are clear. Scholars have understood for some time that the prohibition of speculation into what preceded the creation of the world is based on reservations in this matter concerning Gnosticism.[10] Therefore, we should not be surprised that the sages looked for support for this important prohibition in the text of the Mishna which they interpreted in the light of it.

We have tried above to establish the claim that the formula 'what is before and what is after' was not originally a matter referring to Jewish Gnosis; rather this facet was given to it only later. We have also tried to show that this process went through two stages: A first stage in which the temporal prohibition was derived from the spatial one; and a second one in which the words 'before and after' were interpreted simply as temporal concepts. A similar development occurred later with the terms 'what is above and what is below'. According to their original meaning, these terms refer to heaven and Sheol, or the abyss; Cf. "Though they dig into Sheol, from there shall my hand take them; though they climb up to heaven, from there I will bring them down" (Am. 9:2), and especially the Apocalypse of Ezra, which connects with the descent to the abyss and the ascent to heaven (which are impossible for mortals) the knowledge of hidden things, in the words of the angel Uriel: "Had I asked thee: How many dwellings are in the heart of the sea? Or how many springs in the source of the deep? Or how many ways above the firmament? Or where are the portals of Hades? Perchance thou wouldst have said to me: Into the deep I have not descended, nor as yet gone down into Hades; neither to heaven have I ever ascended" (IV Ezra 4:7-8).

Here also it seems that we may adduce corroborative evidence from a parallel Akkadian text in which Marduk boasts: *[KI]MINA ša šamê(e) ru-qu-u-ti mi-la-šu-nu ḫi-i-ṭu [KI]MINA ša ḫu-bur pal-ka-ti šu-pu-ul-šá*[11] *i-di*

---

[10] See Ch. Albeck, *Tractate Moed*, Jerusalem 1952, pp. 510-511, (in Heb.), and the literature cited there.

[11] W.G. Lambert, *AfO* 17 (1955-56), p. 312, A. ll. 8,9.

'*[I, Marduk,]* who scans the height *[or rather: the high-waters]*[12] of the distant heavens. *[I, Marduk,]* who knows the depth of the broad Hubur-river (= the river by which one enters the underworld)'. We may suppose that already in the Mishnaic Period these terms had lost their original meaning. Proof of this is found in the aforementioned halakhic midrash from the Palestinian Talmud, which deals with what is above the heavens and below the abyss. These definitions are the result of thought which approaches philosophy and are foreign to the naive introspection of the Ancient Near East which limited itself to speculations on the heavens above and the abyss below, but did not raise at all the question what was outside of them. We should not, however, discover in this formulation any special connection with the specific world of the Gnosis. But here also Jewish Gnosticism brought about a transformation of a set of ideas, which is already felt in the Talmudim and in the Gaonic writings, but which did not reach a clear and unambiguous formulation until Rashi who interpreted: "'What is above' - from the firmament above the heads of the living creatures, and 'what is below' - below them" (Hagiga 11b, on the Mishna). This definition is based purely on the teachings of the *Merkaba* in Jewish Gnosticism. A cursory look at this definition shows that its first part is close to the plain meaning of the Talmudic formula, since the place which is above the firmament and above the heads of the living creatures is automatically above the earth. However, the second part of Rashi's definition actually reverses the plain meaning of the Mishna, since it is clear that even the world which is below the heavenly creatures is above the earth and not below it. This strange development is only to be understood in the light of the fact that the Gnostic interest centered in the upper worlds which have no parallel in lower worlds below the earth. The roots of this exegesis may be already clear-

---

[12] The noun *mīlašunu* which we translated 'their height', means literally 'their fullness'. *[*Contrast v. Soden, *AHW*, s.v. *mīlu(m) Hochwasser, Fülle*. Perhaps the opposition between the high-waters of heaven and the subterranean waters of *Ḫubur* is intended.*]* This Akkadian noun is perhaps one of the predecessors, of the Gnostic expression πλήρωμα which signifies the upper spiritual world, which is separated from the lower world, i.e. the world of the aeons cf. e.g.: G.F. Dellwig in *Theologisches Wörterbuch zum Neuen Testament*, Band 6, Stuttgart 1956, pp. 298-300. The Christian Gnostic term πλήρωμα is paralleled in the book *Bahir*, 4, by the term *m^elo'* of Hebrew Gnosticism. See: G. Scholem, *Encyclopaedia Judaica* 3 (1929), p. 974.

ly recognized in the Talmudic and Gaonic literature. The Babylonian Talmud quotes in the name of R. Aha b. R. Jacob the following explanation: "There is still another Heaven above the heads of the living creatures, for it is written: 'And over the heads of the living creatures there was likeness of a firmament, like the color of the terrible ice, stretched forth over their heads above' (Ez. 1:22). Thus far you have permission to speak, for so it is written in the Book of Ben Sira: 'Seek not things that are too hard for thee etc.' (Ecclus. 3:21f.)" (Hagiga 12a). This interpretation is attached to the verse in Ben Sira and not to the words of the Mishna, but since the Mishna also deals with the prohibition of seeking things which are too hard, the idea of explaining it also in the light of this interpretation immediately comes to mind. We find that R. Juda b. Barzilai of Barcelona testifies in his commentary on *Sepher Yeṣira* to the following explanation of R. Hai Gaon: "And the firmament which is above the living creatures is not a wheel but it is His seat of honour, and above it you have no right to seek from the Biblical verses, and we are unable *to look* by our own speculation".[13] R. Hai Gaon's language is clearly influenced by that of the Mishna, and the way from it to Rashi's explanation is not far. The connection of Rashi's explanation in its second part, i.e. the explanation of the phrase 'and what is below' which has no natural interpretation within the framework of the *Merkaba* mysticism, is looser. The Babylonian Talmud comments on the Mishna: "... nor (the work of) the chariot in the presence of a single person" as follows: "R. Hiyya taught: But the headings of chapters may be transmitted to him. R. Zera said: The headings of chapters may be transmitted only to the head of a court and to one whose heart is anxious within him." (Hagiga 13a). This topic is found in a responsum of R. Sherira Gaon in the following manner: "And concerning what is below the work of the chariot the Rabbis said: 'R. Hiyya taught: But the headings of the chapter etc.'"[14] Here we clearly find the term 'below', but even from R. Sherira Gaon's responsum it is clear that the seeking of what is below the chariot is not forbidden with the same strict prohibition that applies to what is above it, and Rashi's explanation adds here a stricture.

---

[13] *Commentary on the book Yeṣirah* of R. Judah of Barcelona, pp. 149-150, quoted here from Levin, *op. cit.* (note 5), p. 55.

[14] Levin, *op. cit.* (note 5), p. 12.

But it is doubtful whether his explanation is simply a sort of hedge which comes to remove man from dangerous thoughts. Rather it seems more likely that his explanation derives from the difficulty in explaining the concept 'below' which has no actual meaning according to the appearance of the world of *Merkaba* mysticism.

To sum up: There is no unambiguous evidence for the origin of the formula 'What is above and what is below, what is before and what is after', but we may hypothesize with a high degree of probability, that its origin is a glorification formula of God who looks everywhere. In the Mishna the glorification of God turns into the censure of the man who dares to compare himself to Him and to seek matters above him. This shows that the Mishna has reservations concerning speculations of a mystical-philosophical nature. There is, however, no basis for the identification of these speculations with Gnosticism. The opposite is true: We may establish with absolute certainty that the concepts 'above and below' do not refer to the Gnostic doctrine of place. The conclusion is then obvious that we should not look for any hint of Gnostic doctrines in the words 'before and after', especially not of the Gnostic doctrine of the creation of the world. This conclusion is affirmed in the light of the linguistic analysis of the formula which shows the preferability of the spatial explanation of the pair of concepts 'before and after', and also in the light of the study of the development of the halakhic midrash which makes it plausible that the spatial explanation is the earlier one. However, in addition it may be established that the formula went through some sort of a process of actualization in the light of Gnosticism. It is not coincidental that the second part of the formula was thrown into the Gnostic melting pot first, since it may be interpreted without any excessive difficulty as a prohibition of speculation into what preceded the creation of the world. For one who transgressed this prohibition not only sought what was above him, i.e. beyond the range of his perception, but also offended the creator by speculating on the Gnostic doctrine of the δημιουργός, the creator of the world of evil. And if Jewish Gnosticism could not accept this doctrine which undermines all the foundations of Judaism - and in fact did not accept it - nevertheless its mark is felt in it as we learn from the famous midrash: "Both R. Johanan and Resh Lakish say: It is like a human king who said to his servants: Build for me a great palace upon the dunghill.

They went forth and built it for him. It is not the king's wish (thenceforth) to have the name of the dunghill mentioned." (Hagiga 16a).

Yāpe^{a}ḥ, Yāpi^{a}ḥ.

In a lecture given in November 1956, Virolleaud[1] gave information on a unpublished Ugaritic document. This document ends with a list of personal names. The last person is called *spr* 'scribe', whereas to the previous names is added the epithet *ypḥ* i.e. 'witness' as Virolleaud has concluded from a comparison of the Ugaritic document with its Akkadian parallels.

On the basis of this discovery, Dahood[2] explained the verse *ki qāmu bi* ^{c}*ede šäqär wipe*^{a}*ḥ ḥāmās* (Ps. 27:12) and established that *y*^{e}*pe*^{a}*ḥ ḥāmās* is nothing but a synonymous term for ^{c}*ed ḥāmās* (Ps. 35:11).

P. Nober, the bibliographer[3] who listed Dahood's article in the bibliography of *Biblica* added that the word *ypḥ* should be explained similarly in the verse *ki* ^{c}*od ḥāzon lammo*^{c}*ed w*^{e}*yāpe*^{a}*ḥ laqqeṣ w*^{e}*lo' y*^{e}*kazzeb* (Hab. 2:3), i.e. the vision which is inscribed on the tablets is a faithful witness to the end of time.

We may add that six verses in Proverbs juxtapose the word *yāpi*^{a}*ḥ* (once written defectively without *yod*) with ^{c}*ed*. The question immediately arises whether this word should also be explained as 'witness'. These verses are close to each other both in content and language, and require a comprehensive discussion. We will list them here in order.

Pr. 6:16-19

There are six things which the God hates
    Yea, seven which are an abomination unto Him.
Haughty eyes, a lying tongue,
    And hands that shed innocent blood.

---

[1] Ch. Virolleaud, *GLECS* 7, 1954-1957, pp. 85f. See now idem, *CRAIBL* 1960, 86f. *[= PRU* 5, text 116*]*.

[2] M. Dahood, *CBQ* 20 (1958), pp. 47f., note 21.

[3] *Biblica* 39 (1958), *Elenchus bibliographicus*, p. 199: *(est) visio diei praestituto testis temporis praefixo infallabilis.*

A heart that devises wicked thoughts

Feet that are swift in running to evil.

yāpi^{a}*ḥ k*^{e}*zābim* ^{c}*ed šāqär*

And he who sows discord among brethren.

Pr. 12:17

Yāpi^{a}*ḥ '*^{ä}*munā* utters righteousness,

w^{ec}*ed š*^{e}*qārim* deceit.

Pr. 14:5 ^{c}*ed '*^{ä}*munim* will not lie

w^{e}*yāpi*^{a}*ḥ k*^{e}*zābim* ^{c}*ed šāqär*.

Pr. 14:25 ^{c}*ed '*^{ä}*mät* saves lives,

w^{e}*yāpi*^{a}*ḥ k*^{e}*zābim* is(?) deceit

Pr. 19:5

^{c}*ed š*^{e}*qārim* shall not be unpunished,

w^{e}*yāpi*^{a}*ḥ k*^{e}*zābim* will not escape.

Pr. 19:9

^{c}*ed š*^{e}*qārim* shall not be unpunished,

w^{e}*yāpi*^{a}*ḥ k*^{e}*zābim* will perish.

This survey puts before us a limited number of phrases in different variations and combinations and gives us an opportunity for a comparative study. The idea *yāpi*^{a}*ḥ '*^{ä}*munā* utters righteousness (Pr. 12:17) is phrased also in the form ^{c}*ed '*^{ä}*munim* will not lie" (Pr. 14:5). This shows that there is no difference at all between *yāpi*^{a}*ḥ '*^{ä}*munā* and ^{c}*ed '*^{ä}*munim*.

Even more instructive is the comparison of the verse *w*^{ec}*ed š*^{e}*qārim* deceit (Pr. 12:17) with *w*^{e}*yāpi*^{a}*ḥ k*^{e}*zābim* is deceit (Pr. 14:25), for we see that *yāpi*^{a}*ḥ kāzāb* and ^{c}*ed šāqär* are free variants. Therefore it is well understood that the same two pairs of words appear also in parallel in the two hemistichs of one verse (Pr. 19:5,9). Moreover, they are found again in parataxis, as a sort of joint concept in Pr. 6:19 which completes the list of things hated by God. Obermann[4] has rightly pointed out that this list contains only general nouns, and the interpretation of *yāpi*^{a}*ḥ* as a verb does not agree with the structure of the proverb. The pair of concepts dealt

---

[4] J. Obermann, *JBL* 70 (1951), pp. 201-207.

with here is so common in Proverbs, that it is even found in a slightly tautological nominal clause in the second hemistich of the proverb: ^{c}*ed ʾ^{ä}munim* shall not lie and *yāpi^{a}ḥ k^{e}zābim* (is) ^{c}*ed šāqär* (Pr. 14:5). Perhaps, the chiastic phrasing of the verse is the cause here.[4a]

We may thus follow Barth[5] and Obermann[6] who thought that *yāpe^{a}ḥ* and *yāpi^{a}ḥ* (in the preceding proverbs) are synonymous forms. We differ from them only in their explanation and attribute to them in the light of the Ugaritic discovery the meaning 'witness'.

The etymology of *yāpe^{a}ḥ, yāpi^{a}ḥ* has not been clarified. Barth[7] and Obermann[8] both thought that *yāpi^{a}ḥ* was a participle of *pwḥ*, even though they explained this participle in different ways. Barth wished to see in this form a metathesis of *pāyi^{a}ḥ*, whereas Obermann brought *yāpi^{a}ḥ* among the few proofs for his contention that in Canaanite existed a participle in the *yaqtil*-form. Both scholars differred on the explanation of the form *yāpe^{a}ḥ*. According to Barth it is a free variant of *yāpi^{a}ḥ*, whereas according to Obermann, it is the result of a mistaken vocalization.

We may also point out that Barth[9] connected *yāpi^{a}ḥ* with the Arabic root *bāḥa* 'to say', 'make known'. If we follow him, then the basic meaning of *yāpi^{a}ḥ* is 'the one who says, makes known', and we may easily understand the semantic development to 'witness'. But there is no proof for this tempting suggestion, since neither a verb *pwḥ* nor a participle with a *y*- prefix are so far attested in Ugaritic. Thus it is impossible to decide whether the root of the word is *pwḥ* or *yph*.

On the other hand, the meaning of the word has become perfectly clear. Moreover, it is no less evident that this ancient term of Canaanite law had become obsolete in everyday speech even in the First Temple Period to remain

---

[[4a] In the verse: *massil n^{e}pāšot* ^{c}*ed ʾ^{ä}mät / w^{e}yāpi^{a}ḥ k^{e}zābim mirmā* (Pr. 14:25), the second stichus does not continue the first. It is obviously synonymous to: *w^{ec}ed š^{e}qārim mirmā* (Pr. 12:17b), which is aptly preceded by: *yāpi^{a}ḥ ʾ^{a}munā yaggid ṣädäq*. It may be supposed that Pr. 14:25b was originally joined to a stichus like: ^{c}*ed ʾ^{ä}munā yaggid ṣädäq*. Pr. 14:25a might have been an old proverb of one stichus only.

[5] Barth, *Nominalbildung*, pp. 189, 233.

[6] Obermann, *loc. cit.* (note 4).

[7] Barth, *Nominalbildung*, pp. 189, 233.

[8] Obermann, *loc. cit.* (note 4).

[9] J. Barth, *Etymologische Studien*, Berlin 1893, p. 24.

only in the high style of Poetry. By the time of the Second Temple the meaning of this word had already fallen into oblivion as evidenced by the Septuagint.

The Septuagint translates *ypyḥ kzbym* three times by ἐκκαίει ψεύδη (Pr. 6:19; 14:5,25), a translation based on an interpretation of *ypyḥ* as the *Hiph^{c}il* of *pwḥ* (cf. Pr. 29:8). The same point of view is seen in the translation ὃς δ'ἂν ἐκκαύσῃ κακίαν (Pr. 19:9). The Septuagint approaches the original correct meaning in Pr. 19:5: ὁ δὲ ἐγκαλῶν ἀδίκως 'the one who accuses unjustly'. But it is clear that this exceptional translation is only a guess from the context. The same applies to the Septuagint to Ps. 27:12: καὶ ἐψεύσατο ἡ ἀδικία ἑαυτῇ from which it seems that they read *wypyḥ ḥms lw* and interpreted *yāpe^{a}ḥ*, as meaning to lie. In Hab. 2:3 they translated *wypḥ* καὶ ἀνατελεῖ 'and he will appear, arise'. Perhaps this is an example of the interchange of *ḥ* and ^{c}, a well-known phenomenon in Second Temple Hebrew. In the light of this we may assume a priori that the Masoretes did understand the noun *yāpi^{a}ḥ* as a *Hiph^{c}il* form. As proof of this we may note that they always vocalize *yāpi^{a}ḥ* (and not *y^{e}pi^{a}ḥ*) *k^{e}zābim*. In spite of this vocalization the meaning of the word *yāpi^{a}ḥ* is entirely clear in the six verses in Proverbs from the parallelism with *^{c}ed* and the same applies to the cstr. form *y^{e}pe^{a}ḥ* (Ps. 27:12) in which *wipe^{a}ḥ ḥāmās* parallels *^{c}ede šäqär*.

In Hab. 2:3 the parallelism between *yāpe^{a}ḥ* and *^{c}ed* is missing in the Masoretic Text, but nevertheless for several reasons it seems that also here *yāpe^{a}ḥ* means 'witness'. First of all, the phrase *w^{e}yāpe^{a}ḥ laqqeṣ w^{e}lo' y^{e}kazzeb* reminds us of the expression *yāpi^{a}ḥ k^{e}zābim* (Pr. 6:19; 14:5; 19:5, 9). It follows that the roots *ypḥ* and *kzb* occur together in the phraseology tradition of the Bible. Moreover, the new interpretation of the word *yāpe^{a}ḥ* reveals the resemblance between the prophecy of Habakkuk and that of Isaiah. In Habakkuk we read: "And the Lord answered me and said: 'Write the vision and make it plain upon the tablets, that a man may read it swiftly. Because *^{c}od ḥāzon lammo^{c}ed w^{e}yāpe^{a}ḥ laqqeṣ w^{e}lo' y^{e}kazzeb*. Though it tarry wait for it, because it will surely come, it will not delay.'" (Hab. 2:2-3). On the other hand we read in Isaiah: "Now go, write it before them on a tablet, and inscribe it in a book that it may be for the time to come *lā^{c}ad ^{c}ad ^{c}olām* for ever in eternity (Is. 30:8). The Masoretic Text reads here *lā^{c}ad*, and this reading lies behind the translation in most manuscripts of the Septuagint (ὅτι ἔσται εἰς ἡμέρας καιρῶν ταῦτα), but other manuscripts understood here *l^{ec}ed* (εἰς μαρτύριον), and this was the opinion of the other ancient versions (TY, Pešiṭta, Vulgate). It is clear that the interpretation of the word *yāpe^{a}ḥ* (Hab. 2:3) as 'witness' and the reading *l^{ec}ed* (Is. 30:8

confirm one another. Both in Isaiah and Habakkuk we find the same idea that the prophecy inscribed on the tablet will serve in the time of fulfilment as testimony to the truth of the prophecy which is slow in coming. We should compare this idea with the verses in Is. 8:16; Dan. 12:4[9a], and the use of *ᶜed* in the meaning 'testimony' with the similar usage of this noun in Gen. 31:44; Jos. 22:27. Moreover, it seems probable that in the original reading of the verse, *yāpeaḥ* was parallel to *ᶜed*. The words *ki ᶜod hāzon lammoᶜed* are obscure and the commentators have always been divided on their interpretation. Ehrlich[10] already pointed out that we should read *ᶜed* and not *ᶜod*, and supported this emendation by the parallelism between *ᶜed* and *yāpiaḥ* in the verses dealt with above. His suggestion was not accepted. But the discovery of the meaning of *ypḥ* clearly proves that he was right. The corruption is easily understood. After the meaning of *ypḥ* was forgotten, the word *ᶜd* was mistakenly understood as a defective spelling for *ᶜod*[11], and this mistaken interpretation was re-inforced by the plene spelling *ᶜwd*. It must be admitted that the antiquity of this corruption is already testified to by the Septuagint reading (ἔτι), as well as by Pesher Habakkuk which also reads *ᶜwd*. The Pesher explains the meaning of the masoretic readings as follows: "that the end of time is far off." (7:7). The second hemistich of the verse - that the coming of the vision will tarry - thus influenced the interpretation of the first hemistich and even its reading.

This is not all. There is an echo of the reading: *ki ᶜod hāzon lammoᶜed* in several expressions in Daniel, which were also obscure until now and caused much dispute among scholars. We read: "Now I have come to make you understand what shall befall your people in the end of days for there is *ᶜwd* a vision for the days" (Dan. 10:14). The same use of *ᶜwd* recurs in another

---

[[9a] The same prophetic idea is clearly reflected in Deut. 31:19-21, 24-29. The song of Moses, respectively the "Tora", are treated in these passages as prophecies which predict the fate of the people to be fulfilled in the distant future. It is for this reason that they were put down in writing, destined to serve as testimony that the events to come had been predicted long before.]

[10] A.B. Ehrlich, *Mikrâ ki-Pheschutô*, Berlin 1901, p. 450, on this verse. I would like to thank Mrs. S. Flusser and Prof. D. Flusser who drew my attention to Ehrlich's suggestion.

[11] In the Masoretic Text *ᶜod* is spelled defectively fourteen times.

verse: "And as for both these kings, their hearts shall be to do mischief, and they shall speak lies at one table; but it shall not prosper, for the end remains *ᶜod lammoᶜed*." (Dan. 11:27). Also: "And some of them that are wise shall stumble, to refine among them, and to purify, and to make white *ᶜad ᶜet qeṣ ki ᶜod lammoᶜed*" (Dan. 11:35). Strobel[12] already recognized that all of these verses are based on Hab. 2:3, and his conclusions fits well the midrash of the wise in Daniel (Chaps. 10-12), which is a midrash on earlier prophecies as H.L. Ginsberg[13] has proved. The wording of all the verses in Daniel is dependent on the Masoretic reading in Hab. 2:3, and hints like it "that the end is far off". It is no wonder that all the commentators of Daniel had difficulty in understanding these expressions whose explanation cannot be arrived at by a regular linguistic analysis, but only on the basis of a clarification of the history of the text in Hab. 2:3, which in its present form is the result of an eschatological midrash, which in turn influenced later interpretations of this type.

---

[12] A. Strobel, *Untersuchungen zum eschatologischen Verzögerungsproblem auf Grund der spätjüdisch-urchristlichen Geschichte von Habakuk*, Leiden-Köln 1961, pp. 49-51. I would like to thank Dr. J. Licht for calling my attention to this study.

[13] *EB* 2, cols. 949-952.

Additions to yāpe^{a}ḥ

Only when this article was in proof did I realize that Prof. N.H. Tur-Sinai had already been aware of the problems dealt with in my article. In his German translation of the Bible, he was the first to translate *yāpe^{a}ḥ* in Proverbs as a term of testimony. Cf. for example, his translation of *yāpi^{a}ḥ 'ä$^{}$munā* (Pr. 12:17) *'Wer Wahrheit ansagt'*.[1] Tur-Sinai also pointed in the *Beilage* to the above translation to the connection between Hab. 2:3 on the one hand, and Dan. 10:14 on the other.[2] However, his explanation there differs from that offered in my article, since he is of the opinion that the word *^{c}od* in all the aforementioned verses is a term of testimony. He translates *w^{e}yāpi^{a}ḥ laqqeṣ* in Hab. 2:3 as *und sagt an das Ende*.

---

[1] N.H. Tur-Sinai, *Die heilige Schrift* IV, Jerusalem 1958, p. 213.

[2] *Beilage* 1959, p. 44.

Further Additions to yāpi^{a}ḥ, yāpe^{a}ḥ

A. Dror in his article[1] "*yāpe^{a}ḥ, yāpi^{a}ḥ*" raised the possibility that the Masoretes considered *yāpi^{a}ḥ* to be a nominal and not a verbal form, even in phrases such as *yāpi^{a}ḥ k^{e}zābim* (Pr. 19:5). His reasoning is that a tone-long *qāmeṣ* can be retained in exceptional cases, even when the tone has been moved forward, as e.g. in the word *šālišim*. This, however, is no proof. True, such a *qāmeṣ* may remain in pl. forms, but is never kept in the sg. cst.; cf. *pāriṣim* (Ez. 7:22), *sārisim* (2 Reg. 9:32) on the one hand, and *p^{e}riṣ ḥayyot* (Is. 35:9) and *s^{e}ris par^{c}o* (Gen. 37:36) on the other. It is thus clear that the Masoretes, like the ancient translators, understood *yāpi^{a}ḥ* as a verbal form. One cannot pose the question: "How is it possible that they did not realize the possibility of the existence of bi-forms *yāpe^{a}ḥ-yāpi^{a}ḥ* even in verses which are close in meaning". But see the dictionaries of Gesenius-Buhl and Brown-Driver-Briggs which also did not recognize the double forms.

I admit that when I wrote my article[2] several things written by my predecessors escaped my attention. As for what Schulbaum wrote, Dror has already corrected my shortcoming. I would just like to point out, that there is no such thing as "*yāpe^{a}ḥ* of Daniel", and he apparently intended to write "*yāpe^{a}ḥ* of Ḥabakkuk". However, I will quote here references to additional literature which has been kindly called to my attention by Prof. H.L. Ginsberg, Prof. I.L. Seeligman, and Mr. R. Weiss.

In 1909, M. Lambert[3] defined *yp(y)ḥ* in Hab. 2:3; Ps. 27:12; Pr. 6:19; 12:17; 14:25 as a noun, and translated it in most of the cases as '*énonciateur*'; in Hab. 2:3 '*témoin*'. Lambert also noted the previous mistaken explanation of *yāpi^{a}ḥ* as a verb, and brought proof from the ancient transla-

---

[1] *Lěšonénu* 27 (1963), p. 72.

[2] See in this volume, yāpe^{a}ḥ, yāpi^{a}ḥ, pp. 137-142.

[3] M. Lambert, *REJ* 57 (1909), pp. 279f.

tions and from the Masoretic vocalization.

In 1912, Ehrlich[4] claimed in his German commentary on Hab. 2:3 that this was a late (!) word and synonymous with *ᶜed*, not only in Habakkuk, but also in Ps. 27:12; Pr. 6:19; 14:5,25; 19:5,9.

Similarly, in 1948, H.L. Ginsberg, explained *yp(y)ḥ* in the verses under discussion as meaning 'witness'. Moreover, he rightly noted that before the writer of Dan. 10:14; 11:27,35 there was the late reading in Hab. 2:3 *ki ᶜod (ᶜwd) ḥāzon lammoᶜed* and not the original: *ki ᶜed (ᶜd)* etc. [Compare now also: P.R. Berger, *UF* 2 (1970), pp. 10-11, 14-17; S.E. Loewenstamm, *Biblica* 59 (1978), pp. 103-104; D. Pardee, *VT* 28 (1978), pp. 204-213.]

---

[4] A.B. Ehrlich, *Randglossen zur Hebräischen Bibel* 5, Leipzig 1912, p. 302.

[5] H.L. Ginsberg, *Studies in Daniel*, New York 1948, pp. 35, 78 notes 17, 29.

The Laws of Adultery and Murder in Biblical and Mesopotamian Law.*

The comparison of Biblical and Mesopotamian laws is at first glance an easy task. Both the Bible and Mesopotamian literature possess collections of laws whose corresponding sections may be conveniently compared. The task of the comparer is to establish in detail the differences, and afterwards to pose the question: What are the distinctive and general ideas underlying the differences in detail?

M. Greenberg has recently employed this methodology in a study of the law of adultery.[1] He notes that the Pentateuchal law (Lev. 20:10; Deut. 22: 22-23) as well as the Mesopotamian laws (Codex Hammurabi § 129; The Assyrian Laws, Tablet 1, §§ 14-16; The Hittite Laws § 198 = Tablet 2, § 84 in Friedrich's edition) impose the death penalty on the adulterer and the adulteress, and points out that the Mesopotamian laws include an additional statute: The punishment of the adulterer is annulled if the husband forgives his wife.

Greenberg has come to some very far-reaching conclusions as a result of this difference. He defines the character of the Mesopotamian law as follows: "The purpose of the law is to defend the right of the husband and provide him with redress for the wrong done to him. If the husband, however, is willing to forego his right and chooses to overlook the wrong done to him there is no need for redress. The pardon of the husband wipes out the crime." This is not the case with the Biblical law which requires the execution of the adulterer and the adulteress in every instance "for adultery is not merely a wrong against the husband, but is a sin against God, an absolute wrong." Greenberg adds that this theological approach is recognizable also in Biblical stories. In the story of Abimelech the text states that God told him: "and so I kept you from sinning against Me." (Gen. 20:6). This

* Compare in this volume, *The Laws of Adultery and Murder in the Bible*, pp. 171-172.

[1] M. Greenberg, *G. Kaufmann Jubilee Volume*, Jerusalem 1960, pp. *[12]*, *[13]*.

same outlook is obvious also in Gen. 39:9; Ps. 51:4. Greenberg does not deny that even the Bible considers adultery an offence against the husband (Num. 5:12), but he thinks that the character of the law of adultery does not depend on this: "Punishment is not designed to redress an injured husband for violation of his rights; the offended party is God whose injury no man can pardon or mitigate". In short the Mesopotamian law of adultery was formulated completely on secular grounds, while in Israel - completely on religious grounds.

This methodology may be criticized on several counts. First of all, when dealing with the Mesopotamian viewpoints on adultery, we should not limit ourselves just to a clarification of the sections of the secular law. To get a complete picture we must look into the religious literature dealing with this subject. Any investigation which ignores this will arrive at unreliable results and will blur the decisive fact that the Mesopotamians also considered adultery to be a religious crime. Several fragments of a bilingual Sumero-Akkadian hymn to Ninurta have been preserved which contain lists of people who sinned against this god, including the adulterer: *ra-ḫu-u aš-ti a-wi-lim a-ran-šu kab-[tum-ma]*.[2] 'He who has intercourse with (another) man's wife, his guilt is grievous'. Ninurta is not the only god who punishes the sin of adultery. We read in a hymn to Šamaš: *sâ a-na al-ti tap-pi-šu iš-šu-û [enê-šu] i-na* u_4*-um la ši-ma-ti û-ša [...]*[3] 'A man who covets his neighbor's wife will ... before his appointed day'. The broken text probably stated that the adulterer will die before his time by the hand of Šamaš. In Šurpu, Tablet II, we find an incantation directed to the great gods in general which asks them not to punish many types of sinners. Included among them is the man who *a-na bît tap-pe-šu i-te-ru-ub a-na aššat tap-pe-ê-šú iṭ-ṭe*$_4$*-ḫi*[4] 'entered the house of his friend, approached the wife of his friend'. This implies that all the great gods were likely to punish this sin. In Tablet IV we find a similar incantation directed to Marduk which asks him to spare the lives of various sinners, among whom is the man who *a-na al-ti ib-ri-šu a-la-ku pu-uz-zu-ru*[5] 'went secretly to his friend's wife'.

---

[2] Lambert, *BWL*, p. 119, l. 4.

[3] Id., *ibid.*, pp. 130f., ll. 88-89.

[4] E. Reiner, *Šurpu*, Graz 1958, p. 14, ll. 47-48.

[5] Id., *ibid.*, p. 25, l. 6.

All this proves that even according to the Mesopotamian outlook the adulterer had sinned against the gods, and they were likely to punish him, even if certain texts give him some hope of receiving their forgiveness. The gods were supposed to punish the man who sinned against them and to bring retribution or even an abnormal death upon him. It was not the function of the courts to act for the gods and to serve as a *bracchium saeculare*. The gods acted by themselves, whereas the court took into account only damage done to the husband's rights.

We now consider the situation in the Bible. There is no doubt that the Bible considered adultery a crime against God. But we have seen that this very outlook does not necessarily lead to the conclusion that the courts will execute the adulterers even against the husband's will. *A priori* there is no reason to deny the possibility that in Israel also there was a fundamental distinction between a punishment meted out by the court and dependent on the husband's will, and a divine punishment which has nothing to do with the courts. A detailed study of the relevant Biblical passages confirms that this, in fact, is the case.

The importance of the husband's decision is reflected in Pr. 6:32-35: "He who commits adultery has no sense; he who ...[6] destroys himself. Wounds and dishonor will he get, and his disgrace will not be wiped away. For jealousy makes a man furious, and he will not spare when he takes revenge. He will accept no compensation, nor be appeased though you multiply gifts."

This warning is unambiguous: Do not deceive yourself - says the text - that the husband will accept ransom. He will be so furious that he will demand your execution. This shows that the author of the proverb considered the husband's perogative to commute the adulterer's execution to be obvious. For if we assume that the Assembly executed the adulterer in every instance

---

[6] *hu' ya*^{ca}*śännā*. 'he will do it'. The accepted vocalization and translation is weak. We may assume that the suffix pronoun refers to the woman, and that the verb ^{c}*śh* is close in meaning to *n'p*, and indicates the act of adultery. Cf.: "They played the harlot in Egypt; they played the harlot in their youth; there their breasts were pressed and their virgin bosoms handled (^{c}*iśśu*)" (Ezek. 23:3); "and they handled (^{c}*iśśu*) her virgin bosom and poured out their lust upon her" (v. 8). This shows that the word should probably be vocalized *y*^{ec}*aśśännāh*.

there is no value in the husband's willingness to be satisfied with ransom.[7]

It cannot be objected that the laws of the Pentateuch contradict the passage in Proverbs and demand the execution of the adulterers in every instance. In their phrasing the laws in the Pentateuch are intended to drive home the seriousness of the punishment for adultery which is death. But they do not answer the question: Who is the prosecutor? The Assembly which avenges the affront against God or the husband who avenges the affront against himself? If we prefer the second explanation then there is no contradiction between the passage in the Book of Proverbs and the Pentateuchal law. For it is clear that the husband who may demand the execution of the adulterers may also waive this right in lieu of payment of ransom or even without it.

We may verify the results of our study by comparing the law of adultery with the law of murder. Consider the following passages: "Whoever sheds the blood of man, by man shall his blood be shed" (Gen. 9:6); "He who fatally strikes a man shall be put to death" (Ex. 21:12); "If a man kills any

---

[7] Perhaps the problem of the adulterer's punishment is connected with the following difficult verse: "Do not despise a thief if he steals to satisfy his appetite when he is hungry. And if he is caught, he will pay sevenfold; he will give all the capital of his house" (Pr. 6:30-31). The difficulties in this verse are obvious: 1) All of chapter 6 speaks of adultery, and it is difficult to understand how the thief does come in here; 2) The verse itself is difficult: A desperately poor person who steals because he does not have money to buy food will certainly not pay sevenfold if he is caught because he does not have what to pay with. It is mockery of the poor person to speak of "all the capital of his house". Since the verse cannot refer to the poor thief it seems better to understand it as referring to the adulterer who is willing to pay the husband "all the capital of his house" in order to save his life. The problem of v. 30 may be explained in two ways: 1) In Biblica Hebraica[3] G. Beer proposes to read as follows: *lo' ya^{ca}zbu laggannāb ki yignob l^{e}malle napšo.gannāb* will then be an epithet for an adulterer who steals his friend's wife to satisfy his lust. 2) We can maintain the text as it is and assume that v. 30 was added from somewhere else. Furthermore, we may even suppose that this insertion resulted from the reasoning of the editor who found disagreement between the two sayings difficult, since one ended in a warning, that the adulterer would have to give "all the capital of his house", whereas the other warned the adulterer that the husband would demand the death penalty and would not agree to any ransom. It is therefore reasonable to assume that the redactor wanted to prevent this contradiction, and that it was for this reason that he added v. 30 from another source. It goes without saying that such proposals are hypothetical and should not be made base on which to analyze Biblical law.

human being, he shall be put to death" (Lev. 24:17). The formulation of these laws is no less absolute than the formulation of the laws of adultery, and in a similar way gives the impression that the execution of the guilty party was the task of the Assembly. Moreover, there is no doubt that the murderer has sinned against God and may expect to be punished by him. (Cf., for example: 1 Sam. 19:5; 25; 31; 2 Sam. 12:9,10; 1 Reg. 2:32; 21:19; 22:38; 2 Reg. 9:7,21; 24:4, and many similar passages). Furthermore, the Bible expresses clearly the idea that God may avenge innocent blood which was not atoned for by the one who shed it by punishing the whole Assembly. The Bible relates that in the time of David God brought a famine upon the land because of the blood of the Gibeonites which Saul had shed (2 Sam. 21:1). In Biblical law this idea found expression in the law of the beheaded heifer (Deut. 21:1-9), and its influence is also recognizable in the conclusion of the laws of murder in Nu. 35:31-34 "You may not accept a ransom for the life of a murderer who is guilty of a capital crime; he must be put to death. Nor may you accept ransom in lieu of flight to a city of refuge, enabling one to return to live on his land before the death of the priest. You shall not pollute the land in which you live; for the blood pollutes the land, and the land can have no expiation for blood that is shed on it, except by the blood of him who shed it. You shall not defile the land in which you live, in which I Myself abide, for I the Lord abide among the Israelite people".

These laws which warn against accepting ransom and which emphasize that the blood will pollute the land conclude a section which is built completely upon the principle of blood vengeance. The laws in Deut. 19:1-13 and Jos. 20:1-9 are based upon the same principle. It is true that the style of these laws makes their understanding difficult. The passages describe separately the trial procedure for a murderer and for a manslayer, but they do not recognize the procedural conception of a person suspected of premeditated murder but who claims that he acted unintentionally.[7a] Furthermore, each of the passages is incomplete. However, it is possible to comple-

---

[[7a] This procedual conception appears only in the Mishna: R. Jose B. Judah says: To begin with, a slayer was sent in advance to (one of) the cities of refuge, *whether he had slain in error or with intent*. Then the court sent and brought him thence etc. (Mishna Makkot, cf. 2:6, Translation by H.L. Lazarus, *Babylonian Talmud, Seder Nesikim*, ed. I. Epstein, London 1935).*]*

te these sources on the basis of each other by noting that until the end of the trial it is uncertain whether the murderer acted with premeditation or not. In this way we may arrive at a comprehensive description of the law. A man who has killed another with premeditation or not, may be put to death without a trial by the blood-avenger as long as the former has not managed to flee to the city of refuge: "Otherwise, when the distance is great, the blood-avenger, pursuing the manslayer in hot anger, may overtake him and kill him; yet he was not guilty of a capital crime, since he had never been the other's enemy." (Deut. 19:6). The killing of the manslayer was an undesirable act. However, if the blood-avenger overtook such a murderer who had not yet managed to get to a city of refuge and he killed him, he did not overstep his legal bounds and was innocent. A murderer who managed to flee to a city of refuge stood at the city gate and told his story to the city elders (Jos. 20:4), i.e., he informed them of the murder and claimed that he had acted unintentionally. Then the elders took him into the city of refuge, i.e., they grant him its asylum without investigating whether the murderer's claims were justified, and they do not hand him over to the blood-avenger who is pursuing him (v. 5).[7b] The latter may turn to the elders of his city and claim that the murderer acted with premeditation, and they send a delegation to take the murderer from the city of refuge (Deut. 19:12). "In such cases the assembly shall decide between the slayer and the blood-avenger" (Nu. 35:24). If there is no proof for premeditation: "The assembly shall protect the manslayer from the blood-avenger, and the assembly shall restore him to the city of refuge to which he fled, and there he shall remain until the death of the high priest ... But if the manslayer ever goes outside the limits of his city of refuge, ... and the

---

[[7b] The Deuteronomic passage Jos. 20:4-5 ⊥ *w^e^yāšab bā^c^ir hahi'* (v. 6) is lacking in Septuagint B and has been added to a priestly law. As it speaks of a refugee who has slain a man in error (not of one who argued that this were the case) it has been interpreted as attributing to the elders of the city of refuge the competence of granting permanent asylum without interrogating the blood-avenger and witnesses. It seems, however, that the declaration of the elders solely served the purpose of precluding to blood-revenge without preceding legal procedure and this kind of protection was conceded by the elders to anyone, who, rightly or wrongly, declared that he had slain in error. It is plausible that in its primary context the passage was followed by a prescription akin to Deut. 19:11-12.]

blood-avenger kills the manslayer, there is no blood-guilt on his account" (vv. 25-27). But if the murder was premeditated: "and they shall hand him over to the blood-avenger to be put to death" (Deut. 19:20). Even in the case where the Assembly had judged the murderer, he is put to death by the blood-avenger.

Three Biblical books - Numbers, Deuteronomy, and Joshua - describe the trial procedure for murder from various viewpoints. But the three of them refer to one and the same complex of laws in which the blood-avenger plays the leading role. On the other hand, we do not find even one law dealing with the execution of a person who killed someone who did not have a blood-avenger or whose blood-avenger did not carry out his task. There is however one story in the Bible in which the king initiates the blood-vengeance. The Bible relates that God brought a famine upon the land during the time of David in the wake of Saul's killing of the Gibeonites. For that reason David considered it necessary to atone for their blood by the blood of Saul's sons (2 Sam. 21:5-15). We should not conclude from this that in David's time the initiative for blood-vengeance had been transferred to the king. The Gibeonites were enslaved to the Israelites, and they therefore did not dare avenge their kinsmen's blood from the Israelites without express permission, even more so when the matter concerned a very high-ranking Israelite family. Note that David did not execute Saul's sons himself but handed them over to the Gibeonites, i.e., the blood-avengers.[7C] It is of course possible that, with the strengthening of the central government during the late monarchy the king took upon himself the blood-vengeance of a victim whose murderer was not put to death by the blood-avenger. This theory, however, lacks proof. In the seventh cent. BCE a family in the Assyrian Empire still demanded blood-vengeance.[8]

In general, we may state that ancient Israelite society left the punishment of the murderer to individual initiative, and there is no reason to think that this society acted any differently in punishing adultery.

[[7C] As generally noted, the legal procedure described is without foundation in the laws of the Torah which do not recognize the punishment of sons for the sins of their fathers. According to the theology, underlying the story, the execution of Saul's sons was urgently required in order to avert divine reprisal from the whole nation. It is instructive that even in such an extreme case of burning divine wrath and national calamity the moment of private bloodvengeance has not been eliminated.*]*

[8] M. San Nicolo, *RLA*, s.v. Blutrache. *[ANET*[3], p. 221.*]*

The difference between the laws of murder and adultery is limited to the fact that the blood-avenger is not allowed to accept ransom[9], while there is no such prohibition limiting the freedom of decision of the adulteress' husband.

It is possible that during the Second Temple Period the punishment for adultery became an absolute punishment which was carried out by the Assembly. We read in the Book of Susannah that two elders testified falsely concerning the alledged adultery of the book's heroine and that the same elders served also as her prosecutors. There is no mention of the fact that her husband demanded her execution. Whatever may be the law reflected in this apocryphal book, it is nevertheless clear that nothing may be learnt from it on the ancient Pentateuchal law.

To sum up: Both in Israel and in Mesopotamia the belief was prevalent that adultery led to divine punishment. This belief had special importance in a case of adultery which went undetected. According to the laws of both lands the execution of the adulterer and adulteress was left to the husband's discretion. The only difference was in the Mesopotamian statute which stated that a husband who chose to let his wife live relinquished the right to demand the putting to death of the adulterer, and consequently the possibility of collecting ransom from him.

The discussion as a whole leads to the conclusion that the comparison of laws requires a large degree of care. Most Biblical laws are succinctly formulated and are intended to instill fear in anyone who plans to transgress them. When we attempt to translate them into practice we must investigate Biblical law and the social structure reflected in it in a comprehensive manner.

---

[9] The prohibition "You may not accept a ransom for the life of a murderer" (Nu. 35:31) addresses the bloodavenger, just as it is clear from the general content of the chapter that only he who may kill the murderer may also waive this right in lieu of payment. The prohibition of taking ransom is probably a lex imperfecta, i.e., the blood-avenger who receives ransom violates an explicit prohibition, but his act is still valid.

Review of W. Schmidt, Königtum Gottes in Ugarit und Israel, Berlin 1961

The problem of the kingdom of God became a subject of scholarly debate because of Mowinckel who in 1922 published his famous theory that the Psalms of the kingdom of God had their origin in the Biblical new year's ritual. According to him this ritual was observed at the time of the enthronement of God who defeated the powers of chaos and created the world.[1]

A second point of departure for the debate was the problem of the antiquity of the idea of the kingdom of God in Israel. The main point of debate in this controversy was Buber's book on the kingdom of God, published in 1932, which puts forth the claim that the nomadic tribes, including nomadic Israel, worshipped their God as a king, whereas the Baals were the gods of the settled land.[2]

A third series of studies began in the thirties in the wake of the decipherment of the Ugaritic literature. The striking relationship with the Bible evoked the question as to what extent the descriptions of the gods of Canaan had influenced the conception of the image of God in the Bible. True, this discussion was not limited to the question of the kingdom of God, but encompassed the problem of the description of God in the Bible in its wider sense. Anyhow, within this general discussion they also dealt with the essence of the kingdom of God, since the Ugaritic texts mention the kingdom of the chief gods of the pantheon.

Schmidt's book deals with the second and third of these topics. His thesis is that the idea of the kingdom of God must be placed later than the conquest of Canaan, and that it is a result of the contact of Israel with the religion of Canaan. According to the evidence of the Ugaritic texts, the Canaanites worshipped their chief gods as kings of the pantheon, and the people of Israel, under their influence, saw in YHWH "a great king over

---

[1] S. Mowinckel, *Psalmenstudien* 2, Kristiana 1922.

[2] See now M. Buber, *Königtum Gottes*[3], Heidelberg 1956.

all the gods" (Ps. 95:3). But Israel in time abandoned this way of thinking and arrived at a complete denial of all the other gods. Thus the kingdom of God lost all of its original content, and this void was filled by a new idea, viz. the idea of the kingdom of God over his people. This theory does not seem plausible. The gods of Ugarit do not take any interest in the fate of Ugarit[2a], and therefore, it cannot be assumed that one of them would be considered the king of Ugarit. This is not the relationship of God to Israel. Even if we assume that the God who took his people out of Egypt was not considered to be a king, this does not detract at all from his being the God of Israel whose whole description is that of his relationship with his people. If the people of Israel afterwards added to their God, who had taken them out of Egypt and had given them the land of Canaan, the title of king, they considered him already from that moment to be the king of Israel, whether they attributed to him in addition the kingdom over the heavenly beings or not.

The author rightly accepts the prevalent view that the image of God in the Bible was especially influenced by the two main gods of the Canaanite pantheon, Il and Baal. As to the title "king", Schmidt points out that it applies in particular to Il, apart from two verses in which the titles "king" and "judge" are attributed to Baal. (*CTA* 3:V:39-41; 4:IV:43-44). Unfortunately, he was unaware of Cassuto's convincing explanation that these titles refer to Il and not to Baal.[3] But even if the title "king" is not

---

[[2a] To be sure, in the meantime two texts have been published, which reveal a special connection between Ugarit and its gods, viz. a) *U* 5, text 2, pp. 551-554, a hymn concluding with the wish that "thine" (probably Il's) glory may dwell upon Ugarit in eternity. See in this volume, *A Ugaritic Hymn in Honour of Il*, pp. 320-332, b) a text published in transcription by A. Herdner, *CRAIBL* 1972, p. 694, which contains an advice to implore Baal if enemies besiege the town (obviously Ugarit). However, even in these documents no god is depicted as king of Ugarit and in the epic the national moment is entirely absent.*]*

[3] Cassuto, *Anath*, pp. 102-103; 150. *[*The passage reads: *tḥmk .mlkn. aliyn bᶜl. ṯpṭn. win dᶜlnh*. Cassuto renders: 'Aliyan Baal O our king, sends thee a message, O our ruler, above whom there is none.' This translation of *tḥmk* 'sends thee' is, however, unsupported. Better Aistleitner (*WUB*, s.v. tḥm): '*Dein Entschluss war, o unser König, dass A.B. über uns Fürst sei.*' But even this translation impairs the parallelism *mlkn/ṯpṭn*. Therefore, we return to Ginsberg's translation (*ANET*[3], p. 133): 'Thy decree is: our king's Puissant Baal etc.' Baal reigns by Il's decree which is proof of Il's wisdom exalted before.*]*

assigned specifically to Baal, we should not doubt his kingship, since it is stated expressly in Ugaritic literature that Baal achieved an eternal kingship. *[CTA* 2:IV:10 cf. ibid. 32.*]*

Most of Schmidt's book deals with the myth of Il and Baal and its reflection in the Bible. In the framework of this review, it is only possible to deal with a few fundamental points.

Baal who is called *rkb* ᶜ*rpt* (*rokeb ba*ᶜᵃ*rābot*) is the god of the fertility of the earth, whose voice thunders and who sends rain upon the face of the earth. He achieved his kingship by his victory over *zbl ym wṯpṭ nhr* 'prince of the sea and ruler of the river', who is aided by the monsters among whom are mentioned *tnn* (Tannin), and *ltn bṯn* ᶜ*qltn*, and *ltn bṯn brḥ (liwyātān nāḥāš bāri*ᵃ*ḥ w*ᵉ*liwyātān nāḥāš* ᶜᵃ*qallāton)*. The author does not stop at just listing the Biblical parallels to this myth, but emphasizes the essential difference, that Baal's war has nothing to do with the creation of the world, whereas at least in some of the Biblical verses, God's war precedes the story of creation (Ps. 74:12-17; 89:10-15) as in the Akkadian epic *Enūma eliš*. But another difference may be emphasized too. There is no mention in the Bible of the prince of the sea and the judge of the river (the prince of the sea is mentioned only in Rabbinic writings), and the text always speaks of the sea and the rivers (in plural!) themselves. These differences are not easily reconciled with the author's view that the people of Israel was influenced by the Ugaritic myth, even if we take into consideration his opinion that in addition to the Ugaritic myth Egyptian and Mesopotamian traditions affected the people of Israel, as well, either directly or through the intermediary of Canaanite culture. The hypothesis seems more probable that the people of Israel did not know Canaanite mythology in its Ugaritic form at all, but rather different forms of this myth which were prevalent in areas closer to Israel from both a geographical and linguistic point of view. Compare in this volume, *The Ugaritic Myth of the Sea* etc., pp. 346-361.

As opposed to the aforementioned myth, the myth of the war of Baal and Mot, which tells of the temporary death of Baal and his resurrection was not accepted by Israel. The theological reason for the rejection of this myth in Israel needs no explanation. Therefore, Schmidt limits himself simply to a discussion of the text of the myth and does not raise at all the question of its reflection in the Bible. Unfortunately, he did not know U. Cassuto's article *Baal and Mot in the texts of Ugarit*[4] which is still the only penetrating study of this story, and in which echoes of this myth in the Bible, are adduced, e.g. the prophecy that in the end of the days God will swallow death forever (Is. 25:8), etc.

Schmidt describes Il as the head of the Pantheon whose static kingship has no beginning and no end, by refuting the theory that Il was deposed from his throne. He is the creator who is described as the one who forms the creatures, the father of gods and men, and his personality as a creator stands out even in the absence of cosmogonic myth. As further attributes of Il mentioned in the Ugaritic texts, Schmidt lists his goodheartedness, his wisdom, and his old age. The parallels to these attributes with the attributes of YHWH are self-evident. Schmidt also emphasizes that Il appears in the assembly of the gods, and that he who approaches him bows down and honours him. To these descriptions he connects the Biblical verses (Is. 6; 1 Reg. 22:19) in which YHWH appears among the gods who were lowered to the rank of angels, and also Ps. 29 in which the sons of the gods bow down before God and honour him. These parallels raise doubts. We do not find in Ugaritic literature that the sons of the gods collectively bow down before Il, and there is no mention of the *Seraphim* or the host of heaven. On the other hand, there is room for a comparison of Il as healer with YHWH. Il asks the gods seven times who will heal the sick Krt, and seven times the gods are silent until Il himself had to create an angel of healing (*CTA* 16: V). Of the many verses which describe God as a healer we may mention only one: "O God, pray heal her!" (Nu. 12:13). This is the only verse in Biblical prose which designates God by the simple epithet *'el* without any other element. To complete the picture a more exact explanation of the concept of creator is required which has several aspects. From what is left of the description of the creation of the angel of healing we learn that Il formed him from clay.[5] The text, therefore, not only recalls Job 33:6 "I, too,

[4] U. Cassuto, *Baal and Mot in the Ugaritic Texts*, *IEJ* 12 (1962), pp. 77-86 [= *BOSt* 2, pp. 168-177].

[5] From the description of the creation only the words *rṯ* ... *yqrṣ* have remained in *CTA* 4:V:66. The obscure word *rṯ* is parallel in *CTA* 17:II:7-8; 22-23 by *ṯiṭ* which has been explained on the basis of Arabic *ṯa'ṭa(t)* as 'wet earth'. In Akkadian texts the material which the god pinches off (*karāṣu*) to create man is called *ṭiṭu*, i.e. clay. See in addition to Gil-

was nipped from clay", but also the story of the creation of man in the Garden of Eden. In the Aqht epic Baal asks Il to bless the righteous Danil, who has no children, with a blessing of fertility, which calls to mind the blessing God bestowed upon Abraham. Furthermore, Il's wisdom cannot be understood comprehensively except in the light of an additional analysis. In the address to Il the words *šbt dqnk ltrsk* (*CTA* 4:V:66) 'may your hoary old age instruct you'[6], are stated together with the explicit mention of his wisdom. Similarly: "In the aged there is wisdom" (Job 12:12). Il's wisdom is the archetype of all wisdom. One of the gods is described as being wise like Il (*CTA* 16:IV:3); cf. in the Bible: "And my lord is wise, like the wisdom of an angel of God" (2 Sam. 14:20). The phrase "angel of God" is just a type of emendation from "God" which comes to remove the comparison of a mortal with God himself. But together with Il's wisdom, we recognize in Il his undeniable weakness, as e.g. in his yielding to the threats of his powerful daughter (*CTA* 3:V:27-37), whereas God YHWH combines the wisdom of the old Il with the bravery of the young Baal.

Up until now we have mentioned the basic outlines of Schmidt's book and have not gone into the large number of details dealt with in it. We should mention only one which the author treats at great length, viz. the problem of Ps. 82. In his opinion this psalm is in the main a Canaanite psalm to which were added in Israel the verses 2-5 and 8. This analysis breaks up connected passages. Furthermore vv. 2-5 call to mind the words of the son of Krt who turns to his father with the request that he relinquish his throne to him, because he has not judged the widow's and orphan's case, nor has he protected the poor and indigent (*CTA* 16:VI:41-54). The Israelite poet raises the same reason to disqualify the sons of the gods from their kingdom. It even is the one who bases his request that God for whom "Jacob, the lot of his inheritance" (Deut. 32:9) "shall inherit all the nations" (Ps. 82:8), i.e. he will inherit the kingdoms of all the sons of the gods. Moreover, even the term "inheritance" of the godhead is known from

---

games I:II:34, also: *BWL*, p. 88, l. 277. From all this it is clear that *rṯ* means approximately 'earth, (wet) clay'. Compare in this volume *Ugaritic Gleanings*, pp. 231-233.

6 *dqn* here means 'old age' and not 'beard' as Schmidt thinks. Cf. also Cassuto's suggestion (above, note 3), p. 43, and the proofs which I have brought to his suggestion in this volume, *Review on Cyrus H. Gordon, Ugaritic Manual*, p. 34.

Ugaritic literature (*CTA* 3:III:27; IV:64, etc.). Echoes of the Canaanite literature are therefore heard even from "the Israelite additions". But in spite of its Canaanite background the psalm is entirely Israelite and describes the assembly of the gods at the very moment when God abolishes their godliness. It thus reflects the same theological approach as the story of the Exodus from Egypt which delays the mentioning of the gods of Egypt until the time that God judges them (Ex. 12:12).

These criticisms do not come to detract from the great value of the research of a young scholar who has successfully summarized the discussions on a research topic in an encompassing and level-headed manner, and has aided even the professional reader by the ample bibliography in his instructive book.

The Ugaritic Fertility Myth - the Result of a Mistranslation.*

The late Prof. U. Cassuto's paper 'Baal and Mot in the Ugaritic Texts' is published in English in the present issue of the *IEJ* [12 (1962), pp. 77-86 = *BOSt* 2, pp. 168-177]. I take this opportunity to corroborate Prof. Cassuto's view by an additional observation.

The current opinion that Mot should be regarded as a symbol of grain is based on the assumption that after his death Mot was sown in the fields.[1] The crucial point in this interpretation is the translation of the Ugaritic verb dr^{c}, generally rendered by sow. It should be observed, however, that this rendering is not cogent, as the corresponding Hebrew verb zr^{c} is twice found in the meaning to scatter (Ju. 9:45; Zech. 10:9). Moreover, it has been pointed out by Driver that the Syriac verb zr^{c} is likewise attested in the sense to disperse.[2] We may add that this double meaning of the root zr^{c} is paralleled by the Greek verb σπειρω, denoting both sowing and scattering. The same applies to the Ugaritic verb dr^{c}. Mot was not sown, but his remains were scattered, and this scattering represents a symbol of utter destruction, comparable to the dispersing of the pounded remnants of the golden calf in Ex. 32:20. The similarity between the two texts may be recognized even in the choice of the verbs used. Like Mot the golden calf was ground (*ṯḥn* in both Ugaritic and Hebrew) and afterwards both were dispersed (dr^{c} in Ugari-

---

* [De Moor, *Seasonal Pattern*, p. 27 remarks that "it was somewhat naive to suggest that the seasonal interpretation would have arisen from a single mistranslation". In a sense de Moor's criticism is justified. Indeed, the seasonal interpretation rather arose from the tendency of interpreting the Ugaritic myth by hook or crook in the light of Frazer's ideas on myth in general. Nevertheless, it remains true that the defenders of this heuristic principle adduce the sowing of Mot as their cardinal proof. Compare also in this volume, *The Ugaritic Fertility Myth - a Reply*, pp. 162-165; *The Making and Destruction of the Golden Calf*, pp. 236-245; *The Killing of Mot in Ugaritic Myth*, pp. 426-432; *The Making and Destruction of the Golden Calf - a Rejoinder*, pp. 503-516.

[1] Against this conclusion, see Th. H. Gaster, *Thespis*², p. 131, who argues that "rigid logic must not be expected in the domain of myth".

[2] G.R. Driver, *Biblica* 19 (1938), p. 179.

tic, *zrh* in Hebrew). Therefore, the Ugaritic dr^c should be interpreted as synonymous with Ugaritic *dry*, Hebrew *zrh* - to winnow, to disperse.

The double meaning of Ugaritic dr^c and Hebrew zr^c solves, moreover, a much discussed phonetic problem. It has been generally noted that in the light of Arabic evidence we should expect zr^c in Ugaritic instead of dr^c.[3] The explanation that the Proto-Semitic root zr^c has been blended with the Proto-Semitic root *dry* - to winnow, to disperse - did not meet with general approval. But this solution gains additional force in the light of the fact that these two roots are synonymous in part, the Ugaritic dr^c in the epic of Mot corresponding exactly to the Hebrew *zrh* in the story of the golden calf. The free interchangeability of zr^c and dr^c in Jewish Aramaic[4] should be explained in the same way.

---

[3] Gordon, *UM*, p. 23; see also A. Dietrich's review thereof in *Orientalia* 26 (1957), p. 64.

[4] M. Jastrow, *Dictionary of the Talmud*, New York, *s.v.*

The Ugaritic Fertility Myth - a Reply*

In his paper *Baal and Mot in the Ugaritic texts* the late Prof. Cassuto[1] challenged the interpretation of the myth of the wars between these two gods as reflecting the cycle of the seasons. In an additional note to that paper[2], I tried to corroborate Prof. Cassuto's view. The thesis challenged has now been forcefully defended by Prof. Kapelrud[3] in his note on *Baal and Mot in the Ugaritic Texts*.

Prof. Kapelrud's deduction rests upon the statement "what happened to Mot is identical with what happened to grain". This statement apparently implies that as grain is a symbol of fertility, Mot should be considered as such a symbol, too. True, grain may be regarded thus symbolically. The grain sown in the field dies, but from the dying grain a new plant sprouts which in its turn bears again. However, a description of grain milled and eaten can hardly be interpreted as symbolizing death and revival and should not be connected with the idea of fertility. I fail to see why this observation of Prof. Cassuto's "hits beyond the mark". Moreover, the text describing the death of Mot[4] does not contain the word grain at all, and what happened to Mot is only partially comparable to what happens to grain. Anat ripped Mot open with a sword. Nobody is supposed to deal with grain in this way. After this we read: *bḫṯr tdry nn*. Prof. Kapelrud follows Driver's translation: 'winnowed him in a sieve'. This rendering is not beyond doubt and has been strongly opposed by M. Dahood.[5] But even if we accept this interpretation, it does not bear out Prof. Kapelrud's conclusions; for in Jer. 15:7,

---

* Compare also in this volume: *The Making and Destruction of the Golden Calf*, pp. 236-245; *The Killing of Mot in Ugaritic Myth*, pp. 426-432; *The Making and Destruction of the Golden Calf - a Rejoinder*, pp. 503-516.

1 *IEJ* 12 (1962), pp. 77-86.

2 *Ibid.*, pp. 87-88; See in this volume "*The Ugaritic Fertility Myth - the Result of a Mistranslation*", pp. 160-161.

3 *IEJ* 13 (1963), pp. 127-129.

4 *CTA* 6:II:30-37.

5 M. Dahood, *Biblica* 38 (1957), pp. 62-64.

we read: "And I have winnowed them with a fan in the gates of the land". The winnowing is here a symbol of destruction, without any reference to fertility, let alone a fertility myth. The following words: *bišt tšrpnn* 'burnt him in the fire' are quite incompatible with the destiny of grain. Prof. Kapelrud's interpretation 'roasted on the fire' is not supported by the meaning of the root *šrp*, which is 'to burn, destroy by fire'. The golden calf was burnt (Ex. 32:20), not roasted! It may be conceded that the following description of the grinding of Mot reminds us of the grinding of grain. But, here again, the same happened to the golden calf, as pointed out in my paper on the Fertility Myth. The next words: *bšd tdr*^{c}*nn* seem at first sight to admit the interpretation: 'sowed him in the field'. In my former paper on this subject, however, I tried to show that we should prefer the translation: 'scattered him in the field'. My proposal is corroborated by the continuation of the text: *širh ltikl* ^{c}*ṣrm* 'verily the birds ate his flesh', - as correctly translated by Cassuto. It is quite evident that flesh may be scattered in a field, but not sown. To be sure, Prof. Kapelrud follows Driver's rendering of *širh* 'the pieces of him'. But Ugaritic *šir* should not be separated from Hebrew *š*^{e}*'er* - flesh, as conclusively proven by RS 22. 225[6], which reads: *tspi širh lbl hrb tšt dmh lbl ks* 'she ate (perhaps better[7]: One had eaten) his flesh[8] without knife, she

---

[6] Ch. Virolleaud, *Un nouvel èpisode du mythe ugaritique de Baal, CRAIBL* (1960), pp. 180-186.

[7] According to Virolleaud's interpretation, the new fragment reports that Anat greedily ate the flesh and drank the blood of Baal before wandering to and fro without aim. But, as pointed out by Virolleaud himself, this interpretation is in contradiction to everything known from the other Ugaritic texts. I should prefer to explain the verbal forms *tspi* and *tšt* as 3 pl. masc. instead of 3 sing. fem. and to render 'they had eaten and drunk', viz. some unspecified person had done so. Apparently, Anat finds her brother killed by Mot and wanders about in search of the murderer in order to avenge Baal.
[Our proposal can not be maintained since the 3 pl. m. of *sp'* should read *tspu*, not *tspi*. E. Lipinski, Syria 42 (1965), pp. 45-73 takes Anat's eating and drinking of Baal's flesh and blood as a metaphor of copulation. Some support for his suggestion may be found in Pr. 30:20 where the eating of an adulteress has a clear sexual connotation (compare also Babli Ketubot 65b). But even from this passage it is still a far cry to the audacious Ugaritic metaphor, posited by Lipinski.]

[8] It is true that Hebrew *š*^{e}*'er* is generally connected with Arabic *ṯa'run* - 'blood revenge'. But this farfetched etymology should be abandoned in the light of Ugaritic evidence, and compare in this volume, *š*^{e}*'er*, pp. 190-191.

drank (perhaps better: one had drunk) his blood without cup'. Mot's flesh, scattered in the field and eaten by birds, is far from being a symbol of fertility. To sum up, Anat's actions convey throughout the idea of utter destruction, and this idea alone.

Prof. Cassuto pointed out the telling fact that in a parallel description of Mot's death we read of his being sown in the sea (*dr^c bym*). In Prof. Kapelrud's opinion, this rendering is outdated by Driver's translation: 'on the day' - not 'in the sea'. But Prof. Cassuto's interpretation is clearly to be preferred. The symbol of scattering in the field in the first text is varied in the second text by the equivalent symbol of scattering in the sea, paralleled by the story of the golden calf. Driver's interpretation is not in accordance with the clear correspondence between the two texts, describing the same event.

Prof. Kapelrud opposes Cassuto's argument that Baal and Mot cannot symbolize two successive seasons of the year, because both live at the same time after their resurrection. In his opinion, a rationalistic argument of this kind is inadmissible in the interpretation of a cultic myth. But objections of this general character hardly carry conviction. We are not entitled to neglect or dismiss clearly stated facts of the myth as irrelevant to its interpretation, without giving more specific reasons.

Prof. Kapelrud imputes to the alleged Ugaritic fertility myth a similar lack of clear thinking, when he argues that even "seasonal myths" do not trouble themselves with counting half years and may count long periods of full years instead. As a "classical example" of seasonal myth, Prof. Kapelrud adduces the Babylonian Creation Myth "which was performed, or in any case recited, on the fourth day of the *Akitu* (New Year) festival." From this statement he proceeds to the contention that "Tiamat was killed and the world created out of chaos each year anew." But this supposition is even more farfetched than the thesis of the Ugaritic fertility myth. The latter may at least point to the empiric fact of the recurrent change of seasons every year. No such empirical fact supports the alleged Mesopotamian conception that the world is created anew every year. The recital of the Babylonian Creation Myth at the New Year festival commemorated an event of the distant past, not its repetition anew.

Prof. Kapelrud stresses the well-known fact that twenty years have passed since Prof. Cassuto's article was originally composed and that much has been written about the Ras Shamra texts since then. But Prof. Cassuto's articles should be judged on their merits, not on their date. Their lasting value is to be found in the author's bold resolve to interpret the Ugaritic epic texts by careful philological exegesis of their wording, rejecting all attempts to read into these texts preconceived ideas about patterns of oriental myth and ritual. This approach is as sound today as it was twenty years ago.

The Formula *me*^{c}*attā w*^{ec}*ad* ^{c}*olām*

The formula *me*^{c}*attā w*^{ec}*ad* ^{c}*olām* 'from now and for ever' is common in Biblical poetry[1] and non-existent in prose. Despite its frequency in poetry, it does not conform to the rules of parallelism and no expression parallels it. Still more puzzling is the lack of conformity between the meaning of the whole formula and that of the sum of its components. Logical analysis demands that the formula refer to a permanent change which has now occurred in the *status quo*: until now things were one way, while from now on they will be different. A cursory glance will show that such is not the case. The passage "Blessed be the name of the Lord, from now and forever" (Ps. 113:2) does not imply that it was uttered by one who previously worshipped other gods and only now has turned to worship the God of Israel. Clearly, one should not understand "from now" literally but only as a rhetorical strengthening of "and for ever". From this it becomes clear how our phrase even may serve to express that which will occur in the future and has not yet taken place such as in Micah's prophecy about the end of days: "And the Lord shall reign over them in Mount Zion from now and for ever". Analysis of the phrase then shows that it is petrified and that its original meaning was not fully felt. Therefore we are confronted with the question of its prehistory.

We should first point out the strong similarity to the language of the Gemara *mywm' dnn wl*^{c}*lm*.[2] This legal formula is also known from the Elephantine documents, many of which contain *lmn ywm' znh w*^{c}*d* ^{c}*lm*[3] which on occasion interchanges with *mnywm' znh* ^{c}*d* ^{c}*lm*[4] or *mn ywm' znh w*^{c}*d* ^{c}*lmn*.[5] [And afterwards appears in Greek documents from Egypt in the form of ἀπὸ τῆς ἐνεσ-

[1] Is. 9:6; 59:21; Mi. 4:7; Ps. 113:2; 115:18; 121:8; 131:3.

[2] Cf. e.g. Babylonian Talmud, *Gittin* 85b.

[3] *AP*, passim.

[4] *BMAP*, text 7:4.

[5] *ibid.*, text 3:11.

τώσης ἡμέρας ἐπὶ τὸν σήμερον χρόνον.[5a]] In addition, the ancestors of this formula have recently become known to us from the Alalakh documents and especially from Ugaritic writings. Legal documents from these cities, written in Akkadian, frequently open *ištu ūmi annim*[6] 'from this day'; and further on in the document are often found expressions of 'for all times' such as *ana dāria*[7], *ana dāri dūri*[8], *adi dāri*[9], *ana dārīti*[10], *adi dārīti*[11], *ana dāriš*[12], *adi dāriš*[13]. In Ugaritic writings, documents may begin *lym hnd*[14] 'from this day' - and in the continuation, at times is written *ᶜd ᶜlm*[15] 'for ever'.

We will now deal with the source of the two components. The second raises no difficulty and it is clear that the transaction described in the document is to be permanent. However, the opening "from now" astonishes the jurist who is looking for a date and finds in its place a cryptic statement - "from this day" - which adds absolutely nothing to clarify the time of the transaction. It seems that this surprising statement must be understood as a relic from the time previous to written contracts. In those days, one party would solemnly declare in the presence of witnesses that from this day forth certain privileges would be granted to the second party; and it is clear that in such a ceremony there is no reason to mention a date. When events were later on recorded in writing, this traditional declaration was registered on a tablet *verbatim* and the act of writing it

---

[[5a] L. Blau, *Festschrift zu H. Cohens siebzigstem Geburtstage*, Berlin 1912, p. 218.]

[6] *Alalakh*, texts 15:2; 73:1; 87:2; 93:1; 102:1; 104:1. [Add 7:33 where the formula appears in a dated verdict.]

[7] *Alalakh*, text 15:8, 12, 24; *PRU* 3, passim.

[8] *PRU* 3, RS 16.248:14, p. 49; RS 15.Z:8,13, pp. 58f.

[9] *ibid.*, RS 15.137:7, p. 134.

[10] *ibid.*, RS 15.119:11', 17', pp. 87f.; RS 15.88:8, p. 88; *ana dārītimma*: RS 16.166:9, p. 48: *ana dāritti*: RS 16.276:19, p. 70; *adārīti* RS 15.37: 11, p. 35.

[11] *ibid.*, RS 16.353:10, 12, p. 113; RS 15.155:18, 25, p. 118.

[12] *ibid.*, RS 16.153:8, p. 147.

[13] *ibid.*, RS 16.162:10, p. 126.

[14] *PRU* 2, texts 6:1; 8:1; 9:1.

[15] *ibid.*, texts 5:5; 8:14, 19, 20; 9:11-12.

down caused no ripple in the form of the announcement.[16]

This archaic form endured, but in the course of time certain changes occurred. The two components "from now" and "for ever" which were in ancient documents separated, joined together into a single continuous phrase reminiscent of the poetic formula "from now and for ever".

The imprint of these judicial formulae is already noticeable in Ugaritic poetry. In the Aqhat epic it is written that Danil found in the innards of an eagle the remains of his son Aqhat and cried in despair *^{c}nt brḥ p^{c}lmh ^{c}nt pdr dr* (*CTA* 19:III: 154, 161-162) 'now he has disappeared for ever, now and for all times'. The formula here retains its original meaning. Only now has Aqhat died and the *status quo* changed. In addition, we find here, as we have already seen in legal documents, that the formula is not continuous, but rather the verb *brḥ* divides up the components. Even more significant is that in the same context we find a curse which closely approximates the Biblical language: *^{c}wrt yštk b^{c}l lht wl^{c}lmh l^{c}nt pdr dr*. (*CTA* 19:IV:167-168). 'Baal shall make you blind from now and for ever, from now and for all times'. It goes without saying that the change spoken about occurs now, but it is fitting to emphasize that the language used here actually is *lht* - 'from now' and that the two components of the phrase are joined.

Comparison of the poetic phrase *me^{c}attā w^{ec}ad ^{c}olām* 'from now and for ever' with the Ugaritic formulae reveals that the first component is parallel to the Ugaritic poetry while the second part parallels the Ugaritic legal formula. This change of formulae serves as certain testimony that there were prevalent in Canaan several expressions parallel to the Ugaritic formula and that the Biblical passage "from now and for ever" was in actuality

---

[16] A similar phenomenon is to be found in the formulation of the ancient letter which is nothing but a verbatim writing down of the command of the letter's sender to his messenger to inform the receiver of a certain matter. The form of the letter which diverges from the simple notice delivered by messenger developed later, cf. S.E. Loewenstamm *EB*, s.v. *Miktab*. The same applies to the form of legal documents which as well is a product of a long evolution, as the Elephantine papyri prove. This is also true of the second century Aramaic documents from Palestine, cf. Bénoit-Milik-De Vaux, *Les Grottes de Murabba^{c}at*. Oxford 1961, pp. 109-112; 137-138. Only in the time of the late Tannaites was the logical claim heard that "from this day forth" should be eliminated because "the date of the deed proves its import." (*Babylonian Talmud*, Gittin 85 b; Baba Batra 136 a).

just one of them. The source is legal terminology whose exacting nature demands emphasizing that the change occurs starting now. However, the normally rigid legal language was adapted to poetry which is not accustomed to such precision. It is understandable that the extent of adaptation should vary from place to place. In Ugaritic literature the adaptation was extensive. The Ugaritic poet was not satisfied only with changing the words in such a way as to remove from the formula its peculiar legal nature, but he also added parallelism in order to incorporate the phrase fully into poetic language. Such was not the case in Biblical poetry. The phrase remains close to its original legal formulation and no parallel stichos has been added. All this more clearly emphasizes the legal origin despite the fact that the words "from now" have lost their meaning.

This is not all. Apart from the ancient formula which we have discussed, there is found in the Bible three times the formula *me^c^olām w^ec^ad ^c^olām* 'from ever and for ever'. In an oral communication J. Heinemann found in this metamorphosis a hint that already in the Biblical period the logical imprecision in "from now ..." was noticed. This suggestion demands further investigation. It is written "Before the mountains were brought forth, and Thou hast formed the earth and the world, from ever to ever, Thou art God." (Ps. 90:2). "From ever" here refers back to the beginning of the verse, "Before the mountains were brought forth" i.e. to times of old and it would be inappropriate to continue "from now". Therefore this verse does not prove the existence of an *overall* trend towards revision of the petrified formula. In addition we find: "But the mercy of the Lord is from ever to ever upon that fear Him, and His righteousness unto children's children." (Ps. 103:17). It cannot be claimed here that the verse itself demands changing the primitive formula. However, the extreme length of the first stichos arouses justifiable suspicion that the verse may have originally read "But the mercy of the Lord is *^c^ad ^c^olām*" 'everlasting'. Support can be found for an overall benediction formula in the prayer (from the Second Temple) attributed to David which begins "Blessed be Thou, O Lord, the God of Israel our father from ever and for ever." (2 Chr. 29:10). We must especially agree with J. Heinemann that a benediction formula is recognizable in the phrase *mehā^c^olām w^ec^ad hā^c^olām* or in the Aramaic influenced min *hā^c^olām w^ec^ad hā^c^olām*, where *^c^olām* is determined by the article.[17] To this group belongs the concluding

[[17] This determination seems to be influenced by the late use of *^c^olām* in the doxology of the first section of Psalms "Blessed be the Lord the God of Israel, from ever and to ever (*mehā^colām w^{ec}ad hā^colām*) Amen, and Amen" (Ps. 41:14) and that of the fourth section "Blessed be the Lord, the God of Israel, from ever and to ever (*min hā^colām w^{ec}ad hā^colām*) and let all the people say, Amen Hallelujah" (Ps. 106:48). It is likely that these doxologies originated in the Second Temple edition of the Psalter. The phrase recurs again in another text which is certainly from that same period: "Then the Levites ... said: Stand up and bless the Lord your God *min hā^colām w^{ec}ad hā^colām*" (Neh. 9:5).

---

sense of world. Cf. TY to Ps. 41:14 which reads: *min ^cāl^emā' hāden w^{ec}ad ^cāl^emā' d^e'āte* 'from this world to the world to come'.*]*

The Laws of Adultery and Murder in the Bible*

In his stimulating paper on *The Concept of Law in Israel and among her Neighbors*[1] M. Weinfeld puts forth the claim "that the prosecution of murderers and adulterers were a matter for the Assembly (*ᶜedā*), a term which in Israel acquired a sacral meaning and not for the adulteress' husband or for the blood-avenger alone". We may conclude from this that the prosecution of murder and adultery were a matter for both the Assembly and the injured party. But if that is the case we may pose the question: How were the legal functions divided between them? Weinfeld does not deal with this point at all.

Especially he does not dwell upon the laws of murder and adultery in the Pentateuch in order to prove his contention that the Assembly (or at least the Assembly too) acted as prosecutor in such trials. He apparently feels that there is no need for such proof, since it is sufficient to point to the religious-sacral character of Pentateuchal justice. But general considerations of this kind are not decisive. Should we assume that in a trial for theft the Assembly appeared as prosecutor and not the owner of the stolen object? How can we explain the laws of the deposit if not as a trial which takes place between the two parties?

A study of the laws of murder clearly shows that the blood-avenger alone represents the prosecution. From this we may suppose with virtual certainty that the prohibition of taking ransom (Nu. 35:32) refers to the blood-avenger and not to the Assembly. This is not at all surprising since it is well known that in all laws which permit the taking of ransom the receiver is the blood-avenger. The laws of adultery do not mention the problem of who takes the adulteress to court, but on the analogy of the laws of murder it appears that the damaged party, i.e. the adulteress' husband, acted here also.

* A reply to M. Weinfeld. I should like to thank Prof. M. Weinfeld for showing me his article before publication.

[1] *BM* 17 (1964), pp. 58-63.

Weinfeld's main proof is from Ez. 16:38-41; 23:45-47. We must admit that these passages clearly show that the Assembly took part in the trials of murderers and adulterers. But the text refers to the execution of the criminal and not to his being brought to trial! See also my comments on these passages in *EB* s.v. *mitot bet din*.

Finally, a few words on Proverbs, ch. 6. Weinfeld here agrees with me that the Book of Proverbs considers the adulteress' husband to be the sole prosecutor, but he adds: "The viewpoint contained in Proverbs, ch. 6, is not one of law. It belongs to the realm of didactic-secular teaching only. Nothing may be learnt from it on the actual legal practice in Israel". This claim is strange, for it is impossible to imagine didactic-secular teaching which is divorced from reality. Anyone who tries to base his teaching on a blatant lie is doomed to failure. We should not suppose that the teachers of wisdom in Israel ever made such pronouncements.

The Trembling of Nature during the Theophany

Among the types of theophany in the Bible an outstanding place is occupied by hymnic glorification of God's appearance which shakes nature. This genre, its roots and evolution has not yet been comprehensively and systematically clarified. This is not to say that scholars have overlooked it completely. Already in the last century Gunkel dealt with this question in connection with his analysis of another hymnic motif in Biblical poetry, viz. the motif of God's war with the sea.[1] But the very fact that his study of the problem of the theophany came in the wake of his clarification of the motif of God's war with the sea impaired his results. His starting-point brought him to differentiate fundamentally between three types of the shaking theophany:

1) The type alluding to the war with the sea;
2) The type which does not allude to this war, but refers at least to the sea itself;
3) The type which does not mention the sea at all.

Obviously Gunkel was able to explain the first type according to his view without patent difficulty. However, in his opinion the two remaining types were strange and required special explanations. Therefore he defined the second type (Ps. 93:3,4; 96:11; 98:7-8 etc.) as "*Nachklänge des Mythus*" and even specified that "*es handelt sich nur um einzelne Züge, die ursprünglich einmal mit dem Mythus in Verbindung gestanden haben, die aber diesen Zusammenhang längst verloren haben und gegenwärtig nur noch als Motive der poetischen Tradition existieren.*"[2] Gunkel thus tried to integrate into the history of the myth of the war with the sea also those verses which mention the thunder of the sea during the theophany, but not God's war against the unruly waters. It is understandable that he did not see any possibility of inserting into this framework the third type, namely, the description of the

---

[1] H. Gunkel, *Schöpfung und Chaos in Urzeit und Endzeit*, Halle 1894, especially pp. 29-114.

[2] id., *ibid.*, pp. 106-107.

trembling which takes hold of the heavens, the earth, and the hills, but not the sea. A priori the content of these verses shows that they have nothing at all to do with the war of the God of heaven against the sea, and therefore Gunkel was forced to look for another source. He states: "*Schilderungen des im Gewitter erscheinenden Jahve sind im AT nicht selten. Sie sind offenbar ursprünglich Ausdruck uralten Glaubens, der in der furchtbaren Hoheit des Gewitters seinem Gott sich nahe fühlte. Der eigentliche Sitz dieser Gewittertheophanieen werden alte Lieder gewesen sein, die von der Moseerscheinung auf dem Sinai handelten. Nachklänge solcher Lieder haben wir Dt. 32_2 f; in Prosa Ex. 19_{18}. Das Motiv wird wiederholt Jud. 5_4; 1 Reg. 19_{11} ff., dann von den Propheten Jes. 29_6, 30_{17} f.; Micha 1_3 f.; Joel 2_2 f., schliesslich Psalmisten 50_1 ff., 97 usw. Charakteristisch für diese Schilderungen ist, dass dabei der Zusammenhang mit dem Sinai mehr oder weniger deutlich festgehalten wird, sodann dass zwar von*

Sausen und Brausen und mächtigem Schall
Wind und Wetter und Flammenlohe Jes. 29_6,

vom Wanken der Erde, vom Reissen der Felsen, vom Zerfliessen der Berge geredet wird, aber nirgends von den Wirkungen des Gewitters auf das Meer. Dies liegt ja auch in der Natur der Sache: in der Sinaiwüste ist ebenso wenig wie in dem Teil Palästinas, den Israel bewohnte das Meer in nächster Nähe."[3] Gunkel's viewpoint is still widely held in Biblical study. In 1950, Weiser[4] noted that no one disputes the dependence of the descriptions of the Biblical theophany on the tradition of the revelation at Mount Sinai. True, Weiser's statement is not exact since already in 1946, Gaster[5] in his study of Psalm 29 claimed that the description of nature's trembling before God continues a Canaanite tradition which described in this manner the appearance of Baal-Hadad, the god of thunder and hail. We will return to his article later on. Gaster's important statements were only incidental to his article and did not change the general approach of research.

As for the subject itself, we should immediately point out that Gunkel had good reason to content himself with the modest claim that the echo of ancient poems is heard through the Biblical poems which exalt God's revela-

---

[3] Gunkel, *op. cit.* (note 1), pp. 104-105.

[4] A. Weiser, *Festschrift Bertholet*, Tübingen 1950, p. 515.

[5] Th. Gaster, *JQR NS* 37 (1946/7), pp. 60-61.

tion on Mount Sinai. In the entire Bible there is not one poem which glorifies the revelation in which God gave His people the law. Even poetical passages which specifically mention the name Sinai are no exception. Deut. 33:2 states "The Lord came from Sinai", but not that He revealed Himself to His people on this mountain. Moreover, there is no mention here of the earth-shaking features which accompany the theophany. True, these phenomena *are* mentioned in a slight connection with Mount Sinai in the Song of Deborah: "Lord, when Thou didst go forth from Seir, when Thou didst march from the region of Edom, the earth trembled, and the heavens dropped, yea, the clouds dropped water. The mountains quaked (*nāz*^{e}*lu*)[6] before the Lord, this is (?) Sinai before the Lord, the God of Israel" (Ju. 5:4-5). The words *zä sinai* rendered here 'this is Sinai' are difficult[7], but whatever they mean, it is in any case clear that the Bible speaks of a God who goes out to war to save His people, and not of the giving of the law. The very assumption that poems on God's revelation on Mount Sinai circulated during Biblical times is no more than a hypothesis for which no proof may be adduced at all.

We must therefore be content with a comparison of prosaic description of nature's trembling during the revelation on Mount Sinai with the poetical passages: "And Mount Sinai was wrapped in smoke, because the Lord descended upon it in fire; and the smoke of it went up like the smoke of a kiln, and the whole mountain trembled (*wayyäḥ*^{ä}*rad*) greatly" (Ex. 19:18). This is preceded by a description of the trembling of the people: "so that all the people who were in the camp trembled" (*wayyäḥ*^{ä}*rad*) (v. 16).

We should not ignore the fact that the verb *ḥrd* 'to tremble' does not recur in descriptions of the theophany in Biblical poetry. In such texts the verb *r*^{c}*š* 'to quake, shake' is common. In addition to the Song of Deborah quoted above we may mention: "and the foundations of the earth quake (*wayyir*^{ca}*šu*)" (Is. 24:18); "I will make quake (*wa'*^{a}*ni mar*^{c}*iš*) the heavens

---

[6] As it is well-known many scholars vocalize here *nāzollu* on the basis of ἐσαλεύθησαν in the Septuagint and Is. 63:19; 64:2. Cf. D. Yellin, *Tarbiz* 5 (1934), pp. 4-6, who assumes an intentional ambiguity between *nāzollu* and *nāz*^{e}*lu*.

[7] As is well-known some scholars delete the words "this Sinai" as being a gloss while others explain it as meaning "of Sinai" on the basis of Arabic *ḏu*. Cf., for example J.H. Allegro, *VT* 5 (1955), pp. 309-312, especially p. 311.

and the earth and the sea and the dry land" (Hag. 2:6). Similarly, in parallel with *mwg* 'to melt': "The mountains quake (*rā^cašu*) before Him, the hills melt (*hitmogāgu*)", (Na. 1:5), and in parallel with *g^cš* 'to reel' and *rgz* 'to be shaken': "Then the earth reeled (*wayyitgā^caš*) and quaked (*wattir^caš*); the foundations of the heavens were shaken (*yirgāzu*)" (2 Sam. 22:8). The verb *rgz* is used in parallel with *plṣ* 'to shudder': "Who shakes (*hammargiz*) the earth out of its place, and its pillars shudder (*yitpallāṣun*)" (Job 9:6); in parallel with *nwṭ* 'to quake' "The Lord reigns; the peoples are shaken (*yirg^ezu*) He sits enthroned upon the cherubim; the earth quakes (*tānuṭ*)" (Ps. 99:1); in parallel with *ḥyl* "to writhe": "When the waters saw Thee, O God, when the waters saw Thee, they writhed (*yāḥilu*), yea, the deep trembled (*yirg^ezu*) (Ps. 77:17). For the use of the verb *ḥyl* cf. also: "The mountains saw Thee and writhed (*yāḥilu*)" (Hab. 3:10); The voice of the Lord makes writhe (*yāḥil*) the wilderness, the Lord makes writhe (*yāḥil*) the wilderness of Kadesh" (Ps. 29:8); and in parallel with *mss* 'to melt': "His lightnings lighten the world; the earth sees and writhes (*wattāḥel*). The mountains melt (*nāmassu*) like wax before the Lord, before the Lord of all the earth" (Ps. 97:4-5). To the long list of verbs which express the shaking of nature before God we should add *rqd* 'to skip': "The mountains skipped (*rāq^edu*) like rams, the hills like lambs" (Ps. 114:4); "He makes Lebanon skip (*wayyarqidem*)[8], like a calf, and Sirion like a young wild ox" (Ps. 29:6); also *r^cd* 'to tremble': "Who looks on the earth and it trembles (*wattir^cad*), who touches the mountains and they smoke" (Ps. 104:32); *zll* 'to quake': "the mountains might quake (*nāzollu*)" (Is. 63:19; 64:2); *rpp* 'to tremble': "The pillars of heaven tremble (*y^eropāpu*), and are astounded at his rebuke" (Job 26:11); *r^{cc}* 'to break', *prr* 'to rent', *mwṭ* 'to shake', *nw^c* 'to stagger', and *nwd* 'to sway': "The earth is utterly broken (*ro^cā hitro^ca^cā*), the earth is rent asunder (*por hitpor^erā*), the earth is violently shaken (*moṭ hitmoṭ^etā*), the earth staggers (*no^{ac} tānu^{ac}*) like a drunken man, it sways (*w^ehitnod^edā*) like a hut" (Is. 24:19-20).

The large list of verbs which are employed in Biblical Hebrew to impress on the reader the trembling of nature during a theophany does not include the

---

[8] The accepted opinion that the verse division is to be moved from the word "calf" to "Lebanon" is correct. The *m* of *wayyarqidem* is not a pronoun but an enclitic *m* as in Ugaritic. Cf. Ginsberg, *KU*, pp. 129-131 and recently: H.B. Hummel, *JBL* 76 (1957), pp. 85-107, and especially p. 93.

verb *ḥrd* found in the story of the revelation on Mount Sinai. Not only is there not even one poem in the Bible on the subject of God's revelation on Mount Sinai, but the poetical descriptions of the earth-shaking theophany differ in their terminology from the prose description of the revelation on Mount Sinai in the Pentateuch. We may point out one additional and important difference which strengthens the argument that the poetical tradition stands by itself.[9] In poetry, we do not find the trembling of nature limited to one place. The sources quoted above - except for Ps. 29 which in addition to Lebanon, Sirion and the wilderness of Kadesh mentions the many waters - do not give topographical names at all. All the other sources define the trembling natural elements in an absolutely general manner. The Bible speaks of heaven and earth, mountains and hills, the sea, etc., but not of one specific place defined by name. In this manner also we recognize the fundamental difference between the theophanies under discussion and the story of the revelation on Mount Sinai.

We must therefore determine the character of the type of theophany which causes nature to tremble by internal analysis without taking into account the tradition on the revelation on Mount Sinai. An unprejudiced study of the Biblical passages immediately shows that they all speak of the magnification of the glory of God at whose terrifying appearance the whole world - and not only the sea alone, His mythological enemy - either trembles or is rent asunder. At the root of the shaking theophany lies the concept of God's image as a warrior. This background stands out especially in those passages which juxtapose praise of God's victory over the sea with the description of the quaking or shattering of the other natural elements. This combination is found in the following cosmogonic verse: "He has described a circle upon the face of the waters at the boundary between light and darkness. The pil-

---

[9] Among all the verses quoted above there is only one which brings to mind the revelation on Mount Sinai, namely Ps. 104:32: "Who looks on the earth and it trembles, who touches the mountains and they smoke." But even here we cannot assume for certain that the verse was influenced by the tradition of the revelation on Mount Sinai. There is room for the alternative explanation that the picture in the verse reflects a general tradition of one of God's powerful acts, namely that at His touch the mountains smoke, and this cosmologic tradition influenced the description of the revelation on Mount Sinai. This alternative explanation is supported not only by the general expression "mountains" without any reference to Mount Sinai, but also by the general character of the Psalm which is a praise of God's cosmic powers.

lars of heaven tremble and are astounded at his rebuke. By his power he stilled (*rāga*ᶜ[10]) the sea; and by his understanding he smote Rahab" (Job 26:10-12). Similar motives come together also in the Book of Nahum: "He rebukes the sea and makes it dry" (Na. 1:4). This is followed by the verses: "The mountains quake (*rāᶜašu*) before him, the hills melt" (*hitmogāgu*) (v. 5); "His wrath is poured out like fire, and the rocks are broken asunder by him" (v. 6). The very juxtaposition of these motives indicates their affinity. This internal affinity is especially brought out in the Prayer of Habakkuk which praises the God who goes out to save His people (Hab. 3:13). At the sight of the divine hero the whole world is seized by trembling. God "stood *wayᵉmodäd*[11] the earth; he looked *wayyatter*[12] the na-

---

[10] U. Cassuto, *Knesset* 8 (1943-44), p. 134 *[= BOSt* 2, p. 94*]*, explained *rāga*ᶜ as meaning pacification, i.e., stilling of the onrush of the sea. But if this is so it is difficult to fit the verse: *roga*ᶜ *hayyām wayyähᵃmu gallāw* (Jer. 31:35). N.H. Tur-Sinai, *The Book of Job*, Tel Aviv 1954, p. 231 (in Heb.), explained *rg*ᶜ by Arabic *rg*ᶜ II meaning 'to turn back'. In any event the parallelism with *mḥṣ* 'to smite' proves that the reference is to military activity.
*[*Is. 51:15; Jer. 31:35 have been interpreted either: 'who stirs up the sea (with the result) that the waves thereof roar (*hmh*)' or: 'who stills the sea when etc.' The second interpretation is suggested by the use of the verb *hmh* in the description of the noisy onrush of the rebellious waters (Is. 5:2) which mostly serves as simile of the onrush of a human enemy (Is. 17:12; Jer. 6:23; 50:42, cf. also Ps. 46:4,7). Is. 51:15; Jer. 31:35 point out that God stilled these rebels, i.e. defeated them and thus put an end to their uproar. The use of *rg*ᶜ should be compared to that of *šbḥ* (*Piᶜel* and *Hiphᶜil*), 'to quiet, calm' in Ps. 65:8; 89:10, which also points to the anything but peaceful quieting of God's enemies. Compare in Latin *pacare* and especially Akkadian *šupšuḫu* 'to calm' in the verse: *[Ti-amat] šu-up-ši-iḫ ina te-e-ka ellu* (*Enūma eliš* II:117) 'Calm Tiamat with thy holy spell'.
Therefore *wayyähᵃmu gallāw* (Is. 51:15; Jer. 31:35) should be interpreted as circumstantial clause, not as a consecutive one. Compare Jer. 51:55 where the roaring of the waves of Babel clearly describes the situation preceding the destruction of the city by the great voice of the Lord and consult David Kimḥi's commentary upon Jer. 31:35.*]*

[11] The word *wayᵉmodäd* is difficult. G.R. Driver in *Studies in Old Testament Prophecy*, Edinburgh 1950, p. 70 derives it from the root *mwd* and compares it with Arabic *māda* 'to be twisted'. W.F. Albright, *ibid.*, p. 14 suggests the reading *yndd* or *ymrr* and compares Arabic *māra* 'to tremble, shake' and Ps. 46:3. The ancient versions already understood *yᵉmodäd* as a term signifying 'trembling'. The Septuagint translates ἐσαλεύθη. Targum Jonathan *wa'ᵃze*ᶜ. But cf. also: "God has spoken in His sanctuary: 'With exultation I will divide up Shechem and portion out (*'ᵃmadded*) the Vale of Succoth.'" (Ps. 60:8). This term refers to the God who goes out to save His people and to proclaim dominion over Shechem and the Vale of Succoth which He will divide and portion out among them, apparently to His people.

[12] The word *wayyatter* is difficult. Cf. Driver, *loc. cit.*, who explains it

tions; then the eternal mountains were scattered, the everlasting hills sank low ... I saw the tents of Cushan in affliction[13]; the curtains of the land of Midian did tremble" (v. 6-7). Similarly, we read further on: "The mountains saw Thee and writhed (*yāḥilu*)" (v. 10). The theophany which shakes the world is explicitely compared here with the mythological war against the sea and the rivers: "Was Thy wrath against the rivers, or Thy indignation against the sea, when Tou didst ride upon Thy horses upon the chariot of victory?" (v. 8). The comparison of the affect of God's theophany which frightens nature with His appearance in the war against the sea and the rivers reveals the source common to both: The description of God as a warrior possessing superhuman strength against whom no one can stand. This characteristic of God is the reason that all tremble at His sight, both those who are His enemies and those who are not. This explains why on the one hand an allusion to the mythological war could be worked into the description of the trembling of nature before God, while on the other hand this combination was not compulsory. The sea may not be mentioned in this context or it may be mentioned among the other trembling natural ele-

---

on the basis of Akkadian and Arabic as the *Hiph^cil* of *ntr* meaning 'to tear to pieces'. On this basis he translated the Ugaritic passage: *bym arṣ wtnn kṯr wḫss yd ytr kṯr wḫss* (*CTA* 6:VI:50-52) 'Kathir - and Khasis threw monster (?) and dragon into the sea, Kathir - and - Khasis cut (them) off' (Driver, *CML*, pp. 114-115). On the basis of Lev. 11:21 Cassuto, *op. cit.* (note 10), p. 133 [= *BOSt* 2, p. 92], interpreted *ytr* in Habakkuk and in Ugaritic as meaning 'to cause to leap, throw'. He claims from this that we find in the Prayer of Habakkuk a reflection of a Ugaritic myth of the throwing of the *Tannin* into the sea. He also compares the Apocalypse of John 20:2-3 καὶ ἐκράτησε τὸν δράκοντα ... καὶ ἔβαλε αὐτὸν εἰς τὸν ἀβύσσον. 'and he took hold of the dragon ... and threw it into the abyss'.
[For the wealth of proposals to explain Ugaritic *ytr* see de Moor, *Seasonal Pattern*, p. 243 (with bibliography); E. Lipinski, *OLP* 3 (1972), p. 109, note 51; Caquot-Sznycer, *Textes* 1, p. 270, note o. Unfortunately even the overall meaning of the text has not yet been clarified. It cannot mean that *kṯr w-ḫss* threw the monsters into the sea in order to destroy them since the sea was their habitat. Rather he removed them for this purpose from their element (*bym = from* the sea); Compare Ez. 29:3-5; 32:2-6. But contrast Ginsberg, *ANET*, p. 141; Caquot-Sznycer, *Textes* I, p. 270 and especially Lipinski, *op. cit.*, pp. 108-110 who look in ll. 50-52 for a description of a cruise of *kṯr w-ḫss* on the sea or on the sea of the Netherworld.]

[13] We may suggest the forced explanation: "As a land which was visited by a misfortune because of its sin I saw ..." For suggested emendations, see, e.g.: Th.H. Gaster, *JBL* 62 (1943), p. 346; W.F. Albright, *BASOR* 82 (1941), p. 48.

ments without any connection with the myth of the cosmic war, e.g.: "Let the sea roar, and all that fills it, the world and those who dwell in it" (Ps. 98:7). A similar phrase is found in Psalm 29, which alludes to the trembling of the waters before God: "The voice of the Lord is upon the waters, the God of glory thunders, the Lord, upon many waters" (Ps. 29:3), and it continues with the description of the trembling of the other natural elements in passages such as: "He makes Lebanon skip like a calf, and Sirion like a wild ox." (v. 6). The absence of any distinction whatsoever between the sea and the other parts of the world stands out particularly in the verse: "I will shake the heavens and the earth and the sea and the dry land." (Hag. 2:6), which is repeated later on in the chapter in a shorter version without any essential change: "I am about to shake the heavens and the earth" (v. 21). The same subjects recur in the psalms which glorify the reappearance of God's powers during the exodus from Egypt, e.g.: "What ails you, O sea, that you flee? O Jordan, that you turn back? O mountains that you skip like rams? O hills like lambs? Tremble, O earth, at the presence of the Lord etc." (Ps. 114:5-7). The description of the trembling of nature in Ps. 77:17-19 is unique: "When the waters saw Thee, O God, when the waters saw Thee, they were afraid, yea, the deep trembled. The clouds poured out water; The skies gave forth thunder; Thy arrows crashed on every side. The crash of Thy thunder was in the wheel[14]; Thy lightnings lighted up the world, the earth trembled and shook." There is no explicit mention here of God's war with the sea or its splitting. But although the sea is merely one of the trembling parts of nature, its trembling is particularly emphasized here in order to allude to the miracle of the splitting of the sea before the Israelites. Before the description of the trembling of nature the text reads: "Thou art the god who workest wonders, who has manifested Thy might among the peoples" (v. 15), and following it: "Thy way was through the sea, Thy path through the great waters; yet Thy footprints were unseen. Thou didst lead Thy people like a flock by the hand of Moses and Aaron" (v. 20-21).

[14] Rashi explained *baggalgal* as *kaggalgal* and many scholars read this way. But there is no point in comparing the powerful sound of thunder to that of a simple wheel. The text apparently refers to the wheel of the heavenly chariot which is the source of thunder. Cf. Ez. 10:2. *[Compare also A.B. Cook, Zeus 2, Cambridge 1923, pp. 830-833 on the thunder caused by the chariot of Zeus.]*

Our conception which explains the trembling of the world before God as a fear of a powerful warring force is confirmed also in the light of those verses which speak of the shaking of nature before other warring forces. First of all we should point out the striking comparison between the picture of the effect of the theophany with that of the appearance of the locusts which are compared to a mighty army. Concerning the locusts we read: "The earth quakes before them, the heavens tremble" (Joel 2:10), whereas the effect of the theophany is expressed in the following way: "Therefore I will make the heavens tremble, and the earth will be shaken out of its place" (Is. 13:13). Furthermore, it is reasonable to assume that this trembling force was also attributed to the sea in accordance with the myth which saw in it the warring force against God, a force which became a symbol of God's enemies and the enemies of His people. We read: "God is our refuge and strength, a very present help in trouble. Therefore we will not fear though the earth should change, though the mountains shake in the heart of the sea (*yammim*); though the waters roar and the foam, though the mountains tremble with its tumult." (Ps. 46:2-4). True, the reading "with its tumult", in the singular, permits the possibility for Rashi's explanation: "In God's glory which is mentioned at the beginning of the Psalm." Modern scholars, however, have rightly claimed that *yammim* is a *pluralis majestatis*, like *'ä̈lohim* 'God', *'ᵃdonim* 'master', and the text speaks of the tumult of the sea.[15] The verse thus means: No matter how long the forces of evil-symbolized by the waters of the sea - run rampant, we will not fear, for God is our refuge and strength. The description of the trembling does not change whether the shaking force is God, the sea, or the locusts. The common denomination is the effect of the appearance of the powerful warring force which is described according to a uniform pattern. It is clear from the start that we should not look for the source of this pattern in the tradition of the revelation on Mount Sinai.

Moreover, the pattern under discussion is common in Akkadian literature and no one would suggest that this literature was influenced by Israelite traditions of the revelation on Mount Sinai. In Akkadian literature

---

[15] Ha-Meiri in his medieval commentary on Psalms already explained the verse in this way. See recently: M. Weiss, *Biblica* 42 (1961), p. 281. On the expression of the swelling of the sea, cf. Ez. 47:5, and especially Ps. 89:10; Job 38:11. See also: Cassuto, *op. cit.* (note 10), p. 130.

the trembling of nature is accompanied by:

1) The appearance of war-like gods such as: Enlil, Marduk, Adad, and Ištar, but not the appearance of the sun god, Šamaš, who is not a hero, but the god of justice;
2) The appearance of the king of Assyria among his troops.

Some of the Akkadian sources are quoted in Tallquist's book of the epithets of the Babylonian gods[16], s.v. *nrṭ* II, 1 and *rwb* II, 1, on which our discussion further on is based. Enlil is called *munarriṭ ḫuršāni* 'shaker of mountains', and apparently the epithet *munarriṭ ša[mê]* 'shaker of heavens' also belongs to this god. Similarly he is called *[rim]u munarriṭ šamê u erṣitim* 'the wild ox who shakes heaven and earth'. Belat Mati, the Ištar of Calaḫ is called *munarriṭi ḫuršāni* 'shaker of mountains' while Ištar is *munarriṭṭi erṣetim* 'shaker of the earth'. Therefore, concerning her the rhetorical question is asked: *erṣetim mannu unarriṭ* 'Who has shaken the earth?' She is also called *muribbat šamê* 'she who angers heaven'. The mention of her name is sufficient to anger heaven and earth: *ana ḫissat šumeki šamê u erṣetim irubbu* 'at the mention of your name heaven and earth are angered'. Similarly, the question is asked about her: *šamê mannu urīb* 'Who has angered heaven?' We may add here texts which are not quoted by Tallquist. Marduk is glorified as a god *ša ana tāḫazīšu šamû irubbu ana utazzumīšu iddalaḫu apsû*[17] 'in whose battle the heavens shake, in his wrath the abyss is stirred up'. The same hymn states: *ina nablīšu utabbatu šadû marṣūti ša tâmtim gallatim isambu' ruppuša* 'with whose flame the evil[18] mountains are destroyed, tosses[19] the width of the ...[20] sea'. Adad is praised in the words: *[ša ina zik]ir pîšu šamû irūbū [erṣetu i]nirruṭu itarruru ḫuršāni*[21] 'at whose thunder the heavens trembled the earth shook, the moun-

[16] K. Tallquist, *Akkadische Götterepitheta, StOr* 7 (1938), pp. 143, 166, 174.

[17] E. Ebeling, *Die akkadische Gebetsserie Handerhebung*, Berlin 1953, p. 94.

[18] The basic meaning of *marṣu* is 'sick'. We may perhaps explain that the mountains which are destroyed from the flame of the god are compared to sick people. Ebeling translates: '*Die "bösen" (steilen) Berge*'. *[*Cf. v. Soden, *AHW*, s.v. *marṣu* 'beschwerlich'.*]*

[19] *sabû* 'to move at high speed'. *[*v. Soden, *AHW*, s.v. *sabā'u* 'wogen, schwanken'.*]*

[20] See *CAD* s.v. *gallu*.

[21] Ebeling, *op. cit.* (note 17), p. 104.

tains quaked.'[22] Further he is glorified: *bēlum ina agagīšu šamû itanarrarusu* ᵈ*IM ina ezezīšu erṣetim inassu šadû rabûti suḫḫupušu*[23] 'In the Lord's anger the heavens will shake, in Adad's anger the earth will tremble[24], the great mountains will crumble'. It should be especially pointed out that we find in texts of this type the verb *ḫâlu*== Heb. *ḥwl, ḥyl*. Adad is the god *[ša ina rigim p]îšu nīšê ušḫarara [itarrara] qirbīte iḫillu ṣêru*[25] 'the one at whose thundering people were benumbed (with fear), the steppes trembled, the field writhed' A praise for a goddess, apparently Ištar, states: *beltum ṣirtu šumki galtu ina šamê izakkarma erṣetim iḫal [... šumki galtu ina erṣetim] izakkarma šamê irubbu*[26] 'Exalted Lady, he will mention your terrifying name in heaven and the earth will writhe ... He will mention your terrifying name on earth and heaven will tremble'.

As we have remarked terms such as these recur also in reference to the kings of Assyria who boast that the world shook during their decisive attack. Tiglathpileser I boasts that he is the king *ša ina tīb kakkēšu ezzūti [...] ušrabbuma iḫillu dadmū*[27] 'at the onslaught of whose raging weapons (the lands) start to quiver and the inhabited regions shake'. Similarly Shalmaneser III claims: *ana tīb taḫāzīšu danni tupqâte ultanapšaqa iḫīlu šadâni*[28] 'at his mighty onslaught in battle the ends of the world are made uneasy, the mountains quiver'. Moreover, Sargon boasts that during his attack *šamû erṣetum ultanapšaquma šadâni u tâmtum iḫillu*[29] 'heaven and earth shook, the mountains and the sea writhed'.

These Akkadian texts indirectly but clearly testify to the character of the Biblical passages which we have discussed. They convincingly show that these passages should not be made dependent on the Israelite tradition of the revelation on Mount Sinai. The opposite is true. The story of the

---

[22] From the root *arāru*.

[23] S. Langdon, *Babylonian Penitential Psalms*, Paris 1927, p. 13.

[24] From the root *nasāsu [*rather from *nâšu*. Cf. v. Soden, *AHW, s.v.]*

[25] Ebeling, *op. cit.* (note 17), p. 98.

[26] Th.J. Meek, *Beiträge zur Assyriologie und vergleichenden Semitischen Sprachwissenschaft* 10 (1913), pp. 37-38.

[27] *CAD*, s.v. *ḫâlu* B.

[28] *CAD, ibid.*

[29] *CAD, ibid.*

fear which seized Mount Sinai and the people reflects the traditional pattern of a warring god. We should not be surprised that this pattern occurs in a story where God appears as a lawgiver and not a warrior, since in Israelite monotheistic religion there is no place for an absolute distinction between the different functions of the god. God does not cease to be a hero even during the giving of the law.[30] The majesty of the great hero is expressed in the trembling which takes hold of everything at his appearance even when he is not acting as a warrior. This explains the trembling of nature during God's enthronement described in Psalm 29, even more so, since - according to the myth - God's coronation is a result of His victory over the sea and the rivers.[31]

Moreover, in Akkadian poetry there is even somewhat of a parallel for the combination of the image of the warrior god who shakes the world with the description of the god as a righteous judge. We refer to the "*Prayer to Ištar*"[32] which begins with the words: *uṣalliki bēlit bēlīti ilat ilāti* 'I pray to you, the lady of ladies, goddess of goddesses'. Among other things, this long hymn praises Ištar as the goddess of war. For example:

> *nanšeat nandiat*[33] *qaritti* ^{d}*Ištar rabû qurdīki*
> *namirtum dipār šamê u erṣetim šarūr kal dadmē*
> *izzit qablu lā maḫar alilat tamḫārī*

---

[30] The motif of the trembling of nature which in the Pentateuch is limited just to the revelation on Mount Sinai is strengthened and enlarged to include the trembling of the entire world in the eschatological passage in 1 Enoch which describes God's revelation on Mount Sinai at the end of days when God will judge mankind to make peace for the chosen ones and to destroy the evildoers (1 Enoch 1:8-9). "And the eternal God will tread upon the earth, (even) on Mount Sinai, and appear from His camp, and appear in the strength of His might from heaven. And all shall be smitten with fear, and the Watchers shall quake, and great fear and trembling shall seize them from the ends of the earth. And the high mountains shall be shaken, and the hills shall be made low, and shall melt like wax before the flame. And the earth shall be asunder, and all that is upon the earth shall perish, and there shall be a judgement upon all (men)." The motif of the trembling of nature before God which in the Pentateuch is restricted becomes more powerful here because of the wide range of the judgement of the nations and its military character.

[31] Cassuto, *op. cit.* (note 10), pp. 135-136 *[= BOSt* 2, pp. 96f.*]*.

[32] Ebeling, *op. cit.* (note 17), pp. 130-137.

[33] On the forms *nanšeat, nandiat*, see: v. Soden, *GAG*, § 102c.

akukūtum ša ana ajābe napḫat šakinat šaḫluqti iqdūti[34]
(ll. 34-37)

'She who raises and lowers, the Lady Ištar, many are your brave deeds,
Brilliant torch of heaven and earth, light of all the inhabited land,
Terrifying in battle she has no equal, the powerful one of battle,
A fire which blazes against the enemies, which destroys the powerful ones.'

It is no wonder that heaven and earth tremble before her. But if we analyze the structure of the prayer we will see that the trembling of the world is not mentioned here in direct connection with the description of the goddess' warlike character, but it is juxtaposed to the praise of her majesty and serves as an introduction to her praise as a righteous judge:

ēkiam lā rabâti ēkī'am lā ṣirāti
^dAnum ^dEnlil u ^dEa ullûki ina ilāni ušarbu bēlūtki
ušašqûki ina napḫar ^dIgigi ušatiru manzāzki
ina ḫissat šumeki šamû u erṣetim irubbu
ilāni irūbu inarruṭu ^dAnunnaki
šumeki rašbu ištammara tenīšēti
attīma rabâti u ṣirāti
napḫar ṣalmat qaqqadi nammaššu tenīšēti idallulu qurdīki
dīn baḫulāti ina kitti u mēšari tadinni atti
tappallasi ḫablu u šagšu tušteššeri uddakam (ll. 17-26)

'Where are you not great? Where are you not majestic?
Anum, Enlil, and Ea raised you up among the gods, increased your sovereignty,
They elevated you among the gods, exalted your place,
At the mention of your name heaven and earth shake,
The gods quaked, the Anunnaki quivered,
People will praise your terrifying name,
You are great and majestic,

---

[34] This follows Ebeling's transcription. But cf. *CAD, s.v. ekdu*.

All the dark headed ones, the throng of humanity will
glorify your valour,
You judge the judgement of mankind[35] with justice and
righteousness,
You look at the oppressed and downtrodden, You provide justice
for him every day.'

From the combination of these motives in the poem it is clear that the connection between the warlike character of Ištar and the trembling of the world at her appearance has become weakened. The main purpose of the description of the trembling of the world is to stress to the utmost the goddess' majesty. From here the poem passes over to her action as a judge of the poor. The general trend of thought reminds us somewhat of the verse: "I dwell in the high and holy place, and also with him is of a contrite and humble spirit" (Is. 57:15).

To sum up: The description of the shaking effect of the warring divinity may turn into a glorification of the greatness of the majestic and terrifying god without any direct connection to that god's military activity. Once again we should point out here that this is the case with warrior gods, but not with Šamaš who is just the god of judgement and does not go out to combat. In every instance the motif of the trembling of nature has its roots in the fear of a powerful warring force. The God of Israel who gives his people the law on Mount Sinai does not appear there as a warrior. But only in the light of his being a warrior may we understand the terrifying impression of his appearance.

The concept of the god as a superhuman warring force is not restricted to Israel, but is common to all the peoples of the ancient Near East. We may therefore assume that the model of the nature-shaking theophany came to Israel from its surroundings. However, we will not easily accept the assumption that Israel borrowed this model directly from Akkadian literature, since this assumption does not agree with the low international status of Akkadian in the Israelite period. We therefore prefer the assumption that the model under discussion passed over from Akkadian into Canaanite at a

[35] *ba'ulāti* - *baḫulāti* 'people who are subject to the rule of a master, *Untertanen*'.

period when Akkadian served as an international language, and to a considerable extent as the language of administration in general, that is to say in the centuries which preceded the Israelite conquest for which the El-Amarna and Ugaritic documents testify. Since, in general, Biblical literature is a continuation of Canaanite literature[36], it follows that it continued to develop this Canaanite model also and applied it to the theophany of the God of Israel.

We are, however, not able to prove this contention decisively from Canaanite literature. Our knowledge of Canaanite hymnology is quite poor[37] while the hymn in honor of the warring god is the *locus classicus* of the descriptions of the trembling of nature. In his above mentioned article on Psalm 29[38], Gaster collected the few relevant passages. Gaster notes the following:

1) The letter of Abimilki, King of Tyre, who praises Pharaoh *ša iddin rigmašu ina šamê kīma Adad u tarkup/b gabbi šadī ištu rigmīšu* (*EA* 149:14-15)
'who thundered in heaven like Adad and ... all the mountains at his thundering'.

The context has led scholars to translate the verbal form *tarkup/b* as 'they trembled', even though there is no proof for this translation either from Akkadian or Canaanite.

2) The Ugaritic text *CTA* 4:VII which speaks of Baal, i.e. the god Hadad.

Gaster[39] tries to find in this text several descriptions of the trembling of nature before Baal. But the tablet is broken, many of the words are obscure, and we cannot consider any of the proofs that Gaster brings from it

---

[36] See e.g.: U. Cassuto, *Biblical and Canaanite Literature, Tarbiz* 13 (1942), pp. 197-212; 14 (1943), pp. 1-10. *[BOSt* 2, pp. 16-59.*]*

[37] On the problem of the fragmentary psalms in the El-Amarna Letters, see A. Jirku, *JBL* 52 (1933), pp. 108-120; W.F. Albright, *JEA* 23 (1937), pp. 196-202.

[38] See note 5. Cf. now also Gaster, *Thespis*², pp. 196-201. There Gaster explains the Ugaritic passage dealt with here as part of the hymn which *kṯr.w-ḫss* says in honour of Baal. He looks for the source of the hymn in the rite of autumn. Gaster also notes there some of the Akkadian hymns in honour of Adad which describe the trembling of nature before him and compares Na. 1:3ff.

[39] Gaster, *loc. cit.* (note 5).

as certain. The only example which is somewhat convincing is in ll. 34-35: *qdmym. bmt. a[rṣ] tṭṭn* 'east (and) west the high places of the earth will shake'.[40] But even this accepted[41] and attractive explanation is not above doubt since:

1) The text before the letters *qdmym* is broken.
2) There is no word divider between *qdm* and *ym*. The separation of the letters *qdmym* into the two words *qdm* and *ym* is uncertain, even more so since the expression *qdm ym* is not otherwise known either from Ugaritic or the Bible (but see: Gen. 12:8; Is. 11:14).
3) The reading *a[rṣ]* is based on a restoration.

With regard to Gaster's other examples the obscure points outweigh the clear ones to such a degree that no proof whatsoever may be brought from them.[42]

To sum up: The motif of the trembling of nature before God has its roots in His image as a warrior whose appearance terrifies the whole world, whether He goes out to war or not. This conclusion is required from analy-

---

[40] Ugaritic *nṭṭ* corresponds to Hebrew *nwṭ, nṭh* (Ps. 73:2). Cf. Cassuto, *Anath*, p. 130.

[41] Cf. H.L. Ginsberg, *ANET*, p. 135; Driver, *CML*, p. 101.

[42] Gaster reads in l. 31 *qlh q[dš yt]r arṣ* 'his holy voice convulses the earth'. On the verb *ytr*, cf. note 12. The restoration *[yt]r* is extremely uncertain. Gaster reads in l. 32: *zrm tḫšn* 'the mountains quake'. But the text reads: *ġrm aḫšn*. While *ġrm* too may be translated 'cliffs, mountains', the reading *aḫšn* precludes Gaster's interpretation. For although confusion of the letters *t* and *a* is possible in Ugaritic there is no place for an emendation in a broken text whose context is not completely clear. *[*But cf. Herdner, *CTA*, p. 29, note 13.*]* There is also no basis for the translation of the verb *ḫwš* as 'quake'. Driver, *CML*, p. 139, translates 'was dismayed' and compares Arabic *ḫāsa* 'was dull', *ḫīsatu* (*ḫys*?) 'grief'. Cf. also de Landberg, *Glossaire Datinois, s.v. ḫ's*, which expresses the meanings *'sentir mal, se gâter'*, and this provides some support for the translation of *ḫwš* as 'to melt'. At the most these doubtful proofs explain the emended reading *tḫšn*, but not the reading *aḫšn*. In the broken l. 33 Gaster reads *rtt*. But the text has *rtq [*Herdner, *CTA*, p. 29, note 14; *rhq ne fait pas de doute]* Driver, *CML*, p. 155, translates 'was perturbed', and compares the Septuagint to Ez. 7:23 which translates *rattoq* as 'disorder, confusion'. But there is no proof that the Septuagint's translation of this difficult verse in anything more than a guess. In l. 41, Gaster translates *ktġḏ arz bymnh* 'Yea cedars quiver at the touch of his right hand'. Here also the meaning of the verb is unknown and the text probably speaks of the cedar in Baal's right hand. See U. Cassuto, *Dinaburg Jub. Vol.*, Jerusalem, 1949, pp. 66-67 (in Heb.); *[= BOSt* 2, p. 191*]* Ginsberg, *loc. cit.* (note 42); Driver, *CML*, p. 101. *[*Compare also de Moor, *Seasonal Pattern*, pp. 164f.*]*

sis of the Biblical material and is confirmed by the Akkadian texts in which we also find the pattern of the trembling of nature before a warrior god or a warrior king. This model probably came into Biblical literature as a legacy of Canaanite literature which borrowed it from Akkadian literature. However, at the moment this last assumption is still in the nature of a hypothesis.[43]

---

[43] While this article was in proof I received C. Westermann, *Das Loben Gottes in den Psalmen*², Göttingen 1961. He also rejects the viewpoint which looks for the source of descriptions of God's revelation dealt with here in the tradition of God's revelation on Mount Sinai (pp. 73-76). *[Cf. now J. Jeremias, Theophanie, WMANT* 10 (1965).*]*

Š^{e}'er

According to the widely accepted opinion the Hebrew noun *š^{e}'er* 'flesh' is etymologically related to the Arabic noun *ṯa'r* 'blood vengeance'. True, scholars felt that the semantic distance between 'blood vengeance' and 'flesh' was great, and they tried to diminish it by supposing that the original meaning of the Arabic noun was 'blood'.

However, in the light of a new Ugaritic text it now appears that the Proto-Semitic root of *š^{e}'er* was different. The text reads: *tspi širh l bl ḥrb tšt dmh l bl ks*. Virolleaud translates: '... *elle déchire sa chair sans (se servir) d'un couteau, elle boit son sang sans (se servir d'une) coupe*'.[1]

From the context of the line it is perfectly clear that *šir* means 'flesh'. Since Ugaritic differentiates between *š* and *ṯ* this proves that the Proto-Semitic root of *š^{e}'er* is *š'r* and not *ṯ'r*.

The Ugaritic line sheds new light also on the Biblical verse: "The violence (*ḥ^{a}māsi*) done to me *uš'eri* be upon Babylon shall the inhabitant of Zion say and my blood be upon the inhabitants of Chaldea shall Jerusalem say" (Jer. 51:35). The noun *š^{e}'eri* in this verse has always been a source of difficulty for the commentators. Rashi explained *ḥ^{a}māsi uš'eri* as "the cry of the violence done to me and *my food* since they ate my flesh (*š^{e}'eri*). R. David Kimḥi quotes his father's explanation: "*š^{e}'eri* - referring to the exiles whom they physically tortured; and *dāmi* - referring to the ones who were killed". Contemporary scholars tend to amend the reading *š^{e}'eri*. The following emendations have been put forth: *šibri*, *šoddi*[2], *šo'āti*[3]. Recently E.Y. Kutscher[4] put forth the view that *š^{e}'eri* should be explained here on

---

[1] Ch. Virolleaud, *CRAIBL* 1960, pp. 180-185. There is no purpose in dealing here with the question of whether the verbal forms in this verse are 3 f. sg., as Virolleaud thinks, or whether it is perhaps better to explain them as 3 m.pl. *[*Virolleaud is clearly right, since 3 m.pl. of *sp'* should read *tspu*, not *tispi.]*

[2] *BH* on this verse.

[3] W. Rudolph, *Jeremia*, Tübingen 1958, p. 288.

[4] E.Y. Kutscher, *Lĕšonēnū* 21 (1967), p. 258.

the basis of the above-mentioned Arabic noun in the sense of 'blood-vengeance' or 'blood'. The explanation 'blood vengeance', however, does not fit the verse. Both *ḥ^a^māsi* and *dāmi* signify the injustice done to Judah and *a priori* it is clear that the same applies to *š^e'eri*. The explanation of the word *š^e'eri* as 'my blood' in itself would make sense but it is based on the derivation of *š^e'er* from Arabic *ṯa'r*. Since we have seen that this etymology is fallacious it then seems probable that *š^e'er* here parallels *dām* as in the Ugaritic line, and that R. David Kimḥi was correct when he offered his own explanation: "*uš'eri* - This refers to flesh as: 'Who also eat the flesh (*š^e'er*) of my people' (Mi. 3:3) and *dāmi* expresses the same idea in different words." Corroboration of Kimḥi's view may be found in the simile *b^e^lā^c^ani kattannin* (Jer. 51:34) 'he swallowed me up like a tannin'.

We should add that in Jer. 51:35 two types of ancient phraseology have merged. Kutscher[5] rightly compared the verse from Jeremiah with Ju. 9:24: "that the violence (*ḥāmās*) done to the seventy sons of Jerubbaal might come, and that their blood (*dāmām*) might be laid upon Abimelech." The word 'blood' (*dām*) in the second hemistich thus parallels 'violence' (*ḥāmās*) in the first, and the Ugaritic verse shows that it could also be paralleled by *š^e'er*.[6] In the phrase *ḥ^a^māsi uš'eri* two traditional parallels of 'blood' (*dām*) are combined.

---

[5] Kutscher, *op. cit.* (note 4).

[[6] The pair *šīru* and *damu* is frequent in Akkadian literature where *šīru* is the only word for flesh. I am indebted for this observation to Dr. Y. Avishur who dealt with this question in his forthcoming book on *Pairs of words in Biblical literature and their parallels in Semitic literatures of the Ancient Near East.*]

The Seven-Day-Unit in Ugaritic Epic Literature

Scholars have long known the typological character of the number seven which was employed as a symbol of completeness in the literature of the Ancient East. This subject was comprehensively treated as early as the year 1907 by J. Hehn[1] in his book on the Sabbath and the number seven. Hehn's study has been supplemented in more recent years by U. Cassuto[2] who especially stressed the recurrence of the role of this number in certain passages in Ugaritic epic literature, describing an action which continues for a period of six days and terminates on the seventh day. However, the particular form that this numerical scheme assumed in the Ugaritic epic has not as yet been investigated. It is this aspect that we wish to clarify in the present paper.

A cursory examination will show that the authors of Ugaritic have borrowed the seven-day unit and all its characteristic features from Akkadian literature. *[*The question is open to doubt. See additions.*]*

In the section of the *Gilgamesh Epic* that deals with the Flood we meet with the following description (XI:141-146):

šadû-u ^{kur}*Ni-ṣir* ^{giš}*elippa iṣ-bat-ma a-na na-a-ši ul id-din*
ištēn^{en} *ūma*^{ma} *šanâ*^{a} *ūma*^{ma} *KI.MIN*
šal-šú ūma^{ma} *ri-ba-a ūma*^{ma} *šadû*^{u} *Ni-ṣir KI.MIN*
ḫanšu^{šú} *šeššu*^{šú} *šadû*^{u} *Ni-ṣir KI.MIN*
sebâ^{a} *ūma*^{ma} *i-na ka-šā-di*
ú-še-ṣi-ma turta^{ḫu} *ú-maš-šir*

Translation:

Mount Niṣir held the ship fast, and did not let it rise

[1] J. Hehn, *Siebenzahl und Sabbath*, Leipzig (1907), pp. 4-44.

[2] U. Cassuto, *Biblical and Canaanite Literature, Tarbiz* 13 (1942), pp. 206-207, notes 31, 32 (in Heb.) *[*= Cassuto, *BOSt* 2, pp. 32-33, notes 31, 32*]*.

One day, a second day, Mount Niṣir held the ship fast and did not let it rise.

A third day, a fourth day, Mount Niṣir held the ship fast and did not let it rise.

A fifth day, a sixth (day) Mount Niṣir held the ship fast and did not let it rise.

When the seventh day arrived, I sent forth and set a dove free ...

It will be observed that by way of introduction the first line of the passage describes the nature of the action that is about to take place for a period of six days. This description is repeated *verbatim* three times, preceded in each instance by a pair of days during which the action is said to take place. Though the numerous *verbatim* repetitions endow the passage with a certain rigidity and archaic character, we may nevertheless sense a tendency in the author to avoid excessive repetitions by not repeating the descriptive sentence after each one of the six days.

The numerical scheme described above is also encountered in Ugaritic composition in the *epic of Aqht CTA* 17:II:30-40.[2a]

	yšlḥm kṯrt	*wyššq bnt [hl]l snnt*
hn ym wṯn	*yšlḥm kṯrt*	*wyš[š]q bnt hl[l] snnt*
ṯlṯ [r]bᶜ ym	*yšlḥm kṯrt*	*wyššq bnt hll snnt*
ḫmš ṯdṯ ym	*yšlḥm k[ṯ]rt*	*wy[ššq] bnt hll snnt*
mk bšb[ᶜ] ymm	*tbᶜ bbth kṯrt*	*bnt hll snnt*

Translation:

Gives food to the kṯrt[3] and drink to the daughters of joyful sound,

---

[2a D. Freedman, *Counting Formulae in the Akkadian Epos, JANES* 3 (1970/71), p. 75, note 53 argues against me that the text cannot be considered the most archaic occurrence of the formula, since it comes within fifty lines of its most sophisticated occurrence in *CAT* 17:I:1-17. His acute remark throws into relief the perplexing literary problem that the same author presents the pattern under discussion in both its most monotonous and its most variegated form. From there it appears that he wanted to demonstrate his mastery in different kinds of style. A relatively late writer made intentionally use of the most archaic form, known to him.

Contrast also in the same epic the simple formulation: *i]rš ksp watnk [ḫrṣ waš]lḥk* (*CTA* 17:VI:17-18) with its enlarged counterpart: *irš ḥym laqht ġzr irš ḥym watnk blmt wašlḥk* (*CTA* 17:VI:26-28).]

3 *Kṯrt*. H.L. Ginsberg, *ANET*, p. 150, renders the 'skilful ones' presumably on the basis of the Akkadian and Hebrew *kšr*. However, since the root *kšr*

the swallows. Behold one day[4] and a second,

He gives food to the kṯrt and drink to the daughters of joyful sound, the swallows.

A third, a fourth day,

He gives food to the kṯrt and drink
to the daughters of joyful sound, the swallows.

A fifth, a sixth day,

He gives food to the kṯrt and drink
to the daughters of joyful sound, the swallows.

Lo, on the seventh day[4a],

Away from his house go the kṯrt.
The daughters of joyful sound, the swallows.

This descriptive scheme is based entirely on the pattern of the Akkadian epic analyzed above. It is apparent, therefore, that the Ugaritic author adopted his scheme from Mesopotamian literature, which was well known in Ugarit. A fragment of the Deluge Epic recently discovered in Ras Shamra[5] confirms this point. This borrowed scheme determined not only the literary structure of the above quoted passage, but also that of all other passages describing an action which goes on for six consecutive days and terminates on the seventh. However, there is at the same time a marked tendency both to modify the archaic style of the scheme and avoid excessive *verbatim* repetitions of the descriptive formula. This tendency led to several varia-

---

also occurs in Aramaic it is quite probable that the Akkadian-Hebrew *kšr* represents a Proto-Semitic *kšr* and not *kṯr* though the possibility of an Aramaic borrowing of *kšr* from Akkadian or Hebrew cannot be completely ruled out. For the Hebrew *košārot* in the probable sense of 'female jubilants' cf. Ps. 68:7. *[*Cf. now M. Margulis, *JANES* 4 (1972), pp. 53-61.*]*

4 On *ym* as denoting the first day see in this volume *The Development of the Term "First" in the Semitic Languages*, pp. 13-16.

*[*4a *bšb^c ymm*, literally in seven days. On this "Canaanism" see M. Liverani, *Ma nel settimo anno, Studi sul' Oriente e la Bibbia*, Genova 1967, p. 51, note 5, who points to its occurrence in the canaanized Akkadian of the *Idrimi* inscription, l. 45 and to its attestations in Phoenician (Friedrich, *PPG* § 315a). Cf. Gen. 7:10; Ex. 19:15. The use seems to be of archaic character, since ordinals represent a later stage in the development of the language than cardinals. In numbers exceeding ten no ordinals at all have been developed in Semitic languages.*]*

5 J. Nougayrol, *U 5*, text 167.

tions of the original scheme, each of which we shall discuss individually.

A minor modification in the descriptive pattern occurs in the story concerning the construction of Baal's palace in *CTA* 4:VI:22-33.

	tšt išt bbhtm	*nb[l]at bhklm*
hn ym wṯn	*tikl išt bbhtm*	*nblat bhk[l]m*
ṯlṯ r!b^c ym	*tikl [i]št bbhtm*	*nbla[t] bhklm*
ḫmš ṯ[d]ṯ ym	*tikl išt [b]bhtm*	*nblat b[qrb? hk]lm*
mk bšb[^c] y[mm]	*td išt bbhtm*	*n[bl]at bhklm*

Translation:

Fire is set to the house, flame to the palace.
Lo, a day and a second, fire consumed in the house, flame in the palace.
A third, a fourth day, fire consumed in the house, flame in the palace.
A fifth, a sixth, fire consumed in the house, flame in the palace.
Lo, on the seventh day the fire departs[6] from the house, the flame from the palace.

The verb *šyt* employed in the introductory clause of the passage has been substituted by the verb *'kl* used in the recurring formula, thus deviating from the rule of the original scheme which requires *verbatim* repetition of the descriptive formula. [The difference goes deeper, *šyt* and *'kl* are not synonymous. Rather *šyt* indicates the cause *'kl* the effect]. Other, even more striking modifications are encountered in the *epic of Aqht CTA* 17:I:1-17.

	[apnk dnil mt rp]i	*apn ġz[r mt hrnmy]*
	uzr ilm ylḥm	*[uzr yšqy] bn qdš*
	yd [ṣth y^cl]	*wyškb yd [mizrt] pyln*[7]
hn ym [wṯn uzr]	*ilm dnil [uzr ilm] ylḥm*	*uzr [yšqy b]n qdš*
ṯlṯ rb' ym	*[uzr i]lm dnil uzr [ilm y]lḥm*	*uzr yšqy bn [qdš*
ḫ]mš ṯdṯ ym	*uzr [ilm] dnil uzr ilm ylḥm*	*[uzr] yšqy bn qdš*
	yd ṣth [dn]il yd ṣth y^cl	*wyškb [yd] mizrt pyln*
	mk bšb^c ymm	*[w]yqrb b^cl*

[6] The translation is *ad sensum*. It is uncertain whether the word *td* derives from the verb *ndy* which means 'to banish' [or rather from the verb *ydy*. Cf. Herdner, *CTA*, p. 76, note 4; H.L. Ginsberg, *JANES* 5 (1973), pp. 132-134].

[7] The text reads *pynl* but has been amended following the suggestion of many scholars based on the parallel wording in the sequence of the passage.

Translation:

Then[8] Danil the Rapha-man, then the hero the Harnamy-man[9]

Gives oblation[10] to the gods to eat[11], gives oblation to drink[12]

---

8 *aphn (apnk)*. Actually 'thereupon, forthwith', cf. Gordon, *UT, Glossary* No. 297 and in this volume, *Notes on the Pronouns*, p. 63.

9 On *hrnmy* see W.F. Albright, *BASOR* 130 (1933), pp. 26-27.

10 On *uzr* see in this volume, *Review on Cyrus H. Gordon, Ugaritic Manual*, p. 36.

11 *lḥm*. The verb apparently belongs to the *D* conjugation, see following note.

12 Some scholars render *šqy* 'to drink' (Gordon, Driver) as opposed to the causative *ššqy* (*Š*) 'to cause to drink'. But a comparison with other Semitic languages shows that in this instance the verb has an identical value in both the *G* and *Š* conjugations. The verb *šqh* occurs in Hebrew only in the *Hiph^{c}il* and in Aramaic only in the *'Aph^{c}el*. In Akkadian the verb *šaqû* in the *G* conjugation denotes 'to cause to drink' and in Arabic the first and fourth conjugations of the verb *sqy* have the same meaning.

This free interchange of the *Qal* in the causative sense and the *Hiph^{c}il* conjugation of the same verb is not particular to the verb *šqy*. Compare e.g. the Biblical use of the word *yld* in the sense of 'to beget' (Gen. 4: 18). In Hebrew the verb which derives from the stem *yš^{c}* occurs only in the *Hiph^{c}il* conjugation yet the personal name *Y^{e}ša^{c}yāhu* attests to the fact that in Early Hebrew the verb also had the same value when it occurred in the *Qal* conjugation, as was pointed out by F. Delitzsch in *Der Prophet Jesaja*^{3} (1879), p. 1. Similar phenomena may be found in other personal names. Cf. M. Noth, *Die Israelitischen Personennamen*, Stuttgart 1928, p. 36. Some verbs occur in the *Qal* conjugation and bear both a causative and non-causative value, whereas in other conjugations these verbs have only a causative value, such as the verb *nḥl* which in the *Qal* denotes both 'to receive an inheritance' and 'to give an inheritance' (Nu. 34:17, 18; Jos. 19:49), whereas in the *Pi^{c}el* and *Hiph^{c}il* conjugations the verb means only 'to give an inheritance'. The antiquity of the causative value of the verb *nḥl* in the *Qal* is now attested by the Mari texts in which the verb *naḫālu* occurs in the *Qal* and means 'to give an inheritance'. For a discussion of this Western Semitic loan-words in the Akkadian texts of Mari see G. Boyer, *ARM* 7, pp. 190-197. Cf. also A. Malamat, *JAOS* 82 (1962), p. 148, who contends that the *Qal* or *Pi^{c}el* form of the verb was determined by the numerical nature of the object. The same is true of the Canaanite stem *mrr*. In Ugaritic literature (*CTA* 2:IV:19) the imperative *mr* recurs twice. The context leaves no doubt that the verb has the approximate value of 'to drive away'. Now, the verb *marāru* in the Amarna letters has the meaning 'to run away, flee' (*EA* 185:66), whereas the same verb when occurring in the *Šaph^{c}el* means 'to cause to run away, to cause to flee' (*EA* 77:24; 103:30 and cf. 185:74). The origin of these letters is Canaan and since the verb *marāru* does not have this value in the texts written in genuine Akkadian, the value of the verb could have been borrowed only from Canaanite usage. In the light of the foregoing remarks, then, it is probable that the Ugaritic imperative *mr* derives from the stem *mrr* and cf. also Gordon, *UT, Glossary*, No. 1556, who connects it with Arabic *marrara* in the second formation, in which it has the value 'to cause to pass'. Cf. *mrrt CTA* 19:156-157. The *Qal* form of the imperative is akin to the He-

to the holy ones.
With[13] his covering[14] he mounts (his couch) and lies with (his) loin cloth and passes the night.
Lo, a day and a second,
Oblation to the gods Danil, oblation to the gods gives to eat, oblations to drink to the holy ones,
A third, a fourth day,
Oblation to the gods Danil, oblation to the gods gives to eat, oblation to drink to the holy ones.
A fifth, a sixth day,
Oblation to the gods Danil, oblation to the gods gives to eat, oblation to drink to the holy ones,
With his covering Danil, with his covering mounts (his couch) and lies, with (his) loincloth and passes the night.
But lo, on the seventh day, Baal approaches ...

Two deviations from the original scheme are evident in this text:

(a) The introductory formula recurs in its entirety only after the third pair of days whereas only the first part of the formula is repeated following each of the first two pairs of days.

(b) The descriptive refrains are not verbatim repetitions. The formula occurring in the opening verses: *uzr ilm ylḥm uzr yšqy bn qdš* has its counterpart in an expanded version of the first colon of the refrains: *uzr ilm dnil uzr ilm ylḥm uzr yšqy bn qdš*. There is a similar difference in the

---

brew imperative *sob* of the verb *sbb*. In any case, the meaning of the verb 'to cause to run away, to flee' in the causative sense is at variance with the linguistic usage of the Amarna letters. The verb *mrr* in Ancient Western Semitic therefore denoted: (a) to run away, (b) to cause to run away. *[In accordance with šqy the verb lḥm*, too, should be explained in this context in a causative meaning i.e. in the same sense as *šlḥm*. The question remains open whether it is to be parsed as a causative *G* or as *D*. As to the latter possibility cf. in Hebrew e.g. the indifferentiated use of the root *'bd* in *Piᶜel* and *Hiphᶜil.]*

13 The word *yd* is generally taken as the imperfect of the verb *ndy* - 'to wear'. However, it is doubtful whether the stem *ndy* bears this meaning. For the word *yd* meaning 'with', see *PRU* 2, p. 209, *s.v.*

14 *ṣth / mizrt*. Cf. Driver, *CML*, p. 105, *s.v.*, who tentatively compares it with the Akkadian *āṣītu* 'cloak'. The word may perhaps be a cognate of the Hebrew *sut* though the interchange between *s* and *ṣ* is unusual when not occurring alongside emphatic consonants or the guttural *ḫ*.

wording of the second part of the formula in the introductory verses, from its sole parallel which occurs after the last pair of days, cf.: *yd ṣth y^cl wyškb yd mizrt pyln* with *yd ṣth dnil yd ṣth y^cl wyškb yd mizrt pyln*. Verses which originally had a simple syntax were rendered more complex by an expansion of their opening cola; this is a familiar literary device in Ugaritic poetic composition, and, as it may be recalled, is also met with in Biblical poetry.

The nature of this syntax has already been pointed out by the Rashbam in his commentary on Ex. 15:6: "Thy right hand, O Lord, glorious in power, Thy right hand, O Lord, dasheth in pieces the enemy". Rashbam remarks: "This verse is similar (in construction) to (the verses) 'The flood have lifted up, O Lord, the floods have lifted up their voice' (Ps. 93:3), 'How long shall the wicked, O Lord, how long shall the wickend exult' (Ps. 94:3), 'For, lo, Thine enemies, O Lord, for lo, Thine enemies shall perish' (Ps. 92:10). The first half-couplet does not complete the statement; it is the second half-couplet which takes it up and completes it. The first half-couplet, however, introduces the subject of the statement."

Contemporary scholars have recognized that this syntax derives from Canaanite poetic tradition.[15] It is by no means fortuitous, then, that the author of the Aqht epic particularly expanded the first colon of the verse but did not alter the simple construction of the second colon; this amplification of a verse is always restricted to its first colon, as examplified by the Ugaritic verse *CTA* 2:IV:8-9: *ht ibk b^clm ht ibk tmḫṣ ht tṣmt ṣrtk*: 'Behold *[now]* thy enemies, Baal, behold *[now]* thy enemies thou shalt shatter, behold thou shalt destroy thy adversaries'[16]; and in the Biblical verse: "For lo, thy enemies, O Lord, for, lo, thy enemies shall perish; all the workers of iniquity shall be scattered" (Ps. 92:10). The literary device of the amplified verse has, then, been adequately recognized. It nevertheless deserves to be mentioned that the present Aqht passage is the only

---

[15] Cf. e.g. U. Cassuto, *Annuario di Studi Ebraici*, 1938, p. 13. For discussion and bibliography, see in this volume, *The expanded Colon in Ugaritic and Biblical Verse*, pp. 281-309.

[16] *srtk nomen unitatis*, that is 'all thine adversaries'. For the parallelism *'oy^ebim // ṣārā* see U. Cassuto, *Lĕšonênu* 15 (1947), p. 98 (in Heb.) *[*= Cassuto, *BOSt* 2, pp. 61-62.*]*

one which cites the same verse in both forms, once in its simple syntax and again in its amplified version, thus heightening the vitality of the verse. In sum, we may note that the author of the Aqht epic diversified the principle of the quadruple repetition scheme with superb artistry.

In the course of time, however, this schematic principle began to break down. The account of the feast of the Rephaim (*CTA* 22B:21-25) is introduced with a lengthy narrative describing the preparations made for the feast, the slaughter of animals and the measures taken to provide wine. Though a great part of this section is unintelligeble, it will suffice to note that at the close of the narrative, reference is made (l. 20) to the Lebanese origin of the wine provided for the feast. The sequence reads as follows:

hn ym wṯn		*tlḥmn rpum tštyn*
ṯlṯ rb^{c} *ym*	*ḫmš ṯdṯ ym*	*tlḥmn rpum tštyn*
bt ikl bpr^{c}	*[...]q birt lbnn*	
mk bšb^{c}	*[ymm]*	

Translation:

Lo, a day and a second, the Rephaim eat (and) drink
A third, a fourth day, a fifth, a sixth day, the Rephaim eat and drink,
In the banqueting hall *[...]* fruit[17] of the wells of Lebanon,
But on the seventh *[day]* ...

In this passage the original scheme appreciably breaks down. It does contain a repetitive formula: *tlḥm rpum tštyn*; but it occurs only in the narrative passage proper and not as an opening section to the passage as a whole. This formula, furthermore, does not recur in the narrative part after the second pair of days (i.e. the third and fourth days). Like the passage in *CTA* 17: I:1-17, the formula is expanded after the third pair of days, but even this augmented part of the formula does not repeat any part of the proceeding text except the single word *lbnn*. The textual characteristics of this passage, then, attest to the desire of the poet to both break the traditional literary bonds and find a richer and more variegated mode of formulation. *[*Nevertheless the ancient standard formulae *hn ym wṯn*

[17] The meaning of *bpr*^{c} is uncertain. Our rendering follows that of Driver, *CML*, p. 196, *s.v. pr*^{c}, who takes it as cognate to the Syr. *par*^{c}*a* 'fruit'.

etc. and *mk b... ymm* are still retained.]

Even those are abandoned in the Keret epic. The Keret epic represents the last stage of the evolvement of the numerical scheme in Ugaritic literature. In this composition we meet with certain passages which recount how the god Il commanded Keret to perform certain deeds for a period of six days until a desired event takes place on the seventh day. These passages are then followed by descriptions relating how Keret executed the commands of Il. Lines *CTA* 14:114-120 in the Keret epic thus read:

dm ym wṯn	*ṯlṯ rbᶜ ym*	*ḫ!mš ṯdṯ ym*
ḥẓk al tšᶜl qrth		*abn ydk mšdpt*
whn špšm bšbᶜ		*wl yšn pbl mlk*

Translation:

Tarry[18] a day and a second, a third, a fourth day, a fifth, a sixth day, send[19] not thine arrows into the city, (nor) thy slingstones[20] to the town.[21] And behold, at the sunrise[22] of the seventh, King Pabel will not sleep.[23]

---

18 From the verb *dmm* 'refrain from acting, from attacking', but cf. Gordon, *UT, Glossary*, No. 484 who assigns to the word the value of 'now, lo'. [Like him Aartun, *Partikeln*, pp. 58, 67. The interpretation of *dm* in *CTA* 14: 114 as an imperative of *dmm* is connected with the question, how we should read *CTA* 14: 218. See Herdner, *CTA*, p. 65, note 8.]

19 *tšᶜl* - is generally taken as *Šaphᶜel* of the verb *ᶜly* 'to go up'. It may however, alternatively be taken as cognate of the Aramaic *ᶜll* - 'to enter'. The translation in both instances nevertheless remains the same: 'send'. [The usual derivation of *tšᶜl* from *ᶜly* is correct, since Aramaic *ᶜll* corresponds to Ugaritic-Arabic *ġll*.]

20 *abn ydk* - is generally taken to be a stone thrown from a sling. Cf. Hebrew *ydh* - 'to throw' and M. Dahood, *Biblica* 40 (1959), pp. 1005f.

21 *mšdpt.* - The derivation of the word has not as yet been clarified. It is probable, however, that it parallels the word *qrt* - 'city'. For another interpretation see F. Rosenthal, *Orientalia* 8 (1939), p. 222; M. Dahood, *loc. cit.* (note 20), p. 1006.

22 *špšm*. The word means either at sunrise or at sunset. I have preferred the former rendering since some support for it may be found in a passage of the *Gilgamesh Epic* that deals with certain actions which lasted for six days and seven nights (Tablet I:IV:21; XII:199). [Cf. also Jos. 6:15.]

23 For the other renderings cf. Gray, *Krt*[1], pp. 39-40 [cf. also *Krt*[2], p. 49].

[As throughout in Keret *ym wṯn* is preceded by a verb, not by *hn* and the seventh day indicated by the words *špšm bšb*^{c}, not *bšb*^{c} *ymm*. *špšm bsb*^{c} may be introduced by *hn* (as here) or by classical *mk* or even by *aḫr*.

In spite of these deep-going differences] this passage continues [in a sense] the line of development already evident in *CTA* 22B. There the descriptive formula is repeated only twice instead of the customary four times whereas in the present passage the repetitive scheme of the descriptive formula has been abandoned completely. The author, however, has been careful to retain the basic system which requires that each of the six days in which the action takes place be expressly mentioned and that the days be enumerated in groups of two. It was in this manner then that the characteristic formula of the Keret epic: *ym wṯn ṯlṯ rb*^{c} *ym ḫmš ṯdṯ ym* evolved.

The execution of the above-mentioned instructions given to Keret is described in the consequent passage by means of verbatim repetition of the phraseology of the command (*CTA* 14: 218-222), thus conforming to the literary style of the Ugaritic epos which frequently employs the device of verbatim repetitions of entire sections of this character.

Il's order not to attack the city of Udum for six days is preceded by another command to undertake a military expedition to that city. This action is also to continue for six consecutive days. Lines 103-109 of the Keret text read as follows:

kirby [t]škn šd *km ḥsn pat mdbr*
lk ym wṯn *ṯlṯ rb*^{c} *ym* *ḫmš ṯdṯ ym*
mk špšm bsb^c *wtmġy ludm rbt!*

Translation:

Like the locusts that dwell on the steppes
Like the grasshoppers on the borders of the desert
march a day and a second, a third, a fourth day, a fifth, a sixth day,
Lo, at the sunrise on the seventh, thou arrivest at Udum the Great.

The execution of this command is also described in a consequent passage. But a surprising thing occurs here: the passage which describes the execution of the command expands the framework of the action which had been delineated in the command itself - a modification which constitutes a revolutionary innovation in the history of Ugaritic literature.[24] Lines 192-210 thus read:

km irby tškn šd *kḥsn pat mdbr*
tlkn ym wṯn
aḫr šp[š]m b[ṯ]lṯ
ym[ġy] lqdš a[ṯrt] ṣrm *wlilt ṣd[yn]m*
ṯm yd[r k]rt ṯᶜ
iiṯt aṯrt ṣrm *wilt ṣdnym*
hm ḥry bty iqḥ *ašᶜrb ġlmt ḥẓry*
ṯnh k!spm atn *wṯlṯh ḫrṣm*
ylk ym wṯn ṯlṯ rbᶜ ym
aḫr špšm brbᶜ
ymġy ludm rbt ...

Translation:

Like[25] the locusts that dwell on the steppe,
Like grasshoppers on the border of the desert
They march a day and a second, afterwards at the sunrise on the third,
They come to the shrine of Asherah of Tyre[26], even that of the goddess of Zidon.[26]
There Keret the Shiite[27] *[or: the noble lord]*[27] vows as[28] Asherah of Tyre exists[28], as the goddess of Zidon,
If Hurriya to my house I take, bring the lass into my court,

---

[24] Cf. the omission of ll. 90-91; ll. 116b-118a in the description of the execution.

[25] *km/k*. In the similar text above the parallelism is *k/km*. The order then is interchangeable.

[26] For other interpretations of the names *ṣrm, ṣdynm*, see Gray, *Krt*¹, p. 45 *[*cf. now *Krt*², p. 56*]*.

[27] *ṯᶜ*. Apparently the name of the family to which Keret was related. For the reasons supporting this opinion and other suggestions, see Gray, *Krt*¹, pp. 43-44. *[*But contrast now J.C. Greenfield, *EI* 9 (1969), pp. 60f., who makes a strong case for the translation 'lord, master'.*]*

[28] *i*. The meaning is obscure. I take the word in the adverbial sense 'where', a word employed when addressing the divinity as in the verse: "Where is the Lord, the God of Elijah?" (2 Reg. 2:14). For other translations, see Gordon, *UT, Glossary* No. 1; Driver, *CML*, p. 233 s.v. In any case it is evident that the meaning of the phrase *i iṯt aṯrt* has a force approximate to that of the Biblical oath: *ḥay YHWH*.

Her double[29] I'll give in silver, and her treble[29] in gold.
He marches a day and a second, a third, a fourth day,
afterwards at the sunrise of the fourth, he arrives at Udum the Great ...

The radical change that occurs in this text is most striking. But before proceeding with the discussion of this passage we wish first to point out a surprising particular. The text recounts that the second part of the action continued for four days; we would therefore expect to read that the new event occurred on the fifth day, yet the text states that the new action took place on the fourth day - the same day on which the previous action had terminated. Noticing this difficulty H.L. Ginsberg proposed to amend the text to read 'five' instead of 'four'.[30] But this would imply that Keret reached Udum on the eigth day and not on the seventh as commanded by Il. This consideration would require, therefore, that we retain the present reading which we believe can best be understood when investigating the numerical scheme of this passage as a whole. The author has here attempted to describe a new but secondary occurrence that took place on the third day in addition to the new and major event that occurred on the seventh day. The second part of the formula should have, therefore, been worded as follows: *ylk ym wṯn ṯlṯ ym aḫr špšm brb*^{c}. The fact that the author did not formulate the second part in this manner is however quite understandable. For as we have observed earlier, Ugaritic literary tradition required that the days in which the action takes place be enumerated in groups of two, whereas the formulation dictated by our own logic must, perforce, isolate the third day in which the action continued to take place and leave it without a chronological partner! The author, then, did not entirely succeed in resolving the new problem and enmeshed himself in difficulties that generally confront all innovators. This does not mean that the authors's in-

---

[29] Scholars differ as to whether Keret vowed to pay twice the weight of Hurriya in silver and three times her weight in gold or whether he vowed to pay two-thirds her weight in silver and one-third her weight in gold, cf. Gray, *Krt*[1], p. 44. The latter interpretation may find some support in that the value of gold exceeds that of silver. However, in the light of Canaanite phraseology the first interpretation is preferable, for there is an ascending numerical parallelism in the verse in which the second numeral exceeds the value of the first numeral by one (cf. also *CTA* 4: I:27-29). Cf. now in this volume, *Bordercases of Ugaritic Comparative Studies*, p. 408, note 6.

[30] H.L. Ginsberg, *ANET*, p. 145, note 19.

novation was a *creatio ex nihilo*. Actually it appears to have been confined to the attempt to superimpose a three-day scheme on the original seven-day scheme. Such a scheme is encountered in one of the *Rephaim texts CTA* 21:6-7 which reads: *alk [........] t̲lt̲m amġ̇y lbt*. Driver's[31] proposed restoration appears to be correct and the restored text should thus read: *alk [ym wt̲n b] t̲lt̲m amġ̇y lbt*.'I shall go a day, and a second, on the third I shall proceed to (my) house'. *[*The restoration is objectionable.[31a]*]* We may also cite *CTA* 20:B:5-6 where Driver[32] correctly reads: *tlkn ym wt̲n! aḫr š[pšm bt̲lt̲] mġ̇y rpum lgrnt* 'They went a day and a second afterwards at the s*[*unrise of the third*]* the Rephaim arrived at the threshing floors'. *[*Cf. also 22:24-26 which, is however, almost undecipherable.*]*

The numerical schemes noted above have also left their mark on Biblical literature. A most interesting development of the old epic seven-days scheme appears in the story of the conquest of Jericho (Jos. 6). Unfortunately this narrative has been revised several times and its literary composition is rather complicated. Nevertheless, the basic story may clearly be recognized. According to it seven priests bearing seven trumpets before the ark of the Lord compassed the city together with the warriors on six days once and on the seventh day seven times. At the seventh procession of the seventh day the priests blasted, the warriors shouted and the walls of the city fell flat. This scheme originated from a combination of two simpler schemes: 1) The Israelites went around the city seven days once; 2) they went around it seven times on one day. Instead of the archaic scheme 'one day and a second, a third day and a fourth, a fifth day and a sixth' the text describes the actions of the first and the second days apart and adds that the Israelites acted in this way six days (Jos. 6:12-14). The processions of the seventh day are described even more summarily: "and compassed the city after the same manner seven times" (ibid. 15). *[*The pattern should be rather reconstructed on ground of vv. 11, 14-15, reading in 11a: *wayyāsobbu 'ät hāᶜir (yom 'äḥād?)* The wording: *haqqep paᶜam 'äḥāt wayyābo'u*

---

[31] Driver, *CML*, p. 66.

[[31a] Contrast Herdner, *CTA*, p. 94, note 5 who reads *t̲lt̲t* and leaves the text without restoration, since there is no possibility of restoring the standard formula *(aḫr) špšm bt̲lt̲.]*

[32] Driver, *CML*, p. 68.

hammaḥ^{a}nä wayyālinu bammaḥ^{a}nä (11b) has been summarized in its repetition to read: *pa^{c}am 'ähāt wayyāšubu hammaḥ^{a}nä* (v. 14). The dawning of the seventh day (v. 15) reminds of the sun-rise of this day, mentioned in the later Ugaritic epic.*]* The radically simplified scheme wherein an action is described as continuing for six days and terminating on the seventh day is met with in the narrative of the Sinaitic theophany: "And the glory of the Lord abode upon Mount Sinai, and the cloud covered it six days; and on the seventh day He called unto Moses out of the midst of the cloud" (Ex. 24:16). Instead of 'one day and a second, a third day and a fourth, a fifth day and a sixth' the passage simply states 'six days'.

The archaic character of the Akkadian-Ugaritic scheme which was modified in the Keret epic has here disappeared completely and is replaced by a brief and simple formula.[33]

*[*I do not feel sure any more that this simple scheme should be regarded as a simplified one, i.e. as derived from a more elaborate pattern. It may have been as ancient in prosaic narration as its more elaborate counterpart in Ugaritic and Akkadian poetry, cf. Liverani, *loc. cit.* (note 4a), who quotes the pattern: Six years ... but in the seventh year twice attested in the Inscription of *Idrimi* (ll. 27-30, 43-47). In the Homeric songs the simple pattern is extant even in poetry.*]*

It should be noted that the same type of formulation encountered in Ex. 24:16 recurs three times in the Odyssey alongside an earlier Greek literary scheme previously found in the Iliad which describes an action as continuing for nine days until its termination on the tenth day.[34] An example of a numerical scheme in which an action is described as reaching

---

[33] The cosmogonic account in Genesis 1 is generally cited as a classical example of the seven-day scheme. But this scheme differs fundamentally from the Akkadian-Ugaritic scheme discussed here in that a new event takes place on each of the six days of creation and each day contains a narrative of its own. In the Genesis passage the seven-day plan has been combined with another scheme which treats six different subjects in detail and then proceeds to mention the principal subject in the seventh and last part. For illustrations cf. S.E. Loewenstamm, *The Development of the Exodus Tradition*, Jerusalem 1965, p. 33 (in Heb.).

[34] I am grateful to Mrs. R. Meridor for calling my attention to the study of G. Germain, *Homère et la Mystère des Nombres*, Paris 1954, pp. 13-15. The scheme which describes an action as continuing for six days and terminating on the seventh occurs in Greek literature in Odyssey 10: 80-81;

its climax on the third day occurs in the story of the sacrifice of Isaac: "On the third day Abraham lifted up his eyes, and saw the place afar off". The Midrash *Genesis Rabbah* (51:1) called attention to the typological character of this verse and compared it, *inter alia*, with such verses as Gen. 42:18; Ex. 19:16; Ho. 6:2; Est. 5:1. The composite scheme in which new events occur both on the third and seventh days is encountered in the Biblical laws of purity as, for example, in the verse: "He that toucheth the dead, even any man's dead body shall be unclean seven days; the same shall purify himself therewith on the third day and on the seventh day and he shall be clean ..." (Nu. 19:11-12; cf. also v. 19 and 31:19).

In conclusion, the scheme wherein an action takes place during a period of six consecutive days until a new event takes place on the seventh day had been adopted by the Ugaritic epic from Akkadian epics together with their rigid and archaic quadruple repetitive formulae describing the six-day action. The Ugaritic epic gradually abandoned these formulae until one single description was employed for the entire six-day action. However even in its last stage the Ugaritic epic retained the Akkadian pattern of enumerating the days in pairs. The Ugaritic epos also evolved a shorter scheme in which an action is described as continuing for two days and reaching its climax on the third day. However, even when this scheme was employed, the two days in which the action takes place were enumerated in a pair. We have also met with an attempt to superimpose the latter scheme on the former.

The imprint of this numerical typology is evident in Biblical literature which was familiar with both the seven-day and three-day schemes and the composite scheme in which the third day occupies a significant position alongside the seventh day. But in striking contrast to the Ugaritic epic there is no reminiscence in Biblical literature of pairs of days. Hence the absence of the cumbersome formula 'one day and a second, a third day and a fourth, a fifth day and a sixth'. In short, the rigidity of the older numerical scheme had been entirely abandoned in Biblical literature. [As already pointed out, it remains a moot question whether the simple numerical pattern of Hebrew prosaic narration should be regarded as the simplification of a complicate numerical pattern, formerly used in poetry.

12:397-400; 14: 249-252. This scheme is confined to days only and has no counterpart which includes years, in contrast to the 'nine ... and ten' scheme, which is employed in the Iliad and Odyssey and embraces both days and years.

This following addition has been inspired by the perusal of E. v. Weiher, *Der Babylonische Gott Nergal, AOAT* 11 (1971), pp. 50f., 53f. Afterwards I realised that my results have been anticipated to a large degree by the paper of D. Freedman, quoted in note 2a.

In its Neo-Assyrian version the myth of Nergal and Ereshkigal exhibits two additional examples of the seven-day unit. IV:9'-14' and VI:36-42. See besides the work of v. Weiher, quoted above the edition of O.R. Gurney, *AnSt* 10 (1960), pp. 118f., 126f.; A.K. Grayson, *ANET*³, pp. 510, 512. The first text reads:

in-na-ad!-ru-ma [aḫ̮ḫi^{meš} *ki-lal- la-an]*
a-na ^{giš}*ma-a-li ši[t-mu-riš i-ter-bu--ma]*
ištēn^{en} *ūma šanâ*^{a} *ūma*^{ma} *ṣal-lu-u[-ma šar-rat* ^{d}*Ereš-ki-gal u* ^{d}*Er-ra]*
[šal-ša^{šá} *ūma*^{ma}*] reba*^{a} *ūma*^{ma} *[KI.MIN]*
ḫ̮anša^{šá} *ūma*^{ma} *šešša*$^{\text{-šá}}$ *ūma*^{ma} *[KI.MIN]*
[sebâ^{a}*] ūma*^{ma} *[i-na ka-šá-di-i]*

Grayson translates:

They *[both]* embraced *[one another]*,
Pas*[sionately they got into]* bed
The first day (verbally: one day), the second day,
they lay, *[queen Ereshkigal and Erra]*;
[The third] day, the fourth day
[they lay, queen Ereshkigal and Erra]
[The fifth day], the sixth day,
[they lay, queen Ereshkigal and Erra];
[When the seventh] day *[came]*

The second text reads:

[i]n-na-an-ad-⌈ru-ma⌉ aḫ̮ḫi^{meš} *ki-lal-l[a-a]n*
⌈a-na ma-a-li šit⌉-mu-riš i-ter-b[u] / išten^{en} *ūma*^{ma}
šanâ^{a} *ūma ⌈ṣal-lu-ma šar⌉*^{ra}*-rat ⌈*^{d}*Ereš-⌉[ki-gal u* ^{d}*E]r-ra*
šalša^{šá} *ūma*^{ma} *KI.MIN*
rebâ$^{\text{a!}}$ *ūma*^{ma} *KI.MIN*
ḫ̮an-šá ūma[^{ma}*]* *KI.MIN*
[sebâ^{a} *ūma*[35] *ina] ka-šá-di-i*

---

[35] Gurney completes: *[VII*^{u} *ūmu*^{mu}*]*. Likewise v. Weiher: *[sebû*^{ú} *u*$_4$*-mu]*. But the parallel text reads: *[sebâ*^{a}*] ūma*^{ma}. Cf. *Gilg.* XI:145: *sebâ*^{a} *ūma*^{ma}*].)*

They both embraced one another
Passionately they got into bed
The first day (verbally one day), the second day they
lay, queen Eresh[kigal and E]rra
The third day they lay, queen Ereshkigal and Erra
The fourth day they lay, queen Ereshkigal and Erra
[The sixth day] they lay, queen Ereshkigal and Erra
[When the seventh day] came

In both texts quoted the pattern apparently concludes with the formula *sebā ūma ina kašādi* which is identical word for word with *Gilg*. XI:145. However, in contradistinction to *Gilg*. XI:145 the introduction describes the preparation of the action which is about to take place, not the action itself. Cf. *CTA* 4:VI:22-33, discussed above, where, however, both formulae differ in a single differentiating word only. More astonishing is the decay of the basic pattern in the second text where the usual counting of days in pairs is restricted to the first two days, whereas the following four days are counted separately.

The Akkadian origins of the Seven-Day-Unit have been strongly contested by Freedman, *loc. cit.* (note 2a), pp. 79-80 who pleads for "the choice of Ugaritic as the source for the Akkadian passage where the counting is done in pairs". It is true that the Akkadian attestations stem from Neo-Assyrian versions of Old-Babylonian texts and may possibly be the creations of Neo-Assyrian poets. It should also be taken into account that the Akkadian attestations of the pattern are very scanty. On the other hand, however, it is rather hard to tell by which channels Ugaritic poetry possibly might have influenced Neo-Assyrian literature. Nothing entitles us to suppose that Neo-Assyrian scribes studied the literature of long ago destroyed Ugarit and the numerous excavations in Mesopotamia have failed so far to yield even one single Ugaritic tablet, whereas a lot of Akkadian tablets have turned up at Ugarit. Should we hypothesize that there existed an oral Old-Aramaic literature, akin to Ugaritic texts and that it was this literature which left its mark upon Neo-Assyrian texts?

As variants of the Seven-Day sequence Freedman mentions Days-Months-Years-Seven Years. On both patterns he remarks ibidem: "In these passages the poet is so eager to get to a new action that he does not want to be bogged down in the normal counting formula". In Ugaritic poetry, however, day-formulae and year-formulae are foundamentally different. The Day-Unit invariably enumerates each of (seven or three) days, whereas the Year-Unit (*CTA* 6:V:7-9; 17:IV:175-177), avoids this monotonous enumeration and proceeds in a variegated progress from days to months, from months to years, from years to the seventh year. This fascinating pattern, attested in the ancient Baal- and Aqhat epics, obviously exists in its own right. There is no point in degrading it to an abridged form of a purely hypothetical formula, supposed to have read: a year, a second, etc. Its abbreviated form in Keret simply reads: *mk bšb^c šnt* (*CTA* 15:III:22). Nowhere in Ugaritic epic a Seven-Day Unit has been reduced to the short wording: *mk bšb^c ymm.]*

Notes on the History of Biblical Phraseology

A

Since the discovery of the Ugaritic texts Bible scholars have dealt with the development of Biblical phraseology from ancient Canaanite phraseology and the recognition that those pairs of roots which are typical to Biblical style were adopted from the Canaanite literary tradition has become more and more established.[1]

In this article we will attempt to expand this study somewhat by not limiting our discussion to just the connection between Biblical and Ugaritic phraseology but will include in our discussion both the Phoenician and Akkadian literary traditions, even though it is *a priori* clear that from their very nature such comparisons are not likely to give as many results as a comparison with Ugaritic. Phoenician literary remains are few and do not include poetry, whereas Akkadian, while possessing a rich literature, is not close to Hebrew in either vocabulary or means of expression. On the other hand, it seems probable that a thorough search of Phoenician literature may turn up at least something of Canaanite phraseology. We may further accept as working hypothesis that Akkadian literature influenced Canaanite literature to some extent in the Pre-Israelite period when Akkadian was the scribal tongue, and that some traces of this influence are still recognizable in the Bible. We begin with a phrase which is common to the Bible and Phoenician.

---

[1] See: U. Cassuto, *Tarbiz* 14 (1943), pp. 1-10 [= *BOSt* 2, pp. 43-56]; id., *Lĕšonénu* 15 (1947), pp. 97-102 [= *BOSt* 2, pp. 60-68]; M. Held, *Lĕšonénu* 18 (1952), pp. 144-160; and cf. also in this volume, *Review of Cyrus H. Gordon, UM*, Rome 1955, pp. 30-38; *Review of Ch. Virolleaud, PRU II*, Paris 1957, p. 88; cf. also R.G. Boling, *JSS* 5 (1960), pp. 221-225.

B

A glance at the Bible shows that Hebrew commonly juxtaposes the roots *yšr* 'to be upright' and *ṣdq* 'to be just' whether in parallel or not. This applies first and foremost to the adjectives *ṣaddiq* 'just' and *yāšār* 'smooth, straight, upright', e.g.: "just (*ṣaddiq*) and right (*yāšār*) is He." (Deut. 32:4); "Just (*ṣaddiq*) art Thou, O Lord, // and right (*yāšār*) are Thy judgements" (Ps. 119:137); "The wicked is a ransom for the just (*ṣaddiq*), // and the faithless for the upright (*yᵉšārim*)" (Pr. 21:18); "Light dawns for the just (*ṣaddiq*), // and joy for the upright in heart (*yišre leb*)" (Ps. 97:11). We find the order of the two adjectives reversed, e.g.: "For the ways of the Lord are right (*yᵉšārim*), and the just (*ṣaddiqim*) walk in them" (Ho. 14:10); "Thou dost make smooth (*yāšār*) the path of the righteous (*ṣaddiq*)" (Is. 26:7). The same connection is found between the nouns *ṣädäq, ṣᵉdāqā* 'righteousness' and the adjective *yāšār* 'upright', e.g.: "For justice will return to righteousness (*ṣädäq*), i.e., the righteous // and all the upright in heart (*yišre leb*) will follow it" (Ps. 94:15); "and Thy righteousness (*ṣidqātᵉkā*) to the upright of heart (*yišre leb*)" (*ibid.* 36:11); "the righteousness of the upright" (*ṣidqat yᵉšārim*)" (Pr. 11:6). In a looser connection: "If you are pure and upright (*yāšār*), surely then He will protect you and bestow welfare upon the habitation of your righteousness (*nᵉwat ṣidqäkā*)"[1a] (Job 8:6). A similar kind of loose connection exists between the adjective *ṣaddiq* and nouns from the root *yšr*, e.g.: "To punish a righteous man (*ṣaddiq*) is not good, // to flog noble men because of righteousness (*yošär*)"[2] (Pr. 17:26); "The way of the righteous (*ṣaddiq*) is smoothness (*mešārim*)" (Is. 26:7). In addition, nouns derived from these two roots may also be a pair of words, e.g.: "Who walks in justice (*ṣᵉdāqot*) // and speaks uprightness (*mešārim*)" (Is. 33:15); "I the Lord speak justice (*ṣädäq*), // I declare uprightness (*mešārim*)" (ibid. 45:19); "And he shall judge the poor with justice (*bᵉṣädäq*), // and decide with uprightness (*bᵉmišor*) for the meek of the earth" (ibid. 11:4); In one instance the verb *yšr* is connected with the noun

---

*[*1a Alternatively: the wife of your rightenousness. Cf. Jer. 6:2; Ps. 68:13; *CTA* 14:12-13. On the precise meaning of *ṣädäq* in this context see note 3.*]*

2 Many scholars are of the opinion that the text should be emended to *ytr* instead of *yšr*. But this suggestion ignores the typical character of the combination of the roots *ṣdq* and *yšr* in the Bible.

ṣ^{e}dāqā: "The justice (ṣidqat) of the blameless keeps his way straight (t^{e}yaššer)" (Pr. 11:5).

The large number of Biblical phrases with the roots ṣdq and yšr is a clear sign that their stylistic affinity has its roots in an ancient tradition. Thus we are not surprised to read in the Krt epic: *at̲t ṣdqh ypq mtrḫ̮t yšrh* (*CTA* 14:12-13). 'The wife of his righteousness he found[2a], the spouse of his uprightness', i.e. he found a wife worthy to his noble character.[3]

[[2a] M. Dietrich - O. Loretz, *AOAT* 18 (1973), pp. 32, 34 derive *yšrh* from a verb *šrh 'vertreiben'* // *ypq* causative *Hiph^{c}il* of *npq 'hinausgehen'*. Contrast, however, O. Loretz - W. Mayer, *UF* 6, pp. 493f. who derive *ypq* from the root *ypq* 'erwerben'.]

[3] [Contrast Ginsberg, *Keret*, p. 14 who translates 'his lawful wife did he find, his legitimate spouse'. Similarly Gray, *Krt*², p. 14.

It is worthwhile dwelling upon the history of the exegesis which ascribes to the amply attested roots ṣdq and yšr in a few sources a secondary meaning 'legitimate' which is highly problematic.

The point of departure is the Phoenician stele of *ytnb^{c}l* from the 3rd century BCE (*KAI* 43). *Ytnb^{c}l* records that he instituted a service of sacrifice to Melqart "for my life and my descendants day by day and *lṣmḥ ṣdq* (l. 11). It is reasonable to admit that the term *ṣmḥ ṣdq* designates the crown-prince. Scholars derived this sense from a supposed basic meaning 'legitimate descendant'. This explanation was transferred to the *ṣämaḥ ṣ^{e}dāqā* or *ṣämaḥ ṣaddiq* of Jer. 23:5; 33:15. From here it was a small step to interpret *yšr* in the same way. In the inscription of *yḥmlk*, king of Byblos this ruler asks the gods to grant him long life *kmlk ṣdq wmlk yšr lpn 'l gbl [h']* (*KAI* 4:3-7), according to many scholars: 'because he is a lawful king and a legitimate king before the gods of Byblos'. Cf. the literature quoted by Gray, *Krt*², p. 31 and by Jean-Hoftijzer, *DISO* s.v. ṣdq III.

But all these explanations of the roots *ṣdq* and *yšr* are farfetched. The oriental king is glorified because of his justice, not because of his being legitimate. Cf. e.g. the introduction of *Codex Hammurapi*, which concludes with the words: "When Marduk commanded me to give justice to the land and to let (them) have (good) governance, I set forth *ki-it-tam u mi-ša-ra-am* throughout the land". *kittum u mīšarum* are the exact equivalents of Hebrew *ṣädäq umišor* (or *mešārim*). The same ideal of the king is attested in 2 Sam. 8:15, Ps. 45:7-8; 72:1. On this background it is perfectly clear, why *Yhmlk* stresses his justice when invoking the gods for long life. Cf. the Proverb: "And justice (ṣ^{e}dāqā) saves from death" (Pr. 10:2; 11:4).

We may easily understand that the future king too was expected to live up to this moral standard. (Is. 11:4-5; 32:1; Ps. 72:1). It is for this reason that he was exalted by the scribes of the court as *ṣmḥ ṣdq*. This simple exegesis is supported by the wording of Jer. 23:5; 33:15 since the *ṣämaḥ ṣ^{e}dāqā* is said to do justice and righteousness (*mišpāṭ uṣ^{e}dāqā*). The plain sense of these verses should not been distorted by the over-sophisticated hypothesis, that they play upon a double meaning of the

This is not an isolated example. We may add interesting evidence from Phoenician mythology as transmitted to us in Greek by *Philo of Byblos* from a euhemeristic approach which turns the gods and demigods into mortals. Among other things his description includes a list of the first inventors who - according to Phoenician mythology - laid the foundations of human culture. He writes in this list: ἀπὸ τούτων γενέσθαι Μισωρ καὶ Συδυκ τουτέστιν εὔλυτον καὶ δίκαιον οὗτοι τὴν τῆς ἁλὸς χρῆσιν εὗρον.[4] 'From them were borne *Mišor* and *Ṣidiq*, that is to say, easy to untie and righteous. They discovered the use of salt'. Philo thus explained Ζυδυκ to mean *ṣaddiq*, and he apparently derived the name Μισωρ from the Aramaic root *šr'* 'to untie'.

For a long time scholars have seen that this explanation does not hold water. Over a hundred years ago H. Ewald[5] gave the correct interpretation of the two nouns by explaining Μισωρ καὶ Συδυκ as *mišor* and *ṣädäq*. But for some reason this suggestion has not met with general approval. Ed. Meyer[6] put forth the far-fetched theory that Μισωρ was considered to be the mythological father of Egypt. There is no reason to deal with this strange opinion after W. Baudissin[7] has already refuted it. The last scholar to deal with the question was O. Eissfeldt.[8] Eissfeldt explained the two names *mišor* and *ṣaddiq*. But the proper noun *mišor* which is a sort of a hypostasis of justice can only be paralleled by the abstract noun *ṣädäq*. From a linguistic point of view it is easy to explain the development of Phoenician **ṣidq* into *ṣidiq* - [by way of *anaptyxis*].[8a] This reasoning is supported by the clear-cut resemblance between the pair Μισωρ καὶ Συδυκ and the names of a pair

---

root *ṣdq*.

The passage of Krt under discussion should be interpreted accordingly, since the Ugaritic ideals are not different from oriental standard concepts. The epos of Krt expresses in clear words the idea that the practice of justice is the only justification of a king's rule. (*CTA* 16:VI:25-54). It never underlines the importance of his legitimate extraction.]

4 Eusebius, *PrEv* I:10:13.

5 H. Ewald, *Abhandlungen der königlichen Gesellschaft der Wissenschaften in Göttingen*, 5 (1853), p. 21.

6 Ed. Meyer, *Geschichte des Altertums*, II, 2, Stuttgart 1931, pp. 162.

7 W. Baudissin, *Kyrios* 3, Gießen 1929, p. 413.

8 O. Eissfeldt, *Taautos und Sanchunjaton*, Berlin 1952, pp. 7, 19f., 40, 58.

[8a But cf. also Friedrich - Röllig, *PPG*, p. 34 on *y* in the transcriptions of Phoenician words.]

of Akkadian gods *kittu u mēšaru* 'righteousness and uprightness', servants of the sun god Šamaš who is considered the god of justice.[9] A final confirmation of this opinion is found in Is. 11:4 quoted above: "He shall judge the poor with righteousness (*b^eṣädäq*) and decide with uprightness (*b^emišor*) for the meek of the earth". It is clear that *ṣädäq* and *mišor* here are those traits which in Phoenician mythology were anthropomorphized and became a pair of demigods. We have thus noted the Phoenician background of Isaiah's phrase which employs the Phoenician form *mišor* synonymous with *mešārim*.[9a]

C

We now come to the question of the parallels of Biblical and Akkadian phrases. First of all, we will mention here a problem which scholars have already dealt with from certain aspects, namely the problem of the parallelism between *leb* and *kābed*. It is true that this parallelism is not actually found in the Massoretic text of the Bible. For a long time however the theory - accepted by most scholars - has been put forward that we should read *kābed* 'liver' for *kābod* 'honour' in several Biblical passages. This is based on the fact that in the Semitic languages the liver is the seat of human emotions.[10] The late U. Cassuto approached the problem from another and more limited point of view in dealing with the following passage from the ᶜnt epic: *tġdd kbdh bṣ̈hq // ymlu lbh bšmḫt* (*CTA* 3:II:25-26) 'Her liver enlarges from laughter // her heart is filled with joy'.[11] Cassuto compared this phrase with Ps. 16:9: "Therefore my heart is glad // and my *kbwd* rejoices." He noted: "Perhaps we should read *k^ebedi*."[12] This note raises a problem which should be investigated in a wider framework. First of all, it should be pointed out that the Ugaritic texts present further evidence for

---

9 See: A. Deimel, *Pantheon Babylonicum*, Romae 1914, No. 1750, 2234.

[9a To the question of Misor and Sydyk cf. M. Liverani, *Studi in Onore di E. Volterra* 6 (1969), pp. 55-74 and in this volume, *Philo of Byblus*, p. 394. On the Ugaritic pair of Gods *ṣdq mšr* see J. de Moor, *UF* 2, p. 228, note 70.]

10 For a detailed bibliography, see: *GB, s.v. kbwd*, 6; add to it: G.R. Driver, *JRAS* 1948, p. 175.

11 Cassuto, *Anath*, p. 119. For the etymology of the Ugaritic verb *ġdd* Arabic *ġdd* 'to be swollen', cf. the Akkadian verb *eleṣu* 'to rejoice' which has the original meaning of 'to be swollen'; and cf. *CAD, s.v.*

12 Id., *ibid.*, p. 120.

the parallelism "heart" // "liver": *il yṣḥq bm lb // wygmḏ bm kbd* (*CTA* 12: I:12-13). 'Il laughs in the heart // and rejoices (?)[13] in the liver'; *tbky pǵt bm lb // tdm^c bm kbd* (*CTA* 19:I:34-35). 'Pǵt weeps in the heart // she sheds tears in the liver'. We should also note an additional Biblical verse: "My heart is steadfast, O God, my heart is steadfast! I will sing and make melody! Awake my *kbwd* etc." (Ps. 57:8-9; cf. 108:2). Even though we do not have here an actual parallel "heart" // "liver", nevertheless it appears that the mention of "heart" attracts after it the word *kbwd*.

This evaluation of the data is doubtful as long as we limit our discussion just to a comparison between the Bible and the Ugaritic texts. One may argue - and perhaps justifiably so - that we should reverse our reasoning: Ugaritic *kbd* should be explained as *kābod* on the basis of the vocalized form in the Bible. This argument falls apart as soon as we look at the unequivocal Akkadian evidence where the juxtaposition of the nouns *libbu* 'heart' and *kabittu* 'liver' is very common. We will limit ourselves here to a few examples: *kī namrat kabtatka u ḫadû libbuk*[14] 'How your liver lights up and your heart is satisfied'; *libbaka linuḫšu kabattaka lip[šahšu]*[15] 'your heart will rest, your liver will be soothed'; *ēliṣ libbašu kabattuš immir*[16] 'his heart rejoiced, his liver shone'. To express anger: *libbi īgugma iṣṣaruḥ kabitti*[17] 'my heart was angry, my liver was furious'. These examples - which could easily be multiplied - clearly prove that the scholars who took Ugaritic *kbd* in parallelism with *lb* to mean 'liver' were right. This in turn is proof for the fact that we should read *kābed* for *kābod* in the Biblical verses dealt with above.

[It is also worth noting that the Vulgate reads in Ho. 13:8 '*interiora jecoris eorum*', i.e. *s^egor k^ebedām* instead of Masoretic *s^egor libbām*. As has been demonstrated by B. Kedar - Kopfstein, *JQR* 65 (1974), pp. 96-97, this

---

[13] The meaning of the verb *gmḏ* is unclear, and I have translated it according to the parallelism. Driver, *CML*, p. 146, translates 'doubled oneself', on the basis of *gms* 'to bend over' in Aramaic and *gmṣ* 'to be crooked' in Ethiopic. But this explanation of *gmḏ* does not fit the context, and it is quite doubtful if we can assume a phonetic shift of Ugaritic ḏ to Aramaic š. Cf. Gordon, *UT* 5.3; E.A. Speiser, *BASOR* 121 (1951), pp. 17-21.

[14] *KAR* 168:I:12, Irra.

[15] S.H. Langdon, *Babylonian Penitential Psalms*, Paris 1927, p. 19, l. 17.

[16] R. Borger, *Esarhaddon*, Graz (1956), p. 6, VII:20.

[17] H. Rawlinson, *The Cuneiform Inscriptions of Western Asia*, 3, 1886, 15, II:13.

version cannot be considered as a free rendering of the *MT*, but rather points to a variant reading in the *Vorlage* of the Vulgate. Compare also M. Dahood, *RSP* 1, pp. 245-246 with bibliography.*]*

D

We may utilize an Akkadian phrase to help clarify to some extent the difficult Biblical verse *mi mānā ᶜapar yaᶜaqob umispār 'ät robaᶜ yiśrā'el* (Nu. 23:10). However, we must first deal with the problems involved in explaining this verse. We begin with the word *mispār*. Scholars have made two attempts to explain this difficult reading. In the last century Ewald[18] tried to understand *mispār* as an accusative of definition, namely: "*etwas zählen nach der Zahl d.i. genau*". This forced explanation which occupied scholars in the last century has long been forgotten. Recently Kutscher[19] has proposed to interpret *mispār* as an infinitive of the *Qal* formed like the Aramaic infinitive of the *G*-stem and employed - as in Biblical Aramaic - to continue the action of a finite verb. Consequently he argues that *mi* has a double force, referring both to the verb *mānā* and the verb *mispār*. In his opinion this linguistic usage comes to characterize Balaam as an Aramean. For the same reason the word *robaᶜ*, which in his opinion is also Aramaic, is used. Concerning the word *robaᶜ* Chief Rabbi Hertz[20] has similarly noted that the use of this Aramaic word in the speech of Balaam the Aramean is natural. Kutscher thus comes to the conclusion that this verse is a mixture of Hebrew and Aramaic, unlike the rest of Balaam's oracles which are composed in pure Hebrew. This assumption is difficult, even more so since the Aramaic character of *robaᶜ* is unclear[21], and we must therefore prefer the widely - held opinion that the text should be read *umi sāfār* 'and who did count'. Support for this is usually brought from the Septuagint καὶ τίς ἐξαριθμήσεται and from some manuscripts of the Samaritan Pentateuch which read *wmy spr*. We may add to this the Samaritan Targum: *wmn mtny* 'and who relates'.[22]

[18] H. Ewald, *Syntax*, p. 283a, apud G.B. Gray, *Numbers, ICC*, 1912, p. 348.

[19] E.Y. Kutscher, *Lĕšonēnu*, 21 (1957), pp. 254-255.

[20] J.H. Hertz, *ET* 45 (1933-34), p. 534.

[21] See infra, note 30.

[22] Z. Ben-Hayyim, *The Literary and Oral Tradition of Hebrew and Aramaic amongst the Samaritans* 2, Jerusalem 1957, p. 538.

This emendation requires close study. Albright[23] has argued that ancient Hebrew orthography did not employ *matres lectionis* at all. This means that in the ancient orthography *my spr* was written *mspr*. When later on *plene* orthography was introduced, this ancient form was misinterpreted as *mispār*. But this theory is forced. It is true that there are many interchanges of defective and *plene* spellings in the Bible, but nowhere do we find *mi* spelled defectively. The consistency of the spelling *my* proves its antiquity. Moreover, as we learn from the *El-Amarna* letters the pronoun "who" was pronounced *mija* in ancient Canaanite. *My* is spelled *plene* even in the defective orthography of the Ugaritic epics.[24] It follows that we cannot rely on the assumption that *my* was spelled defectively in ancient Hebrew.

The real solution to the problem was discovered by J.N. Epstein.[25] Epstein showed that in Tannaitic texts *mi* is occasionally written procliticly in both *plene* and defective spelling. Epstein also noted that in manuscripts of the Samaritan Pentateuch three readings are found in the verse under discussion: 1) *wmy spr*; 2) *wmyspr*; 3) *wmspr*. We thus find here one alongside the other the three spellings of the word *mi* known from Rabbinic literature. It seems then that the three spellings point to the same meaning and this is corroborated by the Samaritan Targum. We may suppose that the first copyist of the Massoretic text who absentmindedly wrote *wmspr* instead of *wmy spr* intended it to be read *umisāpar*. However, it is clear that this opened the way for a misunderstanding of the text as the Vulgate testifies: *et nosse numerum stirpis Israel* 'and to know the number of the race of Israel'.

After this orthographic investigation we return for a moment to our main subject, namely the study of the traditional pairs of words. Scholars have for a long time compared the parallelism between the verbs *mnh* and *spr* in our verse to a phrase in the Book of Kings containing the same words: *'ašär lo' yimmānä w^e^lo' yissāper merob* 'that cannot be numbered or counted for multitude' (1 Reg. 3:8, and cf. 8:5). We may now add that the two roots

[23] W.P. Albright, *JBL* 63 (1944), p. 213.

[24] E.Y. Kutscher, *The Language and Linguistic Background of the Isaiah Scroll*, Jerusalem 1959, p. 136 (in Heb.); and in this volume, *Notes on the Pronouns in Ugaritic in the Light of Canaanite*, pp. 56-58.

[25] J.N. Epstein, *Mavo le-Nosah ha-Mišna*, Jerusalem 1948, p. 1218.

spr and *mnh* are already employed together in the Ugaritic texts: *hn bpy sprhn // bšpty mnthn* (*CTA* 24:45-47). 'Lo in my mouth is their number // On my lips, their counting'.

We now turn to the explanation of the parallel terms *ᶜāpār* and *robaᶜ*. *ᶜāpār* does not pose any real problem since this is a known symbol of a multitude which cannot be counted (Gen. 13:16; and cf. 28:14). We should not accept Guillaume's suggestion[26] who compares this noun with Arabic *ᶜfr* 'hero' and who in addition finds an allusion to it in Gen. 13:16. His proposal implies that the noun *ᶜāpār* is a figure of speech like what is called in Arabic *tawriya*. But there is no reason to attribute a second meaning for which there is no proof in the Northwest Semitic languages to an amply attested and well understood Hebrew word. Moreover, we cannot be sure that Gen. 13:16 is earlier than Nu. 23:10. In any event, Balaam's oracles belong to ancient Hebrew poetry and we should not look for learned allusions to other verses as was the case in later style.

The words *'ät robaᶜ* are difficult even if the difficulty in the reading *'ät* was felt only in recent years (see *infra*). TO took *robaᶜ* as a numeral and translated it 'one of the four camps of Israel'. Similar translations are given in TY and the Pešiṭta. Thus they found in this verse the idea that the number of Israelites was so great that it was impossible to count even a fourth of them. This exegesis was still accepted by Gesenius.[27] According to this explanation we should derive *robaᶜ* from the Proto-Semitic root *rbᶜ*. However, Rashi explains: "Their copulations (*rᵉbiᶜotehäm*) the seed which results from their sexual relationships". Already Saadia Gaon apparently referred to the same derivation in his translation of *robaᶜ* as *d̲urriyya* 'seed'. According to this explanation *robaᶜ* is derived from the Proto-Semitic root *rbḍ*. But Proto-Semitic *ḍ* parallels Hebrew *ṣ* - not ᶜ - and ancient Aramaic *q* which became ᶜ only in the 5th cent. BCE. All scholars are in agreement that Balaam's oracles cannot be assigned to such a late date. In the nineteenth century the feeling became strong among scholars that the ancient explanations did not settle the problem of the verse and therefore

---

[26] A. Guillaume, *VT* 12 (1962), pp. 335-337.

[27] Gesenius, *Thesaurus*, s.v. *rbᶜ*.

the emendation *ribbot*[28] was proposed which was replaced later on by the conjecture *r*^{e}*bābot* 'myriads'.

Twentieth century exegesis was begun by F. Delitzsch[29] who compared *roba*^{c} with Akkadian *turbu'u* which he wrongly translated as *'Getümmel'*. In the meantime it has become clear that this word means 'a dust cloud'. After him B. Jacob[30] noted that the Samaritan Targum to Gen. 18:27 translates ^{c}*āpār by rbw*^{c}, and pointed out that in Christian-Palestinian Aramaic *rbwḥ* is often used to translate ^{c}*āpār*. He also established that in this language ^{c} often became *ḥ*. H.L. Ginsberg[31] clarified the root of all these words by comparing them with the rare Arabic word *rbġ*[32] 'dust', which occurs also in the metathesized forms *ġbār*[33], *ġbrt*, and *ġbr*. All these studies therefore showed that *roba*^{c} should be derived here from the root *rbġ* and not from the roots *rb*^{c} or *rbḍ*. This seemed to mark the end of the study of this problem. But W.F. Albright[34] raised additional questions. First of all he pointed out the difficulty of the use of the word *'ät* which does not fit the ancient poetical style. Albright also stressed that most manuscripts of the Samaritan Pentateuch read *mrb*^{c}*t* instead of *'t rb*^{c}, and he argued that the correct form of the Akkadian noun was not *turbu'u* but *turbu'tu*.[35] On the basis of all these considerations he suggested reading here *trb*^{c}*t* instead of *'t rb*^{c}.

---

[28] I have found this emendation in A. Knobel, *Numeri, Deuteronomium and Josua*, Leipzig 1861, p. 139. However, I do not know if he was the first to suggest it.

[29] Friedrich Delitzsch, *Assyrische Lesestücke*, Leipzig 1900, p. 184.

[30] B. Jacob, *ZAW* 22 (1902), p. 111. This word has not been found in any other Aramaic dialect and was perhaps borrowed into Christian-Palestinian Aramaic from Hebrew; cf. note 35.

[31] H.L. Ginsberg, *ZAW* 51 (1933), pp. 308f.

[32] On this word, see also: D.W. Thomas, *ET* 46 (1934-35), p. 285.

[33] On this word see also B. Landsberger, *Die Fauna des alten Mesopotamien*, Leipzig 1934, p. 123.

[34] Albright, *loc. cit.* (note 23).

[35] Albright suggested considering *turbu'tu* as an Aramaic loanword whose original form was *tarbu'tu*. In the meantime the Old Babylonian form *tarbu'um* has turned up, and an Old Babylonian word cannot be considered an Aramaic borrowing at all.

Since Albright wrote his article, the Akkadian lexicographer W. von Soden[36] has studied the forms of the Akkadian word and surveyed all its variants with the following result. The Old Babylonian form is *tarbu'um*, whereas in late texts the forms *turbu'u, turubû, turubu,* and *turbu'tu* interchange. A further clue for the explanation of *'ät roba*^{c} has been provided in the meantime by the Bar Kosba letters[37] which show that *'ät* in late Hebrew could be written proclitically without *'*. In the light of these data we will attempt to formulate our conclusions. Albright's claim that the use of *'ät* in the pure ancient poetical language is suspicious seems plausible. The absence of the word *'ät* in the Samaritan Pentateuch strengthens this suspicion and makes way for the assumption that the words *'t rb*^{c} developed from the reading *trb*^{c}. This implies that the copyist interpreted the difficult word *trb*^{c} as a popular writing for the simpler words *'t rb*^{c}. But even if we concur with this assumption we should not emend the text to read *trb*^{c}*t*. We have seen that in Akkadian the *t* is missing at the end of the word in most of the forms. No proof for original *trb*^{c}*t* can be adduced from the form *mrb*^{c}*t* in the Samaritan Pentateuch. Not only do some manuscripts of the Samaritan Pentateuch read *mrb*^{c}, but there is no reason to agree with the attempt to explain the Massoretic and Samaritan readings as deriving from one and the same original reading. It appears that in ancient Hebrew various noun patterns interchanged freely, and that at the root of the Massoretic reading is the noun pattern *tqtl*, while the Samaritan Pentateuch reflects the noun pattern *mqtl(t)*.[38]

We have treated at length the interpretation of this verse whose exegetical history forms an instructive and fascinating chapter in the history of Biblical textual study. We have, however, not summarized the material for its own sake, but in order to illustrate the prehistory of word-pairs in Biblical Hebrew. We have already pointed out above the traditional cha-

---

[36] W. von Soden, *Orientalia* 23 (1954), pp. 343ff.

[37] J.T. Milik, *RB* 60 (1953), p. 277. There we find: *m*^{c}*yd 'ny* ^{c}*ly tšmym* 'I invoke upon myself heaven (= *'t šmym*)' and likewise *š'ny ntn tkblym brglkm* 'That I will place shackles (= *'t kblym*) on your legs'. According to Milik there are additional examples of this spelling, known also from Punic, in another letter. The same spelling is found in mistakes in the spelling of Israeli school children.

[38] Cf. on the one hand: *maḥ*^{a}*lā, moṣā', miqwā, marbit*, and on the other: *taḥ*^{a}*luim toṣā'ot, tiqwā, tarbit.*

racter of the combination of the roots *mnh* and *spr*. We may add to this a surprising example of the stylistic affinity of the roots ^{c}*pr* and *rb*^{c} from an Old Babylonian literary text, viz. an incantation to the female demon Lamaštum which reads: *ep-ra-am pī-ki ta-ar-bu- 'a*^{4} *-am pa-ni-ki saḫlâ da-qa-tim ù-ba-lu i-ni-ki*[39] 'may one dry up your eyes with the dust of your mouth, (with) the dust of your face, (with) pounded mustard'. The magic purpose of this formula escapes us. But anyhow its wording clearly attests to the affinity between the roots ^{c}*pr* and *rbġ* which parallel each other in a document antedating Hebrew literature by centuries.[40]

Rabin[41] connects ^{c}*āpār* with Arabic *ġafīr* 'great, large' and *roba*^{c} with Arabic *rbġ* 'a multitude'. We agree with Rabin that the meaning of the words ^{c}*āpār* and *roba*^{c} are 'multitude', but there is no reason to separate ^{c}*āpār* from the Proto-Semitic root *^{c}*pr* and to assume here a *hapax legomenon* derived from the Proto-Semitic root **ġpr*. ^{c}*āpār* 'earth' is a usual symbol of a multitude of people. The same applies to *roba*^{c}, from the Proto-Semitic root *rbġ* meaning 'dust' and having the secondary meaning 'multitude'.

---

39 v. Soden, *op. cit.* (n. 36), p. 338f.

40 Guillaume's proposal (see note 26) to take *roba*^{c} on the basis of Arabic *rb*^{c} 'camp, people of the camp' as a term for 'people' is connected with his second proposal to take ^{c}*āpār* out of its regular meaning and translate it 'warriors', since 'people' is not a fitting parallelism to 'heros'.

41 Ch. Rabin, *Tarbiz* 23 (1964), p. 114; Rabin's study reached me after this article had gone to press, and I have added this remark in proof. During the final proofs I received Dahood's article (M. Dahood, *Mélanges Tisserant*, 1964, p. 99). Dahood reads ^{c}*opär* instead of ^{c}*āpār* and translates 'the stags/warriors'.

On New Texts in Ugaritic

In 1962, Virolleaud[1] described the contents of some new Ugaritic texts which were discovered in the course of excavation of recent years. In his description he included some citations in the original. I intend to deal with some of them in this article, especially with those having a bearing on the study of Biblical Hebrew.

1. In a text concerning an incantation against snakes, the sun goddess says to her daughter: *ytt nḥšm mhrk bn bṯn itnnk.*[1a] Virolleaud rightly translates: '*je te donne les serpents pour ta dot, les fils du reptile pour ton cadeau*'.

The words *nḥš*[2] and *itnn* are found here for the first time outside of Hebrew.

The Ugaritic noun *nḥš* is written with the pharyngal *ḥ*. In the same Ugaritic text we find the words *mlḫš*[2a] 'snake charmer'[2b] written with the palatal *ḫ*. This invalidates Lagarde's theory[3] which connected the Hebrew roots *lḥš* and *nḥš*. For the parallelism between *nḥšm* and *bn bṯn*, cf. the parallelism between *nḥš* and *ptn* in Ps. 58:5. The parallel between *nḥšm* in the first hemistich and *bn bṯn* in the second fits Ugaritic poetic style; cf. *ilm* ('gods') // *bn qdš* ('sons of holiness', *CTA* 17:I:3-4, 8-9, 13-14); *ilm* // *bn aṯrt*

---

[1] Ch. Virolleaud, *CRAIBL* 1962, pp. 105-113 [now published in *U* 5].

[[1a] *U* 5, text 7:75-76, pp. 568, 572.]

[2] The only known parallel to Hebrew *nāḥāš* is Arabic *ḥanaš* with metathesis and irregular phonetic correspondence of Hebrew *š*.

[[2a] *U* 5, text 7:5 et passim, pp. 565, 567.]

[[2b] Ps. 58:6. Cf. also Jer. 8:17; Ecc. 10:11. Contrast E. Lipînski (*U* 6, pp. 169, 172) who interprets 'hissing (serpent)' and resorts to Midrash *Tanḥuma*, section *wā'erā'* IV.]

[3] P. de Lagarde, *Übersicht über die im Aramäischen, Arabischen und Hebräischen übliche Bildung der Nomina*, Göttingen 1889, p. 188.

('sons of Asherah', *CTA* 8:3-5); *aḫym* ('my brothers' or 'brothers') // *bnm umy* 'sons of my mother', *CTA* 7:VI:10-11). Similarly in the Bible: "Your brothers"// "the sons of your mother" (Gen. 27:29); "his foal" (*ᶜiro*) // "his ass's colt" (*bᵉni 'ᵃtono, ibid.* 49:11). Cf. also Nu. 23:18, 19.

The Ugaritic noun *itnn* sheds new light on the etymology of the Hebrew noun *'ätnān*. We may conclude from Ugaritic that this noun is not to be derived from the root *ntn*, which does not exist in Ugaritic, but from the Ugaritic - Phoenician root *ytn*. Therefore the form *itnn* is another form of *ytnn*; cf. *yḥd* and *'ḥd*. The root *ytn* may have existed in southern Canaanite as well; cf. the place name *yitnān*[4] (Jos. 15:23). It should also be emphasized that Ugaritic *itnn* parallels **mhr** 'bride price', unlike Hebrew *'ätnān* which always denotes what is given to a harlot. In the light of Ugaritic this specific meaning of the Hebrew noun seems to be secondary; cf. the personal name *'ätni* (1 Chr. 6:26), which is apparently a shortened theophotic name meaning 'the present of the god', as in the name *mattanyā*.

2. The two snakes mentioned in the text are called *šmrr*[4a] and *ᶜqšr*.[4a] On *šmrr*, cf. "it is the poison (*mᵉrorat*) of asps within him" (Job 20:14). The prefix of the word *šmrr* was previously known in Ugaritic only from the name of the healing messenger *šᶜtqt* (i.e., the one (f.) who removes the sickness). It is the prefix with a causative meaning related to the Ugaritic *Š*-stem. This shows that the name means approximately 'the poisoner', a fitting name for a snake.[5] The name *ᶜqšr* brings to mind Hebrew animal names such as *ᶜaṭallep* 'bat', *ᶜakkābiš* 'spider', *ᶜakbār* 'mouse', and *ᶜaqrāb* 'scorpion'. No nouns of this type have yet been found in Ugaritic, but cf. the noun *ᶜṣr* 'bird', which is a shortened form of **ᶜṣpr*; cf. Arabic *ᶜuṣfūr*. By way of hypothesis we may connect the root *qšr* with Arabic *qaswar, qaswara* 'strong', which is also used as a designation for a lion, and Hebrew *mᵉquššarot* (Gen. 30:41) 'strong (f. pl.)'.

---

[4] On the name of this city see S.E. Loewenstamm, *EB, s.v. yitnān* (in Heb.).

[[4a] *U* 5, text 7:4-5 *et passim*, pp. 565, 567. The interpretation of *šmrr* and *ᶜqšr* as names of two serpents (or rather two bi-names of one serpent) is open to discussion and depends upon the overall-interpretation of the dubious passage. Cf. J.C. de Moor - P. van der Lugt, *BiOr* 31 (1974), p. 13; E. Lipinski, *loc. cit.* (note 2b). Th.H. Gaster, *JANES* 7 (1975), pp. 41-42.]

[5] We should perhaps explain it more exactly as the verbal noun "poisoning". Cf. v. Soden, *GAG*, § 561.

3. Anat's epithet *b^{c}lt šmm rmm*[5a] 'Mistress of the lofty heavens' is also interesting. This epithet recalls Ps. 78:69: "And He build His sanctuary like the heights (*k^{e}mo rāmim*), like the earth which He has founded forever." The noun *rāmim* is difficult and the emendation *kimromim* - in one word based on Ps. 148:1 - is generally accepted. But in the light of the new Ugaritic text it is possible that *rāmim* is short for *šāmayim rāmim*.

4. Of special interest is the mention of the *^{c}r^{c}r* tamarisk which is called *^{c}ṣ mt*[5b] 'the tree of death'. This epithet of the tamarisk deepens our understanding of the background of Jeremiah's phrase: "For he shall be like a tamarisk (*^{c}ar^{c}ār*) in the desert, and shall not see when good comes, but shall inhabit the parched places in the wilderness, a salt land and not inhabited" (Jer. 17:6). Moreover, this tree stands in contrast to "a tree planted by the waters, and that spreads out its roots by the river, and shall not see when heat comes, but its foliage shall be luxuriant; and shall not be anxious in the year of drought, neither shall cease from yielding fruit" (v. 8).

We may, however, ask whether that same tree planted by the waters, as opposed to the *^{c}ar^{c}ār*, the tree of death, is none other than the tree of life. True, Jeremiah does not describe this tree as a giver of life to the one who eats of its fruit, but only as a symbol of life. However, it seems that these two viewpoints are originally interrelated, viz. that the tree of life was originally a tree which was entirely vitality. From this the conception developed that such a tree could impart to others from its strength of life. Moreover, we should also look at Ps. 102:18: "When he has regarded the prayer of *hā^{c}ar^{c}ār*." According to the accepted opinion *^{c}ar^{c}ār* here means 'naked'. But this explanation leaves us unnecessarily with a *hapax legomenon*. Is is possible that the poet compares himself with the tree of death, i.e. to the tree which does not give fruit and is destined to die. Cf. in the same Psalm: "I am like a pelican of the wilderness; I am become as an owl of the waste places" (v. 7).

[5a] *U* 5, text 2:Verso:7, p. 552f.*]*

[5b] *U* 5, text 7:65, pp. 568, 571. *^{c}r^{c}r // ^{c}ṣ mt.]*

'ānoki 'ᵃḥaṭṭännā

In his dispute with Laban Jacob put forth the claim: "That which was torn by wild beasts I did not bring to you; *'ānoki 'ᵃḥaṭṭännā*; of my hand you required it, whether stolen by day or stolen by night" (Gen. 31:39). The verse implies that Jacob acted beyond the line of strict justice which cleared him of any responsibility in such a case (cf. Ex. 22:12) and paid Laban even for one torn by wild beasts. The context of the verse therefore requires the explanation: *'ᵃḥaṭṭännā* 'I shall pay for it'.

This explains the rendering of the Septuagint: ἐγὼ ἀπετίννυον 'I paid (for it)'. The same explanation is found in the Vulgate with an additional clarification: *ego omne damnum reddebam* 'I paid all damage'.

But we may ask: How can we find this meaning in the word *'ᵃḥaṭṭännā*, which is at first glance, a *Piᶜel* form of *ḥṭ'*? This difficulty led the Aramaic translations away from a literal translation. The clearest of the Aramaic Targums is Pseudo-Yonathan *dᵉ'in 'ᵃnā' ḥāṭe bah* 'that if I sin against it'. Pseudo-Yonathan was thus forced to explain *'ānoki 'ᵃḥaṭṭännā* as the *protasis* of a conditional clause. Targum Onkelos is quite incomprehensible: *dahᵃwat šāgyā' min minyānā'* 'which was lost from the number'. The root *šgy* designates both the concept 'to be missing' and the mistake which one makes. It thus seems that the interpretation of the verse as 'if I have caused a loss through my mistake' underlies the Targum's rendering. The translation in the Fragmententargum derives from this Targum: *Kol ḥᵃdā' minhon dahᵃwā ᶜarqa' min minyānā' 'ᵃnā' hāwenā' mᵉšallem*. Completely unintelligible is the Pešiṭta's rendering: *'enā mᵉnaṭṭar (h)wet leh* 'I guarded it'. *[*Actually it is rather the Fragmententargum which provides the clue for the analysis of Targum Onkelos. The words *'ᵃnā hāwenā' mᵉšallem* - 'I used to pay for it' reflect the same interpretation of *'ānoki 'ᵃḥaṭṭännā* as the Septuagint. The additional preceding words *kol ḥᵃdā' minhon dahᵃwā ᶜārqa' min minyānā'* - 'everyone which ran off from the counting' - add a midrashic legal specification. Compare also the virtually identical text of Targum Neophyti. In other Targumim, it was only this specification which was retained, whereas the words 'I used to pay' were omitted as redundant, since in the following "of my hand thou didst require it" Jacob's payment is implied. One of them is a Palestinian Targum, published by P. Kahle, *Die Masoreten des Westens* (*BWAT* 8) II (1928), p. 8 which reads: *wᵉ'aidā' dahᵃwat ṭāᶜyā' män minyānā'* - 'and which had gone astray from the counting.' The other is Targum Onkelos, where *šāgyā'* should be explained as 'deficient'. Compare Targum Onkelos on Nu. 31:49].

All the medieval commentators explained *'ᵃḥaṭṭännā* as being equal to *'ᵃḥaṭṭä'nnā*, with the loss of the *'aläp*, and each one dealt in his own way with the problem of reconciling the meaning of this root with the context in this verse. Ibn Janah[1] connected *'ᵃḥaṭṭännā* with *ḥāṭā'u* (Job 24:19) and explained that 'they refer to robbery and oppression'. His explanation is difficult since we cannot say here that Jacob admitted to an act of robbery and oppression. Perhaps he meant to say that Jacob acted as if he had stolen, i.e. he paid. Rashi's explanation is more understandable: 'It has the same meaning as in 'Sling stones at a hair-breadth and not miss (*yaḥᵃṭi'*) (Ju. 20:16) and 'I and my son Solomon shall suffer the loss of it (*ḥaṭṭā'im*)' (1 Reg. 1:21), i.e., "shall be lacking. I was short of it. If it was missing, it was missing to me because you required it of my hand". Rashbam following him explains: "I have suffered a loss from my own property." Ibn Ezra arrived at the same result in a different way: "If there was one torn by beasts the sin (*ḥeṭ'*) was upon me and I paid according to it". Similarly R. David Kimhi[2]: "The sin (*ḥeṭ'*) shall be upon me and I will pay you".

Most modern scholars have followed their medieval predecessors. Gesenius in his *Thesaurus, s.v. ḥṭ'* explains: '*ego luebam illud, damnum praestabam pro 'ᵃḥaṭṭä'nna'*. Gesenius-Buhl explains: '*Das verloren Gegangene ersetzen*' = 'to pay indemnity for the loss', and claims that the verb is denominative. However, there is no noun from the root *ḥṭ'* denoting indemnity for a loss.

BDB also explains: 'I bare the loss of it, lit. I counted it missing?'

---

[1] *Sepher Haschoraschim, Wurzelwörterbuch der hebräischen Sprache* von Abulwalid Merwan ibn Ganah (R. Jona), aus dem Arabischen ins Hebräische übersetzt von Jehuda ibn Tibbon, ed. W. Bacher, Berlin 1896, *s.v. ḥṭ'*.

[2] Rabbi Davidis Kimchi, *Radicum Liber sive Hebraeum Bibliorum Lexicon*, ed. Jo. H.R. Biesenthal et F. Lebrecht, Berolini 1847.

But it adds in parentheses: 'I was made to miss it poss. rd. *'ᵃḥuṭṭännā*?' This explanation has recently been taken up in Koehler's lexicon: 'To bear the loss of a thing'.

Two attempts have been made to depart from the medieval exegesis. One is that of Ben-Yehuda, who in his dictionary derived the form *'ᵃḥaṭṭännā* from the verb *ḥṭh* and attributed to this verb the meaning: 'he returned to him what someone has lost; what someone has taken from another, he has given him its value'. Ben-Yehuda tried to find support for his proposal in the Arabic verb *'dy* 'to return something which has been lost'. However, it is clear that a Hebrew root *ḥṭh* cannot be connected with an Arabic root *'dy*.

On the other hand, J. Rabinowitz[3] has attempted to solve the problem on the basis of an Akkadian root. Rabinowitz pointed out that in the documents form Susa the verb *ḫaṭu* (*sic*!) is found in the meaning 'to weigh, pay'. He thinks that the Hebrew verb *ḥṭ'* and the Akkadian verb have the same original meaning: 'to cleanse, purify'. In his opinion it is from this basic meaning that in both languages developed the sense 'to pay'.

Rabinowitz' note called my attention to the Akkadian parallels of *'ᵃḥaṭṭännā*. A cursory glance at the Akkadian lexicon shows that we should distinguish between two verbs: 1) *ḫaṭû* 'to sin'; 2) *ḫâṭu* (<*ḫiātu*) 'to weigh, to pay indemnity'.[4]

In the light of this finding it seems clear that *'ᵃḥaṭṭännā* should be derived from the root *ḥyṭ* and not from *ḥṭ'*. We should therefore vocalize: *'ᵃḥiṭännā*, a *Qal*-form, meaning 'I shall pay for it', as the Septuagint translates.[5] This verb, which is common in Akkadian, is a *hapax legomenon* in the Bible, and it is no wonder that the Massoretes, who did not recognize it, conflated it with the common Biblical verb *ḥṭ'*.

---

[3] J. Rabinowitz, *EI* 3 (1964), p. 133.

[4] *CAD*, vol. 6, *s.v.* *ḫaṭû*, pp. 156-158; *s.v.* *ḫâṭu* (4), pp. 161f.

[5] There is, of course, no proof from this that the Septuagint knew the verb *ḥyṭ*. The translation is most likely according to the context.

Ugaritic Gleanings

ḥrš qṭn

In Ugaritic texts listing craftsmen of different categories, we meet several times with the term *ḥrš qṭn*.[1] Eissfeldt[2] connects *qṭn* with the Hebrew adjective *qāṭān* 'small' and explains *ḥrš qṭn* 'a craftsman who manufactures small products'. However, Ugaritic *qṭn* has not yet been found in any other context and therefore it is an open question whether it can mean 'small' in Ugaritic at all. Because of the analogy of *ḥrš bhtm*[3] (or *btm*[4]) 'house-builder', *ḥrš anyt*[5], 'ship builder', *ḥrš mrkbt*[6] 'chair-maker', *ḥrš qšt*[7] 'bow-maker' Ugaritic *qṭn* should be taken as a noun designating the product of a kind of specialized workmanship. *[*Perhaps even a somewhat closer definition may be attained. *qṭn* is an unequivocal singular *b(h)tm* a no less unequivocal plural. If we parse the doubtful forms *anyt, mrkbt* and *qšt* as plurals as well this would mean that *qṭn* serves as a wide, abstract term applying to a variety of different, but congenerous products with each of them bearing a special name.*]*

If we follow this line of speculation, a new interpretation may be propounded for the phrase: *kol k^{e}le haqqāṭān mikk^{e}le hā'aggānot w$^{e c}$ad kol k^{e}le hann^{e}bālim* (Is. 22:24). It is current opinion that *kol k^{e}le haqqāṭān* means: 'all the small (or very small) vessels and that haqqāṭān is to be

[1] *CTA* 122:9; *PRU* 2, text 39:7; *PRU* 5, texts 11:23; 52:12.

[2] O. Eissfeldt, *FuF* 28,3 (1954), p. 84.

[3] *CTA* 73:10; 75:6; 85:II:2; *PRU* 2, text 39:I:1; *PRU* 5, texts 11:18; 52:8-9.

[4] *PRU* 5, text 67:14. The tablet has been found among others like it in a kiln for the baking of tablets. The tablets remained unfinished because of the destruction of the town. The text thus belongs to the latest documents from Ugarit and seems to prove that the regular Ugaritic form *bhtm* turned into *btm*. Should we ascribe to Hebrew *bāttim* the same prehistory?

[5] *PRU* 2, text 40:1.

[6] *CTA* 73:8; 122:6,8; *PRU* 2, text 39:13; *PRU* 5, texts 11:28; 68:16.

[7] *PRU* 2, text 37:1-2.

parsed as an adjective, serving as a *rectum* of a construct instead of a noun which normally fulfils this function.[8] However, Ugaritic *qṭn* suggests that *qāṭān* should be taken as a noun designating a certain type of vessels. Two of these vessels are explicitly mentioned in the passage, viz. The *'aggānot*, wide and round containers of liquids and *n*^{e}*bālim*, jars, pitchers. This definition contributes in its turn to the understanding of the Ugaritic term *ḥrš qṭn* which designates a craftsman who fashions - at least *inter alia* - different kinds of containers subsumed in Isaiah under the comprehensive term *qāṭān*.

[Dr. Y. Avishur drew my attention to N.H. Tur-Sinai, *Ha-lashon we ha-sepher, Ha-sepher*², Jerusalem 1959, pp. 258-260. Tur-Sinai anticipated my argumentation that in the light of Ugaritic *ḥrš qṭn qāṭān* in Is. 22:24 should be taken as a noun, designating a product of craftsmanship. This noun he connected with an alleged Akkadian *quttinitu* 'a kind of chair'. I failed to trace this noun in the dictionary of v. Soden. It may also be observed that the formulation *min ... w*^{c}*d* points to the specification of something mentioned before.

A. Cohen, *Lěšonénu* 34 (1970), p. 154 connects Ugaritic *qṭn* and Hebrew *qāṭān* in Is. 22:24 with Arabic *qaṭāna(t)* 'pot' and *qar*^{c} *yaqṭīnī*, or in short *yaqṭīn*, 'a gourd having the form of a bottle' (in Latin *Lagenaria*), used as a container of water.]

ysr, gnn, gngn

The *G*-formation of the verb *ysr* is attested at in Asherah's address to Il: *lḥkmt šbt dqknk ltsrk*[9]: 'Thou art wise. Thy hoary old age[10] instructs thee'. As is well-known *ysr* means in Ugaritic 'to instruct' and it is worth stressing that even Hebrew *ysr* has the same sense, not only in Is. 28:26, but in Ps. 16:7; 94:10,12 as well and compare also the noun *yāsor* (1 Chr. 15:22), 'instructor, the man in charge'.

---

[8] *GK*, §§ 128w; 133h; Joüon, *Gr*. § 141f.

[9] *CTA* 4:V:65-66.

[10] On *dqnk* 'old age' not 'beard' see in this volume *Review of Cyrus H. Gordon, Ugaritic Manual*, p. 34.

It is further common opinion that the *D*-formation of this verb appears in the introduction of the speech of *Yṣb* who is about to speak to himself. *wywsrnn ggnh.*[11] The difficult noun *ggn* has been connected by Ginsberg[12] with *gngn*, found as parallel to *npš* in the introduction to the words of Mot: *yqra mt bnpšh ystrn ydd bgngnh.*[13] Gray was the first to realise that not only the noun *gngn* reappears in this verse, but even the verb *ysr* in the *Gt*-formation, i.e. to say 'he instructed himself'. After these clarifications there remains the difficulty to explain the noun *gngn/ggn*, translated by Gray[14] as 'inwards'. Obviously we should look for a sense parallel to one of the meanings of *npš* and it appears that the most suitable one is 'throat'[15], and compare: *qra' b^{e}gāron* (Is. 58:1). This consideration suggests the hypothesis that *gngn* should be regarded as a variant of *grgr*[16], in Hebrew *gargärät*, and compare: *w^{e}yihyu ḥayyim l^{e}napsäkā w^{e}ḥen l^{e}garg^{e}rotäkā* (Pr. 3:22). Therefore, the text about Mot should be translated: 'may Mot call in his throat, may the friend instruct himself in his gullet'. That means: may he instruct himself by the voice coming forth from his throat, may he make plans whatsoever. [De Moor, *Seasonal Pattern*, p. 169 correctly argues against this view that *ystrn* "cannot be a *Gt*-stem of *ysr* ... since the inevitable vowel between *t* and *s* (**yittasiru*) would prevent metathesis." I considered for a moment the possibility of parsing *ystrn* as *tD* (cf. Gordon, *UT, Grammar* 9.32), but admit the weakness of this suggestion. Against the widely accepted connection of *ystrn* with Biblical *str* 'to hide' see Caquot-Sznycer, *Textes* 1, p. 218, note *t* who translate *'m'affronte'* in the wake of F. Løkkegaard, *AcOr* 22 (1959), p. 24, note 7 who takes *ystrn* as *Gt* of *srr* 'to be rebellious' known from the Bible. Yet the Hebrew verb never governs an object, not even an indirect one. Compare also Akkadian *sarāru* rendered by v. Soden, *AHW*, *s.v.* *'unbeständig, falsch, unwahr, lügnerisch sein'*, which governs an object only in the *D*-Stem *'belügen'* (Even in Jer. 6:28 the sence of the root may be rather 'to be mendacious' than 'to rebel'). As a possible

---

11 *CTA* 16:VI:26.

12 Ginsberg, *Keret*, p. 48.

13 *CTA* 4:VII:47-49.

14 Gray, *Krt*^{2}, pp. 76f.

15 For this sense of *npš* in Ugaritic see e.g. *CTA* 5:I:7, for the same sense in the Bible Hab. 2:5.

16 On the variations between *reš* and *nun* see *GB*, p. 476.

etymon of *ystrn* we should like to mention *Talmudic str* 'to destroy (a building), to refute (a statement)'. With our suggestion to connect *g(n)gn* with Biblical *gargärät, gāron* compare especially the different, alternative proposals propounded by E.Y. Kutscher, *Lĕšonénu* 31 (1966), p. 36 and A. Herdner, *Textes* 1, p. 571 and note *t* there, who develops Kutscher's idea to connect *g(n)gn* with Arabic *ǧin* '*démon*', translates '*son démon intime*' and comments *la voix intérieure, le démon au sens du Grec daimôn*. But are we really entitled to look for such a *daimôn* in an ancient Semitic text? For additional proposals consult de Moor, *op. cit.*, pp. 169-170*]*.

rṯ, qrṣ

The noun *rṯ* appears in the Ugaritic epics in two contexts. 1) In the enumeration of the services which a faithful son is expected to render to his father. The text reads: *ṭḥ ggy bym ṯiṭ rḥṣ npṣy bym rṯ*[17] 'who plasters my roof on the day of mire washes my garment on the day of ...' 2) In a mutilated text which deals with Il's creating of a healing angel called *šctqt*. The text is commonly read: *ymlu nᶜm rṯ [ ] yqrṣ.*[18] Because of the lacuna, the possibility can not be ruled out with certainty that the letters *rṯ* are only the beginning of a longer word. Even the reading of the first letter *r* has not been established with certainty and Herdner[19] transliterates *k/rṯ*, thus considering as alternative reading *kṯ*.

The interpretation of *rṯ* is controversial. Ginsberg[20] and Driver[21] interpret *bym rṯ* 'at the time when it (i.e. the garment) is soiled', connecting *rṯ* with Arabic *rṯṯ* 'to be worn out'. Yet the transition from this meaning to that of 'to be soiled' is hard to grasp. Aistleitner[22] renders 'mire, excrements' referring to the same etymon and this suggestion meets with even greater difficulties. Gray[23] suggests 'excrements of animals' adducing Ara-

---

[17] *CTA* 17:II:22-23; cf. *ibid*. I:33-34; II:6-8.

[18] See e.g. *UT*, text 126:V:28-29.

[19] *CTA* 16:V:28-29.

[20] *Keret*, p. 48.

[21] Driver, *CML*, p. 155.

[22] Aistleitner, *WUS*, No. 2556.

[23] Gray, *Krt*², p. 74.

bic *rwṯ*. Yet this explanation fails to fit the context. Gordon[24] follows Yasin in connecting *rṯ* with Arabic *raṯīṯ* 'a heavily wounded man', that is to say that the son washes the father's garment which has been stained with blood in battle. This proposal, too, compels us to suppose a very far-reaching process of semantic development. We rather rely for the explanation of *rṯ* on its obvious parallel *ṯiṭ*, compared by all scholars with Arabic *ṯa'ṭa(t)* 'mire, dark clay'.

This explanation is confirmed by the *epic of Krt*. The correct thesis[24a] that the text deals there with the creation of a healing angel by Il is not only borne out by the context in general, but also endorsed by the use of the verb *qrṣ*, aptly compared by Ginsberg[25] to the *Gilgamesh epic* I:II:34-35 which reads: *[dA]-ru-ru im-ta-si qātā-ša ṭi-ṭa ik-ta-ri-iṣ it-ta-di ina ṣēri [ ] dEN-Ki-Du ib-tan-ni qurādu*. 'Aruru washed her hands, pinched off clay and cast it on the steppe ... created valiant Enkidu'. This use of the verb *karāṣu* is known also from other Akkadian texts. In a Babylonian work, dealing with the justice of the gods[26], we read:

šar-ri qád-mi dnar-ru ba-nu-u a-pa-a-t[um]
šar-ḫu dzu-lum-ma-ru ka-ri-iṣ ṭi-iṭ-ṭa-ši-na
šar-ra-tum pa-ti-iq-ta-ši-na šu-e-tu dma-mi

'Narru, king of the gods, who created mankind majestic Zulummar, who pinched off their clay and mistress Mami, the queen who fashioned them.' The remark on the god Zulummaru is somewhat difficult. We are told about him only that he pinched off their clay (i.e. the clay necessary for their creation), not that he really created them. It seems, however, that the phrase should be interpreted as a brachylogy, indicating creation as well. This interpretation is borne out by *Ludlul bēl nēmeqi*[27] 4:40 defining mankind as *šu-ut dAruru ik-ru-ṣu ki-ri-is-sin*, verbally 'those whose off-pinched (pieces) Araru has pinched off', i.e. for whose creation A. has pinched off lumps of clay. Most obviously the sense of this phrase is not restricted to the preparatory acts of creation, but calls to mind the final act of creation

---

24 Gordon, *UT, Glossary* No. 2360.

[24a See especially H.L. Ginsberg, *JANES* 5 (1973), pp. 132f.]

25 Ginsberg, *Keret*, p. 48.

26 Lambert, *BWL*, pp.88:276-278.

27 *ibid.*, pp. 58:40.

proper as well. On the background of this literary tradition the passage *meḥomär qoraṣti gam 'āni* (Job 33:6) can easily be interpreted as well. Its literal translation should read: 'I, too, was pinched off from clay', but actually the passage says: 'I, too, was created from clay'.

We dwelt here upon the terminology of the Akkadian myth and in the light of this myth even the noun *rṯ* can be clarified. A text from the Old-Babylonian period[28] tells about the god Ea: *rūšam ša ṣuprišu adi 7 sibīšu iqqur qātiššu ilqe ēpīšu Ṣaltam ibtani* '(Ea) scraped out the dirt from (under) his finger-nail seven times, took it into his hand (and) baked it, thus he created Ṣaltu'. The phonetic correspondence between Ugaritic *ṯ* and Akkadian *š* does not call for comment and in addition it may be noted that *rṯ* and *rušu* both indicate the raw material of a divine creation.

For this reason we confidently may stick to the reading *rṯ*. Even in the Aqhat text we suggest to explain *bym rṯ* 'on a day of mire', i.e. on a rainy day on which the garments are soiled by mud. This exegesis is corroborated by the above mentioned parallelism between *bym rṯ* to *bym ṯiṭ*, also a day of mud on which the roof leaks and its plastering becomes an urgent necessity.

The noun *rṯ* is not clearly attested in the language of the Bible. However, it is perhaps hidden in the verse *^{c}ad lo' ^{c}āšā 'äräṣ w^{e}ḥuṣot w^{e}ro'š ^{c}aprot tebel* (Pr. 8:26). The difficulty of the noun *ro'š* in this context has long been felt and given rise to the emendation *r^{e}sise* for which some support from Cant. 5:2 is claimed. Those scholars who maintain the Masoretic text, explain *ro'š* or in the sense 'first', 'beginning' or in that of 'totality'. But perhaps we should rather delete the *'āläp* and try to explain the two remaining letters *rš* as a designation of the material forming the *^{c}aprot tebel* - 'the earth of the world'. Although this proposal is but a tentative one, some confirmation may be found in the fact that *ro'š* appears in a reference to divine creation.

yd^{c}

In a letter of the Great King of the Hittites to Ammurapi, the last

---

[28] *CAD, s.v. ṣupru* A I. 2'b.

king of Ugarit we read in ll. 13-16[29]

ht[.--.] špš. b^{c}lk
yd^{c}m.l. yd^{c}t
^{c}my. špš. b^{c}lk
šnt. šntm. lm. l. tlk

The last two lines are correctly rendered by Virolleaud to say: *Auprès de moi (que je suis) le Soleil ton maître pourquoi pendant un an ou deux n'est-tu pas venu?* That is to say: why did you not fulfil the duty of vassalage to appear at the Hittite court, to prostrate before me and to deliver your tribute?

Less clear is the meaning of the first lines. V. renders: '*Voici [ce qu'a dit] le Soleil ton maître. Je ne sais rien.*'

Yet this translation fails to yield a plausible sense, as it is hard to grasp for which possible reason the Great King wanted to emphasize that he knew absolutely nothing. Therefore, it seems preferable to parse *yd^{c}m. l. yd^{c}t* as second person and to translate: Now *[.--.]* the Sun your Lord you did not know. The verb *yd^{c}* implies here the concepts of obedience and of readiness to comply with orders. Compare in the Bible: *ubne ^{c}eli b^{e}ne b^{e}liyā^{c}al lo' yād^{ec}u 'ät YHWH* (1 Sam. 2:12), i.e. they failed to perform His precepts. Cf. also Ho. 2:22; 5:4; Job 18:21, Ps. 79:6. In the lacuna we may restore the word *lm*. This yields the rendering of 11.13-16. 'Why did you not know (i.e. recognize, honour) the Sun your Lord? To me your Lord a year, two years, why did you not come?' *[*On the semantic range of *yd^{c}* see also in this volume '*A Ugaritic Drinker's Burlesque*', pp. 364-365.*]*

Formulas of Prostrations

*[*For the main content of this chapter the reader is referred to the article *Prostration from afar*, this volume, pp. 246-248.*]*

The formula of seven and seven prostrations *[*Letters from El-Amarna and Ugarit*]* has been reduced to one of seven prostrations only in letters of Akizzi, king of Qatna.[30] The formula of these letters is paralleled by

[29] *PRU* 5, text 60.

[30] *EA* 52:3-4; 55:3.

the custom described in the passage: "And he bowed himself to the ground seven times." (Gen. 33:3). *[On prostration in the Bible consult also M. Grintz, Lĕšonénu* 31 (1967), pp. 79f.*]*

The Making and Destruction of the Golden Calf*

The account in Ex. 32, which describes the making and destruction of the Golden Calf (vv. 4,20,24) presents, it may be recalled, various difficulties. The obscure phrase *wayyāṣar 'oto bahäräṭ* in v. 4 may be interpreted in a number of ways. Aaron's description of the production of the calf in v. 24 presumably alludes to the fact that the calf emerged self-produced, whereas v. 4 asserts that it was Aaron who made it. Both these verses, on the other hand, which refer to the making of a golden calf, appear to be contradicted by v. 20 which states that Moses burnt the calf, contrary to the fact that gold does not burn.

The first to deal with the last, but major, difficulty pointed out above was the eleventh century lexicographer, Ibn Jannaḥ, who, in his commentary on Ex. 32:20, wrote: "'And he burnt it with fire' (that is to say) he melted it with fire, for gold does not burn but melts".[1] Bochartus[2], an exegete of the seventeenth century, similarly suggested that we take the verse to mean that Moses melted the calf, but he nevertheless endeavored to justify the use of the verb *śārap* in the verse by contending that since the form of the calf had been destroyed by the fire it may, for all purposes, be described as having been burnt. Abarbanel[3] (late fifteenth century), on the other hand, went to great lengths to explain that Moses did not burn

* Compare also in this volume, *The Killing of Mot in Ugaritic Myth*, pp. 426-432, *The Making and Destruction of the Golden Calf - a Rejoinder*, pp. 503-516.

[1] Jonah Ibn Jannaḥ, *Sefer Hariqma, Hebrew translation by R. Judah Ibn Tibbon*, ed. M. Wilenski, Jerusalem 1964, p. 308. *[*Cf. also the interpretation of the *Midrash Haggadol*, ed. Margolioth, Jerusalem 1956, p. 690 (in Heb.), which reads: "He melted it with fire and crushed it". The compilation of this Yemenite Midrash was completed in the thirteenth century, and we may assume that it was influenced by Ibn Janaḥ's book written in Arabic. The problem, solved by Ibn Janaḥ's exegesis is unknown to ancient sources, viz. to Jewish Hellenistic literature, to the ancient layers of the Midrash and to the fathers of the church.*]*

[2] S. Bochartus, *Hierozoicon*, Editio Quarta, Lugduni Batavorum 1712, pp. 350ff.

[3] Commentary on Ex. 32:4.

the calf itself but other cultic objects employed in its worship. Improving on this line of thought, Michaelis[4], in 1771, presented a brilliant and novel solution of the difficulty. The calf could have burned, he suggested, if it consisted of wood and had had only a gold overlay like the "golden altar" mentioned in Ex. 39:38 and described in Ex. 35:25-28 and the idolatrous images referred to in Is. 40:19-20. Michaelis concluded his discussion with the assertion that it was the wood which burned and the gold overlay which Moses ground to powder. Michaelis' explanation was widely accepted by commentators, and by 1780 it already formed the basis of H. Hezel's[5] discussion of the Biblical account. Hezel, however, sensed the difficulty in Michaelis' distinction between the different methods by which the wood and gold were respectively destroyed. He, therefore, explained simply that Moses ground the charcoal remains of the calf which were left by the fire. Hezel's interpretation of the destruction of the calf was later adopted by J. Holzinger[6] and U. Cassuto.[7] However, the inherent difficulty of this interpretation is that it predicates the supposition that the textual description of the making of the calf relates only to the calf's gold overlay, whereas the description of the calf's destruction refers only to the wooden core of the calf.

Some scholars[8] sought a way out of the dilemma by having recourse to the Documentary Theory. The section dealing with the production of the calf, it is argued, belongs to a tradition which related that the calf consisted of pure gold, whereas the section dealing with the destruction of the calf belongs to a second tradition which recounted that the calf was a wooden structure with a gold overlay. This explanation, however, fails to account

---

[4] J.O. Michaelis, *Deutsche Übersetzung des Alten Testaments mit Anmerkungen für Ungelehrte*, Der dritte Teil, Göttingen 1771, pp. 99-103. [Michaelis' proposal answers anti-religious polemics of the eighteenth century. His discussion of the verse relating the burning of the Golden Calf is introduced by the revealing passage: "*Dies sind die Worte, in denen die Feinde der Religion einen so wichtigen, ich weiss nicht wie oft wiederholten Einwurf gegen Mose zu finden vermeint haben, denn, sagen sie, Gold lässt sich nicht verbrennen.*"]

[5] W.F. Hezel, *Die Bibel Alten und Neuen Testaments mit vollständig-erklärenden Anmerkungen*, Erster Teil, Lemgo 1780, pp. 422-425.

[6] H. Holzinger, *Exodus*, Tübingen 1900, p. 110.

[7] U. Cassuto, *A Commentary on the Book of Exodus*, Jerusalem 1967, p. 419.

[8] Cf. e.g. H. Gressmann, *Mose und seine Zeit*, Göttingen, 1913, p. 205; S. Lehming, *VT* 10 (1960), pp. 16-50.

for the same difficulty met with in the Deuteronomic parallel of the story which is a manifestly homogeneous composition and yet explicitly states that Moses burned a calf of molten gold (Deut. 9:16, 21).

We have previously noted that the question concerning the burning of the calf was not raised in exegetical literature before the eleventh century, a fact which would indicate that the problem is actually the making of a non-historical approach to the Biblical account.

This contention can be substantiated by Ugaritic epic texts dealing with the killing of Mot, the god of Death. The account of Mot's destruction has survived in two versions in Ugaritic literature. The first, in a complete text which recounts how Anat revenged the death of her brother, Baal; and the second, in a broken text, relating how Mot, having returned to life, complains to Baal of the outrages he suffered at the time of his murder. The first version (*CTA* 6:II:30-37) reads as follows:

tiḫd bn ilm mt
bḥrb tbq^{c}*nn*
bḫṯr tdrynn
bišt tšrpnn
brḥm tṭḥnn
bšd tdr^{c}*nn*
širh ltikl ^{c}*ṣrm mnth ltkly npr*

'She seized Mot, son of gods (or: of Il)
ripped him open with a sword
[winnowed him with a sieve][9]
burnt him in fire
ground him with millstones
scattered[10] him in a field
his flesh[11] the birds ate ... the fowl made an end (of it)'.

---

[9] See M. Dahood, *Biblica* 38 (1957), pp. 62f.; [Herdner, *CTA*, p. 42, note 1. Interpret in the light of Jer. 15:7; Is. 41:16.]

[10] On this translation of the verb *dr*^{c} see in this volume, *The Ugaritic Fertility Myth - the Result of a Mistranslation*, pp. 160-161.

[11] On *šir* see in this volume, *The Ugaritic Fertility Myth - a Reply*, pp. 163-164, and *Š*^{e}*'er*, pp. 190-191.

Though the meaning of some of the words is still uncertain, the section as a whole is intelligible. The parallel broken text (*CTA* 6:V:12-15) reads as follows:

^{c}lk pht šrp bišt

^{c}lk [pht ṭ]ḥn brḥm

'Because of you, I have suffered [literally: seen] burning by fire
Because of you, I have suffered [literally: seen] grinding by millstones'.

To these Mot adds three further grievances of which only the third is intelligible:

^{c}lk pht dr^{c} bym

'Because of you, I have suffered scattering in the sea'.

Mot's complaint ends here without any mention of the fact that his flesh was eaten.

These passages shed clarifying light on the descriptive pattern of the calf's destruction employed in the Biblical account. Disregarding the uncertain phrase *bḫṯr tdrynn* in the first Ugaritic text, the series of actions performed on Mot is clear: (1) Anat cleaves Mot with a sword; (2) she burns him with fire; (3) grinds him with millstones and, (4) strews him upon the field. The process of Mot's destruction is terminated when the birds consume the flesh of Mot until the last of its vestiges disappear. The series of destructive acts, however, is described with complete disregard of common realistic considerations. Though Mot is patently conceived as having a human form, his body is described as being ground between millstones - an act which is never performed on a human body. Furthermore, one may ask how the author could speak of fowl consuming the flesh of Mot once he had already stated that Mot's body has been consumed by fire. His intention obviously was, then, to depict Mot's total annihilation by employing a certain series of tangible images, regardless of whether the different images employed were realistically compatible. The parallelism between the account of Mot's destruction and the destruction of the golden calf is also apparent in the details of the two narratives. In both Ugaritic versions, as in the Biblical account, the body is first described as being burnt *šrp* and then ground *ṭḥn*. In the Ugaritic versions the grinding is performed with millstones, in Ex. 32:20 the instrument is left unspecified whereas the Deuteronomic account (Deut. 9:21) takes the verb *ṭḥn* in a metaphoric sense denoting 'crushing' and thus evades the difficulty raised by the use of the verb *ṭḥn* with reference to gold. The water motif in the Exodus story has its analogue in the sea motif in the second Ugaritic version. The scattering of the calf's ashes[12] upon the water is paralleled by Mot's remains being strewn upon the field in the first Ugaritic version and upon the sea in the second version; and the Israelites drinking the water with the scattered ash recalls the fowl consuming Mot's remains in the first Ugaritic version. However, as the agents who destroy the vestiges of the calf in the Biblical episode are the same persons who had previously worshipped the statue, their act also implies a religious repudiation of the calf.[13] Nevertheless, this motif is omitted in the parallel account of the golden calf in the book of Deuteronomy, as is its Ugaritic counterpart in the second Ugaritic version. The omission in the Deuteronomic parallel may, however, also be due to the author's rational conception of the episode. He had earlier accounted for the presence of water near the desert mountain by explaining that "a brook descended from the mountain" (Deut. 9:21). The swift current of a descending mountain-brook, however, would have swept away the calf's ashes before the Israelites could have possibly drunk them.

In view of the parallel Ugaritic motifs observed above we may conclude then that the Biblical description of the Golden Calf constitutes an Israelite development of an early literary pattern that was employed in Canaan to describe the total annihilation of a detested enemy.

---

*[*12 To be sure, the calf's ashes scattered upon the water are mentioned in the Deuteronomic version only, whereas in Exodus it is the calf which is scattered. The text of Exodus is thus clearly akin to the paradoxical description of Mot's annihilation, whereas the text of Deuteronomy bears a more rationalistic character.*]*

13 Many exegetes interpret the drinking of the water to be an act of ordeal of some sort, cf. *Liber Antiquitatum Biblicarum*, 12:7, ed. G. Kisch, Notre Dame 1946, p. 148, TY, *Midrash Haggadol*, ed. Margolioth, Jerusalem, 1956, p. 690; the Palestinian Talmud, *Abodah Zarah*, ch. 3, halakha 3; the *commentaries of Rashi, Rashbam, and Ibn Ezra* and, more recently, A.B. Ehrlich, *Randglossen zur Hebräischen Bibel*, Vol. 1, Leipzig 1908, p. 305; H. Holzinger, *op. cit.* (note 6), p. 111; S. Lehming, *op. cit.* (note 8), p. 23. Against this view see R. Dussaud, *Les origines canaanéennes du sacrifice israélite*², Paris 1941, p. 245; W. Beyerlin, *Herkunft und Geschichte der ältesten Sinaitraditionen*, Tübingen 1961, pp. 150ff. and particularly R. Gradwohl, *ThZ* 19 (1963), pp. 50-53.

Turning now to the Biblical account of the calf's making, we find ourselves confronted with the problematical phrase *wayyāṣar 'oto bahärāṭ* (Ex. 32:4). Commentators have variously taken the phrase to mean, (1) that Aaron fashioned the gold with a graving tool[14], or, (2) a casting mould, (3) that he bound the gold in a cloak, or, (4) a bag. The earliest exponent of the first interpretation is the Septuagint, which translates the phrase. 'And he fashioned it with a letter-engraving instrument'. This rendering has won wide acceptance and is supported by analogous Biblical passages which employ the verb *yṣr* in the sense 'to fashion' (1 Reg. 7:15; etc.) and the noun *ḥärāṭ* in the sense of stylus or engraving tool (Is. 8:1). This interpretation, however, had already been rejected by Bochartus[15] on the grounds that molten images are not produced with engraving instruments but with casting moulds. Clericus[16] dismissed this argument with the assumption that Aaron used the tool after the calf was made to smooth its coarseness, whereas Dillmann[17] contended that the term *massekā* does not denote a *Gusswerk* - the coarse product that results from casting metal, but *Gussbild* - the finished statue which Aaron might have completed with a graving tool. These tortuous explanations, however, failed to explain a further difficulty that Bochartus found in the Septuagint translation: it contradicts Aaron's account of the making of the calf (Ex. 32:24) which makes no mention of the fact that Aaron played any greater role in the calf's production than collecting the gold and casting it into the fire.

The earliest evidence for the second interpretation is Targum Onkelos which renders the phrase: "And he fashioned it *b^ezipā*" 'with a casting mould', *zipā* being, as was pointed out by Friedrich Delitzsch[18], the Aramaic

---

[14] H. Hezel, *op. cit.* (note 5), interprets the phrase to mean that Aaron fashioned the wooden core of the calf with a sculpting instrument. This interpretation was taken up by E.F.C. Rosenmüller, *Scholia in Vetus Testamentum*, Pars prima, Lipsiae 1795, p. 628, and P. Heinisch, *Das Buch Exodus*, (*HAT* I/2), Tübingen 1934, p. 231. However, the supposition that the calf consisted of a wooden core is not supported by the text.

[15] Bochartus, *op. cit.* (note 2), pp. 334-336.

[16] J. Clerici, *Exodus*, Altera Editio, Amsterdam 1709, pp. 178ff.

[17] A. Dillmann, *Die Bücher Exodus und Leviticus*, Leipzig 1880, p. 336.

[18] F. Delitzsch, *Prolegomena eines neuen hebräisch-aramäischen Wörterbuchs zum Alten Testament*, Leipzig 1886, p. 86. I am indebted to my colleague, Prof. Joshua Blau, for calling my attention to Delitzsch's comments on the term. Cf. also *CAD, s.v. ze'pu*.

cognate of the Assyrian *zīpu* which in the Sennacherib inscriptions denotes casting moulds for bronze vessels. This interpretation is also met with in the Pešiṭta, the Midrash *Leqaḥ Tob*[19] and has been advanced in modern times by A. Ehrlich[20] and H. Schneider.[21] However, as was already noted by Bochartus[22], there are no linguistic grounds to sustain this interpretation for the word *ḥäräṭ*.

The third interpretation combined with the second is found in TY which renders the phrase in question *w^e ṣār yāte b^e šošipā ur^e mā yāte b^e ṭupsā* - 'And he bound it in a cloak and cast it with a casting mould'. This sense 'cloak, garment' is also ascribed to the word *ḥ^a riṭim* (Is. 3:22) in the Palestinian Talmud, Sabbath, ch. 6, p. 8b and was suggested by Rashi as an alternative rendering which, he notes, is supported by the form *h^a riṭim* in Is. 3:22 and the construction *ṣwr baḥäräṭ* in 2 Reg. 5:23. A modern view favouring this interpretation has been recently advanced by C. Rabin[23] who calls attention to the word *kh(ar)rāte* in Syrian spoken Arabic denoting a '*sorte de combinaison en jersey*' which he believes is a colloquial pre-Islamic term. A variation of this interpretation rendering the word *ḥäräṭ* 'bag' instead of 'cloak, garment' is encountered in the *Zohar* (II:192:2) and presumably originated among Arabic-speaking Jews. In Al-Fasi's *Hebrew-Arabic Dictionary of the Bible*[24] the word *ḥäräṭ* of 2 Reg. 5:25 is associated with the Arabic *ḫry'ṭ* 'bag'. This interpretation was defended by Bochartus and more recently by M. Noth[25] who suggests emending the word in Ex. 32: 4 to *ḥāriṭ*.

The various possibilities of interpreting the phrase *wayyāṣar 'oto baḥäräṭ* may consequently be reduced to two broad alternatives: (1) that Aaron fashioned the golden calf with a sculpting tool and, (2) that he had

---

19 *Midrash Leqaḥ Ṭob*, ed. S. Buber, Wilna 1884, p. 202.

20 A.B. Ehrlich, *op. cit.* (note 13), p. 390.

21 H. Schneider, *Das Buch Exodus* ("*Echter Bibel*" I), Würzburg 1955, p. 245.

22 Bochartus, *op. cit.* (note 2), p. 334.

23 C. Rabin, *Tarbiz* 33 (1964), pp. 112-114 (in Heb., with English summary).

24 F.L. Scoss, *The Hebrew-Arabic Dictionary of the Bible, known as Kitāb Jāmi al-Alfāẓ* (*Agron*) of David bin Abraham al-Fasi, New York 1936, vol. 1, p. 584.

25 M. Noth, *VT* 9 (1959), pp. 419-422.

bound the gold in a cloak or bag. We have already noted Bochartus' objections to the first alternative: molten images are not produced with sculpting tools but with casting moulds. To assume that Aaron might have used a graving tool after the calf had been cast requires a forced reading of the text and contradicts Aaron's description of the making of the calf in v. 24. The interpretation that most commends itself, therefore, is that Aaron had collected the gold in a cloak or bag.[26]

The crux of the entire account, however, lies in the nature of the relationship between the narrator's and Aaron's description of the making of the calf. How are we to explain the tension between the narrator's statement that Aaron made the gold a molten calf (v. 4) and Aaron's assertion that he threw the gold into the fire "and there came out this calf" (v. 24)? Is Aaron's claim to be taken as a crass falsification of what the narrator described happened? This assumption, however, finds no support in the text; there is no allusion on the part of the narrator that this was so, nor is Aaron punished or reprimanded. This tension between the verses has been frequently discussed in Midrashic literature[27], and the various Midrashic passages discussing these verses leave no doubt that the prevailing view in Midrashic literature is that the calf did, as Aaron claimed emerge self-produced - despite averseness to accept the resulting heretical corollary that the calf possessed an innate vitality. Thus, for example, we read in *Pirkei Rabbi*: "Scripture does not state *umuṣā'* - 'and it was taken out' but *wayyeṣe'* - 'and it came forth' to inform us that it emerged by itself".[28] Since Bochartus[29], however, Biblical scholars have invariably ignored the Midrashic commentaries as irrelevant to the natural interpretation of the verse. U. Cassuto[30] proved the exception among them and discussed these Midrashic commentaries in an article on the building of Baal's palace in Ugaritic literature. In the same paper Cassuto concluded that in ancient Canaan there ob-

[[26] The interpretation 'cloak' is supported by the story of the *ephod* made by Gideon (Ju. 8:24-27). See in this volume, '*The Making and Destruction of the Golden Calf - a Rejoinder*, pp. 509-510.]

[27] For reference see S. Lieberman, *The Tosefta*, Part V, Order Moed, New York 1962, pp. 1218f. (in Heb.).

[28] Cf. id., *ibid*.

[29] Bochartus, *op. cit.* (note 2), p. 336.

[30] U. Cassuto, *Orientalia* 7 (1938), pp. 274, 286-288.

tained the belief that cultic objects were produced by themselves and not by human workmanship. He finds support for this view both in the account of the construction of Baal's palace in Ugaritic literature and in the Midrashic commentaries on the Biblical accounts of the erection of the Tabernacle and the construction of the Solomonic Temple. In Ugaritic literature Baal's palace is described as having been completed after a fire had acted six days upon the gold and silver that Baal had provided for the construction of his palace.[31] Cassuto rightly contends, therefore, that the passage remains unintelligible unless it is supposed that the narrator of the epic believed that on the seventh day the metals acquired the desired form by themselves, whereupon Baal proclaimed that he had completed the construction of his palace as he had provided the building materials and the fire. Cassuto compares this passage with various Midrashic comments on the story of the erection of the Tabernacle and the construction of the Solomonic Temple. Thus, for example, we read in Exodus Rabba 52:4: "... the Holy Spirit rested upon him *[Moses]* and he erected the Tabernacle. You must not say that it was Moses who erected it, for miracles were performed with it and it rose on its own accord for it is stated that, 'the Tabernacle was reared up'" (Ex. 40:17). The Midrash continues with similar comments on the construction of the Solomonic Temple.[32] It is patent, therefore, that the author of the Midrash sensed no inherent contradiction in asserting, on the one hand, that Moses erected the Tabernacle and, on the other hand, that the Tabernacle had erected itself. To his mind, the part played by Moses and the fact that the Tabernacle had erected itself were one integral act so that one factor as well as the other could be described as the author of the result. Thus when viewed in the light of these ancient conceptions of the making of the cultic objects the tension between verses 4 and 24 disappears. To the mind of the Biblical narrator the calf was produced both by Aaron and by itself just as the author of the above Midrash asserts that the Tabernacle was both erected by Moses and that it had erected itself. When viewed thus, verse 4 is complemented and explained retrospectively by verse 24. Aaron bound (*ṣwr*) the gold in *ḥäräṭ* - a cloak or bag - and made

---

[31] *CTA* 4:V:22-38.

[32] Cf. *Midrash Tanḥuma*, ed. S. Buber, Wilna 1885, Pekude VIII; *Pesikta Rabbathi*, ed. M. Friedmann, Wien 1880, ch. 6, and Rashi on Ex. 39:31 (all in Heb.).

the calf (v. 4) by casting the gold into the fire, whereupon the calf emerged by itself (v. 24).

It is interesting to note that the *Liber Antiquitatum Biblicarum* 12:3[33] attributes the making of the calf not to Aaron but to the Israelites: "And they *[*the Israelites*]* cast them *[*the gold noserings*]* into the fire and they assumed a form and a molten calf emerged". Though the author transfers the blame from Aaron to the Israelites he, nevertheless, states that the calf was self-produced and emerged by itself. It is evident, then, that a variation of this sort ascribing to the Israelites[34] what the MT ascribes to Aaron could not have arisen if the account of the calf emerging from the fire was not taken to be true. The author, moreover, did not sense any contradiction in stating both that the Israelites had made the calf and that the calf was self-produced.

To summarize: the story of the making and destruction of the calf may be taken as a homogeneous account and in its literal sense, if we ignore the difficulties created by our own modern conceptions and give mind to the patterns of thought that obtained in ancient Canaan.

*[*After my article *The Making and Destruction of the Golden Calf* had been accepted for publication in Biblica, F.E. Fensham published a paper *The Burning of the Golden Calf and Ugarit* in *IEJ* 16 (1966), pp. 191-193. In this paper Fensham draws consequences for the interpretation of Exodus from views suggested by the present writer in *IEJ* 12 (1962), pp. 87f. Fensham states correctly "that it does not matter whether the material of which a god is made, could burn or not". But I wonder whether the obliteration of the Golden Calf was "bound to a fixed ritual act". The relevance of the question if gold could burn may hardly be denied, if the destruction was actually performed in a ritual act. It may be brushed away as irrelevant only on the supposition that we deal with a fixed literary pattern. Furthermore, I fail to see textual support for Fensham's contention that the birds which devoured Mot's remnants were regarded as cursed animals. They just finished Mot's complete destruction, stressed in the epos.*]*

[33] G. Kisch, *op. cit.* (note 12), p. 147.

[34] Cf. also Ps. 106:19 and Philo, *Vita Mosis*, 2:32.

Prostration From Afar in Ugaritic, Akkadian and Hebrew*

In the Akkadian letters from the archive of the royal palace of Ugarit, published by J. Nougayrol, we thrice meet with the formula: *a-na šēpē*^{meš} *bēli-ya iš-tu ru-qiš 2-šú 7-šú am-qut.*[1] The editor translates correctly: *Au pied de mon maître, de loin, 2 fois 7 fois je m'effondre*. An exactly corresponding formula appears in one of the Ugaritic letters from this archive published by Ch. Virolleaud: *l p*^{c}*n b*^{c}*ly t̲nid šb*^{c}*d mrḥqtm qlt*[2], "at the feet of my lord I bow down twice seven times from afar". This pattern of expression is a slight variant of the simpler *l p*^{c}*n adty šb*^{c}*d wšb*^{c}*id mrḥqtm qlt*[3], "at the feet of my lady I bow seven times and seven times from afar", i.e., seven times on the belly and seven times on the back.

In this pattern the words "from afar" may seemingly be accounted for

---

* Cf. now F.B. Knutson, *RSP* 2, pp. 421-422.

[1] *PRU* 4 *RS* 17.383:4-5, p. 221; *RS* 17.391:4-5, p. 226; *RS* 17.393:5-6, *ibid.*

[2] Virolleaud, *PRU* 5, text 115:5-8. The editor explains: "Le serviteur se prosterne 'deux fois et sept fois'". But it should read: "deux fois sept fois" without "et".

The letter has been discussed by H.L. Ginsberg, *BASOR* 72 (1958), pp. 18f. His treatment of *mrḥqtm* as dual-form is outdated by the publication of the above-mentioned parallel *ištu ruqiš*. For a grammatical analysis of this adverbial expression cf. now Gordon, *UT, Grammar*, 11. 5. Ginsberg's proposal to translate *šb*^{c}*d w šb*^{c}*id* "seven times in the one way and seven times in the other way" has been accepted by A.M. Honeyman, *VT* 11 (1961), p. 349, and by Gordon, *UT, Grammar*, 7.68. But the expression *t̲nid šb*^{c}*d* "twice seven times" shows that the verbal translation should read: "seven times and seven times". Cf. also *t̲lt̲id* (*CTA* 19:79), "thrice". *[*The morphology of *mrḥqtm* remains doubtful. Pleonastic *ištu ruqiš* (preposition *ištu* + adverbial termination *iš*) instead of standard Babylonian *ruqiš* (without *ištu*) is peculiar to the Ugaritic documents (cf. v. Soden, *AHW*, s.v. *ruqiš*). Its interpretation as loan-translation from Ugaritic would not only imply the explanation of the second *m* as an adverbial one, but even that of the first *m* as the preposition *min*. Compare Dahood, *UHPh*, p. 30. But contrast J. Blau, *Lĕšonēnu* (forthcoming) who denies the existence of a preposition *min* in Ugaritic and emends *mab* in *wum tšmḫ mab* (*PRU* 2, text 15:10-11) to read *mad.]*

[3] *CTA*, 52:6-11.

by the simple consideration that the sender of a letter is usually far away from its addressee. But the idea of anybody prostrating himself at a distance of many miles is not convincing at all. The expression makes better sense and is more picturesque if we assume that the sender figuratively represents himself as entering into the presence of his lord and doing homage to him from a distance, which lays additional stress on his reverence.

Our interpretation is born out by the *Gilgamesh Epic*, VI:153-155. The passage reads:

iš-tu a-la i-na-ru lib-b[a-šu] i-na[-sa-ḫu]
a-na pân ^{d}*Šamaš iš-tak-nu*
i-ri-qu-nim-ma a-na pa-an ^{d}*Šamaš [u]š-kin-nu*

The usual translations of this passage fail to bring out the exact meaning of *i-ri-qu-nim-ma*. E.A. Speiser translates:

When they had slain the bull, they tore out his heart,
Placing it before Shamash.
They drew back and did homage before Shamash.[4]

The same interpretation has been adopted by W. von Soden, who renders the crucial line 155: *Sie traten zurück voll Ehrfurcht vor Schamasch*.[5] But v. Soden was not happy about his translation of *i-ri-qu-nim-ma* - *sie traten zurück*, and italicized these words. A comparison of the passage with its Ugaritic parallels shows that the verb is equivalent to the adverbial expression *ištu ruqiš* = *mrḥqtm*. Therefore we may translate: "From afar they bowed down before Shamash."

A further confirmation of the practice discussed here is provided by the Divine command to Moses: "Come up to YHWH ... and bow low from afar" (Ex. 24:1). The unity of this verse has been disputed, and it has been argued that the Divine command involves an inner contradiction, because on the one hand Moses and his companions are asked to come up to the Lord, i.e. to draw near to Him, but on the other hand they are required to bow down from afar. Owing to this alleged inconsistency, the qualification "from afar" has been regarded as a spurious addition to the text "*aus späterer*

[4] E.A. Speiser, *ANET*², p. 85.

[5] A. Schott - W. v. Soden, *Das Gilgamesch-Epos*, Stuttgart 1966, p. 58.

Scheu". But in the light of the ancient oriental parallels cited above, this criticism turns out to be gratuitous. Moses and his companions are expected to appear before the Lord and to prostrate themselves before Him in accordance with accepted rules of ceremony.

---

[6] H. Gressmann, *Mose und seine Zeit*, Göttingen 1913, p. 181. For another critical approach see M. Noth, *Exodus*, Chatham, 1962, p. 197: "... only Moses was to go up really near to God while the other members of the deputation were merely to throw themselves down from afar."

The Noun ṣ^c^r (K^e^tib) ṣā^c^ir (Q^e^re)

Zech. 13:7 reads: "Strike the shepherd, that the sheep be scattered; I will turn my hand against *hasso^ca^rim*". The accepted opinion has long been that *ṣo^c^er* is related to *ṣā^c^ir* 'young' and commentators have only differed on whether the text referred to the young shepherds or to the young sheep. Prof. Tur-Sinai[1] challenged this view with reference to the statement in *Mechilta d^e^Rabbi Ishmael* on the word *me^c^immo* in Ex. 22:11: *l^e^hābi' 'ät hasso^c^er ulhoṣi' 'ät d^e^me hannoqed*. 'This excludes the *ṣo^c^er* and includes the payment for the shepherd'. True, this law is unclear.[2] Nevertheless, it is evident from the text that just like *noqed*, so also *ṣo^c^er* denotes one who works with flocks and not simply a young person. Furthermore, we must conclude from here that there is a difference of status between them. The term *noqed* definitely denotes a high status since it is even given to Mesha, king of Moab (2 Reg. 3:4). This seems to imply that *ṣo^c^er* means the simple shepherd who tends his sheep in the meadow in the employ of the *noqed*.[3]

Zech. 13:7 may be easily understood according to our suggestion. The *ṣo^ca^rim* are simply the assistants and helpers of the shepherd. The moral is clear. The text refers to the smiting of the head of the people and turning of the hand on its nobles. Compare the parallel between the king and nobles in Is. 32:1; Ho. 7:3.

Moreover, Prof. Tur-Sinai put forth the opinion that the term *ṣo^c^er* is to be found also in the following verse: "Even *ṣ^ec^ire* of the flock shall be

---

[1] N.H. Tur-Sinai, in Ben-Yehuda, *Thesaurus, s.v. ṣo^c^er*, note.

[2] The *Yalqut* ad loc. reads: *l^e^hābi' 'ät hannoqed ulhoṣi' ät hasso^c^er*. But here also the *ṣo^c^er* and the *noqed* are names of a class and a profession.

[3] Otherwise Prof. Tur-Sinai who thinks that the *ṣo^ca^rim* "are the *śo^ca^rim* (spelled in Talmudic literature *so^ca^rim*) who count the flock and especially those who come to shear the flock for the owner, i.e. to take the hair (*śe^c^ār*), the shearing of the wool which is their due from the production of the flock".

dragged away; surely their fold shall be appalled at their fate" (Jer. 49: 20).

This proposal seems likely since there is no reason to say that the enemy will carry off only the young sheep, or even the young sheep along with the other. But a description of the retribution brought upon the *ṣo^{ca}rim* who shepherd the sheep in the meadow does make sense. Prof. Tur-Sinai also included in his study the following verse: "Her nobles (*w^{e}'addirehäm*)/ send *ṣ^{c}wryhm* (*Q^{e}re*: *ṣ^{ec}irehäm*) for water" (Jer. 14:3).

This suggestion is based on the interpretation of *'addir* as a brevilocution of *'addire hasso'n* (Jer. 25:34-36), and is supported also by the *K^{e}tib ṣ^{c}wryhm* which in itself indicates that the text does not refer simply to young people. This spelling is found in another verse: "Moab is destroyed; *ṣ^{c}wryh* (*Q^{e}re*: *ṣ^{ec}irähā*) have let out a cry" (Jer. 48:4). Here also the distinction between young and old people is not satisfactory, and therefore, the text is usually emended to *ṣo^{ca}rā*.[4] However, it seems that the reading *ṣo^{ca}rähā* is preferable; cf. "Hark, the cry of the shepherds" (Jer. 25:36). This explanation is likely from a factual point of view as well, since the verse deals with Moab which prided itself on its large number of sheep (2 Reg. 3:4). It goes without saying that our explanation of Jer. 48:4 agrees with the explanation we have offered for Jer. 49:20. Both contain the same motif of the destruction which falls upon the meadow and its *ṣo^{ca}rim*.

A linguistic support for this explanation of *ṣo^{c}er* is supplied by Ugaritic. Three words for 'shepherd' occur in Ugaritic: 1) *r^{c}y*[5] (Heb. *ro^{c}ä*); 2) *nqd*[6] (Hebr. *noqed*); 3) *sġr* or *s_2ġr*.[7] The relation between the profession of the *sġr* and that of the shepherd becomes clear from an administrative document (*PRU* 5, text 72) which begins with the words: *r^{c}ym dt bd iyltm*

[4] This emendation is based on 1) the Septuagint's translation ἀναγγείλατε εἰς Ζογόρα 'Report to *Ṣo^{c}ar*'. 2) On Is. 15:5. Some support for this emendation is found also in a comparison of Jer. 48:3-4 with ib. v. 34: *miṣṣo^{c}ar ^{c}ad ḥoronayim*. But we should note also v. 4^{a}: "Moab is destroyed", which speaks of Moab in a general way. As continuation of the verse fits here: *ṣo^{ca}rähā* (i.e., all the *ṣo^{ca}rim* of Moab) let forth a cry".

[5] Gordon, *UT, Glossary* No. 2340.

[6] id., *ibid.* No. 1694.

[7] id., *ibid.* No. 1787.

ḫyrn ws₂ġrh 'shepherds who are under the control of PN[7a]; PN_2 and his *sġr*'. the same word *sġr* recurs seven times in the document in similar phrases. This shows that it refers to a shepherd who is subordinated to another shepherd possessing a higher status. *Prima facie* we may suppose that just as *r^cy* and *nqd* are common to both Ugaritic and Hebrew, so also is the word *sġr*. The hypothesis that Ugaritics s_2 = *s* became *ṣ* in Hebrew is not far-fetched. The linguistic change *s* > *ṣ* in the vicinity of the emphatic consonants and *ḥ* has long been known[8], and it it not too daring to suggest that the same change took place in the vicinity of *ġ*. [Even the semantic affinity of 'young man' to 'servant' should be considered, cf. Hebrew *na^car*, English boy, French *garçon*. Therefore] perhaps the process defined by Fraenkel[9] as attraction took place here, where one word affects the form of another which is close to it in meaning. We have seen that *sġr* is a low-ranking shepherd, a sort of subordinate. We can now understand how the word, *ṣā^cir* 'young man' influenced the word **so^cer* and changed it to [defectively written] *ṣ^cr*. Finally, the form *ṣ^cr* was occasionally mistaken for a defective spelling of *ṣā^cir*.

We have tried to base our hypothesis that the etymology of *ṣo^cer* is from the root *sġr*, originally different from *ṣġr*, the Proto-Semitic root of *ṣā^cir*, and that the two roots were later conflated only in Hebrew. The possibility that the root *sġr* is not even Semitic, as opposed to common-Semitic *ṣġr* - *ṣā^cir* should be taken into consideration. Support for this is the spelling *s₂ġr* found alongside *sġr*. The letter s_2 is distinguished from the other letters of the Ugaritic alphabet in that: 1) it is extremely rare; 2) it is the last letter of the alphabet. Scholars have perceived for a long time that it was appended to the alphabet at a late date.[10]; 3) the letter has no parallel in any other Semitic alphabet. Gordon has claimed for a long time that the use of s_2 tends to be limited to Non-Semitic loanwords.[11] The

---

[[7a] Cf. *b^eyad* ... 'under the authority of' (Ex. 38:21; Nu. 7:8; 10:13; 31:49; 2 Sam. 18:2).]

[8] *GB*, p. 533.

[9] S. Fraenkel, *Beiträge zur Assyrologie* 3 (1898), p. 61. I would like to thank my friend, Prof. J. Blau, who called my attention to this article.

[10] For bibliography cf. in this volume, *New Light on the History of the Alphabet*, pp. 7-12.

[11] Gordon, *UM*, *Grammar*, 3.1.

origin of Ugaritic *ks₂u* = *ksu*[12] from Akkadian '*kussu*', Sumerian '*guza*' is well known. So is the deriviation of Ugaritic s_2ps_2g[13], 'glaze' from Hittitic *zapzagai*.[13] ks_2m = *ksm*[14] 'spelt' is Akkadian '*kisimmu*', borrowed from Sumerian[15], and the noun s_2s_2w = *ssw* is borrowed from Indo-European.[16] The meaning of the noun $ḫs_2wn$ = *ḫswn*[17] which designates a merchandise (apparently a type of plant) has not been completely clarified, and no cognate has been found in another language. However, there are three common nouns (as opposed to personal names) with s_2 which are considered to be Semitic words, and it is doubtful whether their spelling with s_2 is sufficient to remove them from this status. These words are: 1) kbs_2 = *kbs*[18] 'launderer'. This root however, does not have an ascertained Semitic etymology. Gesenius-Buhl expressed doubt whether Arab. *kbs* 'to knead, to tread' should be coṇnected to Hebr. *kbs* or rather to Hebr. *kbš*. 2) prs_2 = *prs*.[19] This word is known as the name of a weight. In *UT* 105:9 this measure is found beside the measure called *lṯ* (perhaps Hebrew *lätäk*). We also find the phrases prs_2 *ḥṭm* (*PRU* 2, text 46:5) and prs_2 *qmḥ* (*PRU* 5, text 36:1). Virolleaud[20] connected this word with $p^{e}ras$ in Dan. 5:25-28 which is a weight. Closer is the meaning of the word *prs* in the Elephantine documents[21] which is a measure of wheat. Scholars connect this word with the Hebrew verb *prs* 'to divide, split', Akkadian *parāsu*. But, of course, it is possible that the connection between the name of the weight *prs* and the Semitic root *prs* is coincidental. 3) $ns_2{}^{c}$ = ns^{c}. Virolleaud[22] wished to find the verb $ns_2{}^{c}$ in the word $ts_2{}^{c}n$ (*PRU* 5,

---

[12] Gordon, *UT, Glossary* No. 1277.

[13] id., *ibid*. No. 1792; Friedrich, *HW*, p. 260.

[14] Gordon, *ibid*. No. 1283. It is generally found in the plural ks_2mm, and at times alongside *ḥṭm*, cf. *CTA* 16:III:9-10, and especially Ex. 9:32; *CTA* 17:I:32; II:4,21. See Aistleitner, *WUS*, No. 1359, but perhaps this refers to food made from spelt.

[15] v. Soden, *AHW*, *s.v*.

[16] Gordon, *UT, Glossary* No. 1780.

[17] id., *ibid*. No. 983.

[18] id., *ibid*. No. 1193.

[19] id., *ibid*. No. 2110.

[20] *PRU* 2, p. 84.

[21] Kraeling, *BMAP*, text 7:20; text 11:3. See also Kraeling's discussion of this word on p. 262 where additional sources are given.

[22] *PRU* 5, p. 139.

text 116:12) which occurs in an obscure text. Even Virolleaud admits that his interpretation of the text is very uncertain. If his explanation is confirmed by new texts this will be convincing proof that s_2 may be found in Semitic words. The connection between *ns*^{c} and Akkadian *nesû* 'to remove (oneself)' and Arabic *nz*^{c} 'to take out, remove' (so also Ethiopic) has been noted for a long time. Even more so, we were able to explain the interchange between Hebrew and Akkadian *s* and Arabic and Ethiopic *z* if we suppose that s_2 testifies to a Non-Semitic phone, differently rendered in various Semitic languages. But at the moment all of this is highly hypothetical.

We have found the letter s_2 in nine Ugaritic common words, and this is a paltry number. This letter is more frequent in personal names. This is not surprising when we note the large number of personal names of Non-Semitic origin in the Ugaritic texts.

Here is a list of the names: *aps*$_2$*ny* = *apsny*[23], *ars*$_2$*w* = *arsw*[24], *ars*$_2$*wn* = *arswn*[24] = *arsuwanu*[25], *brs*$_2$*m*[26], *ḫps*$_2$*ry*[27] = *ḫpsry*[28], *ys*$_2$*d* = *ysd*[29], *s*$_2$*bl*[30], *s*$_2$*gn*[31] = *sigina*[32], *s*$_2$*gryn*[33] [= *sgryn*[34]], *s*$_2$*dn*[35], *s*$_2$*w*[36] = *sw*[36], *s*$_2$*wn*[36] = *swn*[36] = *suwana*[37], *s*$_2$*z*[38] [= *szw*][38], *s*$_2$*nd*[39], *s*$_2$*s*$_2$[40], *s*$_2$*s*$_2$*w*(?)[41] = *ssw*[42],

---

[23] Gordon, *UT*, *Glossary* No. 310.

[24] id., *ibid*. No. 368.

[25] *PRU* 3, *Repertoire*, p. 242.

[26] *PRU* 2, text 57:11.

[27] Gordon, *UT*, text 147:2.

[28] *PRU* 2, text 140:2.

[29] Gordon, *UT*, *Glossary* No. 1118.

[30] id., *ibid*. No. 1731.

[31] *PRU* 5, text 15, Rev. 6.

[32] *PRU* 3, *Rèpertoire*, p. 255.

[33] *PRU* 5, text 71:6.

[[34] *CTA* 135:4.]

[35] Gordon, *UT*, *Glossary* No. 1743.

[36] id., *ibid*. No. 1745.

[37] *PRU* 4, text 17.252:20, p. 233.

[38] Gordon, *UT*, *Glossary* No. 1747.

[39] *PRU* 5, text 24:7.

s_2rn[43] = *srn*[43] = *suranu*[44], *$s_2\dot{g}r$*[45], *pls_2*[46] = *pls* = *pilsu*[46], *$pls_2b^{c}l$*.[46]

The Non-Semitic character of most of the names stands out clearly. The name *s_2bl* may be given a Semitic etymology. But the word *sbl* occurs also in a Hurrian text from Ugarit.[47] The Semitic character of *$pls_2b^{c}l$* is clear as the element *$b^{c}l$* shows. Compare also the Phoenician name *plsmlqrt*[48], and the Phoenician word *pls*[49] which designates a certain type of craftsman. The name of this craftsman is generally connected to the Hebrew verb *pls* or to the Hebrew noun *päläs* 'scale'. But the root *pls* does not have a clear etymology outside the realm of the Canaanite languages, and perhaps the Canaanites borrowed this element from a Non-Semitic language. The same applies to the name *ys_2d*, which is apparently the Punic name *ysd*[50] and represents the well-known Hebrew root *ysd* which is used in Ugaritic too. But this root also does not have an etymology outside the above-mentioned area, and it can be connected with Arabic *wisād*, Aramaic *'äsādā'* 'pillow' only with great difficulty.

To sum up: The rare letter *s_2* found exclusively in the Ugaritic alphabet and added to it only at a late time, probably represents a Non-Semitic phone. Most of the words in which it is found are either clearly Non-Semitic or Semitic loanwords. The number of words written with *s_2* which may be considered of Semitic origin is extremely small, and the question may be posed whether their spelling with *s_2* does not disprove the supposition of their Semitic origin. Anyone who thinks that this statement is too bold

---

40 *PRU* 5, text 54:19.

41 *PRU* 5, text 33:1; text 83, Rev. 3.

42 Gordon, *UT, Glossary* No. 1780.

43 id., *ibid*. No. 1797.

44 *PRU* 3, *Répertoire*, p. 255.

45 Gordon, *UT, Glossary* No. 1787.

46 id., *ibid*. No. 2053.

47 *CTA* 166:8.

48 N. Slouschz, *Thesaurus of Phoenician Inscriptions*, Tel-Aviv 1942, text 140, l. 3.

49 *Ibid*., text 70, l. 1; text 137, l. 9.

50 *Ibid*., text 431, l. 3.

51 Gordon, *UT, Glossary* No. 1117.

will have to assume that in Semitic also a variant of *s* occurred as a rare or dialectical phenomenon. But even if we do not deny in principle the possibility that a Semitic word may be written with s_2, nevertheless it is clear that such a possibility is remote. Since the root s_2*ġr* = *sġr* does not have any Semitic etymology we may assume with a large degree of probability that it is a foreign word which was only later blended with the semitic root *ṣġr*.

On Stylistic Patterns in Biblical and Ugaritic Literatures

Mission and Letter Formulae in Ugaritic Literature

In 1918, Schroeder[1] proved in a basic study that the introductory formula of the Akkadian letter from the Bronze Age goes back to the oral message formula which antedated the invention of writing. The literature on this topic has grown since then.[2]

We should therefore a priori assume that this rule, or a similar one would apply to Ugaritic literature dating from the 14th - 13th cents. BCE.

The opening formula of a Ugaritic letter has two forms:

1.[3] *tḥm* (= message) *X* *l-Y rgm* (= say)
2.[4] *l-Y rgm* *tḥm X*[4a]

On the other hand, we find in the ancient epic literature the mission formula:

---

[1] O. Schroeder, *BZWA* 33 (1918), pp. 411-417.

[2] C. Westermann, *Grundformen der prophetischen Rede*, München 1940, pp. 71-75 with literature. Cf. S.E. Loewenstamm, *EB s.v. miktāb* (in Heb.).

[3] *UT* 138:1-3; *PRU* 2, text 15:1-3; *PRU* 5, text 127:1-3 *[CTA* 53:1; *PRU* 5, text 60:1*]*.

[4] *CTA* 50:1-4; 51:1-4; 52:1-5; 55:1-3; *PRU* 2, text 14:1-4; *PRU* 5, text 159: 1-3; *[*text 8:1-3*]*.

[[4a] From the classical pattern deviate:
a) *l Y bᶜly rgm* (*PRU* 5, text 114). Most obviously the omission of '*tḥm X*' does not impair the character of the formula as an adress of the messenger.
b) *tḥm X l Y* (*PRU* 2, text 19) or even *X l Y* (*PRU* 2, text 20). Two alternative explanations may be considered α) Message of X to Y. β) Message of X. To Y (say). Cf. the following.
c) *tḥm X ᶜm Y bᶜlh* (*PRU* 5, text 62). Message of X to (*ᶜm* not *l*!) Y his (not mine!) lord. Here the receiver of the message is directly addressed.
d) The same applies when the introductory formula is omitted altogether (*PRU* 2, text 21).*]*

wrgm l-Y (name of the recipient)	*ṯny*[4b] *l-Y_1* (epithet of the recipient)
tḥm X (name of the sender)	*hwt X_1* (epithet of the sender)
'And say to Y,	tell to Y_1
Message of X,	word of X_1'

For example we may quote text *CTA* 4:VIII:29-35 - *CTA* 5:II:8,11.[5]

wrgm lbn ilm mt	*ṯny lydd il ġzr*
tḥm aliyn b^{c}l	*hwt aliy qrdm*
'Say to the son of the gods[6] Mot,	Declare to Il's beloved, the hero,
The message of the strong one Baal,	The word of the strongest of heroes.[7]

A variation of this formula is found in *CTA* 2:I:16-19

wrgm lṯr ab[h/y il	*ṯny lpḫr] m^{c}d*
tḥm ym b^{c}lkm	*adnkm ṯ[pṭ nhr]*
'And say to the Bull his/my father Il,	Declare to the convocation of the assembly,
The message of the sea, your lord,	Of your master, Judge River.'

We can recognize here two differences: 1) In the second hemistich of the first line we find instead of Il's epithet the phrase "convocation of the assembly". This difference stems from the fact that the message is received by two addressees and not one, as is usually the case. 2) In the second hemistich of the second line the word *hwt*, which generally comes in

[[4b] *ṯny* (*D*?). For a close semantic parallel cf. *lu-ul-lik šum-ki lu-ša-an-ni a-na šar-ra-ti ^{d}E[reš-ki]gal* (*Descent of Ištar* l. 24). 'I will go down and announce thy name to the queen *Ereš-kigal*.*]*

[5] Cf. in addition *CTA* 3:III:8-11; VI:21-25. In standard style the delivery of the message was introduced by the formula: *tḥm X hwt X_1*. See *CTA* 3:IV: 51-52; 5:I:13-14; 6:IV:33-34; 14:VI:305-306.

[6] *ilm* may be either plural or singular with enclitic *m*. *[*According to the first reading, adopted in our translation, the phrase means: member of the pantheon, god. Cf. e.g. *bän hāraqqāḥim* (Neh. 3:8) - member of the guild of oilmakers - oilmaker. According to the second reading it would mean 'son of Il'.*]*

[7] *qrdm* recalls Akkadian *qurādu* 'hero' a common epithet of gods and kings.

parallel with *ṯḥm*, is missing. This hemistich contains just a chiastic parallel to *ym bᶜlkm*.[8]

In *CTA* 14:V:248-249 the very form of *parallelismus membrorum* completely disappears:

wrg[m lkrt ṯᶜ]
ṯḥm [pbl mlk]

An even shorter form is found in Pbl's words before his messengers in *CTA* 14:III:125

ṯḥm pbl mlk.[9]

We may *a priori* suppose that all the formulae brought here either reflect a formula of mission or a formula derived from one of mission. We will attempt to follow the development of this matter:

1. If we disregard for the moment the shortened formula in *CTA* 14:III:125, we may state that in epic poetry the formula *wrgm l-Y* precedes *ṯḥm X*, whereas in the letters we note a free variation between *l-Y rgm - ṯḥm X* and *ṯḥm X - l-Y rgm*. The order found in the epic poetry is the original order of the mission formula. The sender of the message, turning to his messenger, always begins with a command to the messenger to go to the recipient. Then he adds: "And say to him: message of X." This order cannot be inverted, and it is clear from this that it was always employed in an orally transmitted mission. Thus the divergent formula *ṯḥm X-l-Y rgm* found in some of the letters digresses from the ancient mission pattern with perhaps the intention of clarifying to the recipient already in the first words who the sender of the letter was. Cf. also in the Akkadian letters the interchange between the formula *ana Y qibima umma X* 'To Y say. Thus (spoke) X', and the formula *umma X ana Y qibima*.

---

[8] Similarly in the words of the messengers in *CTA* 2:I:33-34:
rgm lṯr abh il
ṯḥm ym bᶜlkm [adn]km ṯpṭ nhr
'They say to the Bull, his father, Il: The message of Sea, your lord, of your master Judge River'.

[9] But cf. also in *CTA* 14:VI:305-306 the words of Krt's messengers: *ṯḥm krt ṯ[ᶜ] hwt [n]ᶜmn [ġlm il]* which retain the classical form.

2. To the poetic formula *wrgm l-Y* corresponds in letters always the formula *l-Y rgm*. The placing of the indirect object before the verb is not in accordance with Ugaritic practice, but it is generally employed in Akkadian, and in particular in the epistolary formula *ana Y qibima*. We may therefore seriously consider the suggestion of my collegue, Prof. J. Blau, with whom I discussed this problem, that the word-order in the letters was influenced by the Akkadian formula which was known to every Ugaritic scribe. From this point of view also the poetic formula seems to be more ancient.

3. On the other hand, the hemistichs *ṯny l-Y*$_1$ (parallel to *rgm l-Y*) and *hwt X*$_1$ (parallel to *tḥm X*) give the impression of an expansion which adapted the everyday mission formula to the poetic principle of *parallelismus membrorum*. This opinion may be supported by *CTA* 2:I:16-17 where the word *hwt* is missing, confirming the assumption that it was not originally part of the mission formula. Moreover, *CTA* 14:V:248-249 abandons the principle of *parallelismus membrorum*, and reads: *wrgm l-Y tḥm X*. This prosaic formula is to be considered an original mission model which was used in everyday life. We should also note the shortened pattern in *CTA* 14:III:125 *tḥm X*. No counterpart of this pattern has yet been found in an actual letter, but a similar formula is attested in a scribal exercise in *PRU* 2, text 19 which begins: *tḥm X l-Y*. Cf. also *EA* 59 which drops the formula *ana Y qibima* and contains only *umma X*. This phenomenon is not found elsewhere and is not to be considered ancient.

To sum up: The original mission formula was *wrgm l-Y tḥm X*. This formula developed in various directions. In the epistolary language it became under Akkadian influence: *l-Y rgm tḥm X*, and from this also the formula: *tḥm X l-Y rgm*. In poetry the original formula was enlarged in conformation with the rule of *parallelismus membrorum*. But *CTA* 14:V:248-249 does not employ this expansion and returns to the simple everyday formula. It is no coincidence that this change appears in the *Krt epic* where we find other signs of the abandonment of the classic epic style, viz. the decline of the seven-day unit pattern[10] and the weakening of the epic repetitive pattern. For even though in principle Keret's journey is related in the same words as Il's command to him to set out on this journey, nevertheless the story of the journey adds a new action which is not included in Il's command[11],

---

[10] See also in this volume: *The Seven-Day-Unit*, pp. 191-204.

[11] Cf. *CTA* 14:IV:194-211 with III:105-111. Note that II:90-91, III:116-117 are not repeated.

and in two places even shortens the description of the performance of the command.[11]

This concludes our survey of the development of the Ugaritic formulae. It is however, only proper that we add a note on the relationship of the prose statement to the poetic verse which developed from it. Scholars have felt this general problem for a long time. We should especially point out what Gemser[12] had to say on the subject in his commentary on Proverbs:

> *Sie setzen ... nicht gemeinsame schriftliche Vorlagen voraus ... zeigen vielmehr, dass das den Weisen vorliegende der einzeilige Spruch war, der von ihnen in ihrem Unterricht auf mancherlei Art zu einem mehrzeiligen ausgebaut wurde.*

From the many examples brought by Gemser I will point out only two of the clearest and simplest ones, viz. Pr. 10:1, as opposed to Pr. 15:20, and Pr. 10:2 as opposed to Pr. 11:4. Here may be added in some detail an example of another type which Prof. I.L. Seeligmann kindly brought to my attention:

hawwot l^{e}'ābiw ben k^{e}sil
w^{e}däläp ṭored midy^{e}ne 'iššā

'A foolish son is the calamity of his fathe
and the contentions of a wife are a continual dropping" (Pr. 19:13).

däläp ṭored b^{e}yom sagrir
w^{e}'ešät midyānim ništāwā

'A continual dropping in a very rainy day,
and a contentious woman are alike'. (Pr. 27:15)

The independence of the saying 'the contentions of a wife are a continual dropping' is clarified in Pr. 19:13 in the light of the weakness of its parallel in the first hemistich: 'A foolish son is a calamity to his father.' Moreover, this saying in the hemistich, enlarged here into a distich by the addition of a hemistich containing a new idea, turns into a distich in Pr. 27:15 by enlarging the wording of the basic saying. In addition, another distich is appended to it (Pr. 27:16).

I may add to the examples quoted from Proverbs one from Jeremiah. Jer. 18:16 reads:

---

[12] B. Gemser, *Sprüche Salomons*, Tübingen 1937, p. 45.

lāšum 'arṣām l^{e}šammā	'To make their land an stonishment,
š^{e}riqot ^{c}olām	a perpetual hissing.
kol ^{c}ober ^{c}ālähā yiššom	Everyone who passes thereby shall be astonished,
w^{e}yānid b^{e}ro'šo	and shake his head'.

On the other hand Jer. 19:8 reads:

w^{e}samti 'ät hā^{c}ir hazzo't l^{e}šammā w^{e}lišreqā kol ^{c}ober
^{c}ālähā yiššom w^{e}yišroq ^{c}al kol makkotähā
'And I will make this city an astonishment and a hissing,
Everyone who passes thereby shall be
astonished and hiss because of all the plagues thereof.'

The development of the poetical formulation from the prosaic one stands out here clearly. Moreover, the poetic development is restricted here to the second hemistich. These few examples are sufficient to indicate that the mission formula in Ugaritic epic poetry raises a general problem in the history of the distich verse.

L^e dōr dōr

In YHWH's revelation to Moses the text reads (Ex. 3:15). "God also said to Moses: 'Say this to the people of Israel, The Lord, the God of your fathers, the God of Abraham, the God of Isaac, and the God of Jacob has sent me to you, this is my name for ever, and this is my memorial *l^edor dor*'." The style of the second part of the verse differs from the first in that it is composed exactly according to the rules of parallelismus membrorum, and this stylistic point gives the immediate impression of a quotation from an ancient saying. This impression is confirmed when we examine closely the expression *l^edor dor* which lacks the *copulative waw*. This formulation is unusual in Biblical Hebrew. Cf. e.g.: "Thy name, O Lord, endures for ever, Thy memorial, O Lord, *l^edor wādor*." (Ps. 135:13).[1] The archaic character of the formulation in Ex. 3:15 seems probable also in the light of the Ugaritic formula: *p^clmh // pdr dr* (*CTA* 19:III:154).

A similar expression recurs only once in the Pentateuch, and it is no coincidence that there also it is in a quotation: "A hand upon the banner of the Lord! The Lord will have war with Amalek *middor dor*"(Ex. 17:16).

We may perhaps include here Pr. 27:24 as well, where the text reads: *l^edor dor* (*Q^ere*: *l^edor wādor*).

The *K^etib* would then be the older form which was corrected in the *Q^ere* according to the later language. The entire saying in Pr. 27:23-27, which reflects the life of the shepherd, differs in content from the framework of the Book of Proverbs. It is not far-fetched to suppose that it belongs to its most ancient portions. [The fact that the Samaritan Pentateuch reads in both places: *dr wdr* is quite instructive. Since the Samaritan Pentateuch represents - as opposed to the Jewish text - a popular text which prefers the later language[2], we may find in this fact confirmation of the author's opinion.

---

[1] Also: Joel 4:20; Ps. 33:11; 77:9; 85:6; 89:2,5; 102:13; 106:31; 119:90; 146:10; Thr. 5:19.

[2] [See e.g.: E.Y. Kutscher, *The Language and Linguistic Background of the Isaiah Scroll*, Jerusalem, 1959, pp. 54-55; 452-453.]

We may also consider whether this addition was a free form, or whether it was inserted into the text under the influence of Hebrew writings having late linguistic characteristics, which have not come down to us. A hint of such writings is perhaps to be found in the phrase *ḥayye ᶜolām* found in Hebrew only in Daniel, but appearing also in Samaritan liturgical poetry.[3] – E.Y. Kutscher.]

---

[3] [Z. Ben-Hayyim, *The Literary and Oral Tradition of Aramaic amongst the Samaritans*, vol. 3, part II, Jerusalem 1967, p. 256.]

^{c}ad ^{c}olām

In my article on the formula *me^{c}attā w^{ec}ad ^{c}olām*[1] I pointed out that the phrase *^{c}ad ^{c}olām* originated in the language of Canaanite law. This origin is still felt in the Bible in verses such as: "For all the land which you see I will give to you and your descendants *^{c}ad ^{c}olām*." (Gen. 13:15). We should therefore not be surprised if this expression is found mainly in the prose parts of the Bible - in all 27 times[2] - while in the prophetic parts only 7 times.[3] Its prose origin is recognizable even there since it generally remains without a parallel. The following verse is exceptional: "*^{c}ad ^{c}olām* they shall possess it, *l^{e}dor wādor* they will dwell in it" (Is. 34:17). This is a clear conflation of the poetic formula *l^{ec}olām // l^{e}dor wādor* with the prosaic formula *^{c}ad ^{c}olām* which comes without a parallel. Rarer still is the penetration of this formula into the language of the Psalms. It is found without a parallel in the following verse: "God may establish it *^{c}ad ^{c}olām* (Ps. 48:9), a benedictory phrase appended to the mentioning of the city of God, as in the late Hebrew phrase added to the name of Jerusalem "May it be built and re-established quickly in our days". The formula recurs without a parallel again in the verse: "Great triumphs he gives his king, and shows steadfast love to his annointed, to David and his descendants *^{c}ad ^{c}olām*" (Ps. 18:51 = 2 Sam. 22:51). It seems probable that the expressions used in prose for proclamations of the everlastingness of the dynasty influenced here.[4] Traces of this tradition of proclamation are evident in Ps. 89 based on Nathan's prophecy: "I will establish your descendants *^{c}ad ^{c}olām*, and build your throne *l^{e}dor wādor*" (Ps. 89:5). Here, however, occurred the same conflation of *^{c}ad ^{c}olām* with *l^{ec}olām // l^{e}cor wādor* which we have already found in Is. 34:17. The final phase in the evolution of the phrase is marked by the verse: *l^{e}dor wādor ^{c}ad ^{c}olām* (Ps. 106: 31). *^{c}ad ^{c}olām* which we previously found as a substitute for *l^{ec}olām* in the first hemistich and in parallel with *l^{e}dor dor* in the second hemistich fuses with *l^{e}dor dor* into a continuous expression and even occupies in it the second place.

---

[1] See in this volume, pp. 166-170.

[2] Gen. 13:15; Ex. 12:24; 14:13; Deut. 12:28; 23:4; 28:46; 29:28; Jos. 4:7; 1 Sam. 1:22; 2:30; 3:13,14; 13:13; 20:15,23,42; 2 Sam. 3:28; 7:13,16 (bis), 24,25,26; 12:10; 1 Reg. 2:45; 9:3; Ez. 37:25 (not in LXX).

[3] Is. 32:14,17; 34:17; Jer. 17:4; Ez. 27:36; 28:19; Mal. 1:4.

[4] 1 Sam. 13:13; 2 Sam. 7:13,16; 1 Reg. 2:45.

b^{e}kol dor wādor // l^{ec}olām wā^{c}äd

The ancient order *l^{ec}olām // l^{e}dor wādor* is fixed in Hebrew. Gevirtz[1] is of the opinion that Ps. 45:18 is an exception to this rule: "I will cause your name to be celebrated *b^{e}kol dor wādor*; therefore the peoples will praise you *l^{ec}olām wā^{c}äd*. According to Gevirtz the poet inverted here the order of the two components of the phrase and in the wake of this inversion he lengthened the phrase *l^{ec}olām* to *l^{ec}olām wā^{c}äd*. This analysis does not seem to be correct. First of all, the classic expression *l^{e}dor wādor* is not found here, and it is replaced by *b^{e}kol dor wādor*. This formula already troubled Gunkel[2] who recognized its late character. Recently A. Hurvitz in his doctoral thesis on the linguistic criteria for the identification of late Psalms has dealt with this problem in detail and has shown that the pattern *b^{e}kol X w-X* is specific to late Biblical passages[3] and to Mishnaic Hebrew. The question then arises: How may we explain the occurrence of an expression typical of the Second Temple Period in a Psalm which - according to consensus - belongs to the First Temple Period? A detailed investigation shows that this is not the only strange thing in the language of this verse. The verse ends with the words *l^{ec}olām wā^{c}äd*. This formula known only from Hebrew recurs in biblical poetry in only eight other places in this form[4], and in five places in the form *^{c}olām wā^{c}äd*.[5] In every instance the formula stands by itself, and no time-expression parallels it except in the late verse, Ps. 145:2. However, in the verse under discussion we find the phrase *l^{ec}olām wā^{c}äd* in parallel with *b^{e}kol dor wādor*. The hemistich "I will cause your name to be celebrated *b^{e}kol dor wādor*" therefore presents two problems: 1) Its Second Temple style; 2) It contains an expression paralleling *l^{ec}olām wā^{c}äd* which generally comes without any parallel. This raises the suspicion that this hemistich is not an original part of the verse, i.e., that the original Psalm concluded with the words: "Instead of your fathers shall be your sons; you will make them princes in all the earth. Therefore the peoples will praise you *l^{ec}olām wā^{c}äd*", i.e. your remembrance will last forever because your sons will reign after you.

---

[1] Gevirtz, *Patterns*, p. 37.

[2] H. Gunkel, *Die Psalmen*, Göttingen 1926, p. 196.

[3] 2 Chr. 28:25; 32:28; Est. 2:11; 3:14; 9:21,28. [See now A. Hurwitz, *The Transition Period in Biblical Hebrew*, Jerusalem 1972, pp. 70-73 (in Heb.)].

[4] Ex. 15:18; Mi. 4:5; Ps. 9:6; 119:44; 145:1,2,21; Dan. 12:3.

[5] Ps. 10:16; 21:5; 45:7; 52:10; 104:5.

Yā'er YHWH pānāw 'eläkā

The priestly benediction reads: *yā'er YHWH pānāw 'eläkā wiḥunnäkkā* (Nu. 6:25). A similar expression recurs in the Bible several times but the preposition *'äl* interchanges there with *ᶜal* (Ps. 31:17; Dan. 9:17), with *'ät* (Ps. 67:2), with *b* (Ps. 119:135), and the expression is even found in an abbreviated form: "*hā'er pānäkā* that we may be saved" (Ps. 80:4,8,20). The common denominator in all these verses is that they refer to God who reveals his grace to men.

A similar phrase is found in a Ugaritic letter. In this letter the messenger relates that he was sent from Ugarit to the court of the great king (of the Hittites?), and that he was kindly received. The text reads: *ᶜrbt lpn špš wpn špš nr by mid.* (*PRU* 2, text 15:7-10) 'I have come before the sun and the face of the sun shone greatly upon me'. *Špš* is a fixed epithet of the great king, and in the Akkadian documents it is preceded by the determinative for a god.

We may suppose from this that the Hebrew expression originated in the Canaanite court style. However, in Israel, only the master of the world was considered worthy of the phrase denoting "causing countenance to shine upon men". *[*But cf. Pr. 16:15.*]*

The Meaning of the Parallelism 'äläp // rebābā

In the Book of Samuel there is a short song which was sung by the women in honour of Saul and David: "Saul has slain *ba'alāpāw* and David *beribebotāw*" (1 Sam. 18:7). The text continues: "And Saul was very angry, and this saying displeased him; he said: 'They have ascribed to David ten thousands (*rebābot*), and to me they have ascribed thousands (*hā'alāpim*)'" (v. 8). This implies *a priori* that David achieved more than Saul. Saul only slew thousands, whereas David slew ten thousands. Gevirtz[1] has now disputed the authenticity of this explanation which the Bible itself gives to the song. According to him we should distinguish between the interpretation of the women's song and that of Saul's words. It is a historical fact that the women sang this song in the time of Saul and David, whereas Saul's complaint is the work of the author of the Book of Samuel who took the words out of their plain meaning, and turned the praise which the women gave equally to both Saul and David into a rebuke which placed David over Saul. Gevirtz arrived at this criticism on the basis of his study of the literary pattern in which *rebābā* is used as a parallel to *'äläp*. He notes that the pattern is already found in Ugaritic literature, e.g.: *yṣq ksp lalpm ḫrṣ yṣqm lrbbt* (*CTA* 4:I:26-29).[2] Is is a matter of course to Gevirtz that both *'alpm* and *rbbt* in this verse represent simply a very large number, and we should not look for any semantic difference between them. The same applies to the Biblical phraseology, i.g.: "may *'äläp* fall at your side, *urbābā* at your right hand" (Ps. 91:7).[3] He brings additional proof for his opinion from the verse: "How should *one* chase *'äläp*, and *two* put *rebābā* to flight" (Deut. 32: 30). Gevirtz raises the question: Why does the second hemistich not read: "and *two* put *'alpayim* to flight"? He retorts that the pattern of increasing number is what counts here. In this pattern *'äläp - rebābā* parallels *'ähād - šenayim*. According to him this proves that also in the women's song *'äläp* and *rebābā* are the same.

Let us reinvestigate the question commencing our discussion with the above-mentioned Ugaritic passage. True, the text does not mean that he

[1] Gevirtz, *Patterns*, pp. 15-23.

[2] Cf. *CAT* 3:I:15-17; 4:V:86,118-119; 14:II:92-93; *PRU* 2, text 19:4-5.

[3] Cf. Mi. 6:7; Dan. 7:10.

moulded silver just by thousands of shekels, whereas he moulded gold by ten thousands. But we should not conclude from this that *alpm* is the same as *rbbt*. Rather the passage means: "He moulded silver and gold by thousands, even by ten thousands." In other words *rbbt* is used here as an ascending parallelism. We may explain Ps. 91:7 simply as: "May a thousand, or even ten thousand, fall at your sides." The ascending parallelism may also be clearly recognized in Deut. 32:30: "How should *one* chase a thousand, and (even) *two* put ten thousand to flight." The second difficulty is greater than the first since the ratio changes from 1:1000 to 1:5000. Gevirtz rightly pointed out that the parallelisms *r^e^bābā // 'äläp* and *š^e^nayim // 'äḥād* go back to a traditional literary pattern; however, this does not justify his conclusion that *'äḥād* = *š^e^nayim* and *'äläp* = *r^e^bābā*. The logical relation of the second hemistich to the first in this verse is no different at all from the ascending parallelism that exists between the two hemistichs in the following verse: "Five of you shall chase a hundred, and a hundred of you shall chase ten thousand" (Lev. 26:8). Here there is no traditional parallelism between "five" and "hundred" or between "hundred" and "ten thousand". Instead of the traditional parallelism of the numerals we find here a chiastic formation which is emphasized by the repetition of the number "hundred", found at the end of the first hemistich and at the beginning of the second. The principle of ascending parallelism however, is retained, since the ratio 1:20 in the first hemistich becomes 1:100 in the second.[4] No one would claim here that "hundred" equals "ten thousand".

Furthermore, the meaning of the typological parallelism of two numbers only is not kept in Hebrew poetry when the text speaks of two persons, e.g.: "If Cain is avenged sevenfold (*šib^c^ātayim*), truly Lamech seventy-sevenfold (*šib^c^im w^e^šib^c^ā*)" (Gen. 4:24). It is clear that the verse does not mean to say that each one will be avenged seven or even seventy-seven times, but the rightly-held consensus is that the verse means that the vengeance upon Lamech is greater than that upon Cain. We should also recall the verse from Moses' blessing: "such are the ten thousands (*rib^e^bot*) of Ephraim, and such are the thousands (*'alpe*) of Manasseh" (Deut. 33:17). In the light of Gen. 48:19 this should be interpreted that Ephraim will be greater than Manasseh. True, the ascending order *'äläp // r^e^bābā* is reversed to *r^e^bābā //*

[[4] In both verses, Lev. 26:8 and Deut. 32:30, the same escalation, 1:5, can be observed.*]*

'äläp because the more important tribe is placed first. But there is no doubt that the basis of this verse, too, is in the pattern of the traditional parallelism between *'äläp* and *r^e^bābā*. From this it is clear that we should not interpret the women's song as "Saul and David smote in their thousands, and even in their ten thousands", but: "Saul smote in his thousands, and David (even) in his ten thousands". This implies that the song was sarcastic. It begins with praise of Saul, but in the same breath adds even greater praise of David. It is no wonder then that Saul was vexed by it. We are unable to determine whether what is told concerning Saul reflects an actual event, or whether it is only a literary composition. In any case, there is no reason to presume that the author of the Book of Samuel did not thoroughly know the manner of Hebrew poetry.[5]

[[5] A different analysis of 1 Sam. 18:7 has been advanced by M. Haran, *Tarbiz* 39 (1970), pp. 123f. Haran reaches at the conclusion "that initially, the song does not intend to deride Saul but to praise both Saul and David. The derision has not come about as any result of a secondary understanding of this song, but derives from an ironic look at this song with its formular structure.
The tension is here not between the song and the narrative surrounding it, rather it exists within the song itself - it is a tension between the song's conventional form and the actual significance of the numbers (which in this case are even high and exaggerated). It is this tension that has been humorously relieved in the narrative."]

Šopeṭ and Šebäṭ

In his article *Šopeṭ and Šebäṭ*, Z. Falk[1] proposed a new etymology for *šopeṭ*. According to him this word is a late derivation from *šebäṭ*, and coincides with it only in one of the latter's secondary meanings, viz. "the holder of the ruler's staff = ruler".[2] The noun *šopeṭ* developed from this to indicate also one who held a judicial position. The background for this semantic development was the period of the Israelite monarchy when the kings began to appoint expert judges.

This proposal leads to far-reaching conclusions. Up until now *špṭ* was considered as a verbal root from which the nouns *šopeṭ* 'judge' (active participle) and *mišpāṭ* 'judgement' (noun-pattern *miqṭāl*) were derived. But from Falk's discussion it follows that the verb *špṭ* is derived from the noun *šopeṭ*. We thus get the following formula: *šebäṭ* 'staff' > šebäṭ 'ruler' > *šopeṭ* 'ruler' > *šopeṭ* 'judge' > *špṭ* 'to judge' > *mišpāṭ* 'judgement'. Furthermore, we learn that *šopeṭ* in the meaning of judge was a creation of the period of the monarchy. If we take into account that the words derived from *šopeṭ* must be even later, then we are to place *mišpāṭ* and its compounds (e.g., *ḥošän mišpāṭ* 'breastplate of judgement') at a very late date. Linguistic study becomes Biblical criticism.

But we should have reservations about such criticism. A Ugaritic text reads: *ydn dn almnt yṯpṭ ṯpṭ ytm* (*CTA* 17:V:7-8) 'He judges the case of the widow, adjudicates the cause of the orphan'. Similarly we find: *ltdn dn almnt ltṯpṭ ṯpṭ qṣr npš* (*CTA* 16:VI:33-34) 'Thou dost not judge the case of the wi-

---

[1] *Lĕšonēnu* 30 (1966), pp. 243-247.

[2] Z. Falk compares the semantic relationship between *šebäṭ* 'staff; ruler' to that between *šaᶜar* 'gate' and *šoᶜer* 'gatekeeper'. But perhaps *šebäṭ* 'ruler' is metaphoric; cf. Is. 11:1. It should also be pointed out that Falk ascribes the same double meaning of Hebrew *šebäṭ* to Akkadian *ḫatru* as well. The Akkadian word however, means '*collegium*'; cf. *CAD* s.v. *ḫadru*; v. Soden, *AHW* s.v. *ḫaṭ(a)ru*.

dow, nor adjudicate the cause of the broken in spirit'.[3] This proves that the verb *špṭ* indicated judicial action of the judge already in the Pre-Israelite period. True, this is not the sole meaning of the Ugaritic root *ṯpṭ* as the following line shows: *mlkn aliyn bᶜl ṯpṭn in dᶜlnh* (*CTA* 3:V:40-41) 'Our king is valiant Baal, our judge, there is none above him'. We should also compare the parallelism *mäläk // šopeṭ* in the Bible (Ps. 2:10): "Now therefore, O kings (*mᵉlākim*) be wise; be warned, O judges of the earth (*šopṭe 'äräṣ*. Cf. also Hos. 7:7; Ps. 148:11). The semantic shift from "to serve in a judicial function" to "to be a ruler" is however easily understood. The judges mentioned in the Ugaritic texts were the heads of the people and their kings, and, in general, the king in the ancient Near East was the chief justice. Moreover, in Ugaritic there is no possibility whatsoever to connect *ṯpṭ* with *šebäṭ*. This word is not found in Ugaritic and in its place we have *ḫṭ*[4], Akkadian *ḫaṭṭu*, which means 'staff' in general, and in particular the staff of authority in the hands of gods and rulers; cf. the expression *tāmiḫ ḫaṭṭa*[5] with its Hebrew counterpart *tomek šebäṭ* 'holder of the scepter' (Am. 1:5,8).

We now come to a clarification of the roots *špṭ* and *šbṭ*. The first consonant of the Hebrew root *špṭ* is Proto-Semitic *ṯ*, as is shown by Ugaritic, Qatabanian[6] and Minaean.[7] This conclusion is not shaken by Aramaic *špṭ* in

[3] *qṣr npš*. Cf. Job 6:11. I would like to thank my student M. Mishor who called my attention to this comparison. Cf. also Ju. 16:16 *[Ugaritic qṣr npš*, obviously the desperate man, not the impatient one. Compare Brockelmann, *LS, s.v. kr', kry* (p. 342) - *brevis fuit, doluit, tristis fuit*. The ancient translations interpret Biblical *qoṣär ruᵃh, qāṣᵉrā ruḥo* or *napšo* in the same way. The only exception is the Vulgate on Pr. 14:29 which renders *qᵉṣar ruᵃh* impatiens, obviously because its parallelism to *'äräk 'appayim*. But even there the Septuagint translates ὁ δὲ ὀλιγυψόχος Syriacus and Targum *dᵉkāriyā' ruḥe*. The real opposition is between the man who, even in disaster, remains hopeful and the one who gives way to despair. The verse: *ma-kkoḥi ki 'ᵃyahel uma-qqiṣṣi ki 'a 'ᵃrik napši* (Job 6:11) should be interpreted: 'What is my strength that I should hopefully wait and what is the time appointed to me (i.e. to my rescue. Cf. Hab. 2:3) that I should remain confident.'*]*

[4] Gordon, *UT, Glossary* No. 950f.

[5] *CAD, s.v. ḫaṭṭu*.

[6] C. Conti Rossini, *Chrestomathia arabica meridionalis epigraphica*, Rome 1931, p. 261.

[7] G. Ryckmans, *Muséon* 50 (1937), pp. 264ff., note 199.

the Bible (Ezr. 7:25), in Elephantine, and in Syriac. This root, not found in Post-Biblical Jewish Aramaic, is extremely rare in the other Aramaic dialects, and for a long time scholars have concluded[8] that it is a loanword from Hebrew. This is not the case with Aramaic *šbṭ'* which is a common word in Jewish Aramaic and in Syriac. Therefore, there is no doubt that the *š* of *šebäṭ* represents Proto-Semitic *š*. Even if we disregard the presumption that the interchange of *b* and *p* is phonematic in the Bible[9], we see that *špṭ* and *šbṭ* are different roots.

On the other hand, it is clear that *šopeṭ* and *šebäṭ* became synonymous when referring to the ruler. This explains why they were apt to interchange in parallel texts.[10] Interchanges of this type are a well known phenomenon, even more so when the phonetic similarity of *šebäṭ* and *šopeṭ* helped to create textual variants. This similarity even led to a play on words in Syriac[11]: *'yk špṭ' bšbṭ' dnw šbṭ'* 'how the judges with staffs judged the tribes'.

---

[8] Brockelmann, *LS*, *s.v.* *špṭ*; F. Rosenthal, *Die aramaistische Forschung seit Th. Nöldekes Veröffentlichungen*, Leiden 1939, p. 54, note 1.

[9] The interchange of *b* and *p* in the same root is rare in the Bible. The clearest example is *nšb* = *nšp*. *bzr* = *pzr* (Dan. 11:24) is an Aramaism. The reading *bizzar* (Ps. 68:31) is doubtful as well as whether *p^{e}qā^{c}im* (1 Reg. 6:18) testifies to the free interchange of the roots *bq^c* - *pq^c*. In any event we may *presume* the phonematic character of the interchange *b* - *p* in the Bible.

[10] Falk compares 2 Sam. 7:7 with 1 Chr. 17:6. Cf. also: Deut. 29:9 with Jos. 24:1.

[11] Apud P. Payne Smith, *Thesaurus Syriacus*, col. 4263.

The Covenant between the pieces.

A traditio-historical Investigation.

In the present text of Gen. chapter 15 the covenant between the pieces clearly serves the purpose of confirming the divine promise of the land, whose validity had been called in question by Abraham, and this same intention of the covenant has been regarded by many critics as its primary one, whereas another group of critics hold the view that the original purpose of this covenant was to reinforce the promise of posterity.[1]

Independently of this dispute there exists the problem, how we are to interpret the ceremony as such and to which period its description may be attributed. In the following lines we shall make an attempt of contributing to the solution of this question.

The story of Abraham leaves the symbolism of the ceremony without explicit definition. Yet already at the end of the eleventh century the classic Jewish exeget Rashi[2] drew attention to the definition, given in Jer. 34:18 where we find the statement that the partner of a covenant who passes between the pieces of the killed animal takes upon himself its fate, if he should trespass the covenant. This concept of the covenant between the pieces as a form of conditional selfcurse, symbolized by the dismembering of an animal has won wide recognition in modern research[3], too, and has been

---

[1] For a bibliography listing the advocates of both opinions, consult J. Hoftijzer, *Die Verheissungen an die Erzväter*, Leiden 1956, p. 17, notes 45-46. In addition see L.A. Snijders, *OTS* 12 (1958), pp. 271-277; E.A. Speiser, *Genesis*, Garden City 1964, p. 115; R. Clements, *Abraham and David*, London 1967, p. 18 who defend the first opinion and A. Alt, *Der Gott der Väter, Kleine Schriften*, München 1953, pp. 66f. who defends the second.

[2] Rashi on Gen. 15:10 and Jer. 34:18.

[3] Cf. e.g. Speiser, *op. cit.* (note 1), p. 112; W. Rudolph, *Jeremia*, Tübingen 1958, p. 205.

supported by Old-Oriental parallels, especially by covenants of the Aramean king *Mati^cel* from the eight century, one written in Akkadian, the other in Aramaic.[4] For the possibility of transferring such a form of obligation to the godhead scholars point to the narratives about a divine oath arguing that even the oath involves a conditional self-curse.[5]

Yet, it can not be denied that the application of this exegetic principle to our story meets with difficulties. Our remark does not refer to scruples of those scholars who, for theological reasons, shrink from the very idea that God could make Himself subject to a conditional self-curse, and seek refuge in arbitrary allegoric exegesis.[6] We rather have in mind the difficulties arising from the fact that certain details of the text have no demonstrable roots in the tradition of the covenant between the pieces, or even seem to be incompatible with the very idea of this covenant. A cursory comparison of the text with its parallel in the book of Jeremiah reveals differences in the ceremony. Whereas the book of Jeremiah speaks of a young ox only, the text in Genesis adds to the young ox four other animals, viz. a she-goat, a ram, a turtle-dove and a young pigeon. (Gen. 15:9). The killing of so great a number of different animals in unparalleled in descriptions of such ceremonies[7] and it can hardly be maintained that this distinctive feature strengthens the idea of a conditional self-curse. Still more astonishing is the stress laid upon the fact that the

---

[4] On the Akkadian text see E.F. Weidner, *AfO* 8 (1932), pp. 17-34, on the Aramaic text M.A. Dupont-Sommer, *Les Inscriptions Araméennes de Sfiré*, Paris 1958, pp. 17-60.

[5] E. Quell, *Theologisches Wörterbuch zum Neuen Testament* 2, Stuttgart 1935, pp. 117f.

[6] B. Jacob, *Genesis*, Berlin 1914, pp. 405f.; Snijders, *op. cit.* (note 1), pp. 271-277.

[7] E.A. Speiser, *Orientalia* 25 (1956), pp. 9-25 claims that the documents from Nuzi provide us with a parallel to the plurality of the killed animals in Gen. 15. In these texts typical payments in the value of 30 shekels are often mentioned which comprehend 1 ox, 1 ass and 10 sheep. In Speiser's view, this modality of payment developed from the custom of dividing different kinds of animals in the ceremony of a covenant. This theory, however, lacks support. The payment in animals is rather a remnant of a primitive stage of Hurrian economy. [Compare Latin *pecunia* from *pecus*.]

killed birds were not dismembered (ibid., v. 10). It is obvious that this strongly emphasized omission of dismemberment can not be derived from the symbolism of a covenant between the pieces. Already in the thirteenth century Nahmanides[8] has been convinced by these striking pecularities that we meet here with allusions to the Pentateuchal laws of sacrifice, all the more as the enumerated kinds of animals are without exception appropriate for sacrifice, and as the dismemberment of the bird sacrifice has been forbidden by explicit legal provision.[9] In modern research Nachmanides' view has occasionally been taken up again.[10] Skinner[11] couches the problem in the cautious terms that the description of the covenant between the pieces be in accordance with levitic custom of sacrifice, although no sacrifice in the strict sense of the term is concerned. This formulation, however, is misleading, since it suggests the idea that the covenant between the pieces be considered at least as congenerous to the offering of a sacrifice. However, actually, the similarity is but one of outward appearance, as the idea of conditional self-curse has nothing in common with the idea of sacrifice and it is with good reason that the Akkadian covenant of *Mati^cel* with *Aššur-nirāri* V explicitly points out that the dismemberment of the ram did *not* take place for the sake of sacrifice.[12] If, nevertheless, both heterogeneous elements are traceable in the present text of Genesis, the hypothesis imposes itself that this internal tension resulted from the revision of an older version. It can be added without further analysis that a more homogeneous narration might easily be reconstructed if we take the lead from the text in Jeremiah and reduce the ceremony of killing to the dismemberment of one young ox. A certain corroboration for this hypothesis may be found in the description of the fiery divine appearance passing between the pieces[13] (Gen. 15:17) which neglects the undivided birds. Although this difficulty possibly could be explained away as a result of the concise style of the story, it is more easily accounted for in the light of our supposition that

---

[8] Nahmanides ad Gen. 15:10.

[9] Lev. 1:17: 5:8.

[10] J. Pedersen, *Der Eid bei den Semiten*, Straßburg 1914, p. 40; M. Buber, *Das Königtum Gottes*², Heidelberg 1956, pp. 93f.

[11] J. Skinner, *Genesis*, Edinburgh 1930, p. 281.

[12] Cf. Weidner, *op. cit.* (note 4), p. 18: *la a-na niqî*.

[13] The pieces are called here *g^ezārim*. Cf. *Sfirê* I A:40.

the original text omitted them and spoke only of the dismemberment of a young ox.

More weight is carried by religio-historical considerations. The transfer of the form, originating from a covenant between men, to a covenant between God and a man meets with serious obstacles of both logical and theological nature. The problems, arising from such a transfer may be illustrated to a certain extent by a close comparison of the texts in Genesis and in Jeremiah. In Jer. 34:18 it is related that the covenant was made *before YHWH*, i.e. that the godhead has been invoked as the guarantee of the treaty.[14] In Genesis a statement of this kind is most conspicuously lacking, clearly not by chance, but because of the fact that the partner bound by the treaty is one and the same as the godhead witnessing and guaranteeing it. It could hardly be said of the divine appearance passing between the pieces that it did so before itself. From a theological point of view it is also worth mentioning that the sense of the ceremony has been explicitly stated in Jeremiah (vv. 19-20), but not in Genesis, as such a statement would have implied that God, as it were, had taken upon Himself the conditional punishment to be dismembered if He should fail to fulfil His promise. The transposition of the covenant from the level of a treaty between men to that of a covenant between God and a man thus most understandably blurred the original idea of this covenant, toning it down. Nevertheless, it can not be denied that the very ceremony of dismemberment preserved in a perspicuous form the primary idea of self-curse despite all moderations.[15] It is

---

[14] Cf. *Sfirê* I A:7-13 where a list of gods is enumerated "before whom" the treaty has been concluded, *[who are its witnesses]* and who are invoked to open their eyes and to see the treaty, i.e. to act as its guarantors. On additional clauses of this type see Dupont-Sommer, *op. cit.* (note 4), pp. 35f.

[15] Clements, *op. cit.* (note 1), p. 34, speaks of an additional difference, namely that in the usual ceremony of the covenant between the pieces, as attested at in Jer. 34:18, both partners pass between the pieces, whereas in Gen. 15 it is God alone. This differentiation, however, is unfounded. In Jer. 34:8 it is told that the covenant has been made between the king and the entire people. Yet, only about the people it is reported that it passed between pieces (v. 19). An analoguous situation prevails in extraisraelite documents. In those documents, too, the dismemberment of an animal symbolizes the conditional self-curse of one partner only. Cf. in addition to the documents mentioned in note 4, D.J. Wiseman, *Abban and Alalakh, JCS* 12 (1958), pp. 129ff.

this palpability of the ancient concept which constitutes the main difference between the confirmation of a divine promise by a covenant between the pieces (attested, hardly by chance, only once) and the ampler attested confirmation by mere oath. True, even the oath implies a conditional self-curse. But in the formula "by Myself I have sworn"[16] this moment was felt less and less, with the result that the divine oath came close to that of a mere solemn promise, whereas in the story of the covenant between the pieces those very pieces counteract the process of spiritualisation. Small wonder, thus, that Jewish tradition never took offence at the reports of a divine oath, but found it hard to integrate the idea of a divine selfobligation by a covenant between the pieces and therefore reveals the clear tendency of assimilating the ceremony to that of offering sacrifices, as both require the killing of animals.

It may be admitted that this step was taken in Genesis only hesitatingly. For this reason later tradition considered it necessary to transform the cautious suggestion of a sacrifice into an explicite statement. This final step was taken in the book of *Jubilees*, which prefaces the account taken over from Genesis, by telling that Abraham erected an altar, sacrificed the animals, and sprinkled their blood upon it (*Jub*. 14:11), afterwards appending to the Biblical account that he offered the pieces and the birds together with their fruit- and drink offerings, which altogether were devoured by the fire (v. 19). In this way the author of the book of *Jubilees* unequivocally defines the covenant between the pieces as the ceremony of a sacrifice and it is easily understood that this concept, which removes all theological misgivings was taken over by the Midrash.[17] Thus, in the history of tradition, the primary concept of the narrative is explained away step by step, with the text in Genesis representing the beginning of this process of reinterpretation, and the book of *Jubilees* its conclusion.

It has already occasionally been pointed out that the basic concept of the narrative has an air of great antiquity about it.[18] This general impression may be corroborated if we fix our attention to that layer of the story

---

[16] Gen. 22:16; Ex. 32:13; Is. 45:23; Jer. 22:5; 49:13.

[17] L. Ginzberg, *The Legends of the Jews* 1, Philadelphia 1942, p. 235.

[18] E.g. H. Gunkel, *Genesis*[3], Göttingen 1910, pp. 183f.; Alt, *op. cit*. (note 1), pp. 66f.

which we tried to prove as secondary. This scrutiny yields as its first result that the present text can not be regarded as dependent on the version of the laws of sacrifice, extant in the Pentateuch. Most strikingly each of the three divided animals is qualified by the attribute *m^e^šullāš*, which means according to the probably correct rendering of the Septuagint - three-year-old.[19] This age of the animals does not agree with the laws of the Pentateuch which - if prescribing an age for sacrifices at all - invariably indicate the age of one year.[20] Even if we make allowance for the doubt whether *m^e^šullāš* really does mean 'three-year-old' there still remains the incontestable fact, that we meet here with a qualification, unattested in the laws of sacrifice. To this material deviation we are to add differences in terminology. The young dove is called here *gozāl*, in the laws of sacrifice *bän yonā*[21], the collective designation for birds is here *ṣippor*, in the laws of sacrifice *^c^op*.[22] Therefore, it is probable at the outset that an older law of sacrifice has left here its vestiges. A clue for the tracing of this law may be found in 1 Sam. 1:24. In the Masoretic text we read there that Hanna brought three oxen to Shilo. The following verse, however mentions the slaughtering of "the ox" as if the forgoing text had dealt with a single ox and, indeed, the Septuagint speaks in 1 Sam. 1:24 of one bullock of three years old, thus attesting at the reading *b^e^par m^e^šullāš* which is synonymous with the reading of the Qumran scroll *[bpr bn] bqr mšlš*.[23] All this demonstrates that at Shilo a three-year-old animal was

---

[19] Different is the rabbinic tradition already attested at in Onkelos which explains *m^e^šullāš* as 'three'. Cf. Mishna Para 1:1 which states that a three-year-old female animal is called *pārā* (cow), not *^c^äglā* (female calf) any longer. [But cf. also S. Lieberman, *Hellenism in Jewish Palestine*, New York 1950, p. 186 who convincingly contends that the Mishna Baba Mezia 5:4 speaks of the rearing of a calf until it has reached the age of three years.] It seems, however, that the linguistic usage of the Bible admits in this case the alternative use of *^c^egäl* and *šor*. Cf. U. Cassuto, *Exodus*, Jerusalem 1967, p. 142. [Cf. in addition M. Weinfeld, *JAOS* 90 (1970), p. 198; *JAOS* 92 (1972), p. 469 who points out that in Akkadian cattle up to the age of three years was called 'calf' (*bīru*) and that the meal of *Šamaš* consisted of three-year old calfs.]

[20] Lev. 12:6; 19:10; 23:12; Nu. 6:12,14; 7:15,21,27,33,39,45,51,57,63,69, 75,81. [To be sure, all these passages refer to the sacrifice of a lamb.]

[21] Lev. 1:14; 5:7,11; 12:6,8; 14:22,30; 15:14,29; Nu. 6:10.

[22] Lev. 1:14.

[23] F.M. Cross, *BASOR* 82 (1953), pp. 15-26.

regarded as a preferable sacrifice, if not as the only admittable one. Thus even the statement that Abraham used animals of three years old reflects laws [or at least customs] of sacrifice, presumably those of Shilo. Therefore we even may ascribe the special terminology in the designation of the birds to the same origin.

To sum up. The archetype of the narrative apparently spoke of the dismemberment of one young ox only. The addition of the other animals belongs to an amplification, secondary from a traditio-historical point of view and perhaps even from a literary one. It results from the tendency of assimilating the ceremony to that of a sacrifice. In all probability it was composed in the period of Shilo [and at this place]. This hypothesis implies of course the supposition that this period should be regarded as the *terminus ante quem* of the original version.

We want to add in short that our thesis opposes the postponement of the traditions dealing with divine promises to the patriarchs to the seventh century. Against this theory, established by Staerk[24] and accepted by many scholars, at last by Hoftijzer[25], militates also the nearly complete lack of Deuteronomic phraseology in the text of promise in Genesis.[26]

[M. Weinfeld[27] opposes our view that the sacrifice should be regarded

---

[[23a] Weinfeld, *JAOS* 90 (1970), p. 198, note 131, concludes from the Akkadian sources which mention three-year-old animals that the mentioning of those animals in Gen. 15 does "not reflect precisely a Shilonite tradition ... It seems that the three-year animal was considered of good quality in general." Anyhow, there remains the fact that the presumably Judaean laws of sacrifice in the Pentateuch never mention a sacrifice of a three-year-old animal, whereas such a sacrifice is attested for Shilo.]

[24] W. Staerk, *Studien zur Religions- und Sprachgeschichte des Alten Testaments* 1, Berlin 1899, p. 47.

[25] Hoftijzer, *op. cit.* (note 1), pp. 52f., 81. Against this view at last Clements, *op. cit.* (note 1), p. 21 who ascribes the narration to the tenth-century source *J*.

[26] As possible exception Gen. 25:5 may be mentioned. [Cf. in this volume, *The Divine Grants to the Patriarchs*, pp. 423-425]. However, no consequences should be drawn from this verse for the age of the preceding narration, let alone the age of the promises to the patriarchs in general. [Evoked in Deuteronomy in a most summary form as facts known of old which do not require any explanation (Deut. 1:8; 4:31; 6:10,18; 9:5; 26:15; 29:12; 30:20; 34:4).]

[27] Weinfeld, *ibid.* (note 23a), p. 198.

as a late element in the tradition of the covenant between the pieces and remarks: "It is true that in the ceremony of Gen. 15 the passing between the parts symbolizes the self-curse ... but this does not nullify the sacrificial nature of the ceremony. On the contrary, the ritual adds solemnity to the oath". His argument makes sense only on the supposition that we equate sacrificial character with religious solemnity. But we rather should not. A sacrifice is a gift, offered to the godhead. It has nothing to do with a conditional self-curse, especially not with that inherent in an oath, let alone in an oath of a godhead. The difference between the killing of an animal in a rite of sacrifice and its killing in a *Drohritus* is thus abundantly clear, and in addition explicitly stressed in the treaty between *Aššurnirāri* V and *Mati^{c}el*, quoted by Weinfeld himself in great detail. I fail to see any reason entitling us to reject this precious testimony of Ancient Oriental theology. It goes without saying that the ceremony of treaty may be accompanied by the offering of sacrifices. But such gifts to the gods should be kept apart from the killing of animals in a *Drohritus.]*

The Expanded Colon in Ugaritic and Biblical Verse*

A. History of the Problem

Rashbam, writing in the twelfth century CE, notes in his commentary to the text:

"Thy right hand, O Lord, glorious in power / thy right hand, O Lord, shatters the enemy" (Ex. 15:6): This verse is similar to "The floods have lifted up, O Lord / the floods have lifted up their voice" (Ps. 90:3), How long shall the wicked, O Lord / how long shall the wicked exult?" (Ps. 93:3), "For lo, thy enemies, O Lord / for lo, thy enemies shall perish" (Ps. 92:10). The first half is incomplete without the second half, which repeats and completes the thought".

Rashbam returns to this matter in his commentary to the passage: "A fruitful bough is Joseph / a fruitful bough by a spring" (Gen. 49:22), where he adds another verse to the list of examples: "Vanity of vanities, says the Preacher / vanity of vanities! All is vanity" (Ecc. 1:2). We do not know why Rashbam should here enter into a stylistic analysis, which is foreign to medieval exegesis, and we can only assume that his remark is directed against exegesis which explained redundance of language as implying an exegetical hint. Compare the homiletical interpretation cited by Rashi for Ex. 15:6: "'Thy right hand ... thy right hand' - twice: when the Children of Israel fulfil the will of the Omnipresent, the left hand becomes as the right. 'Thy right hand, O Lord, glorious in power' to save Israel, and 'Thy' second 'right hand' ... shatters the enemy."[1]

---

* It is my pleasant duty to express my thanks to my friend and colleague, Prof. J. Blau, whose advice was of assistance in the preparation of this article. I also wish to thank my students, N. Gubrin, A. Dagani, and G. Brin, for their useful remarks.

[1] It should be noted that Rashi accepted his grandson's innovation and called these verses *Samuel's verses*, after his grandson. Compare S. Poznanski, *Kommentar zu Ezechiel und den XII Kleinen Propheten von Eliezer aus Beaugency*, Warsaw, 1913, p. XIV (in Heb.).

In contrast to this, modern research, in discussing these and similar passages, takes as its starting point the theory of *parallelismus membrorum*. According to the analysis of Lowth, a relationship of synonymous, antithetic, or synthetic parallelism exists between the cola of a Biblical verse. Lowth himself did not hesitate to regard the passages under discussion as a special case of *parallela synonyma*, and in his discussion of this type of parallelism he remarked: *Fit nonnumquam parallelismus per iterationem partis alicuius prioris membri.*[2] He cites the following verses in illustration of this statement: "Thou God of vengeance, O Lord / thou God of vengeance, shine forth" (Ps. 94:1); "How long shall the wicked, O Lord / how long shall the wicked exult?" (ibid. v. 3). But scholars have long felt that this definition does not exhaust the subject, and have considered it necessary to supplement Lowth's analysis by the use of the term *climactic parallelism*. The definition advanced by S.R. Driver[3] is clearly similar to that of Rashbam: "Here the first line is itself incomplete, and the second line takes up words from it and completes them." But even though his definition is similar, Driver actually meant a more general type than Rashbam, as becomes apparent from one of his examples: "The voice of the Lord shakes the wilderness / the Lord shakes the wilderness of Kadesh" (Ps. 29:8). True enough, in this verse too words are repeated, but in the repetitive formula the order of words has been changed.

D. Yellin[4] dealt with this problem in 1939, in his study of repetition in Biblical poetry. He writes:

"There is a unique type of poetic repetition which is used only in elevated and solemn style, and appears in the following manner: Part of the phrase is begun and not ended; then comes the name of the person spoken to, in the form of an address; afterwards, that part of the phrase which has already been stated is repeated and completed."

The innovation in this definition is the stress laid upon the existence of an intervening formula which is phrased as an address. Therefore Yellin's definition excludes Gen. 49:22 (included by Rashbam) and Ps. 29:8 (included by Driver). Yellin goes on to state:

---

[2] R. Lowth, *De Sacra Poesi Hebraeorum Praelectiones*, Praelectio XIX.

[3] S.R. Driver, *Introduction to the Literature of the Old Testament* 1897, pp. 363f.

[4] D. Yellin, *Selected Studies* 2, Jerusalem, 1939, p. 37 (in Heb.).

"But sometimes the first part expresses a complete idea, and the second part of the verse, which repeats the beginning of the first part, adds something else to the preceding idea and strengthens its meaning".

As examples he cites, inter alia, Ps. 67:4,6; Cant. 4:9; 5:9.

With the discovery of the Ugaritic texts this problem again came under discussion. Already in 1935 H.L. Ginsberg[5] had briefly pointed out the striking resemblance between the Biblical verse *ki hinne 'oyebäkā YHWH / ki hinne 'oyebäkā y'obedu yitpāredu kol pocale 'āwän* 'For lo, Thy enemies, O Lord / for lo, Thy enemies shall perish / all evildoers shall be scattered' (Ps. 92:10), and the Ugaritic verse: *ht ibk bclm / ht ibk tmḫṣ / ht tṣmt ṣrtk* (*CTA* 2:IV:8-9) 'Lo[5a], thy enemies, O Baal / lo[5a], thy enemies shalt thou shatter / lo[5a], thou shalt destroy thy oppressors'.[6]

In 1938[7] he went into slightly greater detail concerning this question, mentioning a special type of tricolon, whose first two cola represent the pattern *abc/abd*; that is to say, of the first three words of the first colon (*abc*) the first two are repeated (*ab*) at the beginning of the second colon, with the addition of a third word (*d*).

Following him, W.F. Albright[8] made a systematic collection of Ugaritic and scriptual material, which he also analysed. This scholar coined the term *repetitive parallelism*. This change in terminology is indicative of the change in the method itself. Unlike Rashbam, Driver and Yellin, Albright did not take into consideration whether the first colon completes itself or not, but rather included in his definition all those verses in which the same words recur in two cola of one verse. Thus, according to his conception, there is also repetitive parallelism in the verse *beqäräb šānim ḥayyehu / beqäräb šānim todica / berogäz raḥem tizkor* 'In the midst of the years re-

---

[5] H.L. Ginsberg, *JPOS* 15 (1935), p. 127.

[[5a] Perhaps rather 'now'. Compare in this volume, *Lexicographical Notes 2, hnny / hlny*, p. 451 and especially *The Expanded Colon - reconsidered*, p. 500.]

[6] On *ṣrt* in the sense of the oppressors collectively, cf. M.D. Cassuto, *Lĕšonēnu* 15 (1947), pp. 98-99 (in Heb.) [= *BOSt* 2, pp. 61f.].

[7] H.L. Ginsberg, *Orientalia* 5 (1936), p. 180.

[8] W.F. Albright in *Studies in Old Testament Prophecy, Presented to Th.H. Robinson*, Edinburgh 1950, pp. 3-9.

new it / in the midst of the years make it known / in wrath remember mercy' (Hab. 3:2), even though the first colon *b^{e}qäräb šānim ḥayyehu* expresses a complete idea, and even though its relationship to the second colon *b^{e}qäräb šānim todi^{c}a* is one of synonymous parallelism. The formula of the verse in Hab. 3:2, according to him, is *abc/abd/efg*, and according to that very same formula he describes the verse *ki hinne 'oy^{e}bäkā YHWH / ki hinne 'oy^{e}bäkā y'obedu / yitpār^{e}du kol po^{ca}le 'āwän* (Ps. 92:10), whose structure is entirely different from that of Hab. 3:2, since the colon *abc* in Ps. 92:10 cannot exist by itself.

In 1957 S. Mowinckel[9] published a book on the problem of the tricolon in the Bible. Although this book refrains from any fundamental discussion of the characteristics of the above-mentioned verses, it does touch on some of them from various aspects, especially that of their textual criticism, which is based on the determination of the rules of the structure of Biblical verse.

The problem of the above-mentioned literary type will here be subjected to a new examination which will include comparison of the scriptural material with its Ugaritic parallels. We shall first present a survey of these latter.

B. The Expanded Colon in Ugaritic

As has been stated, the discussion of the Ugaritic material began with the verse: *ht ibk b^{c}lm / ht ibk tmḫṣ / ht tṣmt ṣrtk* (*CTA* 2:IV:8-9). The structure of the first two cola is quite obvious. After the first two words the poet interrupts his continuous flow of words with an address [which, in this case, contains the subject of the sentence], repeats the first two words, and completes the sentence with its predicate. In this sentence, therefore, we can observe: (1) *a repetitive formula* made up of the two words *ht ibk*; (2) *an intervening formula* of one word, *b^{c}lm*; (3) *a complementary formula tmḫṣ*, also of one word. We shall indicate this pattern of the first two cola by means of the abbreviated formula 2-1-2-1. It may be further ob-

---

[9] S. Mowinckel, *Real and Apparent Tricola in Hebrew Psalm Poetry*, Oslo 1957.

served that the third colon *ht tṣmt ṣrtk* parallels the two first cola and especially the second colon *ht ibk tmḫṣ*, and that the omission of the first colon does not impair the meaning of the verse. Therefore we may define the first two cola as *one expanded colon*. Corroboration of this view will be adduced in the following.

Similar to this is the following: *yṯbr ḥrn ybn / yṯbr ḥrn rišk / ᶜṯtrt šm bᶜl qdqdk* (*CTA* 16:VI:54-57): 'May Horon break, O my son / may Horon break thy head / Ashtoret Name-(?) of Baal thy crown'.[10]

*[*In this sentence the addressed person is not its subject, but in all other respects*]* the structure of the expanded verse corresponds exactly to that of the verse discussed above, with but one exception - here the expanded verse is completed by the direct object *rišk*.

The same pattern is also represented by the verse: *a[ṯt tq]ḥ ykrt / aṯt tqḥ btk / ġlmt tšᶜrb ḥẓrk // tld šbᶜ bnm lk / wṯmn tṯtmnm* (*CTA* 15:II: 21-24): 'The woman thou takest, O Krt / the woman thou takest to thy house / the girl thou bringest to thy court // will bear seven sons unto thee / yea, even eight'.

The complementary formula *btk* is, in this case, the complement of the predicate *tqḥ*. Moreover, it should be noted that the expanded colon together with its complement *ġlmt tšᶜrb ḥẓrk* does not make a complete sentence, but merely the subject of the complete sentence. Even so, here too the expanded colon in itself is constructed according to the pattern 2-1-2-1.

Special attention should be given to the verse, *irš ḥym laqht ġzr / irš ḥym watnk / blmt wašlḥk* (*CTA* 17:VI:26-28): 'Request life, O Aqht the hero / request life and I shall give (it) to you / immortality, and I shall bestow it upon you'.

The pattern 2-2-2-1 is but slightly different from the pattern 2-1-2-1 that we have observed up to now. Indeed, the first colon *irš ḥym laqht ġzr* here constitutes a complete sentence, containing subject, predicate and object. Even so, this clause is not independent, but is rather an unconnected *protasis*, whose *apodosis* is *watnk* (that is to say: "If you request life, I

---

[10] Cf.: *yṯb[r ḥrn ... / yṯbr ḥrn] rišk / ᶜṯtrt [šm bᶜl qdqdk]* (*CTA* 2:I:7-8).

shall give it to you"), and therefore it cannot exist separately. Thus what we have here is chiefly the phenomenon described above. Here too it is easy to distinguish the interruption of the continuous flow of words *irš ḥym watnk*, an interruption accompanied by a new beginning, and here too the formulation of the idea ends in the complementary formula only. We might add that the reconstruction of the basic unexpanded sentence is in this case not merely a matter of conjecture, as the same text states some lines before: *šm^c m^c [laqht ġzr / i]rš ksp watnk*! / *[ḫrṣ waš]lḥk* (*CTA* 17:VI:16-18): 'But listen, O Aqht the hero / request silver and I will give it to you / gold, and I will bestow it upon you'.

Thus we can observe the process of formation of the expanded colon from this simple formulation. The address *laqht ġzr* which precedes the simple colon turns into the intervening formula of the expanded colon, which separates the first two words from their repetition.

The following verse deviates from those discussed up to now: *qrn dbatk btlt ^cnt / qrn dbatk b^cl ymšḥ / b^cl ymšḥ hm b^cp* (*CTA* 10:II:21-23): 'Thy horns of strength[11], O virgin Anat / thy horns of strength Baal will anoint / Baal will anoint them in flight'. The pattern[12] 2-2-2-2 is not surprising. But the beginning of the third colon is unusual, for it repeats, without an intervening formula, the complementary formula *b^cl ymšḥ* of the second colon, with a certain addition. If so, then the third colon too is part of the structure of the expanded colon and not a parallel colon. This too can be explained in two ways, neither of which contradicts the other. The whole

[11] *dbat* is apparently related to *dob'ä* (Deut. 33:25) and like it is unclear. The LXX has ἰσχύς 'strength' and the Targum *tuqpā'* 'strength', which also suits the Ugaritic text. *[*Cf. also *wattārām kir'em qarni balloti b^eš̌ämän ra^ca nān* (Ps. 92:11), where *bll* should be interpreted as an intransitive verb. So correctly *RV* 'but my horn Thou hast exalted like (the horn) of a wild-ox. I am anointed with fresh oil'. The context suggests that the text point to an anointing of the horn before battle.*]*

[12] Prof. Z. Ben-Ḥayyim has called my attention to the possibility of understanding the construct state as one word. We would then have the pattern 1-1-1-2. But in all the Ugaritic verses the repetitive formula is composed of two words. This leads us to conclude that even such a combination as *qrn dbatk* was understood as two words.

verse can be considered as the expansion of the *basic* formula *qrn dbatk b^{c}l ymšḥ b^{c}p*. Alternatively, it can be interpreted as the expansion of the formula *qrn dbatk btlt ^{c}nt qrn dbatk b^{c}l ymšḥ b^{c}p*. In this formula, the complementary formula is composed of three words: *b^{c}l ymšḥ b^{c}p*. But, as Ugaritic poetry cannot tolerate such a long complementary formula, it separates the adverbial expression *b^{c}p* from the complementary formula and turns it into a complete colon: *b^{c}l ymšḥ hm b^{c}p*.[13]

In all the above-mentioned examples the intervening formula appears as an address. The pattern is mostly 2-1-2-1, but the patterns 2-2-2-1 and 2-2-2-2 also appear once each, and there is even an uncertain example of the 2-1-2-2 pattern (discussed in note 13). The variation is extremely slight. We have also seen that a colon which is expanded into two cola is generally paralleled by an additional colon in synonymous parallelism, constructed according to the usual rules of syntax. But we have also seen an example of the expansion of one colon into three cola (*CTA* 10:II:21-23), where the parallel colon is absent.

In many cases the intervening formula is the subject of the sentence [without being an address]. One has to bear in mind that in Ugaritic (as in other Semitic languages) the finite verb contains its subject-pronoun in itself, and the noun, serving as subject, may be interpreted as the apposition to the subject-pronoun contained in the verb. Accordingly, a sentence like *y^{c}n ḥtkh krt / y^{c}n ḥtkh rš / mid grdš ṯbth* (*CTA* 14:I:21-23) may be interpreted: 'He saw his descendants, Krt / he saw his descendants destroyed / his dwelling-place utterly crushed', and not as: 'Krt saw his descendants, etc.'

The complement of the incomplete beginning is the second object *rš*. The pattern 2-1-2-1.

The same pattern recurs in the epic of Aqht in two expanded sentences,

---

13 Cf. also *CTA* 3:V:27-29. The reading is very doubtful. A. Herdner, suggests reading *[bnt] bh[tk] yilm / bnt bh[tk] a[l tš]mḫ / al tšmḫ br[m h]kl[k]*, 'In the building of thy house, O Il / in the building of thy house thou shalt not rejoice / thou shalt not rejoice in the raising of thy palace.' The pattern is 2-1-2-2. If this restoration is accurate, then here too the beginning of the third colon repeats the ending of the second, which is a complementary formula. But in spite of this *concatenation* there can be no doubt that the third colon is in any case a kind of parallel colon, and the existence of a colon which expands into three cola need not yet be assumed.

in which the intervening formula is the subject of the complementary formula which contains the predicate. The two sentences are first quoted in the epic as regular sentences and are expanded only upon their repetition. The first unexpanded text reads:

[apnk dnil mt rpi]	*ap[n ġzr mt hrnmy]*
uzr ilm ylḥm	*[uzr yšqy] bn qdš*
yd ṣth y^{c}l	*wyškb yd [mizrt p] yln!*
	(*CTA* 17:I:2-6)[14]

'Then Dnil, the man of Rpi	Then the hero, the man of Hrnmy
Offerings to the gods he gave to eat	Offerings he gave to drink to the holy ones
With his garment he ascended	And he lay with his waistcloth and slept.'

This text is afterwards repeated in expanded form:

[ḫ]mš ṯdṯ ym
uzr [ilm] dnil / uzr ilm ylḥm / [uzr] yšqy bn qdš
yd ṣth dnil / yd ṣth y^{c}l / wyškb [yd] mizrt pyln
(ibid. lines 12-16)

'A fifth. a sixth day
Offerings to the gods, Dnil / Offerings to the gods he gave to eat /
Offerings he gave to drink to the holy ones /
With his garment, Dnil / with his garment he ascended / and he lay
with his waistcloth and slept.'

In addition, we may note the *anaphora* of the parallel colon by the repetition of the word *uzr*.

Further development of the expanded colon can be observed in the following verse: *tšu knp btlt ^{c}n[t] / tšu knp wtr b^{c}p* (*CTA* 10:II:10-11): 'She spread her wings, the virgin Anat / she spread her wings and ...[15] in flight.'

The pattern of the expanded sentence itself, 2-2-2-2, has long been known to us, but it should be noted that the beginning, *tšu knp btlt ^{c}nt*,

---

[14] On the problem of text and translation see in this volume, *The Seven-day Unit in Ugaritic and Biblical Literature*, pp. 196-197.

[15] Gordon, *UT*, *Glossary* No. 1153.

is a complete sentence, and the definition of the words *wtr b^cp* as a complementary formula is rather loose, as these words indicate an additional action. However, this additional action is the direct result of the action described previously, and Anath's spreading her wings and taking to flight can be described as two stages of the same action, where the second completes the first. It is thus possible to say that the words *wtr b^cp* stand in the middle between a complementary formula and a colon paralleling the expanded colon. The resemblance of the complementary formula to the parallel colon thus explains the absence of a parallel colon from the verse. Even with all the unique characteristics of this verse, there can be no doubt that here also we are able to reconstruct the simple, basic formula *tšu knp wtr b^cp*; and here also we find the same method of interrupting the utterance and beginning it anew.

The structure of the expanded verse becomes more complicated in the following verse: *wyšu ^cnh aliyn b^cl / wyšu ^cnh wy^cn / wy^cn btlt ^cnt* (*ibid*. lines 13-15): 'And he lifted up his eyes, the hero Baal / and he lifted up his eyes and saw / and he saw the virgin Anat.'

This verse, which has been expanded into a tricolon, has the following sentence as its basis: *wyšu ^cnh wy^cn btlt ^cnt*. This also describes two consecutive actions which fuse into a kind of single action. But while the expanded sentence is generally interrupted once, and begins anew once, here this happens twice. The first interruption falls into a known category. Two words which function as a subject, *aliyn b^cl*, separate between *wyšu ^cnh* and its repetition; but the second time the repetitive formula contains only one word - *wy^cn* - which does not have any intervening formula between it and its repetition. The one colon ends with the word *wy^cn*, without indicating what Baal saw. The next colon begins with the same verb and adds its object. The following verse is phrased according to the very same pattern: *wtšu ^cnh btlt ^cnt / wtšu ^cnh wt^cn / wt^cn arḫ* (*ibid*. lines 26-28): 'And she lifted up her eyes, the virgin Anat / and she lifted up her eyes and saw / and she saw a cow.[16]

---

[16] The usual wording for vision in the Ugaritic epic is *bnši ^cnh wyph(n) CTA* 17:V:9; 19:II:105, III:120,134-135). 'Upon lifting up his eyes he saw'. Similarly, the feminine *bnši ^cnh wtphn* (*CTA* 3:II:12; 17:VI:10; 19:28-29, 76). These expressions are an additional indication that "lifting up of the eyes" is merely the beginning of the action, and requires completion through the description of seeing.
There are Biblical expressions which resemble the formula in *CTA* 10:II:

The similarity of this pattern to that of *CTA* 2:II:21-23, which was discussed above, should not be ignored. There, too, we have a tricolon construction which includes two repetitive formulas, and the first pair of repetitive formulas is separated by an intervening formula, whereas the second pair is not.

[The text should be quoted to a greater extent: *wtšu ᶜnh btlt ᶜnt / wtšu ᶜnh wtᶜn / wtᶜn arḫ wtr blkt / tr blkt wtr bḫ*(?)*l* (*CTA* 10:II:26-29).

13-15, such as "And he lifted up his eyes and he saw". See M.D. Cassuto, *Tarbiz* 14 (1943), pp. 9-10 (in Heb.) [= *BOSt* 2, pp. 20-22].
[These expressions recur 12 times in the patriarchal legends. In the simplest and earliest form of the phrase the object appears immediately after the predicate "see", as in Gen. 24:64: *wattiśśā' ribqā 'ät ᶜenähā watterä' 'ät yiṣḥāq* 'And Rebekah lifted up her eyes and she saw Isaac'; and also in Gen. 43:29: *wayyiśśā' ᶜenāw wayyar' 'ät binyāmin* 'And he lifted up his eyes and saw Benjamin', and cf. also Gen. 13:10; 22:4; 33:5. The phrase sometimes becomes a formal expression of command: *śā' nā' ᶜenäkā ur'e kol hāᶜattudim.* 'Lift up your eyes and see all the goats' (Gen. 31:12). In the more developed form of the expression, the name which is the object of the predicate "see" is replaced by an object which begins with the deictic word *hinne* - 'behold' -, for example: *wayyiśśā' ᶜenāw wayyar' weᵉhinne šᵉlošā 'ᵃnāšim niṣṣābim ᶜālāw* 'And he lifted up his eyes and saw, and behold, three men stood in front of him' (Gen. 18:2); cf. Gen. 22:13; 24:63; 31:10; 33:1. Instead of a direct object an adverbial determinative occurs: *śā' nā' ᶜenäkā ur'e min hammāqom 'ᵃšär 'attā šām ṣaponā wānägbā wāqedmā wāyammā* 'Lift up your eyes, and see from the place where you are, northward, and southward, and eastward and westward' (Gen. 13:14).

In the other Biblical narratives this phraseology is infrequent (Nu. 24:2; Jos. 5:13; Ju. 19:17; 1 Sam. 6:13; 2 Sam. 13:34; 18:24; 1 Chr. 21:16. Cf. Samar. et Vers. to Ex. 14:10).

In the addresses of Jeremiah it occurs once as a simple imperative: *śᵉ'i (Qᵉre śᵉ'u) ᶜenekäm ur'i (Qᵉre ur'u) habbā'im miṣṣāfon* 'Lift up your eyes and see those who come from the north' (Jer. 13:20). With insertion of an indirect object of *nāśo' ᶜenayim* before *rᵉ'e*: *śᵉ'i ᶜenayik ᶜal šᵉpāyim ur'i* 'Lift up your eyes to the bare heights and see' (Jer. 3:2). With the same technique of insertion in the rethorical style of Deuteronomy: *upän tiśśā' ᶜenäka haššāmayᵉmā wᵉrā'itā* 'And lest you lift up your eyes unto heaven and see ...' (Deut. 4:19). Likewise *wᵉśā' ᶜenäkā yāmmā wᵉṣāponā wᵉtemānā umizrāḥā ur'e bᵉᶜenäkā* 'Lift up your eyes westward and northward and southward and eastward, and see with your own eyes' (Deut. 3:27). It may be noted that this breaking up of the time-honoured pattern *naśā' ᶜenayim wᵉrā'ā* is clearly distinct from the earlier style of Gen. 13:14 quoted above. The expression occurs in Deutero-Isaiah, with the insertion of the indirect object of *nāśā'* between *nāśā'* and *ᶜenayim*: *śᵉ'i sābib ᶜenayik ur'i* 'Lift up round about your eyes and see' (Is. 49:18; 60:4). Likewise: *śᵉ'u mārom ᶜenekäm ur'u* 'Lift up on high your eyes and see' (Is. 40:26). Even further removed from the older mode of expression is the verse: *śᵉ'u laššāmayim ᶜenekäm wᵉhabbiṭu* 'Lift up to the

'And she lifted up her eyes, the virgin Anat / and she lifted up her eyes and saw / and saw a cow and moved(?) in walking / moved(?) in walking(?) and moved(?) in a whirl(?)'. The text reveals a chain of three subsequent expansions and may be reduced to the basic formulation: *wtšu* ᶜ*nh wt*ᶜ*n arḫ̮ / wtr blkt bḫ̮l*. The first of the expansions is due to the intervening formula *btlt* ᶜ*nt*, the two others to expansions of complementary formulas. Furthermore, it should be observed that this extraordinarily expanded text reechoes in structure and wording preceding less expanded verses. The repetition of an end of a colon at the beginning of the following one without intervening formula in ll. 27-28 (*wt*ᶜ*n wt*ᶜ*n*) and with a slight variation in ll. 28-29 (*wtr blkt tr blkt*) is anticipated in ll. 14-15 (*wy*ᶜ*n wy*ᶜ*n*) and in ll. 22-23 (*b*ᶜ*l ymšḥ b*ᶜ*l ymšḥ*), ll. 25-28a recall in structure and wording ll. 13-15, l. 28 is in both respects similar to l. 11. Lines 26-29 make then the impression of a carefully prepared climax.

A very special case of double expansion is now attested in a text of offerings RS 34.126:20-22, preliminarily published by A. Caquot, *ACF* 75 (1974-1975), pp. 427-430. The text reads: *at̠r [b]*ᶜ*lk lksh/at̠r b*ᶜ*lk arṣ rd/ arṣ rd/w špl* ᶜ*pr*. 'After your husband (or lord) to his lot (verbally cup) / after your husband to the Netherworld go down / to the Netherworld go down / and lower yourself to the dust.'[16a]

Although the technique of twofold duplication is a long known phenomenon, the structure of the verse shows surprising features. In contrast to the above mentioned twice-expanded cola, the subject of the sentence is addressed. Therefore we expect that the intervening formula should contain the name of the addressed person. Actually, however, there appears instead *lksh*, i.e. an adverbial completion of the complementary formula *arṣ rd*. That is to say that the intervening formula in neither an address (being the subject of the sentence or not) nor a subject which is not an address. The ba-

---

heavens your eyes and look' (Is. 51:6).

In the night visions of Zechariah the ancient phrasing becomes the introductory formula of the apocalyptic vision: *wā'äśśā' 'ät* ᶜ*enay wā'erä' wᵉhinne 'arba*ᶜ *qᵉrānot* 'And I lifted up my eyes and saw, and behold, four horns' (Zech. 2:1; and cf. 2:5; 5:1,9; 6:1). Once this changes to an imperative *śā' nā'* ᶜ*enäkā ur'e* 'Lift up your eyes and see' (Zech. 5:5). The same usage of the expression at the beginning of the apocalyptic vision also recurs twice in Daniel as follows: *wā'äśśā'* ᶜ*enay wā'är'ä* 'And I lifted up my eyes and saw' (Dan. 8:3; 10:5).

sic formula of the first three cola should be reconstructed to read: *aṯr bᶜlk arṣ rd*. This is borne out by the exact parallelism of this formula with the fourth colon: *w špl ᶜpr* since *arṣ // ᶜpr* (see M. Dahood in *RSP*, pp. 124f.), *yrd // špl* (see Is. 32:19). Although both *lksh* and *arṣ* are adverbial completions of *rd*, it is only *arṣ* which can be attributed to the basic formula, whereas *lksh* represents an additional concept, interrupting the flow of speech. The resulting three first cola are paralleled by a fourth. The outcome is thus the transformation of a bicolon into a tetracolon.*]* The repetition of a verb which concludes one colon at the beginning of the second colon without a preceding expansion by an intervening formula is present by itself in only one verse: *tbrk ilm tity / tity ilm lahlhm / dr il lmšknthm* (*CTA* 15:III:17-19). 'The gods blessed and they went / the gods went to their tents / the godly assemblage to their tabernacles.' *[*But see additional examples, adduced by J. Avishur, *UF* 4 (1972), pp. 8ff.*]*

The verses discussed above differ from the usual style by the interruption of the utterance and its resumption, which gives it tension and solemnity. These verses are fundamentally different from those verses in which the repetition of the same words in two cola does not serve this object, and in which it is impossible to distinguish any expansion of a shorter and simpler formula. To this category belongs, for example, a verse which Albright classes with his examples of repetitive parallelism in Ugaritic: *knp nšrm bᶜl yṯbr / bᶜl ṯbr diy hmt* (*CTA* 19:114-115): 'The wings of eagles may Baal break / may Baal break their pinions.'

[[16a] In our opinion the speaker is Shaphash whose address is introduced by the words: *ᶜln špš tṣḥ* (l. 19) 'above Shaphash cries'. Cf. *CTA* 6:VI:22-23. Contrast Caquot who connects *ᶜln špš* with preceding *ṭbt*, disconnects it from following *tṣḥ* and proposes for ll. 19-20 the rendering: *Sois-nous favorable, Shaphash. Tu luiras*(?) *à la suite de ton Baal, sur sa coupe etc.* In order to prove his point that the text deals with the descent of Shaphash after Baal Caquot invokes *CTA* 6:I:7-10; VI:42-52. However, no personal pronoun may be affixed to a personal proper name and, therefore, *bᶜlk* can only mean your lord or your husband. Baal is not mentioned in the text at all, let alone his death. Add to this that Caquot's rendering of *ṭbt ᶜln* and *tṣḥ* lacks linguistic support and that the connection of *tṣḥ* with the following text impairs the pattern of the expanded colon. We admit that the ceremonial meaning of the passage escapes us. The address may have been directed to a widow, whether to a deceased widow who is really asked to follow her dead husband into the Netherworld or even a living one who is supposed to perform a symbolic act of descent.*]*

It is true that the wording *bᶜl ṯbr* in the second colon corresponds to *bᶜl yṯbr* in the first.[17] Here, however, there is no interruption of the utterance, but an unbroken and continuous utterance. The first colon, *knp nšrm bᶜl yṯbr*, fully describes the subject, and the second colon does not complement it but merely repeats it. This repetitive parallelism is nothing but a special type of synonymous parallelism, being fundamentally different from the phenomenon of the expanded colon which we have described, following Rashbam, Driver, and Yellin.

We may now summarize the results of our discussion of the various types of usages of the expanded colon in Ugaritic. First of all, we should note one type in which a formula serves as an intervening address between two repetitive formulas, [whether the addressed person is the subject of the sentence or not.] A complementary formula comprises the conclusion of the colon. The pattern is 2-1(2)-2-1(2). The colon, which has been expanded into two cola, is followed by an additional, unexpanded colon of the type usual in synonymous parallelism. There is one exceptional case in which one basic colon is expanded into three cola, and lacks a parallel colon. In this case the subject of the third colon repeats the ending of the second colon without any intervening formula (*CTA* 10:II:21-23). More flexible and varied is another type, in which an intervening formula serves as the [not addressed] subject. Here too the pattern is 2-1(2)-2-1(2). In this

---

[17] For the parallelism *yṯbr* // *ṯbr* see M.D. Cassuto, *Tarbiz* 14 (1943), pp. 9-10 (in Heb.) [= *BOSt* 2, pp. 57-59]; M. Held, *Studies and Essays in Honour of A.A. Neumann* (Leiden, 1962), pp. 281-290. Both authors explain this form of parallelism as one existing between the *yaqtul* and *qatala* forms in two cola of one verse. True, this kind of parallelism is well attested in Biblical poetry. Nevertheless it remains a moot question whether *ṯbr* should be parsed as *qatala* or as *qatālu*. Cf. the verse *tṯᶜr ksat lmhr* / *ṯᶜr ṯlhnt lsbim* (*CTA* 3:II:20-22). If the poet had intended to use the *qatala* form, he should have written *ṯᶜrt* and not *ṯᶜr*. We must, therefore, necessarily define *ṯᶜr* as the absolute infinitive. Cf. also M. Dahood, *Psalms* I (New York, 1966), p. 177, and in this volume, *Remarks upon the Infinitive Absolute in Ugaritic and Phoenician*, pp. 366-368.

In any case, the fact remains that both in Ugaritic and Biblical poetry there exists a type of parallelism between the *yaqtul* and another form of the same verb in the two cola of a verse. Such repetition does not change the structure of the verse, and is therefore fundamentally different from the repetition present in the expanded colon.

type also the expanded colon is not always followed by another colon in synonymous parallelism. We have observed one case in which the parallel colon is lacking (*CTA* 10:II:10-11), this being the case where the complementary formula describes an additional action which, together with the first, forms one continuous action. Here the result is a bicolon. Moreover, we have observed a third type which resembles the second (*ibid.*, lines 13-15; lines 26-28). The additional and continued action is indicated in the complementary formula only by a verb, and the third colon, which describes this action in detail, begins with the same verb that concluded the second colon, without any intervening formula. Thus the result is again a tricolon. But this verse differs in structure from the tricolon which we have observed in the cases of the regular expanded cola. [This applies to ll. 13-15 only. In ll. 26-29(!) the expansion effected by an intervening formula is followed by two expansions in the other way and the resulting unit is a tetracolon.] We have noted another verse (*CTA* 15:III:17-19) without any intervening formula, in which the first colon ends with the same verb with which the second colon begins, by way of describing the action in detail.

C. The Expanded Colon in the Bible

In the Bible the most conspicuous type of expanded colon is that in which the intervening formula serves as an address. This type is more diversified and developed than in Ugaritic poetry.

Here too we may make a distinction between those passages in which the first colon requires a complement by the very nature of its grammatical structure, and those passages in which it requires a complement by virtue of its content alone. As an example of the first type we may cite *'itti mill^ebānon kallā / 'itti mill^ebānon tābo'i* 'With me from Lebanon, O bride / with me from Lebanon, come' (Cant. 4:8). The following verses belong to the same category: Ex. 15:6; Hab. 3:8; Ps. 29:1; 92:10; 93:3; 94:3; Pr. 31:4. An example of the second type is the verse *rā'ukā mayim 'ᵃ̈lohim ' rā'ukā mayim yāḥilu* 'The waters saw Thee, O God / the waters saw Thee, they trembled' (Ps. 77:17), i.e. 'The waters trembled when they saw Thee'. It is as if seeing and trembling are one action, and it is clear that the first colon is nothing but the expansion of the second, which is the basic one. Similarly, *yāsaptā laggoy YHWH / yāsaptā laggoy nikbādtā / riḥaqtā kol*

qaṣwe 'ārāṣ 'Thou hast increased the nation, O Lord / thou hast increased the nation, thou art glorified / thou hast enlarged all the borders of the land' (Is. 26:15), i.e. 'Thou art glorified by increasing the nation'. In like manner, ^{c}*uri* ^{c}*uri d*^{e}*borā* / ^{c}*uri* ^{c}*uri dabb*^{e}*ri šir*. 'Awake, awake, Deborah / awake, awake, utter a song' (Ju. 5:12). Here also it is possible to distinguish a complementary formula *dabb*^{e}*ri šir*, for Deborah's "awakening" is nothing else than an awakening to song. Likewise, *šubi šubi haššulāmit / šubi šubi w*^{e}*näḥ*^{ä}*zä bāk*. 'Return, return, O Shulamite / return, return, and we will look upon you' (Cant. 7:1) means 'Return, so that we may look upon you'. Sometimes the complementary formula is a consecutive clause: *ma-ddodek middod hayyāpā bannāšim / ma-ddodek middod šäkkākā hišba*^{c}*tānu* 'What is your beloved more than another beloved, O fairest among women / what is your beloved more than another beloved, that you thus adjure us?' (Cant. 5:9); or an adverbial clause *libbabtini '*^{a}*ḥoti kallā / libbabtini b*^{e}*'aḥad* (*Q*^{e}*re*: *b*^{e}*aḥat*) *me*^{c}*enayik* 'You have ravished my heart, my sister, my bride / you have ravished my heart with a glance of your eyes' (Cant. 4:9); or even apposition: *yodukā* ^{c}*ammim '*^{ä}*lohim / yodukā* ^{c}*ammim kullām* 'Let the peoples praise Thee, O God / let the peoples praise Thee, all of them' (Ps. 67:4,6).

From this we proceed to the cola which parallel each other, each one expressing a complete idea, such as: ^{c}*ad ya*^{ca}*bor* ^{c}*amm*^{e}*kā YHWH /* ^{c}*ad ya*^{ca}*bor* ^{c}*am zu qānitā* 'Until Thy people pass by, O Lord / until the people pass by whom Thou has ransomed' (Ex. 15:16). If the verse had read: ^{c}*ad ya*^{ca}*bor* ^{c}*am YHWH /* ^{c}*ad ya*^{ca}*bor* ^{c}*am zu qānitā* 'Until the people pass by, O Lord / until the people pass by whom Thou hast ransomed' [alternatively: ^{c}*ad ya*^{ca}*bor* ^{c}*amm*^{e}*kā YHWH* ^{c}*ad ya*^{ca}*bor* ^{c}*amm*^{e}*kā qānitā* 'Until Thine people pass by, O Lord / until *Thine* people pass by whom Thou hast ransomed'], we would have had an expanded colon in which the complementary formula ^{c}*am zu qanitā* would have served as the determination of the subject, as in Ps. 67:4. But here the subject of the repetitive formula is determined by the personal pronoun (^{c}*amm*^{e}*kā* Thy people), thus turning the expanded colon into a verse of two parallel cola, each of which is complete and comprehensible in itself, even if the origin of this verse from the expanded colon is quite obvious. Still further removed from the pattern of the expanded colon is *mi kāmokā bā'elim YHWH / mi-kkāmokā nä'dār baqqodäš* 'Who is like unto Thee, O Lord, among the

Gods? / Who is like Thee glorious in holiness?'[17a] (Ex. 15:11): *ᶜad šaqqamti dᵉborā / šaqqamti 'em bᵉyiśrāel* 'Until you arose, O Deborah / until you arose, a mother in Israel' (Ju. 5:7) *[*better: 'O mother in Israel'*]*.

There are more patterns in the Bible than in Ugaritic. Both have in common the pattern 1-2-1-2 (Ps. 67:4,6; 77:17; 93:3; Cant. 4:8) and 2-2-2-2 (Ex. 15:6), but in regard to the latter pattern it must be added that the repetitive formula and the intervening formula deviate from the normal. As a rule, it is the address that intervenes between the repetitive formulas. Here, however, the address proper (*YHWH*) is part of the repetitive formula *yᵉminᵉkā YHWH*, and the intervening formula *nä'dāri bakkoᵃḥ* is in apposition to the address.[18]

[[17a] For an alternative analysis of this verse see S.D. Luzzatto in his *commentary on Exodus ad loc.* (in Heb.) who explains the verse as an abbreviated version of: *mi kāmokā ba'elim YHWH mi kkāmokā ba'elim nä'dār baqqodäš*, i.e. in our terminology as an expanded colon in which the repetitive formula has been shortened. As example of such a verse he quotes: *'ᵃšär ḥerᵉpu 'oyᵉbäkā YHWH 'ᵃšär ḥerᵉpu ᶜiqqᵉbot mᵉšiḥäkā* (Ps. 89:52) 'Wherewith Thine enemies have reproached, O Lord, wherewith they have reproached the footsteps of Thine anointed'. Luzzatto's analysis of Ps. 89:52 is doubtlessly correct since the first colon lacks the object and the second colon has as its subject *'oyᵉbäkā*. Less cogent, however, is his interpretation of Ex. 15:11. There each colon might be understood as a complete sentence.

Anyhow, Luzzatto was the first to discuss the modified forms of the expanded colon, cf. also note 28. My thanks are due to Dr. Y. Avishur who drew my attention to Luzzatto's pertinent remarks.*]*

[18] It has been suggested that *nä'dārā bakkoᵃḥ* be read here (*GK* § 90 1), or *nä'dori* (W.L. Moran, *The Hebrew Language in its Northwest Semitic Background*, in *The Bible and the Ancient Near East*, ed. G.E. Wright, New York, 1965, p. 60). These suggestions would turn the expanded colon into two parallel cola. At first glance it would seem possible to support this suggestion with the passage *ᶜad yaᶜᵃbor ᶜammᵉkā YHWH / ᶜad yaᶜᵃbor ᶜam zu qānitā* 'Until Thy people pass by, O Lord / until the people pass whom Thou hast ransomed' (Ex. 15:16), for there the expanded colon structure is breached even in the Masoretic Text, and turns into a construction of two parallel cola. But here the modified repetition of the words *ᶜad yaᶜᵃbor ᶜammᵉkā* causes the two cola to consolidate into a unified idea, in spite of the breaching of the pattern of the expanded colon. The suggested readings *nä'dori, nä'dārā* produce two cola in which the parallelism is forced and stilted. *[*Consult also Ch. Cohen, *JANES* 7 (1975), pp. 13-17.*]*

Not certainly attested in Ugaritic (see above note 13) is the Biblical pattern 2-1-2-2 (Pr. 31:4; Ju. 5:12; Cant. 7:1). The last two examples bear a striking resemblance to one another in the structure of the repetitive formula. Both of these have a double imperative, whose repetition gives rise to four equal imperative expressions. Moreover, at times Biblical poetry prefixes an unaccented, monosyllabic particle to the two principal words of the repetitive formula; this means that the Bible is not as strict as Ugaritic poetry in having the repetitive formula composed of just two words, and admits its composition of three words bearing two stresses, cf. *ki hinne 'oy^e bäkā* (Ps. 92:10) with *ht ibk* (*CTA* 2:IV:8). In this way the patterns 3-1-3-1 (Ps. 92:10; 94:3) and 3-2-3-2 (Cant. 5:9) are formed, and we have observed once even the entirely exceptional pattern 1-2-1-2 (Cant. 4:9). Special consideration is merited by the passage *h^a binhārim ḥārā YHWH / 'im bann^e hārim 'appäkā*, literally 'Against the rivers did it burn, O Lord / if against the rivers Thy anger?' (Hab. 3:8). Here the poet casts off the chains of tradition, which would have required the wording *h^a binhārim ḥārā YHWH / h^a binhārim ḥārā 'appäkā* 'Against the river did it burn, O Lord / against the rivers did Thy wrath burn?', and allows himself the liberty of changes during his repetition of the formula preceding the address. For this change of the repetitive formula in the expanded colon cf. Ps. 29:5,8 and see below.[19]

The tendency of the Bible freely to develop ancient patterns, which makes itself evident in the very structure of the expanded colon, becomes even more prominent in the structure of the complete verse. In the Ugaritic epic, after the expanded colon possessing an intervening formula in the form of an address, there everywhere appears a short, synonymous colon, except in the text *CTA* 10:II:21-23, where the third colon repeats the content of the preceding cola with a certain addition; whereas the Bible has a large number of variants of this form, and only some of the verses are exactly like the Ugaritic pattern in this respect. Some examples follow: *rā'ukā mayim 'ä lohim / rā'ukā mayim yāḥilu / 'ap yirg^e zu t^e homot* 'The waters saw Thee, O God / the waters saw Thee, they trembled / yea, the depths shook' (Ps. 77:17); *ki hinne 'oy^e bäkā YHWH / ki hinne 'oy^e bäkā yo'bedu / yitpār^e du kol*

[19] Cf. also above, note 17a. The verses cited there, whose cola are in synonymous parallelism, tend to have a repetitive formula of the type customary in the expanded colon. But during the repetition the poet varies the formula which he is repeating.

poᶜᵃle 'āwän 'For lo, Thy enemies, O Lord / for lo, Thy enemies shall perish / all evildoers shall be scattered' (Ps. 92:10); *hᵃbinhārim ḥārā YHWH / 'im bannᵉhārim 'appäkā / 'im bayyam ᶜäbrātäkā* 'Against the rivers did it burn, O Lord / if against the rivers Thy wrath / if against the sea Thy indignation?' (Hab. 3:8).

But sometimes the Biblical verse will have no parallel colon, whether the first part of the expanded colon requires a complement by the very nature of its grammatical structure, as: *yᵉminᵉkā YHWH nä'dāri bakkoᵃḥ / yᵉminᵉkā YHWH tirᶜaṣ 'oyeb* 'Thy right hand, O Lord, glorious in power / Thy right hand, O Lord, shatters the enemy' (Ex. 15:6)[19a], or whether it requires a complement by virtue of its content, as: *ᶜuri ᶜuri dᵉborā / ᶜuri ᶜuri dabbᵉri šir* 'Awake, awake O Deborah / awake, awake, utter a song' (Ju. 5:12; cf. Ps. 67:4,6; Cant. 5:9; 7:1).

On the other hand, the expanded colon pattern may develop in various directions. The verse *'itti millᵉbānon kallā / 'itti millᵉbānon tābo'i / tāšuri mero'š 'ᵃmānā* 'With me from Lebanon, bride / with me from Lebanon, come / journey from the peak of Amana' (Cant. 4:8) essentially fits the ancient pattern; but unlike the parallel colon it goes on enthusiastically in flowing style and language: *mero'š śᵉnir wᵉḥärmon mimmᶜonot 'ᵃrāyot meharᵉre nᵉmerim* '... from the peak of Senir and Hermon, from the dens of lions, from the mountains of leopards'.

The creation of a new literary form can be observed in the verse *nāś'u nᵉhārot YHWH / nāś'u nᵉhārot qolām / yiś'u nᵉhārot dokyām* 'The floods have

[[19a] Contrast M. Dahood in *Ras Shamra Parallels* 1, Rome 1972, p. 98 and Ch. Cohen, *op. cit.* (note 18) who join Ex. 15:6-7a into one verse, i.e. regard 7a as a stichos parallel to 6, not to 7b. From this proposal Cohen draws the unavoidable consequence of connecting 7b and 8a to one verse, although he concedes that the parallelism between these stichoi is anything but obvious. He argues, however, that "only by assuming such parallelism can we understand the juxtaposition of *ḥāron* 'anger' and its synonym *'ap* 'fury' as a case of breaking up of the composite phrase *ḥᵃron 'ap* 'furious anger'." But *'appäkā* appears here as the *rectum* of the construct *bᵉruᵃḥ 'appäkā* and therefore no breaking up of *ḥᵃron 'ap* can be assumed. Pay attention also to the parallelism between *mayim* (8a) and *nozᵉlim* (8b) and compare Is. 44:3; Pr. 5:15; Cant. 4:15.]

lifted up, O Lord / the floods have lifted up their voice / the floods lift up their roaring' (Ps. 93:3), as the parallel colon begins here with the perfect of the verb which, in the expanded colon, recurs in the imperfect form; and even though parallelism between two forms of the same verb is not unknown to the style of Ugaritic poetry[20], it does not occur there in connection with expanded cola, while the Biblical poet combined the two stylistic measures, thus inventing a sort of triplet of the repetitive formula. Not just a *sort* of triplet, but an *actual* triad of this formula can be seen in the verses *hābu laYHWH b*^{e}*ne 'elim / hābu laYHWH kābod wā*^{c}*oz / hābu laYHWH k*^{e}*bod š*^{e}*mo // hištaḥ*^{a}*wu laYHWH b*^{e}*hadrat qodăš* 'Ascribe to the Lord, O heavenly beings / ascribe to the Lord glory and strength / ascribe to the Lord the glory of His name // worship the Lord in holy array' (Ps. 29:1-2). The third colon is connected with the expanded colon itself by tripling the repetitive formula *hābu laYHWH* and this *anaphora* is reinforced even more by repetition of the noun *kābod*. The three cola thus combine into a tricolic unit which is paralleled by the fourth colon *hištaḥ*^{a}*wu laYHWH b*^{e}*hadrat qodăš*.[21]

In conclusion we may state that the form of the colon which has been expanded to two cola with an intervening formula in the form of an address is much more flexible in the Bible than in Ugaritic poetry.

---

[20] Cf. above, note 17.

[21] A certain connection of the third colon to the preceding ones by *anaphora* can already be seen in *CTA* 2:IV:8-9, where the first word of the repetitive formula (*ht*) serves as the beginning of the third colon. Cf. also *CTA* 17:I:10-11 and the case of *anadiplosis* in *CTA* 3:V:27-29, discussed in note 13.
For a different analysis of Ps. 29:1, see Mowinckel, *op. cit.* (note 9), pp. 22-23. Compare the verse under discussion also with *hābu la YHWH mišp*^{e}*hot* ^{c}*ammim / hābu la YHWH kābod wā*^{c}*oz / hābu la YHWH k*^{e}*bod š*^{e}*mo / ś'u minḥā ubo'u l*^{e}*ḥasrotāw / hištaḥ*^{a}*wu la YHWH b*^{e}*hadrat qodăš / ḥilu mippānāw kol hā'āräṣ* 'Ascribe to the Lord, O families of the peoples / ascribe to the Lord glory and strength / ascribe to the Lord the glory of his name / bring an offering and come into his courts / worship the Lord in holy array / tremble before him, all the earth' (Ps. 96:7-9). This psalm is composed of ancient hymnic material. But its author, who rightly or wrongly thought the heavenly beings of Ps. 29 to be the gods of the nations, did not think it proper to address these insufficient gods, and therefore addressed the nations themselves, and even explained to them the meaning of the command *hābu la YHWH kābod wā*^{c}*oz / hābu la YHWH k*^{e}*bod š*^{e}*mo* by explicitly saying *ś*^{e}*'u minḥā ubo'u l*^{e}*ḥasrotāw*. Thus the colon *hištaḥ*^{a}*wu laYHWH b*^{e}*hadrat qodăš* was removed from its original context, and the isolation of the colon caused in turn the addition of the parallel colon *ḥilu* ***mippānāw kol hā'āräṣ***.

Not everywhere does the Biblical poet observe the rule, followed in Ugaritic poetry, that the repetitive formula must include just two words, for at times he allows himself to add a monosyllabic short particle to this formula (Ps. 92:10; 94:3; Cant. 5:9; cf. also Hab. 3:8). He does not even shrink from daring to begin the address already at the end of the repetitive formula (Ex. 15:6). Even more important he does not everywhere observe the rule of literal repetition (Hab. 3:8). We have also observed the tendency to triple the repetitive formula, once literally (Ps. 29:1-2), once with a slight change (Ps. 93:3).

Especially interesting is the question of the place of the expanded colon in the verse in its entirety. In the Ugaritic epic the bicolic expanded colon is complemented by one additional synonymous colon, forming a tricolon, a phenomenon which is also present in the Bible. But here there are exceptions, for at times such a colon is absent (Ex. 15:6; Ju. 5:12; Ps. 67:4,6; Cant. 5:9; 7:1, as at times also in the Ugaritic epic, when the *[*non-addressed*]* subject serves as an intervening formula, and there is also a passage in which two cola are added (Ps. 29:1). It can indeed be asked whether perhaps it is only by chance that all the Ugaritic verses containing an expanded colon, whose intervening colon is in the form of an address, are composed of precisely three cola. *[CTA* 10:II:26-29 is a tetracolon. See above.*]* In Canaanite-Biblical poetry we have found verses of one, two, and three cola. As is known, the most common form is that of the bicolon. Now the expansion of the first colon of the bicolon will, in any case, cause the formation of a tricolon *[*except the case of a double expansion of the first colon to three cola, where the result is the transformation of a bicolon to a tetracolon*]*. Thus, for example, a verse such as *ki hinne 'oy^{e}bäkā yo'bedu / yitpār^{e}du kol po^{ca}le 'āwän* (as in the Septuagint B translation of Ps. 92:10) becomes a tricolon: *ki hinne 'oy^{e}bäkā YHWH / ki hinne 'oy^{e}bäkā yo'bedu / yitpār^{e}du kol po^{ca}le 'āwän*. But the same thing can also happen to the monocolon. Thus, for example, the monocolon *y^{e}min^{e}kā YHWH tir^{c}aṣ 'oyeb* is the base from which is formed the bicolon *y^{e}min^{e}kā YHWH nä'dāri bakko^{a}ḥ / y^{e}min^{e}kā YHWH tir^{c}aṣ 'oyeb* (Ex. 15:6). Such a process can also happen to the tricolon, which in this way becomes a tetracolon. The verse *hābu laYHWH kābod wā^{c}oz / hābu laYHWH k^{e}bod š^{e}mo / hištaḥ^{a}wu laYHWH b^{e}hadrat qodäš* becomes the tetracolon *hābu laYHWH bne 'elim / hābu laYHWH kābod wā^{c}oz / hābu laYHWH k^{e}bod š^{e}mo / hištaḥ^{a}wu laYHWH b^{e}hadrat*

qodäš (Ps. 29:1-2).

From here we proceed to the question of the textual criticism of the tricolon. Ugaritic scholars have already pointed out that the tricolon can appear anywhere in the Ugaritic epic, even among the bicola. Therefore, there is no reason to cast doubt upon the originality of the text of a tricolon in a Biblical poem which is written in bicola.[22]

Nevertheless Mowinckel, in his study mentioned above, innovated a method of textual criticism based on the criterion of the number of cola, and claimed that any tricolon among bicola, and likewise any monocolon, is properly suspect.[23] This rule served as his guidepost in his study, even though here and there he was forced to admit that a tricolon in a bicolon poem was original after all, and he gave Ps. 68:28 as the most certain example of this.[24] In line with the general tendency of his study, Mowinckel disputes the originality of the text in Ps. 92:10, and reads: *ki hinne 'oy*^{e}*bäkā yo'bedu / yitpār*^{e}*du kol po*^{ca}*le 'āwän*, relying on three Masoretic manuscripts and on the Septuagint MS B.[25] In his opinion, the received text stems from dittography. But this assumption is not sufficient to explain the address *YHWH*, which is exactly in line with an ancient stylistic tradition, whereas the shorter version may easily have arisen from a homoeoteleuton. Mowinckel also takes issue with the Masoretic Text of Hab. 3:8, reading instead *h*^{a}*binhārim ḥārā 'appäkā / 'im bayyam YHWH* ^{c}*äbrātäkā*. In Mowinckel's opinion the corruption is proved by the difference between the reading *h*^{a}*binhārim ḥārā* and its repetition *'im bann*^{e}*hārim 'appäkā*.[26] But this in no way explains how the word *YHWH* happened to be dislocated in the Masoretic Text. Besides, his reading itself is unacceptable, as the basic, unexpanded reading here is *h*^{a}*binhārim ḥārā 'appäkā / 'im bayyam* ^{c}*äbrātäkā* without address.[27] This becomes apparent upon comparison

---

22 See Ginsberg, *op. cit.* (note 7), p. 171; Albright, *op. cit.* (note 8), p. 3; cf. also Gordon, *UT, Grammar* 13.107, note 2, and 13.109.

23 Mowinckel, *op. cit.* (note 9), p. 97.

24 id., *ibid.*, p. 34.

25 id., *ibid.*, p. 100.

26 id., *ibid.*, pp. 55-56.

27 This text has been proposed as emendation by *BH*^{3}. Its expansion in classical style yields the text *h*^{a}*binhārim hārā YHWH / h*^{a}*binhārim hārā 'appäkā*. The modification of this classical pattern in the actual text gave rise

of the expanded formulas with their short parallels in the Ugaritic epic. As for Mowinckel's main argument, we have already seen that the Biblical poets varied the ancient patterns in different ways, and have especially pointed out the diversification of repetitive formulas in expanded cola and in parallel cola, the style of which is influenced by that of the expanded cola.

We have seen above that in the Ugaritic epic even the subject [which is not an address] may also serve as the intervening formula. It is doubtful whether this pattern appears in the Bible even once. In the verse *'el n^{e}qāmot YHWH / 'el n^{e}qāmot hopi^{ac} / hinnāśe' šopeṭ hā'āräṣ / hāšeb g^{e}mul ^{c}al ge'im* (Ps. 94:1-2) the form *hopi^{ac}* would appear to be past tense, and so the Septuagint understood it to be, but it can also be regarded as an irregular form of the imperative.[28] This is supported by the imperative forms *hinnāśe'* and *hāšeb* in the continuation of the verse. It has even been suggested to read *hopi^{c}ā(h)*, like the imperative form in Ps. 80:2 (haplography before *hinnāśe'*); but it cannot be decided one way or another. If we consider *hopi^{ac}* to be a past tense, then the repetitive formula *'el n^{e}qāmot* is a regular subject, and the intervening formula is in apposition to the subject. The expanded colon appears without any parallel colon, which means that we have before us a bicolon, like those which we have seen

---

to the current interpretation which regards *YHWH* (not *'appäkā*!) as subject of *ḥārā*. Cf. *RV* which translates: 'Was the Lord displeased against the rivers? Was Thine anger against the rivers?' Likewise e.g. the standard lexica of *BDB*, *GB* and *Baumgartner s.v. ḥārā*. But *ḥārā* without *'ap* is nowhere else attested, *ḥārā 'ap b* ... 29 times. The short emended text removes this difficulty. But so does our interpretation of the traditional reading. Cf. also the Septuagint which reads: μὴ ἐν ποταμοῖς ὠργίσθης, κύριε, ἢ ἐν ποταμοῖς ὁ θυμός σου. The Septuagint (or its *Vorlage*) then realized that *YHWH* is a vocative, but not that *'appäkā* is the subject of *ḥārā*. Therefore it turned *ḥārā* into *ḥāritā*.
The first to advance this explanation of the verse was S.D. Luzzatto in his commentary upon Ex. 15:11 (in Heb.). There he remarks: "The first part lacks the word *'appäkā*, the second part the word *ḥārā* and it is impossible to explain in accordance with the accents of the Massora. This interpretation would require the reading: *ḥārā 'ap YHWH*, since *ḥārā YHWH* is not found anywhere". Recently the interpretation has been proposed by P.R. Berger, *UF* 2, p. 343, note 26 who aptly translates: *'Ist denn gegen die Ströme entbrannt YHWH, etwa gegen die Ströme oder gegen das Meer dein Grimm'.]*

[28] See *GK*, § 53m.

in Ugaritic verses. These are expanded cola in which the subject serves as the intervening formula. But if we explain *hopi*^{ac} as an imperative form, then the doubled formula *'el n*^{e}*qāmot* is an address and the intervening formula *YHWH* is in apposition to the address; cf. Ex. 15:6, in which the intervening formula *nä'dāri bakko*^{a}*ḥ* is in apposition to the address *YHWH*, which concludes the repetitive formula. In addition, we can explain the cola beginning with *hinnāše'* and *hāšeb* as paralleling the expanded cola, thus giving us a tetracolon. In any case it is clear that the expanded colon constructed according to the pattern 2-1-2-1 is exceedingly close to the ancient patterns.

In contrast to this, considerable deviation from the traditional forms is shown by the verse *'ānoki la YHWH / 'ānoki 'āširā / '*^{a}*zammer la YHWH '*^{ä}*lohe yisrā'el* 'I, to the Lord / I will sing / I will make melody to the Lord, the God of Israel' (Ju. 5:3).

Some scholars have explained this combination as *casus pendens*, meaning the isolation of the logical subject.[29] The verse would then mean: 'As for me, I will sing'. If, however, the first *'ānoki* were *casus pendens*, the second only would serve as grammatical subject. But it seems rather unlikely to attribute to these two *'ānoki* different functions. Moreover, the prominent emphasis on the subject is out of place here, as it is not the habit of one who sings in honour of his God to make himself stand out; cf. *'āširā laYHWH ki gā'o gā'ā* 'I will sing to the Lord, for He has triumphed gloriously' (Ex. 15:1).[30] Therefore not only is the complete expression *'ānoki la YHWH 'ānoki 'āširā* difficult, but even the simple combination *'ānoki 'āširā* is strange, as in Biblical Hebrew *'ānoki* is prefixed to a finite verb only when the subject is to be emphasized. If so, it would seem that the function of the personal pronoun here is specifically to expand the expression *'āširā laYHWH*. However, the results of this expansion exceed what would normally be expected. The intervening formula *laYHWH* is the indirect object,

---

[29] S.R. Driver, *Treatise on the Use of the Tenses*, Oxford, 1892, p. 269.

[30] Cf. also Is. 5:1; Ps. 13:6; 27:6; 57:8; 89:2; 101:1; 104:33; 108:2; 144:9; the wording *wa'*^{a}*ni 'āšir* (Ps. 59:17) is in contrast with *hemmā y*^{e}*ni*^{c}*un* (*Q*^{e}*re*, v. 16). In Ugaritic too *ašr* 'I will sing' (*CTA* 24:38,40) appears without a personal pronoun.

and the repetitive formula is limited to one word[31] as in Cant. 4:9.

The Bible also has a type of expanded verse in which the intervening formula is absent, [but not the type of two consequent expansions, one with intervening formula followed by a second without it.] An example which is close in form to the Ugaritic epic is the verse *YHWH zᵉkārānu yᵉbārek yᵉbārek 'ät bet yiśrā'el* 'The Lord has been mindful of us, He will bless / He will bless the house of Israel' (Ps. 115:12). This verse is reminiscent of those Ugaritic verses in which one colon ends in a verb lacking a complement, while the next colon begins with the same verb and adds the details of the action. Also similar to this is the passage *lipne YHWH ki bā' / ki bā' lišpoṭ hā'äräṣ* 'Before the Lord, for He comes / for He comes to judge the earth' (Ps. 96:13), which repeats not only the verb but also the conjunction *ki*. But this slight variation in the repetitive formula is not sufficient to prevent its being in harmony with the common style. Thus here also the received text is to be maintained, being confirmed also by the Septuagint, even though the repetition of the words *ki bā'* is lacking not only in the parallel text of 1 Chr. 16:33, and in a similar version of Ps. 98:9, but also in some MSS of Ps. 96:13. Also to be classified here is the verse *wᵉnātan 'arṣām naḥᵃlā / naḥᵃlā lᵉyiśrā'el ᶜammo* 'And He gave their land as a heritage / a heritage to Israel His people' (Ps. 135:12 and cf. also Ps. 136:21,22), in which the first colon ends with the second object *naḥᵃlā* and the second colon begins with the same noun *naḥᵃlā*, the meaning of which is explained by the addition of the indirect object *lᵉyiśrā'el ᶜammo*.

In contrast to this, much more removed from the ancient patterns is the verse *qol YHWH šober 'ᵃrāzim / wayᵉšabber YHWH 'arze hallᵉbānon* 'The voice of the Lord breaks the cedars / and the Lord has broken the cedars of Lebanon' (Ps. 29:5). The clear meaning of this verse is that the voice of the Lord breaks the cedars of Lebanon. *Lᵉbānon* thus serves as a complementary formula coming at the end, and in the repetitive formula that pre-

---

[31] A. Weiser, *ZAW* 71 (1959), p. 73, has explained *'ānoki laYHWH* as meaning 'I belong to the Lord', assuming that a new sentence begins afterwards. The basis for this explanation is the clear difficulty in translating the expanded verse in the Song of Deborah into a foreign language to whose spirit the syntactical construction of this verse is foreign.

cedes the complementary formula there occur changes, such as we have already observed in other verses. The same type of expanded sentence recurs in the same psalm, as follows: *qol YHWH yāḥil midbār / yāḥil YHWH midbar qādeš*. 'The voice of the Lord shakes the wilderness / the Lord shakes the wilderness of Kadesh' (v. 8).

At the beginning of the article we mentioned that Rashbam classifies with the type of verses discussed also the passages *ben porāt yosep / ben porāt ᶜale ᶜāyin* 'A fruitful bough is Joseph[32] / a fruitful bough by a spring' (Gen. 49:22), and *hᵃbel hᵃbālim 'āmar qohälät / hᵃbel hᵃbālim hakkol hābäl* 'Vanity of vanities, says the Preacher / vanity of vanities, all is vanity' (Ecc. 1:2). These verses differ from all the verses discussed up to now in that they are noun clauses, whereas up to now we have dealt only with verb clauses. Now this difference is of fundamental importance. We had established a rule above that the expanded colon was created from a nucleus, which is the formula following the intervening formula, and whose verb includes the subject of the sentence. But the words *ben porāt ᶜale ᶜāyin*, which follow the intervening formula *yosep*, do not form a complete sentence, as they lack a subject. We are thus compelled to state that the basic formula is in this case *ben porāt yosep ᶜale ᶜāyin*. This type of expanded sentence is not at all present in the Ugaritic texts, and is quite rare in the Bible. Thus it seems likely that it is a new pattern that has been formed under the influence of the usual pattern. Perhaps we may even allow ourselves to conjecture that the type providing the influence is that very colon in which the intervening formula serves as the subject,

---

[32] *ben porāt* (here translated with *RV* 'a fruitful bough') is difficult. See, apart from the commentaries on Genesis and the dictionaries, N.H. Tur-Sinai, *Ha-lashon we Ha-sepher, vol. Ha-sepher*², pp. 211-212 (in Heb.); also J.M. Allegro, *ZAW* 64 (1952), pp. 249f. However, this problem is not the concern of an analysis of sentence structure.
[Most recently Gen. 49:22 has been treated by St. Gevirtz, *HUCA* 46 (1976), pp. 35-49 who propounds the rendering:
'A son of a wild she-ass is Joseph
A son of a wild she-ass at a fountain
(A son of) wild asses by a *šur*'.
Gevirtz remarks that my analysis of the two first cola "is marred in large part by the failure to recognize the structural significance of the verses' third colon" (p. 40, note 28). Yet even in his interpretation the first two cola form a selfcontained statement whose structural analysis does not depend upon the third colon.]

and not as the address. It is true that we have found no certain example of a subject as the intervening formula in the Bible; but as this phenomenon is quite common in the Ugaritic texts, it is likely only by chance that no verses of this type were preserved in the Bible.

The verse in Ecclesiastes is even further removed from the classical scheme, as in this case the intervening formula is a complete sentence *'āmar qohälät* a case which is exceptional.

D. The Original form of the Expanded Colon

The original form of the expanded colon cannot be determined with certainty. Of the expanded cola having an intervening formula, the type appearing to be the most original is that in which the subject of the verse is [a person] addressed [whose name appears in the intervening formula], such as the Ugaritic verse *ht ibk b^{c}lm / ht ibk tmḫ̣ṣ* (*CTA* 2:IV:8-9), and the Hebrew verse *hābu laYHWH b^{e}ne 'elim / hābu laYHWH kābod wā^{c}oz* 'Ascribe to the Lord, O heavenly beings / ascribe to the Lord glory and strength' (Ps. 29:1). Both verses contain an invitation, directed at the possessor of the intervening name, to do something, and it is possible that this formal invitation is the source of the form.[33] [Only in one expanded Ugaritic colon where the addressee is the subject of the sentence, urged to do something, his name is substituted by another expression (RS 34.126:20-22. See *supra*, pp. 291-292. This variation of the pattern should be regarded as secondary.] Apparently less original are those forms in which the intervening formula is an address not directed at the subject of the sentence. To this type belongs, for example, the Ugaritic verse *qrn dbatk btlt ^{c}nt / qrn dbatk b^{c}l ymšḥ* (*CTA* 10:II:21-22). Here the intervening formula is addressed to Anat, while the subject of the sentence is Baal. The same construction appears in the Bible, for example, in the verse *ki hinne 'oy^{e}bäkā YHWH / ki hinne 'oy^{e}bäkā yo'bedu* (Ps. 92:10) and also *rā'ukā mayim '^{ä}lohim / rā'ukā mayim yāḥilu* (Ps. 77:17). Here the sentence does not contain an invitation but

[[33] This definition neglects verses which do not contain an invitation though having an intervening formula in which the subject of the verse is addressed such as Is. 26:15; Cant. 4:9; 5:9. Verses of this type, however, are rare in the Bible and are not attested to in Ugaritic literature at all. They probably represent a later stage in the development of the pattern.]

an announcement, which has been influenced in its solemnity by the form of the invitation. Seemingly less original is that form in which the intervening formula is not an address, but rather the [not-addressed] subject of the sentence, as in the Ugaritic verse *y^{c}n ḥtkh krt / y^{c}n ḥtkh ṛš* (*CTA* 14: I:21-22), and perhaps also the Biblical verse *'el n^{e}qāmot YHWH / 'el n^{e}qāmot hopi^{ac}* (Ps. 94:1), if we explain *hopi^{ac}* as past tense. In this type the contents describe a deed in every case. The example of such verb clauses is apparently followed in the noun clause *ben porāt yosep / ben porāt ^{ca}le ^{c}āyin* (Gen. 49:22), cf. also Ecc. 1:2, in which a complete sentence is used as an intervening formula. The historical placement of those few expanded expressions which lack an intervening formula is entirely unclear, and it cannot be decided whether to consider them as an outgrowth of those expanded cola in which the intervening formula serves as the subject, or to regard the simplicity of form as evidence of extreme antiquity.[34]

The vast majority of the Biblical verses discussed belong to the type of address or, more exactly, to the two types of address, which in Biblical poetry rid themselves of the rigid formal rules to which they were subjected in the Ugaritic epic. In the Bible they develop into such a large amount of variations that almost every verse is a unique form. But there is also a type of expanded colon in which there is no intervening formula, and there is even a verse which breaks all the accepted rules. This is the verse *'ānoki laYHWH / 'ānoki 'āširā* (Ju. 5:3). Thus in the present subject also the Bible constitutes a developed stage in the history of Canaanite literature, a stage which is clearly distinguished from the rigidity of the simple and archaic forms of the Ugaritic epic.

[[34] The second alternative seems to be preferable. In verses having a repetitive formula without an intervening one, the repetitive formula invariably appears the first time at the end of a stichos. The opposite holds true for expanded cola in which an intervening formula serves as subject, since there this formula is always found at the beginning of a colon, even if the subject is not addressed. This basic difference disproves a genetic relation between the two patterns. We should also pay attention to the fact that in Biblical poetry the simple repetition is clearly attested, but not the repetition as consequence of an intervening formula which serves as unaddressed subject. This is not easily understood on the supposition that the second pattern preceded the first.]

It would appear that the style of the expanded colon cannot be ascribed fundamentally to one literary genre. In Ugaritic we have observed it in the epic, in the Bible, mostly in hymns in honour of the Lord, but sometimes also in the love songs of the Song of Solomon and once in a proverb from the Wisdom Literature (Pr. 31:4). This ancient pattern has left its impression also on the noun clause in the Blessing of Joseph (Gen. 49:22), less so in the later passage Ecc. 1:3.[35]

[The present paper has been supplemented by Y. Avishur, *Addenda to the Expanded Colon in Ugaritic and Biblical Verse, UF* 4, pp. 1-10. His additions include hitherto overlooked phenomena of principal interest, e.g. a certain variation in the repetition of a repetitive formula of *three*(!) words in Ugaritic (*CTA* 6:III-IV:25-26) and the appearance of an intervening formula, comprehending a complete sentence, within enlarged verb clauses in the Bible (Ps. 124:1-5; 129:1-2).

In note 54 of his stimulating paper "*Verse - Patterns in Ugaritic, Akkadian and Hebrew Poetry*", *UF* 7, pp. 483-492, W.C.E. Watson points to the verse: *atûme pita bābka / pita bābkama lûruba anāku*. 'Porter open your door - open your door so that I can come in.' (*Ištar's Descent*, 14-15) and remarks that the verse may be an example of the expanded colon. It may indeed be regarded as an expanded colon without intervening formula in spite of the slight variant *bābka, bābkama* and thus be adduced as a proof that

[[35] E. König, *Stilistik, Rhetorik, Poetik*, Leipzig, 1900, subsumes the phenomena dealt with in this paper under other categories which fail to do justice to the extended character of the formulations under discussion.

The expanded colon, containing a vocative as intervening clause, is characterized in his book as *anaphora* or *epizeuxis* (pp. 298f.). According to his definition, in the *anaphora* the repeated words form the basis of a new moment of the descriptions as in Ps. 94:3, whereas in the *epizeuxis* the repeated words are only divided by a vocative as in Ps. 92:10. However, Ps. 92:10 and Ps. 94:3 are of obviously identical structure. The term *anaphora* should be restricted to independent sentences, introduced by the same expression, as Deut. 27:16-25, the term *epizeuxis* to simple duplications of words, laying stress on the duplicated word as Gen. 22:11 which do not imply the extension of one colon into two. The expanded colon without intervening clause is subsumed by König under *anadiplosis*, i.e. as the repetition of the end of a sentence at the beginning of the following one. It might be conceded to him that in those cases the beginning of the second sentence does take up the end of the preceding one. But in order to avoid confusion the name *anadiplosis* should be confined to an expression concatenating two independent sentences as in Ez. 18:20,b-c, where the actual text cannot be cut short without impairing its very sense.]

the expanded colon should not be regarded as a distinctive feature of North-Western Semitic poetry. It seems, however, that this affinity between North-Western Semitic and Akkadian poetry is restricted to those bordercases where both the repetitive and the complementary clause preserve the appearance of complete and independent sentences as here where the two sentences "open your door" and "I may come in" are still clearly discernible.]

Postscript.

The explanation of Ps. 92:11 propounded on p. 286 note 11 should be abandoned. See the present writer, *Balloti b^ešämän ra^canān, UF 10*, pp. 111-113.

The Numerals in Ugaritic

This paper was read before the publication of C.H. Gordon's *Ugaritic Textbook*, Rome 1965 (= *UT*), which contains a highly valuable up-to-date discussion of the Ugaritic numbers in the light of the texts that have been published in recent years.[1] It goes without saying that the present writer's analysis conforms to a considerable degree to Gordon's new grammar. Nevertheless, the reader will not fail to note a certain amount of new proposals.

As in all Semitic languages, the Ugaritic numbering is based on the decimal system. But it seems that this statement requires some qualification. Beside the normal numbers, which belong to the decimal system, Ugaritic preserves a few remnants of a more primitive mode. Though Ugaritic has a specific word to denote the number six, we do find once that it employs a dual form of *ṯlṯ* to indicate the number six: *ṯlṯtm b*^{c}*lm*[2] - six workmen.[2a] Moreover, the number twelve is also expressed occasionally by the dual form *ṯṯtm ḫzr*[3] - twice six workmen.[4] These irregular dual forms of three and six call to mind the regular dual forms ^{c}*šrm* - twenty, *mitm* - two hundred, *alpm* -

---

[1] *PRU* 2 and *PRU* 5.

[2] *PRU* 5, text 80:6-7 (bis).

[[2a] Ugaritic *b*^{c}*l* 'worker', probably *bā*^{c}*ilu*, a substantivized participle of the verb *b*^{c}*l*, 'to work' (*PRU* 2, text 24:rev. 6,8), which should be differentiated from the noun *b*^{c}*l* = *ba*^{c}*alu*, 'lord'. Cf. in Talmudic Hebrew *po*^{c}*el* 'worker', although the verb *p*^{c}*l* is not attested in this sense.]

[3] *PRU* 2, text 24:rev.:7,9 (bis). The exact meaning of *ḫzr* is unknown, but it appears from the context that it denotes some kind of workman and not pig. Possibly it is identical to *ḫnzr // ġlm* known from *CTA* 5:V:9. For the free interchange of *ḫāziru* and *ḫanziru* cf. *CAD, s.v. ḫāziru*.

[4] Cf. also *ṯlṯt w ṯlṯt* - six (*PRU* 2, text 127:13) and *ṯṯ ṯṯ* - twelve (*PRU* 2, text 127:5); cf. also the defective and obscure text: *ṯn ḥblm alp alp m [ ] ṯmn ḥblm šb*^{c} *šb*^{c} *ma [ ]* (*PRU* 2, text 128:30-31). Gordon's interpretation of these numbers as two thousand and fourteen (Gordon, *UT, Grammar* 7.24,42) should be regarded as a tentative proposal only, pending further evidence.

two thousand. It should be observed that these normal dual forms are restricted to the basic numbers of the decimal system. Therefore, it may be argued that the abnormal dual forms *ṯlṯtm* and *ṯṯtm* should be regarded as the remnants of an old and archaic arrangement, in which three and six occupied the place of basic numbers. It may be pertinent to quote Bloomfield here[5]: 'The Khan-Bushmen are said to count by simple numbers only to three and to use two and two for four and so on.' The use of the numbers six/six to represent the number twelve reflects a later stage of the history of the language, a stage that is a consequence of the coming into use of a special number for six, but precedes the decimal system.

I should like to point out another archaic feature which belongs to the system of ordinal numbers. It may be recalled that there is no common Semitic root which denotes the concept 'first'. We may, therefore, conclude that the words which denote it came into use in a relatively late period. This would justify our assumption that, in the oldest stage of language, the concept 'first' was not expressed at all. As a matter of fact, in the Ugaritic epos, we find the opposition 'the first day' as against 'the second day' expressed by *ym* - day, as against *ṯn(ym)* - second (day).[6] So much for our remarks concerning the vestiges of archaic usage.[6a]

Let us now turn to those regular cardinal numbers which exhibit some remarkable features. The form *ṯn* - two, perhaps *ṯina*, like Akkadian *šina*, occurs not only in status constructus but in status absolutus as well[7], e.g., in the verse *aṯr ṯn ṯn hlk*[8] - they went two after two, or in an administrative text: *ṯn b ulm*[9] - two in the town Ullami. *Ṯnm*[10] is attested

---

[5] L. Bloomfield, *Language*, London 1935, p. 279.

[6] E.g. *CTA* 4:VI:24. Cf. in this volume, *The Development of the Term 'First' in the Semitic Languages*, pp. 13-16.

[[6a] For the archaic use of a cardinal instead of an ordinal number in the standard phrase *mk bšbᶜ ymm* see in this volume, *The Seven-Day-Unit*, p. 194, note 4a.]

[7] Cf. now also Gordon, *UT*, *Grammar*, 7.9.

[8] *CTA* 14:94.

[9] *PRU* 2, text 61:2. Cf. *ibid*. 1; *PRU* 5, text 40:33.

[10] *CTA* 18:II:22.

in the meaning 'twice' only and may be compared to Hebrew *'arba^{c}tayim* - four times. The feminine form *ṯṯ* is attested in our texts in *status constructus* only. But we may conjecture that the form remains the same whether occurring in the *status absolutus* or in the *status constructus*, and cf. in Akkadian the absolute forms, *šina, šitta,* as against the Hebrew *š^{e}nayim, š^{e}tayim* and the Arabic *'iṯnāni, 'iṯnatāni*. The number six also presents special problems. It is commonly assumed that the Proto-Semitic root of this word is *šdṯ*. In the Ugaritic ordinal 'sixth', this root becomes *ṯdṯ* by regressive assimilation of the *s* to the *ṯ*. The cardinal number in standard Ugaritic occurs in the form *ṯṯ* as a result of the assimilation of the *d* to the following *ṯ*. But it may be argued that the Ugaritic epos has retained an older archaic cardinal form *ṯdṯ*. We meet with the verse: 'He baked bread for *ḫmš*, provision for *ṯdṯ yrḫm*.'[11] In this verse the rendering of the fifth and the sixth month is forced and not in accordance with the scheme x//x+1 prevalent in Ugaritic and Biblical poetry.[12] Consequently, the numbers are best taken as cardinal forms and the *m* of *yrḫm* as the plural termination and not as enclitic *m*. Our view is corroborated by South-Arabian, where two forms for the cardinal six are attested, an older form which preserves the Proto-Semitic *d* and a later form in which the *d* has been assimilated to the following *ṯ*.[13] It should be added that the Ugaritic form *ṯṯ* may very well have some bearing upon the explanation of the development of the Biblical Hebrew *šeš*, as the possibility cannot be excluded that Hebrew *šeš* is directly derived from *ṯṯ* and not from a form closer to Proto-Semitic.

In the cardinal *ṯmn, ṯmnt* - eight, the ending *y* has been lost. But it reappears in *ṯmnym* - eighty, as opposed to the forms *^{c}šrm, ṯlṯm*, etc. with-

[11] *CTA* 14:83-84. *[*Contrast de Moor, *Seasonal Pattern*, pp. 61f., especially note 78. De Moor argues that "the King Krt had to bake bread during the fifth and sixth month". This argument implies that the Ugaritic months were numbered by ordinals like in Hebrew. But Ugaritic had special proper names for each month (cf. Gordon, *UT*, p. 534) and no alternative Ugaritic system of counting the months by ordinal numbers is attested so far. De Moor argues that Krt is not supposed of having prepared "bread for five/six months because the campaign was not intended to last that long". This argument, however, fails taking into account the hyperbolic style of the description, highlighted by the immense number of the soldiers.*]*

[12] Cf. e.g. W. Roth, *VT* 12 (1962), pp. 300-311.

[13] Hoefner, *ASG*, p. 131.

out *y*.

As has been pointed out by Gordon in his *Manual*[14], the numbers between three and ten may be used in either gender, that is to say, that even before masculine nouns the numerical form does not necessarily have to take the *t*-ending. This confirms the correctness of Hebrew *way*^{e}*hi k*^{e}*mišloš ḥ*^{o}*dāšim* (Gen. 38:24). Gordon correctly states that in a single case *ṯn* even *precedes* a feminine noun.[15]

Numbers between eleven and nineteen occur in Ugaritic in very manifold forms and we may be in a better position to analyze them if we start with the simpler analysis of the compound numbers between twenty-one and ninety-nine and deal with the numbers between eleven and nineteen afterwards.

The compound numbers between twenty-one and ninety-nine are divided into two different types. The first corresponds exactly with that found in modern English usage, e.g. *ṯlṯm ṯṯ*[16] - thirty-six. As a rule, in this type, the smaller number follows the greater asyndetically. Thus far, I have found only one exception to this rule, i.e. the number *ṯlṯm w šb*^{c}[17] - thirty and seven with conjunctive *w*.[18]

The structure of the second type, of compound numbers between twenty-one and ninety-nine, has no parallel in other Semitic languages. The unit precedes and is connected with the decade by *l*, e.g., *šb*^{c} *l* ^{c}*šrm*[19] - twenty-seven, *šb*^{c}*t l ṯlṯm*[20] - thirty-seven.

The first type is attested in the epos once only[21], the second six ti-

---

[14] Gordon, *UM, Grammar*, 7.5. Cf. *UT* 7.6.

[15] Gordon, *UM, Grammar*, 7.5. Cf. *UT* 7.6. *ṯn šurtm* (*CTA* 137:Y:3,8,17) 2 *šurt's* (dual). His argument is cogent, if we accept the likely supposition that the dual *šurtm* is derived from the singular.

[16] *PRU* 5, text 105:4.

[17] *PRU* 5, text 54:rev. 23.

[18] Cf. *ṯlṯt w ṯlṯt* (supra, note 4).

[19] *PRU* 2, text 135:6.

[20] *PRU* 5, text 54:3.

[21] *CTA* 4:VII:10.

mes.[22] In administrative texts, the first type is found twenty-two times[23], the second fourteen.[24] Of the fourteen examples, twelve occur in connection with the twenty[25], whereas of the twenty-two examples there are only four compounds with twenty.[26] The second type requires some words of explanation. It appears that in this construction with *l* the tens are felt as *rectum*; and cf., e.g. the Hebrew *b^{e}'āḥād laḥodäš* (Gen. 8:5) - at the first of the month, or *bišnat šeš me'ot šānā l^{e}ḥayye no^{a}ḥ* (Gen. 7:11) - in the six hundredth year of Noah's life. That is to say, the *l* expresses the belonging of the digits to the tens. This cumbersome device creates a more archaic impression than the simple and easier one of the English type thirty-five; this may also be deduced from its frequent use in epic language.

To return now to the numbers from eleven to nineteen. Here two questions need discussion.

1. The number ten is expressed in three different ways, by *^{c}šr, ^{c}šrt* and *^{c}šrh*.
2. The connections of the digit and the ten occur in various patterns.

Let us take the second question first. As a rule, the digit precedes the ten asyndetically, e.g., *ṯn ^{c}šr*.[27] This rule conforms to Hebrew and general Semitic usage. But there are exceptions. We find the forms *^{c}šr ṯn*[28], *^{c}šr arb^{c}*[29], *^{c}šrt ḫmš*[30], *^{c}šrt ṯṯt*.[31] These may be explained as formations analogous to the *^{c}šrm ṯlṯ* type. Only once do we encounter a form of the

---

[22] *CTA* 4:VII:9; 5:V:20-21; 12:II:49-50; 25:3.

[23] *CTA* 67:6; 157:4-5; *PRU* 2, text 28:9-10; 29:11; 31:14; 84:4,7,11,14,19, 21; 89:13; 111:9; *PRU* 5, text 13:7,19; 91:8; 97:1; 101:7; 105:4; 107:6; 120:1.

[24] *CTA* 35:43; *PRU* 2, text 25:3,5; 30:8; 84:9; 88:2; 135:6; *PRU* 5, text 11: *en marge*; 49:6; 54:3,17, rev. 20; 97:6; 113:33.

[25] The two exceptions are: *[š]b^{c}t l ṯlṯm* (*PRU* 5, text 54:3) and *ṯmn l arb^{c}m* (*PRU* 2, text 25:5).

[26] *CTA* 67:6; 157:4-5; *PRU* 2, text 28:10; *PRU* 5, text 101:7.

[27] *CTA* 67:2,9; *PRU* 2, text 87:1; *PRU* 5, text 103:5.

[28] *PRU* 2, text 81:4; 111:10.

[29] *PRU* 2, text 81:18.

[30] *PRU* 2, text 131:8.

[31] *PRU* 2, text 131:7.

type *ḫmšt l* ᶜ*šrt*[32], a clear analogy to the formation *ḫmš l* ᶜ*šrm*.

Discussion of the three forms ᶜ*šr*, ᶜ*šrt*, ᶜ*šrh*, is, to our regret, seriously handicapped by a blank in our knowledge. We are not in a position to point to even one clear example of these numbers in connection with feminine nouns: they all occur in connection with nouns which are either clearly masculine or at least of doubtful gender.[33] In the numbers between thirteen and nineteen, the correspondence between the digits and the decades is determined by fixed rules. The short form ᶜ*šr* is always connected with the short form of the digit without *t*, e.g., *t̲lt̲* ᶜ*šr*[34] - thirteen, *arb*ᶜ ᶜ*šr*[35] - fourteen. This rule is demonstrated by eighteen examples.[36] It also applies to ᶜ*šrh*, e.g., *arb*ᶜ ᶜ*šrh*[37] - fourteen, a type of which we find thirteen instances.[38] On the other hand, ᶜ*šrt* is connected with the *t*-form of the digits, e.g., *[ar]b*ᶜ*t* ᶜ*šrt*[39] - fourteen, *ḫmšt l* ᶜ*šrt*[40] - fifteen. The rule is confirmed by fourteen examples[41] against a single exception: ᶜ*šrt ḫmš*.[42] But even that exception is doubtful, because the scribe corrected the text and had no space left to add the *t* of *ḫmšt*. It may be pointed out that the structure of these numbers differs basically from the Hebrew and the Arabic, where the short form of the ten is connected with the long form of the unit, e.g., *ḥᵃmiššā(h)* ᶜ*āśār* and likewise *ḫamsata* ᶜ*ašara*. Forms like *arb*ᶜ*t* ᶜ*šrt* have no parallel in the Hebrew, which does not employ the form ᶜ*aśārā(h)* in numbers between eleven and nineteen, or

---

32 *PRU* 5, text 54:7.

33 The only probable exception is *t̲mn* ᶜ*šr šurt* (*CTA* 137:1). Cf. supra, note 15. But even this exception is not beyond doubt, because of the form *t̲n šurtm*.

34 *PRU* 2, text 29:7; *PRU* 5, text 38:2.

35 Cf. *supra*, note 29.

36 *CTA* 66:7; 67:3-4,7,11-12; 137:A:1; 137:B:10; *PRU* 2, text 28:2; 84:1; 128:29; *PRU* 5, text 38:5,10; 76:6; 81:1. For additional cases, see above, notes 29 and 33.

37 *PRU* 2, text 79:1; 83:1.

38 *CTA* 34:9-10; 68:5,8; *PRU* 2, text 30:2; 88:3; 99:2; 106:14; 126:5; *PRU* 5, text 48:4; 97:2; 105:1; cf. *supra*, note 36.

39 *PRU* 2, text 144:6; *PRU* 5, text 54:13; 100:16.

40 Cf. *supra*, note 32.

41 *PRU* 2, text 83:8,14; 108:8; 131:4-7; *PRU* 5, text 54:8; rev:7; 100:6; 101:15. Cf. *supra*, notes 32 and 39.

42 *PRU* 2, text 131:8.

in the Arabic, which connects the short form of the unit with the *t*-form of the decade. The difficult form *ᶜšrh*, whose similarity to the spelling of Hebrew *ᶜăśre(h)* is obvious, has not as yet been satisfactorily explained. In the Hebrew form, the ending *e* is generally regarded as a derivative of the feminine ending *ai*. But it is difficult to explain the Ugaritic *h* in the same manner because we have no reason to doubt its consonantal character. Consequently, the Ugaritic form remains unelucidated and the question concerning the derivation of the Hebrew form *ᶜăśre(h)* has become more problematic than ever.[42a]

Special attention should be given to the Ugaritic forms *ᶜšt ᶜšr*[43] and *ᶜšt ᶜšrh*[44] - eleven, which recall Hebrew *ᶜašte ᶜāśār* and *ᶜašte ᶜăśre*. As is well known, two explanations of the Hebrew *ᶜašte* have been suggested: (a) that it is a late borrowing from Akkadian *ištēn*; (b) that it is an old dialectical form of Canaanite origin. In the light of Ugaritic evidence, the second explanation is to be preferred. Hebrew usage conforms in three respects with Ugaritic usage as opposed to Akkadian: (a) in both Ugaritic and Hebrew, *ᶜašte* is restricted to the connection with ten and is never used to represent the simple number one, whereas *ištēn* denotes one, without any necessary connection with ten[44a], (b) *ištēn* has the ending *n*, whereas the Ugaritic and Hebrew word has not; (c) the *ᶜ* in Hebrew is difficult to explain, if the form has been borrowed from the Late Akkadian, but it presents no difficulties if we regard the Hebrew *ᶜašte* as an old Canaanite form.

Now to discuss the greater numbers. The number *mit* - hundred, has been explained phonetically as *mi'tu* or as *mi'atu* with a short *a*. Be that as it may be, the number *mitm* - two hundred, is patently a dual form which derives from the singular form, as is demonstrated by forms like *t̲lt̲ mat, t̲alāt̲u mi'āti*, with a long *a*.

[[42a] Contrast now: J. Blau - S.E. Loewenstamm, *UF* 2, p. 31.]

[43] *PRU* 2, text 24:rev:7; *PRU* 5, text 103:7.

[44] *PRU* 2, text 83:4; *PRU* 5, text 11: *en marge*:2.

[[44a] *ᶜšty* representing the simple number 'one' without connection with ten appears now in RS 34.126:27. See A. Caquot, *ACF* 75 (1974-75), p. 428.]

The compound numbers, connected with a hundred and tens, occur in two types, of which both have been encountered earlier in this paper, viz. the type *mit ṯlṯm*[45] and the type *ṯlṯm l mit*.[46] The units always appear at the end of the numerical series, in the second type as well as in the first, e.g., *mit* ^{c}*šrm ṯn*[47] - a hundred twenty-two, and likewise *ḫmšm l mit arb*^{c}.[48] The same rules also apply with respect to the number *mitm*. Here, too, we come across the two types *mitm ṯṯm*[49] - two hundred sixty, and *šb*^{c}*m l mitm*[50] - two hundred seventy.

In the numbers from three hundred one onwards, only the descending type of compound numbers is found, viz. the one in which the hundreds precede the smaller numbers, asyndetically, e.g., *ṯlṯ mat ṯlṯm*[51] - three hundred thirty. Numbers of this type have thus far been found in eleven instances.[52] We may consequently assume that compound numbers over three hundred are always represented by this later type exclusively. Our assumption is borne out by the compound numbers over a thousand, represented thus far by seven examples[53], which all conform to the same principle, e.g., *alp ḫmš mat* - one thousand five hundred, *alp ṯṯm* - one thousand sixty, *arb*^{c} *alpm mitm* - four thousand two hundred.

It remains to make some observations concerning the syntactic use of the cardinal numbers in Ugaritic. It seems that after the number two the noun generally appears in the dual form, cf. *ṯlṯ qšt*[54] - three bows with

---

[45] *PRU* 5, text 95:3; 97:9. Cf. *PRU* 2, text 84:6,25-26,28; 143:9,11,13; *PRU* 5, text 92:3.

[46] *PRU* 5, text 107:9; cf. *PRU* 2, text 29:14; 98:3,7-8,12-15,24-25; 107:3; 127:3-4; *PRU* 5, text 13:3; 107:9.

[47] *PRU* 5, text 91:3. With units only: *PRU* 2, text 111:4; 143:7; *PRU* 5, text 101:7.

[48] *PRU* 2, text 96:4-5. Cf. *ibid.*, text 30:10; 31:17.

[49] *PRU* 2, text 157:2. Cf. *PRU* 5, text 91:1; 92:6; 95:5.

[50] *PRU* 2, text 98:44. Cf. *ibid.*, 96:2.

[51] *PRU* 2, text 94:1.

[52] *PRU* 2, text 87:2; 94:1; 95:1-2; 129:6-7(?); *PRU* 5, text 12:11; 13:6,11, 16; 95:1; 96: *en marge*; 106:10.

[53] *PRU* 2, text 60:rev:8; 129:3-4(?); *PRU* 5, text 51:2-3; 97:20; 109:1,3; 111:2.

[54] *CTA* 119:III:5,21. Cf. *ṯmn qšt* (*CTA* 118:14).

ṯt qštm[55] - two bows. The same is true for the adjective: *ṯt aštm adrtm*[56] - two noble women. But this rule admits exception, as shown by the expression *ṯn kst*[57] - two bowls, in which the noun takes the simple plural as in the Hebrew. In accordance with its adjectival character, *ṯn* does not take a suffix. In the verse: 'Both of them travail and bear children'[58], the word 'both' is expressed by *klat*. Cf. the Arabic *kilāhumā, kiltāhumā*, and contrast the Hebrew *šᵉnehäm, šᵉtehäm*, where *šᵉnayim* is treated like a noun.[59]

The numbers from three onwards are connected with the plural or the singular. The attempt to clarify this problem runs into grave trouble. We cannot differentiate the singular and plural of feminine nouns ending with *t* and we are faced by the same difficulties with the masculine noun in the construct state. In many cases, the number refers to a *singulare tantum* as *ṣin* - a head of small cattle, and very often *kbd*[60] - a weight. In expressions like silver sheqel or gold sheqel, the word sheqel is frequently omitted and the word *ksp* - silver, or *ḫrṣ* - gold, is, of course, in the singular. The designation *kd yn* - jar of wine, or *kd šmn* - jar of oil, may be abbreviated to *yn* or *šmn* respectively. Nevertheless, we have approximately a hundred examples which demonstrate the rule that the numbers three to ten are connected with the plural[61] against three exceptions to the rule,

---

55 *CTA* 119:I:2-3,26-27,31; III:3-4,6,8,10,12,15-16,18-19,22,33. *ṯt qšt* (ibid., I:29; IV:16) is a patent *lapsus calami*. Cf. *ṯt qšm* (*ibid.*, III: 34) instead of *ṯt qštm*. Cf. also *ṯt mrkbtm* (*PRU* 2, text 121:6).

56 *PRU* 2, text 119:7. Contrast: *ṯlṯ ašt adrt* (*ibid.*, l. 16).

57 *PRU* 5, text 50:2.

58 *CTA* 23:57-58.

59 But even *ṯn* may be substantivized when used in a multiplicative sense 'double', and may then take suffixes. See *CTA* 14:205-206. Cf. Ginsberg, *Keret*, p. 40; [and in this volume, *Bordercases of Ugaritic Comparative Studies*, p. 408, note 6].

60 Cf. the noun *kubdu* in *ARM* 13, letter 3:6 and the editor's note, p. 157. [But cf. now M. Liverani, *UF* 2, pp. 89-108 who demonstrated that *kbd* means 'in total'].

61 *CTA* 3:III:39; IV:19; 14:8-9,84,285; 15:23; 16:II:84; 33:7,26; 35:52; 39: 17; 66:6,8,10; 77:1-2,3-4; 86:4; 100:I:3; 119:II:45; III:3,21; 144:1; 145:9; 147:5; 206:7-8,12-13,15; *PRU* 2, text 24: rev:5; 28:1,3,5-8; 29: 1-4,9-10; 30:1 (*bis*),3-4; 50:3,6,8-9; 97:1; 99:3; 100:2; 110:2; 114:1-2; 117:1; 121:8; 122:10-11; 123:4,7; 127:19; 128:21; 138:2; 141:1; 151:15; *PRU* 5, text 12:18; 38:1; 51:4; 52:6; 76:9,11-14,16-18,22,33-34,37-39; 80:2-4,6-7; 101:2,14,18; 102:4; 103:2; 168:2.

ṯlṯ šd (*bis*)[62] - three fields, and *ṯmn ḫzr*[63] - eight workmen. This clear prevalence of the plural after the numbers three to ten conforms with Hebrew usage. In relation to the numbers eleven to nineteen, I found six examples for plural[64] against seven for singular.[65] This inconsistent usage is also to be seen in Biblical Hebrew. After tens, from twenty to ninety, there are twenty examples for singular[66] against nine for plural.[67] Five of the nine instances occur in the same epic text. As to the other numbers, clear examples are very rare, so that no conclusion can be drawn from them.

To sum up. The material touching on Ugaritic cardinal numbers at our disposal gives a nearly complete picture of the whole numerical system and very few questions are left unanswered. The principal question, to which no satisfactory solution has as yet presented itself, concerns the numbers between eleven and nineteen. In that respect we still cannot ascertain which numerical form was employed in connection with feminine nouns.[67a]

---

62 *PRU* 2, text 79:3,6.

63 *PRU* 2, text 24: rev. 4.

64 *CTA* 66:7; *PRU* 2, text 28:2; 29:7; 30:2; *PRU* 5, text 49:3; 81:1.

65 *CTA* 68:10; *PRU* 2, text 24: rev:7 (*bis*); 79:1; 98:4; 99:2; *PRU* 5, text 38:5.

66 *CTA* 64:20; 137:B:6; 140:9; 141:8; 142:5; *PRU* 2, text 97:3; 98:16,18,21, 23,27; 99:31; 100:5; 109:2; 123:9; 126:1-2; 127:22; *PRU* 5, text 101:16; 111:1.

67 *CTA* 6:18-20,24,26,28; *PRU* 2, text 30:7; 84:16; 100:1; *PRU* 5, text 54:6.

[67a On the question in which case stood the counted noun consult J. Blau, *IOS* 2 (1972), pp. 78f.]

A Ugaritic Hymn in Honour of Il.

A cursory glance upon the new Ugaritic texts, published by Virolleaud in *Ugaritica* V immediately reveals the fascinating appearance of two fragmentary tablets, numbered there 2[1] and 3. In contradistinction to the epical texts the lines are divided from each other by horizontal strokes and the letters are of outstanding size. Each of both texts depicts a deity being seated in heaven and glorified by song in the heights. This godhead is in text 2 Il[1a], in text 3 Baal. In this paper we shall restrict our discus-

---

[1] *U* 5,2 RS 24.252, pp. 554-557.

[[1a] Along with other scholars (recently C.E. L'Heureux, *HTR* 67 (1974), pp. 489f. *BASOR* 221 (1976), pp. 83-85) we adhere to Virolleaud's proposal to regard *rpu mlk ᶜlm* and *ilṯpṭ* as epithets of Il. The issue is controversial.

De Moor, *New Year* 2, pp. 24f. assigns both bi-names to Baal. He argues that in the epic it is Baal not Il who is glorified as *ṯpṭn* (*CTA* 3:V:40; 4:IV:44), and the words *rpu bᶜl* (*CTA* 22:B:8) characterize Baal as both healer and shade (in the Netherworld) as in the broken Phoenician inscription *CIS* I 41:3 the words *bᶜl mrp'*. In de Moor's opinion Baal was given the epithet *rpu* because of his journey to the Netherworld. For the relation between chtonic deities and healing de Moor refers to M.C. Astour, *Hellenosemitica*, Leiden 1965, pp. 225ff. To these arguments the prayer to Baal, published by A. Herdner, *CRAIBL* 1972, p. 164, could now be added. Nevertheless, de Moor's arguments are open to objection: 1) The explanation of Phoenician *bᶜl mrp'* as *baᶜal mᵉrappe'* 'Baal the Healer' is not cogent. The words may as well be read *baᶜal marpe'* (noun) 'the Healer' (verbally: 'The possessor of Healing'). 2) Ugaritic *rpu bᶜl* is commonly understood to mean 'the *Rpu* (a class of minor gods or of men) of Baal. 3) The Ugaritic root *rp'* is nowhere attested in the unequivocal sense of 'to heal'. Compare Hebrew *rᵉpā'im* who are never described as healers. 4) *CTA* 16: V strongly stresses that the celestial god Il is the only healer among the gods. 5) Baal has no chtonic aspects. The descent of vanquished Baal to the Netherworld results in the temporary cessation of his rule as a celestial deity, not in the beginning of a new function as a chtonic god. 6) Even de Moor does not assert that the merry banquet of the gods took place in the Netherworld. The concept of the Netherworld does not come into the picture at all. 7) Also the title *ilṯpṭ* does not prove de Moor's point. The use of the root *ṯpṭ* is not restricted to Baal. There exists the title *ṯpṭ nhr* and the phrase *ḫṭ mṯpṭk* (*CTA* 2:III:18; 6:VI:29) which relates to the scepter of Mot's rule. The roots *ṯpṭ* and *mlk* are a synonymous pair (see M. Dahood, *RSP* 1, pp. 267f.) and point to the general idea of ruling which suits Il who bears the title *mlk* (*CTA* 4:IV:48 etc. Cf. in detail W. Schmidt, *Königtum Gottes in Ugarit und Israel,*

sion to the text composed in honour of Il, more precisely to its beginning and end, because only these parts of the song have been preserved in a more or less complete state.

Virolleaud characterized the text as mythological. To our mind it would be more exact to define it as a hymn.[1b] The epithets of the gods are different from those which are usual in the epic and even the style is rather

---

BZAW 80 [1961], pp. 18-21). The description of Il as *il*ṯ*p*ṭ is not surprising in a song which attributes to the gods epithets, not attested in the epic. In our opinion it is in honour of Il that Baal is singing and playing on instruments, not in honour of himself nor for mere pleasure.

S.B. Parker, *UF* 2, pp. 247-249 considers *rpu mlk* ᶜ*lm* as the proper name of a special deity, not mentioned either in the epic or in the lists of gods. It is, however, *a limine* improbable that such an obscure deity should have been represented in the song as the foremost personality of the pantheon and the protective deity of Ugarit.

M. Dietrich - O. Loretz - J. Sanmartín, *UF* 7, pp. 115-119 suggest in the broken context of l. 15 the reading *ršp* (***) and tentatively suggest that *Rpu* may be an epithet of *Räšäp* whose positive aspects have been brought out by modern research. But notwithstanding these aspects (cf. also S.E. Loewenstamm, *EB*, *s.v. Räšäp*) his role in the Ugaritic pantheon is clearly inferior to that of Il.

The identification of the central deity of the song can not be disconnected from the interpretation of the concluding invocation of this god that "thy strength etc. might be within Ugarit" *lymt špš wyrḫ wln*ᶜ*mt šnt il*. 'the days of Sun and Moon and the good years of Il'. At the first sight one might be tempted to argue that the phrase *n*ᶜ*mt šnt il* contradict the identification of the addressed deity with Il, since on this supposition we rather should expect the phrase *wn*ᶜ*mt šntk*. But this argument does not hold water. The eternity of Sun and Moon is a stock-symbol for the longevity of a king or a dynasty, well-known from Sumerian, Akkadian, Phoenician and Hebrew sources (see Sh.M. Paul, *JNES* 31 [1972], pp. 351-355). But only in the Ugaritic song the names of Sun and Moon are paralleled by that of an additional god. We suggest that this variation of the common pattern was motivated by the intention to conclude the song with the name of the god, glorified in it.

An invocation of Il as a protective deity of Ugarit makes excellent sense in the light of the epic representing Il as surpassing all gods in his willingness and capacity to take care of mortal men. As noted above Il is the only healer of an ill person. It is his privilege to bless a childless man with the blessing of offspring (*CTA* 15:II:16-28; 17:I:35-38). He appears to the desperate king Krt in a dream and instructs him how to regain his happiness (*CTA* 14:I:35ff.). The expression of the wish, that his glory may dwell upon (the king of ?) Ugarit is thus well understood.]

[[1b] On the suggestion to define the song as a prayer, see the addition to this paper.]

peculiar. In the epical poetry the device of the *parallelismus membrorum* is clearly dominant whereas its application in the hymn is rather limited and the style is inferior to that of the Biblical hymns. Nevertheless the text reveals a number of features which were hitherto known from the hymns of the Bible alone and thus contributes to the clarification of their prehistory.

At the beginning of the first line Virolleaud reads *[aph]n*[1c], 'then'. The second word *yšt* means 'drinks'.[1d] The three following words *rpu mlk* ^{c}*lm* introduce an epithet of Il, repeated afterwards thrice in the preserved part of the tablet. The clearest component of this epithet is the well-known *mlk* 'king'. Il bears this title in the epic as well.[2] The compound term *mlk* ^{c}*lm*, however, appeared in Ugaritic texts so far only as the title of Pharao *Nimmuriya*, better known under the name Amenophis III.[3] The title reminds of *mäläk hā*^{c}*olām* 'king of the world', the well-known designation of God in Talmudic Hebrew. However, the term ^{c}*bd* ^{c}*lm* 'eternal slave', common to Biblical Hebrew and Ugaritic[3a], rather favours here the rendering 'eternal king'. This strong stress, laid upon Il's eternity, is on all fours with the reference to Il's eternity at the conclusion of the hymn. It hardly needs emphasizing that the glorification of the Lord's eternity occupies an important place in the Bible, especially in hymns, e.g. *YHWH mäläk* ^{c}*olām wā*^{c}*äd* (Ps. 10:16) 'YHWH is king for ever and ever'. The noun *rpu* brings to mind the Biblical *r*^{e}*pā'im*. It has already been found in Ugaritic texts and its interpretation has been the subject of prolonged discussions.[4] Here we shall content ourselves with the short remark that the present text lends additional force to Aistleitner's[5] explanation '*Fürst*'.

At the beginning of the second line Virolleaud plausibly restores *il*, connects *gṯr* with Akkadian *gašru* 'strong', and explains the words *wyšt [il]*

[[1c] Contrast B. Margulies (Margalit), *JBL* 89, (1970), pp. 292-304: *[h]n*; de Moor, *New Year* 2, p. 24: *[y]n.]*

[[1d] On the suggestion to parse *yšt* as a jussive, see *infra* the addition to this paper.*]*

[2] See *supra*, note 1a.

[3] *PRU* 5, text 8:9.

[[3a] Cf. A. Herdner in *Textes* 1, p. 511, note e.*]*

[4] J. Caquot, *Syria* 37 (1960), pp. 75-93. *[*Compare also *supra*, note 1a and S.E. Loewenstamm, *EB, s.v. r*^{e}*pā'im.]*

[5] Aistleitner, *WUS, s.v.*

gṯr to mean 'and Il the strong drank'. However in l. 6 we read: *wtšt ^{c}nt gṯr* and there we hardly can admit the translation 'and Anat the strong drank', since a fem. adjective should read *gṯrt*. Therefore it appears that *gṯr* might rather be the name of a beverage, presumably a sort of wine.[5a] Thus we propound the translation: 'Then drinks the mighty man the eternal king and drinks Il wine' a solemn amplification of the simple sentence: 'And Il drank wine', as borne out by the sentence: 'And Anat drank wine'. Anyhow the text obviously describes a banquet of the gods. The motif is well known from the epic[6] and appears now also in a burlesque didactic text.[7]

In lines 4-6 we suggest the translation: 'And Il, seated (on his throne) was glorified[7a] by Astarte, Il the judge by Hadad the shepherd who sing

---

[[5a] Our proposal has been accepted by Margalit, *op. cit.* (note 1c) and taken into consideration by J.R. Parker, *UF* 4, p. 102, note 42 who points to Akkadian (*karānu*) *dannu*. Most scholars follow Virolleaud and read in l. 6 *gṯr<t>.]*

[6] *CTA* 3:I; 4:III, VI.

[7] *U* 5, RS 24.258, pp. 546-548.

[[7a] Contrast Virolleaud *U* 5, p. 553: *[le dieu] fort et majestueux (le dieu) Il est assis à côté de Astart etc*. Similarly most scholars.

The crucial question is whether *yṯb b* may be interpreted in this way. My paper silently denied this possibility. A.J. Ferrara - S.B. Parker, *UF* 4, pp. 37-39 explicitly stress the lack of linguistic support for this rendering, point, however, for its confirmation to the descriptions of seating arrangements in divine banquets in Sumerian texts. The only Ugaritic example adduced by them reads: *t^{c}db ksu wyṯṯb lymn aliyn b^{c}l* (*CTA* 4:V:108-110). 'A chair was readied and he was seated at the right hand of Aleyan Baal'. But this verse, closely paralleled by 1 Reg. 2:19 (cf. also Ps. 110:1), hardly contributes to the clarification of *yṯb b*. Compare, however: *wayyešäb b^{e}'elone mamre'* (Gen. 13:18), perhaps: 'and he settled by the terebinths of Mamre'. Compare also *b^{e}'elone mamre'* in Gen. 14:13; 18:1. But perhaps the name *'elone mamre'* rather denotes a wood or a district (called after this wood) *in* which Abraham settled down. Anyhow, *yšb b* is not attested at in the use 'to sit next to (a person)'.

Margalit, *op. cit.* (note 1c), pp. 293f. translates: 'The Honor of El sits (enthroned) in Ashtarot El rules in Edrei'. This rendering, however, leaves the relative pronoun *d* in *dyšr* (l. 3) without antecedent. Margalit tries to explain away this difficulty arguing: "The relative pronoun *d* - which has been deleted in translation *elegantiae causa* - is here employed conjunctionally". This sophisticated supposition has *a limine* a suspicious air about it. A closer scrutiny shows that the proofs for the possibility of a conjunctional use of *d* fail to stand the test. In his opinion *d* is used as conjunction in *dbḥlmy* (*CTA* 14:150) as borne

and play *[or: who sings and plays]* the lyre and the *ṯlb* (an unidentified instrument[7b]) the timbrel and the cymbals.

The affinity of this description to that of the Biblical psalms is obvious. The latter represent the Lord eight times as seated[8] *[i.e. enthroned]*, sixteen times as judge[8], e.g. in the verse: "Thou satest on the throne, righteous judge"[9] (Ps. 9:5). The epithet shepherd is known from Egyptian, Sumerian, Akkadian and Biblical sources as designation of kings and gods[10] and is twice attributed to the Lord also in the Psalms.[11] Especially instructive is the use of the verb *ḏmr*, i.e. the Hebrew verb *zmr* whose use in the Bible is peculiar to hymns and appears in them no less than forty two times.[11a] In Ugaritic we meet with this verb for the first time here, hardly by chance in a text belonging to the same *Gattung*. This correspondence is the more striking as *ḏmr* is preceded by *šyr* and the related Biblical pair of words *šyr* and *zmr* (in the *D*-formation) is attested at in Biblical hymns twelve times.[12] In addition *[like Ugaritic ḏmr]* even Biblical *zmr* governs the preposition *b* before the name of the instrument as e.g. in *zam-m^eru le'lohenu b^ekinnor* (Ps. 147:7).[13] To be sure, only two of the four in-

---

out by the parallel text which reads instead *wbhlmh* (*CTA* 14:35). However the unproblematic structure of the passage *CTA* 14:142-150 makes it perfectly clear that *d* in *dbḥlmy* is nothing else than a regular relative personal pronoun (whom in my dream Il gave) and moreover, this text is not parallel to l. 35 at all. More persuasive seems Margalit's second example which reads: *dl ytn bt lb^cl* (*CTA* 3:IV:11). Contrast, however, Herdner's reading -(?)*d. lytn* etc. which treats *d* as the last letter of a longer word. Compare also M. Görg, *UF* 6, pp. 474f., who argues that the place-name *'ädrä^ci* should have been read in Ugaritic *udr^cy*.

Our proposal connects the enigmatic *b* with *yqr* interpreted as verb: "Il (who is) sitting (on his throne) is honoured by Astarte. Il the judge by Hadad the shepherd."*]*

[7b See now J. de Moor, *UF* 1, p. 177; *New Year* 2, pp. 24, note 107, who translates oboe and refers to Akkadian *šulpu* and to the iconographic evidence collected by F. Ellermeier, *Sibyllen, Musikanten, Haremsfrauen*, Herzberg 1970, pp. 10ff. (not accessible to me).*]*

8 Ps. 2:4; 9:5,12; 29:10; 47:9; 80:2; 99:1; 123:1.

9 Ps. 7:9,12; 9:5,9,20; 26:1; 35:24; 43:1; 50:6; 51:6; 58:12; 67:5; 75:8; 81:2; 96:13; 98:9.

10 D. Müller, *ZäS* 86 (1961), pp. 126-144.

11 Ps. 23:1; 80:2.

*[*11a See in this volume *The Lord is my Song and my Glory*, pp. 333-340.*]*

12 Ps. 21:14; 27:6; 57:8; 68:5,33; 101:1; 104:33; 108:2; 144:9; 1 Chr. 16:9.

13 Likewise Ps. 33:2; 71:22; 98:5; 149:3.

struments enumerated in the Ugaritic song are known from the psalms of the Bible *[viz. tp = top, knr = kinnor]*, the name *ṯlb* does not occur in the Bible at all and the mention of *m^{e}ṣiltayim* is, for reasons unknown to us, confined to the prose of the later books.

In lines 4-5 we read: *bmrqdm [*some scholars divide: *bm rqdm] dšn*. Il, honoured by Astarte and Baal and in addition by dancers is *dšn*, i.e. vigorous, of fresh appearance in spite of his old age.[13a] Compare *^{c}od y^{e}nubun b^{e}šebā d^{e}šenim w^{e}ra^{ca}nannim yihyu* (Ps 92:15). 'They shall still bear fruit in old age be vigorous and fresh'.

In *[*the continuation*]* of l. 5 *[bḥbr kṯr ṭbm]* appears *kṯr*, the craftsman of the gods who in *CTA* 6:VI:48 is called Baal's *ḥbr*, i.e. comrade. If we take the *m* of *ṭbm* as the *m* of the plural, we attain the translation 'by *Kṯr*'s good comrades'. But the *m* of *ṭbm* may be enclitic as well. Therefore the translation: 'by *Kṯr* the good comrade' can not be excluded. The word *ṭbm* may even be related to Il in parallel to *dšn*, i.e. that Il is honoured by *Kṯr* while being in a happy state of mind.[14]

Notwithstanding the uncertainty as to the exact interpretation of the text the general picture is clear and instructive. Il's worship in the celestial society obviously corresponds to his worship in the Ugaritic cult and this worship has features common to the Lord's worship as reflected in the Psalms of the Bible, at least as far as the musical part is concerned, because it is a moot question whether dancing of men is recorded in the

[[13a] De Moor, *New Year* 2, p. 24 renders *mrqdm dšn* 'anointed dancers', Dietrich-Loretz-Sanmartín, *op. cit.* (note 1a) *'geschmückte Tänzer'*. M. Dahood, *RSP* 1, p. 168f. points to the parallelism between the roots *dšn* and *ṭwb* in Is. 55:2; Jer. 31:14; Ps. 65:11 and translates the words *bmrqdm dšn // bḥbr kṯr ṭbm* 'Among the plump dancers // amid the merry companions of Kôshar'. All these suggestions force upon us the explanation of *dšn* as a noun in the singular which serves as a *rectum* and fulfils the function of an adjective (in Hebrew translation: *m^{e}raqq^{e}de dāšān* instead of *m^{e}raqq^{e}dim d^{e}šenim*). Dahood's interpretation thus implies a parallelism between the singular of the noun *dšn* with the plural of the adjective *ṭb*. But perhaps both *dšn* and *ṭbm* should be parsed as singulars of adjectives and this would yield the translation: 'Glad among the dancers, happy among etc.' Compare also in a broken context *ltm mrqdm dš* (*CTA* 19:189), according to Virolleaud's reading: *[m]ṣltm mrqdm d šn*. Caquot-Sznycer, *Textes* 1, p. 455, note t read thus in our text, too, and render: *'cymbales, castagnettes d'ivoire'*. On the proposal to render *mrqdm* 'castanets' see also Margalit, *op. cit.* (note 1c)*.]*

[14] Cf. Is. 3:10; Jer. 44:17; Ps. 112:5; Thr. 3:26; 4:9.

Psalms. True, the noun *māḥol* (Ps. 149:3; 150:4) [and the related verb form *ḥolel* (Ps. 87:7)] are mentioned in the Psalms, but we can not be sure whether the reference is to dancing or to the playing of the flute.[15]
Two differences between the Ugaritic poem and its Biblical counterparts may be pointed out 1) As a rule the Bible depicts human worship. But this statement requires qualifications and sometimes even there the Lord's worship in the heights of heaven is described. Compare Ps. 29; 69:35; 103: 20-21; 148. and especially the verse *halᵉlu 'el bᵉqodšo halᵉluhu birqiᵃᶜ ᶜuzzo* (Ps. 150:1). 'Praise God in his sanctuary praise Him in the firmament of His strength', a verse which stresses the correspondence between the Lord's praise in His sanctuary on earth to His praise in Heaven. 2) Stricter is a second difference. In the Ugaritic hymn singing and playing of instruments are referred to in the same way as in the epic, i.e. as things which took place. In the Bible the singer proclaims that he is about to sing (e.g. Ju. 5:3) or invites others to sing (e.g. Is. 12:5). The description of a cultic procession: "The singers went before, the minstrels followed after, in the midst of the damsels playing with timbrels" (Ps. 68: 26) is of exceptional character in the Psalms.

Line 6 proceeds to a description of Anat who also is depicted as drinking. Her [otherwise unknown] epithets are *bᶜlt mlk* 'Mistress of kingdom' (*mlk* kingdom in Phoenician, too) and *bᶜlt drkt* a noun which serves in Ugaritic as a standard parallel to *mlk* (in the abstract sense of kingdom). In addition she is designated as *bᶜlt šmm rmm* 'the Mistress of high heaven'. Compare in the inscription of *Bdᶜštrt* king of Zidon, the name *šmm rmm*, the name of a sanctuary or of a quarter of Zidon[15a] and compare also: *wayyibän kᵉmo rāmim miqdāšo kᵉ'äräṣ yᵉsādāh lᵉᶜolām* (Ps. 78:69). 'And he built His sanctuary like the heights like the earth which He has established forever'. It appears that *rāmim* in this context should be interpreted as an abbreviation of *šāmayim rāmim*.[15b] Unexplained in line 8 is *bᶜlt kpṯ*.[16] In the fol-

[15] J. Licht. *EB* s.v. *māḥol*.

[[15a] *KAI*, Nr. 15.]

[[15b] The widely accepted emendation *kimromim* may be dismissed.]

[16] Virolleaud connects *kpṯ* with Akkadian *kapāšu*, Hebrew *kbš* ['to tread down' and explains '*le sol que l'on foule aux pieds*' in contrast to heaven]. However, the Arabic *kbš* proves that the root of Hebrew *kbš* is Proto-Semitic *kbš* and not *kbṯ*. [For the correct interpretation of *bᶜl kpṯ* '*Turbanträger*' (Akkadian *bēl kubši*) see M. Dietrich - O. Loretz, *OLZ* 62 (1960), p. 547.]

lowing text of line 8 we probably should delete *di* as dittography[16a] (Prof. H.L. Ginsberg orally) and explain the remaining text: *w^c nt dit rḫpt*. 'And Anat flies (with outstretched wings) and hovers'.

I shall not deal with the broken text of the following lines, but rather content myself with the remark that the words *wyšt il* are repeated in l. 10.

Let us proceed to the reverse l. 8 *[The following discussion includes some outdated hypotheses, corrected later on in this paper]*. In this part only two words are incompletely preserved. The letters *lr* at the end of l. 8 are followed by a lacuna of two letters at the beginning of l. 9 and the letter *l.* at the end of l. 9 is followed by the lacuna of one letter and by the letters *ak* at the beginning of l. 10. We suggest to complete both words to read *lrak* i.e. 'may fear thee'. The resulting text *l[rak] arṣ ^c zk d̲mrk* means: 'May fear thee the land of thy strength and thy song'. The affinity to the style of the Psalms is close. With *arṣ ^c zk* compare *'^a ron ^c uzzäkā* (Ps. 132:8), *birqi^ac ^c uzzo* (Ps. 150:1). With the parataxis of *^c oz* and *zimrā* compare: *ki ^c ozzi w^e zimrāt YĀ* (Ex. 15:2 etc.) and also the nearness of the roots *^c zz* and *zmr* in *^c uzzi 'eläkā '^a zammerā* (Ps. 59:18) and in favour of our completion *lrak* it should be remarked that the root *yr'* is used to describe the fear of the Lord forty-two times in the Psalms. Let us continue in ll. 9-10 "May fear thee *ḥtkk*". *ḥtk* appears in Ugaritic in the sense of 'offspring'. The meaning of *nmrtk* is dubious. Virolleaud connects it with Akkadian *namurtu*, 'splendour' and suggests 'thy splendour'. But perhaps we rather should compare the above mentioned letter which speaks of *nmryh mlk ^c lm*, and hypothesize that his proper name turned into a title designating emperor, as the name of Caesar. The resulting translation would be 'thy emperorship'. The word *btk* has been explained by Virolleaud to mean 'within'. We prefer the rendering 'thy house' and consequently render: 'May fear thee the land of thy strength glorified in song, may fear thee thy offspring, thy emperorship, thy house Ugarit'. *[The foregoing discussion overlooked the correspondence between b^c z [rpi m]lk ^c lm bd̲mrh bl[- - h] bḥtkh*

[[16a] A.F. Rainey, *JAOS* 94 (1974), pp. 187f. takes *di* as an imperative 2nd f. sg. His proposal is morphologically impeccable fails, however, to fit the context. Dietrich-Loretz-Sanmartín, *loc. cit.* (note 1a), read *di* <*y*> *'Vogel'*. For a description of Anat's flight in different terms see *CTA* 10:II:10-11.

bnmrth (Rev. 6-8) with *^{c}zk ḏmrk l[- -]k ḥtkk nmrtk* (Rev. 9-10). This correspondence, correctly pointed out by R. Borger, *UF* 1, p. 3, refutes our restoration *lrak* in 8-9 definitely and lets it appear improbable in 9-10. After studying the cast of the tablet L.R. Fisher, *HThR* 63 (1970), p. 490, note 20, cautiously suggests the reading *l[a]*nk*. In *UF* 3, p. 356, the same author states without reservations: "The last letter of l. 9 is clearly an *'a* and the first letter of l. 10 is *n*" and thus the text has been read by Dietrich-Loretz-Sanmartín, *loc. cit.* (note 1a), too. In 8-9 de Moor suggests the reading *lr[pi]*. Dietrich-Loretz-Sanmartín even read *lr[p]*i*".

De Moor renders *^{c}z* and *ḏmrt* as 'protection and guard'. However Ugaritic *^{c}z* is obviously derived from Proto-Semitic *^{c}zz* 'to be strong' and should be kept apart from Arabic *^{c}wḏ* 'to take or seek refuge'. On *ḏmr* see in this volume *The Lord is my Strength and my Glory*, pp. 333-340, where *ḏmr* has been explained as 'song', the pair *^{c}z* and *ḏmr* as a hendiadys in the sense 'strength glorified by song'. If we prefer the interpretation of the pair as a synonymous one the rendering should be: 'strength and force'. The noun *lan* has generally be derived from the root *l'y* 'to be mighty, forceful'. For *ḥtk* de Moor convincingly suggests the rendering 'patronage' (derived from the meaning father). On the enigmatic noun *nmrt* see also S.B. Parker, *UF* 2, p. 266, who parses it as a *mqtl* base noun from *mrr* 'bless, strengthen' with dissimilation of the initial *m*. The hypothetical reading *lr[p]*i arṣ* has been taken by Dietrich-Loretz-Sanmartín as vocative addressing the god, formerly called *rpu mlk ^{c}lm*. However, *rpi* is *casus obliquus* and its use in the *regens* remains unexplained. Contrast the vocative in Arabic, where the *regens* appears with the ending *a*. De Moor interprets 'for the healers of the land'. We should prefer the rendering 'for the mighty of the land' taking *rpu arṣ* as the earthly counterpart of *rpu mlk ^{c}lm*, i.e. the king who is *rpu arṣ par excellence, rm btk rpi arṣ* (*CTA* 15:III:3,14), alternatively 'for the mighties of the land', i.e. the dynasty of Ugarit. Our hypothesis is supported by Paul's[16b] comprehensive proof that in all the literature of the Ancient Near East the permanence of sun and moon is invoked for the one purpose to express hyperbolically the long rule of the king or his dynasty. An interpretation of the Ugaritic song in accordance with this amply documented rule has a well-founded claim to probability. This king reigns of course

[[16b] Paul, *loc. cit.* (note 1a).*]*

at Ugarit and Virolleaud's rendering of *btk ugrt* 'within Ugarit' should be maintained.*]*

The last words of the song clearly say: "For the days of Sun and Moon and the good years of Il". A parallelism between days and years has been found in Ugaritic so far only in a letter expressing the wish that the receiver may live a thousand days and ten thousand years.[17] In the Bible this parallel occurs in twelve passages[18], seven of them in Psalms, e.g. *śamm^e-ḥenu kimot ^cinnitānu š^enot rā'inu rā^cā* (Ps. 90:15). 'Make us glad according to the days wherein Thou hast afflicted us, and the years wherein we have seen evil'. To the very idea expressed in the concluding words of the Ugaritic text compare: *Yirā'ukā ^cim šämäš w^eyāre^aḥ dor dorim* (Ps. 72:5). 'Let they fear Thee like the sun and as the moon through all generations'[18a], a passage which looks like a variant of its Ugaritic counterpart. Sun and moon are easily comprehensible symbols of eternity and compare Ps. 89:37-38.[18a] In our text the days of sun and moon are paralleled by the days of Il[18b], the eternal king, verbally by the goodness of the years of Il, i.e. his good years[19] and compare the Hebrew blessing: *l^c'oräk yāmim ṭobim* 'for the length of good days'.

The fragments of the Ugaritic psalm are of great importance for the research of the Ugaritic pantheon. According to a widely held view Il has to be characterized as *deus otiosus*, a god who enjoys a peaceful life, undisturbed by activity. Some scholars even argued that his sons had dethroned and exiled him. Yet here it becomes clear that the gods, his children sing and play in his honour and that even the people of Ugarit fear him, and that the term fear expresses an emotional relation to a deity whose

---

17 *PRU* 2, text 19:2-6. (The correct explanation of *ymt // šnt* has been given before me by C.H. Gordon, *Supplement to the Ugaritic Textbook*, Roma 1967, p. 555. His interpretation came to my knowledge after my lecture).

18 Deut. 32:7; Ez. 22:4; Mal. 3:4; Ps. 61:7; 77:6; 78:33; 90:9,15; Job 15: 20; 32:7; 36:11. Compare also Gen. 25:7; Ecc. 6:3 etc. *[*Compare M. Dahood, *RSP* 1, pp. 203-205, 207, who points also to Phoenician inscriptions. For a comprehensive treatment including Akkadian see now Y. Avishur, *UF* 7, pp. 39f.*]*

*[*18a On the textual and lexical problems of Ps. 72:5; 89:37-38 see Paul, *op. cit.* (note 1a).*]*

*[*18b On the parallelism *šmš, yrḫ // il* see note 1a.*]*

19 Cf. *CTA* 6:II:19-20 *ln^cmy arṣ dbr* 'to the goodness of the land *Dbr*, i.e. to the good land *Dbr*'.

activity is a manifestation of strength. In addition we meet here with the national aspect of Ugarit religion which is entirely absent in the epic.

From a literary point of view special attention is due to the postponement of the national aspect to the end of the song. The song begins with the description of events happening in the world of the gods, and Ugarit does not come into the picture at all. But the conclusion surprisingly throws into relief the relation which prevails between Il and the people of Ugarit. The closing formula is thus congenerous to the phenomenon called in the terminology of Biblical criticism cultic addition. As most obvious analogy Ps 29 may be mentioned which begins with the honour and strength given by the gods to the Lord in the heights of heaven and closes with the words: "YHWH will give strength to His people YHWH will bless His people with peace".

[Addition:

De Moor, *New Year* 2, pp. 24f., defines the song as a prayer accompanying the presentation of a cultic meal to the gods which was given on the occasion of the New Year Festival. He has been followed by Dietrich-Loretz-Sanmartín, *loc. cit.* (note 1a). His main arguments are: 1) The text ends with the wish that the year to come be a most happy one. 2) The persistent use of the short form *yšt* advocates its interpretation as a jussive, viz. the maker of the offering says: May the god so and so drink (from the vine presented to him). 3) De Moor adduces as a decisive confirmation of his exegesis the Assyrian parallel *KAR* 214 (see R. Frankena, *Tākultu*, Leiden 1954, pp. 25-28), which has the unequivocal imperatives *[ši]-ti* ^{d}*En-lil ši-ti* ^{d}*A-nu*, etc.

It can not, however, be conceded that the Ugaritic song expresses wishes for the New-Year. It rather invokes eternal blessing. As to *KAR* 214 it does not contain any allusion to the occasion on which the *tākultu* ceremony was celebrated. The general question whether the date of this ceremony was the New Year Festival, has not yet been definetely settled. Compare E. Ebeling, *Orientalia* 20 (1951), pp. 400f. Also the typological parallelism of the Ugaritic song with the prosaic text *KAR* 214 is open to discussion.

Let us outline the structure of the Assyrian text in short. The above mentioned invitation to drink, directed to some principal gods is followed by a dry and lengthy enumeration of all the gods and temples of Assyria. Throughout, no epithets of the gods are stated and no description of the banquet is given. The text ends with a prayer that 1) he who has arranged the banquet for the gods (i.e. the king) may enjoy, health, mighty rule and long life; 2) all those who hear these words (i.e. all participants in the ceremony that hear the words of the officiating priest) may have all necessaries of life and enjoy health and happiness; 3) the ceremony of *tākultu* may persist in the land of *Aššur*; 4) the god *Aššur* may bless the king *Aššur-etelli*, the giver of this *tākultu*. The fourth section may well be a late Neo-Assyrian addition to a more ancient standard text of prayer. Anyhow, *KAR* 214 makes it perfectly clear that it was the king who had arranged the *tākultu* meal for the gods, and that the gods are asked to bestow their reward for this meal upon him and all participants in the ceremony. This straightforward notion is bluntly stated without any embellishment. No word is wasted in order to extol the gods nor does the text care to describe the splendour of their meal. Nothing in this prosaic text is reminiscent of hymnal style.

In sharp contrast the Ugaritic text throughout glorifies *rpu mlk* ^{c}*lm*. The vivid description of the banquet of the illustrious gods in honour of *rpu mlk* ^{c}*lm* arises doubts, whether a human invitation do drink ('may the god drink' not: 'the god drank') would fit into the picture. True, Dietrich-Loretz-Sanmartín, go a step further than de Moor, reading in l. 9 *št* (Virolleaud *mšt*) and explaining in this line *aklt* and *št* as two imperatives directed to the goddess Anat (*esse, trinke*!). However, *aklt* can hardly be parsed as an imperative and therefore even *št* (*si vera lectio*) which precedes a lacuna should be left unexplained. It should also not be overlooked that, at least in the preserved part of the song, no sacrifice to the gods is recorded at all. Nor is it clear whether human wishes are referred to. To be sure, the word *iršt* (rev. l. 5) might point to such a wish and Dietrich-Loretz-Sanmartín read *ltštk liršt[k]* rendering: '*Er gewähre dir nach deinem Wunsche*'. However, the words are preceded and followed by lacunae and it can not be made out whether they belong to one and the same sentence, and anyhow *ltštk* can not be parsed as 3rd sing. masc. All we can assert with certainty is the prevalence of the hymnal element even in the prayer that the glorious attributes of the god may eternally be within Ugarit (apparently for the king). No specified benefits are demanded, let alone a recompense for a sacrifice. This consideration adds to our doubts, whether we should look in such a hymn for a human invitation to the gods to drink the wine presented to them by men.]

"The Lord is my Strength and my Glory"

The verse *ᶜozzi wᵉ zimrāt Yā(h)* appears for the first time in the Song of Moses (Ex. 15:2), a psalm of thanksgiving. It reappears *verbatim* in Ps. 118:14, a psalm of the same literary genre and again in Is. 12:2, a chapter recognized for its hymn-like quality, with the secondary addition of the *Tetragram* after *Yā(h)*.[1] Therefore the formula seems to be a standard feature of hymn writing which has been in existence from very early times since the fossilized pair of words *ᶜozzi wᵉ zimrāt* has been preserved in this set context only.

This interpretation of this expression is known to present difficulties. *Prima facie ᶜozzi* means 'my strength', *zimrāt* 'song' (not my song!), the suffix of the first person found in *ᶜozzi* being conspicuously absent in *zimrāt*. Moreover the ideas of strength and song seem to be utterly disparate: they are neither synonymous nor even congeneric.

To a certain extent the solution of this second problem depends upon the solution of the first. Scholars emending *zimrāt* to read *zimrāti*[2] maintain the traditional rendering of *ᶜozzi* as 'my strength' and its derivation from the wellknown root *ᶜzz*, 'to be strong'. On the other hand those who would retain the suffixless form *zimrāt*, deny that the *yod* in *ᶜozzi* is suffixed personal pronoun, and consequently explain this yod, as the third radical of a supposed Hebrew root *ᶜzy*, relating *ᶜozzi* to Arabic *ġāzīn* 'warrior' *ġazā* 'go forth to war'[3] or to Arabic *ᶜazā* 'patience, consolation'.[4]

---

[1] The Tetragram may have been here a *varia lectio* of the less usual divine name *Yā(h)*. MT is probably a conflation of both readings.

[2] E.g. F.M. Cross-D.N. Freedman, *JNES* 14 (1955), p. 243.

[3] TH. Gaster, *ET* 48 (1936-7), p. 45; 49 (1937-8), p. 189; D. Winton Thomas, *ET* 48 (1936-7), p. 478; J. Barr, *Comparative Philology and the Text of the Old Testament*, Oxford 1968, p. 29.

[4] Ch. Rabin, *ScHi* 8, Jerusalem 1961, p. 361. Cf. Barr, *op. laud.* (note 3), p. 30.

A higher degree of unanimity has been reached in the interpretation of the root of the noun *zimrāt*. The opinion clearly prevailing to-day is that Hebrew *zimrā* represents two different Proto-Semitic roots, viz. Proto-Semitic *zmr* 'to sing, to play upon an instrument' and *ḏmr*, variously explained as 'strength'[5] or 'protection'[6] both interpretations resorting to different meanings of the Arabic root *ḏmr*. It is further claimed that Proto-Semitic *ḏmr*, 'protect' is attested in South-Arabian, Amorite and Hebrew personal proper names.[7] The choice is then between the following interpretations. 1) My strength and my might. 2) My strength and my protection. 3) Warrior and protection. 4) Consolation and protection.

The basic assumption here is that in Hebrew *zmr* we are to distinguish between two Proto-Semitic stems, viz. *zmr* and *ḏmr*. For Proto-Semitic *zmr* 'to sing, to play upon an instrument' Baumgartner[8] adduces Ugaritic *zmr*. There is an Ugaritic word *azmr*, but its interpretation is entirely obscure and Gordon[9] quite correctly leaves it untranslated. Furthermore Baumgartner quotes Arabic *zmr* and Barr[10] stresses that "Arabic words cognate with 'make music' have the first consonant /*z*/ not /*ḏ*/". This evidence for Proto-Semitic *z* in *zmr* however overlooks Schwally's[11] argument that Arabic *zmr* 'to play the flute' is a loanword from Syriac, where *zmr* is attested in this special sense in addition to its general meaning known from Hebrew. Therefore Syriac *zmr* (not *dmr*!) remains as the only indication for Proto-Semitic *zmr*. But even this should not be considered as a conclusive evidence because the Syriac verb *zmr* might in turn have been borrowed from Hebrew or Canaanite like the Syriac noun *mezmōr*.

---

[5] Cross-Freedman, *loc. cit.* (note 2); Baumgartner, *HAL, s.v.* II *zimrā(h)*.

[6] Gaster, *loc. cit.* (note 3); Winton Thomas, *loc. cit.* (note 3); Barr, *op. laud.* (note 3), p. 29.

[7] G. Ryckmans, *Les noms propres sud-sémitiques* I, Louvain 1934, pp. 70, 85, 222, 260; D. Diringer, *Le Iscrizioni Anticho-Ebraiche*, Firenze 1934, pp. 43, 211f.; H.B. Huffmon, *Amorite Personal Names*, Baltimore 1965, pp. 187f.; Barr, *op. laud.* (note 3), p. 182.

[8] Baumgartner, *HAL, s.v.* I *zmr*.

[9] C.H. Gordon, *UT, Glossary*, No. 823.

[10] Barr, *op. laud.* (note 3), p. 29.

It can now be convincingly shown that this is in fact the case: in an Ugaritic hymn in praise of Il we read: *dyšr wyḏmr bknr wṯlb btp wmṣltm*[12] 'who sings and plays upon harp and [flute][12a] upon timbal and cymbals.' This text admits a thoroughly verbal rendering into the language of the Hebrew Psalms, which would read: *'ᵃšär yāsir wizammer bᵉ kinnor ... bᵉtop umṣiltayim*. In this wording we recognize the Biblical pair of words *šir* and *zammer*. (Cf. Ju. 5:3; Ps. 21:14; 27:6; 57:8; 68:5, 33; 104:33; 108:2) and the construction ... *zammer bᵉ* 'to play upon an instrument' (Cf. Ps. 33:2; 71:22; 98:5; 147:7; 149:3). Therefore the identity of *zmr* in the Psalms with Ugaritic *ḏmr* may be regarded as firmly established. It follows that we cannot distinguish in Hebrew between two Proto-Semitic roots *zmr* and *ḏmr*. There remains of course the possibility of two homonymous roots, both derived from Proto-Semitic *ḏmr*. Yet even if this were possible, the generally claimed wide distribution of *ḏmr* 'protect' cannot be verified. This applies especially to the use of *ḏmr* in South-Arabian personal names, where it is commonly assumed to mean 'protect'. But this assumption lacks support in South-Arabian texts in which *ḏmr* has the meaning of '*solemniter pronuntiare*' like *azmara* in Ethiopic.[13] Therefore the usual explanation of *ḏmr* in these names is unfounded and it goes without saying that no conclusions can be drawn from South-Arabian to support the interpretation of *zimr* in Amorite personal names or the personal name *bᶜlzmr* documented in the Samaritan ostraca. The meaning of all these names is entirely obscure and they are unlikely to elucidate the Hebrew root *zmr*. More relevant is a passage in the above mentioned Ugaritic hymn addressed to Il and describing Ugarit as: *arṣ ᶜzk ḏmrk*.[14] [The words *ᶜzk ḏmrk* should be disconnected from *arṣ*. See in this volume *A Ugaritic Hymn in Honour of Il*, pp. 327-328.] The

---

[11] F. Schwally, *ZDMG* 52 (1898), pp. 133f.

[12] *U* 5, p. 552, text 2R°:3-4.

[[12a] Cf. J. de Moor, *UF* 1, p. 171.]

[13] A.F.L. Beeston, *Muséon* 62 (1950), pp. 265, who discusses also the problematic *mḏmr*, usually translated as 'strong man'. Baumgartner, *HAL*, *s.v.* III *zmr* writes: '*asa. ḏmr schützen, Schutz* (Conti 129)'. In Conti Rossini, *Chrestomatia Arabica meridionalis*, Roma 1931, p. 129, however no such meaning is indicated. Conti Rossini defines: '*solemniter proclamavit, publice praedicavit*' and exemplifies: *yḏmrn 'mr'hmw ᶜṯtr 'exaltent eorum domini Attarum.'* In the light of this translation the question arises of whether South-Arabian *ḏmr* should be connected with Hebrew *zmr* 'praise in cultic song'.

[14] *U* 5, p. 554, text 2 V°:9.

close affinity already demonstrated between this Ugaritic hymn and the language of the Hebrew Psalms makes it virtually certain that the Biblical pair of nouns ᶜ*oz* and *zimrā* reflects the same tradition of hymn writing as the Ugaritic pair ᶜ*z* and *d̲mr*.

Firstly it is quite obvious that Ugaritic ᶜ*zk* represents the well-documented Ugaritic noun ᶜ*z*[15] 'strength', derived from the Ugaritic stem ᶜ*zz* 'to be strong', not the roots *ġzy* or ᶜ*zy*.

Therefore Hebrew ᶜ*ozzi*, too, can only mean 'my strength'. Less evident is the explanation of Ugaritic *d̲mr* in this context. At first sight we may be tempted to interpret *d̲mr* here as a synonym of ᶜ*z* and translate: 'the land of thy strengh and thy might.'

Moreover some corroboration for this view might be adduced from the Ugaritic noun *d̲mr*[16] 'a kind of soldier'. This noun has been tentatively connected with Arabic *d̲amir* 'brave, gallant'. But on the other hand we should not reject out of hand the alternative possibility of relating the noun *d̲mr* (in the expression ᶜ*zk d̲mrk*) to the verb *d̲mr* which appears in the same hymn. True, this interpretation conflicts with the objection above mentioned that the concepts of 'strength' and 'song' are thoroughly disparate. But we shall try to demonstrate that this apparent incongruity disappears in the light of the closer scrutiny of hymnical style.

First of all we draw attention to the verse ᶜ*uzzi 'elekā 'azammerā* (Ps. 59:18) 'My strength, I sing to Thee' where the noun ᶜ*oz* is closely connected with the verb *zmr* 'to sing'. This single observation is further supported by an examination of ᶜ*oz* and *zmr* in the tradition of hymnic poetry. The use of the verb *zmr* 'to sing' is restricted in the Bible to hymns; it occurs forty-two times and always denotes 'to praise the Lord in song and the playing of instruments' (which is identical with the meaning of the Ugaritic term). Therefore we may define *zimrā* as the praise of God in cultic music. This meaning is confirmed by the use of the noun in Psalms (Ps. 81:3; 98:5) and elsewhere (Is. 51:3; Am. 5:23).[17] Therefore it seems

---

[15] Gordon, *UT, Glossary*, No. 1835.

[16] id., *ibid.*, No. 727.

[17] Unclear *mizzimrat hā'āräs* (Gen. 43:11). The context requires the explanation: 'from the best products of the land'. Baumgartner, *HAL, s.v.* II

rather unlikely that this term, deeply rooted in hymnic tradition should take on another meaning when it appears in songs of this kind. Now, one of the main functions of this *zimrā* was to extol the Lord's ^{c}*oz*, 'His strength', which manifests itself in His mighty deeds (Ex. 15:13; Ps. 21: 14; 63:3; 66:3; 77:15; 89:11; 93:1; 96:6). Moreover the praise of the Lord's ^{c}*oz* in cultic music may be described as giving Him ^{c}*oz* (Ps. 29:1 = 96:7; 68:35). From this it appears that the two concepts of ^{c}*oz* and *zimrā* have affinity in the Hebrew text of the Psalms, although this is not felt in their translation into European languages. This conclusion is not invalidated by the observation that the verse ^{c}*ozzi w*^{e}*zimrāt Yā(h)* does not deal with the ^{c}*oz* and *zimrāt* given to the Lord in cultic music, but rather with the ^{c}*oz* and *zimrāt* bestowed upon the Psalmist by his God. This argument fails to observe the reciprocity of the relationship between the Lord and the worshipper, formulated in Deut. 26:17-18 and also recognizable in the terminology of the Psalms. The same verb *brk* is applied to the worshipper blessing his God (Ps. 16:7; 26:12; 34:2 etc.) and to the Lord blessing His worshipper (Ps. 5:13; 28:9; 29:11 etc.). The term *t*^{e}*hillā* mainly denotes the praise given by the worshipper. But the Lord is also the source of *t*^{e}*hillā* for those who adore Him, and the Psalmist can say: From Thee is my *t*^{e}*hillā* in a large community (Ps. 22:26. Cf. Ps. 71:6). There is no doubt that when the terms are reversed in this way they undergo certain semantic changes. When describing actions emanating from the Deity, the words retain only those connotations which are appropriate to God, and lose those which are not. E.g. the glory given to the Lord in the *t*^{e}*hillā* implies the cultic song, whereas the *t*^{e}*hillā* bestowed by the Lord upon His worshipper is without such an implication. With these criteria in mind, let us return to the use of ^{c}*oz* and *zimrā* in the text under discussion. The God to whom ^{c}*oz* is given in the cult, gives ^{c}*oz* to those who sing in His praise (Ps. 68:36. Cf. Ps. 28:8; 29:11; 30:8; etc.) and His people may be described as ^{c}*uzzo* (Ps. 78:61). The noun *zimrā* primarily denoting the glory given to

---

zimrā derives this interpretation from a supposed basic meaning '*Stärke*'. Targum Onqelos: *middimšabbaḥ b*^{e}*'ar'ā* 'from the praiseworthy in the land.' Cf. also the Midrash upon Deut. 8:8 which calls the seven kinds of fruit mentioned in this verse as growing in the land of Israel *šib*^{c}*at hamminim ha'*^{a}*murim b*^{e}*šäbah hā'āräs* (M. Friedmann, *Sifré*, Wien 1864, p. 127 b), 'the seven kinds mentioned in the praise of the land'. Perhaps the expression *zimrat hā'āräs* points to the existence of songs mentioning the most excellent products of the land in its praise.

God in cultic song, may also be applied to the glory bestowed by the Lord upon those who glorify Him. But here too the inverted application of the term involves a certain spiritualisation of its contents. The notion of praise in cultic music becomes reduced to that of glory, pure and simple. It follows that the pair of words denotes the Psalmist's strength and glory, the source of both he finds in his God. If we apply this to Ugaritic *arṣ ᶜzk ḏmrk* we may translate: The land of thy strength and thy praise.' But here it is hard to decide whether the exact interpretation should be: 'The land which giveth thee strength and praise (in song)' or 'the land to which thou giveth strength and glory'. Perhaps the words suggest both ideas.

There remains the lack of congruity between the suffixed form *ᶜozzi* and the unsuffixed one *zimrāt*. We may recall that defenders of the Masoretic reading are compelled to relate *ᶜozzi* to an otherwise unknown Hebrew root *ᶜzy*[18], whereas the Ugaritic parallel makes it virtually certain that *ᶜozzi* is the well-documented Hebrew noun *ᶜoz*, derived from the stem *ᶜzz*, with the addition of the pronominal suffix of the first person. This conclusion tips the balance in favour of the emendation *zimrāti*, which eliminates the troublesome *absolutus* and produces a perfectly satisfactory reading: 'The Lord being my strength and my glory has wrought salvation unto me.' It may be conceded that it is easier to justify the reading *zimrāti* than to explain how this simple and clear form might have been corrupted to the difficult form *zimrāt*. Cross-Freedman's[19] tentative solution that *zimrāt* should be regarded as the outcome of a defective writing of *zimrāti* seems farfetched because such exceptional writing is highly unlikely after the normal plene writing of *ᶜozzi*. Their alternative explanation that the *yod* of *zmrty* might have been omitted before *Yā(h)* as the result of a haplography would imply that the same scribal error had occurred in three books.[20]

---

[18] The obvious lack of congruity between suffixed *ᶜozzi* and unsuffixed *zimrāt* compelled the classical Jewish interpreter Rashi at the end of the eleventh century to explain the *yod* of *ᶜozzi* as *paragogicum*. See his commentary upon Ex. 15:2.

[19] Cross-Freedman, *loc. cit.* (note 2).

[20] A similar proposal has already been made by S. Talmon, *VT* 4 (1954), pp. 206-208. In his opinion the original text contained the Tetragram, later on abbreviated to read *Yā(h)*. In the last stage the *yod* of *zimrāti* was amalgamated with *Yā(h)* by a process of progressive haplography.

The same objection must be levied at Hommel's[21] hypothesis that the text of *MT* has been corrupted from *zimrātih* in which *h* represented an abbreviation of the Tetragram. Therefore it appears that we should revert to Geiger's approach. In a chapter dealing with the divine name *Yā(h)*, Geiger[22] shows that at a certain period there was probably a theological tendency to absorb the divine name *Yā(h)* into the preceding word, a tendency which was later reversed and the divine name restored. The earlier movement yielded, in his opinion, the reading *zmrtyh*, which is actually found in some manuscripts of the Samaritan text; the reversed tendency caused the division of *zmrtyh* into *zmrt yh*.

It is true that this hypothesis, too, assumes a kind of haplography during the first stage in which *zimrāti Yā(h)* is supposed to have been changed into *zimrātyā(h)*. But this haplography would not result from a simple error but rather be the outcome of conscious theological principles. Consequently the same principles may have prevailed in the copying of three different books.

[The above paper initiated a discussion which concentrated upon the root and meaning of *zimrāt*, whereas the explanation of *ᶜozzi* has met with silent, but general consent.

E.M. Good, *VT* 20 (1970), p. 358, concurred with my proposal and correctly remarked, that I should have defined *ᶜozzi wᵉzimrāt* as hendiadys. B. Childs, *Exodus, OTL* 1974, pp. 240, 242 accepted my view hesitatingly. Most scholars rejected it, explicitely or silently. J. Blau - J.C. Greenfield, *BASOR* 200 (1970), pp. 11-12 argued "that *zmr* 'to chant' according to the testimony of the other Semitic languages reflects Proto-Semitic *z* rather than *ḏ*" and raise the question: "Is Ugaritic *ḏ* in this root a blend of two roots (as is the case probably with Ugaritic *drᶜ*) or is it simply a scribal error?" I tried to answer the argument drawn from other Semitic languages in my above paper and should like to add here only the observation that Syriac *zmr* may be a loan not only from Canaanite *zmr*, but from Akkadian *zamāru* as well.

---

[21] F. Hommel apud F. Perles, *JQR NS* 2 (1911-2), p. 115, note 41.

[22] A. Geiger, *Urschrift*, Breslau 1857, pp. 274-278.

S.B. Parker, *VT* 21 (1971), pp. 373-393, took issue with my explanation of *zimrāt* without touching upon the problem of its Proto-Semitic root. His main argument is the indisputable frequency of synonymous wordpairs in Hebrew and Ugaritic. So far so good. But he even questions my interpretation of *zimrā* as cultic music in praise of God. My indication that the Biblical verb *zmr* denotes in hymns invariably (42 times!) the praise of God in cultic music met with his objection that "to derive a definition of a cognate in another wordclass is methodologically unsound". This thesis is as original as unfounded. Parker's interpretation of *zimrā* as music pure and simple is lacking textual support. Am. 5:21-24 clearly opposes righteousness to two kinds of cultic worship, sacrifices and *zimrā*. In Ps. 81:13 *ś'u zimrā* continues the invitation to praise God and in Ps. 98:5 the exhortation to *zimrā* is included between two exhortations to acclaim God (vv. 4,6). The Hebrew root *zmr* is part and parcel of hymnal passages dealing with God's praise in music and it is equally clear that extolling God's *ᶜoz* is a favourite theme of such praise. Both words thus belong to the same semantic field and their connection in a hendiadys can readily be accounted for. The alternative explanation of *zimrāt* as synonymous with *ᶜoz* implies the hardly probable supposition that two homonymous terms *zimrā* served in the same genre of Biblical poetry. It would even be more perplexing to meet with two homonymous roots *ḏmr* in one and the same Ugaritic hymn. On the exegesis of this text in detail see in this volume, *A Ugaritic Hymn in Honour of Il*, pp. 320-332. Cf. now also J. Blau, *Hebrew Annual Review* 1 (1977), pp. 82, 83.*]*

The Cumulative Oath of Witnesses and Parties in Mesopotamian Law

Among the legal documents published by J. Nougayrol in *Ugaritica* 5 there is a procedural judgement of the king of Carcemish from the thirteenth century which provides us with useful information on the use of oaths in the Mesopotamian law of evidence.[1] After the judgement has set out the origin of the debtor's (D) indebtedness, it continues: "And D spoke as follows: 'The 800 shekels of the creditor C which I owed, I have payed to C and my witnesses thereto, W^1 and W^2, are present.' If his witnesses now say: 'It is paid. D. has paid the 800 shekels to C', then D must swear together with his witnesses and C forfeits his claims.[2] And if D's witnesses do not confirm (his statement)[3], C must swear together with his witnesses and D must pay his money."

The words "C must swear together with his witnesses", grammatically speaking may have two meanings: 1) C must swear with his own witnesses (*cum testibus suis*); 2) he must swear with his, i.e. D's witnesses (*cum testibus eius*). However, an analysis of the content shows that only the latter explanation is satisfactory. It is of course clear that D bears the burden of proving that his debt has been paid. Accordingly he has named witnesses, whose examination is ordered in the judgment. On the other hand there is understandibly no mention in the judgment of C naming witnesses, since he in any case does not bear the burden of proof. Such a thing is also hardly conceivable, since non-payment of a debt could not be evidenced by witnesses.

Accordingly, the following picture of trial procedure appears to emerge: the court first examines the witnesses named by D, and imposes the oath

---

1 RS 20.22:5-34, pp. 94ff.

2 On *qāt PN elû* cf. *CAD, s.v. elû*, 3 b 3'.

3 *inakkiru, nakāru* 'to deny, contest' is also used in particular in contrast to *kunnu* 'to establish, give evidence of'. See v. Soden, *AHW, s.v. nakāru* 5.

on the party in whose favour they have pronounced, as well as on the witnesses themselves, meaning repetition of their statement in a special sacral procedure before a god.[4] However, a closer examination raises doubts as to the accuracy of this description. It presumes, of course, that the witnesses will maintain their statements in court in the sacral oath procedure. That will indeed have generally been the case, but it cannot be taken as a matter of course. Refusal by a witness to swear would naturally reverse the state of the evidence. One might therefore suppose that the court ordered an oath by the party only after first examining the witnesses in the oath-proceedings, and that the king's instructions to the court confined themselves to a summary description of the procedure.

It is easy to see the sense of this *modus procedendi*. The duty of the witnesses to take an oath is some safeguard for the inculpated party against the possibility of false evidence. The vindicated party must afterwards corroborate this oath with his oath, which represents on additional safeguard for his opponent against a misjudgment. In this way, all steps have been taken to guarantee ascertainment of the truth.

Cumulation of oaths by witnesses and parties is therefore quite significant. But to the best of my knowledge it was only known up till now through one single Old-Babylonian document[5], whose interpretation has caused no little difficulty. In this document we are told that the female plaintiff (P) has brought an action against the female defendant (D) in the matter of the appointment of an heir, and has claimed that D and a man (apparently D's husband) appointed her heir, which D now disputes. It is to be presumed that the man died and that his death is the occasion for this case. It is further stated in the document that the judges made their witnesses (*šībišina*) swear before the gods, meaning literally the witnesses of the two women litigants. In the context, however, this must refer to the witnesses of P, who has the burden of proof. The witnesses have now

[4] This proceeding, well-known from the Old-Babylonian law of procedure, may be supposed for the period of the Ugaritic documents as well. Cf. *U* 5, text 52:28-30, pp. 142f., 396, where imposition of the oath is formulated as follows: "They must go into the temple".

[5] M. Schorr, *Urkunden des altbabylonischen Zivil- und Prozessrechts*, *VAB* V, Leipzig 1913, text 260.

stated under oath that they know nothing of a gift to P from D and the man. The document continues: *u dajānu šībi ul imguru*, which Schorr[6] translates: '*Jedoch waren die Richter von den Zeugen nicht befriedigt*', while Walther[7] interprets it: '*Die Richter hörten nicht auf die Zeugen*'. These words, to whose explanation we shall return, serve as an introduction to the judges' demand to D: "As the witnesses have sworn, so must you also swear", which D does. With this the case is settled.

The grounds for this behaviour on the part of the judges, characterised by Walther as rejection of the witnesses' statements, have not been satisfactorily explained up till now. Schorr attributes it to the vagueness of the witnesses, who had confined themselves to stating that they knew nothing of the matter. In reality no vagueness is shown, since the witnesses have categorically denied the knowledge attributed to them by the party on whom the burden of proof lies. After a longer discussion Walther arrives at the conjecture that the judges considered the witnesses unreliable. The solution should rather be sought in the judges' demand to D that she swear "like the witnesses". This formulation leads one to suppose that here, as well, the party's oath is to corroborate the oath of the witnesses. We may thus return to the phrase discussed above: *u dajānu šībi ul imguru* whose literal translation reads: 'And the judges did not concur with the witnesses.' Its meaning in the context must therefore be that it was not on the basis of their statements *alone* that the judgment favoured the witnesses' evidence. By this interpretation, the words hardly amount to a rejection of the witnesses' evidence. It is rather to be supposed, on the analogy of the procedural judgment from Carcemish, that in this trial as well the content of the witnesses' statements determined which party would have to take the corroborating oath. [Their evidence, however, was in favour of D, and it was in fact on her that the judges then imposed the oath.] It is also of interest to note that an oath by the party is only ordered after the witnesses have taken the oath. We have already supposed the same in our interpretation of the trial instructions given by the procedural judgment at Carcemish. It is striking that there is no mention of a judicial examination of the witnesses preceding the oath procedure. But it can-

---

[6] id., *ibid*.

[7] A. Walther, *Das altbabylonische Gerichtswesen*, Leipzig 1917, p. 253.

not be taken for granted that no such examination took place. Rather it may have remained unmentioned for the sake of brevity, having been superseded by the witnesses' statements under oath.

This view is supported by another Old-Babylonian document[8], in which P relied on a contract for the division of an inheritance. D objected that this contract had been cancelled by a later one and produced witnesses to support his claim. The document continues: "After the judges had examined their statement that there existed a later contract to divide the inheritance, the judges ordered them to lay their evidence before the moon-god." Therefore examination of the witnesses before the court, not under oath, preceded the order to examine them under oath in a sacral proceeding. This was by no means a pointless formality, as the report of the rest of the trial shows: "P voluntarily (*ina mitgurtišu*) declared: 'I will not have the witnesses go before the moon-god.' Because P did not have the witnesses go before the moon-god, D voluntarily (*ina mitgurimma*) gave P 1 1/2 shekels." In other words, after the unsworn statements of the witnesses, [confirming the statement of D] the parties came to a settlement, P accepting a trifling sum. With this, the case was of course closed and there was no longer room for a judicial requirement of a corroborating oath by the party.

In a further Old-Babylonian trial[9] the matter rested with an oath by the witnesses, without the parties taking an oath, because only the witnesses had first-hand knowledge of the circumstances, while the party vindicated by their evidence did not. To clarify this point, the only one of importance in the context of our discussion, we shall confine ourselves to a short and simple outline of this long and complicated document, which has been minutely analysed by Schorr and Walther. The situation is basically that P, who was born to his fathers' divorced wife after the fathers' death, is suing his fathers' brothers for transfer of the paternal estate, and brings evidence by witnesses, who are examined at first unsworn before the Court, later under oath before a god, that his filiation was established in

---

[8] M. Schorr, *op. cit.* (note 5), No. 298. Cf. E. Cuq, *Etudes sur le droit babylonien*, Paris 1929, pp. 345-349.

[9] M. Schorr, *WZKM* 29 (1915), pp. 74-96; cf. Walther, *op. cit.* (note 7), pp. 161-168.

law by a proper *ventris inspectio*. It is obvious that a corroborating oath by P could contribute nothing to the ascertainment of the facts, since no-one has first-hand knowledge of the circumstances of his birth.

The documents analysed here may therefore be interpreted as varied applications of a uniform rule of procedure. In spite of the limited number of examples one can recognize the tendency to try to ensure ascertainment of the truth through cumulative oaths by the witnesses and the parties.

The Ugaritic Myth of the Sea and its Biblical Counterparts

It is common knowledge today that the Bible contains many allusions to ancient traditions which tell of the war of the God of Israel against the rebellious aquatic forces. It should, however, be pointed out that at the beginnings of modern research scholars did not discern these allusions because they concentrated their attention on source criticism. There was a second reason for this disregard which was inherent in the Bible itself: The Biblical passages on this subject are mere references to the sea myth but never amount to a consecutive and complete description. Thus we should not be surprised that it was only the discovery of the Babylonian epic poem *enūma eliš* which brought about a turning point in the history of research on this subject. The description of the creation of the world following Marduk's victory over the representatives of the aquatic forces opened Gunkel's[1] eyes to perceive traditions of the war of the God of Israel as they are reflected in the Bible. In 1894, he published the first analysis of this important topic in Biblical research, and even aptly included in his treatment evidence on these traditions from the apocryphal literature. From that time on many scholars have dealt with this question. *Facile princeps* among them has been U. Cassuto[2] who offered a systematic and comprehensive description of the motives which make up this myth in the Bible, and who even devoted much attention to the characteristic expression of each of these motives in Hebrew literature. He, too, took up the subject under the influence of extra-Biblical texts, namely the Ugaritic epic poems - which were discovered after Gunkel's time, and the Rabbinic legends which Gunkel was not familiar with.

---

[1] H. Gunkel, *Schöpfung und Chaos in Urzeit und Endzeit*, Göttingen 1894, pp. 3-170.

[2] U. Cassuto, *The Israelite Epic*, *Knesset*, 8 (1943), part III, pp. 121-138 (in Heb.) *[= BOSt* 2, pp. 80-102*]*.

Thus, we may easily understand that both Gunkel and Cassuto emphasized the common features of the ancient near eastern myths, and that occasionally they even tended to overshoot the mark when explaining one myth in the light of another. There is no point today in criticizing Gunkel on this account, since in any event the discovery of the Ugaritic texts has removed from scholarly discussion the overemphasis on the connection of Bible and Mesopotamian literature. However, we must still examine Cassuto's writings on Ugaritic mythology and its relationship to the Bible because of his tendency to prefer synthetic above analytic observation, which led him to too comprehensive definitions which obscure the specific character of Ugaritic myth.

Cassuto[3] summed up the Ugaritic sea myth in the following terms: "The Prince of the Sea who always craved to flood the dry land with his waters became the ally of Mot against Baal." Two assumptions are included in this basic definition:

1) The God of the sea was the ally of Mot, the god of death; 2) The god of the sea wished to inundate the dry land.[4] We will treat these two assumptions in order.

The epic poetry relates the wars of Baal against the god of the sea and Mot, but does not describe any cooperation between Baal's two rivals. Moreover, there is no evidence for such cooperation in any other text from the Ancient Near East. Furthermore, Baal's war with the god of the sea is different in its outcome from his war with Mot. The god of the sea is invariably defeated, whether by Baal himself or by Anat, Baal's sister and ally.

The same applies to the monsters who aid the god of the sea. All those are vanquished in every instance. This is not, however, the case with Mot. True, Anat overpowers him and kills him, but in so doing she avenges her brother who was previously killed by Mot and brought down into the nether world. This important difference is not coincidental. The waters or their

---

[3] Cassuto, *Anath*, p. 67.

[4] This and similar viewpoints have been prevalent among scholars during the past few years. See, e.g. Gray, *Legacy*², p. 22.

representatives are defeated not only in the Ugaritic texts, but also in the other myths of the Ancient Near East. The main myth of the Ancient Near East attributes to the roaring waters the desire to inundate the entire world, as they did before the creation of the world when one of the gods restricted the extent of their rule in face of their fierce resistance.[4a] In fact the very existence of the earth shows clearly that the god of the earth has thwarted their plan. Observation of nature thus shows their downfall.

It appears that the Ugaritic myth took form on this general background, and Baal is called *zbl bᶜl arṣ* (*CTA* 3:I:3-4; 5:VI:10; 6:I:42-43; III:3, 9, 21; IV:29, 40) 'Prince, Lord of the Earth' for good reasons. Quite different is the case with Mot, since life experience shows that every living being eventually dies; therefore, it is not easy to imagine a myth in which Mot is always defeated.

Let us now turn to the second part of Cassuto's definition according to which the god of the sea always strives to inundate the dry land. We have already pointed out that this claim is in accordance with the original and main form of the sea myth, and it may thus be hypothesized that the Ugaritic myth also developed from this point of view. But no supposition can blur the perplexing fact that this desire of the sea is never mentioned in Ugaritic epic poetry. This merits investigation, and therefore we will reconsider the Ugaritic mythological texts. In this study we will first examine those texts in which the god of the sea appears alone, without his accompanying monsters, and afterwards, the texts which deal with these monsters, both in connection with the god of the sea and without such connection.

[[4a] Our characterisation of the basic myth needs some modification in the light of the ancient Sumerian tradition, summed up by W.G. Lambert, *JTS*, 16 (1965), p. 296. This tradition speaks of the mighty waters which began to rise and inundate the land, until they were checked by the dragon-killer Ninurta who built a wall and finally succeeded in containing them. Lambert convincingly argues that this myth reflects the yearly inundations of Mesopotamia. Therefore, it appears that this inner-wordly version of the myth precedes its projection into the primeval *Urzeit*. It follows that the aim of the waters to conquer the dry land should not be regarded just as an attempt at *reconquest*.]

The first type is found in the texts *CTA* 2:I; III; IV. Two questions must be answered here: What are the names of the god of the sea and what are his actions? *CTA* 2:I speaks everywhere of *ym // ṯpṭ nhr*, *CTA* 2:III - as a reconstruction of this broken text shows - of *zbl ym // ṯpṭ nhr*. On the other hand there are many variants in *CTA* 2:IV where we find *zbl ym // ṯpṭ nhr* (14-15, 16-17, 22, 24-25, 29-30), *ym // ṯpṭ nhr* (27), *ym // nhr* (12-13, 19-20), *zbl ym* (7), and *ym* (22, end). The free interchange of these names in one text shows that *(zbl) ym // (ṯpṭ) nhr* should not be viewed as two separate gods, but the names of just one god. The title *zbl* is common to the god of the sea, to Baal (see above), and to *yrḫ*, the moon god (*CTA* 19:164). It is even possible that this title was common to all the gods, since all the thrones of the gods are called *kḫṯ zblhm* (*CTA* 2:I:23-24). We may then conclude that *zbl* was a general title of authority. Albright's suggestion[5] to derive the Ugaritic word *zbl* from the Proto-Semitic root *zbl* known from Arabic and Akkadian in the meaning 'to carry' in Hebrew *nś'*, and to parallel it with the Hebrew title *nāśi'* prince has been rightly accepted. As to the title *ṯpṭ* ('judge') Albright[6] explained it in the light of the judicial function which the river played in Mesopotamian law. In fact, the absence of this title in connection with the other gods supports his suggestion. On the other hand, however, there is no proof that this god served in any judicial capacity even among the West-Semitic peoples. So perhaps it is preferable to explain *ṯpṭ*, in parallelism with *zbl*, as simply a term of authority too. Cf. the Ugaritic parallelism *mlkn // ṯpṭn* (*CTA* 3:V: 40; 4:IV:43-44), and the Hebrew parallelism *mäläk // šopeṭ* (Ho. 7:7; Ps. 2:10; 148:11). The titles *zbl* and *ṯpṭ* thus define the god of the sea as a ruler of the gods, a term which recalls the Midrashic title *śar šäl yam* 'prince of the sea'. This definition is emphasized to the greatest extent in the full phrase *zbl ym // ṯpṭ nhr*, but it applies also to the shorter (and more ancient?) expression *ym // ṯpṭ nhr*. True, this does not fit the expression *ym // nhr*, and plain *ym*, but the context clearly shows that we should understand these expressions as abbreviations of the longer ones, which add titles of authority. What is told of this god reveals his desire for kingship, but does not show him anywhere as connected with the cosmic element of water. *CTA* 2:III is so broken that the question of its restora-

---

[5] W.F. Albright, *JPOS*, 16 (1936), pp. 17-20.

[6] id., *ibid*.

tion and interpretation have led to wide differences of opinion.[7] Nevertheless, it appears from it that both the god of the sea and the god ᶜṯtr want to build a palace for themselves, and this desire - which implies an aspiration for kingdom - leads to the conflict between them. The claim of the god of the sea to erect for himself a palace places him on the same plane with ᶜṯtr, his rival, and brings to mind Baal who spares no effort in order to get his own palace. In this respect the god of the sea is not different from ᶜṯtr and Baal except in name only.

A similar picture is formed from *CTA* 2:I; IV from which complete and understandable sections are preserved. The texts are well-known, and we may therefore content ourselves here with a short synopsis of their main content. *CTA* 2:I relates that the god of the sea sent his messengers to the assembly of the gods headed by Il, and in the statement of his mission he declared himself the master of the gods and demanded the handing over of Baal. The bewildered gods did not pay heed to Baal's words of encouragement, and the frightened Il gave in to the demand of the god of the sea. But Baal rose in an outpouring of fierce anger and attacked the messengers of the god of the sea. True, the aggressive boastfulness of the god of the sea and the faintheartedness of the other gods remind us somewhat of the terrifying impression which the roaring sea evokes, and in particular, what is related of the fear of the gods in *enūma eliš*.[8] But we may imagine such behaviour in any other son of Il who tries to establish the kingship for himself, and it is just the name of the god of the sea which draws the reader's attention to the connection with the cosmic element of the water. *CTA* 2:IV also does not diverge from this framework. This text speaks of *kṯr wḫss*, the artisan of the gods, who encouraged Baal to expel the god of the sea from his throne and supplied him with two weapons with which he smote his enemy on the shoulder and head. Here also there is no reference whatsoever to the waters of the god of the sea, and there is not even any indication of his description as a monster. The text speaks of a duel between two high-ranking members of the pantheon who are described as humans. This formulation of the sea myth is unique. Admittedly we also may discern in sour-

---

[7] See e.g. A. Caquot, *Syria* 35 (1958), pp. 45f., O. Kaiser, *Die mythische Bedeutung des Meeres in Ägypten, Ugarit, und Israel*, Berlin 1959, pp. 44-47.

[8] Gray, *Legacy*², p. 123.

ces outside the Ugaritic texts a personal element, but there is no other source in which the personal element eliminates the cosmic and monstrous features of the ancient myth to such a degree. A phrase like "Am I the sea, or *Tannin* (a sea monster), that Thou settest a guard over me?" (Job 7:12) gives the sea a personality to some extent like the sea monster mentioned alongside it. But as everywhere in the Bible, the sea is mentioned here without any epithet to emphasize its personality and in spite of the personal coloring, the limitations of the water's realm are clearly understood. Furthermore, the mention of the sea monster preserves the monstrous element of the myth. The same applies to the Midrash, even though it gives the sea the title "prince of the sea". For example: "At the time when the Holy One, blessed be He, desired to create the world, He said to the prince of the sea: 'Open thy mouth and swallow all the waters of the world'. He said unto Him: 'Lord of the Universe, it is enough that I remain with my own'. Thereupon, He struck him with His foot and killed him; for it is written (Job 26:12): 'He stirreth up (or: stilleth)[8a] the sea with His power and by His understanding He smiteth through Rahab (Baba Bathra 74b). A comparison with *enūma eliš* is also instructive. True, in this epic the battle between Marduk and Tiamat is a personal battle, except that Tiamat is a monster and the story of her slaying ends with the creation of the world from her body. But even in this description the cosmic element of the war with the water breaks forth in the famous line: "He pulled down the bar and posted guards, he bade them to allow not her waters to escape" (IV: 139-140).

On the other hand, in the stratum of the Ugaritic myth under discussion the cosmic as well as the monstrous element of the water is missing, and there is no reason to distinguish between the figure of *zbl ym // ṯpṭ nhr* and the figure of the other young gods, all of whom are the sons of Il, belonging to one social plane.

We should admit that this conclusion does not at all fit our expectations of the myth on the aquatic powers and monsters, and it is no wonder that Kapelrud[9] ascribes the lack of the cosmic element to a lacuna in the

[[8a] Compare in this volume, *The Trembling of Nature during the Theophany*, note 10, p. 178.]

[9] A.S. Kapelrud, *Norsk Teologisk Tidskrift* (1960), pp. 249f. I have not seen this article, it is known to me from Gray, *Legacy*[2], pp. 29-30.

text. He proposed the theory that *CTA* 2:IV concluded with a description of the creation of the world from the body of the defeated god of the sea. The war between the sons of the old god Il over the kingdom of the world which existed from old becomes - in Kapelrud's view an introduction to a cosmogonic description. But this attempt to graft onto the court-story of the Ugaritic texts a creation story motif similar to *enūma eliš* is not convincing at all. Gray already criticized him and showed[10] that in the Ugaritic texts only one god has the traits of a creator, namely Il, the father of the pantheon, and no other, especially not Baal. This argument is decisive, Il is well-known as *bny bnwt* 'Creator of Creatures' (*CTA* 4:II:11; 6:III:5, 11; 17:I:25), or *ab adm* 'Father of Humanity' (*CTA* 14:37, 43, 136, 151, 297). Il is the only god who is capable of creating a healing messenger (*CTA* 16: V)[10a] and Baal turns to him when he requests a son for a childless man (*CTA* 17:I:24-27). This implies that Baal is not the creator of man, and even more so not the creator of the world.[10b] We can now understand why he needed the intercession of his mother *Aṯrt* and of his sister Anat in order to receive permission from Il to build his temple. It is inconceivable that the creator of the world would have to ask for permission from another god for such a thing. Thus, there is no reason to doubt the image of the god of the sea in our texts. The god of the sea is not a monster, but one of the ambitious sons of the old Il who claim the kingdom of the world for themselves. The text speaks of his throne and not of his waters, and therefore not of his desire to inundate the world. In the milieu of the Ugaritic court cosmic mythology became a clear court epic.[11] This society was interested in the quarrels over authority among the royal family, and its poets were able to give the ancient mythology a new form which captured the hearts of their listeners more than the ancient legends.

However, texts in which elements of the ancient mythology are more conspicuous have also been preserved, such as the reference to the victory

---

10 Gray, *Legacy*², p. 22.

[10a Consult H.L. Ginsberg, *JANES* 5 (1973), pp. 132-134.]

[10b Baal is no more the creator of the world than Ninurta, who defeated the roaring waters. See note 4a.]

11 On the question of the antiquity of the royal court tradition at Ugarit, see J. Nougayrol, *PRU* 3, pp. XL-XLIII; Cl. Schaeffer, *CRAIBL* (1962), pp. 204.

of Baal over a monster known from the Bible by the names *liwyātān nāḥāš bāriᵃḥ* 'Leviathan the fleeing serpent' and *liwyātān nāḥāš ᶜᵃqallāton* 'Leviathan the twisting serpent'. This allusion is found in the words which Mot's messengers present to Baal:

k tmḫṣ ltn btn brḥ
tkly bṯn ᶜqltn
šlyṭ d šbᶜt rašm (*CTA* 5:I:1-3; 27-30)

'Though thou didst smite *Lotan*, the writhing serpent didst destroy the crooked serpent, the ruler[12] of[13] seven heads'.

The following lines are not sufficiently clear, and therefore it is impossible to establish with certainty for what purpose Mot mentions this victory of Baal. Nevertheless, the widely and rightly held opinion is that the general tenor of the text is as follows: Even though you have defeated this monster you have no hope of standing up against me.[14] Kapelrud[15] expressed the opinion that the god of the sea and *Lotan* are identical. But Gaster already criticized him and showed[16] that *CTA* 3:III:35-39 clearly distinguishes between them. Therefore, the question arises: What is the relationship between the tradition of the war against the god of the sea and the tradition of the war against Lotan? The Ugaritic texts do not give a clear answer to this question. In *CTA* 5 Baal's victory over *Lotan* is men-

[12] According to many scholars the word *šlyṭ* is derived from the root *šlṭ*. It should be admitted that until now no satisfactory explanation has been given for the *y* in this word. There is no reason to explain the form *šlyṭ* as a diminutive form like the Arabic noun-pattern *qutail*. But cf. Ugaritic nouns such as *pḫyr, mrym, sdynm* in which the *y* does not belong to the root. Perhaps Ugaritic had a noun-pattern in which consonantal *y* was added to the root but did not indicate the diminutive. Some scholars explain *šlyṭ* as coming from *lwṭ* (Š), a root known from Aramaic, and translate it 'The cursed one'. Even according to this opinion the problem of the explanation of the *y* still remains. As far as the text is concerned the first explanation is preferable over the second, since we do not find any example of a derogatory epithet in Ugaritic. For another explanation, see: Gray, *Legacy²*, p. 30, note 1. *[Cf. also* J. Blau - S.E. Loewenstamm, *UF* 2, p. 28.*]*

[13] On d as a pronoun of possession, see in this volume, *Notes on the Pronouns in Ugaritic in the Light of Canaanite*, pp. 67-75.

[14] See, e.g. M. Held, *JAOS*, 79 (1959), p. 172, note 57. For another opinion, see Gaster, *Thespis²*, p. 201.

[15] Kapelrud, *Baal*, p. 102.

[16] Gaster, *Thespis²*, p. 145.

tioned without any connection with his victory over the god of the sea, whereas in *CTA* 3:III:35-39 the war of Anat against this monster is connected with her war against the god of the sea. If we identify *Lotan* with the sea monster *Tunnanu* we may state that the battle with him is mentioned after the battle with the sea also in *PRU* 2, text 3 (see *infra*). The Bible also raises similar problems (see *infra*). We may establish by way of supposition that *Lotan* was originally one of the helpers of the god of the sea, and in the text *CTA* 3 and *PRU* 2, text 3 a trace of this tradition was preserved, while in *CTA* 5 the tradition concerning *Lotan* became an independent and selfcontained theme. In any event, it seems likely that in the figure of the seven headed monster[17] an old myth was preserved in its original form, unlike the figure of *zbl ym // ṯpṭ nhr* who became a figure of one of the princes among the gods of the pantheon.

We have already mentioned incidentally the important text in which Anat boasts of her victories over her brother's enemies. This text reads as follows:

mn ib yp^{c} lb^{c}l
ṣrt lrkb ^{c}rpt lmḫšt mdd
il ym lklt nhr il rbm
lištbm tnn...[18]
mḫšt bṯn ^{c}qltn
šlyṭ dšb^{c}t rašm
mḫšt mdd il ar[š?]
ṣmt ^{c}gl il ^{c}tk
mḫšt klbt ilm išt
klt bt il ḏbb (*CTA* 3:III:34-43)

'Who[19] is the enemy (who) has arisen against Baal, / Or foe[20] against

---

[17] For comparative material on the seven heads of *ltn*, see Cassuto, *Anath*, p. 134.

[18] On the question of the reading, see Herdner, *CTA*, p. 17, note 2.

[19] The usual translation is "what enemy". But see in this volume, *Notes on the Pronouns in Ugaritic in the Light of Canaanite*, p. 59.

[20] On *sarā* in the meaning of all the enemies, see U. Cassuto, *Lěšonénu* 15 (1947), pp. 98f. *[= BOSt 2, pp. 61f.]*

the rider of the clouds. / I crushed[21] the beloved of Il, Sea, / I destroyed the great[22] river of Il, / I muzzled[23] *Tunnanu* ..., / I crushed the writhing serpent, / ruling-one of seven heads, / I destroyed the beloved of Il *Arš*(?)[24], / I destroyed the calf of Il *ᶜtk*, I crushed the bitch of Il fire, / I destroyed the daughter of Il flame (?)'.

The enumeration of Baal's enemies in this text surpasses all that we know from other sources. Therefore, the absence of Mot, Baal's bitter enemy, who was also defeated by Anat, stands out. This omission permits us to hypothesize that the text belongs entirely to the realm of the myth dealing with the war of Baal against the god of the sea and his helpers, and that the enemies are enumerated here according to the order of their importance: The text begins with the god of the sea, and afterwards enumerates *Tunnanu* a synonym of *Lotan*, which is mentioned afterwards and in

---

[21] See W.F. Albright, *BASOR*, 84 (1941), p. 16, note 21. Albright explained *mḫš* as a metathesis of *ḫmš*; cf. Akkadian *ḫamāšu*. On this verb, see recently *AHW, s.v. abknicken, vernichten*. Held, *op. cit.* (note 14), p. 143, derives *mḫšt* from *mḫṣ* and surmises that the *ṣ* of the root shifted to *š* by partial assimilation to the following *t*. But such a phenomenon is not known either in Ugaritic or in any other West-Semitic language.

[22] The explanation of the words is disputed. Cassuto, Anath, pp. 93, 133f., translates 'the great rivers of Il' basing himself on the parallelism 'sea // rivers' in the Bible. But in Ugaritic the parallelism (*zbl*) *ym* // (*ṯpṭ*) *nhr* appears in the singular. The parallelism *ym // nhrm* is found only in *CTA* 4:II:6-7, where the text speaks of a natural phenomenon and not of a god. Even there we may explain the word as *nhr-m*, a singular form. Ginsberg (*ANET*, p. 137) translates: 'El's flood *Rabbim*', but there is no proof for a noun '*Rabbim*'. Moreover, *nhr* itself is a noun. Driver, *CML*, p. 78: 'The mighty god *Nahar*', and similarly Kaiser, *op. cit.* (note 7), p. 58: '*Strom, den grossen Gott*'. The translation given here follows Albright, *op. cit.* (note 5): 'River-of-El, the Chief'. According to him, *nhr il* is a construct phrase like the epithets *mdd il, klbt il, bt il*.

[23] On the muzzling of the *Tunnanu*, see Cassuto, *op. cit.* (note 2), p. 133; and in this volume, *The Muzzling of the Tannin*, pp. 91-92; *[Anat's Victory over the Tunnanu*, pp. 465-470].

[24] Albright, *op. cit.* (note 21), p. 16, reads: *ar[ṣ]*, and translates: 'The Underworld Dragon beloved of El'. But such a monster is unknown from the Ugaritic texts. Cassuto, *Anath*, pp. 92, 134f., reads like him and translates 'beloved of the mighty of the Underworld'. But according to this suggestion, this enemy of Baal is indicated solely by his epithet, whereas the other enemies are called by name. Kaiser, *op. cit.* (note 7), p. 75, and Gray, *Legacy*², p. 31, read - following Gordon - *arṣ mt*. According to this reading Anat boasts of her victory over Mot. But from a graphic point of view there is no room for this reading. Cf. Herdner, *CTA*, p. 17, note 3, who mentions, in Gaster's name, the suggestion to read *ar[š]*, based on *CTA* 6:VI:50.

parallelism with it. This monster's importance is attested by its being mentioned in the Bible and in other Ugaritic texts. Afterwards *Ar[?]* is mentioned. If we restore *Ar[š]* and see in *Arš* in *CTA* 6:VI:50 the name of a monster, then this enemy is mentioned once again in the Ugaritic texts. In any event, he is not attested at in the Bible, indicating that his importance was less than that of *Lotan - Tunnanu*. The other monsters are not known from any other sources.

The brevity of the text which only alludes to Anat's war does not permit us to define the exact character of the god who is called here "beloved of Il *ym* // the great river of Il". True, the words *mdd il* remind us of the honorific epithet *naram AN* (The beloved of a god) in Akkadian texts. But nothing may be learnt from it of the character of the god of the sea since this epithet is also given to *Arš*, and the epithets *nhr il*, *ᶜgl il*, *klbt il*, *bt il* are similar to it, though their exact meaning is unknown to us. Nevertheless, we may establish that the war against the god of the sea is mentioned here together with the war upon a complete group of monsters which are not mentioned in the description of Baal's war with *zbl ym* // *ṯpṭ nhr*. We may probably conclude from this that here also the god of the sea has a monstrous nature, and it is thus possible to state with certainty that the ancient myth is recognizable here to a much greater extent, and that it has not yet become a court story. In spite of all this we cannot neglect the fact that the text does not mention the water at all. Thus, the monstrous aspect of the myth was kept, but not its cosmic aspect.

Important additional material for our knowledge of the war alluded to in *CTA* 3:III is included in *PRU* 2, text 3 which - according to a reasonable suggestion of Virolleaud[25] - presents a fragment of a description of Anat's war with the sea and the monsters. We will content ourselves here with a discussion of the continuous text in ll. 3-10, since the single letters in the other lines are not explainable. The text reads as follows:

...[25a] *un barṣ*
mẖnm ṯrp ym

---

[25] Ch. Virolleaud, *PRU* 2, p. 12. [On the interpretation of this text see now in this volume, *Anat's Victory over the Tunnanu*, pp. 465-470].

[[25a] Virolleaud has suggested the reading *[tš]un*. No less probable is the reading *[tb]un*.]

lšnm tlḥk
šmm tṯrp
ym ḏnbtm
tnn[26] *lšbm*
tšt trks
lmrym lbt

A cursory study of the text reveals that the sea is mentioned first, and afterwards the *Tunnanu* whose muzzling was previously known from *CTA* 3: III:37. We may thus assume that the text speaks of the war with the sea and the *Tunnanu*. The context then suggests for the words *tṯrp ym* the approximate meaning 'she crushed the sea'. The exact explanation of the verb runs into difficulty since the root *ṯrp* is not known, either from Ugaritic or from the other Semitic languages. But we may put forth the hypothesis that this root is simply a metathesis of the Proto-Semitic root *prṯ*[27] known from Arabic, which means - *inter alia* - 'to split'. The root *prt* occurs in the *Pešiṭta*[28] as a translation of the Biblical verb *bqᶜ* which is frequently mentioned in connection with the splitting of the Red Sea (Ex. 14:16,21; Is. 63:12; Ps. 78:13; Neh. 9:11).

Let us now return to the beginning of the document. Virolleaud saw in the word *mḫnm* the name of a country, and in fact his suggestion is supported by the parallel phrase *arṣ dbr* in *CTA* 6:II:19. We may therefore suggest the translation: '... from the land of Mahanayim to split the sea', and suppose that it was Anat who came forth from this land. Virolleaud translated the following words *lšnm tlḥk šmm* as '*les langues lèchent les cieux*'. From a linguistic point of view we may also translate 'with a tongue she (i.e. Anat) licks the skies'. But it is difficult to assume that such a monstrous description fits Anat, and we must say that the description applies to the sea. This explanation, however, raises a linguistic difficulty since due to the absence of a possessive pronoun in the word *lšnm* it is difficult to explain the words under discussion as an asyndetic subordinate clause, namely: 'whose tongue(s) lick(s) the skies'. Therefore

---

26 Text: *tan*. On the confusion of *a* and *n*, see Gordon, *UT*, *Grammar*, 4. 13.

27 Cf. e.g. the West-Semitic root *brk* with Akkadian *karābu*; regular Aramaic *rgl* with *lgr* in the *Panamu* inscription and Mandaic.

28 Brockelmann, *LS*, *s.v.*; and cf. Jastrow, *Talmud Dictionary*, *s.v.*

it seems that the phrase is an independent sentence, a cry of amazement at the act of the sea: 'tongue(s) lick(s) heaven'. Virolleaud has rightly pointed out that this bold picture recalls Mot's action in *CTA* 5:II:1-2: *[špt la]rṣ špt lšmm [... l]šn lkbkbm* '[A lip to ea]rth, a lip to heaven, [and to]ngue to the stars'. There are, in fact, four signs missing before the letters *šn*[29], but the restoration *lšn* is confirmed from the Biblical parallelism *śāpā* 'lip' // *lāšon* 'tongue'.[30]

We offer the following translation for the rest of the text: 'The tails[31] of the Tunnanu (which) she placed into a muzzle, she tied to the height[32] of the house of ...', i.e. Anat placed a muzzle into the mouth of *Tunnanu* and hung him by his tails from the height in a place whose exact definition is lacking due to a lacuna in the text. This fragment is very important for the study of Ugaritic mythology. The text speaks here of "sea", without any epithet, and this sea is a terrible monster, whose tongue licks heaven, and whose dimensions are indeed cosmic. But even here there is no mention of his waters. The poet wishes to hold his listeners' attention with dramatic scenes, and not with the cosmic question of the existence of the earth.

This completes our survey of the Ugaritic texts which describe the war with the sea and its helpers, except for *CTA* 6:VI:50-52 which is so obscure that nothing definite may be learnt from it.[33] When we come to

---

29 See *CTA*, p. 33.

30 Is. 28:11; 33:19; Ez. 3:5-6; Ps. 12:5; 34:14; 120:2; Pr. 17:4.

31 Concerning Tiamat, *enūma eliš*, Tablet V:59 states: *egir zibbassa* 'he twisted her tail'. Apparently the sea monster fights especially with its mouth and tail. [For a fuller discussion of this verse see in this volume, *Anat's Victory over the Tunnanu*, p. 469].

32 Virolleaud, *PRU* 2, p. 12, casts doubt on the accepted translation of *mrym* as 'height' because of the difficulty in explaining the *y* in *mrym*. But see *supra*, note 12, and cf. *mrym* in Sabean.

33 The text reads: *bym arš wtnn kṯr wḫss yd ytr kṯr wḫss*. Ginsberg, *ANET*, p. 137, translated: 'on the sea of monster and dragon proceedeth *Kothar wa Khasis, Kothar wa Khasis* does journey'. This shows that he derived *yd* from *ndd* and *ytr* from *twr*. [For a similar interpretation see E. Lipiński, *OLP* 3 (1972), pp. 106-109.] But the text remains obscure. The rendering of J. Aistleitner, *Texte*, p. 23, is completely meaningless. Others find here a reference to the act of *kṯr wḫss* who threw the monsters *arš* and *tnn* into the sea. See, e.g. Driver, *CML*, p. 115: 'Kathir and Khasis threw monster (?) dragon into the sea, Kathir and Khasis cut

draw conclusions about Ugaritic mythology we should remember that every new text is likely to change them. Nevertheless, we may suppose that the cosmological element had degenerated, and that only the names of the god of the sea and his desire to rule the world had remained. This is not the case with regard to the monstrous elements which still stand out in the descriptions of Anat's wars with the sea and its helpers and also in the allusion to the war of Baal with the *Lotan*. These elements disappeared also in the myth of Baal's war with *zbl ym // ṯpṭ nhr* which became a court epic in which the sons of this old king fight among themselves for power. These changes are apparently reflected in the names of the god of the sea. *PRU* 2, text 3 which preserved - as no other text - traditions on the battle with monsters calls the god of the sea simply *ym*. From this we may understand that in the court text *CTA* 2:IV the full name *zbl ym // ṯpṭ nhr* could be abbreviated to just *ym*. We may also establish with certainty that it is no coincidence that the full name only appears in the stratum of the court texts.

In the light of all that has been said above, we may ask: In what measure may the Ugaritic poems and the Biblical passages clarify one another? Here we must preface a fundamental statement: The Biblical passages make us aware of the cosmological element in Ugaritic mythology which in the milieu of the Ugaritic court had so weakened that we would not have been able to discern its roots were it not for the large number of allusions to the cosmological mythology found in the Bible and in its parallels in Mesopotamian literature and the Midrash. This forces us to the conclusion

---

them off'. Driver apparently derived *yd* from *ndy* and *ytr* from *trr* which he explained from Arabic *tarra* (p. 153, note 8). Gaster, *Thespis*², p. 230, translates: 'Even that same Sir Adroit-and-Cunning who can hurl both Monster and Dragon into the sea, even that same Sir Adroit-and-Cunning who can toss them therein'. However, the first line has no parallel in the original text, and I do not know from which root Gaster derived the word *ytr*. Similarly, Cassuto, *op. cit.* (note 2), p. 133, claimed that the text deals with throwing (literally: to make spring) into the sea. He derives *ytr* from the root *ntr* 'to spring', comparing *rā'ā wayyatter goyim* (Hab. 3:6), and he even quotes the Apocalypse of John 20: 2-3. But we cannot understand the reason for throwing the *Tunnanu* into the sea when in any event he is already there. The subject is not the same as that in the text of the Apocalypse of John which speaks of the throwing of a monster into the abyss and its imprisonment there. *[Perhaps* *bym* should be rendered 'from the sea', that is to say that *kṯr wḫss* removed the sea-monsters from their element in order to destroy them. Cf. Ez. 29:3-5; 32:2-6.*]*

that we should not see in Ugaritic mythology an immediate predecessor of its Biblical counterpart, but rather look for the origin of the common elements in West-Semitic traditions which not only pre-date the Bible, but also the Ugaritic texts. An unequivocal proof for this common background may be found in the names *tnn*, and *ltn bṯn brḥ // ltn bṯn* ^{c}*qltn* in the Ugaritic texts. Moreover, the war with this monster is also mentioned in the Bible, sometimes in connection with the war with the sea[34], and sometimes without any connection with it.[35] This is additional support for the common background of the Bible and the Ugaritic epics in the Ancient West-Semitic tradition. Still we should not discount the possibility that this tradition took on different forms among the West-Semitic tribes, and that the Biblical tradition developed from a West-Semitic version which was different from the Ugaritic one. Thus *Lotan* is called in Ugaritic *bṯn brḥ* and *bṯn* ^{c}*qltn, liwyātān* in Hebrew *nāḥāš bāri*^{a}*ḥ* and *nāḥāš* ^{ca}*qallāton*, although *nḥš* is common to both Hebrew and Ugaritic[36] and Ugaritic *bṯn* parallels Hebrew *ptn*. Still more important is the absence of the monster *Rahab* in the Ugaritic texts even though in Biblical mythology it holds a most important place. We cannot explain its absence by the assumption that the Ugaritic texts which mention it have by chance not come down to us, since in the text which relates Anat's victory over the sea and its helpers these monsters are enumerated in great detail.[37]

We arrive at the same conclusions from a study of an additional parallel between the Bible and the Ugaritic texts. Cassuto[38] already stressed the fact that the Ugaritic parallelism *(zbl) ym // (ṯpṭ) nhr* is repeated in the Bible with a slight change *yam // n*^{e}*hārot* 'sea // rivers'.[39] Today

---

[34] Ps. 74:13-14; Job 7:12; Is. 51:9-10.

[35] Is. 27:1; Ez. 29:3; 32:2. On the development of an independent myth on the Leviathan see also the following verses: Ps. 104:26; Job 3:8; 40:25-32.

[36] See in this volume, *On new Texts in Ugaritic*, p. 222.

[37] It should be noted that some of the monsters mentioned in Anat's speech do not occur in the Bible, and it is possible that they were not known in all variants of West-Semitic tradition. But perhaps it is just coincidental that they are not mentioned in the Bible, since even at Ugarit they were not the most important.

[38] Cassuto, *op. cit.* (note 2), p. 129, quotes Na. 1:4; Hab. 3:8; Ps. 74:13-15; 93:3-4.

[39] The parallelism "sea // river" in Ps. 66:6 should also be pointed out. True, in the Ugaritic texts *ym* and *nhr* are identical. But this is not so

we may add the comparison of *PRU* 2, text 3 with those Biblical verses which mention just the sea without referring to the rivers.[40] But with all the similarity we should not ignore the above mentioned difference between Hebrew and Ugaritic which lead to the conclusion that the Bible and the Ugaritic texts evolved from two kindred but not identical forms of West-Semitic tradition. As to the Bible, the supposition of a West-Semitic background is not shaken even in the light of the parallels between the Biblical and the Mesopotamian tradition. True, a verse such as "Am I the sea, or a *Tannin*, that thou settest guard over me" (Job 7:12; and cf. 38:8-11) reminds us of *enūma eliš*, IV:139-140. But the sea and the sea monster, dealt with in Job 7:12 are mentioned one after the other in exactly the same terms in *PRU* 2, text 3. If we have here Mesopotamian influence, then it probably penetrated into Israel through the Late Bronze Age Canaanite culture, or - to be more exact - from one of the forms of the Canaanite myth which - as opposed to the Ugaritic texts - preserved an ancient motif or a war with the waters which threaten to inundate the earth.

---

in Ps. 66:6 where the splitting of the Red Sea and the dividing of the Jordan are alluded to. On the other hand, it is probable that the tradition of the splitting of the Red Sea and the dividing of the Jordan itself developed from the myth. See S.E. Loewenstamm, *The Tradition of the Exodus from Egypt in its Development*, Jerusalem 1965, pp. 101-129 (in Heb.). It is not surprising that in Israel even the river alone became a symbol of the enemy's power which God fights against (Is. 59:19).

[40] See e.g.: Is. 17:12-13; 51:15; Jer. 5:22; 31:35; Ps. 46:4; 65:8; 104:5-9; Job 7:12.

Ugaritic Formulas of Greeting*

The greeting *ilm tġrk tšlmk*[1] attested in Ugaritic letters has been the subject of much discussion ranging from H.L. Ginsberg's[2] pioneer treatment in 1938 to the remarks of M. Dietrich and O. Loretz[3] in 1968. The most detailed inquiry into this question has so far been made in 1967 by B. Hartmann[4], whose paper contains also an exhaustive bibliography.

Taking up the problem again we may first of all point to congener formulas of greeting in letters, especially to the short greeting *yšlm lk*[5] and the complex formula *yšlm lk. ilm tġrk tšlmk*[6], literally 'May welfare be upon thee. May the gods watch over thee and give thee welfare', i.e. may they watch over thy welfare.

All these more or less standardized patterns are by now known as well from Akkadian letters found in Ugarit. The complex blessing reads in Akkadian: *lu šulmu ana muḫḫika ilānu*^{meš} *ana šulmāni liṣṣurūka*.[7] This basic pat-

---

* Compare in this volume, *Who is afraid of the Linguistic Method? (tġrk again)*, pp. 433-439.

[1] *UT* 138:4-5; *CTA* 51:7-9 and especially the exceedingly solemn greeting in *PRU* 2, text 19:2-6 *ilm tġrk tšlmk tᶜzzk alp ymm w rbt šnt bᶜd ᶜlm*, where the standard formula has been enlarged by the additional wish 'and might they give strength to thee a thousand of days and a myriad of years forever'. For *bᶜd* in the meaning *ᶜd* cf. Am. 9:10. Compare also in this volume, *Review of PRU* 2, note 27a, p. 88. For the parallel *ymm / šnt* see *U* 5, text 2:verso:11-12, pp. 554-555; Deut. 32:7; Mal. 3:4; Ps. 61:7 etc.

[2] H.L. Ginsberg, *BASOR* 72 (1938), p. 19. *[*Contrast id., *BASOR* 95 (1944), p. 28, note 14.*]*

[3] M. Dietrich - O. Loretz, *WO* 4 (19-7-68), p. 307, note 26.

[4] B. Hartmann, *VTS* 16 (1967), pp. 102-105.

[5] *CTA* 53:4.

[6] *PRU* 5, texts 9:4-5; 10:4-6; 59:4-5; 61:4-5; 65:1-2. Cf. also *PRU* 2, text 16:4-6, where the sequence of verbs is reversed to read: *tšlmk [tġ]rk*.

[7] *PRU* 3, RS 15.77:4-6, p. 6; RS 11.730:4-6, p. 12; *PRU* 4, RS 17.286:4-5, p. 180; RS 17.78:4-5, p. 196; RS 17.424 C:6-7; *U* 5, *passim*.

tern admits variations. Either part may be enlarged[8] or the second part may be shortened to: *ilānu*^{meš} *liṣṣurūka*.[9] As in the Ugaritic letters the first[10] part or the second[11] can be omitted.

The use of the noun *šulmu* in the first part of the formula as opposed to the impersonal construction of the Ugaritic verb *šlm* in *yšlm lk* corresponds to normal Hebrew usage. Cf. e.g. *šālom lākäm* (Gen. 43:23, not *yišlam lākäm*!) literally 'welfare upon you!' or *šālom yihyä li* (Deut. 29:18, not *yišlam li*!), literally 'welfare will be unto me.' The impersonal use of the verb *šlm* 'to be in a state of welfare' is not found in Hebrew at all and even its personal use is restricted to Job 9:4; 22:21. A still closer parallel between Ugaritic and the language of the book of Job appears in the second part of the formula. In the hendiadys *tġrk tšlmk* the second verb has been correctly parsed as the *D*-form of *šlm* denoting 'to bestow welfare'. It is worthwhile stressing that this usage is not standard Hebrew (cf. Lev. 26:6; Is. 45:7; 66:12; Hag. 2:9; Ps. 72:3; 147:14; Job 25: 2) and restricted to Job 8:6. This observation lends additional force to H.L. Ginsberg's contention that Biblical *yā*^{c}*ir* and *šillam* in Job 8:6 and Ugaritic *tġrk tšlmk* represent the same traditional pair of words and strengthens his conclusion that we should admit a Hebrew root ^{c}*yr* 'preserve', derived from Proto-Semitic *ġyr*. We may add that further support of this view has been forwarded by Hartmann's remarks upon the Safaitic noun *ġyrt*, 'help, protection', paralleled by *slm*. Therefore the derivation of the Ugaritic verb from *nġr*, Proto-Semitic *nẓr*, defended still by Dietrich and Loretz, can hardly be sustained. It may be conceded that in a

---

8 For an enlargement of the first part see *U* 5, text 56:2'-5'; for an enlargement of the second *PRU* 3, RS 15.33:4-6, p. 15; RS 15.24+50:4-8; *PRU* 4, RS 17.116:1'-4', p. 132; RS 17.152:4-5, p. 214; RS 17.83:4-7 and especially the solemn wish in *U* 5, text 55:4-12, pp. 147f., 397. The formula *li-ši-bu-ki ši-bu-t[a]* (l. 10) reminds of Ps. 91:16. Cf. also Gen. 35:29; Job 42:17; 1 Chr. 29:28.

9 *PRU* 3, RS 11.723:5-6; *U* 5, text 41:4-5, p. 124; text 43:4-5, p. 128. Cf. *PRU* 4, RS 17.152:4-5, p. 214.

10 *PRU* 3, RS 16.111:4-6, p. 13; RS 15.63:4, p. 20; *U* 5, text 25:4-5, pp. 90, 384.

11 *PRU* 3, RS 16.03:4, p. 3; RS 8.333:4, p. 7; RS 12.33:4, p. 14; RS 15.11: 4, p. 19; *PRU* 4, RS 17.292:5, p. 188; RS 17.394+427:4, p. 220; *U* 5, passim. For an Assyrian variant in a letter from *Alašia* see *ibid*., text 22:5-6, p. 83. For a solemn enlargement in letters from Ugarit addressed to kings (always after a formula of prostration) see letters from

minority of cases Ugaritic *ġ* corresponds to Proto-Semitic *ẓ* and that the well-attested Ugaritic *nġr* 'watchman' could easily be explained in this way. But no forcible conclusion can be drawn from these premisses to the effect that Ugaritic *tġrk* stems from Proto-Semitic *nẓr*, and should be treated as different from Hebrew *yāᶜir*, which certainly cannot be explained as being derived from *nẓr*.[12] The seeming difficulty raised by Ugaritic *nġr* may be solved either by Hartmann's suggestion to differentiate between a Ugaritic root *nġr* > *nẓr* and another root *ġyr* preserving Proto-Semitic *ġ*, or by the alternative explanation of *nġr* as a variant of *ġyr*. Cf. in the Bible *gyḥ* to *ngḥ*, *pwš* to *npš*, *pyḥ* to *npḥ*, *qwr* to *nqr* and Biblical *nsṡ* to Rabbinical *nwṣ*. In any case it should not be denied that the figure of speech in Job 8:6 is rooted in an ancient Canaanite pattern of blessing.

Less convincing appears Ginsberg's and Hartmann's proposal to explain *yāᶜir* in Deut. 32:11 in the same way as in Job 8:6 and not in its normal meaning 'to stir up', although in the Song of Moses *yāᶜir* does not appear as a part of a traditional pair of words. The proposed translation 'as an eagle protects his nest soaring over his youngsters' hardly yields good sense, because it remains obscure who is supposed to assault an eagle's nest. Neither may this explanation account for the following verse telling

---

The King of Ugarit to the Hittite Great King, *PRU* 3, RS 16.112:5-8, p. 4; RS 15.14:4-8, p. 5; *U* 5, text 28:5-8, pp. 97-98, 386; text 29: 3-5, pp. 100, 386; a letter to the king of Alašia, *ibid.*, text 21: 3'-9', pp. 81, 382. Cf. also a letter to Pharaoh, *ibid.*, text 36:5, pp. 111, 389 [and *EA* 49:5-7, which is also a letter from Ugarit, see W.F. Albright, *BASOR* 95 (1944), pp. 30-33. The addition of the formula of greeting to that of prostration calls for comment, since in principle the former belongs to the style of correspondence between equals, whereas the latter indicates the inferiority of the sender. A combination of both formulas points to a rank of the sender which observes the mean between these positions. Even within this range an additional nuance can be discerned. When addressing the Great Kings of the Hittite and Egyptian empires the king of Ugarit designates the receiver of the letter as his lord, himself as his servant, whereas in the letter to the king of Alašia he uses less servile language and turns to the addressee as a son to his father. On all these questions compare S.E. Loewenstamm, *EB* 4, col. 969-970 and in this volume *I am thy servant and thy son*, p. 382-383; *The formula 'I am thy servant and thy son' in a letter from El-Amarna*, p. 445; A. Altman, *ABIU* 13 (1976), pp. 1-15.]

[12] Hebrew ᶜ never derives from Proto-Semitic *ẓ* and Hebrew *n* is never assimilated when preceding a laryngal.

that the eagle takes the youngsters on his wings. Instead we should rather expect him to put up a fight. It appears that the only satisfactory interpretation of these verses has been given by G.R. Driver[13], who interpreted them as a hint to the way in which the mother-eagle teaches her young to fly by throwing them from their nest, swooping down afterwards and letting them alight on her out-spread wings. This procedure may be adequately described as 'stirring up of the nest'.

[13] G.R. Driver, *PEQ* 19 (1958), pp. 56-57.

Remarks upon the Infinitive Absolute in Ugaritic and Phoenician

In his stimulating paper "Studies in Ugaritic Grammar" I (*JANES* 1, No. 2 *[1969]*, pp. 55-61) D. Marcus *inter alia* rejects my view that *ṯʿr* in *tṯʿr ksat lmhr[m] ṯʿr tlḥnt lṣbim* (*CTA* 3:II:20-22) is necessarily an infinitive absolute[1] and parses this form as a perfect. In contrast to U. Cassuto, M. Held and G.R. Driver Marcus interpretes *ṯʿr* as a stative verb, and argues that an agreement between such a verb and its noun subject is not required.

This rule, however, is not borne out by the examples of Marcus' paper. In a sentence like *šmḫ btlt ʿnt* (instead of *šmḫt* etc.) *šmḫ* lends itself to the explanation of a third masculine singular for the sole reason that the predicate precedes the subject, not because *šmḫ* is a stative verb. The same applies to all sentences adduced by Marcus in order to illustrate the alleged special use of the stative verbs *šmḫ, ṣḥq, ark*. None of them verifies the possibility of a lack of congruence between a stative and its *preceding* subject.

The explanation of *ṯʿr* as infinitive absolute admits of some corroboration from Phoenician forms like *yrdm 'nk* 'I brought them down' *[Yiphʿil* of *yrd* or rather 'I dominated them', *Yiphʿil* of *rdh]*, parsed by Marcus as perfects incongruent with their subsequent subjects. But this explanation is highly improbable in view of Hebrew in which the person of the verb invariably does correspond to its subject. *Yoridem 'ānoki [*more aptly in this context: *horidām* or *rādām 'ānoki]* instead of *'oridem 'ānoki [*More aptly *horadtim* or *rᵉditim]* in obviously incompatible with Hebrew usage, as the possible lack of congruence is strictly limited to gender and number. An explanation of these forms as participles encounters no less serious difficulties, correctly pointed out by Marcus himself. Therefore, the most plausible solution is to regard these forms as infinitives. The consequences

[[1] See in this volume, *The Expanded Colon*, note 17, p. 293.*]*

for the parsing of Ugaritic *ngš ank* and Hebrew *šabbe*^{a}*ḥ '*^{a}*ni* are self-evident.

[In his reply, attached to my note, Marcus points out that he "was not positing incongruence as a rule for stative verbs, but only where they precede the subject". My incorrect rendering of Marcus' view in this point was due to his statement that "the lack of agreement between the verb involved and the noun subject ... can be explained simply as being due to the fact that the verb involved is a stative (i.e. *qatila* or *qatula*) *or* because congruence is not necessary when the predicate precedes the subject". The author obviously wanted to say: "when the predicate is a stative verb *and* precedes the noun subject".

Marcus overlooks my central argument that the predicate *ṯ*^{c}*r* is preceded by the subject ^{c}*nt*. To be sure, in the sentence *CTA* 2:II:20-23 the subject is not mentioned at all. Yet the entire column is dealing with Anat's military action and her name, the subject of all sentences, has already been mentioned in ll. 4 and 7. Therefore the rule, stated by Marcus, fails to justify the parsing of *ṯ*^{c}*r* as *qtl* 3rd. m., even if we follow Marcus in the rendering of *ṯ*^{c}*r* as a stative verb meaning 'imagine'. It may, however, be added that this interpretation has little to commend itself. Why should Anat have imagined that the chairs were heroes, the tables warriors and the footstools troops, and how is this alleged imagination supposed to have influenced the way of her action? All other proposals propounded for the rendering of the difficult verb *ṯ*^{c}*r* take the furniture as its direct object. Compare e.g. Aistleitner, *WUS*, *s.v.*; E. Lipiński, *UF* 2, p. 78; de Moor, *Seasonal Pattern*, p. 69f.

Marcus adduces support for his above discussed interpretation from *CTA* 23:33-35 which reads: *tirkm yd il kym / wyd il kmdb. ark yd il kym / wyd il kmdb*. This text is rendered by him: 'The 'hand' of Il is a long as the sea / long as the flowing water. The 'hand' of Il is long as the sea / long as the flowing water'. In his opinion the sequence *tirkm - ark* is congenerous to *tṯ*^{c}*r - ṯ*^{c}*r*. However, even a cursory look reveals the difference that *ark* precedes the subject, *ṯ*^{c}*r* does not. A closer scrutiny revels even more deepgoing differences since the forms *tṯ*^{c}*r - ṯ*^{c}*r* appear in *parallelismus membrorum*, *tirkm - ark* do not. The parallel stichos to *tirkm yd il kym* clearly reads *wyd il kmdb*, not *ark yd il kym*. The relation between the verse *tirkm yd il kym / wyd il kmdb* to the following verse *ark yd il kym / wyd il kmdb* rather resembles the correspondence between Danil's prayer *knp hr[g]b b*^{c}*l yṯb* <r> */ b*^{c}*l y[ṯb]r diy [h]wt* (*CTA* 19:122-123) 'the wings of Hrgb may Baal break / may Baal break the pinions of him' to the subsequent verse: *knp hrgb b*^{c}*l ṯbr / b*^{c}*l ṯbr diy hwt* (*CTA* 19:128-129) reporting that Baal granted Danil's request. In other words. The form *tirkm* should be interpreted as a jussive which expresses the wish of the women, *ark* as a report that their wish was fulfilled. Only this interpretation renders account of the fact that the difference between the two verses is restricted to the form of the verb, whereas in all occurences of a *yqtl / qtl* sentences within the two stichoi of one and the same verse additional differences between the wording of the stichoi exist.

As to the question of Phoenician *yrdm 'nk* (where the verb precedes the subject) Marcus refers to his former paper. In this paper he urged the rule that an inf. abs. can not take a suffix. It certainly can not in Hebrew. Yet a phrase like *horidām* (or *rādām*) *'ānoki* is no less incompatible with Hebrew grammar. Compare also Friedrich-Röllig, *PPG*^{2}, pp. 267f., where Friedrich abandons his former explanation of the verb forms under discussion as 3rd. m. and accepts the view, that they should be parsed as infinitives*]*.

A Didactic Ugaritic Drinkers' Burlesque

Among the Ugaritic texts published in *U* 5 we find in RS. 24.258[1] the burlesque description of a series of banquet scenes, in which Il becomes drunk, falls into excrement and urine and gets altogether into a wretched state. This is followed, separated by a horizontal line, by the characterization, in general terms, of the miserable condition of the drunkard, whereupon medical advice is given how to prevent this evil.

The motif of the banquet of the gods has been known for a long time from the Ugaritic epos[2] and is also to be found in a recently published hymn in honour of Il.[3] However, in the text under consideration, we have a specific kind of didactic literature. Here, practical advice forms the conclusion of a realistic tale presented in the rough tone of a comedy, which clearly differs from the exalted style of epic and hymnal poetry. Accordingly, the epithets of the gods, which in other texts lend the accounts of their feats a dignified solemnity, are here missing. The stylistic principle of *parallelismus membrorum* is recognizable here and there, but is certainly not consistently applied, so that the impression is rather that of prose. This may suggest a relatively late composition. Two peculiarities in spelling, which can most easily be explained as unhistorical phonetic ways of writing, point in the same direction. In recto line 16, we find *sb*^{c} [but contrast now note 4][4] as a variant of the normal *šb*^{c}, found in line 3, which corresponds to the proto-semitic *śb*^{c}, Hebrew *śb*^{c}, 'to be satiated'. The irregular spelling *sb*^{c} is easily understood in view of the

---

[1] Ch. Virolleaud, text 1, pp. 545-551.

[2] *CTA* 3:I; 4:III; VI:39-59; 22 B; Cf. 4:IV:31-38, V:106-109.

[3] *U* 5, text 2, pp. 551-555, 557.

[[4] Contrast, however, Loren R. Fisher, *UF* 3, p. 356 who remarks after studying the cast of the text: "1. 6 has *s* in the autograph but it should be a *š* as Virolleaud's transliteration indicates". Compare also A.F. Rainey, *JAOS* 94 (1974), p. 185, who points to the difference between Ugaritic *š*, representing Proto-Semitic *ś* and Ugaritic *s* in Egyptian transcriptions.]

well-attested change from *ś* to *s* in Hebrew and Aramaic. Furthermore, it may prove that the Ugaritic *š* was a homophon for Hebrew *š* and *ś*, thus supplying a further argument in favour of the opinion that the Masoretic differentiation between the two pronunciations of שׁ goes back to an ancient tradition. A second example of late phonetic spelling is found in recto line 18 in *h̤ṭrh*, which should be taken with Gordon[5] as a variant of *h̤ẓrh* 'his court'. Like *h̤ẓr* in the Ugaritic epos[6] it appears here in the second half of the verse as a parallel to *bt* 'house'.[7] The spelling *h̤ṭrh* thus points to the fact that in spoken late Ugaritic the transition from *ẓ* to *ṭ*, known from Aramaic, was already completed.

The text is damaged in a number of places and the end of the tablet is broken off, thus presenting great difficulties to the interpretor. Not only do certain details remain doubtful, but even the course of action is only partly understandable. Therefore, the present study is intended as an attempt at a critical discussion of Virolleaud's (hereafter V.) interpretations, and it can claim to have reached a clear understanding of the text only in a few passages.[7a] We start with presenting the text in transcription.

Recto

il dbḥ .bbth . mṣd . ṣd . bqrb
hklh ṣḥ . lqṣ . ilm . tlḥmn*
ilm . wtštn . tštn y <n> ^{c}d šb^c
trṯ . ^{c}d . škr . y^{c}db . yrḫ
gbh . km . [klb?] yqṯqṯ . tḥt
ṯlḥnt . il . dyd^{c}nn
y^{c}db . lḥm . lh . wdl yd^{c}nn

---

5 Gordon, *UT*, *Glossary* No. 852a.

6 *CTA* 2:III:19; 4:I:50-51, IV:62, V:63, 90-91; 14:132-133, 203-205, 279-280; 15:II:21-23.

7 V. differs, explaining *h̤ṭr* as a variant of *ḥdr* 'room'. However, a parallel between *bt* and *ḥdr* is nowhere attested. In addition, the change of *d* to *t* is here hardly understandable. With the variants *qdš* > *qṭš*, *ṣdqšlm* > *ṣṭqšlm* there is a partial assimilation of the *d* with emphatic *q̣*.

[7a Compare the recent treatment by M. Dietrich - O. Loretz - J. Sanmartîn, *UF* 7, pp. 109-114 with bibliography.]

bmṣd
ylmn . ḥṭm . tḥt . ṯlḥnt
bqr^{c}*
^{c}ṯtrt . w^{c}nt . ymġy
^{c}ṯtrt . t^{c}db . nšb lh
w^{c}nt . ktp [?] bhm . yg^{c}r ṯġr
bt . il . pn . lmgr lb . t^{c}bdn
nšb . linr . t^{c}dbn . ktp
bil a*b*h. g^{c}r . yṯ*b . il . kb
a - - - il yṯb bmrzḥh
yšt[n . y]n . ^{c}d sb^{c} . trṯ . ^{c}d škr
il . hlk . lbth . yštql
lh̤trh . y^{c}msn . nn . ṯkmn
wšnm . w <y> ngšnn . ḫby .
b^{c}l . qrnm . wḏnb . ylšn
bḫrih . wṯnth . ql . il
il . kyrdm . arṣ . ^{c}nt
w^{c}ṯtrt . tṣdn
- - - - - ḅ - - - - -

Verso

[^{c}ṯ]trt . w^{c}nt -----
r*bhm . tṯṯb -- dh
km trpa . hr*n* ^{c}*r
----
dyšt . llṣbh ḫš ^{c}r klb
[b?]h* riš . pqq . wšrh
yšt . aḥdh . dm zt . ḫrpnt

Commentary

Recto 1-2a

Here the "ballast variant" (so called by Gordon) *b//bqrb*[8] reminds us of the style of the epic as does the standard parallel *bt//hkl*. There may be differences of opinion about the division of the verses in halves. V. ta-

[8] Gordon, *UT, Grammar* 13. 116.

kes *dbḥ* to be a verbal predicate and assigns to it two synonymous substantival objects, *mṣd* and *ṣd*. If so, the first verse would conclude with *mṣd*. It seems more acceptable to regard *ṣd* as the verb, to which *mṣd* forms an inner object. In this case, the first verse would consist only of the words *il dbḥ bbth*, where *dbḥ* might possibly be understood as a verb. However, it may be more plausible to accept here too the parallel between the nouns *dbḥ* and *mṣd*[9], which exists in *CTA* 14:78-79, 169-170, thus reading 'Il, a banquet is in his house'. Thus Il is understood as the logical subject placed at the head of the sentence and referred to again in the suffix of the adverbial local determination *bbth*. There is no clear Semitic parallel for *ṣd*. V. places *ṣd* with Hebrew *ṣwd* 'to hunt' and deduces that the gods ate venison. Although the sacrifices consisted of domestic animals, in his opinion the gods served venison at those meals which they prepared themselves. Against this speaks the fact that in the above mentioned passages of the Krt epos *mṣd*, in parallel to *dbḥ*, designates the oblation, which the king sacrifices to Baal. Furthermore, the epic descriptions of the gods' meals mention only meat of domestic animals.[10] Gordon's[11] comparison with Hebrew *ṣedā* too does not lead any further, as *ṣedā* designates provisions for a journey, similar to Accadian *ṣidītu*. However, these difficulties of derivation do not influence the explanation of the word, as it follows from the Ugaritic texts themselves that *mṣd* is a synonym to the well-known *dbḥ*. Thus perhaps: 'A banquet he made in his palace.'

2b

V.: '*Il crie pour rêveiller les dieux.*' This interpretation assumes that

---

[9] This suggestion is supported by the fact that *dbḥ* appears in the epic only as a noun. *[*We suppose that a simple sentence *dbḥ bbt il* 'a feast of slaughtering is in *Il's* house' has been transformed into the phrase *il dbḥ bbth* '(As to) Il a feast of slaughtering is in his house.' Such a construction, though common in Hebrew, is admittedly unusual in Ugaritic. It fits, however, with the noticeable wordorder *mṣd ṣd* 'a banquet he arranged' instead of regular *ṣd mṣd* 'he arranged a banquet'. The formulation of the second colon throws the noun *mṣd* into relief and requires as parallel a stressed noun in the first colon. On the supposition that *dbḥ* be a verb, *mṣd* would be redundant. Compare Dietrich-Loretz-Sanmartîn, *loc. cit.* (note 7a), who adhere to the commonly accepted parsing of *dbḥ* as a verb and consequently delete *mṣd als überzählig und überflüssig*. Compare also in this volume, *mṣd*, note 10, pp. 421-422.*]*

[10] *CTA* 1:IV:30-32; 3:I:6-8; IV:85-86; 4:V:107-108; VI:40-43, 56-58.

[11] Gordon, *UT, Glossary* No. 2152. Compare in this volume, *mṣd*, pp. 419-422.

the banquet took place at such an early hour that the participants had to be aroused from sleep. The basis for this rather improbable explanation is the Hebrew *Hiph^{c}il hqṣ* 'to rouse, to awake', which, however, has its root in Proto-Semitic *qyẓ*. Therefore we should expect an Ugaritic *Š*-form of *qyẓ*, i.e. *šqẓ* instead of *qṣ*. But *qṣ* is already known as a synonymous parallel to *ṯd* 'breast'[12] from epic descriptions of banquets and there it describes the food of the gods. Therefore, it may be assumed that here *qṣ* as *pars pro toto* designates the meal and the line should perhaps be translated: 'He called the gods to the meal'.

2c-4a

The following words are according to V. supposed to be the invitation to the meal: 'Eat and drink!' But then the description of the meal itself would be missing. As we have found the invitation to the meal already in 2b, we prefer to understand 2c-4a as a description of the banquet: 'The gods ate and drank.'[12a] The unexplicable form *tštny* has been read correctly by V. as *tštn y<n>*, whereby the parallelism *yn/trṯ* attested in l. 16 is here restored. The repetition of the verb *tštn*, closing one verse and opening the next, can be compared with *tbrk ilm tity tity ilm lahlhm dr il lmšknthm* (*CTA* 5:III:17-19). This then results in: 'The gods ate and drank, drank wine until they were satiated, young wine until they were drunk'. Here appears for the first time the central theme of the text, the drunkeness.

4b-5a

According to V., the subject of the sentence is *Il*, who organized his feast called *yrḫ gb*, where *gb* is supposed to be related to Accadian *gabbu* 'all'. This explanation which takes *Il* as subject, presupposes, of course the interpretation of the preceding words as his speech and is impossible, if we see in them a report on the banquet of the gods. The subject of the sentence might be the moongod *yrḫ* of whom it is said that he made his back

[[12] *CTA* 3:I:6-8; 4:VI:56-58. Cf. J. Blau - S.E. Loewenstamm, *UF* 3, p. 20, note 8, who point to Arabic *qaṣṣ* 'breast'.]

[[12a] Rainey, *loc. cit.* (note 4) adds the morphological argument that the verbal forms under discussion are "*yaqtulu* - indicative 3rd c. pl. as demonstrated by the *n*-sufformative". However, from a purely morphological point of view, the forms could be parsed as energic as well.]

(cf. Hebrew *gb*) like a ... The following gap takes up the space of three letters. We suggest tentatively the completion *klb*, which will be explained below.

5b-6a

The verb *yqṯqṯ* describes an action of *yrḫ* under the tables. In Middle-Hebrew *qšqš* occurs frequently meaning 'to move (something) to and fro'. From here it is not far to the meaning 'to move to and fro'. We assume that the drunken moongod bends his back like a dog and crawls on all fours under the tables.

6b-8

V. explains: "*Le dieu qui sait prêpare un mets de gibier pour lui, et celui qui ne sait pas [glisse?] les bâtons sous la table*." However, this translation does not take into consideration the suffix in *ydᶜnn* and overlooks the fact that *ylmn ḫṭm* obviously means 'hits him with the stick'.[13] The person in question is thus someone who receives, according to the circumstances, either food or a thrashing. The person in question can obviously only be *yrḫ*, who busies himself under the tables (we suggest - like a dog). What happens to him in each instance, depends apparently on the changing moods of *Il*, who sometimes smiles on him and at other times frowns on him. This meaning of *ydᶜ*, which is suggested by the context, is easily derived. As early as in 1908, Baumann[14] pointed out that the Hebrew *ydᶜ* often expresses *eine persönliche Verbindung, auf Grund deren ein persönlicher Verkehr stattfindet, ein Austausch nicht nur von Wissen, sondern von Achtung, Liebe, Fürsorge, Wohltaten, Diensten u.s.f.* We mention here only one of the examples given by him, i.e. Ho. 13:5, where the God of Israel *betont, dass er es gewesen sei, der sich des Volkes in der Wüste, im dürren Lande angenommen, ihm Speise, Trank und anderes mehr gegeben habe*. The question has been taken up again most recently by Huffmon[15], who, however, limits the

[13] With reference to *ylm* (from *hlm*), cf. Gordon, *UT*, *Grammar* 9.49. With the adverbial use of *m* in *ḫṭm*, cf. *mtm tgrš* (*CTA* 3:III:15) 'with the staff she drives away' and in particulȧr: *ylm b[n. ᶜ]nk ṣmdm* (*UT* 1001:16) 'with the mace he hits your forehead'.

[14] E. Baumann, *ZAW* 28 (1908), pp. 30-41, 110-143.

[15] H.B. Huffmon, *BASOR* 181 (1966), pp. 31-37. Cf. also H.B. Huffmon - S.B. Parker, *BASOR* 184 (1966), pp. 36-38.

importance of the positive relationship in a much too one-sided manner to the mutual recognition of the partners to a treaty. He even argues in a very forced manner that the divine care for the people in the wilderness (as hinted at in Ho. 13:5) is an allusion to the covenant of Sinai. But *yd*^{c} really means, in its emotional sense, quite generally: 'To feel and act towards somebody else in a positive way.' Thus we arrive at the interpretation: 'Il[15a], who means him well (i.e.: if he etc.), prepares food for him, and who means him ill, hits him with the stick under the tables.' Beneath the words *lḥm* and *ylmn* there are interlinear glosses in small script, *lḥm* is explained by *bmṣd* 'of the meal', *ylmn* by *bqr*^{c}[15b], which may be translated as 'at the scolding', following Arabic *qr*^{c} II. Scolding and hitting go together.

9

Here a new scene begins, of which only the first line is understandable. Ashtoret and Anat arrive.[15c] The verb *mġy* is known from the epos as a stereotype formula for the introduction of a new person into the action and corresponds in this function to Accadian *kašādu*. Cf. e.g. *CTA* 17:V:25. However, in this epos the description is much more eleborate and artistic. There we are told first of all how the host sees the arriving guest while he is still far away and makes arrangements for his reception. Next we are told that - after the guest arrived - the host did this, that, and the other. Here, however, the text contents itself with the simple statement that the two goddesses have arrived. In connection with this, the form *ymġy* is interesting, as it is the first instance of the use of *yqtl* (*yaqtula*?) as 3rd pers. fem. dualis.[15c]

10

'Ashtoret prepares for him a *nšb*.' *nšb* is already known[16] from other

[[15a] Contrast Rainey, *loc. cit.* (note 4), p. 186, who renders *il* 'the deity' and translates in 6-8: 'The god who knows him ... but the one who does not know him ...'.]

[[15b] Contrast Dietrich-Loretz-Sanmartín, *loc. cit.* (note 7a), who read *bqr* and translate '*kontrolliere*!', an order to the scribe to verify the correctness of the text.]

[[15c] Contrast Rainey, *ibid.*, who interprets that *Yrḫ* comes to Ashtoret and Anat.]

[16] Gordon, *UT*, *Glossary* No. 1710.

texts as designation of an edible part of an animal, but is not defined more precisely. More disturbing is the uncertainty, for whom Ashtoret prepared the *nšb*, for Il or for *Yrḫ*.

11a

'and Anat a shoulder'. The certainty of the textinterpretation is impaired by a possible lacuna of one letter between *ktp* and the following *bhm*, a letter which may have belonged to the preceding (e.g. *ktp[h]*) or the following (e.g. *[a]bhm*).

11b-12a

On the basis of reading *bhm* we may translate with V.: *Le portier de la maison de Dieu les gourmande (en ces termes)* (cf. *CTA* 2:I:14), where *bhm* (instead of *bhn*) may be explained as a form of the feminine dual.[17]

12b

V. derives *pn* from a verb *pny* = Hebrew *pnh* and compares *mgr lb* with Accadian *migir libbi* 'obedience, devotion'. This interpretation results in the translation: *'Prenez garde à la règle'*. Alternatively, we might think of Hebrew *māgor* 'terror'. This would result in: 'Turn to terror, i.e. look what terrible things have happened.' Both interpretations seem quite uncertain.[17a]

12c-13

inr is known from *CTA* 16:I:2-3, 15-17; II:100-101 as parallel to *klb* 'dog'.[18] V. understands *t*ᶜ*bdn* as an order, i.e. prepare (for *Il*) *nšb* (as did Ashtoret), for the dog the shoulder (and not for Il, as Anat did).

Following this interpretation, however, the doorkeeper should have scolded only Anat. The completion "for *Il*" too is without foundation. The interpretation depends on the alternative whether *lh* in line 13 refers to *Il* or to *Yrḫ*. According to the first interpretation, the doorkeeper was

---

[17] Gordon, *UT*, *Grammar* 6.10.

[[17a] D.R. Hillers, *BASOR* 198 (1970), p. 46, suggests the reading: *h*(!)*n*. *lm*.(!) *k*(!)*lb* instead of *pn. l mgr lb*. Cf. also Rainey, *loc. cit.* (note 4), p. 186.]

[18] Different, but not convincing. Gray, *Krt*², p. 64.

shocked by the goddesses, because they prepared the meat not for *Il*, but for *Yrḫ*, according to the second he said that one should prepare *nšb* and *ktp* for the dog (and not for *Il*, to whom the breast is due).

14a

V.: *Il (le portier) gourmande le Dieu, son père. ab* is rather uncertain and the scolding of the doorkeeper remains without motivation.

14b-15a

V. reads: *yṯb il b* [15]*aṯ[rt]* and explains *(Alors) le Dieu s'assied à côté*(?) *de Ašerat*. However, at the end of line 14, a well recognizable *k* precedes the *b*. At the beginning of line 15, only *a* is legible, followed by a lacuna of four (not three!) letters. Furthermore, Ashera is not mentioned anywhere in the text. Therefore the question whether *yṯb b* ... means 'to sit on the side of ...' is irrelevant. The text cannot be restored.

15b

Il sits in his thiasus. The word *mrzḥ* is known from texts found at Ugarit[19] as well as from the Hebrew, Phoenician, Punic, Nabatean and Palmyrene.[20] Here it is found for the first time as a designation of a thiasus in which a god in person takes part, but it remains doubtful what is meant by the sitting of Il in his thiasus. In the following we are told that Il went from there to his house. Therefore it is obvious that previously he should have left his house in which the banquet of the gods took place, but there is no mention of this in the extant text.

16

V. completes *yšt [.il. y]n*. But the space in the lacuna is insufficient for this. Read: *yšt[n.y]n*.[20a] 'He drinks wine until he is satiated, new wine until he is drunk'.

---

19 J. Nougayrol, *PRU* 3, pp. 234-235, *PRU* 4, p. 261.

20 Jean-Hoftijzer, *DISO*, *s.v.*

[20a Dietrich-Loretz-Sanmartín, *loc. cit.* (note 7a), note a word-divider after *yšt* and read: *yš*t*.[y]n*.]*

17-18a

'Il went to his house, reached[21] his courtyard.' Here we have a slight variant of the standard formula of the going home, which precedes the description of the special circumstances of the way home.

18b-19a

The verb *^{c}ms*, which V. declares as incomprehensible within the context, is to be understood in its common meaning 'to carry, to load'. The God *ṯkmn* and *šnm* loads him[22], i.e. he takes the drunken *Il* on his shoulder, in order to carry him home. In the Aqht-epos it is said of the son, who fulfils his duties towards his father: *aḫd ydh bškrn m^{c}msh kšb^c yn* (*CTA* 17:I:31-32, cf. ibid. 20:II:5-6) 'who takes his hand in his drunkeness, carries him, when he is satiated with wine'. It may not be by chance that it is the god *ṯkmn* and *šnm* who fulfils here this task, as *ṯkm* means 'to carry on the shoulder'.[23]

19b-20a

V.: "*et il rencontre le ḥby du Ba^{c}al à deux cornes et à queue.*" But there is no mention here of any Baal. *b^{c}l qrnm wḏnb* simply means 'the horned and tailed'. Cf. *hā'ayil ba^{c}al haqq^{e}rānayim* (Dan. 8:6) 'the horned ram'. *ḥby* is probably the proper name of the demon who is documented here for the first time. The suffix *<y>ngšnn* probably refers to *Il* as does the preceding pronoun *nn*. The subject of the verb is thus *ḥby*. *Ngš* is mostly placed with Hebrew *ngš* 'to approach'. This would result in '*ḥby* approached him'.

---

21 *hlk // yštql* is a variant of the common parallel *mġy // yštql*. See Gordon, *UT, Glossary* No. 2472. Gordon correctly drew from this the conclusion that *yštql* cannot mean 'to go/proceed to', as otherwise the parallelism would be an anticlimax. Therefore in our text the following scene must take place directly in front of Il's house.

22 The combination *y^{c}msn. nn* needs a special explanation. J. Aistleitner, *AOH* 7 (1957), pp. 283-286, explains the *nn* in forms like *tštnn* as a combination of the verbaffix-*una*, found in the Amarna Letters from Byblos, with the energetic form of the accusative suffix *-nhu*: *-una* + *-nhu* > *-unannu*. The frequent separation of *nn* from the preceding verb, which changes the first *n* into part of a pronoun, is therefore the result of a metanalytical process. Because of this process, an afformative *-n* = *una* could again be added to the preformed verbal form.

23 Gordon, *UT, Glossary* No. 2675.

However, it might be preferable to accept the view of Ullendorff[24], who compares the Ugaritic *ngš* with Hebrew *ngś* 'to oppress', with Arabic *ngš* 'to press, to beat', and with Ethiopian *ngš* 'to rule'. He retains the meaning 'to approach' for Ugaritic *ngṯ*, on the basis of Ugaritic *mgṯ* (*CTA* 16: VI:18,21) 'victim', which would correspond to Hebrew *mgš* (Mal. 1:11). *[*But contrast in this volume, *The Sending of Messengers to the Land of no Return*, p. 535, note 39.*]* Thus translate perhaps: 'He used him ill, *ḥby*, the horned and tailed'.

20b-22a

V. completes *ql il* <*ql*> *il* and explains: '*il patauge dans sa fiente et son urine. (Alors) la voix de Dieu [la voix] de Dieu (est faible comme) la voix de ceux qui descendent dans la terre*.' The repetition of the words *ql il*, obtained by means of textual conjecture is, however, without any function. *ql* should not be understood as the noun the voice, but as the verb he fell.[25] Thus translate: '*Il* fell into the excrement and urine. *Il* resembles those who descend to the Netherworld'[26], i.e. he is in a most

---

[24] E. Ullendorff, *JSS* 7 (1962), p. 340. *[*Ullendorff's proposal to explain Ugaritic *ngš* everywhere as Proto-Semitic *ngś* 'to oppress' is disproved by *CTA* 23:68, where this verb clearly means 'to approach'. For the same reason Ugaritic *ngṯ* cognate of Arabic *ngṯ* 'to search' should be disconnected from Hebrew *ngš* 'to approach'*]*.

[25] Gordon, *UT, Glossary* No. 2231. Cf. W. von Soden, *VTS* 16 (1967), p. 295, who places the Ugaritic verb with Accadian *qiālu* 'to fall'.

[26] For parallels to this phrase, cf. following V. *CTA* 4:VIII:7-9; 5:V:14-16; 6:I:7-8. *[*Cf. *wrd bt ḫpṯt ars tspr byrdm ars* (*CTA* 4:VIII:7-9; 5:V:14-16) and also: *aṯr b^{c}l ard barṣ* (*CTA* 5:VI:24-25); *aṯr b^{c}l nrd barṣ ^{c}mh trd nrt ilm špš* (*CTA* 6:I:7-9). The descent of the dead to the depth of the earth is frequently mentioned in the Bible as well (see below) and even the wretched condition of a living man may be highlighted in the Bible by comparing him with those who went down to the Netherworld (Ps. 28:1 = Ps. 143:7. Cf. also Jon. 2:7). In the Bible, however, the indirect object of *yrd* is never designated by the unqualified term *'äräs*. The term nearest to Ugaritic literature is *'äräs taḥtit* (Ez. 31:18. Cf. Ez. 31: 14, 16) or *'äräs taḥtiyot* (Ez. 32:24. Cf. Ez. 26:20; 32:18). The other terms used in this connection are: 1) *š^{e}'ol* (Gen. 37:35; 42:38; 44:29; Nu. 16:30, 33; 1 Sam. 2:6; 1 Reg. 2:6, 9; Is. 14:11, 15; Ez. 31:15, 17; 32:27; Ps. 55:16; Job 7:9. 2) *bor* (Is. 14:15; 38:18; Ez. 26:20; 31:14, 16; 32:24-25, 29-30; Ps. 28:1; 30:4; 88:5; 143:7; Pr. 1:12. Cf. Is. 14: 19. 3) *šaḥat* (Ez. 28:8; Ps. 30:10; Job 33:24. Cf. Ps. 55:24. 4) *dumā* (Ps. 115:17). 5) *qiṣbe hārim* (Jon. 2:7). 6) *^{c}āpār* (Ps. 22:30). 7) *māwät* (Pr. 5:5).
The first five of these nouns (including *š^{e}'ol*!) are not attested in Ugaritic at all, *^{c}pr* not in this context. Only to the use of *māwät* a far

wretched state. Cf. Ps. 28:1; 143:7. The difficult verb *ylšn* prepares, no doubt, the scene of *Il's* fall. Thus we may suggest: 'He (*ḥby*) dropped excrement and urine.' Cf. Middle-Hebrew *lšlšt* which is documented in the context meaning 'chicken excrement', but which may go back to a more general basic meaning.

22b-23a

Here begins a new scene, with Anat and Ashtoret again as the central figures, of which only single words remain. Therefore it cannot be decided, whether *tṣdn* means 'they ramble about' or 'they hold a banquet'.

Verso 1-3

Here too the text deals with these two goddesses. Perhaps the verb *trpa* suggests that they have cured Il.

4a

Here begins, under the dividing line, 'the moral of the story'. *lṣb* has until now been documented only in the phrase *yprq lṣb wyṣḥq* (*CTA* 6:III: 16), where Ullendorff[27] places it with Arabic *lṣb* VIII 'to be narrow' and explains: "He divides 'the narrow straits between two ridges of the teeth' and laughs." One may also think of the opening between the lips instead of that between the rows of teeth. In any case it is evident that the phrase points to the opening of the mouth. Therefore, we may presume here: 'He who drinks into his mouth', which may indicate - as an idiomatic phrase - rather strong drinking.

---

analogy might be detected in the expression *lrt bnpš bn ilm mt* (*CTA* 5:I: 6-7).
These farreaching differences corroborate the contention, that Biblical literature should not be regarded as a later stage of Ugaritic literature, but rather a later form of a South-Canaanite brand of tradition, which was akin, but different from the tradition preserved in the Ugaritic texts.*]*

[27] E. Ullendorff, *Orientalia* 20 (1951), pp. 271-272. Ullendorff furthermore compares ἕρκος ὀδόντων in the Homeric standard phrase: ποιόν σε ἔπος φύγεν ἕρκος ὀδόντων in which he takes ἕρκος ὀδόντων as the gap formed by the two rows of teeth. But ἕρκος does not mean 'slit, narrowness'. Generally it is understood as the fence of the teeth, which should have prevented the escape of the words, while Hesychius explains ἕρκος ὀδόντων as a paraphrase of the lips. *[*Compare now also Caquot-Sznycer, *Textes* 1, p. 204, note f for the view that in the light of the unedited text 24.247 *lṣb* should be rendered 'forehead'.*]*

4b

The following words seem to describe the state of the drunkard who feels 'miserable like a dog'. In the above mentioned passages of the Krt-epos, the dangerously ill king is also compared with a dog. Cf. also the Hebrew phrase *käläb met* (1 Sam. 24:15 a.o.).[28] Therefore in the words *ḫš* *^{c}r* we should look for a description of the pitiable state of the dog. Cf. following J.C. de Moor, *UF* 1, p. 174 Arabic *ḫassa*, to be contemptible, weak. The description of the miserable state of the drunkard reminds us of the lament about the dangerously ill king Keret (*CTA* 16:I:2-5, 15-19; II:100-104). In both texts we find the letter groups *klb* and *ḫš*. Perhaps one should translate there: 'Like a dog, who was driven out of your house, even like a cur is your pitiable state. And your pitiable state became the lamentation of a woman.'

5

It seems that at the beginning of the line a narrow letter is missing. Of the following letters, only a horizontal wedge at the top remains, which may be interpreted most likely as the remainder of an *h*. The words *riš pqq* are pretty clear. *pqq* means in Middle-Hebrew 'to stagger, to totter', and is related to Biblical *pyq* which has the same meaning. At the beginning of the line one may complete *[b]h*. Cf. *bh p^{c}nm tṭṭ* (*CTA* 3:III:29-30), literally: 'In her the legs totter'. Thus one should translate freely: 'His head turns.' *šrh* has been found up to now only in the difficult verse *šrh larṣ brqm* (*CTA* 4:V:17), where we might render *šrh*, according to the context, perhaps as 'to hurl'. Here the verb could be understood as an intransitive or passive form. The drunkard falls down violently.

6

The last line has been explained correctly by V. as an advice given to the drinker. *'il boit, à la fois, le sang de l'oliver.'* *ḫrpnt* is possibly an adverbial construction, comparable to Hebrew *'^{a}ḥorannit, q^{e}dorannit*, which may be compared with Accadian *ḫarpiš* 'early, quickly'. The drinker should not hesitate to take quickly the necessary steps against drunkenness.

---

[28] For analogous phrases in Akkadian cf. R.H. Pfeiffer, *State Letters of Assyria, American Oriental Series* 1935, p. 35, No. 39:6-7; p. 178, No. 255:5-7.

I am Thy Servant and Thy Son*

In his article *The King's Son at Ugarit and among the Hittites*[1], A.P. Rainey dealt, *inter alia*, with *EA* 44:1-4, where it reads "To the Lord, King of Egypt, my father, say: 'So says Zida the king's son, thy son'." Rainey notes "In addressing Pharaoh as 'my father' and in calling himself 'thy son', he is merely following international protocol for salutations of letters sent from one of lower rank to his superior."

I have not come to dispute Rainey's contention but to add to it the qualification that "my father" was customary only in addressing the greater of two equals (*primus inter pares*). Otherwise, the inferior uses "my Lord" and entitles himself "thy servant". I have dealt with this distinction and its implications in letter formulation in the entry *Miktab* in *EB*.[1a] To the list of examples which I brought there, it is possible to add Rainey's letter. As he indicated, the letter was sent to Pharaoh by the appointee over Hittite - Egyptian international relations who was, very significantly, the brother of the Hittite king. It is known that the king of the Hittites and the king of Egypt were of equal rank and that both bore the title *šarru rabû* - 'great king', implying that they would address each other as "my brother". The brother of the Hittite monarch was, therefore, on one hand from the same social stratum as Pharaoh, but, on the other, Pharaoh was superior to him by his royal title. Consequently, his relationship to Pharaoh is equal to that of a son to the father in that the son is obligated to honour his father and at the same time he is his relative.

On this opportunity I should like to point out that salutation formulae became so devoid of their original meaning to the extent where it became possible to combine two of them for the sake of exact clarification of the relationship with regard to rank between the two sides. We have found

---

* Compare in this volume, *The Formula 'I am Thy Servant and Thy Son' in a Letter from El-Amarna*, p. 445.

[1] *Lěšonênu* 33 (1969), pp. 306-307.

[[1a] *EB* 4, col. 969f.*]*

in a Ugaritic letter that the sender calls himself "thy brother, thy father" and the receiver "my son, my brother".[2] Another composite and well-balanced formula is found in the Bible. Here we read "So Ahaz sent messengers to Tiglath-pileser king of Assyria saying 'I am thy servant and thy son, come up and save me etc. ...'" (2 Reg. 16:7). In the formula "thy servant" the king of Judah announces that he will receive upon himself the yoke of the king of Assyria. But, even while doing so, he softens his submission and calls himself "thy son" - the lesser among equals.

---

[2] The formulas are *aḫy bny* (*UT* 138:3, 10-11, 15-16), *laḫk ladnk* (ibid.:18-20). *adn*, here means 'father' as in *CTA* 24:33-34 in which *adn* parallels *um* 'mother'. In the dictionary: Ugaritic *a-da-nu*, Akkadian *a-bu* (*U* 5, text 130:9, pp. 232f.).
*[*Compare now also R. Gordis, *'immi wa'^{a}ḥoti w^{e} 'aḥāb, Lěšonénu* 36 (1972), pp. 71-72.*]*

Review of R. Yaron, *The Laws of Eshnunna*. Jerusalem 1969.

The *Laws of Eshnunna* (= *LE*) antedate the *Code of Hammurabi* (= *CH*) and constitute the oldest law code which has come down to us in Akkadian. The *editio princeps* of this important source for the study of Babylonian law was published in 1948 by A. Goetze along with a transliteration, an English translation and a commentary. In 1956 a revised edition was published. Since then studies on this text have appeared. On the philological side many new suggestions have been offerred for the transliteration of the text, restoration of lacunae, and lexicographical interpretation. On the legal side the clarification of the content of the laws and their place in legal history has advanced. The literature on the subject is scattered over a large number of publications in various languages, and the time has come for a comprehensive summary of these discussions. Now, Reuven Yaron, who has been one of the foremost researchers in this field, has undertaken this task.

Following an introduction the book begins with a transliteration of the Akkadian text and a synoptic English translation. The purpose of this translation is to serve the reader as much as possible in lieu of the Akkadian text. As a result the author is careful to translate in every instance each Akkadian word by the same English equivalent, and when the Akkadian text is ambiguous, he gives two alternative translations. In addition he quotes in the notes all the suggested readings, restorations, and lexicographical interpretations with full bibliographical references. The main part of the book is the commentary on the text itself. Unlike Goetze's commentary Yaron's commentary does not follow the order of the laws, but is divided into chapters which are of the author's own making. This method enables him to survey in one place general problems such as the structure of the code, modes of expression, legal procedure, and social classes. This applies also to the chapters which analyze the single legal statutes. They too are not arranged according to the order of the laws, rather each deals with one complete subject, such as property and contract, delicts, etc. This method of strict consolidation of the difficult material adds much to its clarification. The book closes with indices of sources, Akkadian words and phrases, and a glossary.

In his commentary Yaron deals with all suggestions which have been put forth, and his treatment is occasionally a sort of a historiography of research. Outstanding among these discussions are lucid monographs, such as his analysis of the formulation of the laws[1], his incisive discussion of the ambiguity of the class term *muškēnum*[2], his survey of the history of the principle of *lex talionis*, and his convincing claim that the term *ṣimdat šarrim* should be taken at its face value to mean a royal ordinance which is in the nature of a *novella*.[3] We see the fine attention to details also in his commentary on minor points. His explanation of the expression *ana bīt emim šasû* (*LE* 25) 'to claim the consummation of the marriage', which is based on a comparison with Babylonian legal documents, is a classical example of the use of such documents to elucidate law.[4] His commentary on the formula "he shall die, he shall not live" (*LE* 12, 13, 28) is also enlightening. He notes that in every instance this formula refers to a criminal who is caught in the act and concludes from this that the formula has the exclusive meaning that the criminal may be killed on the spot without a trial.[5]

In his introduction Yaron mentions the many difficulties encountered in writing a commentary on an ancient legal code and apologizes for the fact that some chapters are inconclusive.[6] The reviewer agrees with this cautious approach and employs it to an even greater extent than the author. As an example let us consider the problem of the law of the man who rapes a betrothed woman. *LE* 26 imposes the death penalty on such a man. *CH* 130 adds that the woman goes free. Yaron concludes from this addition that the woman is subject to the death penalty if there was no rape. This implies that she is considered in *CH* like an adulteress, and he like an adulterer. In the light of this basic concept, Yaron argues, we should interprete *LE*,

---

[1] pp. 59-71.

[2] pp. 83-95.

[3] pp. 71-79.

[4] pp. 123-129.

[5] p. 173.

[6] p. VIII.

too.[7] It appears, therefore, that the Mesopotamian law coincides with the law of the betrothed woman in Deut. 22:23-27, which imposes the death penalty on both parties in the case of consent. This, however, seems rather daring. *LE* imposes the death penalty on a man who rapes a betrothed woman. Yaron adds that the same applies in the case where the woman gives her consent. Both are subject to the death penalty. As said before Yaron's starting point is *CH*, which states that in the case of rape the woman goes free. Yaron explains that it is in this case *only* that the woman goes free, but not if she consented. The legitimacy of such an inference is doubtful as may be seen from a study of the law of the goring ox. Both *LE* 54 and *CH* 251 impose punishment on the forewarned owner of an ox who had killed a man. *CH* 252 explicitely adds that the owner of a first gorer goes free, whereas *LE* does not. The absence of the liability of the owner of the first gorer in *LE* derives from the fact that the law makes the punishment of the ox's owner dependant on forewarning. In such cases we should not speak of the incompleteness of the law.[8] The most complete lawcode does not enumerate all the legally irrelevant cases just to emphasize their irrelevancy as *CH* did in this instance. We may imagine that a similar difference in formulation should be recognized in the case of a man who rapes a betrothed woman. *LE* did not see the need to emphasize that the woman goes free, whereas *CH* explicitely prescribes her acquittal in spite of the fact that this prescription was dispensable. From the expanded formulation we cannot learn with certainty anything of the law of a woman who was not raped. Moreover, we should note that according to our assumption the law of marriage may be more easily explained. *LE* 27 and *CH* 128 state that without a marriage contract a woman is not considered to be married. These sections are an introduction to the law of adultery. But we may ask: What is the meaning of the marriage contract from the point of view of criminal law if the laws of adultery apply to a woman before marriage? Yaron, who felt this difficulty, limits the validity of the sections concerning marriage to the case where marriage was not preceded by betrothal.[9] This limitation is, however, not alluded to in the formulation of the law and is therefore doubtful. I should point out here a perplexing point in the formulation of the laws dealing

---

[7] pp. 186, 187, 189.

[8] p. 198.

[9] p. 189.

with betrothed and married women. It is a matter of common sense that the problem of rape is the same with regard to both the betrothed and married woman, and that the latter too should go free in the case of rape (cf. *MAL* A 12). Nevertheless, *LE, CH* and the Pentateuch all mention just the case of the rape of a betrothed woman. This phenomenon may be easily understood if we assume that the Mesopotamian law of the betrothed woman imposed the death penalty only on the rapist whereas it acquitted the man in the case where the woman gave her consent, and that a law like this antedated even the Pentateuch which is more stringent in this case but is nevertheless influenced in its formulation by the earlier law. Still we should not ignore the incompleteness of the ancient laws a fact which leaves room for the possibility that the Mesopotamian law in spite of all argument adduced coincided with the Pentateuchal law. The final result in this matter is inconclusive.

We have previously referred to the laws of marriage. *CH* 128 formulates this subject in a concise and exact manner: "If a man has taken a (woman to) wife and has not drawn up a (marriage) contract for her, that woman is not a wife." On the other hand *LE* 27 formulates the law more expansively: "If a man took a man's daughter without asking her father and?/or? her mother, and also did not fix marriage feast and?/or? contract for her father and?/or? her mother - should she (even) dwell in his house the days of one year (she is) not a wife." We may pose here the following question: Are all the parts of the protasis relevant or does the law perhaps reflect a precedent and relates at length the details of an actual case? The woman dwelt in the house of a man for a long period of time perhaps even for exactly one year - but the man did not act properly before marrying her: He did not ask her parents, nor did he make the marriage feast, nor the contract. Now, his wife has had sexual relations with another man and the question arises whether this is adultery or not. The text gives the impression that we should not look for legal niceties in it, otherwise we would have to conclude that if the woman dwelt in a man's house for more than one year she would automatically become his wife. Therefore, we may imagine another explanation which radically disregards the special circumstances indicated in this text and defines the legal kernel of *LE* 27 in accordance with *CH* 128.

Yaron looks for the golden mean between these two interpretations of *LE* 27 mentioned above. He thinks that the woman becomes a wife after a year when the man marries her with the consent of her parents, but without a contract or feast.[10] This compromise however has no basis either in the formulation of *LE* or *CH*. Yaron refers to section A 24 of the Assyrian Laws which states that the widow who dwells in the house of a man without a marriage contract becomes his wife automatically after two years.[11] But this law makes the impression of an amendment to *CH* whose purpose is to lessen the need for a marriage contract in the case of the marriage of a widow. We can not be sure that *LE* applies the same rule to the marriage of a widow and there is no reason whatsoever to suppose the applicability of such a principle to the marriage of a virgin in Old Babylonian law. With regard to the period of one year which is mentioned we may imagine that this is either just a precedent or a formulation indicating a long period of time. In short, we do not have sufficient data to permit an authoritative explanation of *LE* 27 and our results again are inconclusive.

The few examples brought above show clearly the importance of the comparative study of *LE* and *CH*. It goes without saying that Yaron is constantly aware of this. But in one instance it seems to me that he went too far in his comparison. *LE* 25 and *CH* 161 require the father of the bride, who annulled the betrothal without a valid reason to pay the groom twice the bride money. Neither of the laws formulates this principle in a general manner, but each law describes a concrete precedent. *CH* 161 is easily understood. A friend of the groom slandered him and therefore the father of the bride told the groom that he would not give him his daughter in marriage. The law which imposes upon the father the payment of twice the bride price in addition forbids the friend from marrying the bride. On the other hand, *LE* 25 is difficult and only Yaron's investigation has clarified that the *protasis* deals with a groom who demanded without success that the father give him his bride, but failed to obtain her since the father did him wrong and gave his daughter to another man in marriage. Yaron sees this injustice in the fact that the father told the groom that he would not give him his daughter. He concludes that the giving of the daughter in marriage to another man is irrelevant.[12] However on this point we do not have to explain

---

[10] pp. 130-133.

[11] p. 133.

[12] p. 129.

LE 25 on the basis of *CH* 161, and perhaps the injustice done by the father is in the fact that he gave his daughter to another man. Suppose, for example, that he had promised the groom who demanded his bride that he would soon marry her off to him, but he did not keep his promise and quickly gave her in marriage to another man. In any event we may ask: What is the law concerning the father who gave his betrothed daughter to another man before the groom had managed to ask him to marry her off to him? No answer is given to this question in *LE*. However, in the light of *CH* 161 we may suppose that even in such a case the father would be required to pay twice the bride price. This implies that the groom's request is irrelevant and reflects the special circumstances of the precedent.

These short notes on the Laws of Eshnunna were added here to the general criticism in order to illustrate to the reader the difficulties encountered in explaining ancient Near Eastern law. Within this tight framework Yaron as one who is at home in Akkadian has worked diligently to explain to the reader the measure of certainty in the readings of the text and in its translation. Furthermore, he has analyzed the various possibilities of understanding the text with the trained eye of a legal historian and has even not neglected the tiresome work of summarizing the scattered studies which are not easily available to one who is interested in the Laws of Eshnunna. This book will undoubtedly serve as the basis of discussion on the Laws of Eshnunna for a long time to come.

Philo of Byblos*

The literature of the ancient Orient sank, during the Roman period, into the abyss of oblivion and nothing remainded of it save the Bible until the rise of nineteenth and twentieth century scholars. Due to their unceasing endeavour, abundant texts in all the cultured tongues of the ancient Orient were discovered, deciphered, and interpreted and our knowledge of the literature of ancient peoples in general, and of their mythology in particular, increased decisively. Such was not the case, however, of Phoenician mythology. It is true that in recent generations a significant number of Phoenician documents have been published. Nevertheless, they contain not a single mythological text and we are still dependent in this area on second hand information scattered throughout Greek literature. The most important of these remnants of Phoenician myth in Greek literature stems from Philo of Byblos, a Phoenician scholar born in 64 CE, who wrote, among other things, a book about the Phoenicians. Unfortunately, this book was lost along with Philo's other books. However, the Church Father Eusebius often dealt with him, even quoting him in his work *Praeparatio Evangelica* in order to prove the futility of paganism. Eusebius's words are based on Philo's book itself. However, at times he relies on summaries of Philo's reports extant in the works of Porphyrius, a pagan philosopher who polemicized against Christianity. Eusebius, therefore, at times painstakingly quoted his writings in order that he might victoriously proclaim that his opponent himself implied that pagan mythology is nothing but superstitious nonsense (I:9:22).

Philo cites as a source for his Greek book a Phoenician work whose author was Σαγχουνιάθων, a name known from the Phoenician as *sknytn*. Eusebius often mentions Sanchuniathon, sometimes in the name of Philo, and sometimes in the name of Porphyrius. In Porphyrius's account, Sanchuniathon was from Beirut, lived in the period of the Trojan war, and gathered his

* Presented before the Schocken Institute on 25 March 1971.

material from various traditions, especially from their temple archives (I:9:20-21). In contrast to this, Eusebius, in the name of Philo, emphasizes Sanchuniathon's dependence on Taautos (I:9:24). This Taautos is a wondrous image with two faces. On the one hand he is considered a god whom Alexandrians called Thoth (*ibid.*). On the other hand he appears as one of the founders of civilization often described by Philo. He invented letters and was the first human to write down traditions (*ibid.*). Philo reports in his praise that he did not simply record the words of the ignorant masses concerning worship of the gods, but scientifically edited them in order to purge the traditions about the origins of all of myth and allegory. It is therefore that Sanchuniathon concerned himself with his writings (I:9:26). The implication is that Sanchuniathon rejected the gods, and he claimed that the imaginary deities were one of two things, either illustrious men who invented the essentials of human existence and were worshipped as gods after their death, or kings after whom were named natural phenomena such as Sun and Moon (I:9:29). The assumption that the natural phenomena were named after mortal kings is at first glance most surprising. However, it serves an important function in that it offers the atheistic writer a chance to save the myths. In other words, it would have been impossible to apply the myth about the god of the heavens solely to the natural heavens, but it could cleverly be applied to a mortal king whose name was "Heavens" and thereby save the essence of the story.

This atheistic approach, which found a way of integrating the myth, reflects the approach of the philosopher Euhemeros, a contemporary of Alexander the Great. It is therefore clear from the start that Philo's book does not transmit actual Phoenician myth but only a reworking in the Hellenistic spirit.

Philo does not specify the cities whose traditions are included in his book. However, we encounter names of cities in stories which are stamped with the mark of local legend. Among the Phoenician coastal cities, especially prominent are Byblos in the north and Tyre in the south. Zidon is mentioned only once and not as a city but as the daughter of Pontos - i.e. Sea - who excelled in the sweetness of her voice and who invented the songs of praise (I:10:28). Beirut occasionally appears in the account of the four generations of rulers who were in reality the chief gods. There we read about Elioum, the first of the four gods who reigned consecutively - who sat alongside Byblos together with his wife whose name is Beirut (I:10:14). A relationship between Beirut and Byblos is also indicated in the story of Kronos (= Elos, a grecised form of the Canaanite name El). Philo reports about Kronos the grandson of Elioum, among other things, that he surrounded his habitation with a wall and founded Byblos as the first Phoenician city (I:10:11). He gave it to Baaltis, the goddess *b^{c}lt gbl* known from the Phoenician Byblos inscriptions - and he gave Beirut to Poseidon, the son of Pontos, and to his friends (I:10:35). The two stories, therefore, indicate that essentially Beirut is nothing but the colony of Byblos.

Outside the realm of the Tyre-Byblian coast lies Mt. Kasion, the modern Jebl-Akra, north of Ras-Shamra. This place is known from Ugaritic literature as Baal's dwelling place and during the Greek period came to be known as the habitation of Zeus-Kasios. Philo mentions this matter as an appendix to his stories about Kronos. He writes: "And at that time[1] the sons of the Dioscurs made a raft and sea-craft and set sail in them. After they were thrown ashore by Kasion they dedicated a temple there (I:10:20)". These very Dioscurs are related in Philo's words to Zydyk, namely Justice, who is either a Byblian or Tyrian figure. In any case, we hear in Philo's words the claim of the inhabitants of the Phoenician coast that they founded the renowned temple on that northern mountain which is a centre for the mixing of Canaanite and Greek culture. Apollodorus Mythographus, in the chapter describing the war between Zeus and Typhon, mentions Kasion and in that same chapter, Zeus is mentioned as ἐπὶ πτηνῶν ὀχούμενος ἅρματι, that is, as he who rides in a winged horse-drawn chariot (I:VI:3). This description of Zeus appearing on a horse-drawn chariot is exceptional in Greek literature *[Contrast in this volume: Bordercases of Ugaritic comparative Studies, pp. 417-418, note 26.]* and its origin must be found in Ugaritic literature which entitles Baal Zaphon *rkb ^{c}rpt* - rider of the clouds. This recurs as a title of the Lord in Ps. 68:5 in the form of *rokeb ba ^{ca}rābot*. These clouds are described, in the language of Habakuk's prayer, as a chariot hitched to horses: *ki tirkab ^{c}al susäkā mark^{e}botäkā y^{e}šu^{c}ā* (Hab. 3:8). This chariot becomes in Appolodor's account a type of Helian chariot.

Mentioned along with these well known places is a settlement named Peraia which is unknown to us apart from a short entry in Stephanus Byzanti-

---

[[1] The secondary formula of connection κατὰ τὸν χρόνον τοῦτον 'at this time' reveals the originally independent character of the story.*]*

us's dictionary stating that Peraia was a village (πολίδιον) in Syria. This village appears in the story of the birth of Kronos's children as the birthplace of Kronos - named after his father, Zeus Belos, and Apollon (I:10:26). These gods do not appear in other parts of Philo's account and it is clear that before us is a fragment of a forgotten local tradition.

The remaining Oriental traditions, whose antiquity is unquestioned, serve as a criterion for judging the antiquity of Philo's traditions. Only a short while ago, research was dependent on Hesiod's *Theogonia* which was written in the eighth century. The obvious parallels between Philo and *Theogonia* raised the question whether we are allowed to look in Philo's writings for Phoenician traditions or whether we are confronted with purely Greek-Hellenistic literature. The situation changed with the discovery of remnants from Hurrian-Hittite and Ugaritic myths. The first scholar to call for reevaluation of Philo in the light of new finds, and the father of research in this area, was Eissfeldt.[1a] Study has revealed that Philo has indeed preserved ancient traditions but, even more apparently, that certain traditions changed so drastically that their original form was largely or totally obliterated. Philo mentions Mout, the son of Kronos whom the Phoenicians called Thanatos or Plouton, namely death[2], and tells about him that he died in the lifetime of his father Kronos (I:10:34). It seems that Mout is none other than Mot the son of Il known from the Ugaritic epic as a monstrous embodiment of the powers of death and the bitter enemy of Baal. Of all this, the only features retained by Philo are the name and the relation to Il. It is even possible that Philo thought that he was called Mout because of his premature death.[3] Most enlightening is a comparison of Philo's account of Chousor with the information contained in Ugaritic writings concerning *Kṯr*. In Ugarit, *Kṯr* is described as the chief artisan of the gods and his dwelling place is Kaphtor. In Philo's report his foreign origin is already forgotten and he is fitted into the genealogy of the first generations of Tyre, the continuation of which mentions two brothers who discovered iron and its applications. Only one of the two is mentioned by name.

[1a] O. Eissfeldt, *Taautos und Sanchunjaton*. Berlin 1952; id., *Sanchunjaton von Berut und Ilumilku von Ugarit*, Halle 1952.

[2] Philo's statement is surprising. The order of his statement should be reversed so as to yield "Plouton or Thanatos whom the Phoenicians call Mout".

[3] Compare his words on Persephone about whom he tells nothing except that she died a virgin (I:10:18).

He is Chousor who composed incantations, conjurations, and prophecies, he is called Hephaistos, and was the inventor of fishing equipment and rafts and the first seafarer. Therefore, after his death he was worshipped as a god (I:10:11). It is therefore clear that the image of *Kṯr* has been blended in these texts with traditions of Tyre dealing with the founders of civilization. However, there has been preserved not only his name Chousor but also a hint of his original nature in that he is identified with Hephaistos, the divine artisan of the Greek pantheon. It should be pointed out that this is not the last of Chousor's transformations in the Canaanite myth. This great artisan even found himself a place in the cosmogony according to Damascius who brings in his book *De primis principiis* 215 the words of Mochos. According to Mochos, in one of the phases of the creation appears Oulomos, (Hebrew *ᶜolām*) who bore from himself two children, the first of them Chousor about whom it is written that he was the first engraver and is even called ἡ νοητὴ δύναμις the intellectual capacity. Misor and Sydyk, who, according to Philo, discovered the use of salt, underwent similar transformations. The true meaning of the names Misor and Sydyk can be seen in Is. 11:4 - *wᵉšāpaṭ bᵉṣädäq dallim wᵉhokiᵃḥ bᵉmišor lᵉᶜanwe 'äräṣ*. Their names indicate that Misor and Sydyk are essentially hypostases of justice, just like the Akkadian god pair *kittu u mēšaru*, namely righteousness and justice, who were servants of *Šamaš*, the sun god, considered in Mesopotamia to be the god of justice. Misor and Sydyk, too, are ancient gods and their names already appear in the god lists of Ugarit.[4] In Phoenicia they were absorbed into the local legends about early inventors and became the discoverers of the use of salt. Even more significant the very meaning of the names has disappeared from Philo and he explains Misor and Sydyk as εὔλυτος καὶ δίκαιος - loose and righteous - and it seems probable that he derived *mišor* from the Aramaic *šrh* 'to loosen'.

Philo has more faithfully preserved the traditions concerning the first four generations of gods, namely Hypsistos (= Elioum, Hebrew *ᶜälyon*), Ouranos (Heavens), Kronos or Elos (El) and Adodos (Hadad) who is called Demarous. Demarous is none other than the Ugaritic name *dmrn* which in Ugaritic writings is a title of *hdd*, i.e. *bᶜl*.[5] The account of these gods surprising-

---

[4] *U* 5, RS 24.271 A:14, p. 583. For the reading *ṣdq mšr* cf. de Moor, *UF* 2, pp. 196, 225.

[5] Cf. U. Cassuto, *Zeus Demarous in Ugaritic Writings*, *Sepher Dinaburg*, Jeru-

ly resembles the Hurrian-Hittite myth which lists as the first god Alalu, the second Anu, the god of the heavens, the third Kumarbi, and the fourth, the storm god. Both myths speak about four generations and in both the representative of the second generation is entitled Heavens. Even more significant. In both myths, the son of Heavens usurps his father's throne and castrates him, and in both myths the fourth god is the god of storms, lightning, and thunder.[6] Moreover, there is certain similarity between the Hurrian-Hittite epic and Philo's description of the last god's pedigree. According to the Hurrian-Hittite myth, Kumarbi, the son of Heavens, bit his father, swallowed his genitals and from the semen swallowed three gods were formed within him, the most important one being the storm god. The result is that the storm god is the offspring of Heaven, the second god, even though he came out from Kumarbi, the third god. This story resembles Philo's account. He also connects the birth of Baal to Kronos' rebellion against Ouranos. According to him, the most beloved of Ouranos' wives was pregnant when Kronos rebelled. At the time of the rebellion Kronos captured this wife and handed her over to Dagon his brother as a wife, and while Dagon's wife she bore Demarous (I:10:18) who is Haddad, alias Baal. As in the Hurrian-Hittite myth, the third god played a role in the birth of the fourth but in both myths the fourth god was not biologically descended from the third god but from the second who is Heavens. The myth in Hesiod's *Theogonia* differs from these myths in two important aspects. a) The first generation is absent and the list of gods mentioned starts with the god of the Heavens. b) Zeus is simply the offspring of Kronos and not of Ouranos.

In marked contradiction to all the myths thus far considered, the Ugaritic myth lacks the second generation, Heavens, and starts right off with Il. He is parallel to Kumarbi of the Hurrian-Hittite myth, to Kronos of Hesiod, and to Kronos-Elos of Philo. The chief representative of the next generation in Ugaritic mythology is *b^{c}l-hdd-dmrn*, who is parallel to the storm god of the Hurrian-Hittite myth, to Zeus of Hesiod, and to Adodos-Zeus-Demarous of Philo. Establishing his pedigree encounters difficulties. The epic poetry describes him as a son of Il, as in Hesiod, but with all

---

salem 1949, p. 65-67 (in Heb.) *[= BOSt* 2, pp. 188-192*]*; Eissfeldt, *Sanchunjaton*, pp. 41-42. Contrast de Moor, *Seasonal Pattern*, p. 166.

[6] For the parallels between the Hurrian-Hittite myth and Philo cf. Eissfeldt, *ibid.*, p. 59-66.

this he is occasionally called the son of Dagan. To this is added a second difficulty. It has already been pointed out that in the order of the gods he is parallel to Kumarbi. We could therefore expect Ugaritic writings to identify Kumarbi with Il and this indeed occurs in a portion of the texts. However, Laroche[8] has already demonstrated that in another portion of the texts Kumarbi is identical with Dagan. There is therefore room for the conjecture of my colleague Abraham Malamat (orally) that Dagan at one time occupied in Ugaritic mythology the place finally occupied by Il, and, if so, it is not in vain that in Philo's version El and Dagon appear together in the account of Adodos' birth. I have already emphasized that Il is not preceded by Heavens in the genealogy of the Ugaritic gods and consequently all the story of El's rebellion against his father is missing. This motif could not be imagined in the Ugaritic myth because Ugaritic Il's character is strikingly different from that of his counter-parts in other myths. In the three other myths El is a vicious fighter and Philo even reports that he killed one of his brothers, one of his sons, and one of his daughters (I: 10:20-21). Very unlike this was Ugaritic Il. His image is that of one called in European languages *le bon Dieu, der liebe Gott*. No hint of belligerence is detectable in him. In our opinion there is room to conjecture that the Ugaritic epic writers intentionally avoided the prevalent myth and formulated a new theological ideal.

Now we shall discuss El's relationship to his sons. According to the Hurrian-Hittite myth, and the Theogonia, the god of the last generation usurped his father's throne. This myth was common in Greece even though Diodor (V:70) has preserved hints of a Greek version in a euhemeristic passage which simply tells that Zeus ruled after his father's death.[9] However, in Philo's report not the slightest hint is to be found indicating that El was ever removed from power. Just the opposite is true. We already pointed out that according to Byblian tradition El enthroned Baaltis over Byblos and Poseidon over Beirut. Similarly, Tyrian tradition contends that the

---

[8] E. Laroche, *U* 5, pp. 532f.

[9] For the Greek tradition which brought Kronos to the Isles of Bliss and fixed his place at the head of those dead who merited life in a quasi-paradise, cf. Pindar, *Olympia* 2:68-83. Also see Hesiod, *Opera et dies*, I:169. However, this line is missing in some manuscripts. I do not know how this tradition described Kronos' death.

great Astarte and Adodos, the king of the gods, ruled upon earth at Kronos' will (I:10:31). Moreover, the basic motif of enthroning young gods by El determined the nature of two stories reflecting the spread of Phoenician settlement outside of Phoenicia. Philo tells that at the time of his journey Kronos handed the reign over Attika to Athene (I:10:32) and over Egypt to Taautos (I:10:38). All these reports point to a major principle of Phoenician mythology that the reign of the young gods derives from El's will[9a] and apparently the Phoenicians saw no contradiction between regional authority of young gods and the all encompassing supervision of El. The antiquity of this Phoenician tradition becomes clear in the light of Ugaritic writings. It is true that certain critics try to find in the Ugaritic myth hints of Baal's rebellion against his father, in that he finally exiled his father to a remote place and there are those who are not satisfied with this and claim that Baal castrated Il.[10] We will not involve ourselves at present with this complex matter but will restrict ourselves to point out some facts clearly listed in the Ugaritic epic poetry. 1) When Baal died, Il mourned[11], and when told of Baal's resurrection, he rejoiced greatly.[12] 2) In the latest of the epic poems, in the Krt epic, Il is the chief divinity. He appears to the king in dreams, commands him what to do, and the King is obedient.[13] In that same poem, Il is described at a gathering of the sons of Il and it becomes clear that Il is the sole creator and healer among the gods.[14] Without going into further detail I would only like to add that we

---

[9a We should also pay attention to the principal difference between the story about Baal and Ashtoret who were appointed by El to rule over the earth, i.e. the whole earth and the accounts on those gods whose investiture by El was restricted to special territories. The all encompassing character of Baal's and Ashtoret's reign calls to mind the universalistic approach of the Ugaritic myth, and cf. especially the passage in which Il appoints *ᶜṯtr* to become universal ruler after Baal's death (*CTA* 6:I:45-55). The other and more amply attested type of stories limiting El's grants to the dominion over one town or land, presumably reflects a later stage in the development of Canaanite theology. On the question of its traces in the Bible, see below, p. 399.*]*

10 Cf. e.g. M.H. Pope, *El in the Ugaritic Texts*, Leiden 1955, and especially U. Oldenburg, *The Conflict between El and Baal in Canaanite Religion*, Leiden 1969.

11 *CTA* 5:VI:11-25.

12 *CTA* 6:III:3-21.

13 *CTA* 15:I:35; V:305.

14 *CTA* V:16.

should not expect in the Ugaritic myth a type of *Titanomachia* of the Greek myth in which Zeus usurped the throne of Kronos his father, because we have already reached the conclusion that it was the Ugaritic epic which radically transformed Il's image from that of a cruel warrior who castrates his father to the prototype of a wise and goodhearted elder.

After this description of the order of the generations of the first gods, we will say a few words about a goddess who interests us also from the standpoint of the Bible, namely Astarte. In this matter there is a clear distinction between the Tyrian and the Byblian traditions. In the latter, Astarte, is one of El's wives and bore him seven daughters and two sons (I:10:23-24). This implies that she belongs to El's generation and her position is not very prominent. However, in the Tyrian tradition, as we have already pointed out, the great Astarte and Baal, the king of the gods, reigned at El's will, and Philo adds here that Astarte put upon her head an ox's head as a sign of her sovereignty. This tradition, which increases Astarte's, greatness and places her next to Baal and not next to El, originates in the *hieros logos* of the temple of Astarte in Tyre. This *hieros logos* relates that Astarte found, while walking upon the earth, a star which fell from the heavens, brought it to the holy island of Tyre, and sanctified it there (I:10:31). This mythology from Tyre casts light upon the passages in Ju. 2:13, 10:6 and 1 Sam. 7:4, 12:10 which accuse Israel of abandoning the Lord and serving the Baals and the Ashtorets. More important with regard to Biblical scholarship is the question whether the Phoenician myth is relevant to the development of Biblical outlooks. It can be assumed from the start that there is some connection between Philo's Elioum and the divine epithet ^{c}*älyon* of the Bible. However, defining the connection encounters various serious difficulties. As has been said, Philo's Elioum is the grand-father of El. However, there are scholars who reject Philo's account of Elioum as reliable testimony to the Phoenician myth and contend that Elioum is nothing but one of El's epithets, substantiating their contention on the basis of a document from the Sefiré inscriptions which lists in a god list *'l w* ^{c}*lyn*. They claim that *'l* and ^{c}*lyn* are a double name of one deity, on the pattern of such double names in Ugaritic as *kṯr wḫss*.[15]

[15] Cassuto, *Anath*, pp. 54f.; F.M. Cross, *HTR* 60 (1962) p. 244; otherwise, R. Rendtorff, *Fourth World Congress of Jewish Studies* I, Jerusalem 1967, pp. 167f.; J.A. Fitzmyer, *The Aramaic Inscriptions of Sefiré*, Rome 1967, p. 37.

This explanation is reasonable, for it seems implausible to assume that a grandfather and his grandson would be recorded as a couple in a god list on the pattern of Marduk and his wife Zarpanit. Anyhow, it seems unlike that we should be entitled to explain the pantheon of Byblos in the light of the pantheon of Sefiré. We should rather keep them apart, since the reliability of Philo's account about Elioum's position in the pantheon is supported by the analogous position held by Alalu in the Hurrian-Hittite myth. The question is no less complex upon turning to the Bible. As well known, both *'el* and *ᶜälyon* serve as epithets for the Lord. However, there are certain exceptions. In Ps. 82:6 we read *'ᵃni 'āmarti 'ᵃ̈lohim 'attäm ubᵉne ᶜälyon kullᵉkäm*. Interpreting 'you are all my sons' has difficulties. The echo of which tradition is audible here? It seems to us that the tradition which identified Elyon with El reverberates here because it is supposed that *bᵉne ᶜälyon* are identical with *ᶜᵃdat 'el* (Ps. 82:1). The same problem appears in the song of Moses in which most critics, in accordance with the Septuagint and the Qumran documents, read *bᵉhanḥel ᶜälyon goyim bᵉhaprido bᵉne 'ādām yaṣṣeb gᵉbulot ᶜammim lᵉmispar bᵉne 'el. ki heläq etc.* (Deut. 32:8-9). Here also it is difficult to explain that the Lord is *ᶜälyon*. However, we cannot look for an echo of Philo's Elioum tradition because the result would be the most unreasonable explanation that *ᶜälyon* divided the earth among the sons of *'el* his grand-son. If we say that *ᶜälyon* is *'el*, we find that *'el-ᶜälyon* divided the earth among his sons, in accordance with Phoenician traditions about El.[16] The hint of henotheism detectable here is not surprising if we pay attention to the second Targum on the verse. Even though this Targum abandons the mythological image of the source it replaces it with a no less mythological image which describes the Holy Blessed be He as casting lots with the princes of the seventy nations of the earth. We will point out on passing that such a motif is already documented in an Old-Babylonian text. The first tablet of the *Atraḫasis* epic (I:11-18) describes the heads of the Babylonian pantheon dividing the cosmos amongst themselves and that motif subsequently recurs in the Iliad 15:184-195. However, in these sources, the gods are pictured as cosmic gods dividing the universe between themselves by lot, while in the second Targum the outlook is nationalistic.

To the account of the gods we will add a few words about the coming into being of the universe. We say "coming into being" rather than "creation" because Philo has no god as a creator of the universe. We will quote this crucial text in its entirety but we will first point out a detail which we are unable to explain. In the text appears the concept of *Mot*. We cannot explain the nature of this name because the context leaves no room for doubt that we cannot consider here *Mot* the god of death, and the suggestion to identify Philo's Mot with the Egyptian Mot - a title of Isis - is totally unfounded.[18] Unfortunately, this cryptic concept recurs twice in the text and the second instance is in an obscure context which rouses the suspicion of a mixing of versions. The description is as follows: "First of all there was dark air like a wind or a gust of dark wind and muddy and dark chaos. This was without boundary and for a long time without end, and it was when the wind fell in love with the beginning of itself that an amalgamation, came into being and that combination (συμπλοκή) was called desire (πόθος) - the beginning of the existence of all. It was not cognizant of its own existence and from the intertwining *Mot* came into being whom some call 'mire' and some 'putrifying watery mixture'. From this came into being the seed of all existence and the origin of all. And there were living creatures without senses from which came into existence intelligent beings named Ζοφασημιν (read Ζοφησαμιν) or watchers of the heavens (in Hebrew *ṣope šāmayim*)". Until this point the text is in order and even more or less comprehensible apart from the term *Mot*. However, the following sentence does not suit the preceeding one and apparently the words of another description of the beginning of the world have crept in. We read: "And it assumed a form like an egg and lit up *Mot* and the sun and the moon and the stars and the great constellations" (I:10:2).[19] The matter of *Mot* and the egg is most disturbing and we believe that a parallel passage was improperly inserted and it should read simply: "and the sun and the moon lit up etc.". In any case, the continuation is again comprehensible. It is written: "And when the air glowed

---

[18] C. Clemen, *Die Phoenikische Religion nach Philo von Byblos, MVAG* 42,3 (1937), p. 36.

[19] It is customary to translate: "And Mot took on the form of an egg and glowed, and so the sun etc." But this translation blurs the difficulty in the text rather than solving it.
[J. Barr, *Philo of Byblos and his Phoenician History, BJRL* 57 (1974), p. 23, note 2, comments upon this difficult Mot: "One is tempted to think of the Hebrew *m^e'orot* the 'heavenly lights' of the Genesis story of creation, especially since in the Greek text the sun and other heavenly bodies appear to be here in apposition with Mot."]

as the sea and land heated up, the winds and the clouds formed, and the great water estuaries came down from the heavens. And after, in the heat of the sun, everything had left its appointed place, they all met again and clashed. Thunder and lightning came out and at the sound of the thunder the aforementioned living creatures were awoken and from the noise they were afraid and they wandered the land and seas, male and female (I:10:4)."

We found here in a vague context the concept of the egg and we speculated that this egg belonged to the words which were added from another cosmogony. We want to point out that this egg is mentioned in a clearer setting in the cosmogony recorded by Damascius in his book *De primis principiis* 215 in the name of Eudemos. In his version there were in the beginning: time, desire (πόθος) and darkness (ὀμίχλη). We can, naturally, disregard the time which is only a philosophical addition and plays no role in the continuation which mentions the mixing of the desire with the darkness from which were made Ἀήρ and Αὔρα, air and wind, and from them the egg was made. The egg reappears in Damascius' description brought in the name of Mochos. According to Mochos Oulomos bore it from himself after he had borne Chousor and from breaking the egg heaven and earth were made. It is clear that this egg occupied an important place in most, if not all, versions of the Phoenician account on the beginning of the world. It is well known that its traces were sought even in the words of the Pentateuch *w^eruaḥ ʾälohim m^eraḥäpät ^cal p^ene hammayim* 'and wind swept across the face of the waters', and some tried to interpret *rḥp* on the basis of the Syriac as '*hatch*'. This suggestion is most doubtful. Water is not like an egg and, furthermore, in the Phoenician myth this egg comes into being only in the advanced stages of the formation of the world while the Pentateuch speaks about the pre-creation situation.

We shall now return to Philo. Philo's description of the formation of the world out of chaos without any creative action of a god may seem strange to us, not only on account of our familiarity with the Pentateuchal creation, but also because in the Babylonian epic, *enūma eliš*, the world was divinely created. We might conclude from this that Philo's description is rooted in his denial of gods. However, this conclusion is invalid. The belief in gods does not at all necessitate the view that one god or another created the world. Just the opposite. A god would only be said to have created the world if he was exeedingly greater than the other gods, as it is indeed said about Marduk in *enūma eliš*, and a polytheistic approach which attributes creation to one of the gods comes near to monotheism. Therefore, Philo's narration cannot be seen as testifying to a later atheistic reworking. His account is like Hesiod's *Theogonia* which also does not recognize a creator god, even though Hesiod's belief in gods is obvious. Nor can we ignore the similarities between the beginning of Hesiod's *Theogonia* and Philo's words. Hesiod also tells about the existence of two elements at the beginning of the world and they are *Chaos* which bore the darkness, and *Eros* which parallels Philo's *Pothos*. It is not without reason that *Eros* and *Pothos* appear in Philo as brothers (I:10:24) because they are similar and the possibility cannot be excluded that we are dealing simply with synonyms. From this it seems that Philo's description originated from ancient tradition. The similarities between his account and that of the Pentateuch are evident. They are: the situation of primeval darkness and chaos, the action of the wind, and emphasis of male and female, even though in Philo the emphasis is all inclusive while in the Pentateuch it is limited to human beings alone (Gen. 1:27).

After the creation, Philo surveys the beginnings of the human culture including the origin of divine worship and the origin of material culture. As primeval innovations, the innovators of which merited eternal renown, are mentioned, on one hand libations and sacrifices to plants worshipped as gods (I:10:6), spreading the hands during prayer in the time of a drought (I:10:7), erection of pillars and guarding the holy staffs in the temple, which recalls Aaron's staff (I:10:10,11 and cf. I:9:29), and fixing of holidays (I:10:11 and cf. 9:29); and on the other hand discovery of the possibility to eat fruit from trees (I:10:7), producing fire (I:10:9), use of animal hides for clothing (I:10:10), brick making and wall building (I:10:12), and more. This chapter is similar in nature to Gen. 4 which deals in its entirety with the beginnings of culture.[20] This central theme is especially notable in the story of the sons of Lamech which lists the fathers of professions, Jabal, the ancestor of tent dwellers and herdsmen (20), Jubal the ancestor of lyre and pipe players (21) and Tubal-Cain, the forger of copper and iron implements (22), and Onkelos certainly was right in trans-

[20] See Cassuto, *From Adam to Noah*, pp. 188, 230, who points out that there are parallels between Philo's description of the origin of material culture and that of Genesis 4.

lating "the ancestor of every forger". If we are precise, we see that the theme covers the entire chapter. It mentions Enoch, the builder of a city (17), and clearly the intent is the builder of the first city. Not only this, but even the story of Cain and Abel is related to this theme, there being no doubt that Cain and Abel were considered the first of shepherds and of farmers (2). Furthermore, we even find in Gen. 4 the beginnings of cult because Cain and Abel were the first to sacrifice from the produce of the earth and the firstlings of the sheep (3-4). From this we can understand the last verse of the chapter which reads: "And to Seth was born a son and he called his name Enosh. Then *huḥal liqro' bᵉsem YHWH* (26). Scholars have found no small amount of difficulty with this verse. However, if we pay attention to the traditional link between the beginnings of material culture and the start of divine worship, the lack of this verse seems to be nearly inconceivable. How would the Bible describe the beginnings of civilization and silently pass over the beginnings of the worship of the Lord which is its main concern.

Among the rest of Philo's words which have relevance to Biblical scholarship, special mention should be made of repeated testimony that in times of trouble the head of the nation would sacrifice his beloved and only son (μονογενής in Phoenician Ἰεουδ = *yᵉḥud* = Hebrew *yāḥid*), as ransom to the demons of revenge (I:10:44; IV:16:11 and cf. IV:16:6). To this belongs, among other things, the following incident concerning El in the Tyrian tradition: "At the time of pestilence and destruction El sacrificed to Heavens his father, his only son, he circumcised his genitals and forced his allies to do similarly" (I:10:33). This shows that the two incidents had the same apotropaic aim. It should be pointed out that circumcision serves the same function of driving off mortal danger in the Biblical story of the "Bridegroom of Blood" (Ex. 4:24-26). Even more interesting is that the two motifs of circumcision and of sacrificing the only and beloved son recur in the stories of Abraham totally divorced from their original meaning. Not only does the binding of Isaac terminate in saving his life, but in both stories Abraham does not act of his own will, but at the command of the Lord, and in both of them the motif of absolute obedience to God's command is the dominant. It is no mere coincidence that the two stories are connected to God's covenant with Abraham which is fulfilled in the person of Isaac. The uniqueness of the Biblical narratives becomes exceedingly evident in the light of comparison with the ancient Phoenician motifs.

In conclusion it should be said that the wealth of new primary sources of ancient Near Eastern mythology which have been discovered in our lifetime have done nothing to detract from studying Philo. On the contrary. Not only do the new finds cast light from time to time on Philo, but at times it is Philo's words that provide the proper perspective for viewing the other sources and their own special nature.

While reviewing my lecture, Prof. M. Plessner pointed out to me the closeness between Taautos and Hermes Trismegistos of the Hellenistic literature. Both were identified with the Egyptian Thoth and both were represented sometimes as gods, sometimes as men who laid the foundations of human civilization. Prof. Plessner's remark is validated by Philo's testimony that the Greeks called Taautos Hermes (I:9:24). Cf. R.P. Festugière, *La Rèvèlation d'Hermès Trismègiste*, [2]Paris 1950, and especially the allusion to Taautos on p. 57; also M. Plessner, *Studia Islamica* 2 (1954), pp. 45-59 and in this volume *Taautos*, pp. 463-464.

Border-cases of Ugaritic comparative Studies

Hebrew of the Second Temple, Talmudic Hebrew, Greek

It is generally accepted nowadays that Ugaritic contains a wealth of comparative information for the study of Old-Hebrew texts. The view that it might likewise be usefully compared with the Hebrew of the Second Temple period is also gaining acceptance. But there has as yet been little discussion of what might come of a comparison with Middle-Hebrew. On the other hand, the astonishing postulate has been voiced that in spite of their total dissimilarity, Ugaritic and Greek should be submitted to comparative research. In this study we shall attempt to deal with some of the questions arising from the latter three heads. We shall concentrate on the little-discussed question of comparison with Greek and Talmudic, and confine ourselves to a few remarks on the problems of comparison between Ugaritic literature and Hebrew of the Second-Temple period, most of which have been solved.

Ugaritic Literature and Hebrew of the Second-Temple Period

Parallels to Ugaritic usage in the literature of the Second Temple period are often seen as archaisms. This cannot be so in every case, however, since an old usage is by no means necessarily an antiquated one. We may begin with the Ugaritic verse: *tġdd kbdh bṣḥq ymlu lbh bšmḫt* (*CTA* 3:II: 25-26) 'Her liver swells[1] with laughter, her heart is filled with joy'. Held[2] long ago pointed out that the Ugaritic parallelism of the roots *ṣḥq* //

[1] Ugaritic *ġdd* is usually compared, with justification, to Arabic *ġdd* 'to be swollen'. For the semantic shift from 'to swell' to 'to rejoice', see Akkadian *elēṣu*, which depicts swelling, particularly of the liver and the heart, but is mostly used in the figurative sense of 'rejoice'. See *CAD* *s.v. elēṣu*.

[2] M. Held, *Lĕšonēnu* 18 (1953), pp. 149, 160 (in Heb.). [We may take the opportunity to point out a loose parallelism of the verbal form *y^{e}śammaḥ* with the substantive *ś^{e}ḥoq* (Ecc. 10:19). This is a later modification of the classical parallelism, since in the ancient Canaanite style, substan-

šmḫt is the same as *śḥq* // *śmḥ*[3] in Pr. 14:13; Ecc. 2:2; 10:19. Nonetheless, it is certainly not a stylistic archaicism of Ecclesiastes, since both roots are not restricted to couplets but are well attested in other usages in the same book. Cf. for *śḥq* Ecc. 3:4; 7:3,6; for *śmḥ* Ecc. 2:1,10,26; 5:19 etc.

It should be mentioned in passing that Dahood[4] has also discussed the same question, being unaware of Held's study. He analysed the verse: *šmḫ lṭpn il dpid / p^cnh lhdm yṯpd / wyprq lṣb wyṣḥq* (*CTA* 6:III:14-16) 'The kindly one El benign is glad, His feet on the footstool he sets, and parts his mouth(?)[4a] and laughs' and concluded, correctly, that the third stichos is parallel to the first, bringing in support Ecc. 2:2. Dahood's study therefore complements Held's, but his conclusions complicate the problem of A and B words, which R.J. Boling[5] first raised in the wake of an unpublished paper of Held. His conclusion may be summarized as follows: in Ugaritic, parallel words are rigidly assigned to either the first or second half of the verse, while in Hebrew this old system is generally but by no means exclusively preserved.

In contradiction to this rule, however, *CTA* 3:II:25-26 begins with *ṣḥq*, as in Hebrew, while *CTA* 6:III:14-16 begins with *šmḫ*. One might at first be tempted to attribute this relaxation of the rule to the peculiar construction of the latter verse, in which the parallel stichoi, instead of directly following one another, include a third by way of *inclusio*. There is, however, a similar variation between *lb / kbd* and all the three verses of this instance have the normal *parallelismus membrorum* without *inclusio*. Cf. for *lb / kbd*, *il yṣḥq bm lb / wygmd̲ bm kbd* (*CTA* 12:I:12-13) 'El laughs in his heart and rejoices(?) in his liver', and *tbky pġt bm lb // tdm^c bm kbd* (*CTA* 19:I:34-35). '*Pġt* weeps in her heart, she sheds tears in her liver'. Cf. also Hebrew *lāken śāmaḥ libbi // wayyāgäl k^ebodi* (Ps. 16:9), where the con-

---

tives correspond to substantives and verbs to verbs. I am grateful to my student Y. Avishur for drawing my attention to this question, on whose systematic investigation he is at present engaged*]*.

[3] Before the discovery of the Ugaritic texts, it was disputed which of the two roots *ṣḥq* and *śḥq* was the older. Cf. *GB s.v. śḥq*.

[4] M. Dahood, *Biblica* 47 (1966) p. 267.

[[4a] Cf. note 14a.*]*

[5] R.G. Boling, *JSS* 5 (1960), pp. 223-226. Cf. also St. Gevirtz, *JNES* 20 (1961), pp. 41-46.

jectural reading *k^e^bedi* is generally accepted. But in *CTA* 3:II:25-26 mentioned above we find surprisingly the reverse order, *kbd / lb*. This is not to deny the existence of Held's and Boling's rule, but it shows that variability of word-order is not a purely Biblical innovation: its beginnings are already discernible in Ugaritic poetry.

We now pass to an example where the preservation of an old usage in a text of the Second Temple period represents a conscious archaicism. In Ezr. 9:9 an extremely solemn phrase is used for the building of the Temple, *l^e^romem 'ät bet '^ä^lohenu*, 'to erect (lit. to lead upwards) the House of our God', in which *l^e^romem* is used instead of the usual *libnot* 'to build'. This form is quite exceptional for Biblical Hebrew, but it has two clear parallels in Ugaritic. Compare the verse, *ḥš bhtm tbn[n] // ḥš trmmn hk[lm]* (*CTA* 4:V:115-116) 'build quickly (or may there be build) houses, quickly lead upwards (or may there be led upwards) palaces'. And cf. also *CTA*:3:V:28-29. The verb *rmm* thus appears in Ugaritic as a B-word parallel to *bny*, and its archaicising usage in the Book of Ezra allows us to suppose that the same applies for Old-Hebrew poetry, although there are no actual examples of it. Further support for this hypothesis may also be derived from Ben Sirah 49: 11b-12a, which also deals with the building of the Temple. Restored from the Septuagint, this verse reads: *['^a^sär bimehäm bānu bayit]*[5a] // *wayyārimu hekal qodäš* - 'in whose days they built the Temple and led upwards the holy palace.' In spite of its obvious similarity to its Ugaritic predecessor, the verse's archaicism is somewhat moderated by the use of the *Hiph^c^il* form of the verbs.[5b]

Ugaritic-Talmudic Parallels

We should be cautious in seeking parallels to Ugaritic texts in the Talmud, not so much because of the gap in time between the two sources as the difference in their literary character. Books like Ecclesiastes and Ben Sirah continue notwithstanding the lateness of their composition the

---

[[5a] But contrast *The Book of Ben Sira*, published by the Academy of the Hebrew Language and the Shrine of the Book, Jerusalem 1973. This edition of the Hebrew fragments indicates in 49:11b the letter *lāmäd*, not contained in the reconstruction according to the Septuagint.*]*

[[5b] S. Lieberman, *H. Yalon Memorial Vol.*, Jerusalem 1974, p. 556 (in Heb.) observes that *rmm* always refers in this use to the erection of temples, i.e. of outstandingly high edifices. Cf. to this remark: *wayyibän k^e^mo rāmim miqdāšo* (Ps. 78:69).*]*

tradition of Old-Canaanite verse, whereas the even later Talmudic texts represent a completely different literary genre. Here and there, however, we can indeed discern in this Middle-Hebrew literature the retention of such a tradition.

In one such instance, the Talmud explains the custom behind a Ugaritic text. The text relates how Krt sets out on a campaign to bring back a king's daughter as his wife and on the way comes to a sanctuary of Ashera, where he vows that if successful: *ṯnh kspm atn wṯlṯh ḫrṣm* (*CTA* 14:205-206) 'her double[6] (i.e. double her weight) will I give in silver and her triple in gold'. Lieberman had already remarked, as Ginsberg noted[7], that this type of vow has Talmudic analogies. We shall examine this parallel more closely. The Mishna (Arakin 5:1) states: "Whoever says 'I owe my weight' gives his own weight. If (he has said) silver, then silver: if (he has said) gold, then gold. Once the mother of Yarmatya said 'I owe the weight of my daughter', and she went up to Jerusalem and they weighed her (scil. the daughter) and she (scil. the mother) gave her weight in gold." The background to this Mishna and the meaning of the practice it describes is made clear by the parallel source Tosephta Arakin 3:1, where it is stated: "Once it befell the mother of Rimatya that her daughter fell sick. Then she said: 'if my daughter recovers from the sickness, I shall give her weight in gold. When she recovered from her illness she went up to Jerusalem and weighed her with gold." We may conclude, therefore, that the Talmudic custom was to offer the simple weight of a person in silver or gold. Krt differs strikingly from the Talmud in both these respects, since the king promises to weigh the maiden in silver as well as gold, and to offer, moreover, multiples of

---

[6] A different view is that *ṯnh* should be translated 'the half of her', *ṯlṯh* 'one third of her'. Cf. Gray, *Krt*[2], p. 57. But the assumption of an ascending progression is stylistically more appropriate to Ugaritic than that of a descending one. On the other hand, it cannot be argued that the weight of the precious gold should be reckoned less than that of the lower-priced silver. Contra cf. *CTA* 4:I:27-29 *yṣq ksp lalpm // ḫrṣ yṣqm lrbbt* 'he poured silver for thousands (of vessels), gold he poured for tens of thousands (of vessels)'.

[7] Ginsberg, *Keret*, p. 40. This important note has regrettably escaped notice. Cf. Gray, *Krt*[2] (note 6), who conjectures that the bride-price is in question here. But the text explicitly mentions a *ndr*, and this term, well-known from the Hebrew, describes the promise to perform a service to the divinity and has nothing to do with payment of private debts.

her weight. In our opinion, there can be no doubt that the Talmudic text approximates reality more closely than the Ugaritic one. In the latter, a true-to-life situation is adapted to meet the needs of Ugaritic verse-construction, namely, the well-known parallelism *ksp // ḫrṣ*, as well as the common stylistic technique of arithmetic progression. The net result of both is the hyperbolic formula before us. There may also have been a desire to emphasize that the king's vow far exceeded that customary among ordinary men. Thus the texts are illustrative of one another. The Ugaritic text demonstrates the antiquity of the Talmudic custom, while the Talmudic sources for their part clarify a practice which in Ugaritic is reflected only in poetic embellishment.

After this digression into the realm of custom we now return to linguistic problems. According to *U* 5, p. 545, text 1:3-4 it is said about the gods: *tštn <y>n* ^{c}*d šb*^{c} *trṯ* ^{c}*d škr* 'they drink wine until they are full, new wine until they are drunk'. Cf. *ibid.* l. 16. H.P. Rüger[8] correctly pointed out that the parallel of roots *šb*^{c} // *škr* is found again in Ez. 39:19 and Hag. 1:6. Here, however, there is a certain limitation. In Ugaritic both substantives relate to the consequences of drinking, while in the abovementioned Biblical verses only the substantives derived from the root *škr* describe the consequences of drinking[8a]; the substantive *šb*^{c}, in contrast, describes satiation caused by eating. Association with *šth* of both the roots *šb*^{c} and *škr* is found in Hebrew only in the Gemara Babli Sukka 49b. Here the fourth century Amoraite Pappa defines the words *šekār lYHWH* (Nu. 28:7) as follows: *šekār l*^{e}*šon š*^{e}*tiyā, l*^{e}*šon š*^{e}*bi*^{c}*ā, l*^{e}*šon šikrut* - '*šekār* signifies drinking, satiation and drunkenness.' It is remarkable how exactly the nexus of the three terms fits Ugaritic. Moreover, the underlying concept in Pappa's definition is clearly of old and stands in flat contradiction to the ancient translations of the Bible, which carefully avoid any expression reminiscent of the concept of drunkenness. The Septuagint is content with a transliteration of *šekār*. TO translates *n*^{e}*sik d*^{e}*ḥ*^{a}*mar* ^{c}*attiq* - 'a libation of old wine' - and the Syriac translation (Pešiṭta) means the same: *nuqāyā' d*^{ec}*atiqā'*. The Vulgate goes furthest, leaving these words completely untranslated, which indicates that they were an embarassment for

---

8 H.P. Rüger, *UF* 1, p. 204.

8a But cf. also Jer. 46:10; Is. 66:11; Am. 4:8.

Hieronymus.[9] R. Pappa's interpretation, which runs counter to all the foregoing, apparently relays an old, suppressed oral tradition, a view also supported by the fact that it is in Hebrew, not Aramaic.[9a]

Another example of the continuity of Canaanite tradition is offered by the Talmudic explanation of the Biblical expression *ben* ^{c}*enäkā* (Ex. 13: 9 etc.). This idiomatic usage is explained as follows in Talmud Babli Menahot 37a: *ben* ^{c}*enäkā zu qodqod, hekā'? 'āmre d*^{e}*be Yannai. māqom šämmo*^{a}*ḥ hattinoq ropes. - 'ben* ^{c}*enäkā* means the skull. On what part? It was said in the school of R. Jannai: where the skull of a babe is still tender'[10] i.e. the fontanel. The authenticity of the first part of this definition is proved by an Ugaritic verse, in which it is stated: *ylm qdqd zbl ym // bn* ^{c}*nm ṯpṭ nhr* (*CTA* 2:IV:24-25) 'he strikes on the skull Sea, the ruler; between the eyes River, the judge.' The same substantive *qdqd* which in the Ugaritic text stands as the parallel to *bn* ^{c}*nm* is used in the Talmud to define this idiomatic expression.

More problematic is the usage *ben yadäka* (Zech. 13:6), which today is generally taken as meaning the breast. The Talmud thinks otherwise, however. In Mishna Makkot 3:10 it is stated: "And how many times does one strike him? Forty less one ... R. Judah says: he receives a full forty strokes, and where is he struck (on the fortieth stroke)? Between his shoulders (*ben k*^{e}*tepayim*)". In the Gemara Babli Makkot 22b R. Isaac poses the question:

---

[9] Unfortunately, there is no list of the expressions left untranslated by Hieronymus. I have come across the following three: 1) *we hammiṣpā '*^{a}*šär 'āmar* (Gen. 31:49); 2) *'*^{a}*šär dibber 'itto* (Gen. 35:13); 3) Gen. 49:32 (*in toto*). In all these three cases the Vulgate omits words which are attested in the Septuagint but queried by modern textual criticism. The problem of their omission in the Vulgata deserves further investigation.
[Compare also the omission of ^{c}*al š*^{e}*ne k*^{e}*bāšim* (Lev. 23:20); *'otām w* (Nu. 26:10), *b*^{e}*yad mošä* (Nu. 27:23). The tendency of revising the text is most tangible in the Vulgate on Lev. 5:23-24 where Masoretic *'ät hagg*^{e}*zelā '*^{a}*šär gāzāl 'o 'ät hā*^{c}*ošäq '*^{a}*šär* ^{c}*āšāq 'o 'ät happiqqādon '*^{a}*šär hopqad 'itto 'o 'ät hā'*^{a}*bedā '*^{a}*šär māṣā'. 'o mikkol '*^{a}*šär yiššāba*^{c} ^{c}*ālāw laššäqär* is corresponded by Latin: *omnia quae per fraudem voluit obtinere*. It seems that Hieronymus substituted here purposely a short all-comprising definition for what seemed to him a cumbersome casuistic enumeration.]

[[9a] On parallel passages in Rabbinical literature and their interpretation see Lieberman, *loc. cit.* (note 5a), pp. 557-558.]

[10] On the root *rps* cf. Z. Ben-Hayyim in *S. Yeivin Jubilee Volume*, Jerusalem (1970), pp. 428-432 (in Heb.).

"What is R. Judah's reason?" The answer is: "Because it is written *ma hammakkot haellä ben yādäkā*". For R. Isaac it is obvious that the expressions *ben yādäkā* and *ben k^e^tepäkā* are synonymous and that the fortieth stroke likewise is given on the back, since *ben k^e^tepayim* undoubtedly refers to the back, and cf. 1 Sam. 17:6.

In Ugaritic we find: *hlm ktp zbl ym // bn ydm [ṯp]ṭ nhr* (*CTA* 2:IV:14-15) i.e. the parallel *ktp // bn ydm*. It might be admitted that in this case the Ugaritic parallel and the Talmudic definition are not in complete conformity, since we read *ben hakk^e^tepayim* in the Talmud, but simply *ktp* in Ugaritic. We should take into account however that the shoulder can hardly represent a synonymous parallel to the expression *bn ydm*; *ktp* should therefore better be understood as a breviloquence for *bn ktpm*, necessitated by the metre (and perhaps also the formal analogy to *qdqd*). The Talmudic definition, given in simple, everyday language, is here more exact than its Ugaritic counterpart, which is modified by the demands of poetic style.[10a]

[[10a] Cf. H.L. Ginsberg, *JPOS* 15 (1935), p. 327; *KU*, p. 73, who already explained *ben yādayim* 'on the back'. Contrast Gray, *Legacy*², p. 27, note 2 who refers to Arabic *bayna yadayhi* 'before' as supporting the interpretation 'on the chest' and G.R. Driver, *JSS* 12 (1967), p. 108, who adduces Akkadian *birti aḫīja imḫasuma* 'they struck me between my arms' i.e. 'on the chest' as proof for this exegesis. Gray and Driver were followed by J.C. de Moor, *Studies in Semitic Lexicography*, Firenze 1973, p. 99, note 2 who argues that the very late Talmudical interpretation cited by the present writer, cannot be regarded as reliable evidence.

After reconsideration it seems to me that a new solution imposes itself. Ugaritic *bn ydm* is paralleled by *ktp* in the very same way as *bn ^c^nm* by synonymous *qdqd*. Therefore *bn ydm* should simply be taken as a synonym of *ktp* 'shoulder', that is to say that *ben yādäkā* (Zech. 13:6) means 'on your shoulder(s)'. In the light of this evidence even Akkadian *birti aḫīja* should be given the sense 'on my shoulder(s)', since the usual explanation 'on my chest' (cf. e.g. *CAD, s.v. biritu*, 3, 2', b. 1') is no more than guess-work. Arabic *bayna yadayhi* 'before' does not designate a part of the body and therefore fails to provide any clue.

In contrast to *ben yādāw, ben k^e^tepāw* hardly can mean 'on his shoulders', although this interpretation would yield sense in 1 Sam. 17:6 and conform with the Gemara Makkot 22b. However, the obvious rendering of 'on his shoulders' in Hebrew would be *^c^al k^e^tepāw* not *ben k^e^tepāw*. The latter expression should either be interpreted to mean 'in the midst of both his shoulders' or as an idiomatic use corresponding to *ben ^c^enāw* and *ben yādāw*. If we prefer the second possibility we are left with the choice between either, 'on his breast' or 'on his back'. The context in 1 Sam. 17:6 tips the balance in favour of the second explanation.]

A further residuum of Old-Canaanite style in the Talmud has recently been pointed out by A. Demsky.[11] Špš threatens Mot who fights Baal with the words: *ik al yšm[^{c}]k ṯr il abk lys^c alt ṯbtk lyhpk ksa mlkk lyṯbr ḫt mṯpṭk* (*CTA* 6:VI:26-29). 'How should not hear of you the bull Il your father? He'll pull out your ... of dwelling, overturn your chair of kingship, break your staff of dominion!' The similarity of this threat to the formula of curse concluding the Old-Phoenician inscription of *Aḥiram* has generally been noticed. Demsky added that one element of this complex formula proved to be very tenacious, viz. the overthrowing of the chair. It returns in Haggai where a prophecy reads: *w^{e}hāpakti kisse' mamlākot* (Hag. 2:22) 'and I will overthrow the chair of kingdoms' and even reappears in a Talmudic source of the third century (Babli, Gittin 35a). The passage deals with a widow who felt herself wronged by a sentence of Rabba Rab bar Huna and cursed the judge with the words: *apkuh l^{e}kurseh*. 'Throw over his chair'. Those present, in order to invalidate the force of this curse, actually overthrew the chair of the judge and immediately set it up again. In spite of this apotropaic measure the cursed man was stricken with feableness from then on.

With this we come to the end of an admittedly small list of Talmudic parallels. It should not be forgotten, however, that we are still far from completing a thorough examination of the Talmudic material in this connection and the results profferred have been obtained only by chance observation.

Ugaritic-Greek Parallels

The progress of research into comparative Ugaritic and Greek literature has most recently been surveyed by P. Walcot.[12] His survey shows that until now only one Ugaritologist has chosen to use this approach in research into the Ugaritic language, viz. E. Ullendorff.[13] His proposals should therefore be accorded the utmost gravity, since they raise the general question of whether research of the Ugaritic language is entitled and bound to take into consideration Greek texts and if so to what extent?

---

[11] *Lĕšonênu* 34 (1970), pp. 185f. (in Heb.).

[12] P. Walcot, *UF* 1, pp. 111-126; id., *UF* 2, pp. 273-275.

[13] E. Ullendorff, *Orientalia* 20 (1951), pp. 271ff.

Ullendorff explains two Ugaritic expressions by reference to Homeric parallels. The first of these describes the state of joyful excitement with the words *wyprq lṣb wyṣḥq* (*CTA* 6:III:16; 17:II:10). He compares the problematic substantive *lṣb* to the Arabic *lṣb* VIII 'to be narrow' and concludes that the Ugaritic usage signifies the dividing or opening of a narrow place. The question, which narrow place is meant, is answered in his opinion by the common homeric phrase: ποιόν σε ἔπος φύγεν ἕρκος ὀδόντων "What word has escaped from the narrowness of your teeth?" Accordingly, the Ugaritic term would relate to the narrow gap which opens between the teeth when a person laughs with joy. Now, it is immediately obvious that the two texts are not entirely on all fours. The Ugaritic text actually talks about joyful excitement, while the Greek does not. On the other hand, Homer expressly mentions the teeth, while this is lacking in the Ugaritic text.

We would therefore have to impute to the Ugaritic poet a somewhat cross breviloquence, since a narrow space between the teeth cannot normally be referred to in brief as 'the narrowness', without further explanation. Moreover, as we have already pointed out elsewhere, the interpretation of ἕρκος as 'narrow place' is not tenable.[14] This finally disproves the assumed analogy between the Ugaritic and Homeric texts. As far as the noun *lṣb* is concerned, we suggested in the same article the meaning 'mouth', which fits the context of both, the text before us and of *U* 5, pp. 548, 551, text 1V°:4, and we explained it in the present text as having to do with the opening of the mouth[14a] in joyful laughter, pointing also to the analogy of the Arabic *prq* 'to divide'.

Ullendorff's second *interpretatio Graeca*[15] concerns the famous epithet of Baal *rkb* ᶜ*rpt*, which is generally interpreted as 'Rider of the Clouds'. Here again Ullendorff combines reference to the language of Homer with Semitic considerations. He points to the fact that Zeus, the Rain-God in Homer, also bears the epithet νεφεληγερέτης 'The Cloud-Gatherer' and that

---

14 See in this volume, *A Didactic Ugaritic Drinkers' Burlesque*, p. 380.

[14a Contrast Caquot-Sznycer, *Textes* 1, p. 204 who translate: "*Il déride le front*" and remark: "*Il est maintenant certain, grace au text inédit 24. 247 que lṣb signifie 'le front'*."]

15 Ullendorff, *BJRL* 46 (1963/4), pp. 243f.

this epithet fits perfectly for Baal, who is likewise known as the bringer of rain. Accordingly, it can be no coincidence that this epithet also appears in those Ugaritic verses concerning this particular characteristic of Baal, as e.g. in the line *[ṭ]l šmm šmn arṣ rbb [r]kb ᶜrpt* (*CTA* 3:II:39-40). 'The dew of the heavens, the fat of the earth, the rain of the cloud-gatherer.' This new interpretation imposed by the subject matter, can be corroborated by an examination of the Semitic root *rkb*: the root actually exists in Ethiopic with the meaning (*inter alia*) 'to put together', and the same is true of Arabic *rkb* II, the *Paᶜel* of the root in Syriac, and its *Hiphᶜil* in Middle-Hebrew. The semantic development of its meaning is explained by South Arabic in which *rkb* means the harnessing of a beast of burden. Furthermore, we should adduce, by way of comparison the semantic range of ξεύγνυμι which also means both 'to harness' and 'to put together'.

The above proposal has provoked a lively discussion. J.P. Brock[16] appends to Ullendorff's arguments the comment that in Arabic the verb designates particularly the gathering of the clouds, citing *tarākaba assaḥāba* - 'the clouds were / became heaped; piled upon one another'. He further maintains that the meaning 'to put together' is also demonstrable in Biblical Hebrew, in which the words *harkeb yādᵉkā ᶜal haqqäšät* (2 Reg. 13:16) require the meaning 'join, combine, grasp' for *harkeb*. As additional evidence for Ancient Hebrew he adduces a document from Arad in which it is stated: *wmᶜwd hqmḥ hr'šn trkb qmḥ lᶜṣt lḥm*. Brock rejects Ben-Ḥayyim's correction of *trkb* to *trbk* 'mix' and translates: 'and from the residue of the first flour scrape together flour to make bread'. He also notes that in Syriac *rkb* is attested as meaning 'to harness'. His conclusion is that the basic meaning of the root *rkb* is 'to put together' and that it receives striking confirmation from comparison of *rkb ᶜrpt* with νεφεληγερέτης. His arguments have been strongly opposed by C.J. Cathcart[17], however, who rightly maintains that *harkeb* in 2 Reg. 13:16 means 'to place on' and suggests that *trkb* in the Arad document should be understood as the denominative of *räkäb* 'the upper millstone' i.e. 'to mill'. For *rkb* in Ugaritic he refers to the verse: *wᶜl lẓr [mg]dl rkb ṯkmm ḥm[t]* (*CTA* 14:II:75), 'climb up onto the tower, be on the shoulder of the wall'. He concludes that the basic meaning of *rkb* is

---

[16] J.B. Brock, *VT* 18 (1968), p. 395.

[17] K.J. Cathcart, *VT* 19 (1969), pp. 121-123.

'to mount' from which developed the secondary meaning 'to construct, pile up'. Accordingly 'the Rider of the Clouds' should be retained as the correct translation.

For the sake of completeness it should be noted that B. Otzen[18] recently interpreted *trkb* in the Arad document as 'loading and transporting', on the basis of 2 Sam. 6:3; 2 Reg. 9:29.[19]

On methodological grounds a discussion of the root *rkb* should omit mention of the Arad document, whose meaning is totally obscure, and concentrate only on the undisputed meanings of the root. Further, it should be stated at the outset that the variant meanings of ξεύγνυμι are of no assistance to the investigation at hand. It is true that the Greek verb can signify 'to put together' as well as 'to harness' but it lacks the meaning of riding on a beast or a chariot. As regards the root *rkb* itself, the assumption of a semantic shift from harness to riding seems rather far-fetched. A more likely point of departure for all meanings of the root are the concepts of carrying up and bringing up. This may be illustrated by the Middle-Hebrew usage, in which *hirkib* means 'to graft', in other words 'the putting of a branch on a tree'. In this way we obtain the semantic shift from 'to put on' to 'to put together', which for its part explains the use 'to harness'. 'To ride' can be derived without difficulty from the basic meaning 'to climb up'. It should be pointed out however that this consideration is not decisive for the interpretation of *rkb* ^{c}*rpt*. One cannot have a rule saying that a root in a doubtful case should be given its basic meaning, when there in fact exists a well-attested secondary meaning that is contextually possible, as is the case in Semitic for the use of *rkb* in the sense of 'putting together'. More important for the answer to our problem is Cathcart's argument, mentioned above, that the only other example of the root in Ugaritic requires the translation 'to be above (something)', which is very close to 'ride'. But this argument is also not absolutely cogent being

---

[18] B. Otzen, *VT* 20 (1970), pp. 239-242.

[19] This explanation was mentioned by Y. Aharoni, *BIES* 30 (1966), p. 34 (in Heb.) earlier than Otzen, but was dismissed by him. *[*But similarly now Y. Aharoni, *Arad Inscriptions*, Jerusalem 1975, pp. 13-14, 1:7 (in Heb.) who argues against Otzen that flour was transported not by cart but rather by ass and therefore explains 'Load (upon an ass)'. Even this proposal is doubtful, since *hrkb* is not attested in the sense 'to load an unanimate object upon an animal'.*]*

open to the objection that *rkb* might possibly appear in Ugaritic in any one of its attested Semitic meanings. Such a possibility could be raised to the level of probability were Ullendorff right in saying that the context of the Ugaritic epic requires the translation 'cloud-gatherer'. But this is not the case. The use of the epithet *rkb* ᶜ*rpt* is actually not restricted to texts in which Baal is portrayed as the giver of rain, but has a much wider currency[20] which cannot simply be dismissed as secondary. A decisive point here is the proximity of the Ugaritic *rkb* ᶜ*rpt* to the Biblical divine epithet *hārokeb bā*ᶜᵃ*rābot* (Ps. 68:5), which therefore deserves to be more closely examined. The meaning of ᶜᵃ*rābot* had already been forgotten in the time of the Septuagint, which **translated** τῷ ἐπιβεβηκότι ἐπὶ τῶν δυσμῶν; following which the Vulgate has *ei qui ascendit super occasum*, and the Syriac translation *l*ᵉ*drākib l*ᵉ*ma*ᶜ*arbā'*. The old translations therefore mistook ᶜᵃ*rābot* for *ma*ᶜᵃ*rāb* - the West. In modern exegesis the translation 'steppe' has been adopted, and P. Haupt[21] was the only modern researcher to sense the true meaning of this substantive, proposing the conjecture ᶜ*ābot* (cf. Is. 19:1). Since the publication of the Ugaritic texts it is generally acknowledged that ᶜᵃ*rābot* means 'clouds', Ugarit ᶜ*rpt* being parallel to Akkadian *erpetu urpatu* 'cloud' and ᶜᵃ*rābot* being nothing more than a variant of ᶜ*rpt*.[22] The variation of *p* in Ugaritic and *b* in Hebrew is rightly regarded as no objection. Cf. the variation of the roots *lbš* and *lpš*, *nbr* and *npr* in Ugaritic, and of the words *nšb* and *nšp* in Hebrew, and the forms *hibqidām* (= *hipqidām*) and *nabš*ᵉ*käm* (= *napš*ᵉ*käm*) in a Hebrew document from Arad.[23] It cannot be argued against the generally accepted identity of the Hebrew and Ugaritic phrases that in Ugaritic *rkb* takes the accusative of the direct object, while in Hebrew it takes a prepositional object, since we are dealing here with a free variant as the Hebrew *rokbe 'ᵃtonot* (Ju. 5:10) proves. Now, the Hebrew phrase, because of the preposition *b*, can only be interpreted as 'the Cloud-Rider'. Here lies the fundamental point. The Ugaritic *rkb* ᶜ*rpt* can be interpreted equally well as 'Cloud-gatherer' or 'Cloud-rider'. The first meaning finds support in the Homeric the second in the Hebrew *hārokeb*

---

[20] *CTA* 2:IV:8,29; 3:III:35; IV:48,50; 4:III:18; 5:II:7.

[21] P. Haupt, *ET*, 22, p. 375. I am quoting from Gesenius-Buhl, since I did not have access to his article.

[22] H.L. Ginsberg, *Orientalia* 5 (1936), p. 110; J. Greenfield, *HUCA* 29 (1958), pp. 226-228.

[23] Y. Aharoni, *EI* 9 (1969), pp. 10-11 (in Heb.).

bāᶜarābot. The superiority of the *interpretatio Hebraica* over the *interpretatio Graeca* is self-evident, since there is literal conformity between Hebrew and Ugaritic on all decisive points.[24]

We have left open until now the question whether the Ugaritic-Hebrew phrase has in mind riding on a beast or on a chariot. Ps. 18:11 can be cited as an example of the former meaning, where God rides on a cherub; for the second Hab. 3:8, which depicts God 'riding' on a chariot drawn by horses. We have no verses in Ugaritic which give a closer description of Baal's riding, and only of the *rpum* is it said: *tᶜln lmrkbthm* (*CTA* 20:B:4) 'they climb into their chariot', but this is no proof for Baal. [But cf. now in the second amulet from Arslan - Tash, verso, ll. 1-2 the words: *bᶜl 'sr mrkbty* 'Baal harnessed his chariot'.[24a]] On the other hand, there seems to be evidence that a Canaanite conception was preserved in Apollodorus Mythographus I:VI:3 in his description of the battle of Zeus against Typhon. It is highly significant that in this tradition ὄρος Κάσιον is mentioned, i.e. Jebl 'Aqraᶜ, situated North of Ugarit, the classical seat of Baal Zapon, which later became the seat of Ζεὺς Κάσιος. It is noteworthy that Zeus is described in this chapter as ἐπὶ πτηνῶν ἵππων ὀχούμενος ἅρματι, i.e., as riding in a chariot drawn by winged horses. This description, reminiscent of Helios the Sun-God's chariot harnessed with winged horses, is unique in the Greek Zeus-myth, and it is a fairly safe hypothesis that the Canaanite myth of Baal riding on his cloud-chariot has here been interwoven into the Greek myth of the Sun-god. Our investigation confirms the conclusions of S. Mowinckel[25], who understood *rokeb bāᶜarābot* of Psalm 68 as the charioter of the cloud-chariot. [The Greek attestation of Zeus' chariot is not confined to Apollodorus.[26] Nevertheless it appears that the story of Apollodorus re-

---

24 This very obvious question has been passed over in silence by Ullendorff, *loc. cit.* (note 15). Brock, *loc. cit.* (note 16), puts forward the daring conjecture that the Hebrew phrase is due to a misunderstanding of the ancient Canaanite. But no misunderstanding of this sort has ever been suggested until now, let alone demonstrated. Cf. also the epithet of Ninurta, *rākib abūbi* (*CAD, s.v. abūbu*), 'the one who rides (or drives) on the storm', and not 'the storm-gatherer'.

[24a See A. Caquot - R. du Mesnil du Buisson, *Syria* 48 (1971), pp. 392, 396.]

25 S. Mowinckel, *VT* 12 (1962), p. 299.

[26 Cf. the detailed descriptions of Zeus' chariot drawn by horses in Iliad 8:41-46; 438-441 referred to in M. Weinfeld's instructive paper '*Rider of the Clouds and Gatherer of the Clouds*', *JANES* 5 (1973), pp. 421-426. Cf. also Platon's description of Zeus as ἐλαύνων πτηνὸν ἅρμα (*Phaedros*

sults from a blend of Greek and Canaanite traditions.*]*

In conclusion it may be said that the only attempts to utilize Homer for the linguistics of Ugaritic texts have failed. Greek texts can be considered a useful aid if their dependence on Canaanite conceptions is clear. Even then they should be employed with extreme caution, since one always has to reckon with a certain adaptation of oriental tradition to the Greek mind.

---

246 E) 'driving a winged chariot i.e. one drawn by winged horses and Pindar's address of Zeus as ἐλατὴρ ὑπέρτατε βροντᾶς ἀκαμαντόποδος (*Olympia* 4:1) 'Driver on high of the tireless footed thunder' and the beginning of a lost hymn of Pindar: ἐλασίβροντα παῖ Ῥέας 'Thunder-driving son of Rhea' and Hesychius commentary that the thunder was thought the chariot of Zeus. See also the discussion of this problem by A.B. Cook, *Zeus*, Cambridge 1, 1914, p. 338; 2, 1925, pp. 830-833.

The question needs further investigation, since it is obvious that Zeus' specific character as the god of thunder and rain is connected with his representation as a driver of a chariot in Pindar's hymns only.*]*

m ṣ d

The publication of text RS 24.258 in *U* 5 (text 1, pp. 545-547) has lead to renewed discussion on the meaning of *mṣd*. Opinions are diametrically opposed. C. Virolleaud[1] prudently refrained from translating the word at all. H.P. Rüger[2] interpreted it as *Wildbret*, J.C. de Moor[3] as 'a sacrifice of game'. I[4] explained the noun as synonymous with *dbḥ* and translated *Bankett* from the context. Similarly, B. Margulis[5] assigned the meaning 'feast'. Finally, de Moor[6] has insisted once more that the word can only mean 'game' or "sacrifice of the spoils of game'. The problem is taken up here again.

The text mentioned above describes a divine banquet held by Il. If, in fact, venison is mentioned in this description, it would be a completely isolated case, as elsewhere in accounts of banquets given by gods only the meat of domestic animals is mentioned. The most detailed list of such animals is *CTA* 4:VI:40-43 which describes Baal's preparations for celebrating the inaugural ceremony of his palace, at which he is host to the gods. The texts referred to by de Moor must be differentiated from such descriptions. Let us consider first the epic text *CTA* 6:I which depicts a sacrifice for the dead by a goddess. The sacrifices are designated by the unexplained term *gmn*. Now these certainly include wild as well as domestic animals. However, there is nothing about a meal here. The peculiar character of this text is already clear in that the wild animals it numbers do not recur in descriptions of divine banquets or in liturgical specifications for sacrifice. Also, de Moor appeals to *U* 5, RS 24.260 (text 11:5, pp. 586-587) the only liturgical prescription for sacrifice from Ugarit, which lists, toge-

---

[1] C. Virolleaud, *U* 5, p. 547.

[2] H.P. Rüger, *UF* 1, pp. 203f.

[3] J.C. de Moor, *ibid.*, pp. 168f.

[4] S.E. Loewenstamm, *ibid.*, pp. 72f.

[5] B. Margulis, *UF* 2, pp. 72f.

[6] J.C. de Moor, *ibid.*, p. 347.

ther with the domestic animals, a sacrificial animal termed *tr*, i.e. the turtledove, known to be a migratory bird. This by itself is certainly interesting, and all the more noteworthy considering that the turtledove is the only wild animal to appear in Biblical prescriptions for sacrifice. We may, therefore, surmise that a relic of an ancient custom has here been preserved, with origins reaching back to one of the eras prior to the domestication of animals. There is, however, no support for the view that turtledoves were served up at banquets for gods, and even so they would only have been a minor part of the meal. Accordingly the conclusion is that the content of such a meal could in no way be flatly denoted 'quarry'.

After this general look at the concrete aspect of the question, let us turn to a literary investigation of both the texts mentioning *mṣd*. The epic sacrificial text in Krt runs: *šrd b^{c}l bdbḥk // bn dgn bmṣdk* (*CTA* 14:II:77-79) - 'Fetch Baal down[7] with your sacrifice // the son of Dagan with your *mṣd*'. Earlier, a lamb and a bird (called *msrr*, an unexplained word) were said to comprise the sacrifice. Even if we adopt the unsupported hypothesis that an undomesticated type of bird is involved, it still remains hard to understand how the whole sacrifice, including the lamb, could be denoted as game. Furthermore, there can be no doubt about the parallelism *dbḥ // mṣd*. The derivation of the noun *mṣd* from the recognised Arabic, Hebrew and possibly Ugaritic root *ṣyd* 'to hunt', leads to a dilemma, also discernible in the words of de Moor. For, either we must keep to the proposed root-meaning 'game', despite the parallelism, or we have to construct a semantic bridge from this meaning to the meaning required by the context and translate 'sacrifice of a captured living animal'.[8] Far more satisfactory is the procedu-

[7] Aistleitner, *WUS*, *s.v.* relates *šrd* to Hebrew *šrt* 'to serve'. Similarly, M. Held, *EI* 3 (1953), pp. 101-103, who also brings Hebrew *bigde ś^{e}rād* into the explanation. To be preferred, however, is the explanation of Ginsberg, *Keret*, p. 37, as *Š* of *yrd*. Cf. in Akkadian: *šu-pu-ur a-na[m] li-ši-ri-du-[nim-m]a* - 'Send that Anu be fetched down' (Lambert- Millard, *Atraḫasis* I:97, p. 48).

[8] This sort of semantic bridge-building is always to be regarded with suspicion. A classical example occurs in the Septuagint of Is. 2:16, where *kol ś^{e}kiyyot haḥămdā* has been transmitted as πᾶσαν θέαν πλοίων κάλλους i.e. the whole spectacle of beautiful ships. The translator related *ś^{e}kiyyot* to Aramaic *śkh*, 'to see' but at the same time realised from the context that the subject matter was ships. Accordingly he combined the presumed root-meaning 'spectacle' with 'ships', the meaning from the context. The problem, as is well known, has been solved through Ugaritic *ṯkt*, 'a kind of ship'. See further J. Barr, *JSS* 12 (1967), pp. 116f. An example of modern semantic

re of H.L. Ginsberg[9] who exclusively adheres to the context and renders *mṣd* 'oblation'.

This conclusion will be further confirmed by text RS 24.258:1-2. It runs: *il dbḥ bbth mṣd ṣd bqrb hklh*. With the exception of myself all the scholars mentioned above divide the first colon off at *mṣd*, that is to say, they interpret *dbḥ* as a verb, and both *mṣd* and *ṣd* as parallel, synonymous nouns derived from the same root. However, parallelism between such nouns would be contrary to style. Realization of this unsuitability is probably what lead Margulis to suggest correcting *ṣd* into *mṣd*. Instead, I have put forward the proposal that the first colon ends with *bbth*; *ṣd* would then be a verb with the noun *mṣd* as its internal object, parallel to *dbḥ*. In favour of the parallelism *dbḥ // mṣd* supposed here is its unquestionable occurrence in the Krt text. To confirm my division I refer to the following examples of *bbt // b(qrb) hkl* where the first colon ends in *bbt*: *ṣḥ ḫrn bbhtk // ᶜḏbt bqrb hklk* (*CTA* 4:V:75-76 cf. 91ß93); *bl ašt urbt bbhtm // ḥln bqrb hklm* (*ibid*. VII:17-19,25-27): *tšt išt bbhtm // nblat bhklm* (*ibid*. VI:22-23; cf. 24-26,26-28,29-31; *in bᶜl bbth* {*t*} *// il hd bqrb hklh* (*CTA* 10:II:4-5); *wykn bnh bbt // šrš bqrb hklh* (*CTA* 17:I:26-27 cf. 43-44). In all these examples (and they amount to more than a few), *bbt* ends the first colon. Examples where the reverse occurs are unknown which suggests a fixed principle of style. From the stichometrical division established here the conclusion must be that it is absurd to translate *mṣd* as 'venison' since it would result in the undeniably bizarre 'he hunted a venison in his palace'. Further, it must be pointed out that in the Krt text *mṣd* is a B-word to *dbḥ*, 'sacrifice', while in the other text it occurs as a B-word to *dbḥ*[10], 'banquet'.

---

constructions of this kind is *tištāᶜ* (Is. 41:10) which used to be analysed as the *Hitpaᶜel* of *šᶜh*, 'to look at' and interpreted 'to look for help' or 'to look anxiously round' to suit the context. However, today no one would question that the Proto-Semitic root *ṯtᶜ*, 'to fear' is involved, as documented in Ugaritic. These examples should serve as a warning against correcting on the basis of etymology where the meaning is clear from the context. *Vestigia terrent*!

[9] Ginsberg, *Keret*, p. 15. Contrast Gordon, *UT*, *Glossary* No. 2151 where *mṣd* is rendered 'provisions' in view of Hebrew *ṣedā*. Even this proposal has no etymological foundation especially as Hebrew *ṣedā* and Akkadian *ṣidītu* denote only provisions for a journey.

[10] Cf. *U* 5, 137:III:6 (pp. 244-245), where the Akkadian equivalent of Ugaritic *da-ab-ḫu* is *i-zi-nu* [Our proposal yields the translation: 'Il a banquet (was) in his house'. This amounts to saying that Il is the isolated logical subject of the sentence. Contrast E.L. Greenstein, *JANES* 6 (1974),

This amounts to saying that *mṣd* corresponds to both meanings of *dbḥ*, also known from Hebrew *zäbah*, and covers the same semantic range. If this is true, then *mṣd* can no longer be understood on these grounds as game. Whether we should posit a Proto-Semitic root *ṣyd* II, synonymous to *dbḥ* and homonymous with Proto-Semitic *ṣyd*, 'to hunt', or prefer to derive *mṣd* from a hypothetical Proto-Semitic root *ḍyd*, is not in question here.

We agree with de Moor that the easiest course is to interpret Punic *ṣd*, occurring in the Marseilles sacrificial tariff in the expression *zbḥ ṣd*, as a synonym of Ugaritic *mṣd*. However, nothing can be ascertained from the context regarding the meaning of *ṣd* and both the etymologising explanations 'food-sacrifice' and 'sacrifice of game' are baseless.[11] Closer to the truth would be to interpret *zbḥ* and *ṣd*, in the light of Ugaritic, as two synonymous nouns in the construct state. That words found in other texts either in parallelism or parataxis (or both) occur together in the construct state is a phenomenon met with more often than commonly recognized. My student Y. Avishur has made a comprehensive study (soon to be published)[11a] of word-pairs in Biblical Hebrew which are also found in the construct relation. For the purpose of the present paper it is sufficient to make brief reference to the expressions *šeʾer bāšār* (Lev. 18:6; 25:49) and *śimḥat gili* (Ps. 43:4).

In sum it may be ventured that to approach *mṣd* via etymology leads to unacceptable conclusions while an analysis based on context guarantees a clear and plausible interpretation.

---

p. 92, who interprets "*dbḥ* in our passage as an intransitive verb or a transitive verb with an elliptical object" and appeals to *CTA* 14:II:76. Compare also M. Held apud Greenstein, *ibid.*, note 27, who suggests the reading: *il dbḥ <dbḥ> bbth*. Contrast in this volume, *A Didactic Ugaritic Drinker's Burlesque*, note 9, p. 372.]

11 *KAI* 2, pp. 84, 86 "*zbḥ ṣd.. entweder 'Speiseopfer' oder 'Jagdopfer'*".

[11a See now *Semitics* 2 (1971/72), pp. 17-81; id., *The Construct State of Synonyms in Biblical Rhetoric*, Jerusalem 1977 (in Heb. with English Summary.]

The Divine Grants of Land to the Patriarchs

In his stimulating and amply documented paper *The Covenant of Grant in the Old Testament and the Ancient Near East*, Moshe Weinfeld[1] dwells upon the parallels between the divine grants of land, priesthood, and kingdom in the Old Testament and analogous human grants attested to in treaties of the ancient Near East. In the following note we shall try to supplement his research on the grants of land with some additional remarks.

In every legal or quasi-legal declaration, one should distinguish between the operative part and eventual concomitant statements. This rule applies to the divine grants of land as well. Let us therefore begin with an analysis of the operative part, i.e. the formula of grant proper. A short glance at these formulas in Genesis reveals the existence of two clearly distinct types:

a. The land is given to the patriarch himself and his seed: (Gen. 13:15; 17:8; 26:3; 28:4,13; 35:12);

b. The grant is restricted to the patriarch's seed (Gen. 12:7; 15:18; 24:7; 48:4).

It is worthwhile mentioning that this difference cannot be connected with the division of sources. In the *El Shaddai* texts, commonly attributed to *P*, one finds three instances in which the donee is the patriarch and his posterity (Gen. 17:8; 28:4; 35:12) and one instance in which it is his posterity alone (Gen. 48:4). In the other texts, ascribed to *JE*, one encounters the first formula twice (Gen. 28:4; 35:12) and the second three times (Gen. 12:7; 15:18; 24:7).

How may these variations be accounted for? It is rather obvious that the clearly promissory formula restricting the grant to the seed of the patriarch is vindicated by the context, as Biblical historiography attributes the possession of the land exclusively to the descendants of the patriarchs, never to the patriarchs themselves. In contradistinction, the other

[1] M. Weinfeld, *JAOS* 90 (1970), pp. 184-203.

formula gives the impression of a transfer of land with immediate effect, although no such transfer is intended. The sources of this puzzling style of formulation should apparently be sought in the profane formula of grant of land, by which possession is invariably bestowed upon the donee and his children for all generations. This standard legal formula of setting up contracts of grant influenced the formulation of the Biblical text, although, in a strict sense, the formula is inappropriate in Genesis.

It has already been noted[2] that in the *El Shaddai* texts the posterity is called *zar*^{ca}*kā 'aḥ*^{a}*räkā* (Gen. 17:8; 35:12; 48:4) 'your seed after you' or *zar*^{ca}*kā 'itt*^{e}*kā* (Gen. 28:4) your seed with you; in the other texts, however, it is simply *zar*^{ca}*kā*. R. Yaron[3] has pointed to the parallels of the expression *zar*^{ca}*kā 'aḥ*^{a}*räkā* in the Elephantine documents of the 5th century BCE. It is worthwile stressing that the Near Eastern analogies to *zar*^{ca}*kā 'aḥ*^{a}*räkā* are limited to these late documents and are never found in older treaties. A parallel to *zar*^{ca}*kā 'itt*^{e}*kā* was not found in ancient Near Eastern texts at all, and in the Bible it is found only in the clearly priestly passages: Lev. 10:15; Nu. 18:11, 19.

After these comments upon the operative part of the formulas, we should like to add some remarks about the concomitant part of the text. As a formulation, connected with the promise to Abraham, Weinfeld quotes "in as much as Abraham obeyed and kept my charge, my rules, my laws and my teachings" (Gen. 26:5). In Weinfeld's opinion, this formula is congenerous with similar Akkadian material and should not be considered as Deuteronomic. Weinfeld admits that *šāma*^{c} *b*^{e}*qol* is very frequently found in the Deuteronomic literature, but denies that this term was coined by the Deuteronomic school and adds that the origin of *šāmar mišmärät* is likewise not Deuteronomic. His proof against the Deuteronomic character of the passage is the combination of *ḥuqqim w*^{e}*torot*, never found in Deuteronomic literature but attested in *JE* (Ex. 18:16). His argument is open to discussion from various points of view. To start with, the passage explains the reason for the grant to Isaac, but does not refer to a grant to Abraham, whose godfearing behaviour

---

[2] Cf. e.g. J. Hoftijzer, *Die Verheissungen an die drei Erzväter*, Leiden 1956, p. 6, note 3.

[3] R. Yaron, *The Law of the Elephantine Documents*, Jerusalem, 1961, pp. 82f.; 165 (in Heb.).

justifies the covenant with his son. Abraham's merits are the foundation of the favour bestowed upon his son. This justification of the grant is anything but typical for the divine grants of land in Genesis and its pious fervour arouses suspicion that it is a later addition. Furthermore, the only expression for which a straight-forward Akkadian parallel can be claimed, is *šāmar mišmärät*. The Deuteronomistic influence upon this text is clearly indicated by the cluster of four appositions, *mišmärät, miṣwā, ḥuqqā, torā*, which is out of line with the style of Genesis, but is in perfect accord with the Deuteronomic style of speech; cf. Deut. 11:1 and elsewhere. Therefore, we may confidently stick to the common supposition that Gen. 26:5 stems from a writer influenced by the Deuteronomic school.

A word may be added about Gen. 15. Weinfeld dismisses our argument[4] that the sacrifice is a late element in this tradition, although he concedes that the passing between the parts symbolizes a self-curse. He argues, however, that the element of self-curse does not nullify the sacrificial character of the ceremony and states that this character disappeared only in the first millenium. We fail to see how the ceremony of a sacrifice to the deity and that of a divine self-curse could possibly have been combined. Moreover, Weinfeld himself points to the *Abba-El - Yarimlim* deed from Alalakh (15th cent. BCE), in which the cutting of the neck of a lamb symbolizes a self-curse, not a sacrifice.[4a]

---

[4] See in this volume, *The Covenant between the Pieces*, pp. 273-280.

[4a] *JCS* 12 (1958), p. 126:39-42.

The Killing of Mot in Ugaritic Myth

Ever since the decipherment of mythological tablets from Ugarit, the seasonal interpretation of this myth has held a foremost place. The pivot of this system of exegesis is a scene describing the killing of Mot by Baal's sister Anat. From the very beginning of Ugaritic research it has been argued that in that scene Anat treated Mot as if he were grain, i.e. a symbol of fertility, whose fate is connected with the seasons of the year.

This idea has been propounded in different ways. Ch. Virolleaud[1] stressed the description of Mot being sown in the field. According to his reasoning this action of Anat points to the destiny of seed which dies but produces a new plant which will in its turn bloom again. In contrast to Virolleaud, R. Dussaud[2] emphasized Mot's destruction which should be considered as symbolizing the sacrifice of the last sheaf, a rite performed in order to preserve the fertility of the field.

Virolleaud's view has been contested by the late U. Cassuto[3] and by the present writer[4] who proposed the thesis that the Ugaritic text under discussion should be considered as the prototype of the Biblical story of the destruction of the Golden Calf since both accounts represent the same literary pattern emphasizing utmost destruction.

---

[1] Ch. Virolleaud, *Journal des Savants* 1931, p. 172. Cf. de Moor, *Seasonal Pattern*, pp. 9-10.

[2] R. Dussaud, *RHR* 104 (1931), pp. 353-408. Cf. de Moor, *op. cit.*, pp. 10-13.

[3] U. Cassuto, *BJPES* 9 (1941/42), pp. 45-51 = *IEJ* 12 (1962), pp. 72-86.

[4] See also in this volume: *The Ugaritic Fertility Myth - the Result of a Mistranslation*, pp. 160-161; *The Ugaritic Fertility Myth - a Reply*, pp. 162-165; *The Making and Destruction of the Golden Calf*, pp. 236-245; *The Making and Destruction of the Golden Calf - a Rejoinder*, pp. 503-516; cf. F.E. Fensham, *IEJ* 16 (1966), pp. 191-193.

Our arguments have been discussed by J.C. de Moor[5] in his important book *The Seasonal Pattern in the Ugaritic Myth of Ba^{c}lu*, pp. 208-215. In his study, de Moor arrives at the conclusion that our arguments are not conclusive and returns to Virolleaud's approach, though in a way which modifies the essence of the interpretation. According to his reasoning, Mot is not the symbol of grain, sown in the fields, sprouting, and blooming again, but rather the symbol of grain, sown in a garden of Adonis where plants are rapidly withering. From this explanation de Moor draws the conclusion that a comparison between the killing of Mot and the destruction of the Golden Calf should not be admitted. In the following lines, his deductions shall be scrutinized. In order to make the issue clear, we shall first of all present his translation of Anat's actions in *CTA* 6:II:30-37, adding the gist of his explanation:

She seized the son of Ilu Motu;

De Moor refrains from explaining this passage in accordance with his system, but he remarks that "when Anatu first seizes him (i.e., Mot) by the hem of his robe (*CTA* 6:II:9-11) this might symbolize the ingathering of the reaped grain, which was done by women".

With the cutting blade she split him;

i.e., with the blades of the threshing-sledge.

With the sieve she winnowed him;

This winnowing becomes understandable in the light of the foregoing explanation.

With the fire she burnt him;

i.e. straw, shaff, weeds.

With the millstones she ground him,
in the field she sowed him;

De Moor tacitly supposes that one part of the grain was ground, the other sown.

The birds did eat his flesh,
the fowls consumed his limbs;

i.e. a part of the grain sown in the field. The other one was left and sprouted in good time.

---

[5] Cf. de Moor, *Seasonal Pattern*, pp. 24-25, 27.

Even in this exerted interpretation, the reaping of the grain remains unmentioned. The alleged hint to its ingathering is found in a scene preceding the killing of Mot by months. Let us recall the setting of this first encounter between Anat and Mot. Anat, being aware of the disappearance of her beloved brother Baal, suspects Mot of being his murderer. She therefore roves through the country in search for him. When encountering him at last, she seizes him by the hem of his robe and enquires of him the whereabouts of her brother. This seizing of the hem then underlines the dramatic character of her calling Mot to account. Nothing in the text could create any association with grain, let alone ingathering of reaped grain. The same applies to the second meeting of Anat with Mot, where she seizes him in order to split him with a *ḥrb*. The clear meaning of *ḥrb* is knife. De Moor adduces Syriac *ḥarbā' d^epaddānā* 'ploughshare' in order to prove that *ḥrb* may denote the cutting blade of a threshing-sledge as well. However, even in Syriac, *ḥarbā'* bears the unqualified meaning of a sword, not a ploughshare; and secondly, a threshing-sledge is not a plough. There is no indication whatsoever that Anat carried a threshing-sledge with her when roaming over the country in order to avenge her murdered brother. But it is quite reasonable to suppose that she was girded with a sword. It is obvious from the text that with one hand she gets hold of Mot and with the other slays him with her sword (cf. 2 Sam. 2:16; 20:9-10). Nothing in the text points to Anat throwing Mot down and afterwards drawing a threshing-sledge over him.

So far, then, no expression is used which could evoke any idea of grain. Admittedly the following winnowing with a sieve could refer to grain when taken by itself, but the very simile of winnowing is well-known from Biblical passages describing utter destruction, without any reference to grain (Jer. 15:7; Is. 41:16). It is further stated that Anat burnt Mot, an additional simile of total annihilation. De Moor's restriction of Anat's burning Mot to the burning of worthless by-products of grain is unwarranted. Everywhere the text speaks of Mot as of an undivided whole and does not differentiate between one part of him being burnt, another ground and a third "sown" in the field. The outstanding feature of this description is the unrealistic accumulation of different acts of destruction, each being a symbol of thorough extermination. This even applies to Mot's being "sown" in the field, because this act of Anat leads to Mot's flesh being eaten by the birds, the premeditated outcome of the "sowing". De Moor's explanation that the birds ate a part of the flesh only, is not borne out by the text. It may be added that the explicit mention of Mot's flesh does not fit the concept of seed, destined to sprout.

Only one word alone in the text seemingly supports de Moor's view, viz. the verb *dr*^{c} ('to sow'). De Moor admits in principle that *dr*^{c} may denote 'to scatter' as well, but argues that this explanation is far-fetched in the context *dr*^{c} *bšd* and adduces the analogy of Lev. 25:3; Ps. 107:37. It is evident, however, that pieces of flesh may be scattered in a field, but not sown. The conclusive proof of this view derives from the parallel text *CTA* 6:V:19, where Mot complains of having been 'sown' in the sea, which cannot mean anything but 'scattered'. In order to evade this obvious difficulty, de Moor draws attention to the "Gardens of Adonis", which were planted in pots and boxes and thrown into the sea after the rapid withering of their plants. We have already alluded to the radical change in the meaning of the supposed grain-myth implied in his proposal. But there is no need to elaborate upon this point. The ceremonial of the cult of Adonis is not attested to in Ugarit and certainly not alluded to in the Ugaritic text discussed here, counting two different symbols of complete disappearance: 1. scattering in the field combined with subsequent consumption by the birds; 2. scattering in the sea. There is no point in combining these two equivalent and alternative symbols by supposing a sowing of grain in a box (called field!) from which the birds pick a part of the seed (called the flesh!) and the ensuing throwing of this box into the sea (an action called 'sowing in the sea'). Only a resolute *eisegesis* can obtain explanations of this kind.

Another trend of exegesis followed Dussaud's concept that Anat's action symbolized the sacrifice of the last sheaf, although no such ceremony is attested neither in Ugaritic nor in Biblical literature.[5a] The last scholar who took up this idea was Hvidberg-Hansen in his article "*Die Vernich-*

[[5a] On the burial of the last sheaf (sic, not its sacrifice!) see Dalman, *AuS* I, 2, pp. 574-579, who describes this rite, observed by the Arabic rural population. In the wake of Frazer's ideology Dalman ascribes to this custom the original(!) aim of preserving the fertility of the earth and even hypothesizes that such fertility rites were observed already in Biblical times. In Dalman's opinion it is due to theological censorship that this heathen practice is not mentioned in the Bible. But why did neither the Bible nor the Talmudical literature include any prohibition?]

tung des Goldenen Kalbes und der Ugaritische Ernteritus", *AcOr* 37 (1971), pp. 1-46.[6] This author combines Dussaud's view with the present writer's thesis that both the story of killing Mot and the account of the destroying of the Golden Calf represent the same literary pattern, viz. the pattern of punishment by way of utmost annihilation. He also admits that no other idea be extant in the story of the Golden Calf, but contends that in the myth of Mot's killing the penalty of complete destruction represents the additional idea of a rite of fertility.

The compatibility of these two lines of interpretation is anything but evident. But let us concentrate upon the indications of a fertility rite, adduced by Hvidberg-Hansen. To start with, he asserts that the *ḥrb* splitting Mot should be considered a sickle. However, the verb *bq*^{c} 'split' describes the action of a sword, not that of a sickle, and the noun *ḥrb* is not attested in the meaning suggested by Hvidberg-Hansen. The winnowing of Mot is compared by the author to Egyptian texts describing the worship of Osiris. In that cult men were burnt and their ashes dispersed by winnowing-shovels. The comparison neglects the fact that the Ugaritic text describes the winnowing of Mot as preceding his destruction by fire. Mot burnt and milled is related to the Biblical law prescribing the offering of first fruit: *'ābib qāluy bā'eš gäräš karmäl* (Lev. 2:14) 'young ears parched with fire and groats of fresh fruit' - an interpretation mixing up *qlh* 'to roast, parch' with *śrp* 'to burn'. The "sowing" of Mot in the field calls to the author's mind the sowing described as a part of the cult of Adonis in Is. 17:10, the eating of the birds the law of the fallow year in Ex. 23:11, which destines to the wild beasts whatever has been left by the poor. The author's explanation of the "sowing in the sea" coincides with de Moor's proposal, discussed above. To sum up: Farfetched associations to heterogeneous sources are welded in order to ascribe to the killing of Mot the sense of a ceremony in a fertility rite, i.e. a meaning thoroughly different from that of a punishment afflicted to a hated enemy.

After this survey let us return to the plain meaning of the Ugaritic text. In considering Anat's role in the myth of Baal's death, we should note that she deals with both, the corpse of Baal and that of Mot. She buries

---

[6] I wish to thank my colleague Dr. A. Rofé for drawing my attention to this paper.

the body of her beloved brother and destroys utterly until its complete disappearance that of his murderer. The antithetic correspondence between these actions is manifest. Our interpretation is corroborated by the scene of Anat's first encounter with Mot after Baal's death, where Mot appears as a fearful monster who boasts of having swallowed up Baal like a lamb. It is under the impact of this hateful speech that Anat finally decides to blot Mot out of existence. Nothing in Mot's behaviour could possibly evoke the association of grain. We therefore fail to see why Anat should relate to Mot's remnants with the positive attitude of men to grain, cultivated in hard toil and necessary for their livelihood.

[E.J. Smit, *The Concept of Obliteration in Ez. 5:1-4, JNWSL* 1 (1971), pp. 46-49, represents Ezekiel's prophecy of doom as resembling to the literary pattern of total destruction discussed above. In this prophecy Ezekiel is told by God to shave off his hair and to divide it into three parts in order to deal with each part in a way which symbolizes the fate of a certain section of the people. It is this text describing the treatment of these three parts of hair which Smit compares to the old pattern of annihilation as follows: "With the three different parts of his hair, Ezekiel is ordered to burn the first with fire (*b^{c}wr tb^{c}r*) to smite the second part with a sword (*tkl bḥrb*) and to scatter the third part to the wind (*zrh lrḥ*). These three concepts precisely are found in Ex. 32:20 ... and are even in the same order. It is only in the second concept that Exodus uses the concept of grinding ... Ezekiel adjusts these concepts to the fall of Jerusalem. The idea of grinding is the same of Ezekiel's smiting, viz. the destruction of the form". Smit adds at some length that the basically identical pattern is already found in the Ugaritic episode describing the killing of Mot.

This argumentation, however, is open to various objections. Let us start with the terminological observation that destruction by fire is expressed in either of the old texts by the verb *śrp*, in Ezekiel by *b^{c}r*. Smiting with the sword is entirely different from grinding. There remains only the identity of the verb *zrh* 'winnow'. But even this verb does not designate in both texts the same thing. Whereas in the old texts the verb means an additonal act of annihilation, the very same verb points in Ezekiel to the dispersal of the exulants, one part of them being destined to life and not to death. With this remark we touch upon the inherent structural difference between Ezekiel's prophecy and the older texts dealing with obliteration.

In those a series of acts each of them involving annihilation is performed on the same undivided object of destruction, here the object is divided into three parts and each suffers its own fate, that of the third part being only a partial destruction. This principal incongruity can easily be accounted for. Ezekiel's attitude to his people, represented by his hair, is obviously unlike the bitter and uncompromising hatred of Anat and Moses. In contrast to those Ezekiel does not act of his own free will but performs God's command and this command was not one of total obliteration. A pattern designed for the purpose to stress the totality of complete annihilation is *ex definitione* not applicable to a story of partial destruction. This deep-rooted heterogeneity should not be smoothed out.

Cf. also P.L. Watson, *The Death of 'Death' in the Ugaritic Texts*, *JAOS* 92 (1972), pp. 60-64, who reaches at the same basic conclusions as the present writer. Our differences of opinion are restricted to the following details:

1) In Watson's opinion the meaning of *ḫṯr* is 'pitchfork'. Our rendering 'sieve' is more probable in the light of Talmudic evidence. Cf. Jastrow, *Talmud Dictionary*, s.v. *ḥašar*, *ḥ^{a}šar*.

2) Watson translates *šir* to mean 'piece'. But this translation is unsupported whereas our rendering 'flesh' is clearly attested in Ugaritic. Cf. also Goliath's taunt to David: "Come to me and I will give your flesh to the birds of the heaven and the beasts of the field" (1 Sam. 17:44). This passage, quoted by Watson, corroborates our interpretation.]

Who is Afraid of the Linguistic Method?

[Ugaritic tġrk-again]

In his note "*Linguistic Method - may they preserve it*" A. Rainey[1] takes issue with the present writer over the explanation of a Ugaritic formula of greeting. For the benefit of those readers who are not conversant with the subject of our dispute I should like to premise some short words of introduction. The excavations at Ras-Shamra yielded a considerable amount of letters, most of them written in Akkadian, some of them in Ugaritic. The typical Ugaritic formulas of greeting patently correspond to their Akkadian counterparts. Therefore the Akkadian letters are of valuable assistance in the interpretation of the Ugaritic greetings. The present writer surveyed these more or less standardized formulas in *BASOR* 194 (1969), pp. 52-54 *[see in this volume, Ugaritic Formulas of Greeting*, pp. 362-365.*]* paying special attention to a very common formula which reads in Akkadian: *lu šulmu ana muḫḫika, ilānu* ^{meš} *ana šulmāni liṣṣurūka*. In literal translation 'Be welfare upon thee. The gods may protect thee for welfare'. This greeting reads in Ugaritic: *yšlm lk ilm tġrk tšlmk*. On the first half of this greeting I remarked: "The use of the noun *šulmu* in the first part of this formula as opposed to the impersonal construction of the Ugaritic verb *šlm* in *yšlm lk* corresponds to normal Hebrew usage. Cf. e.g. *šālom lākäm* (Gen. 43:23, not *yišlam lākäm*), literally 'welfare upon you' likewise *šālom yihyä li* (Deut. 29:18), not *yišlam li*). The impersonal use of the verb *šlm* 'to be in a state of welfare' is not found in Hebrew at all and even its personal use is restricted to Job 9:4; 22:21". On this statement Rainey remarks: "Loewenstamm was apparently not aware of the fact that we are met here with an additional difference - Hebrew and Ugaritic do not make use of the same formula." I freely confess that I fail to see his point, since I made the issue perfectly clear. Furthermore, Rainey argues against me that the Akkadian formulae under discussion were attested in Cassite documents and consequently independent of West-Semitic usage. Again, his criti-

[1] *Lĕšonênu* 35 (1970), pp. 11-15.

cism surprised me since I did not deal in my note with the origin of the Akkadian formula, but rather with its comparison to Hebrew and even had noted in another article that the formula is already found in the Cassite period.[2]

So far then we are in full agreement. The actual subject of our dispute is the derivation of the Ugaritic form *tġrk* in the second half of the formula. There exists no doubt that the translation of this sentence should read: 'The gods may protect thee and bestow welfare upon thee'. It is, however, controversial whether we are to derive *tġrk* from the verb *nġr* or from a verb *ġyr*. Rainey accepts the first solution, whereas the present writer prefers the second.

I have no intention to recapitulate here the prehistory of this controversy, but shall rather confine myself to a summing up of Rainey's arguments. Rainey stresses the existence of a Ugaritic verb *nġr* = Hebrew *nṣr* and argues that not only Hebrew *nṣr*, but even Ugaritic *nġr* reflect PS *nẓr*, since Ugaritic *ġ* sometimes corresponds to PS *ẓ*. From this root we may easily derive the form *tġrk*. No objection against this result should be raised because of the Hebrew passage: *'im zak wᵉyāšār 'attā ki ᶜattā yāᶜir ᶜāläkā wᵉšillam nᵉwat ṣidqäkā* (Job 8:6). 'If thou art pure and righteous than he will protect thee and bestow welfare upon thine beautiful wife who befits thine justice' (my translation. S.L.).[2a] The form *yāᶜir* should be parsed in this context as the *Hiphᶜil* of the Hebrew root *ᶜyr* / *ᶜwr*, attested in Ugaritic in the *Polel* *ᶜrr*, spelt with *ᶜ* and not with *ġ*. In other words - the spelling of the Ugaritic *tġrk* with *ġ* rather than with *ᶜ* proves that we are to disconnect it from Hebrew *ᶜwr*. This result is confirmed by literary considerations as well, since the Ugaritic formula is a translation from Akkadian. Therefore it may be supposed that both Ugaritic and Akkadian make use of the same PS root *nẓr*. It seems more reasonable to take as point of departure for the explanation of the Ugaritic formula its Akkadian counterpart than to look for parallels in the Bible.

I should like to point out in advance that I paid attention to Ugaritic *nġr* in my former paper and even pointed out that its derivation from

---

2 *EB, s.v. Miktāb* vol. 4, col. 969 (Hebrew).

[2a See in this volume, *Notes on the History of Biblical Phraseology*, note 3, pp. 212-213.]

PS *nẓr* cannot be excluded. Moreover, I discussed the possibility of relating *tġrk* to this root. I dismissed, however, this solution as improbable and am maintaining even now my view for different mutually corroborative reasons:

1. As shown by Hartmann[3], the root *ġyr* is clearly attested in Safaitic. This fact has not been disputed by Rainey.
2. It is possible that *yāᶜir* in Job 8:6 is related to this root rather than to Hebrew *ᶜwr* which J. Barth[4] connected with Arabic *ᶜrr* VI. According to this line of thought we would have to differentiate between Hebrew *ᶜwr*, Arabic *ᶜrr*, Ugaritic *ᶜrr* on the one hand and the Safaitic noun *ġyrt*, Ugaritic *ġyr* and Hebrew *ᶜyr* on the other hand.
3. This supposition is supported by the juxtaposition of the verbal forms *tġrk* and *tšlmk* in Ugaritic corresponding to the pair of words *ġyrt* and *slm* in Safaitic and still more evidently to the parallelism of the verbs *ᶜyr* and *šlm* in Job 8:6.
4. The use of the *Piᶜel* of *šlm* in Job 8:6 is unparaleled in the Bible because only here it serves instead of the standard phrases *ntn* or *śym šālom*. This deviation from normal Hebrew conforms to Ugaritic without doubt. Therefore one may argue that this exceptional meaning of the *Piᶜel* of *šlm* has been preserved in the Bible here because the roots *šlm* and *ᶜyr* form an ancient petrified pair.[5] This supposition is quite legitimate because a considerable number of common word-pairs is to be found in both the Biblical and the Ugaritic literatures.

---

[3] B. Hartmann, *VTS* 16 (1969), pp. 102-105.

[4] J. Barth, *Ethymologische Studien*, Berlin 1893, p. 70.

[5] This answers Rainey's argument that the pair *šlm* - *nṣr* is found in the Bible as well. Rainey adduces additional proof from Ps. 31:24 and Is. 26:3. Yet Ps. 31:24 is not a case in point at all since *šlm* means here 'to pay retribution' rather than 'to give welfare'. True, in Is. 26:3 we do find the pair of words *nṣr* and *šālom* (well being). Both words, however, belong to the stock of Biblical language and their nearness in one single passage does not conclusively prove the standardized character of their combination. Quite different is the matter in Job 8:6 where both the *Piᶜel* of *šlm* meaning 'to give welfare' and the verb *ᶜyr* meaning 'to protect' are unparalleled in the Bible. Therefore we may conclude that the combination of the two extraordinary words derives from the Canaanite formula of greeting attested in Ugaritic letters.

[As demonstrated by my student Y. Avishur in his doctoral thesis on pairs of words in ancient Semitic languages we should speak of pairs of words only provided that the words concerned appear in a limited number of mu-

This explanation raises of cause the question how we are to understand the relation between the Ugaritic verbs *nġr* and *ġyr*. In my former paper I pointed out that this problem admits two alternative solutions, viz. either we may follow Hartmann who differentiates between a Ugaritic root *nġr* < *nẓr* and another Ugaritic root *ġyr* reflecting PS *ġyr*, or we may disconnect Ugaritic *nġr* from PS *nẓr* and regard *nġr* as a variant of *ġyr* assuming an interchange of roots which would be analogous to the alterations *gwḥ* - *ngḥ*, *pwṣ* - *npṣ*, *pwḥ* - *npḥ*, *qwr* - *nqr*, *ṣwp* - *nṣp* in Hebrew. In favour of the second alternative one may argue that the correspondence of Ugaritic *ġ* to PS *ġ* is in accordance with the rule, its correspondence to PS *ẓ* restricted to exceptional cases only.

After this survey of details let us return to the methodological aspect of the dispute. Rainey stresses that the linguistic method permits us "an approach to the verses of the Bible only after a comprehensive analysis of the Ugaritic evidence based upon Ugaritic itself". That is to say in our case that the attestation of a Ugaritic verb *nġr* tips the balance and excludes the option of turning to other languages. This argument is sound provided that we are dealing with a single word but not if a pair of words common to Ugaritic and Hebrew is concerned and even less if the Hebrew pair of words is unusual and calls for the hypothesis that it were a remnant of an ancient idiomatic usage.

No more valid is Rainey's argument that the Ugaritic letters imitate the style of the Akkadian epistles and that for this reason the latter provide us with a starting point for a "literary" comparison. There is no escape from the statement that the Ugaritic writer gave a free rendering since the Akkadian nominal sentence *lu šulmu ana muḫḫika* turns into the Ugaritic verbal sentence *yšlm lk* and the Akkadian *ana šulmāni liṣṣurūka* into the hendiadys *tġrk tšlmk*. True, one might even so be tempted to object that the Ugaritic writer presumably preferred the root *nġr* since this root is nearer to *naṣāru* than the root *ġyr*. But this argument fails to take into account the fixed character of the pair of roots *ġyr* and *šlm* which is decisive in

tual relations, as e.g. in *parallelismus membrorum, parataxis, status constructus* etc. The relation between predicate and its object existing between *nṣr* and *šālom* in Is. 26:3 does not constitute a pair of words at all.]

our case. The linguist is not entitled to neglect the stylistic aspect and to aspire to a pure linguistic one, disqualifying literary considerations.

After these methodological considerations let us deal in short with Deut. 32:11. Rainey argues that *yā*^{c}*ir* in this verse makes a fine parallel to *yiṣränhu* in v. 10 and tries to show that here as well the *Hiph*^{c}*il* of the root ^{c}*wr* were attested in the meaning 'to protect'. Yet even if we were to accept his translation of *yā*^{c}*ir* in Deut. 32:11, we could nevertheless parse it as *Qal* of ^{c}*yr*. But his very explanation of *yā*^{c}*ir* is not satisfactory. It should be remarked that the verbal forms *yā*^{c}*ir* - *yiṣränhu* do not appear here in *parallelismus membrorum*. In v. 11 a new topic is introduced, viz. a simile of God's providence leading the people in the wilderness as shown by the tenor "YHWH alone lead it" (v. 12) and the vehicle of the simile means "as the eagle stirs up his nest" which illustrates in all its details, as shown by G.R. Driver[6] a realistic description of the life of the eagles.

At last some short remarks on a form of greeting dealt with by Rainey in passing. He mentions the greeting *ilānu šulumka šulum bītīka liš'al* (*EA* 96:4-6) 'god(!) may ask thine welfare' and the similar formula, found in a letter from Taanach: *ilānu liš'alū šulumka šulum bītīka mārīka* 'the gods may ask thine welfare, the welfare of thine house and thine sons'. He adds: "The clause *yiš'al l*^{e}*šālom* is attested in the Bible and has now be found in the letters of Arad as well where it reads *YHWH yš'l lšlmk*". This statement makes the impression as if in the Bible we also meet with the greeting formula that YHWH might ask for somebody's welfare. But this is not so. True, we do find clauses like *wayyiš'*^{a}*lu 'iš l*^{e}*re*^{c}*ehu l*^{e}*šālom* (Ex. 18:7) 'And they asked one for the welfare of the other'. But nowhere in the Bible a person expresses the wish that God might ask for the welfare of another person. The lack of such an attestation is worth mentioning since it now has become clear that greetings of this kind were used in the Hebrew of the Biblical period as well. In contrast to the Bible the greeting under discussion is quite usual in the Elephantine papyri, e.g. *šlm mrn 'lh šmym yš'l* (Cowley 30:1-2).

[E.Y. Kutscher[7] calls attention to the fact that in the Elephantine formula

---

[6] G.R. Driver, *PEQ* 19 (1958), pp. 56f.

[7] E.Y. Kutscher, *Current Trends in Linguistics* 6, pp. 363f.

šlm ... yš'l the object always precedes and argues that for this reason the formula should be considered as *Reichsaramäisch* i.e. as Eastern Aramaic. He adds: "This assumption is confirmed by the fact that the formula is paralleled exactly by the same introductory formula of the letters of the Neo-Babylonian, Neo-Assyrian and Late Babylonian periods" and refers to E. Salonen.[8] The basic pattern of the formulas quoted by Salonen reads: *DN* (*name of a god*) *and* DN_2 *šulum ša PN liš'alū*. Salonen remarks that the writing *šu-lum* (not *šul-mu*) points to a relatively late date. This late Akkadian formula, however, differs from the formula in the Aramaic Elephantine letters in the crucial point that it is the subject which precedes, not the object and leaves the peculiar order of words in the documents of Elephantine without explanation. Anyhow it seems reasonable to suppose that this pattern of greeting originated in ancient Canaanite and penetrated into Late Akkadian via the Aramaic.

The formula *YHWH yš'l lšlmk* has some bearing upon the interpretation of greeting formulas like *wayyiš'alu lo lᵉšālom* (Ju. 18:15). It is commonly supposed that the translation should read: 'and they enquired about his wellbeing'. Cf. the English greeting formula "How do you do". This interpretation is supported by the verse *wayyābo' 'uriyyā 'elāw wayyiš'al dāwid lišlom yo'āb* (2 Sam. 11:7), where the context makes it perfectly clear that David required information about the wellbeing of Joab. On the other hand, however, it is hardly possible to translate the formula *YHWH yš'l lšlmk* 'YHWH might enquire about your welfare'. Obviously the meaning must be that God might look for your welfare. Therefore also the formula in Ju. 18:15 seems to express good wishes for the welfare of the man addressed. The same holds good for analogous Akkadian formulas as *PN šulum* PN_2 *bēlīšu lišal* (Salonen, *op. cit.*, p. 86). Salonen translates: *'PN erkundigt sich nach dem Wohlbefinden seines Herrn'*. The translation *'Wünscht Wohlbefinden seinem Herrn'* seems to be more appropriate.*]*

---

[8] Kutscher refers to E. Salonen, *Die Gruss- und Höflichkeitsformeln in babylonisch-assyrischen Briefen, StOr* 38 (1967), pp. 78ff., especially pp. 99-102. Actually the formula under discussion is adduced there on p. 110 only.

Addition:

After completing this note I became aware of Dahood's[9] and Kselman's[10] proposal who read in Job 8:6 *ᶜulǟkā* 'thine children' instead of *ᶜālǟkā* pointing out that Ugaritic *ġyr* is followed by the direct object. In this respect, however, free variants are frequent in Hebrew, e.g. *šmr* is normally used with the direct object, but nobody will be tempted to amend for this reason verses as *lo' šᵉmartǟm ᶜal 'ᵃdonekǟm* (1 Sam. 26:16) or *tišmor ᶜālǟkā* (Pr. 6:22).

[On the question whether Ugaritic *tġrk* should be derived from a root *nġr* or *ġyr* see now also J. Blau, *Hebrew Annual Review* 1 (1977), pp. 70-72.]

---

9 M. Dahood, *Biblica* 46 (1965), p. 483.

10 J.S. Kselman, *CBQ* 32 (1970), pp. 571.

Postscript to Who is afraid of the Linguistic Method?

Gilgamesh III:9 reads: *ᵈEN-KI-DU ib-ri li-iṣ-ṣur tap-pa li-šal-lim 'Enkidu* shall protect the friend, safeguard the companion'. In this verse we doubtlessly meet with the PS verbs *nẓr* and *šlm* (in *D* formation) appearing as a pair which in Rainey's opinion is attested in the Ugaritic formula of greeting as well. Nevertheless I stick to my view, since Ugaritic *ġ* is *in dubio* PS *ġ* rather than PS *ẓ* and since Ugaritic is nearer to Hebrew than to Akkadian.

The Lord Shall Rule Over You (Judges 8:23)

In her article *Gideon and the Beginning of the Monarchy*, Y. Dishon[1] accepts the opinion of those who claim that Gideon became a king of Israel, and tries to further substantiate the claims of her predecessors. However, even after her full explanation, there is still room for discussion and even dissent.

1. Anyone who deals with this problem should pay strict attention to the absence of any explicit statement that the people of Israel made Gideon king. For if this were really the case, the author should have recorded the fact in clear and unambiguous words just as the scribes did who described the enthronement of Abimelech, Saul, David, and Solomon.

2. Those who accept the enthronement of Gideon from the Biblical verses rely on Abimelech's words when he turned to the people: "Which is better for you, that all the sons of Jerubbaal, who are seventy, rule over you, or that one rule over you?" (Ju. 9:2). They conclude from this that it was obvious to the people that Gideon's rule would pass to his descendants, and the only question was which one would be the ruler. However, this passage proves just the opposite. In general, after the death of a king, the previously appointed heir-apparent rules. On rare occasions, two of the deceased's sons claim the crown and fight over it. But it never occurs that all the sons establish a sort of oligarchy and reign together.

3. Mrs. Dishon explains in detail that the author of the Gideon stories evaluates the deeds of his hero in a positive manner. This proof is not to the point. A positive appraisal is one thing, and an enthronement is another. Moreover, the storyteller disapproves of Gideon's final act. It is related that he made an *ephod* which all Israel worshipped and that the *ephod* was a pitfall for him and his house (Ju. 8:27). This *ephod* recalls the golden calf (which was also made from nose-rings), and what is written about it prepares the reader's mind for the stories of the calamities which

---

[1] *Tarbiz* 41 (1972), pp. 255-268.

befell Gideon's sons after the death of their father.[2]

4. Mrs. Dishon tries to remove a pitfall from the way of those who see in Gideon a king of Israel. This pitfall is Gideon's answer to the people of Israel who offered him the kingship: "I shall not rule over you, neither shall my son rule over you the Lord shall rule over you." (Ju. 8:23). All Biblical commentators see in these words a rejection of the monarchy. Those scholars who nevertheless assumed that Gideon became king, considered his words to be a late addition, or resorted to an even more forced explanation, viz. that Gideon changed his mind on his refusal. Not so Mrs. Dishon who interprets Gideon's declaration as a promise that the rule of Gideon's house will not impinge on God's rule over Israel, a promise which would imply that Gideon bowed to the people's will. However, there is no hint in the context of this verse which permits to remove it from its plain meaning, which puts us up against two alternatives: A human rule over Israel or a divine rule. This opposition is not unique to Israel, but is mentioned also in Akkadian literature. In a description of the beginning of the world we read (*VAT* 8830, ll. 7-8):[3]

> *ina pāna*[na] *šar-ru-tu ina mātāte*[meš] *ul ba-ši u be-lu-tu a-na ilāni*[meš] *šar-ka-at*
>
> 'Formerly kingship did not exist in the lands (i.e. on earth), and the rule was given to the gods'.

Here we see the Mesopotamian view that the kingship of the gods preceded terrestrial kingship, and that some time passed until kingship descended from heaven to earth, a descent which is mentioned in Sumerian texts on the ancient antideluvian and later kingship.[4] In Mesopotamia where kingship was ensconced in an ancient glory, this idea did not contain an argument against the terrestrial institution of kingship. The situation in Israel, where the very establishment of the new institution of the monarchy was up

---

[2] Mrs. Dishon refers this verse to a footnote, and explains that the verse comes "to demonstrate the lack of human perfection as opposed to divine perfection, that even the man most fit to rule is just a man with all his frailties, and he must submit to the kingship of God" (*ibid.*, p. 259, note 29).

[3] Lambert, *BWL*, p. 162:7,8.

[4] Th. Jacobsen, *The Sumerian King Lists*, Chicago 1939.

for discussion, was different. Here the viewpoint that "the kingdom of the earth" was a replacement of "the kingdom of heaven" became a slogan of the anti-Monarchist theology in the period when conservative groups opposed a change in the social structure. This idea leads to the extreme formulation in 1 Sam. 8:7, that the people which requests a king rejects the kingship of God. The same idea is expressed in the Gideon story in more moderate terms.

The Phrase X (or) X plus one in Biblical and Old Oriental Laws

MAL A 24 deals with a wife who, having deserted her husband, entered another's house and stayed with its mistress "three (or) four nights". G. Cardascia[1] regards the formula "three or four" as "*imprécis*". This characterization has been challenged by R. Yaron.[2] The latter correctly states that the phrase "X (or) X plus one" occurs not infrequently in legal texts. As examples he points to *MAL* A 41 which deals with a veiling ceremony before "five (or) six" neighbours and to sec. 37 of the Hittite law "if anyone elopes with a woman and an avenger goes after them, if two men or three men die, there be no compensation (the reason being) thou hast become a wolf". From Biblical law Yaron adduces Deut. 17:6; 19:15 requiring the testimony of two or three witnesses, and the formula of Ex. 21:21 "if he survive a day or two".

Yaron argues that the legally relevant number is invariably "X" and not "X plus one" and adds that the seemingly superfluous number "X plus one" had been added "to forestall an argument ... that a given formulation be strictly interpreted as referring only to a particular, exactly defined number - not only less, but also not more", i.e. as an archaic *abundans cautela* comparable to the Roman formula *terni pluresve* - three or more children.

This interpretation, however, meets with difficulties. Sec. 37 of the Hittite code excludes compensation if two or three men have been killed. In this case the relevant number is obviously "X plus one". Even if the number of killed men reaches three, there is no compensation, *a fortiori* - not if their number was less. The supposition of an *abundans cautela* is unwarranted in this case, since such a formula should also mention the killing of one man. In the other paragraphs mentioned above, the legally decisive number is really X. But even there the addition of "X plus one" can hardly be accoun-

[1] G. Cardascia, *Les Lois Assyriennes*, Paris 1969, p. 146.

[2] R. Yaron, *Biblica* 51 (1970), p. 553.

ted for as an *abundans cautela*, since such a cautela would require the formula "X plus an indefinite number" like *terni pluresve*, not just "X plus one". Therefore we return to Cardascia's definition of the formula as "*imprécis*". This lack of precision is rooted in the careless way of every-day speech, not in archaic overprecise terminology, a priori not to be expected in Old Oriental Law.

*[*Compare B. Jackson, *Two or Three Witnesses, Essays in Jewish and Comparative Legal History*, Leiden, 1975, pp. 153-171.

Jackson suggests a new interpretation of sec. 37 of the Hittite code. In his opinion the law prohibits the substitution of the death penalty by composition if at least two men had been killed. It seems, however, rather improbable that the law should have insisted upon the execution of the death penalty for homicide in a brawl, so much the more as the homicide was committed under mitigating circumstances as the eloper and his helpers were obviously in the wrong. At least we might expect such a stern law to inculate its ruling by an explicit command to put the delinquent to death.

Jackson admits that the formula 'X or X-1' should not be regarded as an *abundans cautela* to forestal a hyperformalistic argument. He makes, however, the point that the formula could neither be characterized as *imprécis*, since there existed no more precise way of expressing 'at least X' or "X or more' in Biblical Hebrew. The redundant addition of 'or X+1' represents in Jackson's opinion rather a tendency of later law towards completeness in formulation.

The present writer prefers the view that the formula under discussion simply reflects the way of every-day speech. Compare "five or six times" (2 Reg. 13:19) 'at least five times'.*]*

The Formula 'I am Thy Servant and Thy Son'
in a Letter from El-Amarna

In a former paper entitled '*I am Thy Servant and Thy Son*'[1] we dealt with the address of Ahaz, king of Judah, to Tiglath Pileser, king of Assyria. Mr. Menahem Kister kindly drew my attention to a much earlier attestation of this diplomatic formula in a letter of Abdi-Ḫeba, king of Jerusalem where we read: *[^{m}]ardu-[ka u ^{m}]māru-ka a-na-ku* (*EA* 288:66). From this text Kister drew the consequence that Ahaz' words were not formulated *ad hoc*, but rather reflect a time-honoured tradition of international etiquette. In addition he points out that in another letter of Abdi-Ḫeba the wording is reduced to the simple formula: *ardu-ka a-nu-ki* (*EA* 287:66).

I should like to add to these observations that, although the letters of Abdi-Heba were directed to Pharaoh, the writer added to both of them a postscript destined to the *tupšarru*, the royal scribe, and that the formulae discussed here, belong to the postscript. Their comparison reveals that Abdi-Ḫeba only hesitatingly dared address the scribe of Pharaoh in the same manner in which Ahaz addressed the king of Assyria himself. This difference may readily be explained. The late kingdom of Judah was more powerful than the early kingdom of Jerusalem and the hold of Egypt over Canaan in the period of El-Amarna was stronger than that of Assyria in the days of Ahaz.

---

[1] [Compare in this volume, pp. 382-383].

Review of the Ugaritic part of R. Labat, A. Caquot, M. Sznycer, M. Vieyra: Les religions du Proche-Orient asiatique, textes babyloniens, ougaritiques, hittites, Paris, 1970.

The Ugaritic section of the volume (pp. 351-458) is the work of two well-known authorities in this field: André Caquot and Maurice Sznycer. After a thoroughly up-to-date introduction to the study of Ugaritic literature the reader is presented with briefly annotated translations of the Baal poems and the 'librettos' of the marriage of the moon-god and the birth of the gods. Each text has been furnished with a special preface.

The interpretation of large passages of the texts remains a matter of guess-work, as rightly stressed by the authors. Their new attempt, therefore, to solve many of the difficult problems of translation is bound to meet with general interest. A detailed discussion of their proposals, however, should be postponed until after their publication of the promised scholarly commentary. For the time being we shall restrict our discussion to their views on general aspects of the Ugaritic myth, passing over in silence the many points of agreement, and concentrating upon some differences in outlook.

The authors lay much emphasis on the epithet of Baal 'son of Dagan' and from this draw the conclusion that Baal was not the Son of Il, although they admit that certain texts point to the assumption that Il, too, was responsible for Baal's existence in some way. Their cautious formulations touch upon a vexing problem of Ugaritic mythology. The following points should be noted: (1) 'The son of Dagan' is one of the main gods of the Ugaritic pantheon, summarily described as the 'sons of Asherat', who is Il's wife. The resulting impression of Il's fatherhood is supported by the description of the mourning rites observed by him after Baal's death. (2) The excavation at Ugarit revealed a temple of Dagan, but no temple of Il. In the poetical texts, however, Dagan appears only in the forementioned epithet of Baal, whereas Il plays a prominent role in them. (3) As amply demonstrated by E. Laroche[1] the Hurro-Hittite god Kumarbi is identified in some texts with Il, in others however with Dagan. (4) Philon of Byblos[2] relates an involved story of the birth of Baal: According to this source, Ouranos' favourite wife was pregnant when his son El dispossessed him of his kingdom. The victorious El gave her in marriage to his brother Dagan, and after this Baal was born to her. All these confused or outright contradictory testimonies point to a blending of different traditions on Baal's paternity. One may conclude that the Ugaritic myth discounting Dagan's role in the pantheon is apparently dominated by the concept that Baal was Il's son and preserves a remnant of the other version only in the petrified epithet of Baal: 'son of Dagan'.

In the exegesis of the myth of Baal and Mot the authors maintain the hypothesis that Baal symbolizes the season of rain, Mot that of aridity. From this basic assumption the authors proceed to the following illustration of their thesis: 'The descent of Baal into the voracious gorge of Mot represents a mythological fable symbolizing the fall of rain which waters the earth, parched by the violent oriental summer which is the season of death' (p. 368). There is nothing new in the seasonal explanation of this myth, maintained by many scholars, although strongly contested by others.[3] But until now the defenders of this theory argued that Baal's death coincides with the end of the rainy period, whereas in the new version of this theory Baal's dying commences with the beginning of this season and is protracted until its conclusion. Baal's reign thus becomes a period of slow demise. It is doubtful whether the thesis of the seasonal myth is more convincing in this new garb.[3a]

---

[1] *U* 5, pp. 523-525.

[2] Eusebius, *Pr Ev* I:10:18-19 [cf. in this volume, *Philo of Byblos*, pp. 394-396.]

[3] Cf. the excellent summary of this question by de Moor, *The Seasonal Pattern*.

[[3a] This concept is apparently influenced by V. & J. Rosensohn Jacobs, *HTR* 38 (1945), pp. 77-109. True, even there we meet with the rather conventional statement: "The death of Baal ... is quite simply the cessation of rain" (p. 93). But on the other hand there appears the idea that "Mot comes up in vegetable growth and Baal goes down in the suffusing rain of heaven" (p. 87). In other words: "Mot ... is Baal's absorber for without the rain he can not come to fruition in the harvest" (p. 108).]

Baal's fight with the god of the sea is expounded in an even less conventional way: 'Baal the protector of men is obliged to defend the coast of Ugarit against the assault of the sea ... and at the same time to defend sea-faring people' (p. 369). The Ugaritic myth, however, contains reference neither to the coast of Ugarit, nor to sailors. This lack of references is hardly surprising, as the corresponding Akkadian, and especially the Biblical myths are clearly cosmological and not limited to a special territory. True, the Ugaritic myth plays down the cosmological element and does not mention the waters of the sea even once. The god of the sea is nothing but one of Il's ambitious sons who aspires to the kingship of the world, differing from his brothers only in his name and in his occasional association with sea monsters. But these distinctive features of the Ugaritic texts only prove that these texts stand midway between a comological myth and a story reflecting the rivalries at the court of Ugarit and have nothing to do with assaults of the sea upon the coast of Ugarit, let alone the perils faced by a sea-faring people.

These strictures on the valuable contribution of Caquot and Sznycer will not surprise anybody who has followed up the differences of opinion in the explanation of the Ugaritic myth. Differences of approach in this respect are unavoidable and do not diminish in any way our gratitude for the important research carried out by the authors.

Lexicographical Notes on

1. ṭbḫ; 2. *hnny/hlny*

1. ṭbḫ

CTA 23:14 reads according to Ch. Virolleaud: *ṭb[ḫ.g]d. bḥlb.annḫ bḫmat*, 'Cook (or they cooked) a lamb in milk a kid in curd'. As early as 1935 H.L. Ginsberg[1] pointed to the importance of this Ugaritic verse for the clarification of the historical background of the famous biblical prohibition to cook a kid in the milk of its mother (Ex. 23:19; 34:26; Deut. 14:21) and this idea has won wide recognition.

Some scepticism, however, has been voiced too. C.H. Gordon drew attention to the uncertainty of the reading *d* in the crucial word *[g]d* and stressed that the proposed meaning of *annḫ* unfortunately depends on the restored and tenuous parallel *[g]d*(?).[2] Another, no less heavy doubt, arises in the light of A. Herdner's[3] corrected reading: *ṭb.*(?) *[g]d. bḥlb. annḫ bḫmat*. It goes without saying that the word-divider after *ṭb* excludes any possibility of restoring *ṭb[ḫ]*. Nevertheless Herdner does not dismiss the time-honoured proposal altogether, but remarks: *On peut toutefois supposer qu'un signe a été omis ṭb<ḫ>*.

All scholars then suppose as a matter of fact that we are entitled to ascribe to the Ugaritic verb *ṭbḫ* the meaning 'cook'. True, Arabic *ṭabaḫa* does mean 'cook'. But Biblical *ṭbḥ* invariably designates 'slaughter', sometimes with the nuance 'butcher animals for food' and only the noun *ṭabbāḥ* has the sense 'cook' because the cook slaughtered the animal. Cf. the Greek

---

[1] H.L. Ginsberg, *JRAS* 1935, p. 72.

[2] Gordon, *UT, Glossary* No. 257, cf. No. 560. *[*On its meaning 'mint' see Aistleitner, *WUS*, No. 1794, de Moor, *New Year* 2, p. 19. On the possibility of explaining also *[g]d* as the name of a plant see J. de Moor, *Orientalia* 37 (1968), p. 214, note 5.*]*

[3] Herdner, *CTA*, p. 98, **especially note 9.**

noun μάγειρος 'butcher, cook'. Since Ugaritic is nearer to Hebrew than to Arabic, the explanation of the Ugaritic verb *ṭbḫ* 'slaughter' seems *a limine* more probable than its rendering 'cook'.

J. Aistleitner[4] indeed interpretes *ṭbḫ 'schlachten'* with the only exception of the verse under discussion where the reading *tb[ḫ]* or *ṭb<ḫ>* is a mere conjecture. In contrast to him Gordon[5] restricts the meaning 'slaughter' to *PRU* 2, text 153:3-4 and renders in all other occurrences 'cook'. The interpretation 'slaughter' seems, however, evident in the verses in which *ṭbḫ* is parallel with *šql*. The text reads: *ṭbḫ alpm ap ṣin šql ṯrm wmri ilm* (*CTA* 22 B:12-13). 'He slaughtered cattle and sheep slayed (verbally causes to fall), bulls and fatlings!' Likewise: *ṭbḫ alpm [ap] ṣin šql ṯrm [w] mria il<m>* (*CTA* 4:VI:40-42). Cf. also *ṭbḫ alp[m ap ṣin šql] ṯrm w[mri]* (*CTA* 1:IV:30-31).

As W. von Soden[6] has shown, there exists in Ugaritic a hollow verb *qyl* corresponding exactly to the Akkadian verb *qiālu* 'fall' and a causative *Š* of this verbal root. Semantically this causative should be compared to the *Hiph^{c}il* of the Hebrew verb *npl* 'fall' well known in the sense 'slay'. Cf. especially: *l^{e}happil ^{c}āni w^{e}'äbyon // liṭbo^{a}ḥ yišre dārāk* (Ps. 37:14) 'to cast down the poor and needy // to slay such as upright in the way'. Here too the causative of a verb denoting 'fall' appears in parallel with *ṭbḥ*. Ugaritic *ṭbḫ* appears further in *CTA* 6:I:18, 20, 22, 24, *[*26, 28*]*. The text deals with a funeral rite observed by Anat after the burial of Baal and apparently describes the killing of different kinds of animals. No funeral banquet is reported.[7] Our interpretation is admittedly less cogent in the verse *ṭbḫ imr wilḥm* (*CTA* 16:I:17-18) since a translation 'prepare a lamb that I may eat' would make sense. But even here the rendering 'slaughter a lamb (in order to prepare it for a meal) etc.' is clearly preferable and supported by ample Ugaritic and Hebrew evidence.

To sum up: A Ugaritic verb *ṭbḫ* 'cook' is not attested and therefore inadmissible in text-restoration.

---

[4] *WUS*, No. 1111.

[5] Gordon, *UT*, *Glossary* No. 1029.

[6] W. von Soden, *VTS* 16 (1967), pp. 295f.

[7] Cf. in this volume, *mṣd*, p. 419.

2. *hnny / hlny*

In Latin letters we meet with the formula: *Si vales bene est ego valeo*, mostly abbreviated to read *S.V.B.E.E.V.* A similar, although less rigidly standardized formula appears in correspondence, found at Ugarit, both in letters written in Ugaritic and in Akkadian. The gist of the formula may be summed up to say: 'I am well. Let me know how your are'.

The examples in Ugaritic language are: *hnny ^{c}mn šlm ṯmny ^{c}mk mnm [š]lm rgm ṯṯ[b]* (*PRU* 5, text 59:6-9) '.. with us is welfare. There with you what what is the welfare?[7a] Send back word.' Similarly: *hnny ^{c}mn [š]lm ṯmny ^{c}[m] bny mnm [šl]m [r]gm [ṯṯb]* (*PRU* 5, text 61:6-8). More expanded is the formula: *hnny ^{c}mny kll mid šlm w ap ank nḫt ṯmny ^{c}m adtny mnm šlm ṯṯb l^{c}bdk* (*CTA* 51:10-18) '... with both of us is most perfect welfare and also I enjoy repose. There with our (dual) mother what is the welfare? Send back word to your servant'. *hnny* alternates with *hlny* in *hlny ^{c}mny kll šlm ṯmny ^{c}m umy mnm šlm ṯṯb ly* (*CTA* 50:9-13) where *rgm* is omitted. *hnny / hlny* and *ṯmny* are left out in *^{c}mny šlm kll w mnm šlm ^{c}m umy ^{c}my tṯṯb rgm*. (*PRU* 2, text 15:14-20), where *^{c}my tṯṯb rgm* 'let her return word to me' corresponds to *ṯṯb ly* in the forementioned text.

In all examples but one the first part of this formula is introduced by *hnny / hlny*, the second by *ṯmny*. [This statement needs correction in the light of the following passage from a letter: *lḥt šlm k lik[t] umy ^{c}my ht ^{c}m[ny]-kll šlm. ṯmny ^{c}m umy mnm šlm wrgm ṯṯb ly* (*PRU* 5, text 9:5-9), rendered by Virolleaud to say: '*La tablette de paix (ou de bonne santê) comme ma mère me l'a envoyée, voici (en rêponse) que chez moi tout va très bien. Là bas, chez ma mère, tout va-t-il bien*?' Virolleaud's rendering of *ht* is correct, since the context proves that, like English 'now', *ht* can be used without temporal force. It could even be argued that in this context *ht* serves as a free variant of *hlny / hnny*, thus providing a clue for the explanation of the latter particles as well. Yet this argument is not cogent, as

[[7a] The words *mnm šlm ^{c}m* ... and their Akkadian counterpart *mi-nu-me šul-mā-nu itti* ... should more correctly be rendered to say: 'Is whatsoever welfare with', i.e. 'is all right with', since *mnm* and *minummê* are indefinite pronouns. So correctly already J. Nougayrol, *PRU* 4, p. 222, ll. 2-3: *est-ce que tout va bien pour ...]*

it could be objected that *ht* introduces here the answer to a question implied in the preceding words.*]* *hnny / hlny* is generally rendered to mean 'here' as opposed to *ṯmny* 'there'. It may be admitted that the opposition of 'here' to 'there' sounds most plausible. The difficulty, however, is that this translation of *hnny / hlny* is disproved by close Akkadian parallels.

The Akkadian counterpart of the formula reads: *e-nu-ma it-ti šarri u it-ti-ja gab-ba šul-mu aš-ra-nu it-ti šarri bēli-ja mi-nu-me-e šul-ma-nu. ṭe-ma li-te-er-ru-ni* (*PRU* 4, p. 222, ll. 6-9). '.. with the king and with me is perfect welfare. There with the king my lord what is the welfare? One may send back[8] me word:' Cf. *U* 5, p. 145, 54:6-8; p. 146, 54:24-28; p. 151, 57:9'-14'. *PRU* 6, text 20:3'-5'. Alternatively: *a-nu-ma i[t-tu šul-mu] aš-ra-nu it[tu* ^{f}*ummi]i-ja mi-nu-um-me-e šul-ma-nu. ṭe-ma te-er-ri a-na mari-ki* (*U* 5, p. 148, 55:Vo 6'-10'. Cf. ibid. R^{o} 13-17) '... with me is welfare. There with my mother what is the welfare? Send back word to your son.' *a-nu-ma* is also clearly attested in the passage *PRU* 6, text 14:6-8 where Nougayrol reads (l. 6) *e*(!)-*nu-ma*.[9] In all these texts the second part of the formula begins with *ašrānu*, which evidently means 'there' (= the place of the recipient of the letter).[10] More problematic is the rendering of *anumma* and *enūma*. Nougayrol translates the first word by *voici*, the second by *tandis que*.[11] His rendering of *anumma* is impeccable since this word is 'used to introduce a message' (*CAD s.v. anumma*), but his entirely divergent rendering of *enūma* raises suspicion. The functional equivalence of *anumma* and *enūma* makes it perfectly clear that *enūma* is here not a conjunction, but rather the adverb, well attested in the Akkadian of Boghazkeui and El-

---

[8] Akkadian *tur D* exactly corresponds to Ugaritic *ṯwb Š*.

[9] The formula concludes *ṭ[e-ma] šu-u[p-r]a* 'send word' (Cf. also ibid. 15: 9) deviating from the standard formulation 'return word'.

[10] Contrast *CAD s.v. ašrānu* 2 which attributes to *ašrānu* besides its ordinary sense of 'there' a second meaning 'here' restricted to El-Amarna and Ugarit. This assumption, however, has convincingly been refuted by A.F. Rainey who arrived at the correct conclusion that "the *CAD* references .. to *ašrānu* in the supposed meaning of 'here' must be stricken from the record" (*UF* 3, p. 161, note 48). The correspondence between Akkadian *ašrānu* and Ugaritic *ṯmny* in the formal under discussion corroborates his view.

[11] Likewise, *CAD*, loc. cit. (note 10), 'while'.

Amarna in the sense 'now, here is' (cf. *CAD s.v.*) i.e. French '*voici*'.[12]

A confirmation of our view may be found in the obvious equivalence of *enūma* and *anumma* in two letters of the king of Carcemish, both announcing the coming of a man from that place. One reads: *a-nu-ma* ^{m}*talmi-*^{d}*tešub* ^{amil}*qar-dab-bu ša* ^{d}*šamši*^{si} *il-la-ka-ak-ku* (*PRU* 4, p. 192, ll. 6-8). Here Nougayrol correctly renders: '*Voici que T. qardabbu de Mon Soleil va aller chez toi.*' In the second letter we find the formulation: *e-nu-ma* ^{m}*mi-iṣ-ra-mu-wa aš-ra-nu it-ti* ^{m}*PAP* ^{d}*šarru-ma a-ša-bi il-la-ka* (ibid.), p. 193, ll. 6-8). Nougayrol translates: '*M. allant habiter sur place* (= *à Ugarit*) *auprès de P.*' It seems, however, that here too we should translate: '*Voici que M. va habiter là-bas*' etc.[13]

It follows that Ugaritic *hnny / hlny* should be interpreted in accordance with the occurences of *enūma* and *anumma* discussed above in the meaning 'behold'.

[Our interpretation of *hlny, hnny* as a presentative particle is corroborated by a document in which the great king of the Hittites imposes upon the king of Ugarit a tribute whose items are enumerated one by one. This enumeration is introduced by the sentence: *h[l]ny* (or *h[n]ny*?) *argmn d[ybl N]qmd lšpš* (ll. 17-18)[14], correctly rendered by Nougayrol: '*Voilà le tribut que [payera N]iqmaddu au Soleil!*' In this case even the context excludes the explanation of *hlny* as a local adverb.

The formula, discussed in this paper, appears now also in a letter, communicated in transcription and translated by A. Caquot.[15]

---

[12] The result of our discussion has been anticipated by Rainey's translation 'now' (*loc. cit.*, note 10).

[13] The amply attested use of *enūma* in the sense of genuine Akkadian *anumma* is readily accounted for. Whoever writes in a foreign language, may easily mix up similar words. This faulty Akkadian is of course a pitfall for modern scholars. Only by systematic comparison of parallel texts this pitfall can be avoided.

[[14] *PRU* 4, p. 45.]

[[15] *ACF* 75 (1974/75), pp. 430-432.]

We quote from his publication.

lp^{c}]n. umy [.qlt]	*aux pieds de ma mère*
	je m'effondre.
]. umy. šlm.[ilm	*Ma mère, salut! Que les dieux*
t]ġrk. tšlm[k	*te gardent (et) te sauvent.*
h]nny. ^{c}mn. š[lm	*Ici, chez nous, cela va bien,*
ṯmny. ^{c}mk. mnm	*là-bas, chez toi, que tout*
šlm. rgm. ṯṯ<b>.ly	*aille bien. Donne-moi réponse.*

We suggest to restore at the beginning of the second line before the word divider the letter *l* and to translate: '*A ma mère salut*'. Yet even this text is suspect, since normal Ugaritic use requires here *yšlm* instead of *šlm*. Therefore the line should be restored to read: *[l]. umy. <y> šlm.* Compare the omission of the letter *b* in *ṯṯ<b>* (l. 6). The formula of ll. 5-6 has been interpreted by Caquot as a good wish for the health of the addressee, not as an inquiry about it. The disposition of the letter, militates against this exegesis. Its first part (ll. 1-3, set apart by a dividing line) comprehends after a formula of prostration two formulas of good wishes. The second part (ll. 4-6) turns to another subject and the writer there says: "I am well, inform me how you are." Compare in a letter from Mari: *ša-al-ma-ku. šu-lum-ka ši-ta-ap-pa-ram* (*ARM* 1, 129:5-6) 'I am well. Send message about your wellbeing.' Likewise: *a-na na-we-em ša Ha-na ù a-na a-lim Ka-ḫa-at^{ki} šu-ul-mu-um. a-bi šu-lu-um-šu li-iš-pu-ra-am* (*ARM* 2, 59:11-15) 'The pastureland of H. and the town K. are well. My father may send message about his wellbeing.'*]*

The origin of the *[Ugaritic]* letter formula remains a matter for further research. *[*Anyhow it appears that the involved and cumbersome Akkadian of the formula in letters from Ugarit can hardly be derived from the simple and straightforward language in which it was couched in the Mari letters. Are we to look for a Ugaritic or even a Hurrian origin?*]*

On the Predicative Use of the Suffix joined to a Subject-Noun in Hebrew and Ugaritic.

The possessive pronoun is employed in all the Semitic languages as an attribute. However, Brockelmann already pointed out that there are exceptions from this rule in some languages including Hebrew. His notes on this exceptional usages in Hebrew will serve us as a starting-point for the analysis of this phenomenon in both Hebrew and Ugaritic.

1. In his discussion of the single-member clause, Brockelmann states that the pronominal suffix of the noun may be employed in it as a predicate.[1] He quotes as a definite example[2] of this phenomenon the verse *y^e^dehäm w^e^lo' y^e^mišun raglehäm w^e^lo' y^e^halleku* (Ps. 115:15) which is clearly equivalent to the more common wording: *yādayim lāhäm etc.*, i.e. 'They have hands and they do not feel, they have feet and they do not walk'. The sentence then has two single-member clauses i.e. *y^e^dehäm* and *raglehäm* and in both the possessive pronoun is used as a predicate and not as an attribute.

This analysis emphasizes the single-member character of the verse. However, there is room also for this exceptional usage of the possessive suffix in a nominal clause which is not single-membered as we shall try to show from a Ugaritic text. In the Baal epic the following words are attributed to Mot, the god of death: *šb^c^ ydty bṣ^c^* (*CTA* 5:I:20-21)[3], literally 'my seven portions are in the plate'. These words of Mot come in the course of his boasting about his large appetite. From this it is evident that Mot does not intend to emphasize that his seven parts are *in a plate* but rather that in his plate there *are no less than seven portions*, i.e. a complete number. Therefore the sentence is equivalent to the more simple wording:

---

[1] Brockelmann, *Grundriss* 2, p. 40.

[2] Id. *ibid.*, hesitantly adds Gen. 22:24.

[3] Scholars are divided over whether to read *ydty bṣ^c^* or *ydt ybṣ^c^*. See Herdner, *CTA*, p. 33, note 6. But in the light of the text RS 24.293:8 there remains no doubt as to the reading *ydty bṣ^c^*. See *U* 5, p. 559.

šb^c ydt ly bṣ^c. *ydty* then means here *ydt ly* 'I have parts' as *y^edehäm* in Ps. 115:15 means *yādayim lāhäm* 'they have hands'. But in contradistinction to Ps. 115:15 the Ugaritic sentence is not one-membered, but adds a numeral (*šb^c*) to the subject, an adverbial clause (*bṣ^c*) to the predicate, contained in the suffix of the predicate. It is, however, clear that this difference does not affect the basic identity of the two phenomena and it is probably only by chance that no verse has been preserved in the Bible whose syntax agrees in all details with the Ugaritic verse.

2. Brockelmann states further[4] that in expressions of belonging (*Eigentumsverhältnisse*) the possessive pronoun sometimes fulfills the function of the preposition *l-* with the pronominal suffixes, e.g. in the verse *lo' tihyä tip'art^ekā ^cal haddäräk '^ašär 'attā holek* (Ju. 4:9) 'You will not have glory on the way etc.'. The possessive pronoun in the word *tip'art^ekā* denotes here the "belonging" of the glory to its possessor which is more usually expressed by the word *l^ekā*.

The two phenomena are described by Brockelmann in different chapters of his book and each is treated as a separate topic. However, the complete separation of the case in which the personal pronoun serves as predicate from that in which it indicates the belonging of its subject is problematic, since in both cases the pronoun has both functions. In *y^edehäm* 'they have hands' the pronominal predicate expresses also the belonging of the hands to their possessor and in the word *tip'art^ekā* 'you have glory' the pronoun designating the belonging of the *tip'ärät* fulfills a predicative function as well. True, in Ps. 115:15 we are dealing with nominal clauses, whereas in Ju. 4:9 we have a verbal clause. Furthermore, in Ps. 115:15 the possessive pronoun of the subject is a complete predicate, whereas in Ju. 4:9 the predicate is a compound and comprises in addition to the personal pronoun the words *lo' tihyä l^ekā ^cal haddäräk* etc., i.e. a verb and an adverbial clause. But we have already demonstrated that there is no essential difference between the case in which the possessive pronoun of the subject acts as complete predicate and the case in which it is merely part of the predicate. This implies that in the subject under discussion we should not differentiate between nominal and verbal clauses. In both cases we are deal-

[4] Id. *ibid.*, p. 263. He notes as further examples Ex. 2:9; Job 6:10 and even the difficult verse Nu. 12:6.

ing with the predicative use of the possessive pronoun attached to the subject of the sentence.

3. To this principal discussion we may append a note on an exact parallel to the syntax of Ju. 4:9 in a Ugaritic text. In the Aqhat epic we read that Baal interceded with El for Danil the righteous judge who had no son. He says: *wykn bnh bbt šrš bqrb hklh*, literally 'And his son will be in the house, a descendant in his palace'.[5] From the story it is clear that Baal did not intend to say that Danil's son (who does not exist as yet) might actually be in the house (and not outside), but that Danil wants to have a son in the house. The words *wykn bnh bbt* then admit the translation into simpler Ugaritic: *wykn bn lh bbt* 'There will be a son to him in the house.' Like in Ju. 4:9, here as well, we are dealing with a verbal clause in which the possessive pronoun of the subject is part of the predicate. Here also the additional parts of the predicate are a verbal expression (*wykn*) and an adverbial expression (*bbt*).

[Special uses of the possessive pronoun, affixed to a noun, have been discussed by M.M. Bravmann, *Muséon* 85 (1972), pp. 269-274; 88 (1975), pp. 449-453, who coined for them the term *pregnant possessive pronoun*. Under this category the author subsumes rather divergent phenomena. Three examples may suffice to illustrate the point:

1) *Muséon* 88, p. 450, he quotes the Judeo-Baġdādi sentence: .... *bhådik - əlwlāyi akū weḥəd qayəbnī ḥōšu* - In that town there was somebody who built "his house", i.e. built a house for himself. Compare Hebrew *bānā beto* (Jer. 22:13; Job 27:18) instead of *bānā lo bayit*. The example demonstrates that

[5] We should of course interprete *wykn bnh bbt(h) // šrš(h) bqrb hklh*, i.e. in both *bnh* and *hklh* the possessive pronoun serves as a double duty suffix. On this phenomenon in Hebrew and Ugaritic see e.g. Dahood, *UHPh*, pp. 38ff. and the literature cited there. What is unique to our passage here is that the phenomenon is found in it twice. 1. In the parallelism *bnh// šrš* in which the pronoun appears only in the first hemistich and acts as a predicate. 2. In the parallelism *bbt//bqrb hklh* in which the pronoun occurs only in the second hemistich and acts as an attribute.
[Contrast J. Obermann, *How Daniel was Blessed with a Son*, New Haven 1946, p. 14, who sensed the difficulty created by the personal suffix in the word *bnh* and remarked: "The couplet ... states that the intercession, if successful, would result in that Daniel would have not 'a son in his house', but rather '*his* son in his house' ... It would thus seem as though the narrator has intended to epitomize the conduct of a good son in anticipation of the list. A good son, the couplet would thus imply, remains in his father's house so that he may discharge his filial duties."]

a predicative personal suffix may be affixed even to the object of a sentence, not to its subject only.

2) Bravmann (*Muséon* 85, p. 271) quotes from *Buḫāri Saḥiḥ*: *fawagiᶜa wagaᶜahu llādi tuwuffiya fīhi* - and he became sick with his sickness (i.e. with the sickness) from which he died'. Compare Hebrew *wä'ᵃlišaᶜ ḥālā 'ät ḥolyo 'ᵃšär yāmut bo* (2 Reg. 13:14). In this pleonastic formulation the personal pronoun determinates the noun instead of the article.

3) In both papers Bravman dwells at length upon the passage: *ᶜal ken yaᶜᵃzob 'iš 'ät 'ābiw wᵉ'ät 'immo wᵉdābaq bᵉ'išto* (Gen. 2:24). 'Therefore a man shall leave his father and his mother and shall cleave unto his wife', i.e. according to his understanding of the passage: 'he shall cleave to a wife (which turns by his cleaving unto her to his wife)'. In the present writer's opinion the passage simply states that a man's connection with his wife should prevail over that to his parents.*]*

Did the Goddess Anat wear a Beard and Side-Whiskers?

The Ugaritic epic of Baal tells of the mourning rites observed after Baal's death by his father Il and subsequently by his sister Anat. One stichus in these passages gave rise to the contention, that Anat were regarded at Ugarit as some kind of *Venus barbata*. It is this perplexing argument which shall be discussed in the following lines.

The text relating to Il reads: *yhdy lḥm wdqn* (*CTA* 5:VI:19) and is exactly paralleled by the text on Anat reading: *thdy lḥm wdqn* (*CTA* 6:I:3).

The word *lḥm* and *dqn* have been variously interpreted to mean 'cheeks and chin' or 'side-whiskers and beard'. Recently the second interpretation has been vigorously defended by de Moor[1] who reached at the result, that Anat represented an androgynous type of goddess, wearing a beard and side-whiskers. His arguments, however, are open to objection.

De Moor explains the verb *hdy* on ground of Arabic *haḏ'a* and *haḏḏa* 'to cut off quickly'. This interpretation of *hdy* excellently fits his translation of *lḥm wdqn* 'side-whiskers and beard' and almost excludes the alternative rendering 'cheeks and chin'. Nobody is supposed to cut off his cheeks and chin, even not when inflicting upon himself wounds in performance of a mourning rite. But the trouble is that Arabic *haḏ'a, haḏḏa* and also *haḏa(w)* are not attested in the sense 'to cut off quickly' but invariably denote 'to cut' especially 'to cut into pieces and to lacerate'.[2] The real meaning of the Arabic etymon of Ugaritic *hdy* then clearly favours the rendering of *lḥm wdqn* 'cheeks and chin'.

Let us proceed to a discussion of *lḥm wdqn* proper. De Moor starts his treatment of this wordpair with its second component, viz. *dqn* and makes a

---

[1] De Moor, *Seasonal Pattern*, p. 193.

[2] I am indebted to my friend Prof. J. Blau who checked for me all occurrences of these Arabic verbs.

case for its interpretation in the sense of 'beard'. He admits that Arabic *ḏaqan, ḏaqn* means not only 'chin-beard', but 'chin' as well; he stresses, however, the argument that in Akkadian and especially in all West-Semitic languages this noun exclusively denotes beard (Akk. *ziqnu*; Phoen. *zqn*; Hebr. *zāqān*; Aram. *da/iqnā'*). From this point of departure he proceeds to the discussion of *lḥm* and remarks: "Then the *lḥm* (dual!) which are certainly related to Arab. *laḥy*, Hebr. *l^{e}ḥi*, Akk. *laḫu* 'jaw, cheek' are probably side-whiskers (cf. Arab. *liḥyah* 'beard')". His argument is inconclusive. According to his survey each of the roots under discussion is attested in two meanings in Arabic, whereas in the other languages, Proto-Semitic *ḏqn* is restricted to the meaning 'beard', Proto-Semitic *lḥy* to the meaning 'cheek'. It is arbitrary to take as starting point the *probable* sense of *dqn* 'beard' and to explain *lḥm* accordingly to mean 'side-whiskers', since one can as well transfer the stress to the fact that *lḥm* denotes *prima vista* cheeks and then arrive at the conclusion that *dqn* should mean 'chin'. We may add that the Lexicon of Brown-Driver-Briggs renders even Hebrew *zāqān* 'chin' in Lev. 13:29-30; 14:9; 2 Sam. 20:9, Ez. 5:1. This interpretation is clearly preferable in Lev. 13:29-30 which reads: "If a man or a woman has an affection on the head or *b^{e}zāqān*, the priest shall examine the affection. If it appears to go deeper[2a] than the skin and there is thin yellow hair in it, the priest shall pronounce him unclean, it is a scall, a scaly eruption of the head or of *hazzāqān*." The text deals with an affection of the skin whose character is indicated by its depth and by thin yellow hair in it, but not with an affection of the hair as such which could easily be removed by cutting off.

We then arrive at the conclusion that from a purely lexicographical point of view both interpretations of *lḥm* and *dqn* are admissable and that the Arabic cognates of Ugaritic *hdy* tip the balance in favour of the translation 'cheeks and chin' since the cognates mean 'to cut, to lacerate'.

This result is corroborated by the context of the stichus. According to the correct view, accepted by de Moor, the preceeding passage as well as

---

[[2a] Contrast Z. Ben-Hayyim, *H. Yalon Memorial Volume*, Jerusalem 1974, pp. 52-54 who assigns to *^{c}āmoq* in Lev. 13 the sense 'strong-coloured'. Pay, however, attention to the synonymous interchange of the roots *^{c}mq* and *špl* in Lev. 13:25-26.]

the subsequent one deal with the self-infliction of wounds.[3] The translation 'He (she) cuts into cheeks and chin' thus perfectly fits in. The alternative rendering: 'He (she) cut off side-whiskers and beard' assumes that a scene of hair-cutting has been sandwiched between two scenes of self-laceration. Therefore de Moor's reasoning would even then not be convincing, if we could accept his characterization of Anat as an androgynous type.

In de Moor's opinion[4] this bold assertion is borne out by the passage *^{c}ṯtrt w^{c}nt ymġy* (*U* 5, pp. 545-546, text 1:9), *[*'Astarte and Anat arrive'[4a]*]* in which the masculine character of the preformative *y* in *ymġy* points to the androgynous character of the goddesses.

It must be admitted that we should really have expected here *tmġy*, the some times attested form *tqtl* of 3 fem. du. whose preformatives correspond to Arabic.[4a] But no strict observances of such rule should be expected in Ugaritic as shown by the 3 masc. du. form *tša* (*CTA* 5:II:16), *tšan* (*CTA* 14: 303) instead of *yša(n)*. Another analogous process of displacement occurred in 3 pl., where Proto-Semitic *y* (common gender) has been supplanted in many cases by *t*.[5] It may be surmised that these processes resulted in a neutralisation of the opposition between *y* and *t* in 3 du., whereas in 3 sing.

---

[3] This interpretation of ll. 20-23 is universally accepted. Most scholars interpret in the same direction, also ll. 17-19 which read: *ġr babn ydy psltm by^{c}r*. Cf. e.g. de Moor's translation: 'he scrapes his skin with a stone using a flint-block as razor'. We should prefer the guess: "He removes his skin with a stone (and) by hewing with thorny bushes'. Cf. Ugaritic *n/ydy // grš* 'to drive away, to remove', *psltm* may be a *nomen actionis* with affixed adverbial *m* 'by hewing', *by^{c}r // babn* 'with thorny bushes'. Cf. Syriac *y^{c}r'*, '*virgulta, vepres*' (Brockelmann, *LS, s.v.*). Cf. also Ju. 8:7,16. For an entirely different exegesis see Driver, *CLM*, p. 199. Partly differing Caquot-Sznycer, *RPOA*, p. 424; *[Textes* 1, pp. 250f. and notes g, h, i there*]* who render: '*Il (se) taillade la peau avec une pierre, il tranche (sa) double tresse au rasoir.*' The second part of this translation assumes an act of haircutting, interrupting the description of self-laceration. But *il tranche* is unparalleled in the Ugaritic verse and the translation of *psltm* 'double tresse' is without support.

[4] J. de Moor, *UF* I, p. 171.

[[4a] But contrast A.F. Rainey, *JAOS* 94 (1974) p. 186 who interprets: 'He (*Yariḫ*) comes to *^{c}Aṯtrt* and *^{c}Anat*'.*]*

[5] Gordon, *UT, Grammar* 9.15.

the original force of *y* (masc.) and *t* (fem.) has been preserved. It is for this reason that the subject *ᶜnt* in sing. invariably governs *tqtl*, never *yqtl*. Therefore the form *ymġy* under discussion is instructive for the morphology of the Ugaritic verb, not for the character of the Ugaritic goddesses.[6]

Last not least we are to pay attention to the words of Krt who praises his future wife. *Ḥry dknᶜm ᶜnt nᶜmh km tsm ᶜṯtrt tsmh* (*CTA* 14:291-293) - 'Ḥry whose beauty is like the beauty of Anat whose fairness is like the fairness of Astarte'. It may not easily be assumed that Krt craved for a wife with side-whiskers and a beard. He rather had in mind the type of an attractive young woman, represented in the famous Ugaritic relief of a warrior goddess. No scrap of archaeological evidence can be produced in order to establish the cult of a bearded goddess at Ugarit.
[Compare now also D. Marcus, *The Term "Chin" in the Semitic Languages*, *BASOR* 226 (1977), pp. 53-60].

---

[6] In addition de Moor refers to his interpretation of Il's address to Anath: *ydᶜtk bt kanšt win bilht qlsk* (*CTA* 3:V:35-36; 18:I:16-17), given by him in *Seasonal Myth*, p. 132: 'I know you my daughter that you are like a man and that in a goddess your scorn would not be.' The interpretation of this verse, however, is just a matter of guesswork.
Cf. e.g. Cassuto, *Anath*, pp. 103: 149-150; Ginsberg, *ANET*³, p. 137; Rin, *Aliloth*, p. 110; Caquot-Sznycer, *RPOA*, p. 400. [*Textes* 1, p. 176 and notes r, s there.]

Taautos*

Taautos is described sometimes as man sometimes as god. It is told of him that he invented the letters of the alphabet and composed the first books (*PrEv* I:9:24; 10:14; cf. 10:36). In particular he appears as a wise man who detached the old beliefs about the gods from their entanglement with myth and superstition and explained them in a scholarly way, i.e. in accordance with Euhemeristic philosophy (*PrEv* I:10:43). On the other hand, however, it is stated that he was a god to whom Kronos had transferred the rule over Egypt and that he was called by the Egyptians Thoyth, by the Alexandrinians Thoth, but by the Greeks Hermes (*PrEv* I:10:14; 10:38). His father is said to have been Misor (*PrEv* I:10:14).

The Phoenician character of the name Misor (= Hebr. *mišor*) makes it clear that Taautos, like all cult-heroes, was regarded by Sanchuniathon as a Phoenician. It is for this reason that Eissfeldt thought him to be a primarily Phoenician image and even compared his name with the Hebrew root *t'w* > *t'h* and with the name of the letter ταῦ - a Phoenician loan - both designating 'sign mark'. But we should rather adapt the commonly held view regarding Taautos as a variant of the manifold vocalized name of the Egyptian god Thot. The notice that Kronos invested Taautos with the rule over Egypt makes the impression that the kingdom of an indigenous Egyptian god has been secondarily attributed here to his investiture by a supreme Phoenician godhead. A clearcut example of such a theological construction is extant in the notice that Kronos appointed his daughter Athene over Attika (*PrEv* I:10:32. Cf. 10:38). In both cases the foundation of Phoenician colonies abroad engendered the tendency to ascribe a Phoenician origin to foreign gods, thus including them into the Phoenician sphere. The image of the god who has turned into a Phoenician under the name Taautos results from a Hellenistic blending of Thot and Hermes, often named Hermes Trismegistos[1]

* Compare in this volume, *Philo of Byblos*, pp. 390-404.

[1] Cf. also *PrEv* I:10:17 where Hermes Trismegistos appears as Kronos' counsellor and assistant. He should be differientiated from Taautos and regarded as another ramification of the Hellenistic tradition about Hermes. [He should rather not. Hermes bears the epithet Trismegistos in the work

who showed a tendency to change from a god into a wise man living in primeval times.

As Thoth of old, the Hellenistic Hermes was considered the inventor of the signs of script and as the author of the most ancient books. For this reason the tendency developed of attributing to him the authorship of all books for which decisive authority was claimed.[2] In addition to this Hermes was celebrated in Hellenistic literature as ἑρμηνεύς[3] in accordance with a popular etymological explanation of the name Hermes, attested already in the writings of Plato.[4] Therefore it is well understood that Taautos appears in the writings of Sanchuniathon as the authentic interpret of ancient popular theology. Thus it happens that the Phoenician transformation of Hermes serves in Sanchunjaton's writings the purpose of providing the Hellenistic reader with an authoritative foundation for the Euhemeristic version of Phoenician tradition.

of Philo only in this passage, whereas in its continuation (I:10:8) he is called Hermes pure and simple as elsewhere and especially in the definitions identifying him with Taautos. His role in the war of Kronos against Ouranos, described in I:10:17-18 is just another testimony to his wisdom.]

[2] R.P. Festugière, *La Révélation d'Hermes Trismégiste*[2], Paris 1950, pp. 74f.

[3] Hekataios of Abdera ap. *Diodor*. I:16:2; Artapanus ap. *Eus*. *PrEv* IX:27:6, who identifies Moses with him.

[4] *Kratylos* 407e.

Anat's Victory over the Tunnanu

In the famous text *CTA* 3:III:35-44 the goddess Anat describes her victories over the god of the sea and a host of monsters. First place among the monsters is occupied by the *Tunnanu*[1], the predecessor of the well-known Biblical *Tannin*. The description of *Tunnanu's* defeat comprises no more than three words, of which only the first two can be deciphered with certainty:[2] *lištbm tnn* (line 37).

The interpretation of the verb-form *lištbm* has given rise to prolonged discussion. Ch. Virolleaud[3] explained it as 'to muzzle' on the ground of Arabic *šabama*. It could, however, be argued against this proposal that the concept of muzzling does not fit into the context. The verb summarizing Anat's actions is the *Gt* of *mḫṣ* (l. 43), which like the *Gt* of *maḫāṣu* in Akkadian means 'fight'. The verbs describing Anat's single actions are *mḫš* (ll. 35, 38, 40, 42), *kly* (ll. 36, 44) and *ṣmt*[4] (l. 41), all meaning 'destroy'. This meaning is obvious for the verbs *kly* and *ṣmt*, well known from Biblical and Ugaritic usage. This holds good even for the difficult verb form *mḫšt*, explained by W.F. Albright[5] as a metathesis of Akkadian *ḫamāšu*

---

[1] Cf. *U* 5, text 137, R° I:8', p. 241: *tu-un-na-nu*, i.e. *tunnanu* or *tunnānu*. Cf. in Arabic the change between *fuᶜāl* or *fuᶜᶜāl* and *faᶜīl* (Ch. Rabin, *Ancient West Arabian*, London, 1951, pp. 33f.) But perhaps *tunnanu* has been blended in Hebrew with *tan* jackal. Cf. *tannin* (Thr. 4:3) 'jackals', instead of *tannim* and *tannim* (Ez. 29:3; 32:2), instead of *tannin*.

[2] On the reading of the third word, see Herdner, *CTA*, p. 17, note 2.

[3] *La déesse Anat*, Paris 1938, p. 53. True, Virolleaud added to the translation *bâillonner* in brackets: "*plus particulièrement d'un chevreau pour le sevrer*". But this restriction has been neglected in later treatments.

[4] Gordon's reading: *mdd ilm ar (41) ṣ mt* has little to commend itself. Cf. Herdner, *CTA*, p. 17, note 3... "*On voit mal pourquoi le scribe qui disposait, à la fin de la ligne 40, d'une place suffisante pour graver encore plusieurs signes, aurait coupé, sans raison, son mot en deux*". Add to this decisive argument the attestation of the verb *ṣmt* in Ugaritic and the lack of a word-divider after *ṣ*.

[5] *BASOR* 84 (1941), p. 16, note 21.

'break (a reed)'[6], and alternatively explained by M. Held[7] as from *mḫṣ*; he supposes that *mḫṣt* became *mḫšt* "through partial assimilation of the emphatic *ṣ* to the following *t*", a phonetic change otherwise unattested in West-Semitic languages. Anyhow, it is clear that *mḫšt* stands in close parallel to *klt*, since in the verses *lmḫšt mdd il ym // lklt nhr il rbm* (ll. 35-36) *mdd il ym* and *nhr il rbm* designate the same god.[8] Therefore it might seem reasonable to suppose that *šbm* also roughly means 'destroy', and so it is easily understandable that C.H. Gordon in his *Ugaritic Manual* tentatively offered this interpretation.[9]

Against this argument the present writer[10] adduced in a paper called *The Muzzling of the Tannin* the beginning of the second column of *Ludlul*[11] which reads:

> *im-ḫa-aṣ rit-ti ma-ḫi-ṣi-a ú-šad-di kakka-šu* ^{d}*Marduk*
> *i-na pi-i gir-ra akili-a id-di nap-sa-ma* ^{d}*Marduk*
> 'Marduk beat the hand of my beater, caused his weapon to fall down; upon (or into) the mouth of the lion about to devour me Marduk put a muzzle.'

Upon this passage the present writer remarked: "This Akkadian text combines the conceptions of beating and muzzling in a way analogous to our Ugaritic text." His exegesis had met with general acceptance.

After the appearance of the above-mentioned paper on the muzzling of the *Tannin*, the new fragment *PRU* 2, text 3, p. 12 was published; in it we read in ll. 7-10 *d̲nbtm tnn*[12] *lšbm tšt trks lmrym*. In a paper on '*The Myth*

---

[6] Cf. *CAD* and von Soden, *AHW*, *s.v.* *ḫamāšu*.

[7] *JAOS* 79 (1959), pp. 169-176.

[8] See in this volume, *The Ugaritic Myth of the Sea etc.*, p. 349.

[9] But in *Ugaritic Textbook* 'muzzle'.

[10] See in this volume, *The Muzzling of the Tannin in Ugaritic Myth*, pp. 91 f.

[11] This paper appealed to a text reconstructed by B. Landsberger. J. Barr, *JSS* 18 (1973), p. 26, communicates that "Lambert had ... found new evidence, as yet unpublished, which shows that the reconstruction proposed by Landsberger was in fact right."

[12] The text actually reads *tan*. The omission of one wedge of *n*, however, is a well-known mistake of Ugaritic scribes. Cf. Gordon, *UT*, *Grammar* 4.13; and the reading *tnn*! has been accepted by all scholars.

of the Sea in Ugaritic Literature and in the Bible' the present writer[13] proposed the translation: 'The tails of the *Tunnanu [*which (i.e. the *Tunnanu*)*]* she had put into a muzzle, she tied to the height.'

The basic assumptions of this exegesis have been forcefully contested in a recent study by J. Barr[14], who argues that the Arabic evidence for a root *šbm* denoting 'muzzle' is extremely thin, since Arabic *šibām* does not denote 'muzzle' in general but has the restricted sense of a muzzle put into the mouth of a kid in order to prevent it from sucking, and the denominative verb-forms *šabama* and *šabbama* mean 'to apply the *šibām*'. He adds that *šibām* has a second meaning 'threads to hold a veil in its place' and that in the light of this second meaning the sense 'muzzle of a kid' cannot be considered as primary.

Barr differs from the present writer also in the evaluation of the *Ludlul* text and remarks that "the application of the *napsamu* ... does not belong to the same conceptual field as the smiting or beating done against the afflicted writer."

Barr's own exegesis is founded upon South Arabian *šbm*, amply attested in personal proper names as well as in names of places and explained by Landberg to mean 'be high'. This meaning, Barr observes, makes excellent sense in *PRU* 2, text 3 where *šbm* can easily be explained as parallel to *mrym*[14a], both denoting 'height'. Upon the difficult *lištbm* Barr hesitatingly comments: "As we have seen, the environing words are distinctly verbs of annihilation and destruction. If the sense of *šbm* were basically something like 'be high', then it is at least possible that the meaning in this line would be something like 'lift up', 'remove', 'get rid of'. This would be comparable with familiar usages of *slq* 'go up' developing into *hstlq* 'be removed, taken away', or Akkadian *elûm* 'go up', but *etlûm* 'go up and away from; get rid of (a thing)'."

II

Barr's criticism of the present writer's paper on the muzzling of the *Tannin* is basically sound, although not all of his objections are of the

[13] *Op. cit.* (note 8), p. 358.

[14] *Op. cit.* (note 11), pp. 17-39.

[14a] On the *y* of *mrym* cf. J. Blau-S.E. Loewenstamm, *UF* 2, p. 28.

same validity. When quoting the text from *Ludlul* the present writer wanted to point out that the Akkadian text ascribed to Marduk both smiting and muzzling. He never thought of a parallel between the muzzling done by Marduk and the beating done to the afflicted writer by his enemy. Stronger, however, are Barr's arguments against the alleged Arabic etymon of Ugaritic *šbm*, especially his contention that Arabic *šibām* is not a general term for 'muzzle'. It could be added to his criticism that in *PRU* 2, text 3 'muzzle' fails to yield a satisfactory sense, since it would hardly be apt to describe the muzzling of a beast as putting into a muzzle. We should rather expect an expression like 'putting a muzzle upon (or into) its mouth'.

Barr's own proposal, however, meets with no lesser difficulties. Landberg's explanation of *šbm* in South-Arabian names as meaning 'be high' lacks textual support and his etymological reasoning, summed up by Barr, proves at the most that *šbm might* have this meaning. True, *šbm* in *PRU* 2, text 3 could easily be interpreted as a parallel to *mrym* 'height'. However, the interpretation of *lištbm* as 'I removed' remains precarious, although *slq* does mean 'remove' in Talmudic Aramaic (and even in Talmudic and modern Hebrew). But *slq* has this meaning only in the *D* form. Similar is the position in Akkadian. *CAD* quotes the sense 'remove' for the *D* and *Š* forms of *elûm*, not for *G* and *Gt* which mean 'lose', 'forfeit', not 'get rid of'.

III

Let us look for a new starting point of analysis and compare both Ugaritic texts under discussion. The general tenor of the first text is Anat's victory over the god of the Sea and a host of monsters of which the *Tunnanu* is the first. Less clear is the overall meaning of the second text, a small fragment, which reads: ... *'un b'arṣ / mḫ̆nm ṯrp ym / lšnm tlḥk / šmm tṯrp / ym ḏnbtm / tnn lšbm / tšt trks / lmrym lbt* ...

The interpretation of this small fragment is beset with many difficulties. But it is clear at first sight that this text, too, mentions the *Tunnanu* after the *ym* and reports that a goddess tied the *Tunnanu* or its tail(s) to the height. These first observations strongly support the commonly held view that we are dealing with an alternative version of Anat's victory over the Sea and the monsters. This persuasive hypothesis becomes even more forcible if we accept the present writer's proposal to explain the enigmatic verb *ṯrp* as a metathesis of Arabic *frṯ*, Syriac *prt* 'split'. In support of this guess it may be noted that *prt* renders in the Syriac version of the Bible the Hebrew verb *bq*^{c} describing the splitting of the Red Sea (Ex. 14: 16, 21; Is. 63:12; Ps. 78:13; Neh. 9:11). On these suppositions it is hardly fortuitous that the rare root *šbm* appears in both texts in relation to the *Tunnanu* and the idea imposes itself that the *Gt* of *šbm* should be interpreted as denominative of *šbm* meaning 'put into a *šbm*', i.e. that both texts describe the same action of Anat with slight differences of wording. True, even this working hypothesis does not provide us with a ready exegesis of the difficult passage *ḏnbtm tnn lšbm tšt trks lmrym*. *ḏnbtm* has been explained as dual of *ḏnb* 'tail'. This interpretation is possible, but not cogent, since *ḏnbt* might be an alternative singular form of *ḏnb*, and cf. Akkadian *zibbatu*. There exists no proof that the *Tunnanu* had two tails in contrast to *Tiamat* who had only one. Cf. *Enūma Eliš* v:59: *e-gir zib-bat-sa dur-ma-ḫ[i-iš] ū-rak-ki-is-ma* 'He (Marduk) bent her (*Tiamat's*) tail, bound (it) to the great band'.[15] The similarity of Marduk's action to that of the Ugaritic goddess is obvious and is even underlined by the correspondence of Akkadian *rakāsu* with Ugaritic *rks*. Therefore it might well be that both texts are akin in content as well. Marduk, however, bound *Tiamat's* tail to the great band only after he had killed her. In the light of this consideration we might take into account the possibility of explaining the *m* of *ḏnbtm* as enclitic *m*, added to the singular form *ḏnbt*, and *lšbm tšt* as an unconnected relative clause. We might then translate: 'The tail of the *Tunnanu*, (which, i.e. the *Tunnanu*) she had put into a *šbm*, she bound to the height.' This, admittedly hypothetical, translation would exactly fit the proposed translation of *lištbm tnn* 'I put the *Tunnanu* into a *šbm*'. A less exact correspondence between both texts would be yielded by the alternative rendering 'The two tails (or the tail) of the *Tunnanu* she put into a *šbm* and bound them (or it, i.e. either the tails or the *Tunnanu*) to the height' or even 'On its tail (adverbial *m*) she put *Tunnanu* into a *šbm*, etc.'. In any case, the *šbm* should denote some fettering device bigger than a muzzle. It is worthwhile stressing that the use of fettering devices in the description of Marduk's struggles is not restricted to *Ludlul*, but plays an important part even in the fourth tablet of *Enūma Eliš*. When fighting with *Tiamat* her-

---

[15] See B. Landsberger - J.V. Kinnier Wilson, *JNES* 20 (1961), pp. 160f., 174f. The translation given here is theirs.

self "the Lord spread out his net to enfold her" (l. 95).[16] Her helpers were "thrown onto a net, they found themselves ensnared" (l. 112).[16] "The whole band of demons that marched on her right, he cast into fetters" (ll. 116-117). "And Kingu, who had been made chief among them, he bound and accounted him to Ugae" (ll. 119f.).[16] As to the *Tunnanu* in particular, cf. the description of the *Tannin's* fate in Ez. 32:3, beginning with the words "I will spread my net over you ... and you will be dragged up in its meshes" (*NEB*).

All these examples demonstrate that the fettering of monsters in this way or another is one of the distinctive features of ancient Near-Eastern texts describing the fight of a god against them. Barr, too, considered the possibility of translating the crucial word *lištbm* 'she puts in a tie, she binds', but rejected it. In the present writer's opinion this rendering, however, points in the right direction, although the exact nature of the fettering device applied defies closer definition. It has the clear advantage of explaining two Ugaritic descriptions of a goddess' struggle with the *Tunnanu* in the same way and solves, moreover, a problem which was the very starting point of Barr's research, viz. the difficulty of assuming a triliteral Semitic verbal root, having *b* in second and *m* in third position. In our view no verbal morpheme is involved here, but rather a primary noun formation and a verb denominated from it.

The relation between *šbm* in Arabic, South-Arabian and Ugaritic remains after all a matter for speculation. We cannot even be sure that any relation exists at all. Barr supposes two homonymous roots, Arabic *šbm* on the one hand, South-Arabian and Ugaritic *šbm* on the other. Even the relation between the two thoroughly divergent meanings of *šbm* in Arabic cannot be explained with confidence. The present writer rather feels inclined to derive both usages from a basic conception of fettering, since the threads holding fast a woman's veil might evoke such an idea as well.

---

[16] Translation by E.A. Speiser, *ANET*, p. 67.

The Rendering of Danil's Garment in the Aqhat Epic

In his paper: *Birds of Heaven and Rending of the Garment - a Motif of Ugaritic Literature and Targum Sheni of the Book of Esther* Y. Avishur[1] points to a feature common to the Aqhat epic and the midrash about King Solomon and the Queen of Sheba, extant in the Second Targum of the Scroll of Esther. In his article Avishur demonstrates that in these texts the appearance of birds announcing disaster is followed by the rending of a garment. Avishur holds the view that in both cases the act of rending has been performed by the person who received the evil omen. Avishur then attains to the result that the correspondence between the Ugaritic text and the midrash should be considered as a perfect one. Danil as well as the Queen of Sheba rent their garments at the sight of the ominous birds.

Let us scrutinize this argument. The exegesis of the Ugaritic text depends upon the interpretation of the crucial words: *tmz*^{c} *kst dnil* (*CTA* 19:I:36). Avishur discusses three explanations which have been proposed:

a) She (i.e. Danil's daughter) rent Danil's garment (*tmz*^{c} active *G*)
b) Danil's garment was rent (*tmz*^{c} passive *G* or *N*)
c) Danil rent (his) garment (*tmz*^{c} *taqattala*, a verb formation extant in Arabic).

Avishur concurs with the third of these proposals. This view, however, meets with decisive difficulties. *Taqattala* is not attested either in Ugaritic or in any other Nord-West Semitic language. Even more stringent is another objection. Arabic *taqattala* indicates a reflexive action and does not take a direct object. That is to say, the explanation of *tmz*^{c} as *taqattala* would result in the translation: 'The garment was rent'. The alternative rendering: 'She (i.e. Danil's daughter) rent the garment' is admissible from a linguistic point of view. Avishur correctly points out, however, that the rendering fails to yield satisfactory sense since in ancient times it was the mourner himself who rent his garment. Therefore it follows

[1] *BM* 60 (1974), pp. 72-75 (**Hebrew with English summary p. 163**).

that the garment was rent of itself. As regards the conception underlying this report, Avishur has already pointed to the narration of the synoptic Gospels that the veil of the Temple was rent (of itself), according to Matt. 27:51; Mar. 15:38 after Jesus' death, according to Luke 23:45-46 preceding it.

To sum up: No perfect correspondence between the Aqhat epos and the midrash about Solomon and the Queen of Sheba can be maintained. Nevertheless the similarity of both texts is striking to such a degree that they may be considered as variations of one motif. In addition we meet here with an analogy between the Ugaritic epic and the New Testament illustrating the conservative character of Ancient Oriental literature.

Ugarit and the Bible. I*

As early as at the very beginning of Ugaritic research scholars have become aware of striking similarities between the Ugaritic texts and the Hebrew Bible, parallels which pertain to the monetary system, the alphabet and the language, and comprehend even the structure of the verse, imagery, customs and concepts of ethical and mythological character. Therefore it is easily understood that very soon first attempts were made to sum up observations of this kind, the first already by H.L. Ginsberg and B. Maisler (Mazar) in *JPOS* 14 (1934), pp. 248f., note 15. Among the many subsequent comparisons we would like to single out U. Cassuto's paper: *Biblical and Canaanite Literatures, Tarbiz* 13 (1942), pp. 197-212; 14 (1942), pp. 1-10 *[= BOSt* 2, pp. 16-59*]* as a well balanced account of the literary aspects of the problem, which reached the closely reasoned conclusion that the Hebrew Bible should be regarded as the continuation of an ancient literary tradition flourishing in the land of Canaan in the period preceding the Israelite conquest. After the appearance of this study new Ugaritic texts have been published and comparative Ugaritic-Biblical studies have been continued with unabated vigour. Therefore, it may readily be admitted that the time has come for a new summing up of this subject which is of paramount importance for the very approach to Biblical research.

This purpose is served by the new comprehensive work *Ras Shamra Parallels* edited by Loren R. Fisher. The work will comprise three volumes, the first of which has appeared in 1972. It contains after an introduction by the editor (XI-XXIII) three contributions: I) *Literary Phrases* by A. Schoors (pp. 1-70); II) *Ugaritic-Hebrew Parallel Pairs* by M. Dahood with the collaboration of T. Penar (pp. 71-382); III) *Flora, Fauna and Minerals* by J.M. Sasson (pp. 383-454). The book concludes with detailed indices (pp. 455-537).

---

* Loren R. Fisher (Editor), *Ras Shamra Parallels*. The Texts from Ugarit and the Hebrew Bible. Vol. I. Assistant Editors: F. Brent Knutson and Donn F. Morgan (*Analecta Orientalia*, 49). xxiii-537 p. 27,5 x 22,5. Roma 1972. Pontificium Institutum Biblicum.

I

A work of this kind, composed by different authors, raises questions of general redaction.

1) A considerable amount of items have been dealt with by two authors. The Ugaritic verse *lḥ[m] bṯlḥnt lḥm št bkrpnm yn* (*CTA* 4:IV:35-37) and its Biblical parallels are discussed in I 15 and again in II 332.335. The famous problem of the kid cooked in milk is treated in I 23 (over three pages!) and a second time in III 30, the question of *ksp // ḫrṣ* and *ksp* and *yrq ḫrṣ* in II 301.302 and once more in III 60.69. This list could easily be continued.

2) The editor states in his introduction "that the project staff has striven for consistency in presentation". In accordance with this principle every item of the bibliography is printed in large letters and occupies a special line. A continuously printed bibliography in small letters would have left more room for explanations. Let us consider the simple case of *dblt* (III 38). There the bibliography takes up six lines, whereas the explanation is restricted to the remark on 2 Reg. 20:7 "Among others, Jacob refers to this passage where Hezekiah's cure is effected by the application of fig-cakes *d^{e}bälät t^{e}'enim* upon boils". A more helpful commentary should read: "Mentioned in hippiatric texts along with *ṣmqm* 'dried raisins'. In the Bible as well *d^{e}belim* are mentioned sometimes together with *ṣimmuqim* (1 Sam. 25:18, etc.). 2 Reg. 20:7 relates that Hezekiah's cure etc.". After this explanation the item *ṣmq* (III 105) could have been cut short to a reference to *dblt*. In the comparison of *[t]l šmm šmn arṣ* (*CTA* 3:II:39) with Gen. 27:28 (II 208) the bibliography (which omits H.L. Ginsberg, *Tarbiz* 4 *[*1932*]*, p. 46) takes up thirteen lines but no remark upon the anything but obvious meaning of the "oil of the earth" is added, although this term has been clarified by W. Zobel's thorough analysis.

3) Schoors most helpfully quotes the texts under discussion and adds their translation. Dahood, however, does so in exceptional cases only and mostly contents himself with references to the sources.

4) In his introduction the editor refers for questions of comparative grammar and lexicography to the studies published by C.H. Gordon and M. Dahood. The insertion of the Chapter *Flora, Fauna and Minerals* is hardly com-

patible with this restriction of scope. Consider for example III 100 dealing in eleven lines with the correspondence of Ugaritic *pr(t)* "bull, cow" to Hebrew *par, pārā*.

5) Less conspicuous, but not less important, are two other questions of general organisation:

a. One of them is the problem of numerical sayings, touched upon in I 14, II 44.200.531.532.602.604.609. The reader wonders whether this sporadic treatment does justice to the widely discussed questions of numerical sayings (see most recently M. Haran, *Tarbiz* 39 [1969], pp. 109-136), whose adequate treatment requires a special chapter. The present book fails to bring out these specific problems. One example may suffice. I 14 (cf. II 609) deals with the Ugaritic verse *ṯn dbḥm šna bᶜl ṯlṯ rkb ᶜrpt* (*CTA* 4:III: 17-18) 'two banquets Baal hates, three the rider of the clouds' in comparison with Pr. 6:16, but does not state: 1. that the formula introduces the specification of three kinds of banquets; 2. that this function of numerical sayings is unparalleled in Ugaritic; 3. that all numerical sayings of this kind in Hebrew (cf. also Akhikar 14-15) belong to the Wisdom Literature and that the solitary use of this form in the Ugaritic epic poses a well-known difficult question. The present writer tentatively proposes the solution that the author of the epic made use of a saying taken from Ugaritic proverbs in order to demonstrate that Baal really shows the reactions ascribed to him in a sapiential saying.

b. Another structural parallel between Ugaritic and Hebrew poetry deserving comprehensive and systematic treatment is the specific kind of verse-structure, dubbed by S.R. Driver *climactic parallelism*, enlarged by W.F. Albright to comprehend all cases of repetitive parallelism and restricted by myself to cases admitting the definition *expanded colon*. The cases covered by the latter definition are confined to Ugaritic and Hebrew and therefore provide us with one of the most distinctive features of Canaanite poetry. I have tried to analyse this form in *Lĕšonênu* 27 (1963), pp. 111-126 and again in a revised version in *JSS* 14 (1969), pp. 176-196, and my survey has been completed by Y. Avishur in *UF* 4 (1972), pp. 1-10. All we find on this important problem in the present volume is a short comparison of *CTA* 2:IV:8-9 to Ps. 92:10 by Schoors (I 29) who erroneously speaks of synthetic parallelism, a term describing since the days of Lowth a verse in which the second colon does not contain either a repetition or a contrast to the first, but supplements or completes it, i.e. the parallelism is merely of form and does not extend to the thought (S.R. Driver, *Introduction to the Literature of the Old Testament* [Edinburgh [9]1913, pp. 362-363). It may be added that Schoors expresses his astonishment at the omission of the words *ki hinne 'oy*^{e}*bäkā YHWH* in the translations of *BJ* and *NEB*, obviously being unaware of the fact that these words are lacking in Septuagint B (probably by *homoeoteleuton*) and that this short reading has been defended by S. Mowinckel, *Real and Apparent Tricola*, Oslo 1957, p. 34.

II

1) Schoors' chapter *Literary Phrases* contains *inter alia* passages which are hardly entitled to this designation, e.g. I 1 where the words *dqt šrp w[š]lmm* (*CTA* 36:7) are taken from a simple list of offerings. The place for the discussion of such an enumeration is clearly in a comparative treatment of Ugaritic and Biblical sacrifices. The items I 5.10.11 deal with the relevance of Ugaritic phrases for the explanations of Hebrew proper nouns. Again, proper nouns are a subject in its own right.

2) A part of the alleged parallels is open to discussion.

a. Schoors (I 49) compares *bšlḥ ttpl* (*CTA* 14:I:20, 21) 'they fell through the spear' with *b*^{ec}*ad haššälaḥ yippolu* (Joel 2:8) 'they burst through the weapons'. Both translations are controversial. M. Tsevat, *VT* 4 (1954), pp. 41-44, 322, explained *šlḥ* as the god of the river of the Netherworld, D. Leibel, *Tarbiz* 32 (1963), pp. 225-227, as the river of the Netherworld itself. *šälaḥ* in Joel has been explained by S.E. Loewenstamm, *Lĕšonénu* 26 (1961), p. 62 as the outer wall of a city (Akkadian *šalḫu*), by D. Leibel (*loc. cit.*) and H. Yalon, *Tarbiz* 18 (1964), p. 404 as 'canal' (Hebr. *š*^{e}*lāḥim*). But even if we prefer Schoors' interpretation of the texts, there remains the obvious objection, that the ideas of falling by a spear and breaking through weapons are patently disparate.

b. Schoors (I 24) reads: *iqnu šmt [b]n šrm* (*CTA* 23:21-22) 'I have zeal for the names of the sons of princes', comparing *w*^{e}*qinne'ti l*^{e}*šem qodši* (Ez. 39:25); consult also II 491. However, the supposition of a Ugaritic verb *qn'* cannot be supported by corroborative evidence, whereas the name *iqnu* 'lapis lazuli' is amply attested. Like *iqnu*, *šmt* is known as the name of a precious stone, and both stones appear together in *PRU* 2, text

106:5-6, 16-17; text 107:1. To these remarks we have to add the undisputed possibility that some words may be missing after *šmt*. It follows, then, that the text defies interpretation.

c. Another case in point is the famous text *CTA* 23:14 made by Schoors (I 23) to read *ṭb[ḫ(?)g]d. bḥlb* 'they cook a kid in milk'. This reading with its interpretation inspired by the famous Biblical prohibition *lo' t^{e}baššel g^{e}di baḥ^{a}leb 'immo* (Ex. 23:19 etc.) has been proposed by Ch. Virolleaud, *Syria* 19 (1933), p. 140 as *simplement conjecturale*, but has nevertheless won in wide circles the renown of an ascertained fact. The full passage reads in Herdner's rendering: *ṭb.* (?)*[g]d. bḥlb annḫ bḫmat*. The word *annḫ* is an unexplained *hapaxlegomenon [*de Moor, *New Year* 2, p. 19 compares Akkadian *ananiḫu* the name of a garden plant*]* and therefore fails to provide us with a clue for the reconstruction of the word preceding *bḥlb* from which only a doubtful *d* has been preserved. Moreover, as pointed out by Herdner, *ṭb* is followed by a word divider which excludes the restoration *ṭb[ḫ]*. Therefore Herdner ponders whether we should read *ṭb<ḫ>*. But this kind of restoration is most precarious in a broken and anyhow unclear text and Sasson's scepticism (III 30) is justified. In a paper in *UF* 5 (1973), pp. 209-210 I tried to show that the Ugaritic verb *ṭbḫ* and its Hebrew counterpart never means "cook", but invariably "slaughter". *[*See in this volume, *Lexicographical Notes*, pp. 449-450.*]*

3) Let us add some selected remarks on different items. Regarding I 6 *nḫlm tlk nbtm* (*CTA* 6:III:7), 'the wadies flow with honey', compared with *w^{e}nah^{a}rotām kaššämän 'olik* (Ez. 32:14) and *w^{e}kol '^{a}piqe yehudā yel^{e}ku māyim* (Joel 4:18), Schoors stresses the similarity in words and formulas to describe the fertility caused by a deity and underlines especially the same use of the verb *hlk*. This is correct, although Akkadian *alāku* is attested in the same use as well. Cf. *CAD, s.v. alāku* 3g. The similarity to Ez. 32: 14 becomes even more evident if we pay attention to the pair of words *šämän* and *nopät*. Consult II 376. Schoors adduces without comment Kapelrud's view that the prophetic texts have their prototype in the description of fertility after Baal is restored to the throne. Kapelrud's view is commendable. The abundant fertility of nature is perfectly adequate to the resurrection of a deity procuring fertility, whereas its connection with the rescue of a people from the yoke of foreign conquerors seems to be secondary.

I 17 *wtn qlh b^{c}rpt* (*CTA* 4:V:70) 'and he gives forth his voice in the clouds'. Schoors considers the difficult *wtn* as infinitive, but fails to adduce any certain example for such a shortened form of the infinitive. Dahood's proposal to regard *wtn* as syncope of *wytn* is preferable.

I 18 Schoors explains the last letter of *yišrehu* (Job 37:3) as an archaic *yaqtulu* ending. This ending, however, is short and could hardly have been rendered in archaic orthography by *w*.

I 20 *bmt [arṣ] tṭṭn* (*CTA* 4:VII:34-35) 'the high places of the earth rocked', in comparison with *tānuṭ hā'ārāṣ* (Ps. 99:1). Schoors explains *tānuṭ* as *yiqtol* of *nṭṭ*. Its derivation from *nuṭ*, however, is impeccable, since the interchange between *mediae waw* and *mediae geminatae* is a well known phenomenon. The Ugaritic verse can be singled out as the only Ugaritic attestation of the motif that the whole of nature trembles at the appearance of a militant deity, whereas this motif is amply attested in Hebrew and Akkadian. See in this volume, *The Trembling of Nature during Theophany*, pp. 173-189; Jörg Jeremịas, *Theophanie* (*WMANT* 10; Neukirchen 1965), especially pp. 75-81, 151.

I 21 *tspr byrdm arṣ* (*CTA* 4:VIII:8-9) 'you will be counted among those who go down to the earth', compared with *w^{e}nähšabti ^{c}im yor^{e}de bor* (Ps. 88:5). Cf. also *inter alia yor^{e}de ^{c}āpār* (Ps. 22:30) *yār^{e}du ... 'äl 'äräṣ taḥtiyyot* (Ez. 32:24). In this connection Schoors also discusses *btḫpṯt* (*CTA* 4:VIII:7) in comparison with *bet ḥopšit* (2 Reg. 15:5) explaining 'infirmary'. Contrast de Moor, *Seasonal Pattern*, pp. 185-186, who convincingly interprets 'house of freedom', a euphemism for prison and *ḥopši* in Ps. 88:6 as 'free' (i.e. imprisoned). Cf. also *w^{ec}äbäd ḥopši me'^{a}donāw* (Job 3:19) where possibly a double entendre is intended i.e. the slave (when imprisoned in the Netherworld) is free from his master.

I 25 *ktmḫṣ ltn bṯn brḥ tkly bṯn ^{c}qltn* (*CTA* 5:I:1-2) 'when you smote Lotan the fleeing serpent, made an end of the twisting serpent' in comparison with Is. 27:1. It is worthwhile pointing out that in both the Ugaritic and the Biblical texts that monster appears in its own right, without preceding reference to the *ym*, in contrast to *CTA* 3:III:38 where *bṯn ^{c}qltn* is mentioned after *ym* and *tnn* as in Ps. 74:14 where *liwyātān* is preceded as well by *yam* and *tannin*. Furthermore the continuation of the Ugaritic text *šlyṭ d šb^c t rašm* (*CTA* 5:I:3) 'the ruler (?) possessing seven heads' could have been compared with *rā'še liwyātān* (Ps. 74:14).

I 26 *^c n kd̲d aylt* (*CTA* 5:I:17). Schoors emends the obscure *kd̲d* to read *kšd*. However, the parallel version of the text in *U* 5, pp. 559f., text 4:8 confirms the reading *kd̲d*.

I 27 *^c bdk an wd^c lmk* (*CTA* 5:II:12) in comparison with Ps. 116:16. Schoors' translation 'your slave am I, yea yours forever' is doubtlessly correct. His definitions of *d^c lmk* as "brachylogy", however, is open to discussion. For another syntactical approach see in this volume, *Notes on the Pronouns in Ugaritic in the Light of Canaanite*, p. 70. To the address *^c bdk an* cf. also 2 Sam. 15:34; 1 Reg. 18:36; Ps. 119:125.

I 28 Schoors quotes the explanation of *at̲r* in *PRU* 5, text 60:34 as a relative pronoun. Contrast A.F. Rainey, *UF* 3 (1971), pp. 161-162.

I 30 *tqḥ mlk ^c lmk drkt dt dr drk* (*CTA* 2:IV:10) 'you will take your everlasting kingdom, your dominion of endless generations' in comparison with *malkut^e kā malkut kol ^c olāmim* (Ps. 145:13). The undeniable parallel becomes even more interesting if we pay attention to A. Hurvitz, *The Transition Period in Biblical Hebrew* (Jerusalem 1972), pp. 70-72 (in Heb.) who conclusively proved the late character of the stylistic pattern *b^e kol X w X*.

I 42,h *mid rm [krt] btk rpi ar[ṣ]* (*CTA* 15:III:13-14). Schoors accepts two translations of *btk rpi arṣ*, viz. J. Gray's 'among the congregation of the land' (dependent upon H.L. Ginsberg), and J. Aistleitner's *'unter den Fürsten des Landes'*. However, it goes without saying that we are dealing here with two mutually exclusive interpretations.

I 43 *wpn špš nr by* (*PRU* 2, text 15:9-10) "the face of the sun shone on me" in comparison with *pānäkā hā'er b^{ec} abdäkā* (Ps. 119:135) and Nu. 6: 25. Schoors comments: "Ugaritic *špš* designates the king, just like *šamšu* in the Amarna letters". It actually designates in Amarna and Ugaritic letters the great king only, i.e. the kings of Egypt and the Hittite empire. In the Bible the simile mostly applies to God. Cf. in addition to Schoors' quotations Ps. 31:17; 67:2; 80:4,8,20; Dan. 9:17. Only once it refers to the king (Pr. 16:15). Compare in this volume, *Remarks on Stylistic Patterns etc.*, p. 266.

I 48 *irš ḥym watnk blmt wašlḥk* (*CTA* 17:VI:27-28) 'ask for life and I will give (it) to you, for not dying and I will bestow (it) upon you' in comparison with *ḥayyim šā'al mimmᵉkā nātattā lo 'oräk yāmim ᶜolām wāᶜäd* (Ps. 21:5). Schoors accepts Dahood's view, that we should infer from the parallel that *ḥayyim* means in the psalm eternal life and adds that the idea of eternal life is expressly formulated in Dan. 12:2. The very late chapter Dan. 12, however, is of no consequence for the exegesis of classical Hebrew poetry. In Ps. 21:5 *ḥayyim* is primarily parallel to *'oräk yāmim*. Cf. the *parataxis ḥayyäkā wᵉ'oräk yāmäkā* (Deut. 30:20). The enlargement of *'orak yāmäkā* by *ᶜolām wāᶜäd* is rooted in hyperbolic court style. Cf. *yᵉḥi 'ᵃdoni hammäläk dāwid lᵉᶜolām* (1 Reg. 1:31).

4) It is difficult to assess the completeness of Schoors' survey, since some literary phrases omitted by him and not representing pairs of words may be treated in the forthcoming second volume under another headline. Therefore, only two obvious omissions may be noted:

a. The phrase *[t]rḥṣ ydh bdm ḏmr* (*CTA* 3:II:34) 'she washes her hands of the blood of warriors' has been compared by M. Dahood in his commentary on Psalms to *pᵉᶜāmāw yirḥaṣ bᵉdam hārāšāᶜ* (Ps. 58:11) explained by him 'he washes his feet of the blood of the wicked'. Dahood adds that the Ugaritic parallel favours the reading *kappāw* attested in Septuagint, Vulg. and Syr. against *pᵉᶜāmāw*. We could even go a step further than Dahood and regard τὰς χεῖρας αὐτοῦ as translation of *yādāw*. Dahood's interpretation of Ps. 58:11 stands to reason although *rḥṣ b* is amply attested in the sense 'to wash in' and *pᵉᶜāmāw* is an unexceptional variant of *yādāw*.

b. A major parallel is the fixation of destiny by a cup (*ks, kos*) held in the hand of a deity. Cf. U. Cassuto, *Or* 7 (1938), p. 283, who refers to *CTA* 3:V:42, where Baal's cup is brought to Il for the fixation of Baal's destiny, and to Ez. 23:31-34; Ps. 11:6; 16:5. To these passages we would like to add *CTA* 15:II:16-20 where Il holds a cup in his hand when blessing Krt (on the restoration of this passage consult Y. Avishur, *UF* 4 *[*1972*]*, pp. 7-8) and perhaps also *CTA* 17:I:35, where we probably should read: *[ks y]iḫd il bdh* (!) *ybrk* (Herdner's reading *il. ᶜbdh* is precarious. There is only one unclear sign between *il* and *bdh* which might be either an ᶜ or a word divider, but not both). *[*On this question see now in detail J.J. Jackson - H.H.P. Dressler, *JAOS* 95 (1975), pp. 99-101.*]* In the Bible cf. Ps 75:9; even the *kos* in the hand of a man blessing God (Ps. 116:13) might be relevant in this context.

III

1) The main contribution to the volume is M. Dahood's programmatic and challenging article on pairs of words. True, the title of his paper does not ring the sound of a revolutionary proclamation. The existence of pairs of words, common to Ugaritic and Hebrew, has never escaped the attention of scholars, and already Cassuto composed provisional lists of such pairs reaching the number of forty, while M. Held compiled an additional list of twenty, combining previous observations of H.L. Ginsberg and U. Cassuto with observations of his own. But in contrast to these modest enumerations Dahood presents us with six hundred and sixteen items. How are we to understand this enormous difference? The reasons are manifold and we shall try to discuss them one by one.

2) a. The addition of new pairs does not reflect in all cases Dahood's specific approach. New texts have yielded new pairs. Cf. e.g. II 18 *aḫ* and *r*^{c} (*PRU* 2, text 19:8,10), II 381 *nḥš* and *bṯn* (*U* 5, pp. 568, 572, text 7:75-76), II 581 *šr* and *ḏmr* (*U* 5, pp. 551f., text 2:3-4) and even the renewed research of texts published before World War II sometimes revealed a hitherto overlooked pair. Cf. e.g. II 26 *akl* and *kly*, II 378 *nhqt* and *g*^{c}*t*.

b. To this we may add some cases of what Dahood dubbed "distant parallelism" (II Intro 6c-f), a phenomenon whose manifold ramifications have been studied in the unpublished dissertation of Y. Avishur, "*Pairs of Words in Biblical Literature and their Parallels in Semitic Literature of the Ancient Near East*".

α) Dahood mentions *inclusio* and adduces *inter alia* the verses Ps. 18: 39-41 included by the pairs of verbs *'ämhāṣem* and *'aṣmitem* and sagaciously remarks that "of the six verbs in these three verses, only the Ugaritic pair stands in the first person singular with the attached plural suffix as the direct object".

β) In the same context Dahood treats a phenomenon which I would like to describe as "command and its performance". David is ordered *m*^{e}*ne 'ät yiśrā'el* (2 Sam. 24:1) and afterwards his performance of this order is referred to in v. 10 by the words *sāpar 'ät hā*^{c}*ām*. Here also belongs the relation between ${}^{c}ms$ and *nša* (*CTA* 6:I:12-14) subsumed in II 431 under the vague category of "collocation". Šapšu tells Anat ${}^{c}ms$ m^{c} (v. 12) and Anat complies *tšu* (v. 14).

γ) Near to this category is the case where the same subject is described in the same text by different words, e.g. in Gen. 24:43-44 where the servant speaks of the same girl in v. 43 as an *^{c}almā*, in v. 44 as an *'iššā*. Although no parallelism can be recognised here (pace Dahood II 86), this kind of repetition should be taken into consideration for the fixing of pairs.

δ) A pair of words in a real "distant parallelism" sometimes can be found in a poetic passage comprehending more than two cola, e.g. the parallelism between *'oyeb* (Ex. 15:6) and *qāmäkā* (v. 7). Here two verses describing God as destroying enemies are parallel to each other and there is no necessity for Dahood's proposal (II 6f.) to change the stichometry of the text by joining v. 7a to v. 6, i.e. by detaching *qāmäkā* in v. 7a from v. 7bc which include the verb *yo'k^{e}lemo* whose suffix refers to *qāmäkā*.

3) All these observations, however, account only to a certain degree for the difference between the classic sixty pairs and Dahood's six hundred and sixteen, and I may point out that Y. Avishur in his above-mentioned recent dissertation counted one hundred and ninety-seven pairs only as common to the Bible and the Ugaritic literature and that even this relatively small number includes thirty-three cases of admittedly uncertain character. The high number, given by Dahood, is due to the following reasons.

a. Cases of reversed sequence of words (cf. II Intro 4) are treated as two items. Till recently it has been common opinion that the sequence of the components of a wordpair was fixed and invariable in Ugaritic and that only the later Biblical style admitted deviations from these rigid, ancient rules. In *UF* 3 (1971), p. 94 I adduced two exceptions to this rule. Systematic studies by Dahood and Avishur yielded the result that the number of variations in the sequence of the components is rather considerable even in Ugaritic, that is to say that variations of this kind do not impair the identity of the pair.

b. In the wake of an unpublished dissertation by R.E. Bornemann *Verbal Parallelism in Ugaritic and Biblical Poetry* Dahood combines a word with its repetition to a pair of words as well (II Intro 3c). The phenomenon of the stylistic affinity of two words (or roots), however, is basically different from the repetition of the same word (or root), and the latter problem calls for special treatment. As an important beginning of such a research we welcome Dahood's valuable comparison of *bntb pš^c // bntb gan* (*CTA* 17:VI:43-44) with *l^{e}ḥop yammim // l^{e}ḥop 'oniyyot* (Gen. 49:13) where in both texts the *regens* is repeated, but the *rectum* varied. Both expressions are aptly compared by Dahood (II Into 10c) although *ḥop* and *ntb* are clearly different words. It is not the identity of repeated words which matters here, but rather the syntactic and stylistic pattern of the repetition.

c. Dahood includes in his list prepositions and conjunctions, i.e. particles whose function is restricted to the connection of words which carry an independent meaning. This problem would better be treated apart.

d. He includes pronomina like *an, at*. True, these pronomina do have an independent sense. But nevertheless they might be omitted in a comparative literary research since their use in parataxis or parallelism is commonplace and can not be adduced as proof for the specific affinity of Ugaritic and Biblical style. There is only one peculiar case which might perhaps deserve discussion even in this framework, viz. *an // ank* in comparison with *'^{a}ni // 'ānoki* (II 51), a phenomenon restricted to Ugaritic and Hebrew, which has even some bearing upon the source criticism of Biblical texts in which *'^{a}ni* and *'ānoki* interchange, since the use of *'^{a}ni* is here widely regarded as a criterion of a later source.

e. As already remarked (above I 5a) numerical sayings should be treated as a special subject.

f. Some items are subject to lexicographical restriction.

α) There is no pair *qšt* and *ql^c* common to Ugaritic and Hebrew (II 507). Ugaritic *ql^c* is a loan from Egyptian and designates 'shield'. Consult B. Landsberger, *AfO* 18 (1958), pp. 279, note 8; A.F. Rainey, *JNES* 24 (1965), pp. 22, and cf. 2 Chr. 14:7. Therefore Ugaritic *ql^c* is to be kept separate from Hebrew *qäla^c* 'sling'.

β) No parallelism *qll / kbd* (II 488) exists, either in Hebrew or in Ugaritic. Ugaritic *tql* (*CTA* 4:IV:25) derives from the root *qyl* 'fall'. Consult W. von Soden, *VTS* 16 (1967), pp. 295-296, Hebrew *qālon* 'shame' from the root *qlh*. Cf. *niqlä*.

γ) There is no necessity of looking in Ecc. 6:12 for a parallel *'ᵃšär // 'aḥar* corresponding to the Ugaritic parallel *uḫryt // aṯryt* (II 20) since *'ᵃšär* can easily be interpreted as the conjunction *'ᵃšär = ki*, *'aḥᵃrāw* in its usual sense 'after him'.

δ) The alleged pair *ᶜm* and *ḥkm* 'to be wise and sagacious' is highly questionable. Ugaritic *ᶜm ᶜlm* (*CTA* 4:IV:42) is commonly explained as a free variant of *ᶜd ᶜlm* 'forever' and this explanation is borne out by the well known use of *ᶜm* as a preposition which designates the direction. (Perhaps even Biblical *ᶜam ᶜolām* (Is. 44:7) should be read *ᶜim ᶜolām*). The verb *ᶜmm* (Ez. 28:3) has been convincingly rendered to mean 'be equal'. Consult Sh.H. Paul, *JNES* 31 (1972), p. 351.

g. Different are the cases in which a word common to both languages is paralleled by interdialectical equivalents of different roots. Incomplete parallels of this kind should be kept apart from the perfect parallels.

α) *ḥy // iṯ* in comparison with *yeš // ḥay* (II 181). *iṯ* and *yeš* stem from different roots. Consult J. Blau, *IOS* 2 (1972), pp. 58-62. Cf. also II 366 where Dahood identifies *mġy* with *mṣa*. The two roots should be differentiated. See Blau, *ibid.*, pp. 67-72.

β) At this opportunity attention might be drawn to the incomplete correspondence between *ṭbḫ // šql* (*CTA* 22:B:12) and *happel // ṭāboᵃḥ* Ps. 37:14, where in both languages *ṭbḫ(ḥ)* 'slaughter' is paralleled by a verb meaning *'fell'*.

h. Dahood goes as far as to deduce the existence of Ugaritic pairs of words from simple administrative enumerations of items, although texts of this kind are far from reflecting literary style. One example (II 386) out of many must suffice. In a long list of persons we read: *annmn w ṯlṯ nᶜrh rpan w ṯn bnh*. Pointing to the nouns *nᶜrh* and *bnh*, Dahood notes: 'child, servant // son', and finds this parallel again in *ki naᶜar yiśrā'el wā'ohᵃbehu umimmiṣrayim qārā'ti libni* (Ho. 11:1) where he parses the possessive suffix of *libni* as that of the third person and translates: 'When Israel was a slave I loved him and from Egypt I called his sons'. However, 1) No parallels can be proved by the simple Ugaritic enumeration; 2) The explanation *nᶜr* 'slave', is purely hypothetical. Contrast A.F. Rainey, *JNES* 24 (1965), p. 21 who renders *nᶜr* 'firstclass experienced fighting man'. 3) Dahood's interpretation does violence to the tender simile of God as a loving father who takes care of his growing son.

i. Dahood regards differences in meaning as irrelevant if the same roots are involved.

α) In II 287 Dahood notes *kll - šlm* (*CTA* 51:11-12; 50:9-10; *PRU* 5, text 9:6-7; text 60:3-4) 'everything and peace', *šlm - kll* (*PRU* 2, text 15:14-15; *U* 5, pp. 286f., text 11:9-10) 'peace and everything', and *kullāh // š^elomim* (Jer. 13:19) 'all of her // wholly'. A closer scrutiny reveals that all the Ugaritic sources but one contain a part of a Ugaritic letter formula *kll šlm* or *šlm kll* 'perfect wellbeing'. Cf. *gabba šulmu* (*PRU* 4, p. 222, l. 2), whereas the interpretation of *šlmm kll* is disputed. The text reads: *š lil bt šlmm kll ylḥm bh* (*U* 5, pp. 586f., text 11:9-10). It has been argued by J. Blau - J. Greenfield, *BASOR* 200 (1970), p. 50, that *šlmm kll* represent the type of sacrifice called in Punic *šlm kll* (*KAI* 69:3ff.). It is, however, more plausible that we should interpret 'A ram for the god of the house as a peace-offering. Everyone may eat thereof' (J. de Moor, *UF* 2, p. 316), since this interpretation yields a good correspondence to l. 8: *wtlḥm aṯt* 'and the wife (of the king) may eat thereof'. That is to say that the words *šlmm* and *kll* are entirely unconnected. In the Biblical example *š^elomim* has nothing to do either with well-being or with a kind of sacrifice.

β) The same methodological question appears in II 12 in a veiled form. There Dahood notes *adn // um* (*CTA* 24:33-34) 'lord, father // mother' and compares the collocation of *'ādon* "lord" and *'em* 'mother' in Ps. 71:5-6. It is, however, clear that in the Ugaritic text *adn* means father, not lord; cf. also the lexicographic text *U* 5, pp. 232-233, text 130:II:9', where Ugaritic *a-da-nu* is equated with Akkadian *a-bu*.

γ) A special case is II 533, where Dahood compares *šbt - dqn* (*CTA* 4: V:66) 'greyness and beard' with the amply attested pair of the Hebrew roots *zqn* and *śyb* pointing to old age and greyness. If we were to accept his interpretation of *dqn*, no common pair could be recognized. It appears, however, that *dqn* should be rendered 'old age'; consult de Moor, *Seasonal Pattern*, p. 112.

j. If a word is parallel to a composit expression Dahood assumes its parallel to each of its components. II 178 and 180 deal with *ḥ̈z // abn* 'arrow // stone' and *ḥ̈z // yd* 'arrow // hand'. Both items refer to ***ḥ̈zk //*** *abn ydk* (*CTA* 14:III:116-117). In the construct *abn ydk*, however, the ***rectum*** *ydk* is only a qualification of the *regens abn* and no Ugaritic parallel *ḥẓ* // *yd* is borne out by this example. Moreover, it is improbable that *yd* here denotes 'hand'. It should rather be derived from *ydy* denoting in Hebrew the throwing of stones (Thr. 3:53) and arrows (Jer. 50:14); cf. also ^{c}*eṣ yād* (Nu. 35:18) and *'äbän yād* (Nu. 35:17).

4) There remains the question, under which conditions different words of one text should be regarded as a pair. Dahood (II Intro 11, b-d) differentiates between parallelism, juxtaposition and collocation, adding that only those words are listed which are strictly parallel either in Ugaritic or in Hebrew. From this rule Dahood purposely deviates only in II 426. The application of these three categories calls for closer scrutiny.

a. As already remarked above (III 2,b) Dahood includes in the category of parallelism the "distant parallelism". The reviewer is inclined in principle to accept this approach. But even then many cases of parallelism remain doubtful.

α) In II 193 Dahood states: *ḥmt* // *nḥš* (*U* 5, pp. 565, 567, text 7:5-6 etc.) 'venom // serpent'. The crucial words there are *lnh ydy ḥmt*, 'from it (i.e. the serpent) he shall remove the venom'. No parallelism between *nḥš* and *ḥmt* is evident.

β) In II 196 Dahood lists *ḥäräb* 'sword knife' // *ta*^{c}*ar* 'scabbard, blade', comparing the collocation *ḥrb* ... *t*^{c}*rt* (*CTA* 19:IV:207) 'sword ... scabbard'. 1 Sam. 17:51 reads: *wayyiqqaḥ 'ät ḥarbo wayyišl*^{e}*pāh mitta*^{c}*rāh* 'and he took his sword and drew it out of its scabbard'; Jer. 47:6 *hoi ḥäräb* ... *he'ās*^{e}*pi 'äl ta*^{c}*rek* 'sword ... betake yourself into your scabbard'. The lack of parallelism between sword and scabbard is evident. The passages are obvious cases of collocation like the Ugaritic passage *tšt ḥrb bt*^{c}*r[th]* (*CTA* 19:IV:207) 'she put the sword in its scabbard'. Ez. 5:1 is irrelevant, because *ta*^{c}*ar* there denotes 'razor'.

γ) Dahood admits the existence of a pair of words even if the real parallel is between two compounds of words in which the alleged parallel words are components, as in Job 36:6, *lo' y*^{e}*ḥayyä rāšā*^{c} *umišpaṭ* ^{c}*aniyyim yitten* 'He will not bestow life upon the wicked and give (i.e. allow) the right of the poor'. In this verse Dahood (II 185) looks for a parallel between *y*^{e}*ḥayyä* and *yitten*. The real antithetic parallel, however, is between *lo' y*^{e}*ḥayyä* and *mišpaṭ yitten*.

δ) Dahood admits parallelism between words in verses exhibiting synthetic parallelism. This procedure is most problematic. It exceeds the scope of the present paper to survey the different categories into which the classic concept of synthetic parallelism has been split up in modern research. Two simple examples may be enough to clarify the point. Let us consider the verse *'ašre hā^{c}ām yod^{ec}e t^{e}ru^{c}ā YHWH b^{e}'or pānäkā y^{e}hallekun* (Ps. 89:16) 'Happy the people who know to acclaim (Thee), O Lord, in the light of Thy face they will walk', i.e. the people who know to acclaim the Lord are happy (statement), since they walk in the light of His face (justification of the foregoing statement). We can hardly follow Dahood (II 222) who assumes in this case a parallelism between *yod^{ec}e* and *y^{e}hallekun*.

The same applies *a fortiori* to verses which describe a person's perception and his reaction to it, e.g. the verse *yšm^{c} aliyn b^{c}l yuhb ^{c}glt bdbr prt bšd šḥlmmt* (*CTA* 5:V:17-19), 'Puissant Baal hears, he makes love with a she-calf in Dbr, with a heifer in Šḥlmmt'. Here Dahood (II 566) supposes a parallelism between *yšm^{c}* and *yuhb*. It is, however, obvious that a synonymous parallelism exists only between the second and the third colon, whereas it remains a question of terminology whether we regard the introductory first colon as an independent unit or as connected with the following cola by synthetic parallelism.

b. Let us contemplate the term "juxtaposition". This term is used by Dahood whenever a word appears beside another, without regard to the syntactical relation between the words concerned. I noted:

α) parataxis II 9. Pair *abn* and *^{c}ṣ*. *'^{a}bānayik w^{ec}eṣayik* (Ez. 26:12)

β) construct II 2. Pair *ab* and *dr*. *dor '^{a}botāw* (Ps. 49:20).

γ) apposition II 36. Pair *il* and *mlk*. *'eli malki baqqodäš* (Ps. 68:25).

δ) subject, predicate II 59. Pair *ar* and *yrḫ*. *ar yrḫ* (*CTA* 24:38). 'The moon was shining'.

ε) predicate and object. II 226. Pair *yld* and *bn*. *tld šb^{c} bnm* (*CTA* 15: II:23) 'She will bear seven sons'.

ζ) predicate and its adverbial determination II 77. Pair *išt* and *šrp*. *bišt tšrpnn* (*CTA* 6:II:33) 'With fire she burns him'.

η) apposition to objet and following subject II 4. Pair *ab* and *ġr*. *tbkyk ab ġr* (*CTA* 16:I:6) 'For You, father, weeps the mountain'.

This treatment raises serious doubts. To start with let us single out the classical case of parataxis (syndetic and asyndetic) as one of the well known hallmarks of pairs, which has been given wide attention as early as in the dictionary of Brown-Driver-Briggs. It has even been argued that all parallelism should be regarded as the breaking up of parataxis. Cf. E.Z. Melamed, *Break-up of Stereotype Phrases as an Artistic Device in Biblical Poetry, ScHi* 8 (1961), pp. 115-153. Anyhow, it is obvious that in both, parallelism and parataxis, words are fully coordinated.

Some other cases of "juxtaposition" might indeed be treated in the same way as Dahood does, i.e. not as full proof but as corroborative evidence. Y. Avishur has explained in great detail the tendency of Semitic languages to turn the coordination of nouns into the subordination of the construct, a tendency steadily growing in strength in the course of time. Whereas its attestations in Ugaritic are still rare they abound in post-Biblical Hebrew. In Biblical Hebrew Avishur (*Semitics* 2 *[1970]*, pp. 17-81 and dissertation) has found nearly two hundred pairs of words, attested in parallelism and/or parataxis which appear in the construct connection as well. This result amply justifies the quotation of word-pairs in the construct as corroborative evidence.

Avishur (Dissertation) is probably also right in his assumption that we should attribute the same value to pairs of subject and predicate in a nominal sentence, as *ṣädäq mišpāṭäkā* (Ps. 119:75). Here the very structure of the sentence reveals the tendency to equate the predicate *ṣädäq* to the subject *mišpāṭäkā*. Both roots are attested in parallelism (e.g. Ps. 72:1-2), in parataxis (e.g. Ps. 89:15) and even in the construct (e.g. Deut. 16:18).

In the same way he evaluates the relation between the components of a simile. Cf. e.g. *w^{e}nogah kā'or tihyä* (Hab. 3:4), to the parallelism between both roots in e.g. Is. 60:3 and their connection in the construct (Pr. 4:18).

The remaining cases of juxtaposition can roughly be divided into two groups: one group in which the consecutive words are related to a pair of words though not forming such a pair themselves, and another group in which the sequence of words is merely incidental.

In a sequence of words *yaḥaloq naḥalā* (Pr. 17:2) we are dealing with a simple sequence of predicate and object and no co-ordination or quasi-co-ordination can possibly be found here. Nevertheless the affinity of this expression to the famous pair of words *ḥeläq weraḥalā* is obvious and we may even surmise that the simple down-to-earth formulation *yaḥaloq naḥalā* may be the source of the pair of words. This source itself should not be quoted as an example of the pair but should be mentioned in its discussion by way of simple reference only: cf. *yaḥaloq naḥalā*. An example of a merely casual connection of words is the above-mentioned verse *ybkyk ab ġr*. Here the casual character of the sequence *ab ġr* is evident. No mountain is normally supposed to bother about the father of anybode.

c. The term "collocation" designates the relation of words which have nothing in common but the fact that both appear in the same text. One example (II 413) must suffice. In his treatment of the alleged pair *ᶜd ᶜlm // ᶜlmt* Dahood quotes as "collocation" *bnh ᶜd ᶜlm šḥr ᶜlmt* (*PRU* 2, text 8:14-15). The words quoted pertain to a text representing a type of documents in which the king of Ugarit bestows landed property upon a man and his sons. Contracts of this kind are amply attested in Akkadian documents from Ugarit, e.g. *PRU* 3, RS 16.138, pp. 143-145. In those tablets the king gives his grant for ever (*adi darīti* or a similar expression) and adds the promise that in future nobody shall take it (i.e. the grant) from the hand of its receiver. The Akkadian term for 'in the future' is *urra(m) šēra(m)*, tentatively explained by E.A. Speiser, *JAOS* 74 (1954), p. 23, as 'day and dawn'. In Ugaritic *ᶜd ᶜlm* stands for *adi darīti*, *šḥr ᶜlmt* (not *ᶜlmt* alone!) for *urra šēra*. The *hapaxlegomenon ᶜlmt* should probably be disconnected from *ᶜlm = ᶜolām* and tentatively explained to mean 'evening', i.e. the time when the sun disappears. Cf. the Hebrew verb *ᶜlm*. But cf. also the enigmatic *ᶜlm* in *U* 5, pp. 588ff., text 12:Obv. 7, Rev. 3,7, tentatively explained by J. de Moor, *UF* 2 (1970), p. 319 in the sense 'the following day'. Anyhow, it cannot be contested that the words *ᶜd ᶜlm* and *ᶜlmt* belong to two different legal formulas and are unconnected. Incidentally it might be remarked that Dahood assumes an actual parallel *ᶜalmot // ᶜad ᶜolām* in Ps. 48, where *ᶜad ᶜolām* in the closing of the first strophe (v. 9) is to his mind parallel to *ᶜalmot* (MT *ᶜal mut*) in the closing of the second (v. 15). This "distant parallelism", however, becomes highly suspect if we pay attention to the undeniable correspondence between *ᶜad ᶜolām* (v. 9) and *ᶜolām waᶜäd* (v. 15).

5) To this general discussion of Dahood's approach remarks on detail might be added:

II 52 Add M. Held, *Lěšonênu* 18 (1953), p. 146.

II 65 *arṣ // kl. wymlk barṣ il klh* (*CTA* 6:I:65)

'and he ruled upon the earth the god of all of it', i.e. 'as the god etc.' Dahood supposes then a breaking up of the phrase *wymlk il barṣ klh*. Unfortunately, the text is broken after *klh* and therefore defies sure interpretation. Dahood himself quotes the alternative translation: 'and he ruled in the land of Il in its totality', defended by B. Couroyer, *RB* 78 (1971), pp. 59-70, by comparison with Egyptian *tꜣ nṯr* 'the land of god', a term designating Syria in the time of the eighteenth dynasty and considered by Couroyer as a loan from Canaanite. True, this hypothesis is highly questionable, not only because of the doubt whether the Ugaritic text really speaks of the land of Il, but also because of Couroyer's own statement that *tꜣ nṯr* designated in the period of the twelfth dynasty a land in Africa. Nevertheless the interpretation of the Ugaritic text defended by Couroyer cannot be ruled out on linguistic grounds. Both interpretations adduced by Dahood have been contested by J. Blau - S.E. Loewenstamm, *UF* 2 (1970), p. 33 who argued that they fail to make sense in the context, and advanced the proposal to explain *klh* as the name of a deity. Moreover the Hebrew examples quoted by Dahood are doubtful. True, in Job 38:18 *kullāh* refers to *'äräṣ* but is logically parallel to *raḥ^{a}be 'äräs*, and in Job 34:13 *kullāh* does not refer to *'äräṣ* but qualifies *tebel*.

II 119 *bny // rm*, cf. in this volume, *Border-cases of Ugaritic Studies*, p. 407. *rāmim* in Ps. 78:69 is possibly an abbreviation of *šāmayim rāmim*. Note the parallelism *k^{e}mo rāmim // k^{e}'äräṣ* and cf. also *šmm rmm* (*U* 5, pp. 551f., text 2:7).

II 152 Add M. Held, *Lěšonênu* 18 (1953), p. 146.

II 208 Add H.L. Ginsberg, *Tarbiz* 4 (1932), p. 116.

II 211 (cf. II 68) *ybl // pr. ybl arṣ // pr ^{c}ṣm*

(*CTA* 5:II:5-6) contains a double pair. Cf. *w^{e}nātan ^{c}eṣ haśśādä 'ät piryo w^{e} hā'äräṣ titten y^{e}bulāh* (Ez. 34:27). In Lev. 27:30 *ybl* of the classic pair has been replaced by *zära^{c}*, in Zech. 8:12 *^{c}eṣ* by *gäpän*. The existence of an independent pair *p^{e}ri // y^{e}bul* is not attested either in Ugaritic or in MT. But Dahood correctly draws attention to the Septuagint in Hab. 3:17 which reads instead of *tiprāḥ // y^{e}bul - tiprä* (καρποφορήσει) // *y^{e}bul*.

II 243 Add H.L. Ginsberg, *KU*, p. 26.

II 250 Add M. Held, *Lěšonēnu* 18 (1953), p. 146.

II 254 Add J. Greenfield, *HUCA* 29 (1958), pp. 226-228.

II 262 Add H.L. Ginsberg, *Or* 5 (1936), p. 172.

II 347g Contrast Friedrich Delitzsch, *Prolegomena eines neuen Hebräisch-Aramäischen Lexikons* (Leipzig 1886), pp. 69-71, who explains *mhs* in Ps. 68:24 on ground of Akkadian *maḫāṣu* '*übergiessen, begiessen*'. Cf. von Soden, *AHW, s.v. maḫāṣu* G. 5 '*besprengen mit (ina)*'.

II 355 Add J. Greenfield, *HUCA* 29 (1958), pp. 207-210.

II 404 Pay attention to the pattern *A // bn B*. On this pattern see for the time being in this volume, *On New Texts in Ugaritic*, pp. 222-223.

II 425 In Hebrew early *lᵉdor dor* should be distinguished from later *lᵉdor wādor*. See in this volume, *Stylistic Patterns*, etc., p. 262. In *ᶜad ᶜolām // lᵉdor wādor* (Is. 34:17) poetical *lᵉᶜolām* is replaced by the originally legal term *ᶜad ᶜolām*. Cf. *ibid*., p. 264.

II 431 Cf. J. Greenfield, *Festschrift W.F. Albright* (Baltimore-London 1971), pp. 260-261, who quotes also *Eshmunazor* 5-6.

II 448 d *btk ġry il ṣpn* (*CTA* 3:III:26) 'in the midst of my towering mountain Zaphon'. The construction of *il* as genitive designating a superlative tacitly supposes the doubtful possibility of a personal suffix in the *regens ġry*.

II 450 *ḥeläb // ṣur* (Ps. 81:17), 'hill // mountain'. This explanation of *ḥeläb* is adduced as a tentative proposal, made by E.Y. Kutscher, *Lěšonēnu* 32 (1968), p. 346. Kutscher, however, did not go as far as that, but rather pointed to the affinity of *ḥeläb ḥiṭṭā* (Ps. 81:17) to *ḥeläb kilyot ḥiṭṭā* (Deut. 32:14) and to *ḥeläb ḥiṭṭim* (Ps. 147:14), where the rendering 'hill' is obviously impossible, and concluded with the tentative proposal of a *double entendre* of *ḥeläb* in Ps. 81:17.

II 452 See now in this volume, *Who is afraid of the Linguistic Method*, pp. 433-439.

II 475 Contrast in this volume, *mṣd*, pp. 419-422, where the equation of *ṣd* with *ṣedā* is contested.

II 476 Add from the present volume, *Notes on the History of Biblical Phraseology*, pp. 211-214, where the affinity of Is. 11:4 to the Phoenician pair of gods Μισωρ καὶ Συδυκ (Eusebius, *PrEv* I:10:13) is pointed out. Cf. now also in Ugaritic *ṣdq mšr U* 5, pp. 583, 585, text 10A:14.

II 500 The meaning of *bt ḫbr* is disputed. See recently A.F. Rainey, *JNES* 24 (1965), p. 18, note 5.

II 519 *rbb // šr*^{c} (*CTA* 19:I:44-45) 'showers // surging' compared with *ś*^{ec}*irim // r*^{e}*bibim* (Deut. 32:2) 'rainfall // showers'. Dahood comments: "Cassuto's equation assumes the metathesis *šr*^{c} > *š*^{c}*r*, but since the *Wortfeld* of Deut. 32:2 is so similar to that of the Ugaritic passage, this *metathesis* is easy to accept". The Ugaritic text speaks of *šr*^{c} *thmtm*. The rendering 'upsurging' for *šr*^{c} is just a guess whose corroboration by Arabic *sr*^{c} 'hasten' (H.L. Ginsberg, *JBL* 57 [1938], p. 212, note 4) is anything but cogent. Even if we are to accept this guess, the difference between 'upsurging' and 'rainfall' should not be glossed over.

II 526 Contrast in this volume, *Notes on the Pronouns in Ugaritic etc.*, p. 76, where *šalm* has been rendered 'claims', and M. Liverani, *Ugaritica* 6 (1969), p. 365 who translated '*debiti*'.

II 527 Compare in this volume, *š*^{e}*'er*, pp. 190-191, where *dām // š*^{e}*'er w*^{e}*ḥāmās* (Jer. 51:35) has been explained as a combination of the pair *dām // š*^{e}*'er* with the pair *ḥāmās // dām* (Ju. 9:24). In a chapter of his dissertation dealing with pairs of words common to three languages, Y. Avishur observes: "The pair *šir // dm*, which is rare in Ugaritic and in Hebrew, is frequently found in Akkadian, since the word *šīru* which is seldom used in Ugaritic and in Hebrew is the usual word in Akkadian". This remark highlights the importance of Akkadian for studies of this kind.

II 549 Add *šimḥat gili* (Ps. 43:4). Consult Y. Avishur, *Semitics* 2 (1971-1972), pp. 37-38.

II 552 Read *BASOR* 97 (!) and add J. Greenfield, *HUCA* 30 (1959), pp. 144-147.

II 553 Add M. Held, *Lĕšonênu* 18 (1953), pp. 147, 160; J. Greenfield, *HUCA* 30 (1959), pp. 143; M. Dahood, *Biblica* 47 (1966), p. 267; and in this volume, *Border-cases of Ugaritic Comparative Studies*, pp. 405-407.

II 556. Add M. Held, *Lĕšonênu* 18 (1953), p. 147; J. Blau - S.E. Loewenstamm, *UF* 2 (1970), p. 29; de Moor, *Seasonal Pattern*, p. 241. De Moor argues that in *š*^{c}*ly dġṯh bšmym dġṯ hrnmy dkbkbm* (*CTA* 19:IV:192-193) "the parallel *dkbkbm* 'those of the stars' requires simply 'those of heaven'". The use of *d* as quasi-noun, however, is extremely rare in Ugaritic whereas it often breaks up a construct. Therefore possibly render: 'He made his incense ascend in heaven, the star incense of the hrnmy'.

II 572j Contrast H.L. Ginsberg, *VTS* 16 (1967), pp. 71-72.

II 577 Add Sh.M. Paul, *JNES* 31 (1972), pp. 351-355.

IV

Sasson's single remarks upon minerals, fauna and flora do not call for general methodological evaluation. Some comments upon details will suffice.

III 26 Sasson defines *bṣql* as "some sort of vegetable" and remarks that many scholars identified *bṣql* with *b^e^ṣiqlon*. It would have been worth mentioning that Cassuto proposed the more specific meaning 'ear (of corn)', pointing in short to the correspondence between *bṣql* and *šblt* in *CTA* 19:II: 61//74 and the aptness of this explanation in 2 Reg. 4:42, if we consider there *b^e^ṣiqlono* a haplography or haplology instead of *bibṣiqlono*. His arguments are convincing since: a) The passage *CTA* 19:II:61-67 reading *bṣql* and the following passage 68-74 reading *šblt* are partly identical and partly synonymous in wording. b) The interpretation 'ear (of corn)' indeed makes excellent sense in Kings. Cf. *^c^äśrim läḥäm ś^ec^orim w^e^karmäl b^e^ṣiqlono* (2 Reg. 4:42) 'twenty barley loaves (literally breads) and fresh corn in its ear' to *w^e^läḥäm w^e^qāli w^e^karmäl* (Lev. 23:14) 'and bread and roasted corn and fresh corn'. This exegesis which refrains from doing violence to MT is preferable to J. Gray's daring emendation *b^e^ṣiqlon karmo* 'plants of his orchard' and to J. Barr's tentative proposal to interpret *b^e^ṣiqlon* as a plot where the *bṣql* are grown.

III 27 Contrast J. Blau - S.E. Loewenstamm, *Thesaurus of the Language of the Bible*, 2 (Jerusalem 1959) *s.v. bḥwn*, who suppose a *double entendre* of *bāḥon* in Jer. 6:271) 'examiner' 2) 'fortification'. Cf. T.O. Lambdin, *JAOS* 73 (1953), p. 248, who compares Egyptian *bḫn* 'fortress' with *bḥyn* (*K^e^tib* Is. 23:13).

III 35 *gpn*. Add J.N.E. Epstein, *Tarbiz* 5 (1934), p. 83 who compares *kapnitā* which designates in Geonic Aramaic a type of saddle.

III 43 *dq(t)*. Delete the brackets. There is no sacrificial animal in Ugaritic texts which is called *dq*. *dqt* appears in the same lists of victims as *gdlt*, overlooked by Sasson. Both terms are obviously akin to the Talmudical terms *b^{e}hemā gassā* 'large cattle' and *b^{e}hemā daqqā* 'small cattle'. It is for this reason that many scholars explain *dqt* in the general sense 'a beast which belongs to the small cattle (including male and female animals)', among others Baumgartner in his Hebrew dictionary, *s.v.* 3, to whom Sasson erroneously ascribes the explanation 'ewe or she-goat'. The latter interpretation, proposed by H.L. Ginsberg, *KU*, p. 111 and defended by B. Levine, *JCS* 17 (1963), pp. 107-108, derives from the consideration that the same sacrificial texts which mention *gdlt* and *dqt* mention also sacrifices of *alp* and *š* and that therefore a semantic differentiation between those designations of sacrificial animals should be assumed.

III 62 In his discussion of *ṭhr* Sasson comments: "Parallel to *iqnim* 'lapis lazuli'", in *ṭhrm iqnim* (*CTA* 4:V:81). In support of this statement Sasson refers to Cassuto and ascribes to him the view that *ṭohar* (Ex. 24:10) occurs in parallel with another precious stone *sappir* just as in the Ugaritic text. Actually Cassuto remarked: "The Ugaritic poems apply to lapis lazuli gems (*iqnu*) the adjective *ṭhrm* (pure, i.e. shining). In the Bible the abstract noun *ṭohar* occurs in parallelism with *sappir* as expressing the characteristic quality of the latter (Ex. 24:10)". Cassuto's correct exegesis has recently been elaborated by J. Blau, *IOS* 2 (1972), pp. 74-77. In a short survey on the substantivized use of adjectives in Semitic languages Blau compared *ṭhrm iqnim* with *ib iqni* (*CTA* 14:III:147), the Ugaritic counterpart of Akkadian *uqnu ebbu* 'pure, shining lapis lazuli'. In contrast to Akkadian, however, in Ugaritic the adjective *ib*, a loan from Akkadian, has been substantivized and turned into the *regens* of a construct. In *ṭhrm iqnim* the indigenous Ugaritic word *ṭhr* has taken the place of the loan word *ib*. In connection with this question Sasson also mentions Dahood's view that the difficult *miṭṭ^{e}hāro* (Ps. 89:45) contains the word 'splendour' (omitting Dahood's comparison of this supposed meaning with Akkadian *melammu*, the terrifying splendour surrounding gods and kings in battle). We have, however, already pointed out that the interdialectical equivalent of Ugaritic and Hebrew *ṭhr* in Akkadian is *ebbu* which describes the delighting appearance of gold and precious stones, not the terrifying manifestation of a mighty warrior. For a more plausible exegesis of Ps. 89:45 consult J. Greenfield, *Festschrift W.F. Albright*, Baltimore-London (1971), pp. 256-257.

III 67 Compare in this volume, *A Didactic Ugaritic Drinker's Burlesque*, p. 381.

III 85 Contrast A.F. Rainey, *UF* 3 (1971), p. 184.

III 99 Contrast J.T. Tigay, *JBL* 92 (1972), pp. 517-522.

III 116 *škm*. Sasson remarks: "In the early days of Ugaritology Bauer identified Ug. *škm* with Hebrew *šiqmā*." His reference is to H. Bauer, *ZDMG* 84 (1930), p. 254. Bauer's proposal which supposes a correspondence between Ugaritic *k* and Hebrew *q* was quite understandable at its time. By now it has become obsolete and should be passed over in silence. [J. de Moor - P. van der Lugt, *BiOr* 31 (1974), p. 26 note that already in 1932 Bauer revised his opinion (*Das Alphabet von Ras Schamra*, Halle 1932, pp. 19, 22) and connected Ugaritic *škm* with Hebrew *sikkim* 'thorns' following P. Dhorme, *RB* 40 (1931), p. 48.]

V

To sum up. The present volume contains an overwhelming wealth of comparative material and will occupy a central position in all future discussions on the relationship between Ugaritic literature and the world of the Hebrew Bible. Its importance is in its stimulating force, not in the drawing up of a balance which summarizes generally accepted results.

The Expanded Colon, reconsidered.

As early as in medieval research a certain type of Biblical verse has been singled out in which the repetition of words in subsequent cola is of expressive, not of informative, character. In our days the interest in this stylistic phenomenon has been enhanced by the publication of Ugaritic texts in which obviously congenerous features can be discerned. In a paper "*The Expanded Colon in Ugaritic and Biblical Verse*" (*JSS* 14 [1969], pp. 176-196) [See in this volume, pp. 281-309] the present writer made an attempt at a comprehensive presentation of the relevant verses and their systematic analysis. His survey was considerably supplemented by Y. Avishur's article "*Addenda to the Expanded Colon in Ugaritic and Biblical Verse*" (*UF* 4 [1972], pp. 1-10). Now the discussion of the problem has been taken up again by E.L. Greenstein in the second part of his article "*Two Variations of Grammatical Parallelism in Canaanite Poetry and their Psycholinguistic Background*" (*JANES* 6 [1974], pp. 96-104). Greenstein adds to the material hitherto discussed but one single example (see the following) and lays the stress rather on questions of methodological approach.

I. In a sense his treatment follows lines of classical research. Like S.R. Driver he speaks of climactic parallelism and restricts the applicibility of this term to verses in which "the last word(s) of the first line separate(s) its initial words from their reproduction at the beginning of the second line". In contrast to the present writer and to Avishur, Greenstein thus excludes from his discussion all passages in which there is no intervening formula at the end of the first line and the first words of the second colon repeat the last words of the first for purely expressive reasons. In order to illustrate his view, he points to the verse *tbrk ilm tity / tity ilm lahlhm / dr il lmšknthm* (*CTA* 15:III:17-19) 'they bless the gods they come / they come the gods to their tents / the assembly of Il to their tabernacles' and argues that this text "is only a tricolon similar in form to such passages as *CTA* 14:62-64", i.e. to the verse *trḥṣ w tadm / rḥṣ [y]dk amt / uṣb[^{c}tk] ^{c}d [ṯ]km* 'do thou wash and rouge thee / wash from thy hand to elbow / from thy fingers up to the shoulder'. This comparison, however, is unconvincing, since in the last mentioned text not a single word is repeated in Ugaritic, whereas in *CTA* 15:III:17-19 the two first words of v. 19 verbally reproduce the end of v. 18 and could be omitted without impairing the information conveyed by the text. To be sure, the words are repeated here in a chiastic order and their repetition is therefore less striking than in a simple case [noted by Avishur] like *ygrš grš ym / grš ym lksih / [n]hr lksi drkth* (*CTA* 2:IV:12-13) Yagruš expel Yam / expel Yam from his chair / Nahar from the throne of his dominion'. But this stylistic nuance is of no consequence for the definition of the phenomenon. In all verses of this structure the repetition has the only function to suspend the giving of the information, thus creating a certain tension. To put it in another way: The first two cola may be defined as the enlargement of the monocolon: *ygrš grš ym lksih.*[1] Cf. in Hebrew: *lipne YHWH ki bā' / ki bā' lišpoṭ hā'ārāṣ* (Ps. 96:13) with *millipne YHWH ki bā' lišpoṭ 'ät hā'ārāṣ* (1 Chr. 16:33). In all these cases a well-defined literary device of suspending enlargement is clearly recognizable.[1a]

II. Let us proceed to the discussion of the pattern characterized by the existence of an intervening formula at the end of the first line separating the first occurrence of a repetitive formula at the beginning of the first line from its second occurrence at the beginning of the second. 1) Here, too, the two lines admit the definition as the enlargement of a single line. Cf. the one line *uzr ilm ylḥm* (*CTA* 17:I:3) 'oblations to the gods gives to eat' with the two lines: *uzr ilm dnil / uzr ilm ylḥm* (*CTA* 17:I:7-8)

[[1] The verse could easily be transformed to read: *grš ym ygrš / grš ym lksih*. Thus we might surmise the short basic formula: *grš ym lksih.*]

[1a] In this context Greenstein discusses the restoration of *CTA* 15:II:18-20. Greenstein follows H.L. Ginsberg who reads:

brkm.ybrk
[ᶜbdh] ybrk. il krt
[ymr]m . nᶜm[n] ġlm. il

Indeed he blesses [his servant] Il blesses Keret / [beatif]ies the belov[ed] lad of Il.

and adduces support from *[--y]ḫd. il. ᶜbdh.ybrk* (*CTA* 17:I:35). The reading *ᶜbdh*, however, is anything but ascertained. Between *il* and *bdh* there is only one unclear sign which may be either a word-divider or an ᶜ. We should probably read: *[ks.y]hd. il. bdh. ybrk* 'A cup takes Il in his hand, he blesses'. [Cf. J.J. Jackson - H.H.P. Dressler, *JAOS* 95 (1975), pp. 99-101.] Ginsberg's proposal supposes an atypical parallelism *brkm ybrk / ybrk / ymrm*. The repetition of *ybrk* in two subsequent cola rather

'oblations to the gods Danil / oblations to the gods gives to eat'. Greenstein introduces his treatment of the pattern by the general remark: "Although most scholars include in this category the climactic parallelism of two lines, we shall consider only the parallelism of three (or more) lines". This restriction of scope can hardly be justified and obfuscates the basic fact that in any case we are dealing with the enlargement of one colon into two, irrespective of whether the basic unexpanded colon was followed by another one or not. Mostly that was so since in unexpanded verses the *bicolon* surpasses the *monocolon* in frequency.[2]

2) Greenstein notes that the repetitive formula is composed of two words and mentions as only exception Cant. 4:9, "in which the accusative pronominal suffix on the verb serves in lieu of a second word". It hardly does. Are we expected to count in the repetitive formula *rā'ukā mayim* (Ps. 77:17) *rā'ukā* as two words? For repetitive formulas of three words see *CTA* 6:IV:25-26; Ps. 92:10.

3) According to Greenstein the intervening formula is either the grammatical subject or a vocative. Let us put it more precisely. In Ugaritic it may be either a vocative with the function of a subject (e.g. *CTA* 2:IV:8-9) or a vocative without that function (e.g. *CTA* 16:VI:54-57) or a subject not

---

points to an enlarged form of speech. A comparison with Baal's address to Il: *ltbrk [krt] ṯ^c / ltmr n^{c}mn [ġ̇lm] il* (*CTA* 15:II:14-16) then justifies Avishur's restoration *brkm ybrk / [brkm] ybrk. il. krt.[ṯ^c]*. Greenstein objects that this proposal "overloads the second line while leaving the first line irregularly light". But short cola of two words are attested. Cf. e.g. *CTA* 14:206, 215; 15:I:7, and so are long cola of five words. Cf. e.g. *CTA* 4:V:89-90; 19:178-179; 23:67-68.

[2] Greenstein remarks: "Loewenstamm claims that the three-line climactic parallelism or staircase evolved from the two liner" and refutes "this evolutionary theory". The present writer never held this view. He only expressed the opinion that *every* enlarged colon should be regarded as the enlargement of one colon into two. Greenstein adds "that Loewenstamm attempted to show another simple-to-complicate development in the seven-day counting formula of Ugaritic and Biblical Hebrew" and objects "that in fact the latest occurrence in the Keret epic is by far the simplest and barest". It should be noted that the present writer actually characterized the seven-day pattern in the Keret epic as the last phase in the break-down of the classical pattern, the beginnings of which are already evident in *CTA* 22 A. See in this volume, *The Seven-Day-Unit*, pp. 199-204.

being a vocative (e.g. *CTA* 17:I:12-13), whereas in Hebrew only the two first-mentioned of these usages are attested (e.g. Cant. 4:8; Ps. 77:17) and in addition the use of a complete sentence (e.g. Ps. 124:1-2).[3]

4) Greenstein does not dwell upon the categories created by the different syntactic function of the intervening formulas, but rather takes interest in the distinction of variant kinds of parallelism resulting from an analysis of the repetitive and the complementary formulas. There he tries to establish three categories:

a. cases of suspended analysis, that is to say of "an uncompleted sentence or idiom in the first line which requires the listener to suspend syntactic analysis of the first line until he has heard the second" (13 cases).

b. cases of "reanalysis". Here we are supposed to meet with" a shift in the syntactic functions of a repeated word which requires the listener to reanalyze the syntax of the first line" (5 cases).

c. a "weak" form of "additive" climactic parallelism, which "psycholinguistically has no special effect of surprise, climax or suspense, because the first line possesses a self-contained statement and the second line reproduces the first words of the first line without a change in syntax or meaning" (10 cases).

a) His definition of the first category comes near to the general description of the phenomenon given by the twelfth-century exegete Rashbam who summed up the problem with the following words: "The first half is incomplete without the second half which repeats and completes the thought". It is evident that in a sense this simple definition indeed does apply to all cases of an expanded colon, since everywhere the full information may be grasped from the second line only, irrespective of whether the first line by itself fails to convey any information or the information provided by it be of an incomplete character. Greenstein's first category then does not call for a closer scrutiny, and we may confine our discussion to his two new categories.

b) It was obviously the psycholinguistically fascinating category of 'reinterpretation' which focused the interest of the author who toiled hard to establish it, although even so he detected only the small number of five

[3] Cf. Avishur, *Addenda*, p. 6.

examples. Let us look at these few test cases one by one.

α) In Ps. 92:10 Greenstein reads: *hinne 'oyebäkā YHWH / hinne 'oyebäkā yo'bedu* and comments that *'oyebäkā* 'Thy enemies' is the predicate of the deictic *hinne* 'behold' in the first line, however, the subject of the nominalized sentence *'oyebäkā yo'bedu* 'Thy enemies shall perish' in the second". Unfortunately, this argument can only be taken into consideration if we neglect with Greenstein the conjunction *ki* 'for' which precedes *hinne* in both colə, since the sequence of words '*for* lo Thy enemies' is most evidently incomplete and far from evoking a *prima vista* understanding: Lo, Thy enemies!

β) *ht ibk bᶜlm / ht ibk tmḫṣ* (*CTA* 2:IV:8-9) 'now thy enemies Baal / now thy enemies destroy'. Again, 'now thy enemies Baal' is a clearly incomplete sentence. To be sure, *ht* has sometimes be interpreted as 'lo, behold'.[4] [And this interpretation has been followed by Greenstein.] But the only clearly attested meaning of *ht* is 'now' (*CTA* 19:IV:167), in Hebrew *ᶜattā(h)*, and already the dictionary of Brown-Driver-Briggs correctly points to the use of *ᶜattā(h)* in addresses of encouragement implying that the time has come for the exhortation or advice to be followed. Cf. Gen. 31:13; Ex. 18:19 etc.[5] [Our statement requires modification in the light of *PRU* 5, text 9:5-9 where *ht* is obviously equivalent to Hebrew *hinne*. Therefore, Greenstein's translation can not be ruled out with certainty. Compare also in this volume, *Lexicographical Notes 2 hnny / hlny*, pp. 451-454.]

γ) *rā'ukā mayim 'ä̆lohim / rā'ukā mayim yāḥilu* (Ps. 77:17). Greenstein divides the second colon in contrast to the Masoretic accents *rā'ukā - mayim yāḥilu* and renders: 'See Thee the waters, O God // (they) see Thee, the waters whirl'. That is to say that *mayim* is the subject of *rā'ukā* in the first line, whereas in the second line *mayim* only serves as subject of *yāḥilu*. Greenstein adds: "Compare Hab. 3:10 *rā'ukā yāḥilu hārim* 'they saw You, the mountains quake' in which we find the same construction as, and nearly identical wording to *rā'ukā mayim yāḥilu*, except that the explicit subject *hārim* 'mountains' follows *yāḥilu*. Thus it unambigously goes with *yāḥilu* 'they quake' not *rā'ukā* 'they saw You'; compare also Ps. 97:4. This

[4] See e.g. Aartun, *Partikeln*, p. 67.

[5] See also J.C. de Moor - P. van der Lugt, *BiOr* 31 (1974), p. 5.

constitutes independent evidence that in the second colon of Ps. 77:17 the clause must be divided *rā'ukā - mayim yāḥilu*." Greenstein then interprets that the waters, respectively the mountains quaked because some undefined "they" saw the God. It is, however, abundantly clear that they did so at the sight of the awe- inspiring God, in grammatical terms, that *mayim* is the subject of both verbs. No mysterious "they" possibly could be found in Ps. 97:4, where the sing. fem. *rāᵃtā* most obviously refers to *hā'āräṣ* and cf. also Ps. 94:3.

δ) *ptḥ bt mnt / ptḥ bt wuba*[6] (*U* 5, text 7:71). Greenstein quotes this example without translation and comment. He evidently took it over from Avishur who translates: 'Open the house *mnt* / open the house and I shall follow'. No reinterpretation is involved at all.

ε) *yᶜn ḥtkh krt / yᶜn ḥtkh rš* (*CTA* 14:I:21-22) 'he sees his offspring Keret / he sees his offspring ruined'. Greenstein argues that *ḥtkh* 'his offspring' is in the first line a direct object, in the second the subject of the nominalized sentence *ḥtkh rš* 'his offspring (is) ruined'. This description omits that here the nominalized clause constitutes an object. The crucial question, however, is whether in the first line *ḥtkh* makes the afterwards corrected impression of a self-contained object. If we isolate the verse, such a psycholinguistic analysis may be admittable. However, the reader of the text has already been informed that Keret's children have perished.

*[*To sum up. From Greenstein's five test-cases of reinterpretation only the single one of *CTA* 2:IV:8-9 can be taken into consideration and even the validity of this lonely example depends upon the doubtful rendering of the particle *ht*. It goes without saying that no psycholinguistic category can be established on such a small basis. The pattern of the expanded colon endows a simple basic phrase with tension and emphasis. This evident purpose can hardly be served by an intricate formulation forcing upon the hearer a confusing reinterpretation.*]*

c. Even the category of "weak" or "additive" climactic parallelism is of doubtful validity. Let us illustrate this problem by two examples:

α) *irš ḥym laqht ġzr / irš ḥym watnk* (*CTA* 17:VI:26-27) 'ask for life, and I'll give it thee'. In this verse the first line contains a grammatical-

---

[6] Cf. L.R. Fisher, *UF* 3 (1971), p. 356.

ly perfect sentence. Nevertheless it is precarious to argue that it possesses a self-contained statement, since the gist of Anat's speech is her offer to bestow immortality upon Aqhat if he should ask for it. That is to say that the relation of the complementary formula *watnk* to the repetitive formula *irš ḥym* comes very near to that of an *apodosis* to its *protasis*.

β) The term "additive" may be more easily justified in the one hitherto overlooked case of an expanded colon where Greenstein reads with H.L. Ginsberg: *^{c}bdk b^{c}l yymm / ^{c}bdk b^{c}l [l^{c}l]m*[7] (*CTA* 2:I:36-37) 'thy servant is Baal, O Yam, thy servant in eternity'. In this verse the complementary formula *l^{c}lm* indeed only completes the information provided by the repetitive formula. But we should not fail to appreciate the stress laid upon this additional information, which intensifies the force of the statement. Here, if anywhere, the term climactic parallelism would be an appropriate characterization of the expanded colon. Ancient verses of this kind should not be depreciated as "imitation of the popular form without recognizing what made this form successful".

---

[7] This restoration is preferable to Herdner's proposal *[ynhr]m*, which substitutes for the complementary formula a second address, parallel to the intervening formula. This pattern is nowhere attested in Ugaritic poetry. To be sure, in Hebrew there are two passages, in which such an interpretation could be taken into consideration. Cf. *mi kāmokā bā'elim YHWH / mikkāmokā nä'dār baqqodäš* (Ex. 15:11) and *^{c}ad šaqqamti d^{e}borā / šaqqamti 'em b^{e}yiśrā'el* (Ju. 5:7). In these verses *nä'dār baqqodäš* and *'em b^{e}yiśrā'el* possibly could be explained as addresses. The verses, at any rate however, deviate from the ancient Ugaritic type of the expanded colon, in which the repetitive formula invariably is repeated in full.

The Making and Destruction of the Golden Calf - a Rejoinder

In a paper entitled "*The Making and Destruction of the Golden Calf*" the present writer had proffered some unconventional explanations of the much discussed verses Ex. 32:4,20,24.[1] His views have been strongly contested in a recent article by Leo G. Perdue[2] arguing that the present writer unduly neglected the application of literary and traditio-historical criticism and tried to make up for these deficiencies by adducing far-fetched Ugaritic parallels.

True, the present writer treated Ex. 32:4,20,24 as belonging to the same source. The expression of this opinion on three verses, however, was not meant to imply a denial of the complicate prehistory of the whole chapter, a problem touched upon by the present writer in two recent papers.[3] The question, therefore, imposes itself whether the assignment of Ex. 32:4, 20,24 to the same source stands the test of a comprehensive analysis of the chapter.

In accordance with a widely held view we may reasonably surmise that the present story of the golden calf was preceded by a cult legend of its worshippers, who regarded its making by Aaron as a meritorious act.[4] This

---

[1] See in this volume, pp. 236-245.

[2] "*The Making and Destruction of the Golden Calf - a Reply*", *Biblica* 54 (1973), pp. 237-246.

[3] "*Review of Herbert Schmid, Mose, Überlieferung und Geschichte*", *Biblica* 50 (1969), pp. 431f. (in German); *The Investiture of Levy, EI* 10 (1971), pp. 169-171 (in Heb.).

[4] See e.g. R.H. Kennett "*The Origin of the Aaronide Priesthood*", *JTS* 6 (1905), pp. 165-167; T.J. Meek, "*Some Religious Origins of the Hebrews*", *AJSLL* 32 (1920/21), pp. 120f., 129; W. Beyerlin, *Origin and History of the Oldest Sinaitic Traditions*, Oxford 1965, pp. 125-136. Cf. also Loewenstamm, "*Review*" and "*Investiture*". For other historico-critical approaches see S. Lehming, "*Versuch zu Ex. 32*", *VT* 10 (1960), pp. 16-50; M. Averbach - J. Smolar, "*Aaron, Jeroboam and the Golden Calf*", *JBL* 86 (1967), pp. 129-137. Both papers defend the view that according to the most ancient version the calf was made by the people. This version was superseded by another attributing the making of the calf to Aaron. In the latest sta-

hypothesis is born out by the historically ascertained fact that the calf occupied a central place in the worship of the northern kingdom from the time of its consolidation unto its downfall.[5] It is hardly conceivable that such an important cult object was lacking a cult legend but rather plausible that in the view of its worshippers Jeroboam just followed Aaron's venerable example. On this supposition it is obvious that the cult legend did not relate either God's or Moses' irate reaction to the making of the calf. In extant Jewish tradition, however, this act has turned into a most severe tresspass which kindled the wrath of both and whose result was radically wiped out. The central figure in this counteraction is Moses who is said to have been absent during the time when the calf was made because on God's command he had ascended His mountain for forty days and forty nights do receive the divine tablets and to descend with them to the people. The actual text of Ex. 32 then presumably welds and transforms two primarily unconnected aetiological traditions, viz. the cult legend of the existing calf and the cult legend of the existing tablets which never had been broken. (Cf. the version of the giving of the tablets Deut. 5:22 and its priestly counterpart in Ex. 25:16; 40:20; both are unaware of any breaking). By this synchronisation an ideal setting for the story of the sin of the golden calf was provided. The contrast between God, Moses and the divine tablets on the one hand, and Aaron, the people and the calf on the other hand, is crystalclear and Moses counteraction nullifying the worship of the calf is motivated with logical and dramatic force. A similar change affected the story of the tablets which were destroyed as well, although the reason for their destruction is different and even opposite to that of the destruction of the calf, viz. that the people were unworthy of the divine tablets in their state of depravation. Two straightforward actiologi-

---

ge a tendency to return to the ancient version allegedly appears in v. 5a interpreted to mean that Aaron saw the calf which was made by the people; vv. 25b, 35b are treated as glosses introducing Aaron into the ancient version. On all these views see the following.

[5] Cf. 1 Reg. 12:28-33; Ho. 8:5. The intricate question what were the roots of Jeroboam's worship of the calf can be left open in the present paper. For the view that Ju. 20:28 is pointing to a historical Aaron living in the period of the Judges who is supposed to have been the eponym of the Bethel priesthood and the founder of the worship of the golden calf see T.J. Meek, "*Aaronites and Zadokites*", *AJSLL* 45 (1929), pp. 149; Beyerlin, *op. cit.* (note 4), pp. 126-135; Perdue, *op. cit.* (note 2), p. 238, note 3 and the additional literature quoted there.

cal stories relating the creation of an existing cult object turned into an intricate narration of their intertwined making and immediately following destruction.

But even after this recasting of the cult legend of the calf a vexing problem was left unanswered. We should expect that in the new version Aaron bore the brunt of Moses' anger. A statement to this effect, however, is conspicuously absent in all sources.[6] Instead, we meet with an outspoken tendency to shift the responsibility from Aaron to the people, apparently because the enemies of the worship of the calf held Aaron in the same high esteem as its worshippers. This reluctance to putting the guilt squarely upon Aaron's shoulders left its unmistakable marks already in Ex 32 and makes headway in later sources. Let us work back from these simplified later texts to the more complex and complicated version of Ex. 32. Philo's detailed report on the pericope of the golden calf ascribes its making to the people and refrains from any reference to Aaron (*Vita Mosis* 2:31).[7] This radical elimination of Aaron already characterizes the postexilic Ps. 106: 19-20, where the sin of the golden calf is shortly mentioned among the people's tresspasses in the wilderness. The same applies even to Deuteronomy (9:7-21,25-29). To be sure, Aaron's sin is alluded to in v. 2o which states that God's wrath was kindled against Aaron as well and that also for him Moses offered a prayer to God. This verse, however, shows clear marks of a later addition, since it is most perplexing in its context which refrains from any hint to Aaron's part in the making of the calf and contains the formula "at that time" which serves in the introductory chapters of Deuteronomy as a criterion of secondary addition.[8] The annotator who derives his knowledge of Aaron's sin from predeuteronomic sources drew the consequence that Aaron needed special divine forgiveness. Even in this unparalleled verse mentioning God's anger upon Aaron the vague allusion to his sin is postponed to the moment of Moses' prayer for him.

---

[6] It has been argued that Aaron's punishment had been reported in our text, but that this passage has been deleted by a redactor. See M. Noth, *Exodus*, London 1962, pp. 244f.; Averbach - Smolar, *op. cit.* (note 2), p. 239. It is however extremely difficult to fit such a hypothetical report into our text, which treats Aaron with outspoken leniency.

[7] Less consequent is Aaron's elimination in Pseudo-Philo's *Liber Antiquitatum Biblicarum* XII where he holds his own in the prehistory of the making of the calf and only the actual making is attributed to the people.

[8] S.E. Loewenstamm, "*The Formula* $b\bar{a}^{c}$*et hahi' in Deuteronomy, Tarbiz* 38 (1969) pp. 99-104 (in Heb.).

After this survey on the later sources let us return to Ex. 32, the only text in which Aaron's part in the events is clearly shown both in the author's relation (vv. 2-5) and in Aaron's words (vv. 21-24). But in contradistinction to these detailed descriptions two short references mention the making of the calf by the people (vv. 8,35a). True, both statements are reconcilable, since Aaron had acted not only with the aid of the people, but in response to its request and on its behalf. Nevertheless vv. 8,35a[9] reveal the tendency of blurring Aaron's part. The verses belong to the passages vv. 7-14[10] and 30-35a which are remarkably similar in outlook. In both we are told that Moses interceded when God's wrath was kindled against the people and He wanted to destroy it completely by immediate divine action. According to the vv. 7-14 Moses succeeded in obtaining full forgiveness as in Deuteronomy, whereas according to vv. 30-35a God only spared the people as such, but smote the sinners among them. Both later additions are basically different from the story in vv. 25-29. Here any straightforward reference to the calf is avoided. It is not the making of the calf by itself which calls for penalty, but the behaviour of the people which has got out of hand, and Moses himself organises the execution of the sinners which is performed by men.

On the supposition that vv. 7-14 and vv. 30-35 are the only additions to the original story of the sin of the calf, Moses performed in this sto-

---

9 The composite character of v. 35 has generally been recognized. For the view that v. 35b should be regarded as an addition to the oldest version which allegedly attributed the making of the calf to the people, see above, note 4. It has even been proposed to regard v. 35b "as an addition to *E* by a later editor to further a polemic against Aaron the Eponym of the Bethel priesthood" (Perdue, *op. cit.* (note 2), p. 238, note 2). In the present writer's opinion v. 35b should be accounted for by the fact that the later version ascribing the making of the calf to the people has never succeeded in completely superseding the older version which attributed this act to Aaron. In 35b an editor just added by way of annotation a short reference to the older version to a text representing the later one. Cf. Deut. 9:20, a more elaborate gloss reintroducing Aaron into a later version from which he had completely been removed. Cf. above, note 8.

10 It might well be that vv. 7-8 belong to a more ancient layer than vv. 9-14. Anyhow vv. 9-14 presuppose vv. 7-8 and therefore vv. 7-14 can be treated for our purpose as one passage. It has often been observed that the depiction of Moses' descent from the mountain loses much of its dramatic force on the supposition that Moses was aware of the situation beforehand.

ry four acts: 1. he broke the tablets; 2. he destroyed the calf; 3. he called Aaron to account; 4. he had the sinners among the people punished. This sequence makes good sense. The breaking of the tablets throws into relief the seriousness of the sin indicating that it amounts to an annulation of God's covenant with Israel. The following destruction of the calf does not call for explanation. But neither does his calling to account of Aaron. We could hardly imagine that Moses were described as turning a blind eye on Aaron. Aaron exculpates himself laying the blame on the people. Moses accepts his answer but realizes that Aaron is not the man to control the situation and proceedes himself to the punishment of the rebels. No inherent difficulty can be detected in this sequence.

True, it could be argued that this general impression does not stand a closer scrutiny which reveals a lack of homogeneity in the text because 1. the tradition of the tablets has its own roots; 2. the same applies to the passage describing the punishment of the sinners containing an aetiological report on the investiture of Levi; 3. Aaron is spared punishment although it was he who made the calf. Let us examine these arguments one by one.

The tradition that Moses received tablets from God on the mountain is indeed in its origin clearly independent of the tradition of the calf. The breaking of the tablets, however, is no less clearly an innovation of the author who regarded the making of the calf as a sin, modified the tradition of the tablets and adapted it to his story. The traditio-historical criticism proves then to be irrelevant for the literary criticism of the story.

The same applies to vv. 25-29. In a paper on the investiture of Levi the present writer[11] has defended the thesis that Deut. 33:8-9 hints at a version of the story of Massah and Meribah in which God tried the Levites requiring them to kill the rebels. The Levites stood the test and were rewarded with their investiture. This ancient aetiology was later transferred to the story of the golden calf, which dealt with a problem felt more

[11] See above, note 3. Cf. already Lehming, *op. cit.* (note 4), p. 42 who remarks: "*Dem Verfasser von Ex. 32:25-29 lag bereits Deut. 33:9 vor.*" The present writer would rather say that the author of Ex. 32:25-29 knows the story hinted at in Deut. 33:8-9.

strongly in the period of the First Temple than the lack of water from which the Israelites had suffered in the wilderness. In its new form this aetiology solved the problem of how the necessary punishment of the sinful people came about.

There remains the difficulty that Aaron, the maker of the calf, was spared. This tension, however, is inherent in the transition from the cult legend glorifying Aaron's making of the idol to a story condemning it, yet shrinking from outright condemnation of Aaron. The immanent tension should not bewilder modern scholarship, although it quite understandably troubled Jewish tradition, which solved the problem by transferring the making of the calf to the people. Here again historio-critical and literary analysis should not be kept apart. All this said, we should be careful not to over-stress this tension, since even the old story tried hard to reduce it.

This even applies to Aaron's making of the calf and his proclamation of the feast. The story relates that in both phases Aaron bowed to the will of the people. He made the calf because the people demanded from him gods (v. 1) and he proclaimed the feast because he realised (v. 5a) that the people acclaimed the calf shouting: These are the gods Israel who brought you up from the land of Egypt. In what follows Aaron's activity ceases altogether. It is the people who celebrate the feast with disgusting noisy revelry whose shocking impression upon Moses is described dramatically (vv. 17-19, cf. v. 6), and this impression rather than the making of the calf as such motivates Moses' action against the rebels (v. 25). True, this action is preceded by Moses' reproachful address to Aaron: What did this people do to you that you brought upon them heavy sin? (v. 21). But even in this question the author's bias for Aaron is discernable since it provides an ideal transition to Aaron's reply that the reason of his misdeed were the wickedness of the people who urged him to make gods for them. It was under this pressure that he asked the people to provide him with gold, a request which was immediately complied with. This gold, Aaron adds, he put into fire and the calf emerged, apparently by itself. All these considerations suggest the hand of one and the same author who welded different elements into one clearly organised composition.

A comprehensive survey on Ex. 32 then tends to show that vv. 4,20,24 belong to the same source. There remains the question whether their detailed examination confirms this result. The crucial words *wayyāṣar 'oto baḥäräṭ* (v. 4) have been explained in different ways. Perdue adopts the translation: 'He formed it in a casting mould'. He feels less sure about the interpretation of v. 24. On p. 239 he accepts the commonly held opinion that Aaron described the calf as self-emerged. On p. 245 however he prefers the view that we are to consider "the placing of the gold into the fire in v. 24 as a reference to the casting process". His second proposal then interprets v. 24 in full accordance with v. 4 leaving no room whatsoever for source criticism. But the same holds good if we prefer his first interpretation of v. 24 taking into account Perdue's view that the author of the text considered Aaron's description as untrue. This amounts to the exegesis that v. 4 reports the real procedure, v. 24 its misrepresentation by Aaron. Again no argument for different sources can be found on this supposition. Let us proceed from these *argumenta ad hominem* to a renewed scrutiny of v. 4. Already S. Bochartus objected to the translation adopted by Perdue because of its lack of linguistic support.[13] This objection still holds good to-day, although our knowledge of Semitic languages has considerably increased in the meantime. The only *raison d'être* of this exegesis is apparently the consideration that a molten image is produced in a casting mould. In his former paper the present writer preferred the translation 'and he bound it in a cloak or bag' and adduced detailed linguistic support. He would like to add here that this interpretation yields a description which is remarkably similar to the report on the making of Gideon's *ephod*. There as well the very making of the idol is described with laconic brevity and simply reads: "And Gideon made it (the material) into an *ephod*" (Ju. 8:27), but is preceded by the statement: "And they spread a cloak (*śimlā*) and put there everyone the noserings of his booty" (v. 25). The verse vividly illustrates the procedure of collecting the material for the idol in a cloak. One may well be tempted to surmise that the same procedure is presupposed in Ex. 32:7 and thus arrive at the interpretation: And he accepted from them and bound it (the material) in the cloak (into which they had put it). Anyhow it appears that the act of collecting the material for the making of

---

[12] A comparison with the story of Gideon's *ephod* (Ju. 8:24-27) suggests that Aaron's request and the people's response stem from the cult legend. This does not apply, of course, to the people's initiative.

[13] *Hierozoikon*[4], Lugduni Batavorum 1712, p. 334.

an idol in a cloak[14] (rather than in a bag!) is an act well worth mentioning in such texts.[15] This parallel is so much the more convincing as both images, the calf as well as the *ephod*, were made of gold procured from adornements called *n^e^zāmim*. The affinity of this anything but harmless trinket to the worship of foreign gods is highlighted by the report that Jacob's children gave to their father the foreign gods which were in their hands and the rings (*n^e^zāmim*) which were in their ears, and that Jacob concealed them under the terebinth in Shechem (Gen. 35:4). No less significant is the Jewish-Aramaic and Syriac name of *näzäm-q^e^dāšā'* defining it as a holy object.

It follows that Ex. 32:4 leaves us without any information concerning the procedure by which the calf was made. This lack however is made up by Aaron's reply to Moses. Aaron just put the material into the fire and out of it the calf emerged by itself. Modern exegesis has ridiculed this answer as an extremely weak excuse, since it implies an obvious impossibility. But neither the author nor Moses stigmatizes Aaron's statement as a lie. On the contrary, the context proves that the author believed in Aaron's words. Aaron is nowhere represented as a liar, and even a liar will never tell things which his contemporaries would regard as impossible thus undermining his credibility. The motif is clearly rooted in the old cult legend and taken up by the author of the present story with the purpose of alleviating Aaron's guilt. The author's condemnation of the worship of the calf did not imply the negation of its supernatural character. Even Deuteronomy distinguishes between the prohibition of worship and the negation of divine character, as appears in its attitude to the host of heavens whose worship is forbidden to Israel, but is incumbent on the other peoples (4:19-20). As to the golden calf in particular, I already drew attention to *Liber Antiquitatum Biblicarum* XII:3 which describes the creation of the calf by the people in the following words: *Et miserunt ea (i.e. inaures mulierum) in ignem et effigiata sunt in figuram et exivit vitulus conflatilis.* This description is the more remarkable as it is presented in the author's

[14] *śimlā* is translated in *TO* on Deut. 22:17 and in the Targum on 1 Sam. 21:10 by *šošipā'*. Cf. *TY* on Ex. 32:4.

[15] I am indebted for this observation to my former student Esther Cohen.

name. The same concept is even to be found in Talmudic sources.[16] There is no real contradiction between this supernatural procedure and the statement of v. 4 that Aaron made the calf, but rather a difference in stress. In the author's mind Aaron made the calf by putting the gold into the fire with the intention of the calf emerging from it self-produced. Cf. also the Midrashic literature in which the explicit statements of the Bible that Moses and Solomon erected cultic buildings are combined with the idea that these buildings arose by themselves.[17] The closest parallel to the making of the calf is provided by the Ugaritic text *CTA* 4:VI:22-35 describing the erection of Baal's palace by fire, after which Baal proclaims that he has built his palace. Perdue objects: "In the case of Baal's temple, we consider the catastrophic fire as referring to the smelting of the Canaanite god of craftsmanship, Kothar wa-Khasis ... Therefore, the argument that the palace of Baal self-emerges lacks validity".[18] But the building of a palace is not a smelting process. True, Kothar wa-Khasis did build the palace on behalf of Baal. But that is to say that he fetched the materials and lit a (not at all catastrophic!) fire which was doing its work for six days until on the seventh day the building was completed by itself. He (alternatively his lord Baal) was the builder of the palace in the same sense and with the same qualifications as Aaron was the maker of the calf.

In his treatment of v. 20 Perdue makes the point that the destruction of the calf "is presented in realistic language." But unfortunately he fails to explain how we are to understand this realistic procedure in concrete terms, although this problem has vexed scholarship for some hundreds of years and yielded a host of tortuous interpretations, surveyed in my former article. By-passing this intricate question Perdue rushes into a comparison of Ex. 32:20 to 2 Reg. 23:6b which depicts Josia's destruction of the Asherah. Both texts depict the annihilation of an idol with the very same verbs *śrp* and *dqq*. Josia's action was actually performed, thus vindicating the realistic character of Ex. 32:20. True, a certain similarity between these verses is obvious. Its evaluation however requires more detailed analysis. To start with, 2 Reg. 23:6b is nearer to Deut. 9:21 than it is to

---

[16] See S. Lieberman, *The Tosephta*, Part V. *Order Moed*, New York 1962, pp. 1218f.

[17] *Midrash Tanhuma*, ed. S. Buber, Wilna 1885, *Pekude* VIII; *Pesikta Rabbathi*, ed. M. Friedmann, Wien 1880, ch. 6.

[18] "Golden Calf", 239.

Ex. 32:20, as born out by the following observations: 1. Ex. 32:20 reads: *wayyiṭḥan ^{c}ad '^{a}šär dāq*. 'and he milled (it) until it was crushed'. Deut. 9:21 uses instead the formulation *wā'äkkot 'oto ṭāḥon heṭeb ^{c}ad '^{a}šär dāq*. 'and I beat it until it was crushed milling (it) well'. Deuteronomy thus explains away the unrealistic milling of a golden idol by taking *ṭḥn* in a metaphorical sense, 2 Reg. 23:6b goes a step further omitting the verb *ṭḥn* altogether; and thus entirely eliminating the time-honoured literary motif of milling, deeply rooted in ancient epic tradition, but highly troublesome from a realistic point of view adopted by Deuteronomistic sources. 2. Ex. 32:20 described the dispersion of the calf (not its ashes!) by the verb *zrh*, whereas both Deut. 9:21 and 2 Reg. 23:6b speak of the throwing (*Hiph^{c}il* of *šlk*) of the idol's ashes (!) into a certain place. In all these respects Ex. 32:20 is remarkably near to *CTA* 6:II:30-37. After Mot has been burnt (*šrp*), it is he who is being milled (not his ashes!) and his (not his ashes!) dispersion is described by the verb *dr^{c}* which in this use is synonymous with *zrh* in Ex. 32:20 (see the following).

To sum up: Ex. 32:20 is related to the unrealistic style of Ugaritic epic, whereas Deut. 9:21 breaks loose from it and still more so does 2 Reg. 23:6b. Moreover, the difference between the wooden Ashera and the golden calf should not be overlooked. Wood burns, gold does not. It follows that the late verse 2 Reg. 23:6b is far from providing us with a starting point for the interpretation of the earlier verse Ex. 32:20. Just the opposite is true. Ex. 32:20 sheds light on Deut. 9:21 which in its turn influenced the formulation of 2 Reg. 23:6b.

In this discussion of Ex. 32:20 we already mentioned the Ugaritic verb *dr^{c}* rendering it by 'to scatter or to disperse'. This view, however, is by no means common opinion and Perdue went to some length to disprove it. The verb has been explained as 'to sow'. From this it follows that the dead Mot was sown in the field. All scholars who regard Mot as a symbol of grain refer to this scene as to one of their main proofs. Contradicting this argument the present writer pointed to the secondary sense of the root *dr^{c}* 'to scatter' adducing evidence from Hebrew and Syriac *zr^{c}* and from Greek σπείρω and tried to establish that only this sense fits the context here.[19]

[19] See in this volume, *The Ugaritic Fertility Myth - the Result of a Mistranslation*, pp. 160-161.

The second part of his deduction has of course met with the opposition of those scholars who adhere to the interpretation of Mot as a symbol of grain.[20] Perdue goes a step further, denying even the linguistic option of understanding Hebrew *zr*^{c} sometimes as meaning 'to scatter' and states categorically that "the meaning of *zāra*^{c} in Ju. 9:45 must be to sow". It goes, however, without saying that no plant could possibly sprout from salt and that consequently salt never can be sown. In Zech. 10:9 he explains away *zr*^{c} 'to disperse' as a methaphorical use of 'sow'. But *zr*^{c} there is exactly synonymous to *zrh* in Lev. 26:33. Another objection raised by Perdue carries more weight. In the aforementioned paper the present writer argued that Ugaritic *dr*^{c} should be interpreted as synonymous with Ugaritic *dry*, Hebrew *zrh* - 'to winnow, to disperse'. Perdue objects that the occurrence of *dry* only three lines before *dr*^{c} points to a difference in meaning of the two words. It really does, and in his recent paper entitled "*The Killing of Mot in Ugaritic Myth*"[21] the present writer has tacitly corrected his former mistake and rendered *dry* by 'winnow', *dr*^{c} by 'to scatter'. Yet this correction does not detract from the force of the argument that both Mot and the calf were scattered. Winnowing as well as sowing involves actions of dispersion. This explains the fact that both verbs under discussion coincide in the secondary sense 'to scatter'. It is the same process of dispersion indicated in the Ugaritic text by *dr*^{c} that is described in the Hebrew text by *zrh*. The interchange between synonymous and phonetically similar verbs does not call for explanation.

To sum up, both texts reveal uniqueness in their general pattern describing the utter extinction of a hateful enemy by a series of unrealistic and mutually irreconcilable acts, and in both, the later acts are directed, as it were, against the enemy himself, not against what has been left of him after the former acts of destruction. Two acts, viz. burning and milling appear in the same sequence and are rendered by the very same words, a subsequent act of scattering by synonymous and phonetically similar verbs. No more could be requested for the proof of identity of pattern, and no conformity in all details should be expected between old Ugaritic epic and much later Hebrew prose.

---

[20] See e.g. de Moor, *Seasonal Pattern*, pp. 210f. Contrast e.g. P.L. Watson, "*The Death of 'Death' in the Ugaritic Texts*", *JAOS* 92 (1972), p. 60, note 3.

[21] See in this volume, *The Killing of Mot in the Ugaritic Myth*, pp. 428-429

Perdue overemphasizes the dissimilarities, arranging a list of Hebrew verbs unparalleled in the Ugaritic text and *vice versa*. The Hebrew verbs are *dqq* and *šqh*. In Ex. 32:20 however *daq* is a verbal adjective, indicating only the result of milling, not an additional act of destroying. True, the *Hiph*^{c}*il* of *šqh* is related to the final disappearance of the calf's remnants and absent from the Ugaritic text which has instead the verb *akl*. But does this difference really constitute a diversity in pattern? In one case the scattered remnants disappear by drinking, in the other by eating, both acts apparently being equivalent. As unparalleled Ugaritic verbs Perdue mentions, besides *akl, aḫd* also *bq*^{c}. Anat took hold of Mot and split him open with a sword. Here, however, we meet with a realistic description of killing, since Mot is represented in the shape of a human being. Therefore the depiction of his killing should be differentiated from that of the following annihilation of his corpse. It is only in this second part that the poet changes over to a typological style neglecting realistic considerations. No parallel to the killing of Mot by a sword should be expected in a text dealing with the destruction of an idol. To be sure there is one difference between the two texts which matters here. Anat winnows Mot with a sieve, another symbol of utter destruction paralleled in Jer. 15:7; Is. 41:16, but not in Ex. 32:20. But even this real difference only proves that Ex. 32:20 presents the pattern in a shorter form. Against the hypothesis that Mot should be regarded as a symbol of grain see the present writer's above-mentioned paper on the Killing of Mot.

Let us conclude this detailed analysis of the making and destruction of the golden calf with some remarks upon the methodology of Biblical exegesis, raised in Perdue's paper.

Perdue attributes to the present writer the attempt to demonstrate the literary dependence of Ex. 32:20 on the pericope of Mot's destruction, that is to say that the Biblical writer had been conversant with Ugaritic epic. The present writer never held such a fanciful view. There is no proof that the literary tablets of far-away Ugarit had ever reached Israel and even if they had, it is hardly conceivable that the Israelites took pains to decipher them and to study the difficult language of those ancient pagan writings. The undeniable specific affinities between the two literatures rather call for the assumption of a common ground underlying the literatures of all Canaanite peoples. The hypothesis imposes itself that there existed a southern version of this tradition which left its imprint upon the Bible. In a paper on the myth of the Sea the present writer has tried to strengthen this contention by the demonstration that the allusions to this myth in the Bible can hardly be explained as references to the Ugaritic epic, but reflect another version of this myth, akin to the Ugaritic one, but nevertheless different from it.[22] In spite of these qualifications (which hold good all the more for Akkadian and Egyptian texts) the impact of Oriental studies upon the exegesis of the Hebrew Bible should not be belittled. In referring to these materials, however, we should be careful not to exceed the limits of sound philological analysis. There is no point in Perdue's speculation about the question whether Aaron's activities included a rite comparable to the opening of mouth attested in Egypt and Mesopotamia, since no hint whatsoever of such a rite can be found in Ex. 32.

Perdue strongly emphasizes the undisputed necessity for literary criticism, adduces ample proof for the composite literary structure of Ex. 32 and arrives at the conclusion that "efforts to find uniformity in vv. 4,20, 24 appear tenuous". *Non sequitur*! In every composite text a certain number of verses will belong to the same source. Furthermore, prudence cautions against literary criticism based upon a problematic interpretation of a difficult verse. In such a precarious instance at least support from the broader context should be required. Ex. 32:4 is a classical case in point. Every explanation of this debatable verse which involves a contradiction between it and v. 24 is *a limine* highly suspect, since v. 24 is an integral part of the passage vv. 20-24 which patently refers to the passage vv. 1-6 and continues its narration satisfactorily. Above all, literary criticism should not be kept apart from traditio-historical analysis, for an uneveness in the text might be accounted for by this kind of analysis rather than by division into sources.

Last but not least, a remark upon the evaluation of Jewish Post-Biblical sources. Perdue passes in silence over all writings of this kind adduced in the present writer's former paper. One may wonder whether he is right in doing so since this literature sometimes preserves most ancient traditions. Its disputes on the issue whether the calf was self-emerged or not reflect

---

[22] See in this volume, *The Ugaritic Myth of the Sea and its Biblical Counterparts*, pp. 346-361.

a most revealing struggle between the tradition that it indeed emerged such a way and the theological criticism of this view. But even those who were prepared to draw all consequences from the disavowal of the idol's vitality realized the difficulty of their position, and even in their words the old tradition sometimes shines through, as in the Midrashic story on Moses who objected to God's wrath, putting to Him the incisive question: "If there is no reality in it (the golden calf), why art Thou wroth? (*Numeri Rabba* 2:15). These Rabbinical disputes shed light on modern exegesis. The text makes perfect sense on the supposition that it attributes to the calf a supernatural character. If we decline this supposition the text is hard to understand and evokes fanciful, textually unsupported devices of exegesis. Nevertheless nearly all modern exegetes acquiesced with this glaring difficulty in order to avoid what seemed to them a theological stumbling-block.

Exodus 21:22-25

The time-honoured debate on Ex. 21:22-25 has been continued in the last few years with unabated vigour. Recently, Sh. Paul's[1] discussion of this enigmatic law has induced B. Jackson[2] to a monographic treatment combining a detailed critical survey on most of the former views with the presentation of a highly original analysis of his own. Jackson's treatment concludes with the reconstruction of an *Urgesetz* from which the actually transmitted law developed by a process of subsequent amendments.

To his mind, the final law occupies itself with two possible consequences of a blow given to a pregnant woman, viz. 1) the case of a miscarriage including perhaps that of a premature birth, and 2) the case of the woman's death. In the first event the trespasser is liable to a fine, fixed in principle by the woman's husband but subject to a kind of judicial assessment; in the second case there applies the death-penalty. This interpretation of the Biblical text differs from anonymous Tannaitic exegesis[3] only by the remark that the first provision of the law might have been applied even in the case of a premature birth.[4] To the present writer this possibility seems remote. A miscarriage causes the loss of a life, a premature birth at the most a temporary inconvenience. It is improbable that the same ruling should have included two obviously disparate contingencies.

The main scope of Jackson's paper is the reconstruction of the *Urgesetz* and of its subsequent amendments. Jackson restricts the *Urgesetz* to vv. 22-23 and discerns even in them vestiges of later redaction. V. 22a describes

---

[1] Sh.M. Paul, *Studies in the Book of the Covenant in the Light of Cuneiform and Biblical Law, VTS* 18 (1970), pp. 70-77, 108f.

[2] B.S. Jackson, *The Problems of Exod. 21:22-5 (Jus Talionis), VT* 23 (1973), pp. 271-304.

[3] *Mechilta d'Rabbi Ismael*, ed. H.S. Horovitz - I.A. Rabin (Jerusalem, 1960), pp. 274-276.

[4] The above-mentioned Midrash (pp. 275f.) remarks: "If there will be no calamity (you might interpret) if no calamity befalls either the woman or the foetus? But on this supposition he (i.e. the husband) even should pay the price of a midwife (to the man who had struck the woman)".

the blow as the result of a brawl between men who hit the woman (*w^{e}nāg^{e}pu*). No indication can be found that only one man is held responsible for the blow. In contrast to this *protasis* the *apodoses* in vv. 22b, 23b prescribe the punishment as that of one single man. Jackson concludes from this inconsistency that the original law held all participants in the brawl responsible, whereas the later redactor rejected this principle of collective responsibility. Jackson further argues that the beginning of v. 22b grants to the husband an unlimited claim, whereas the subsequent words *w^{e}nātan bipli=lim* subject his claim to the approval of assessors and should be regarded as an addition. These modifications, however, did not affect the legal meaning of the crucial term *'āson* translated by Jackson as 'calamity', and explained by him in the *Urgesetz* as the death of the foetus. Nor did the above-mentioned modification result in a change of the original meaning of the punishment *näpäš taḥat näpäš* which intended substitution, as borne out by a comparison with Lev. 24:18. The *Urgesetz*, then, distinguished between premature birth and miscarriage. In the first case the husband was entitled to an unlimited fine, in the second to substitution.

The slightly revised *Urgesetz* underwent radical transformation by the insertion of the late, probably Deuteronomic, principle of talion in v. 24, enlarged in the final stage by the addition of v. 25. The direct effect of the added ruling "an eye for an eye, etc." was a change in the meaning of the formula *näpäš taḥat näpäš* which in its new context clearly prescribed the death penalty. But the recasting of the law was more farreaching. The words "a tooth for a tooth" failed to yield sense with respect to a foetus and were meaningful only when related to the corporeal integrity of the woman. Therefore, the term "calamity" was interpreted at this stage as a reference to the woman's death. On this supposition, however, the punishment for causing a birth which involved no calamity could hardly be restricted to the event of a premature birth, but acquired the (additional?) meaning of a miscarriage.

Jackson then reconstructs an *Urgesetz*, dealing with the contingencies of a premature birth and a miscarriage and omitting the eventuality of the woman's death. This hypothetical law, however, is blatantly different from the corresponding old oriental laws. Two[5] deal with miscarriage alone;

---

[5] The Sumerian tablet *YBC* 2177, rev. IV, 1-2, see J.J. Finkelstein, *ANET*³, p. 525, and the *Hittite Laws* 17-18.

three[6] add the case of the woman's death. None of them occupies itself with premature birth. Jackson tries to play down this difficulty by adducing a Greek document from Egypt, drawn up in the year 89 BCE, which possibly might allude to such a ruling. Unfortunately, however, this possibility is rather remote even in that late post-Biblical text. The plaintiff there is a pregnant woman who was given many blows and complains: "The blows caused me to be laid up with sickness and my life is endangered. I inform you in order that T. be brought up and secured until my case be ascertained in the appointed period, so that, if anything happens to me, she may be treated according to the enactments concerning such conduct, and, if I survive, I may obtain satisfaction from her as is right". The document does not mention the eventuality of a premature birth at all. It is perfectly clear that the plaintiff was entitled to compensation under all circumstances including that of a normal birth since she was laid up with sickness as a result of the blows. To sum up, there is no evidence of even a late oriental law imposing a fine in the event of a premature birth.

Let us scrutinize the hypothetical *Urgesetz* in some greater detail. Jackson surmises that the *Urgesetz* entitled the husband to assess the fine for a premature birth according to his own unfettered discretion. The present writer wonders whether any law might provide for an unlimited claim. To be sure, Jackson invokes the law of the goring ox whose owner is liable to any sum imposed upon him as ransom for his life (Ex. 21:30). But the case of the goring ox is clearly different. The formulation of that law in the passive voice fails to answer the question who determines the ransom, the judge or the plaintiff. Even according to the second interpretation the situation is a very special one, since then the plaintiff is primarily entitled to insist upon death penalty and therefore might freely state the conditions under which he is prepared to waive this right. No comparable situation exists in the case of a premature birth, where at the most a simple claim for a modest sum of money could be imagined.

Jackson argues that the *Urgesetz* considered the injury inflicted upon the woman as the outcome of a brawl between men and that the law held all

---

[6] The Sumerian text *UM* - 55 - 21-71, III ll. 2'-13'. See M. Civil, *Assyriological Studies in Honor of B. Landsberger* (1965) (= *AS* 16), pp. 4-6; *CH* 209-214; *MAL* A 50-52.

the men collectively responsible. Even in this respect the *Urgesetz* is unparalleled in ancient oriental laws, which invariably deal with the responsibility of one single person who did harm to the pregnant woman. It is hard to explain for which reason an ancient Hebrew law would have omitted this simple case and substituted for it a complicated and far-fetched one. At least we might expect some explanation how it came about that a brawl between men ended with an assault on a pregnant woman. Such badly needed clarification, however, is conspicuously absent in the law under discussion, and Jackson quite correctly states that it cannot be gained by reference to Deut. 25:11.

Let us consider the alleged process of redaction. Jackson argues that the original principle of collective responsibility was later rejected. His reasoning implies the doubtful explanation of the *protasis* that not all participants in the brawl actually struck the woman but only one of them whose action was considered by the *Urgesetz* as if all the men had hurt her. Jackson's analysis shows in some detail that this ruling indeed makes excellent sense in such an event; it fails, however, to adduce any reason for its rejection. Moreover, Jackson's thesis constrains us to admit that the redactor performed his work with remarkable inaptness, since he contented himself with changes in the *apodoses* but failed to correct the statement of the *protasis* that the woman was hit by a plurality of men.

Still more perplexing is Jackson's proposal that the very tenor of the old law has been transformed by the insertion of the principle of talion, regarded by him as a late one without a single change in the wording of vv. 22-23. That is to say, not only that the words *näpäš taḥat näpäš* turned from a ruling for substitution into one for the death-penalty, but that the addition of v. 24 even redefined the basic term "calamity" which originally adumbrated the death of the foetus, in the revised version, however, that of the woman. The present writer wonders whether any example of such a sophisticated technique of amendment can be adduced from the history of law.

Jackson is guided by his concept that the principle of talion has been introduced into Hebrew law at a late stage, and points to Deuteronomy as its possible origin. His tentative assumption that Deut. 19:21 should be regarded as the source of the principle in Biblical law fails to stand the test of a closer scrutiny. Deut. 19:16-21 deals with the crime of a deceitful witness and states his punishment in v. 19a which reads: "You shall do to him as he intended to do to his fellow-man". From a strictly legal point of view, this ruling would have been quite sufficient. Actually, however, Deuteronomy adds in vv. 19b-21 some admonitions, impressing the observation of the law, which conclude with the words: "Your eye should not look with compassion, life for life, eye for eye, tooth for tooth, hand for hand, foot for foot" (v. 21). A legal principle which in its origin applies to corporeal damages is quoted here in a different legal context in order to reinforce the abstract formulation of v. 19a by reference to an ancient concrete wording sounding the pathos of an emotional appeal. If the formula "an eye for an eye etc." had been a Deuteronomic innovation, it would have appeared in rulings on corporeal damages. In its actual context, however, it is patently intended to call to mind a commonly known principle, generally accepted at its time. Deuteronomy then provides us with a clear *terminus ante quem*. No *terminus post quem* is evident.

To the present writer's mind a plausible point of departure for the interpretation of Ex. 21:22-25 may be found in a comparison of old oriental legal provisions with the interpretation of the Biblical law extant in the anonymous Tannaitic Midrash which should be kept apart from those Midrashic interpretations which are added to the bulk of the Midrash in the name of their authors. Such a comparison reveals at the first glance that one Sumerian law, the codex of Hammurabi, the Middle Assyrian law and the Midrash deal firstly with a miscarriage and subsequently with the woman's death. In the light of this striking coincidence it might a limine be admitted that the Biblical *Urgesetz* did not differ in this respect. True, this general statement is far from solving all problems of interpretation. There remains first of all the difficulty that the Bible speaks of a plurality of men who hurt the woman, the non-Israelite laws of a single person only. But even this special feature of Biblical law becomes obliterated in old Tannaitic exegesis. The anonymous Tannaitic Midrash reads:[7] "And if there is a strife between men - for which reason is this passage said? Because scripture says: If a man acts intentionally (Ex. 21:14) - we heard only that the death-penalty applies to a man who intended to kill his enemy and killed his enemy, but we did not hear about a man who intended to kill his enemy

---

[7] *Op. cit.* (note 3), p. 274.

and killed his friend. Therefore it is written: And if there is a strife between men". That is to say that Tannaitic exegesis was aware of the difficulty involved in the interpretation of v. 22a and therefore raises the question of the reason why the law does not simply speak of one man who hurt a pregnant woman. The answer is that the roundabout formulation of the law implies in addition to a ruling for this uncomplicated case a hint of the solution of the problem of *aberratio ictus*. A wanted to hit B, but missed and struck C. According to this exegesis the law implies three rulings, viz. 1) if a man hurts a pregnant woman etc. 2) The same applies even if he intended to hurt a man. 3) An analogous principle holds good in every case of *aberratio ictus*. The first of these three rules is clearly paralleled in ancient oriental legislation; the two additional rules are not. Ancient oriental legislation formulates simple, typical circumstances and does not concern itself with abstract speculations on general theory of penal law as the divergence between the trespasser's intention and the result of his action. The Tannaitic law already did face questions of this kind and read the solution of the problem of *aberratio ictus* into v. 22a. But this astute *eisegesis* reached a very remarkable result, viz. a law providing in its main meaning for the event that one man struck a pregnant woman. It is exactly this case which is dealt with in ancient oriental legislation.

We venture to surmise that this Tannaitic exegesis reflects the practice of Biblical law with greater fidelity than the actual wording of the law in the Bible does, where the text of a law dealing with a blow given to a pregnant woman has become mixed up with the text of another law providing for the consequences of blows which men dealt upon one another in a brawl. By the supposition of a textual confusion we can also easily account for the above discussed inconsistency between the *protasis* of v. 22 and the *apodoses* of vv. 22 and 23. Even the provisions of vv. 24-25 make plausible sense only when related to damages which men inflicted upon one another in a brawl. To be sure, the possibility cannot be excluded that a stroke given to a pregnant woman deprived her of an eye, but in that case her pregnancy is irrelevant - compare also Jackson's plausible reasoning that the loss of one tooth could hardly be qualified as a calamity.[8]

---

[8] Already H. Cazelles, *Études sur le Code d'Alliance* (Paris, 1946), p. 56, advanced the view that v. 22a is derived from the law of talion, not from the law of the pregnant woman and remarked: "*Mais la liaison de lois du*

Let us proceed to a scrutiny of the wording of the law in some detail. Its proposition *w^{e}yāṣ^e'u y^{e}lādähā w^{e}lo' yihyä 'āson* (v. 22a) is not easily understood. Jackson advances two arguments in order to prove his point that the difficult text intended a premature birth, not a miscarriage: 1) it fails to make clear that the child was stillborn; 2) on the supposition that it wanted to say that the woman stayed alive, it should simply read *w^{e}lo' tāmut hā'iššā*, "and the woman will not die", instead of making use of the ambiguous term *'āson*. His arguments are remarkable, but hardly decisive. The noun *'āson* appears in the Bible outside the law of the pregnant woman in Gen. 42:4,38; 44:29, all three passages relating to Jacob's apprehension that an *'āson* might happen to Benjamin if he joined his brothers on their journey to Egypt. We concede to Jackson that the precise meaning of *'āson* remains without definition in Gen. 42:4. Gen. 42:38 and 44:29, however, leave no doubt about Jacob's fear that Benjamin might be put to death, and thus explain the meaning of this term in Gen. 42:4 as well. That is to say that *'āson* is attested only as a reference to the death of a person. The extremely limited occurrence of the noun tends to show that its use was restricted to a certain Hebrew dialect and that the law of the pregnant woman comes from the same surroundings as the passages dealing with Jacob's opposition to Benjamin's journey. It appears that the draftmanship of that milieu did not reach the same degree of perfection that is usually found in Biblical law. A formulation "if there will be no calamity", which fails to describe whom this calamity shall befall, lacks the degree of explicitness expected in a law. It is the same lack of exact definition which makes itself felt in the absence of an outspoken statement that the child was stillborn, at least if we interpret the strange plural *y^{e}lādähā* as "children" rather than as a term for a foetus that is not viable. It is hardly by chance that the interpretation of the words *w^{e}nātan biplilim* meets with

---

talion avec le cas de la femme enceinte paraît remonter à la rédaction même du code. A la différence des autres législations, le code d'alliance rattache curieusement le coup porté à la femme enceinte à une rixe entre hommes. C'est me semble-t-il, en vue justement d'amener la loi du talion qui fait suite à ce cas." Cazelles then regards the combination of both laws as the result of a redaction, not as that of a scribal error. The main difference between Cazelles and the present writer concerns the term *'āson*. Cazelles holds the view that *'āson* is a "*dommage corporel quelconque*" and that the term "*a été utilisé pour faire la liaison entre les cas particuliers et l'énoncée de cette loi très générale*" (i.e. the law of talion), whereas to the present writer *'āson* means the woman's death and has no connection with the law of talion.

similar difficulties. The term *p^e^lilim* is a *hapax legomenon* apparently belonging to the same dialect as the word *'āson* and obviously denotes some procedure of objective assessment. Again the formulation is cumbersome and even appears to be self-contradictory as stressed by Jackson. Nevertheless, the overall meaning of the text is clear. The law prescribes in highly untechnical terms that the husband's claim be subject to an objective assessment.[9]

More questionable is the interpretation of the formula *näpäš taḥat näpäš* (v. 23), "then you shall give a life for a life" in the original law of the pregnant woman, since the formula prescribes in Deut. 21:19 talion, in Lev. 24:18 substitution in kind or money. Two considerations favour its interpretation as death-penalty even if we disregard vv. 24-25, which presumably do not belong to the original law of the pregnant woman. 1) The transition from the quiet formulation in the third person to the pathos of an address in the second, indicating that the punishment in the event of the woman's death is incommensurably more stringent. 2) If we were to interpret the ruling " a life for a life" as prescribing substitution, this substitution should be imposed in addition to the fine due for the death of the foetus. The formulation of the law, however, clearly favours the view that the penalty "a life for a life" is meant to be an exclusive one. This interpretation is expressly stated in a lengthy anonymous Midrash.[10] It may suffice to quote here its beginnings and its concluding passages: "If there shall be no *'āson* he shall pay a fine. Consequently if there shall be an *'āson* he shall not ... This is the general ruling: Everybody who has become liable to the death-penalty and a fine by one act will be condemned to the death-penalty and absolved from the fine". This principle is undisputed in Talmudical law[11] and apparently already underlies Biblical legislation, although its abstract formulation is due to the rabbis. We can hardly follow Jackson who contests the applicability of this rule to

---

[9] H. Yalon, *Tarbiz* 6 (1935), pp. 223f., has demonstrated that *plpl* means in Talmudical Hebrew "upturn an object in order to find a thing hidden in it". This sense comes near to "investigate".

[10] *Mekhilta d' Rabbi Šim^c^on b. Yochai*, ed. J.N. Epstein - E.Z. Melamed (Jerusalem, 1955), p. 176.

[11] Cf. e.g. the sentence: "Everyone liable to death-penalty is absolved from payments" *Mechilta d'Rabbi Ismael* (note 3), p. 276, and the discussion in Babli Ketubot 35a.

Biblical law by reference to the *MAL* A 50 which recognizes the substitution for the foetus (probably in money) in addition to the death-penalty for the loss of the woman's life.[12] The Assyrian ruling, however, can hardly be considered as a clue for the interpretation of Biblical law. It restricts the principle that the death-penalty and a fine are mutually exclusive (cf. *MAL* A 10; B 2) to the event that a criminal act has one result only. This restriction is in accordance with the tendency of Assyrian law to multiply punishments for one delict, a tendency foreign to Biblical law. The simple Tannaitic ruling, less differentiated than that of Assyrian law, can hardly be regarded as the innovation of a later jurisprudence, more sophisticated than Biblical law.

To sum up, the Biblical law of the pregnant woman should be interpreted in accordance with the ancient basic layer of Tannaitic sources, reflecting the actual practice of that law even in Biblical times. The corruptions of the text were of no consequence for that practice.

---

[12] The correctness of Jackson's view is borne out by the second sub-para. of *MAL* A 50, which reads: "However, if that woman died, they shall put the seignior to death; he shall compensate for the foetus with a life (*napšāte umalla*)". If the second clause were a general statement of the principle underlying the punishment meted out in the first (as explained by Driver-Miles), it should read instead: "He shall compensate for the woman's life with a life". Cf. also G. Cardascia, *Les Lois Assyriennes* (Paris, 1965), who rejects the opinion of Driver-Miles in his commentary upon para. 52 (p. 244), whereas he accepts it in his commentary on para. 50 (p. 242). Cf. also Paul, *op. cit.* (note 1), pp. 72f., note 6, who correctly interpretes *napšāte umalla* as related to a payment of a fine for the loss of the foetus.

The Sending of Messengers to the Land of no Return (*CTA* 4:VIII)

When, for the first time, Baal is sending his messengers Gpn w- Ugr[1] to his enemy Mot he takes care to provide them with most detailed instructions for their approach. The involved structure of his long-twined speech vividly illustrates the qualms of the author of the epic who struggled hard with the intricate task of finding an adequate formula for the paradoxical tenor of Baal's order to Gpn w- Ugr to descend into the Netherworld, approach there the god of death in person and return afterwards to their sender, to the land of the living. In this paper we shall try to analyse the author's attempts to reach a solution of this perplexing problem. The text reads according to our division[2]

a

idk al ttn pnm — Then[3] set[4] your face[5]
^{c}m ġr trġzz — toward[6] the mountain Trġzz[7]

---

[1] *Gpn w-Ugr* two gods, not the double name of one deity. See H.L. Ginsberg, *BASOR* 95 (1944), pp. 25-30.

[2] The end of the column *CTA* 4:VII is not readible. Therefore it may be that Baal's address began with the formula: *tb^{c} wl tṯb ilm* (cf. *CTA* 5:II:13). 'Depart and do not tarry (verbally: sit, from the root yṯb) gods.' On this formula see H.L. Ginsberg, *JAOS* 70 (1950), p. 160.

[3] On *idk* consult Aartun, *Partikeln*, p. 5.

[4] H.L. Ginsberg, *JCS* 2 (1948), p. 140.

[5] Reminiscent of: *wayyāśäm 'ät pānāw har haggil^{c}ād* (Gen. 31:21). Cf. Cassuto, *BOST* 2, pp. 22f. In the Bible itself *śym hoq* (Ex. 15:25) is synonymous with *ntn ḥoq* (Ez. 20:25), *śym šālom* (Nu. 6:26) with *ntn šālom* (Hag. 2:9).
ttn pnm = *ttn pnkm*. Compare: *widk pnk al ttn* (*CTA* 5:V:12). The affixed personal pronoun may be omitted if it can be supplemented from the context. Cf. also in the text treated in this paper, l. 5: *śa ġr ^{c}l ydm*, i.e. *^{c}l ydkm*

[6] The preposition *^{c}m* is used here in lieu of *tk*. It is *tk*, not *^{c}m* which usually precedes the name of a place. See *CTA* 3:VI:12-13; 5:V:11-13; 10: II:8-9; *U* 5, text 7:63, p. 568, whereas *^{c}m* precedes the name of a person. See *CTA* 3:IV:81; 4:IV:20; 4:V:84-85; 5:I:9-10; 6:I:32-33; 6:IV:31-32; 14: VI:301-302; 17:VI:46-47; 18:IV:5-6. This difference is especially conspi-

ʿm ġr ṯrmg	toward the mountain Ṯrmg[7]
ʿm tlm ġṣr arṣ	toward the great[8] the ruler[8] of the Netherworld
(5) *śa ġr ʿl ydm*	Lift[8a] the mountain upon your hands
ḫlb lẓr rḥtm	the elevation[9] upon your palms
wrd bt ḫpṯt arṣ	and descend to the house of freedom[10] of the Netherworld

---

cuous if the two prepositions appear in parallelismus membrorum as in: *[idk pnm] al ttn ʿm pḫr mʿd t[k ġr ll]* (*CTA* 2:I:13-14). 'Then direct your face toward the assembled body toward the mount Ll'. *Idk lytn pn* <m> *ʿm bn ilm mt tk qrth* (*CTA* 5:II:11-13). 'Then they directed their face toward the son of Il Mot toward his city'. It is very difficult to account for the use of *ʿm* instead of *tk* in *CTA* 4:VIII:2-3 if we take even *tlm ġṣr arṣ* (*ibid*., l. 4) as the designation of a place. It could more easily be explained if we regard these words as an epithet of Mot (see note 8), since on this supposition at least in l. 4 *ʿm* conforms to the rule and we may assume that the author intended the triad *ʿm* ... *ʿm* ... *ʿm* which creates a stylistic effect. It is perhaps for the sake of this effect that the common differentiation between *ʿm* and *tk* has been neglected in this verse.

7 The names of the two mountains are not otherwise attested. Their Hurrian character has already been pointed out by Ginsberg, *KU*, p. 40.

8 Current opinion regards *tlm* as cognate with Hebrew *tel*. This supposition serves as starting-point for the search after the meaning of the difficult *ġṣr*. See e.g. Ginsberg, *KU*, p. 42; Caquot-Sznycer, *Textes*, p. 107. In our opinion the context requires the explanation of *tlm ġṣr arṣ* as an epithet of Mot. It is this epithet to which the affixed personal pronoun in the word *qrth* (l. 11) 'his city' refers back. Consult also note 6. We hypothesize that *tlm* is the Hurrian word *talm(i)* 'great'. See E. Laroche, *U* 3, pp. 127-129. Cf. also note 7, on the Hurrian character of the names of the mountains mentioned here. As Hurrian words in Ugaritic we adduce:

kḫṯ 'seat'. See J. Friedrich, *AfO* 14 (1944), pp. 329-331.
mišmn 'seal'. See W. von Soden, *VTS* 16 (1967), p. 294.
kmn a surface measure. See note 21.
šiy in the verse *špk km šiy dm* (*CTA* 18:IV:22-24). Compare the Hurrian word denoting water, transcribed by J. Friedrich, *Hethitisches Wörterbuch*, Heidelberg 1952, p. 324 as *šeia*, by E. Laroche, *PRU* 3, p. 31 as *šiye* and cf. on this word also *CAD, s.v. bâ*. Therefore we suggest the translation: 'He spilled his blood like water'. Compare *šap*^{e}*ku dāmām kammāyim* (Ps. 79:3) 'They spilled their blood like water'. Cf. also TO on Deut. 32:14e *w*^{e}*dam gibbārehon it'*^{a}*šad k*^{e}*mayyā'* and in an inscription of *Šamaši-Adad* V, quoted in *CAD, s.v. damu* l. 3' c: *dame-šû-nu kīma mê nāri talbīt ālišunu lu ušardi* 'I let their blood run down the surroundings of their city like water'. The difficult *ġṣr* can readily be compared with *zä yaʿaṣor beʿammi* (1 Sam. 9:17), where the context requires the rendering: 'This one shall rule over my people'.

8a *śa*, probably a dual of the imperative; cf. note 1.

9 On the root *ḫlb* in Ugaritic and Hebrew consult E.Y. Kutscher, *Lĕšonēnu* 31 (1967), p. 36; 32 (1969), p. 346.

10 On *bt ḫpṯt* see in this article in the following.

tspr byrdm arṣ	be counted among those descending to the Netherworld

b

(10) *idk al ttn pnm*	Then set your face
tk qrth hmry	toward his city Hmry (Pit)[11]
mk ksu ṯbth	low[12] is the throne of his sitting
ḫḫ arṣ nḥlth	hole[13] the land of his inheritance

---

[11] The name of the Netherworld *hmry* is obviously cognate with the common noun *mhmrt* in the verse: *lyrt bnpš bn ilm mt bmhmrt ydd il ġzr* (*CTA* 5: I:6-8) 'O, descend unto the gullet of the son of Il Mot, unto the ... of the beloved of Il the illustrious man.' Scholars correctly compare: *yappilem bᵉmahᵃmorot bal yāqumu* (Ps. 140:11) 'One may cast them unto ... lest they not rise up'. In addition one can adduce: *bšptyw ytmhmh ṣr wblbw yḥšwb mhmrwt ᶜmwqwt* (Ben Sira 12:16) 'With his lips hesitates (?) the enemy (but) in his heart he devises deep *mhmrwt*', obviously deep pits in order to cast into them his killed adversaries. In the Palestinian Talmud (Moed katan, ch. 1, halakha 5; Sanhedrin, ch. 13, halakha 12) *mhmwrwt* are mentioned as places where the dead were buried provisionally until their flesh was gone. All these sources obviously deal with pits within the earth, dwelling places of the dead. Contrast de Moor, *Seasonal Pattern*, p. 171 who renders *mhmrt* as libation-pipe. But notwithstanding the Arabic root *hmr* 'to pour' it appears that Hebrew *mahᵃmorā*, Ugaritic *mhmrt* have no connection with the pouring out of fluids. Cf. also M. Held, *JANES* 5 (1973), p. 188.

[12] Ginsberg, *KU*, p. 42 *šāpel*, i.e. deep; Caquot-Sznycer, *Textes*, p. 220 '*ruine*' and compare the Hebrew roots *mkk*, *mwk*. Some scholars look even here for the presentative particle *mk*, e.g. Aartun, *Partikeln*, p. 72 who translates '*Hmri, siehe, ist der Thron seines Sitzes*'. But this particle is only attested as the first word of a passage describing the decisive change which took place on the seventh day or in the seventh year (9 attestations!). See in this volume, *The Seven-Day-Pattern*, pp. 193-202, 209. *mk* is obviously stronger than *hn* and out of place in the text under discussion. Also the comparison with *CTA* 3:VI:14-15 confirms our view that no presentative particle should be expected here. Compare also in the following note 13.

[13] Many scholars render *ḫḫ* as filth and appeal to Akkadian *ḫaḫḫu*. See de Moor, *UF* 1, p. 174, note 54. But *ḫaḫḫu* denotes cough or slime, not filth. Gordon, *UT*, *Glossary* No. 942 compares *ḥᵃwāḥim* (1 Sam. 13:6), seemingly crevices, places within the earth and such or a similar meaning conforms to *mk*, if explained as deep. Cf. also Held, *loc. cit.* (note 11), pp. 188-190 who explains *mk* and *ḫḫ* as masculine participles of stative verbs preceding feminine nouns, and attributes to both verbs the meaning 'to be deep'. Alternatively both *mk* and *ḫḫ* may be interpreted as names or epithets of the Netherworld. Cf. *CTA* 3:VI:14-16. Even on this supposition the meaning of both names probably belongs to the same semantic field as *mhmrt*, i.e. they denote places within the earth.

c

wnġr ^{c}*nn ilm*	and beware servants[14] of the gods
al tqrb lbn ilm mt	approach not the son of Il[15] Mot
al y^{c}*dbkm kimr bph*	lest he make you like a lamb in his mouth
klli bṯbrn qnh	like a kid in his throat[16]
ṯḫtan	(lest) you will be overwhelmed[17]
nrt ilm špš	(even) the torch of the gods Špš[18]
ṣḥrrt la šmm	which makes bright[19] the gleam[19] of the heaven
byd mdd ilm mt	is in the hand[19] of Il's beloved Mot

d

ba lp šd rbt kmn	(Cross)[20] over thousand šiddu[21] a myriad kumanu[21]

---

[14] The meaning of ^{c}*nn* is open to discussion. On the different proposals see van Zijl, *Baal*, pp. 22, 102-104.

[15] For the justification of this translation see J. de Moor, *UF* 1, p. 187. Nevertheless the alternative rendering 'son of the gods' i.e. a member of the pantheon, divine, can not be ruled out. Cf. for instance *bän hāraqqāhim* (Neh. 3:8), 'a member of (the guild of) the perfumers, a perfumer'. Cf. also Herdner, *CTA*, p. 143, note 2, who reads in *CTA* 6:VI:30 *bn ilm* <m> *t*.

[16] The exact meaning is not ascertained. Ginsberg, *KU*, p. 42 *b*^{e}*pätaḥ qānehu*. That means that he understands *ṯbr* (= Hebrew *šäbär*) as opening, *q̊n* as *oesophagus*. (But *qānä* in Talmudic Hebrew '*trachea*'). Contrast M. Dahood, *CBQ* 17 (1955), pp. 180-183; J. Delekat, *UF* 4, p. 18 and pay attention to the *varia lectio* (or the corrupted reading) *ṯbrnqy* (*CTA* 6:II:23).

[17] This translation follows W.F. Albright, *BASOR* 52 (1941), pp. 46-49. Contrast W.A. Ward, *JNES* 20 (1961), p. 35. On the syntactical disconnection of *ṯḫtan* from the foregoing words see in this article in the following.

[18] As well known, *šämäš* in Hebrew is common gender. It follows that different ideas about the sex of the deity of the sun existed in Southern Canaan.

[19] On this translation see in this article in the following.

[20] Contrast Ginsberg, *ANET*[3], p. 135 who translates: "from a thousand etc." and adds the remark "from a safe distance" (*ibid.*, note 29). In the same way Ginsberg renders *CTA* 3:VI:17-18 (*ANET*[3], p. 138). But there Baal despatches his messengers to *Kṯr* and with good reason Ginsberg expresses his astonishment "that this precaution should be necessary with Kothar who is otherwise an obliging deity and a friend of Baal" (*ibid.*, note 20). Our interpretation is borne out by the passage: *idk lttn pnm* ^{c}*m b*^{c}*l mrym spn balp šd rbt kmn shq btlt* ^{c}*nt tšu gh wtsh* (*CTA* 4:V:84-88). Here Ginsberg (*ANET*[3], p. 133) renders: "There, she is off on her way,

lp^{c}*n mt hbr wql*	To Mot's feet[22] bow[23] and fall down[24]
hštḥwy wkbd hwt	prostate you and show him honour
wrgm (30) *lbn ilm mt*	and say unto Il's son Mot
ṯny lydd il ġzr	Declare[25] unto Il's darling the illustrious man[26]
tḥm aliyn b^{c}*l*	message of puissant Baal
[hw]t aliy q(35) *rdm*	word of the mightiest of heros

A cursory glance over the text reveals that the introductory formula of l. 1 is repeated in ll. 10-11.

Therefore lines 1-9 should be treated as a distinct unit. In the continuation of the epic its formula is paralleled by the order given to Baal himself to go down to the Netherworld (*CTA* 5:V:11-16) with the only difference that instead of the long description ^{c}*m ġr trġzz* ^{c}*m ġr ṯrmg* ^{c}*m tlm ġṣr arṣ* (*CTA* 4:VIII:2-4) we meet here with the short indication *tk ġr knkny* (*CTA* 5:V:11-16). The exact meaning of *knkny* has not been clarified.[27] Nevertheless it is reasonably sure to suppose that the text deals with Baal's descent to the Netherworld and that this descent involves his death, and

---

unto Baal upon Zaphon's summit, o'er a thousand fields ten thousand acres. Laughing the Maiden Anath lifts up her voice and cries." In his treatment of this text, Ginsberg correctly connects the formula *balp šd rbt kmn* with the preceding passage. When travelling to Baal, Anat crossed immense areas. Only after her arrival she addressed him. In our opinion the same stereotype appears in *CTA* 3:VI:18. Like Anat, the messenger too crossed an immense area on his way to *Kṯr*. Only after having reached his destination he prostrated with him. The same interpretation should be given to the standard formula of crossing the areas even in *CTA* 4:VIII:24-25. Its meaning becomes immediately obvious, if we disregard section *c* whose insertion creates difficulties, since there the messengers are instructed not to draw near to Mot. On this problem see in this article in the following.

21 The Akkadian term *šiddu* and its Hurrian counterpart *kumanu* (Nuzi, Alalakh, Ugarit) designate the same surface measure. Cf. in this volume, *The Alalakh Tablets*, pp. 21-22; M. Dietrich - O. Loretz, *UF* 1, pp. 61f.

22 On the Ugaritic nouns *p*^{c}*n, pam* and their relation to Hebrew *p*^{c}*m* see A. Schlesinger, *Sepher A. Schlesinger*, Jerusalem 1962, p. 31 (in Heb.).

23 On *hbr* see J. Blau, *VT* 7 (1957), pp. 183f., who compares Is. 47:13.

24 On *ql* see W. von Soden, *VTS* 16 (1967), pp. 295f. who compares Akkadian *qiālu* 'to fall'.

25 On the root *ṯny* see M. Tsevat, *HUCA* 29 (1958), p. 125.

26 On *ġzr* see A.F. Rainey, *AOAT* 22 (1973), pp. 139-142.

27 In *CTA* 19:III:147 Virolleaud reads: *yqbr nn bmdgt knkn*(?). On the doubt-

correctly de Moor[28] pointed out that *bt ḫpṯt* should be translated 'the house of freedom' and taken as a euphemism for the house of eternal imprisonment. With even a higher degree of certainty we may assert that *arṣ* denotes the Netherworld as in the lament of Il who exclaims after Baal's death *aṯr* *bᶜl ard barṣ* (*CTA* 5:VI:24-25). 'After Baal I shall descend into the Netherworld.' Already Cassuto[29] observed that Il utters here a standard phrase of mourning which still reappears in the words of Jacob: "I will descend mourning to my son into Sheol" (Gen. 37:35). Compare also the portrayal of Il's desperate situation which reads: *il kyrdm arṣ* (*U* 5, text 1:22, p. 546). 'Il is like them that descend to the Netherworld'; a simile paralleled by the Biblical verse: *wᵉ nimšalti ᶜim yorᵉde bor* (Ps. 28:1) 'and I became like them that descend into the pit'. Likewise: *wᵉnäḥšabti ᶜim yorᵉde bor hāyiti kᵉgäbär 'en 'ᵃ̈yāl. bammetim ḥopši kᵉmo ḥᵃlālim šokᵉbe qäbär* (Ps. 88: 5-6) 'I am counted with them that descend into the pit. I am as a man who has no strength, free (i.e. closed up) among the dead like the slain that lie in the grave'. We thus may assume that *CTA* 5:V:14-16 reflects a traditional formula which in its primary use describes the death of a man, here the death of Baal, and we can hardly follow de Moor[30] who opposes this interpretation and tries to establish the thesis that Baal was spared real death when descending to the Netherworld, whereas it was a twin-brother of Baal that was swallowed up by murderous Mot and buried by *Špš*. Yet the very existence of a twin-brother of Baal is highly hypothetical, and there is no point in differentiating between the fate of a person that goes down to the Netherworld, on the one hand, and the lot of somebody that is devoured by Mot, on the other hand. The two concepts, viz. that Mot kills a man by devouring him, and that the dead descends into the Netherworld, are

---

ful reading *knkn* see also Herdner, *CTA*, p. 90.
Knkny may be the name of a mountain, alternatively a general noun + the suffix of the 1st person sing. De Moor, *Seasonal Pattern*, pp. 170f. appeals to Akkadian *kankannu* 'potstand', but nevertheless suggests the lexically unsupported translation 'my libation pipe' (libation pipe in Akkadian *arūtu*!)

28 De Moor, *Seasonal Pattern*, pp. 185f. Cf. also in this volume, *Review of Ras Shamra Parallels* 1, p. 478.

29 Cassuto, *BOSt* 2, p. 35.

30 De Moor, *Seasonal Pattern*, p. 195 mentions E. Largement's suggestion that Il's words may be an indecisive question, because Il does not go down into the earth. This exegesis fails to take into account the typically hyperbolic character of the mourner's utterances.

found side by side and even intertwine, as for instance in Mot's address to Baal: *lyrt bnpš bn ilm mt // bmhmrt ydd il ġzr* (*CTA* 5:I:6-8). 'Thou shalt descend unto the gullet of the son of Il Mot // unto the pits (see supra note 11) of Il's beloved the illustrious man'. In this speach no distinction is made between Baals descent into hollow places within the earth and his descent into Mot's gullet, the latter being a clear indication of Mot's intent to swallow Baal up. Both similes are connected in the Bible too as in the description of the end of Korah's people which reads: "and the Netherworld opened its mouth and swallowed them up ... and they descended living into Sheol" etc. (Nu. 16:32-33) and thus in a prophetical symbol of disaster: "Therefore Sheol has enlarged her throat and opened her mouth without measure, and there descend their glory and their multitude" etc. (Is. 5:14). Wisdom literature puts in the mouth of the wicked the declaration: "let us swallow them up alive as Sheol and whole, as those that go down into the pit". (Pr. 1:12). It hardly needs mentioning that no contradiction was felt between the descent of the dead into the Netherworld and his burial. Rather the opposite is true as borne out by Ez. 32:22-26 where the Netherworld perfectly coalesces with the graves, and the same blend of concepts led in Ps. 88:12-13 to the parallelism *qäbär // 'ᵃbaddon // ḥošäk // 'äräṣ nᵉšiyyā*. The realistic notion that the dead was buried and the mythological imagination that he went down to the Netherworld were felt as complementary aspects of one process rather than as mutually exclusive ideas.[31]

[31] According to the exegesis of de Moor, *Seasonal Pattern*, pp. 183f., the speaker in *CTA* 5:V:4-17 is *Špš* who advises Baal to outwit Mot by begetting a twin-brother before going down to the Netherworld himself. This twin-brother will be mistaken by the god of death for Baal and devoured by him instead of his father = twin-brother and only he, not Baal will be buried. De Moor's main arguments are 1) Baal begot a *mṯ* (*CTA* 5:V:18-22). Cf. Akkadian *māšu* 'twin-brother'. 2) The speaker anounces: *aštn bḫrt ilm arṣ* (ll. 5-6). 'I shall lay him down in the grave of the gods of the earth'. In de Moor's opinion it is *Špš* who declares here that she will bury the twin-brother. The verse "must correspond to *CTA* 6:I:17-18 *tštnn bḫrt ilm arṣ* where ᶜAnatu or both ᶜAnatu and Šapšu may be the subject ... But ᶜAnatu would seem to be excluded ... since she did not know beforehand what had happened to Baᶜalu (*CTA* 5:VI:25ff.)", according to de Moor's premisses more exactly, since she mistook Baal's dead twin-brother for himself. Both arguments fail to convince. 1) Ugaritic *mṯ* and Akkadian *māšu* should be kept apart, since *mṯt dnty*, the wife of Danil and *mṯt ḥry* Krt's wife were hardly twin-sisters. Still more weight carries the simple consideration that nobody can beget his own twin-brother. 2) It seems that the burial under discussion was performed by Anat alone. Anat had asked *Špš* to put the dead on her shoulder and *Špš* complied. (*CTA* 6:I:11-15). Since the dead god is now on Anat's shoulder, it

To sum up. There is no distinction in Oriental thought between the fate of a man that was devoured by Mot[32], brought to burial and thus really died and the lot of his fellow-man who managed to escape death and merely went down to the Netherworld.

Moreover, we meet even with an explicit definition of the meaning of Baal's descent in the words: *wtd*^{c} *ilm kmtt* (*CTA* 5:V:16-17) 'And thou will know god (or the gods will know) that thou hast been killed'.[33]

After this excurse let us return to Baal's address in *CTA* 4:VIII:1-9. Its very wording evokes the idea that the messengers are doomed to death, whereas Baal expects them to return to him. The continuation of the text proves that the author of the epic became aware of this incongruency. It is therefore that he puts into Baal's mouth a second address which reflects the pattern of an ordinary diplomatic mission, i.e. a mission to one of the rulers of the earth.

---

is clearly she alone who brought him up to his mountain, bewailed and buried him (ll. 15ff.), not *Špš* and even not both goddesses together. Last not least. The author himself reports in outspoken words that it was Baal whom *Špš* put on Anat's shoulder. We should not distort this plain testimony by interpreting Baal as Baal's twin-brother, mistaken for himself by Anat, though not by *Špš*.

32 Another simile of Mot's murderous activity appears in his words: *b*^{c}*l [t]*^{c}*n it*^{c}*nk* (*CTA* 5:I:26) 'Baal, I surely shall pierce thee. Compare *m*^{e}*ṭo*^{ca}*nė häräb* (Is. 14:19) 'pierced with a sword'. So correctly already A. Goetze, *JAOS* 58 (1938), p. 304, note 191. Cf. also Aramaic *m*^{e}*ṭa*^{ca}*nin* in TY as translation of Hebrew *m*^{e}*duqqārim* in Jer. 37:10 (Dr. Y. Avishur, orally). Its etymon is Arabic *ṭ*^{c}*n* 'to pierce', not Hebrew *ṭ*^{c}*n* as in *ṭa*^{ca}*nu 'ät b*^{ec}*ir*^{e}*käm* (Gen. 45:17) 'load your beasts', where Hebrew *ṭ*^{c}*n* irregularly corresponds to Arabic *ẓ*^{c}*n*, whose normal correspondence in Hebrew is *ṣ*^{c}*n* (Is. 33:20). In Gen. 45:17 *ṭ*^{c}*n* is reminiscent of normal Aramaic *ṭ*^{c}*n* 'to load', whether we regard this form as an Aramaism pure and simple or ascribe it to a northern Hebrew dialect in which *ṭ* corresponded to Proto-Semitic ẓ as in Aramaic. Anyhow, it appears that in Ugaritic this root should read *ẓ*^{c}*n*. Contrast E.Y. Kutscher, *Lĕšonēnu* 31 (1967), p. 36 who follows C.H. Gordon in explaining Ugaritic *ṭ*^{c}*n* 'to load' and concludes that *ṭ*^{c}*n* in Gen. 45:17 "is not a loan from Aramaic" but that rather "there existed two roots near in form and sense". However the Ugaritic context points to an action of killing.

33 On the reading *ilm* see Herdner, *CTA*, p. 36, note 1. Most exegetes follow Virolleaud's first proposal to read *ill*. Compare e.g. J. de Moor, *BiOr* 26 (1969), p. 107 who explains *ill* as weakness, *mtt* as an abstract noun with a concrete collective meaning and translates: "thou wilt experience weakness like the dead" (i.e., in de Moor's opinion, not really die). To our mind *mtt* should be parsed as 2nd person sing. masc. perfect of *mwt* in the *Polal* formation. (Cf. the Hebrew *Polel motet-kill*), *ilm* as *il*

With these remarks in mind, we may turn to the interpretation of *CTA* 4:VIII:10-35. Even this text is longer than the usual formula of mission since here a detailed warning is inserted not to approach Mot. The warning which begins with the word *wnġr* (l. 14) and ends with the word *mt* (l. 24), requires special scrutiny. For this reason we postpone its interpretation and start with an exegesis of the remaining basic text, i.e. of the sections, marked here as *b* and *d* which can be read as a consecutive text.

These sections are paralleled by the wording of the text describing the mission of Ashera's fisherman to *Kṯr* (*CTA* 3:VI:12-25)

idk al ttn pnm	'Then set thy face
tk ḥqkpt il klh	toward ḥqkpt (toward) the god Kulla[34]
kptr ksu ṯbth	Kptr is the seat of his sitting
ḥkpt (15) *arṣ nḥlth*	Ḥkpt the land of his inheritance
balp šd rbt kmn	(cross) over thousand šiddu a myriad kumanu
lp^{c}*n kṯr hbr wql*	to Kṯr's feet bow and fall down
ḥšth (20) *wy wkbd hwt*	prostrate thee and show him honour
wrgm lkṯr wḫss	and say unto Kṯr w-Ḫss
ṯny lhyn dḥrš ydm	declare unto Hyn[35] the man[36] of craftsmanship[37]
tḥm al[iyn b^{c}*l]*	message of puissant Baal
(25) *ḥ[wt aliy qrdm]*	word of the mightiest of heros'

The identity of pattern is striking. Even in the description of the receiver of the message the same stereotype ... *ksu ṯbth* ... *arṣ nḥlth* can be observed. Sections *b, d* of Baal's address to Gpn w-Ugr thus reflect the very pattern of an ordinary mission. Therefore it is easily understood that

---

with enclitic *m* in the meaning god. Our interpretation can be maintained even if we prefer the reading *ill*. Cf. Akkadian *illilu* 'deity of highest rank'.

34 This translation follows Cassuto's suggestion (*Anath*, pp. 153f.) to interpret *klh* as the name of the Mesopotamian god *Kulla*, identified at Ugarit with *Kṯr*. On this and other proposals see in this volume, *Review on Ras Shamra Parallels* 1, p. 490 with bibliography. Add Ginsberg, *ANET*^{3}, p. 138; Caquot-Sznycer, *Textes*, p. 178.

35 *Hyn*, an epithet of *Kṯr*. Cf. Gordon, *UT*, *Glossary* No. 761.

36 On the use of the particle *d* in this connection see in this volume, *Notes on the Pronouns in Ugaritic*, pp. 70-75.

37 To *ḥrš* in the abstract meaning workmanship compare Phoenician and Ugaritic *mlk* in the sense 'kingdom'.

we do not meet here with the phrases describing the descent of the dead as going down into the house of freedom of the Netherworld and of being counted with them that go down to the Netherworld. Nevertheless, even here it was impossible to omit a definition of the messenger's destination which is given in *CTA* 4:VIII:11 (*tk*) - 14 (*nḥlth*)[38] and its frightening impression induced the author to add the warning, found in section c (l. 14 *nġr* - l. 24 *mt*). The warning proper (l. 14 *nġr* - l. 17 *mt*) is an unparalleled innovation, its motivation (l. 17 *al* - l. 24 *mt*), however, reflects Mot's words in which he describes to Anat the killing of Baal (*CTA* 6:II:21-24).

ngš ank aliyn bᶜl	I approach[39] puissant Baal
ᶜdbnn ank imr bpy	I make[40] him like[41] a lamb in my mouth
klli bṯbrnqy	like a kid in my throat
ḫtu hw	He is overwhelmed
nrt ilm špš	The torch of the gods Špš
ṣḥrrt la šmm	which makes bright the gleam of the heaven
byd bn ilm mt	is in the hand of the son of Il Mot

[38] The text of *CTA* 4:VIII:10-14 reappears in the short description of the messenger's second approach to Mot in *CTA* 5:II:13-16 without any additional details. The text neither notes that the messengers observed rules of precaution when addressing Mot nor mentions their prostration with him. Due to lacunae in the epic we can not be sure whether their first approach to Mot was reported in the same laconic style. Even the text of the second mission of Baal's messengers to Mot has not been preserved, and therefore it eludes our knowledge whether Baal then repeated his first address to them in full.

[39] It appears that *ngš* should rather be parsed as *N* formation like Hebrew *N ngš* than as *G* formation like Akkadian *G nagāšu* 'hingehen', (v. Soden, *AHW, s.v.*). For the meaning of *ngš* consult *CTA* 23:68 where the context makes its rendering 'to approach' compulsory. This interpretation is plausible even in the text under discussion. Roving Mot approaches Baal before devouring him. Compare also *CTA* 4:VIII:15-20, where Baal's messengers are admonished not to draw near to Mot lest he devours them. Therefore no Ugaritic root *2 ngš* (< Proto-Semitic *ngš*) 'to oppress' should be posited. Compare also J. de Moor, *UF* 1 (1969), p. 173.

[40] In *ᶜdbnn* the lack of an *'a* at the beginning of the word is noticeable. Gordon, *UT, Grammar*, 5.38 quotes examples for the loss of *'a* before *ᶜ* and considers these forms as *Sandhi*. Yet the form *ᶜdbnn* stands at the beginning of a sentence and therefore this reason does not hold good.

[41] Perhaps we should read *<k>imr* and suppose that the *k* was omitted by haplography (H.L. Ginsberg, *Orientalia* 5 *[1936]*, p. 186). But contrast M. Dahood, *UF* 1, p. 28 who attributes to the *k* of *klli* a double duty.

The last two lines are extremely difficult and scholars[42] disagree not only as to their syntax and lexicography but even in their overall explanation. And indeed, it is hard to grasp for which reason the goddess of the sun should be mentioned in this context.[43] Our proposal looks for a hint in another text connecting the fate of *Špš* with Baal's death, viz. Anat's lament: (*CTA* 6:I:7-9): "After Baal we will descend to the Netherworld, with him will descend the torch of the gods *Špš*." This implies that even *Špš* will be in Mot's hand[44] and that the light of the sun will eclipse. This darkness which befalls the world in the hour of mourning is described in God's words in the prophecy of Amos: "I will cause the sun to go down at noon, and I will darken the earth in the clear day. And I will turn your feasts into mourning, and all your songs into lamentation" (Am. 8:9-10).[45] Therefore, it is a reasonable guess that in the polytheistic poetry of Ugarit this idea appears in the form that at the time of the funeral even the torch of the gods *Špš* is in the hand, i.e. the power, of the god of death and that the words *nrt ilm špš byd bn ilm mt* are the mainstay of this ver-

---

[42] For bibliography see de Moor, *Seasonal Pattern*, p. 114; J.A. Emerton, *AuJBA* 2 (1972), p. 65; Caquot-Sznycer, *Textes*, p. 175.

[43] The formula is attested another time at the conclusion of Il's answer to Anat who invades his palace and threatens to kill him. The text reads: *nrt ilm špš ṣ[ḥrrt la šmm by]d bn ilm mt* (*CTA* 3:V:25-26). We hypothesize that l. 24 ended with the words *ḫtu ank* and that in the preceding words Il expressed his apprehension that he would be killed.

[44] Ch. Rabin, *JJS* 6 (1955), pp. 111-115 suggests to distinguish between an ancient mono-consonantal root *d* which has been preserved after prepositions only and the later du-consonantal root *yd*. However, the form *byd* appears not unfrequently in epic texts (*CTA* 2:I:39; 4:VIII:23; 6:II:25; 15:II:17; 16:I:41, 47; 18:I:14). Likewise *bydh* (10:II:6; 14:III:160; *U* 5, text 3, verso 6, pp. 556, 558) beside *bd* (*CTA* 1:IV:13, 15, 21, 23; 3:I:19; 4:I:25; 6:III:160; 16:I:5, 19; 16:II:104; 17:V:26); *bdy* (*CTA* 19:IV:216); *bdk* (*CTA* 4:II:32; 16:V:7); *bdh* (*CTA* 23:8), whereas in every day language *byd* appears only one single time (*PRU* 2, text 5:14), beside very frequent *bd* (*PRU* 2, texts 8:19; 9:14; 24:27; 34:2; 50 *passim*; 51:3, 4, 6; 94:5; 109:7; 110:2, 5; 121:9; 128:34; 134:3, 5, 7; *PRU* 5, text 28 *passim*; 29 *passim*; 123:7). Therefore *byd* seems to be an archaic orthography. *Bd* presumably emerged from *biyad* by the elision of the unstressed heterosyllabic diphtong *iy* before stressed *a*. The result was the form *bad* known from a gloss in an Akkadian letter, written at Jerusalem (*EA* 245:35).

[45] Dr. Y. Avishur kindly drew my attention to Luke 23:44-45 where the failing of the sun's light at the time of Jesus' death is described. He further pointed out to me that the same motif reappears in Ibn Gabirol's poem *rᵉ'e haššämäš bᵉᶜet ᶜäräb*. See Solomon Ibn Gabirol, *Secular Poems*, ed. H. Brody and J. Schirmann, Jerusalem 1945, p. 83.

se as has been suggested by H.L. Ginsberg long ago.[46] We thus refute as improbable the many proposals founded upon the division of the text into two sentences, viz. 1) *nrt ilm špš ṣḥrrt* = The light of the gods *Špš* beams or is hot or becomes dust-coloured; 2) *la šmm byd bn ilm mt*. Heavens slackened or were strengthened or became dust-coloured by (or by the love of) the god Mot. Consequently we accept even Ginsberg's further proposal to look in the difficult words *ṣḥrrt la šmm* for an apposition of the name *špš*. However, our attempt to guess the meaning of this apposition is guided by the conjecture that even the apposition belongs to a lament over the disappearance of the sun's light. Therefore we look here for a description of the sun's normal function to illuminate the day, and connect *ṣḥrrt* with Hebrew *ṣḥr* 'white', Aramaic *ṣḥr* 'reddish' (cf. also the change between the personal proper names *ṣoḥar* [Ex. 6:15] and *zäraḥ* [Nu. 26:13]) and regard *ṣḥrrt* as the participle of a verb denoting 'illuminate'[47], *la* as the accusative of a noun **lu* 'gleam'[48] which is cognate to Arabic *l'l'* 'to gleam'. Our suggestion thus tries to reconstruct a standard formula of lament, traditionally affixed to the announcement of death and quoted here by the author of the epic without any attempt to adapt it to the parallelismus membrorum of Ugaritic verse.

We even venture to go a step further attributing to the lament also the words *ḫtu hw*, which, in our opinion, should be taken as an independent

---

[46] H.L. Ginsberg, *BASOR* 95 (1944), p. 38, note 13.

[47] Dr. Y. Avishur kindly drew my attention to the discussion of *ṣḥrr* by E. Deist, *JNWSL* 1 (1971), pp. 168-170. Deist derives both Ugaritic *ṣḥrr* and Hebrew *zrḥ* from a hypothetical Proto-Semitic root **ḍḥr*. It can, however, not be made out whether Ugaritic *ṣḥrr* reflects the Proto-Semitic root *ṣḥr* or *ḍḥr*. The connection of Hebrew *zrḥ* with Proto-Semitic **ḍḥr* postulates not only a metathesis, but even a change between Proto-Semitic *ḍ* and Hebrew z. The sole example known to me is the alleged change between Hebrew *ṣrb* and *zrb*. But the connection of Hebrew *ṣrb* with Arabic *ḍrm* is doubtful, and not less doubtful is the explanation of the difficult *zrb* as a bi-form of *ṣrb*. It would be easier to hypothesize Proto-Semitic **ṣḥr*. Compare the interchange *ṣ^{c}q / z^{c}q, ^{c}lṣ / ^{c}lz, ṣhb / zhb* where Proto-Semitic *ṣ* is involved. But even this hypothesis is tenuous. My friend Prof. J. Blau kindly pointed out to me that Hebrew *zrḥ* has been compared to Aramaic *dnḥ*, i.e. that the *z* of *zrḥ* has been explained as corresponding to Proto-Semitic *ḏ*.

[48] A.F. Rainey, *Lĕšonénu* 34 (1970), pp. 182f. parses *la* as the 3rd person singular of a verb which precedes the plural (not dual!) *šmm*. From a purely linguistic point of view the possibility of this analysis can not be refuted. But *la* may be the accusative of a noun as well.

short sentence denoting: 'he is overwhelmed'. This division yields for the foregoing sentence the perfectly satisfactory text: 'I made him like a lamb in my mouth // like a kid in my throat'. The addition of the unparalleled words *ḫtu hw* to the second colon spoils the verse. Even the syntax of a sentence which includes *ḫtu hw*, would be confusing. As long as the reader has not reached the words *ḫtu hw*, he will connect the words *imr bpy* with ^{c}*dbnn* and understand: 'I made him ... like a kid'. Only when reaching the words *ḫtu hw* we would become aware of his error and realise that the words *imr bpy* should rather be related to *ḫtu hw* - 'like a kid ... he is overwhelmed'.

Let us return to the general characterisation of Baal's address to his messengers, discussed in this paper from different aspects. We tried to substantiate our thesis that the text is made up from different components and that its intricate structure truly reflects the perplexity of an author who struggled with the difficult task of describing the paradoxical, if not self-contradictory, order to go down to the land of no return and to bring back from there a report to the land of the living. Small wonder thus that a clear tension makes itself felt between the one instruction not to draw near to Mot and the other one to bow down to his feet. The second of the two phrases repeats the traditional pattern of an official mission to a ruler, the first is the author's innovation.
[Addition: Am. 8:9-10 (quoted above, p. 536) was recited in a lament for R. Joḥanan, who on his part had explained the verse as a prophecy of the death of King Josiah (Moed katan 25b)].

Publications in which first appeared the writings collected in this volume.

Read not *'ᵃrubbotenu* but *'armᵉnotenu, BJES* 13 (1946), pp. 16-19 *[Translated from the Hebrew]*.

New Light on the History of the Alphabet, *BIES* 16 (1952), pp. 32-36 *[Translated from the Hebrew]*.

The Development of the Term "First" in the Semitic Languages, *Tarbiz* 24 (1955), pp. 249-251 *[Translated from the Hebrew]*.

Notes on the Alalakh Tablets, *IEJ* 6 (1956), pp. 217-225.

The Cypress as a Symbol of the Life - Giving Force, *Sepher Biram* (*ISBR* 2, 1956), pp. 199-200 *[Translated from the Hebrew]*.

Review of Cyrus H. Gordon, Ugaritic Manual, Rome 1955, *Tarbiz* 25 (1956), pp. 468-472 *[Translated from the Hebrew]*.

Review of A. Goetze, The Laws of Eshnunna (AASOR 31, 1956), *IEJ* 7 (1957), pp. 192-198.

Beloved is Man in that he was created in the Image, *Tarbiz* 27 (1957), pp. 1-2 *[Translated from the Hebrew]*.

Review of Ugaritica 3, ed. C.F.A. Schaeffer, Paris 1956, *IEJ* 8 (1958), pp. 138-140.

Notes on the Pronouns in Ugaritic in the Light of Canaanite, *Lěšonēnu* 23 (1959), pp. 72-81 *[Translated from the Hebrew]*.

The Hebrew Root *ḥrš* in the Light of the Ugaritic Texts, *JJS* 10 (1959), pp. 63-65.

Review of Ch. Virolleaud, Le Palais Royal d'Ugarit 2, Paris 1957, *Tarbiz* 28 (1959), pp. 244-250 *[Translated from the Hebrew]*.

The Muzzling of the Tannin in Ugaritic Myth, *IEJ* 9 (1959), pp. 260-261.

The Flood, *Sepher Tur-Sinai* (*ISBR* 8, 1960), pp. 3-26 *[Translated from the Hebrew]*.

What is Above, What is Beneath, what Before, what After, *Yehezkel Kaufmann Jubilee Volume*, ed. M. Haran, Jerusalem 1960, pp. 112-121 *[Translated from the Hebrew]*.

Yāpeªḥ, yāpiªḥ, yāpi(y)ªḥ, Lĕšonēnu 26 (1962), pp. 205-208, 280; *Lĕšonēnu* 27/28 (1964), p. 182 *[Translated from the Hebrew]*.

The Laws of Adultery and Murder in Biblical and Mesopotamian Law, *BM* 13 (1962), pp. 55-59 *[Translated from the Hebrew]*.

Review of W. Schmidt, Königtum Gottes in Ugarit und Israel, (BZAW 80, 1961), *Kirjath Sepher* 36 (1962), pp. 191-193 *[Translated from the Hebrew]*.

The Ugaritic Fertility Myth - the Result of a Mistranslation, *IEJ* 12 (1962), pp. 87-88.

The Ugaritic Fertility Myth - a Reply, *IEJ* 13 (1963), pp. 130-131.

The Formula *meᶜattā wᵉᶜad ᶜolām, Tarbiz* 32 (1963), pp. 313-316 *[Translated from the Hebrew]*.

The Laws of Adultery and Murder in the Bible, *BM* 18-19 (1964), pp. 77-78 *[Translated from the Hebrew]*.

The Trembling of Nature during the Theophany, *Sepher Ben-Gurion* (*ISBR* 15, 1964), pp. 508-520 *[Translated from the Hebrew]*.

Šᵉ'er, Lĕšonēnu 27/28 (1964), p. 295 *[Translated from the Hebrew]*.

The Seven-Day-Unit in Ugaritic Epic Literature, *IEJ* 15 (1965), pp. 122-133.

Notes on the History of Biblical Phraseology (The pairs of roots *ṣdq* and *yšr*; *leb* and *kābed*; Nu. 23:10), *Sepher Zvi Segal* (*ISBR* 17, 1965), pp. 180-187 *[Translated from the Hebrew]*.

On new Texts in Ugaritic, *Lĕšonēnu* 29 (1965), pp. 6-8 *[Translated from the Hebrew]*.

'ānoki 'ªhaṭṭännā, Lĕšonēnu 29 (1965), pp. 69-70 *[Translated from the Hebrew]*.

Ugaritic Gleanings, (*ḥrš qṭn*; *ysr, gnn, gngn*; *rṯ, qrṣ*; *ydᶜ*; Formula of Prostration), *Lĕšonēnu* 30 (1966), pp. 85-80 *[Translated from the Hebrew]*.

The Making and Destruction of the Golden Calf, *Biblica* 48 (1967), pp. 481-490.

Prostration from afar in Ugaritic, Akkadian and Hebrew, *BASOR* 188 (1967), pp. 41-43.

The Noun *ṣ^{c}r (K^{e}tib), ṣā^{c}ir (Q^{e}re), Tarbiz* 36 (1967), pp. 110-115 *[Translated from the Hebrew]*.

Stylistic Patterns in Biblical and Ugaritic Literatures (Formulas of Mission and Correspondence; *l^{e}dor dor; ^{c}ad ^{c}olām; b^{e}kol dor wādor // l^{ec}olām wā^{c}ed; yā'er YHWH pānāw 'eläkā; the meaning of 'äläp // r^{e}bābā*), *Lĕšonēnu* 32 (1968), pp. 27-35 *[Translated from the Hebrew]*.

Šopeṭ and *Šebäṭ, Lĕšonēnu* 32 (1968), pp. 172-174 *[Translated from the Hebrew]*.

The Covenant between the Pieces - A Traditio-Historical Investigation, *VT* 18 (1968), pp. 500-506 *[Translated from the German]*.

The Expanded Colon in Ugaritic and Biblical Verse, *JSS* 14 (1969), pp. 176-196.

The Numerals in Ugaritic, *Proceedings of the International Conference on Semitic Studies, Jerusalem 1965*, Jerusalem 1969, pp. 172-179.

A Ugaritic Hymn in Honour of Il, *Proceedings of the fourth World Congress of Jewish Studies, Jerusalem 1965*, Jerusalem 1969, pp. 62-67 *[Translated from the Hebrew]*.

The Lord is my Strength and my Glory (The phrase *^{c}ozzi w^{e}zimrāt yā*), *VT* 19 (1969), pp. 464-470.

The Cumulative Oath of Witnesses and Parties in Mesopotamian Law, *Jura* 20 (1969), pp. 539-542 *[Translated from the German]*.

The Ugaritic Myth of the Sea and its Biblical Counterparts, *EI* 9 (*William F. Albright Volume*, 1969), pp. 96-101 *[Translated from the Hebrew]*.

Ugaritic Formulas of Greeting, *BASOR* 194 (1969), pp. 52-5 .

Remarks upon the Infinitive Absolute in Ugaritic and Phoenician, *JANES* 2 (1969), p. 53.

A Didactic Ugaritic Drinker's Burlesque, *UF* 1 (1969), pp. 71-77; *UF* 2 (1970), p. 355 *[Translated from the German]*.

I am thy Servant and thy Son, *Lĕšonēnu* 34 (1970), pp. 146-147 *[Translated from the Hebrew]*.

Review of R. Yaron, The Laws of Eshnunna, *Mishpatim* 2 (1970), pp. 203-206 *[Translated from the Hebrew]*.

Philo of Byblos, *Perakim* 2, Jerusalem 1971, pp. 315-327 *[Translated from the Hebrew]*.

Border-Cases of Ugaritic comparative Studies (Hebrew of the Second Tample, Talmudic Hebrew, Greek), *UF* 3 (1971), pp. 93-100 *[Translated from the German]*.

Mṣd, UF 3 (1971), pp. 357-359.

The Divine Grants of Land to the Patriarchs, *JAOS* 94 (1971), pp. 509-510.

The Killing of Mot in Ugaritic Myth, *Orientalia* 41 (1972), pp. 378-382.

Who is afraid of the Linguistic Method (Ugaritic *tġrk* again), *Lĕšonénu* 36 (1972), pp. 67-70, p. 316 *[Translated from the Hebrew]*.

The Lord shall rule over you, *Tarbiz* 41 (1972), pp. 444-445 *[Translated from the Hebrew]*.

The Phrase X (or) X plus one in Biblical and Old Oriental Laws, *Biblica* 53 (1972), p. 543.

The formula "I am thy Servant and thy Son" in a Letter from El-Amarna, *Lĕšonênu* 36 (1972), p. 316 *[Translated from the Hebrew]*.

Review of Les religions du Proche-Orient asiatique, R. Labat, A. Caquot, M. Sznycer, M. Vieyra, Paris 1970. Deuxième Partie, Les textes Ougaritique par A. Caquot et M. Sznycer, *IEJ* 22 (1972), pp. 55-57.

Lexicographical Notes on 1. *ṭbḫ*; 2. *hnny/hlny, UF* 5 (1973), pp. 209-211.

On the Predicative Use of the Suffix joined to a Subject-Noun in Hebrew and Ugaritic, *Lĕšonĕnu* 38 (1974), pp. 149-150 *[Translated from the Hebrew]*.

Did the Goddess Anat wear a Beard and Side-Whiskers?, *IOS* 4 (1974), pp. 1-3.

Taautos, *Paulys Realencyklopädie der Classischen Altertums-Wissenschaften, Pauly-Kroll-Ziegler, Supplement* 14, 1975 col. 593-594 (§ 2 of the article Sanchunjat(h)on, ibid., col. 593-598). [Translated from the German].

Anat's Victory over the Tunnanu, *JSS* 20 (1975), pp. 22-27.

The Rending of Danil's Garment in the Aqhat Epic, *BM* 62 (1975), p. 361 *[Translated from the Hebrew]*.

Publications in which first appeared the writings collected in this volume

Ugarit and the Bible 1 (Review of Ras Shamra Parallels 1, ed. L.R. Fisher, Roma 1972), *Biblica* 56 (1975), pp. 103-119.

The Expanded Colon, reconsidered, *UF* 7 (1975), pp. 261-264.

The Making and Destruction of the Golden Calf - a Rejoinder, *Biblica* 56 (1975), pp. 330-343.

Ex. 21:22-25, *VT* 27 (1977), pp. 352-360.

The Sending of Baal's Messengers to the Land of no Return, *EI* 13 (*H.L. Ginsberg Volume* 1978, pp. 1-6). *[Translated from the Hebrew]*.

Publications not included in the present volume

hamm^egillot säl ^cen päšḥa *[The Scrolls from Ras Feshkha]*, *BJPES* 15 (1950), pp. 40-44.

maṭṭe hā'ᵃlohim *[The Rod of God]*, *World Congress of Jewish Studies, Jerusalem 1947*, vol. 1 Jerusalem, 1952, pp. 207-210.

lᵉtorat hammibnä hakkiasti bammiqrā' *[Observations on Chiasmus in the Bible]*, *Sepher Auerbach* (*ISBR* 1), Jerusalem 1955, pp. 27-30.

yᵉsodot hammusār bᵉsippur hammabbul, *[The Ethical Elements in the Narrative of the Flood]*, *BM* 1 (1956), p. 21.

Review of R. North, Sociology of the Biblical Jubilee, Roma 1954, *ibid.*, pp. 27-28 (in Hebrew).

mot mošä, *Tarbiz* 27 (1958), pp. 142-157 Enlarged English edition: The Death of Moses, *Studies in the Testament of Abraham* ed. by George V.E. Nickelsburg Jr., *SCS* 6 (1976), pp. 185-217.

naḥᵃlat YHWH *[The Heritage of the Lord]*, *Sepher Dim*, (*ISBR* 5), Jerusalem 1958, pp. 120-125.

ᶜedut bihosep *[The Bearing of Psalm 81 upon the Problem of Exodus]*, *EJ* 5 (1958), pp. 80-82 (with English Abstract, p. 88*).

Review of R. de Vaux, Les Institutions de l'Ancien Testament 1, Paris 1958, *Kirjat Sepher* 34 (1959), pp. 45-49 (in Hebrew).

yᵉᶜabbᵉṭun = yᵉᶜawwᵉtun ?, *Lĕšonênu* 24 (1960), pp. 107-108.

ᶜbṭ = ᶜrb ?, *Lĕšonênu* 25 (1961), pp. 111-114.

ubᵉᶜad haššälaḥ yippolu (Joel 2:8), *Lĕšonênu* 26 (1961), p. 62.

yᵉṣi'at miṣrayim *[The Exodus from Egypt]*, *BM* 13 (1962), pp. 121-125.

Review of W. Beyerlin, Die Herkunft und Geschichte der ältesten Sinaitraditionen, Tübingen 1961, *IEJ* 12 (1962), pp. 160-164.

Review of S. Mowinckel, The Psalms in Israel's Worship, Oxford 1962, *Kirjat Sepher* 39 (1963), pp. 48-53 (in Hebrew).

An Observation on Source Criticism of the Plague Pericope (Ex. 7-11), *VT* 24 (1964), pp. 374-378.

k^{e}lub qayiṣ, l^{e}ṭipologiā šäl ḥ^{a}zon hann^{e}bu'ā [k^{e}lub qayiṣ, an Observation on the Typology of the Prophetic Vision], *Tarbiz* 34 (1965), pp. 319-322.

The Death of the Upright and the World to come [Nu. 23:10b], *JJS* 16 (1966), pp. 183-186.

^{c}ābar l^{ec}ābar b^{e}iwrit šäl ḥazal [The Plusquamperfect in Talmudic Hebrew], *Lĕšonénu* 31 (1966), pp. 21-22 (with English abstract).

kitbe 'ugārit, hahistoriā šäl ^{c}am yiśrā'el 2, hā'ābot w^{e}haššop^{e}ṭim, Tel Aviv 1967, pp. 9-16, 304-306 = Ugaritic Writings, *The World History of the Jewish People*, Vol. 2 The Patriarchs, ed. B. Mazar, Tel-Aviv 1970, pp. 9-23; 250-252.

hammišpaṭ [Biblical Law], *ibid.*, pp. 272-283, 363-365.

^{c}al 'immot q^{e}ri'ā b^{e}'ugāritit [Matres Lectionis in Ugaritic], *Lĕšonénu* 32 (1968), pp. 369-373.

māsorät y^{e}ṣi'at miṣrayim b^{e}hištalš^{e}lutāh [The Tradition of the Exodus in its Development], 151 pp., 10 pp. English Summary, Jerusalem 1968, Second Edition 1972.

r^{e}'uben wihudā b^{e}maḥzor sippure yosep [Reuben and Judah in the Joseph-cycle], *Fourth World Congress of Jewish Studies Jerusalem 1967*, Vol. 1, Jerusalem 1969, pp. 69-70 (with English abstract, p. 257).

kitbe 'ugārit w^{e}siprut hammiqrā' [Ugaritic Texts and Biblical Literature], *Qadmoniot* 2 (1969), pp. 83-88.

hayyod k^{e}'em q^{e}ri'ā b^{e}'ugāritit [The Yod as Mater Lectionis in Ugaritic], *Lĕšonénu* 33 (1969), pp. 111-114 (with English abstract).

liš'elat 'o šä [A Remark on the Question of 'o šä], *ibid.*, p. 319 (with English abstract).

näšäk and t/marbit, *JBL* 78 (1969), pp. 78-80.

Kritik über Herbert Schmid, Mose (BZAW 110), Berlin 1968, *Biblica* 50 (1969), pp. 429-432.

Zur Frage der scriptio plena im Ugaritischen und Verwandtes (with Joshua Blau), *UF* 2 (1970), pp. 19-33.

'ugāritit ṣly 'qillel' (with Joshua Blau) [Ugaritic ṣly 'to curse'], *Lĕšonēnu* 35 (1970), pp. 7-10 (with English abstract).

haqdāšat lewi la^{ca}bodat YHWH b^{e}māsorät hattorā [The Investiture of Levi in the Traditions of the Pentateuch], *EI* 10 (1971), pp. 162-172 (with English abstract, XIV-XV).

Isaiah 1:31, *VT* 21 (1971), pp. 246-248.

Esther 9:29-32: The Genesis of a late Addition, *HUCA* 42 (1971), pp. 117-124.

pārāšat motām šäl 'ābot hā'ummā b^{e}sepär b^{e}re'šit [The Death of the Patriarchs in the Narratives of the Book of Genesis], *Bible and Jewish History*, Studies in Bible and Jewish History dedicated to the Memory of Jacob Liver, ed. B. Uffenheimer, Tel-Aviv 1971, pp. 104-123 (with English abstract XIV-XV).

The Number of Plagues in Psalm 105, *Biblica* 52 (1971), pp. 34-38.

māsorät sippur hitnaḥ^{a}lutām šäl b^{e}ne gād ubne r^{e}'uben [The Relation of the Settlement of Gad and Reuben in Nu. 32:1-38 - its Background and its Composition], *Tarbiz* 42 (1972), pp. 12-26 (with English abstract II).

^{c}e(y)n ya^{ca}qob [Deut. 33:28], *BM* 64 (1975), pp. 152-153 (with English abstract, p. 169).

^{c}al haṣṣā^{c}ot ḥ^{a}dāšot l^{e}nittu^{a}ḥ pārāšat hammakkot [New Proposals to analyze the Composition of the Plague Pericope], *Shnāton*, An Annual for Biblical and Ancient Near Eastern Studies 1 (1975), pp. 183-188 (with English abstract, p. XV).

k^{e}tobät 7 me'ostrāqā'ot ^{ca}rād, ^{c}edut l^{e}biṭṭul m^{e}lā'kā b^{e}ro'š ḥodäš? [Ostrakon 7 from Arad, attesting the Observance of the New Moon Day?], *BM* 66 (1976), pp. 330-332 (with English abstract, p. 494).

The Testament of Abraham and the Texts concerning the Death of Moses, *Studies in the Testament of Abraham*, ed. by George W.E. Nickelsburg Jr., *SCS* 6 (1976), pp. 219-225.

ḥ^{a}lušā, *Lĕšonēnu* 42 (1977), p. 78 (in Hebrew).

Ugarit and the Bible 2 (Review of Ras Shamra Parallels 2, ed. L.R. Fisher, Roma 1975), *Biblica* 59 (1978), pp. 100-122.

Review of A. Toeg, mattan torā b^{e}ṣinai [Lawgiving at Sinai], Jerusalem 1977, *BM* 74 (1978), pp. 387-398.

'ānoki '^{a}ḥaṭṭännā, *ZAW* 90 (1978), p. 410 (in German).

balloti b^{e}šämän ra^{ca}nān, *UF* (in press, in English).

^{c}am s^{e}gullā - ^{c}am ^{c}äbäd? [The meaning of ^{c}am s^{e}gullā], *Sepher Ben-Ḥayyim* (in press).

riq^{c}o hahistori šäl Targum haššib^{c}im lithillim 29:5-6 [The Septuagint Version of Ps. 29:5-6 and its historical background], *Sepher Seeligmann* (in press).

Zur Götterlehre des Epos von Keret, *Schaeffer-Festschrift* (in press).

Die Geburtsgeschichte Moses, Studies in Jewish Religious and Intellectual History in Honour of Alexander Altmann, University of Alabama Press (in press).

'osar l^{e}šon hammiqrā' [Thesaurus of the Language of the Bible] with Joshua Blau Volume 1 ('āb - '^{a}tārim), Jerusalem 1957, Volume 2 (b - wasti), Jerusalem 1959, Volume 3 (z^{e}'eb - zetar only), Jerusalem 1968.

Encyclopaedia Biblica, Volume 1, 'āb - '^{a}ṭārim, Jerusalem 1950

'ābel m^{e}ḥolā 1, 38f. - - 'ābel miṣrayim, 39 -- 'ābel haššiṭṭim, 39f. - - 'äbän hā'äzäl, 46 - - 'äbän y^{e}qārā [precious stones], 48f. - - 'obot, 69f. - - 'äglayim, 78 - - '^{ä}dom 'aḥ^{a}re ḥurban habbayit hāri'šon [Edom after the destruction of the First Temple], 98f. - - yihuse b^{e}ne '^{ä}dom [genealogy of the Edomite clans], 99-102 - - malke '^{ä}dom [the kings of Edom], 102-103 - - 'odäm [precious stone], 110 - - 1. '^{a}dāmā [earth], 110f. - - 2. '^{a}dāmā [place], 111 - - '^{a}dāmi hannäqäb, 112 - - 'addān, 'addon, 113 - - 2. 'addār [place], 116 - - b^{e}ne 'ah^{a}ron (with E.S. Hartum), 131-134 - - 'ulay, 146f. - - 2. 'on [place in Reuben], 148 - - 'upāz, 163 - - 1. 'or [light], 168f. - - '^{a}ḥiyyā(hu), 213f. - - 'aḥlāmā, 228 - - 'izäbäl, 255 - - 'elim [place], 268 - - 'itāmār, 276 - - 1. 'akzib, k^{e}zib [place in Juda], 278 - - 'älgābiš, 292f. - - ^{c}emäq hā'elā, 296 - - 'elā [person], 296f. - - 'āluš, 333 - - '^{ä}liāb, 334f. - - '^{ä}liäzär, 346f. - - '^{ä}liṣāpān, älṣāpān, 349f. - - '^{ä}liqā, 350 - - '^{ä}lyāqim, 359f. - - '^{ä}lišäba^{c}, 351f. - - '^{ä}lišu^{ac}, 353 - - '^{ä}lyāšib, 353f. - - '^{ä}lišāmā^{c}, 354f. - - '^{ä}lišā^{c} [the name], 358 - - '^{ä}lišāpāt, 358f. - - 'älmodād, 361 - - 'älnā^{c}am, 366 - - 'äl^{c}ād, 368 - - 'äl^{c}ādā, 368 - - 'äl^{c}uzay, 369 - - 'äl^{c}āzār, 369f. - - 2. 'äl^{c}āšā [place], 371 - - 'älpā^{c}al, 415f. - - 'älqānā, 417f. - - 'āmon [the name], 422f. - - 3. '^{a}mānā [river], 436 - - 'amṣi, 437 - - 1. 'immer [person], 439f. - - 2. 'immer [place], 440 - - 'imri, 448f. - - '^{a}maryā(hu), 449 - - '^{a}mittay, 450 - - 'ani^{c}ām, 459 - - 'assir [person], 475 - - 'āsir, 'assir, 'āsur [prisoner], 476-478 - - 'āsāp, 482f. - - 'aspātā', 484 - - '^{a}peq '^{a}piq, 501-503 - - 'epär, 504 - - 'appiryon, 504f. - - har 'äprayim, 513 - - ya^{c}ar 'äprayim, 513 - - 2. 'äprayim [place], 513f. - - 2. 'äprātā [person], 516 - - 'āṣal, 517 - - 'eṣär, 518 - - 'äqdaḥ, 518 - - '^{a}rubbot [place], 526f. - - 'arba^{c}, 527f. - - 'argob, 528f. - - 'argāmān, 529f. - - 'āraḥ, 555f. - - 'äräk, 564-567 - - 'arki, 567 - - '^{a}ram nah^{a}rayim, 581f. - - paddan '^{a}rām, 583f. - - 'armoni, 595f. - - '^{a}rān, 596 - - 2. 'orän [person], 597 - - 'arnon, 598 - - 'arpakšad, 602 - - 'äräṣ taḥtim ḥodši, 742f. - - 'ašbel, 749 - - 'äšba^{c}al, 749f. - - 'šd, '^{a}šedot, 750 - - 'ašdot happisgā, 752 - - 'ašḥur, 760f. - - 'äškol, 762 - - 'ašk^{e}naz, 762f. - - 'ašnā, 768f. - - 'äš^{c}an, 769 - - 'äštā'ol, 788f. - - 'äšton, 789

- - '^{a}śar'el, 790 - - '^{a}śar'elā, 790 - - 'aśri'el, 790 - - 'ittay, 791 - - 'etām, 792f. - - 'ätni, 793 - - 'ätnān [person], 793 - - '^{a}tārim, 794 - -

Encyclopaedia Biblica, Volume 2 b - zetar, Jerusalem 1954

b^{e}'er 'elim, 6 - - b^{e}'er laḥay ro'i, 6 - - b^{e}'era, 8 - - b^{e}'eri, 9 - - bigway, 32 - - bed^{e}yā, 34 - - b^{e}dān, 36 - - bidqar, 36 - - bohan, 40 - - bunā, 41 - - boṣes, 41 - - bizyotyā, 43f. - - b^{e}ṭonim, 50 - - 1. bet 'el [topography, history and archeology], (with I. Ben David), 56-63 - - bet 'arbe'l, 68 - - bet haggan, 70 - - bet hārām, 71 - - bet ḥābär, 72 - - bet ḥoglā, 72 - - bet ḥoron, 73-75 - - bet hakkäräm, 84f. - - bet l^{e}bā'ot (with M. Avi-Yona), 85f. - - bet l^{ec}aprā, 89 - - bet marze^{a}ḥ, 89f. 947 - - bet ^{ca}not, 95f. - - bet rāpā', 102 - - bet tappu^{a}ḥ, 119 - - bäkär, 128 - - bokru, 129 - - bikri, 129 - - b^{e}korat, 129f. - - bilgā, 130f.; 947f. - - 1. bilhā, 132 - - bilhān, 132 - - bäla^{c}, 133 - - bil^{c}am [person], 133-135 - - bālāq, 135f. - - belša'ṣṣar, 136f. - - bimhāl, 153 - - bāmot ba^{c}al, 153 - - bän - [in personal proper names], 154 - - bän-'^{a}binādāb, 154 - - bän-däqär, 155 - - bän-h^{a}dad, 155-158 - - bän-zoḥet, 158 - - bän - ḥayil, 158f. - - bän - ^{c}ammi, 169 - - b^{e}not ṣ^{e}lopḥād 170f.; 948 - - bāni, 171f. - - bunni, 172 - - b^{e}ne ta^{ca}rubot [hostages], 197 - - b^{e}nāyāhu), 262f. - - b^{e}ninu, 281 - - bin^{c}ā', 281 - - b^{e}sodyā, 282 - - besay, 282 - - b^{ec}or, 282 - - bo^{c}az [person], 282f. - - 2. ba^{c}al [person], 285f. - - ba^{c}al ḥānān, 298 - - ba^{c}al p^{ec}or, 289f. - - ba^{c}al ṣ^{e}pon, 291f. - - ba^{ca}lā, 294f. - - b^{ec}alyā, 299f. - - ba^{ca}lis, 300 - - ba^{ca}lāt, 300f. - - ba^{ca}nā', 301 - - ba^{ca}nā, 301f. - - ba^{c}šā', 303f. - - b^{ec}ašt^{e}rā, 304 - - ba^{ca}śeya, 304f. - - beṣay, 305 - - boṣqat, 308 - - 2.3. bäṣär [places], 308f. - - biq^{c}at ^{c}āwän, 311 - - biq^{c}at durā', 311 - - biq^{c}at hall^{e}bānon, 311f. - - biq^{c}at miṣpä, 312 - - bäräd, 337 - - barzillay, 342f. - - b^{e}ri^{c}ā, 346f. - - ^{c}emäq b^{e}rākā, 361f. - - bära^{c}, 363 - - bāräqät, bār^{e}qat, 365f. - - birša^{c}, 366 - - bišlām, 366 - - bāšān, 366-370 - - bat par^{c}o, 378f. - - b^{e}tu'el, 380f. - - bitron, 386 - - g^{e}'u'el, 389 - - gibbor ḥayil, 397f. - - gabbay, 400 - - gebim, 400f. - - gib^{c}on, 416-418 - - gib^{c}at 'ammā, 419f. - - gib^{c}at hā^{ca}rālot, 420 - - gibbār, 420 - - gabri'el, 420f. - - gibb^{e}ton, 421f. - - gād [person], 423 - - gudgod, 431 - - gādi, 435 - - gaddi, 435 - - gaddi'el, 437 - - giddel, 437 - - g^{e}dor [person], 446 - - gob, 448 - - gozān, 450-456 - - goy, 457 - - golān, 458 - - guni, 458 - - gur ba^{c}al, 459 - - gorāl [lot] (with H. Gevaryahu), 459-461 - - gzh, gizzoni, 463f. - - gāzez, 464 - - gazzām, 465 - - gaḥam,

474f. - - gaḥar, 475 - - ge(') bän-hinnom, 476f. - - ge yiptaḥ'el, 477 - - ge hā^{c}obrim, 477f. - - ge hass^{e}bo^{c}im, 478 - - ge ṣ^{e}pātā l^{e}mārešā, 480 - - gid hannāšä, 480f. - - 1. giḥon [Gen. 2:10, 13], 481f. - - ginat, 483f. - - gilbo^{ca}, har haggilbo^{ca}, 486 - - gallim, 508 - - gālāl (with M. Plessner), 509f. - - 3. gil^{c}ād [district] (with S. Yeivin), 512-516 - - 4. gil^{c}ād [town], 516 - - gullot, 516 - - gammādim, 518f. - - gāmul, 519 - - g^{e}malli, 524f. - - 2. gomär [people], 525-527 - - g^{e}maryā(hu), 527 - - g^{e}nebā [theft], 536f. - - g^{e}nebat halleb ["stealing of the heart"], 537f. - - g^{e}nubat, 539 - - g^{e}nāzim [treasury], 539 - - gerā', 549f. - - garmi, 558 - - gorän b (with C.Z. Hirschberg), 559f. - - gorän hā'āṭād, 560 - - b^{e}ne geršom, b^{e}ne geršon, 565-567 - - g^{e}šur, g^{e}šuri, 568 - - gäšäm, gašmu 568f. - - 1. gošän [district in Egypt], 569f. - - do'eg, 577f. - - 2. d^{e}bir [person], 587f. - - d^{e}bir [town], 588-590 - - d^{e}birā, 590 - - dibri, 596 - - dāb^{e}rāt, 619f. - - dabbäšät, 620 - - dodānim, 626f. - - dod, dodā, 627f. - - dodo, 646 - - dodāwāhu, 646 - - 3. dumā [place in Juda], 648 - - di zāhāb, 649f. - - dibon [place in Juda], 651f. - - d^{e}lāyā(hu), 655f. - - dil^{c}ān, 656 - - dimnā, 671f. - - dannā, 685 - - dinhābā, 685f. - - d^{ec}u'el, 697 - - dopqā, 700 - - d^{e}rišā 'äl hammetim [necromancy], 710f. - - dātān, 773f. - - hāgār, 782-784 - - hagri, hagri'im, 784f. - - 2. h^{a}dad [persons], 790f. - - h^{a}dadrimmon, 792 - - hidday, 795 - - hohām, 798 - - hoqā^{c}ā [kind of execution], 798-800 - - hotir, 806f. - - hemān, 808f. - - b^{e}ne hemān, 809f. - - helām, 850 - - hena^{c}, 852 - - haṣlälponi, 852f. - - hor hāhār, 853f. - - hārā', 855 - - hārum, 855 - - horām, 855 - - hārāri, 856f. - - hāšem, 860 - - wāheb, 873 - - wopsi, 888 - - zabdi, 892 - - zabdi'el, 892 - - z^{e}buddā, z^{e}bidā, 894f. - - z^{e}bulun [the name], 900f. - - 1. zäbaḥ [person], 901 - - zabbay, 906f. - - z^{e}binā, 907 - - 1. z^{e}bul [noun], 907f. - - 2. z^{e}bul [person], 908 - - zaham, 909 - - zuzim, zamzummim, 909f. - - zizā('), 911 - - zi^{ac}, 911 - - zakkur, 919f. - - zakkay, 920 - - zākär, 920 - - z^{e}karyā(hu) [person], 921-923 - - zilpā, 929 - - zimmā, 929f. - - z^{e}mirā, 930f. - - zimri, 931-933 - - zimrān, 933 - - z^{e}nunim, z^{e}nut [harlotry], 935-937 - - zäraḥ, 941f. - - zetām, 946 - -

Encyclopaedia Biblica, Volume 3, ḥobāb - y^{e}tet, Jerusalem 1958

ḥ^{a}baṣṣinyā, 6 - - ḥäbär, ḥebär, 10f. - - ḥag, ḥaggim umo^{ca}dim [feasts], 21-24 - - ḥaggi, 27 - - ḥ^{a}dad, 28 - - ḥādid, 28f. - - ḥiwwi, 45-47 - - ḥupām, ḥuppim, 52f. - - ḥuqoq, 55 - - ḥur (with S. Yeivin), 56 - - haḥori b^{e}'äräṣ yiśrā'el [the Horite in the land of Israel], 61-63 - - ḥušā, 64 - - ḥušim, 65f. - - ḥotām [person], 67f. - - ḥ^{a}zāel, 87f. - - ḥ^{a}zi'el, 89 - - ḥäzyon, 89f. - - ḥ^{a}zir [boar], (with E. Billik), 90-94 - - ḥezir, 94f. - - gib^{c}at haḥ^{a}kilā, 124 - - ḥ^{a}kirat qarqa^{c} [lease of land], 124-127 - - ḥäl'ā, 134 - - ḥeläd, ḥälday, 140 - - ḥuldā [person], 142 - - ḥeläm, 157 - - ḥolon, ḥilen, 158f. - - ḥeläp, 159 - - ḥäläṣ, 159f. - - ḥeläq, 160 - - ḥälqat, ḥälqāt, 162 - - ḥälqat haṣṣurim, 162 - - ḥām, 162-164 - - ḥämdān, 164 - - ḥammu'el, 164 - - ḥ^{a}muṭal, ḥ^{a}miṭal, 165 - - ḥammon, 165f.; 961 - - 1. ḥammat [person], 192 - - ḥammot do'ar, 200f. - - ḥenādād, 201f. - - ḥannā, 202f. - - ḥānun, 211 - - ḥanni'el, 215f. - - ḥ^{a}nam'el, 216f. - - ḥosā, 223f. - - ḥopni, 251f. - - ḥopši [noun], 256f. - - ḥāṣer, ḥ^{a}ṣerim [noun], 273f. - - ḥ^{a}ṣar gaddā, 274f. - - ḥ^{a}ṣar šu^{c}āl, 275 - - ḥāṣer hattikon, 276 - - 1. ḥäṣron [person], 276 - - ḥ^{a}ṣerim [place], 277f. - - ḥ^{a}rumap, 281 - - ḥoronayim, 285 - - ^{c}emäq häḥāruṣ, 285 - - ḥarḥur, 286 - - ḥarḥ^{a}yā, 286 - - ḥārip, 289 - - ḥorim, 289f. - - ḥeräm [ban], 290-292 - - 1. ḥārān [person], 300f. - - ḥarnäpär, 303f. - - ḥäräš, 308 - - ḥ^{a}šabyā(hu), 313f. - - ḥ^{a}šabn^{e}yā, 315 - - ḥāšum, 316 - - ḥošän hammišpāṭ [pouch of judgement], 318f. - - ḥ^{a}śupā', 319 - - ḥätlon, 357 - - ḥ^{a}ṭat, 360 - - ṭāb'el, 361f. - - ṭäbaḥ, 363 - - ṭäbaḥ, ṭibḥat, 363 - - ṭ^{e}balyāhu, 365 - - ṭob, 366 - - ṭäläm, 390f. - - ṭipsār, ṭapsār, 408 - - ya'^{a}zanyā(hu), 413-415 - - dātām šäl y^{e}hude yeb [The religion of the Jews at Elephantine], 439-444 - - yibbum, yābām wibāmā [levirate marriage], 444-447 - - yibḥar, 448f. - - yābin [the name], 451 - - yibl^{ec}ām, 452f. - - yibn^{e}yā, 455 - - yig'āl, 461 - - yigdalyāhu, 462 - - yogli, 463 - - yid'^{a}lā, 464 - - yiddo, yaddo, yadday, 465 - - yādon, 465 - - y^{e}dutun, y^{e}ditun, 467f. - - y^{e}didā, 468 - - y^{e}didyā, 468f. - - y^{e}di^{ca}'el, 469 - - yādā^{c}, 469f. - - y^{e}da^{c}yā, 470f. - - yah^{e}dāy, 471f. - - y^{e}hudiyyā, 472 - - y^{e}hudā [person], 487-489 - - y^{e}hudi, 510 - - y^{e}hudit [person], 510 - - y^{e}hozābād, yozābād., 518 - - y^{e}hoyārib, yoyārib, 530f. - - y^{e}hukal, yukal, 531f. - - y^{e}ho^{c}addā, 535 - - y^{e}ho^{c}addān, y^{e}ho^{c}addin, 536 - - y^{e}hoṣādāq, yoṣādāq, 536 - - yah^{a}lom, 571 - - yahaṣ, yahṣā, 571f. - - yo'āb, 572f. - - yo'el [person], 574f. - - yobāb, 577f. - - 2. yobel [legal institution], 578-582 - - yoḥā', 590 - - yokäbäd, 592 - - yom hakkippurim [Day of Atonement], 595-600 - - yāwān, 603-605 - - yosipyā, 617f. - - yušab ḥäsäd, 620f. - - yošibyā, 621 - - yošawyā, 621 - - yotām, 621-624 - - y^{e}zu'el, 624 - - yāziz, 625 - - yizli'ā, 625 - - yizrāḥ, zarḥi, 625f. - - yizraḥyā, 626 - - yizr^{ec}ä'l [the name], 626f. - - yaḥdo, 634 - - yaḥdi'el, 634f. - - yäḥd^{e}yāhu, 635 - - yaḥ^{a}zi'el, 635f. - - yaḥz^{e}yā, 636 - - yaḥzerā, 655 - - y^{e}ḥi'el(i), 656f. - - y^{e}ḥiyyā, 660 - -

yaḥl^{e}'el(i), 660 - - yaḥṣ^{e}'el, yaḥṣi'el, 671 - - yaḥat, 671f. - - yākin [person], 682 - - yam suf, 695-699 - - b^{e}qi^{c}at yam suf [the splitting of the Red Sea], 699f. - - y^{e}mu'el, 700f. - - yimlā('), 702 - - yamlek, 702 - - yimnā, 703 - - yimnā^{c}, 703 - - yānoaḥ, 704f. - - yānum, yānim, 705 - - yiskā, 707 - - ya^{c}beṣ, 708 - - yä^{c}do, yä^{c}di, 708f. - - y^{ec}uš, y^{ec}iš, 709 - - ya^{ca}zi'el, 709f. - - ya^{c}zer, 710-712 - - yam ya^{c}zer, 712 - - y^{ec}i'el, y^{ec}u'el, 712f. - - 1. yā^{c}el [person], 713f. - - ya^{ca}lā', ya^{c}lā, 715f. - - ya^{c}lām, 716 - - ya^{ca}nay, 716 - - ya^{c}rā, 735 - - ya^{c}re 'or^{e}gim, 735f. - - ya^{c}aśi'el, 736 - - yipd^{e}yā, 743f. - - y^{e}punnä, 745 - - yäpät, 745f. - - b^{e}ne yäpät, 746-748 - - 1. yiptāḥ [person], 748-750 - - yiṣhār(i), 751f. - - y^{e}ṣi'at miṣra=yim [the Exodus from Egypt], 754-759 - - y^{e}quti'el, 762 - - y^{e}qamyā, 764 - - yir'iyyā, 770 - - y^{e}rubba^{c}al, 771 - - midbar y^{e}ru'el, 787f. - - y^{e}rusā(') [person], 788 - - y^{e}ruššā [law of heritage], 788-791 - - y^{e}roḥām, 859f. - - yārib, 863f. - - y^{e}riyyā(hu), 864 - - y^{e}rimot, 864f. - - y^{e}ri^{c}ot, 865 - - y^{e}remot, 867 - - yirm^{e}yā(hu) [person], 867f. - - yirp^{e}'el, 885f. - - yor=q^{ec}ām, 890 - - yäšäb'āb, 890 - - yošb^{e}qāšā, 893 - - yāšub(i), 893f. - - 1. yešu^{ac} [place], 895 - - yišay, 899 - - yiššiyyā(hu), 900f. - - y^{e}šišay, 901 - - yišmā', 901 - - y^{e}ša^{c}yā(hu) [person], 908 - - yāš^{e}pe, 936f. - - yišpā, 937 - - yešär, 937 - - y^{e}śimi'el, 938 - - yiśrā'el, 938-943 - - 1. yśśkr, yiśśākār [person], (with S. Yeivin), 944 - - yātom, 962f. - - yitlā, 953 - - yatni'el, 953 - - yitnān, 954 - - yitro, 954-957 - -

Encyclopaedia Biblica, Volume 4, kābed - mältāḥā, Jerusalem 1962

kabbon, 8 - - konanyāhu, 49 - - kozbi, 74 - - kidon [person], 102 - - kal=kol, 184 - - k^{e}lāl, 184 - - kimhām, kimhān, 186 - - k^{e}nanyāhu, 192f. - - k^{e}sut ^{c}enayim, 220f. - - k^{e}sil [place], 221 - - 3. kopär [ransom], 231-233 - - kāri, 310-312 - - karmi, 322 - - kāret, hikkāret [punishment], 330-332 - - k^{e}reti, 332 - - k^{e}reti upleti, 332-334 - - käśäd, 365 - - kittim, 394-398 - - kitliš, 398 - - lā'el, 412 - - 1. l^{e}bonā [place], 418 - - lābān [the name], 421 - - lud, ludim, 438f. - - loḥeš, 447 - - loṭ, 447-449 - - läḥi, 486f. - - laḥmās, 495f. - - laqqum, 530f. - - läšäm, 531f. - - mabbul [the Flood], 597-610 - - m^{e}bušim [Deut. 25:11-12], 610f. - - m^{e}dān, 695 - - mohar [purchase-price of a wife], 702-706 - - har mo^{c}ed, 737f. - - moṣā', 738 - - muśāgim ge'ogrāpiyim bammiqrā' [Geographic terms], (with Y. Aharoni), 742-754 - - māwät [death], 754-763 - - māḥoz, 785-787 - - māḥol [person], 788 - - m^{e}ḥidā, 792 - - m^{e}ḥir [person], 793 - - maḥli, 800 - -

maḥ^{a}ne dān, 805 - - m^{e}ḥoqeq, 811f. - - maṭṭä [rod], 825-832 - - maṭred, 834 - - me zāhāb, 834 - - middā k^{e}nägäd middā [talion], 840-846 - - mikā'el [angel], 881-882 - - mayim [water], 909-917 - - hammitos hakk^{e}na^{ca}ni [the Canaanite myth], 943-946 - - mitot bet din [execution of criminals], 946-950 - - makke 'ābiw w^{e}'immo [Ex. 21:15], 951f. - - makkot miṣrayim [the Plagues of Egypt], 952-959 - - miktāb [letter], 966-974 - - malqot [corporal punishment], 1160f. - - l^{e}bānon [addition], 1166 - -

Encyclopaedia Biblica, Volume 5, m^{e}mukān - sitri, Jerusalem 1968

mamzer [bastard], 1-3 - - mān [manna], 7-10 - - mānaḥat, 33f. - - 1. m^{e}naššä [different persons], 40f. - - massā umribā, 57 - - mass^{ec}e b^{e}ne yiśrā'el [the migrations of the Israelites in the wilderness], 167-170 - - hammispār hammudrāg [the ascending number], 185f. - - mipqād [muster of the people], 218-221 - - m^{e}sobāyā, 225 - - m^{e}ri', 455f. - - (me) m^{e}ribat qādeš, 456-458 - - 'äräṣ hammoriyyā, 458-460 - - m^{e}rāri, 475 - - b^{e}ne m^{e}rāri, 475-477 - - mošä, 482-495 - - m^{e}šobāb, 497 - - miškan YHWH [the tabernacle], 532-548 - - mišpaṭ hammiqrā' [the law of the Bible], 614-637 - - bän-mäšäq, 638 - - no^{a}ḥ, 799f. - - naḥal miṣrayim, 813f. - - naḥ^{a}lā, 815f. - - naḥaš [animal], (with Y. Ahitub), 821f. - - nissāyon [temptation], (with Y.S. Licht), 879-883 - - näšäk w^{e}tarbit [usury], 929f. - - soṭā [unfaithful wife], 1003f. - - ma^{ca}mad har sinay [The theophany at Sinai], 1027-1033 - - sepär hammiqnä [document of purchase], 1092f. - -

Encyclopaedia Biblica, Volume 6, ^{c}äbäd - ṣar^{e}tan, Jerusalem 1971

^{c}äbäd ^{c}iwri [the Hebrew slave], 13f. - - ^{c}äglā ^{ca}rupā [Deut. 21:1-9], 77-79 - - ^{c}ed [witness], 81-83 - - 2. ^{c}edut [as designation of covenant], 89 - - ^{ca}dat 'el, 96-98 - - ^{c}ir hannidaḥat [Deut. 13:13-19], 217f. - - 2. ^{ca}nāt [Canaanite goddess], (with S. Aḥitub), 314-317 - - ^{c}ārob, 344f. - - ^{ca}rebut [surety], 367-370 - - ^{ca}rāyot [forbidden marriages], 388-390 - - ^{c}aštorät, 406-412 - - pilon migg^{e}bal [Philo of Byblos], 457-462 - - pārā '^{a}dummā [Nu. 19:1-10], 579-581 - - pätän, 641f. - - ṣ^{e}bi [gazelle], (with E. Bilik), 661-663 - - ṣādoq, 673-677 - - ṣalmunnā^{c} (with I. Ephal), 736f. - - ṣ^{e}lopḥād, 738 - -

Encyclopaedia Biblica 7, qā'āt - š^{e}lišiyyā, Jerusalem 1976

qādeš, 35f. - - q^{e}dešā, 62-66 - - 1. q^{e}hāt, 84 - - 2. b^{e}ne q^{e}hāt, 84-87 - - qāṭāb, qoṭāb, 109f. - - qayin wāhābāl, 119-124 - - qayiṣ wāḥoräp [summer and winter], (with Y.S. Licht), 174f. - - qelāyā, 184f. - - 1. qoraḥ, 255 - - 2. b^{e}ne qoraḥ, 255-259 - - qoraḥ, dātān wa'^{a}birām, 259-262 - - 1. r^{e}'u=ben [person], (with Y. Zakovitch), 285-287 - - rāḥel, 358-360 - - r^{e}kilut [slander], 371f. - - ra^{c}aš [earthquake], 401-403 - - r^{e}pā'im, 404-407 - - 1. räšäp [god], 437-441 - - š^{e}'ol [netherworld], 454-457 - - š^{e}'er, k^{e}sut w^{ec}onā [Ex. 21:10], 459f. - - š^{e}bu^{c}ā [oath], 479-491. 719f. - - šedim [demons], 524f. - - sepär šop^{e}ṭim [Judges, book], (with Y. Zakovitch), 583-598 - - šor naggāḥ [the goring ox], 602-607 - - šoḥad [bribery], 617-619.

INDEXES

A. Index of Authors

B. Index of Sources

1. Ugaritic Texts

2. Bible

3. Ancient Bible Translations

Septuagint

Vulgate

TO

TY

Second Targum (= Fragmententargum)

Palestinian Targum BWAT NF (8) II, p. 8

Pešiṭta

4. Sumerian, Akkadian, Hittite Texts

5. Egyptian Texts

6. Northwestsemitic Epigraphy

7. South-Arabian Epigraphy

8. Apocrypha, Qumran

11. Samaritan Literature

12. Arabic Literature

13. Classical Literature

C. Index of Names

1. Gods

2. Persons

3. Places

D. Index of Words

1. Hebrew Words

2. Ugaritic Words

Ugaritic in Syllabic Writing

3. Phoenician, Punic Words

4. Aramaic Words (including Syriac)

5. Akkadian Words

Ideograms

Hurrian Words

6. Arabic Words

7. South-Arabian Words

8. Greek Words

E. Subject Index